# Institutional Economics

# Institutional Economics

## An Introduction

**JOHN GROENEWEGEN
ANTOON SPITHOVEN
and
ANNETTE VAN DEN BERG**

palgrave
macmillan

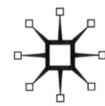

© John Groenewegen, Antoon Spithoven and Annette van den Berg 2010

All rights reserved. No reproduction, copy or transmission of this publication may be made without written permission.

No portion of this publication may be reproduced, copied or transmitted save with written permission or in accordance with the provisions of the Copyright, Designs and Patents Act 1988, or under the terms of any licence permitting limited copying issued by the Copyright Licensing Agency, Saffron House, 6-10 Kirby Street, London EC1N 8TS.

Any person who does any unauthorized act in relation to this publication may be liable to criminal prosecution and civil claims for damages.

The authors have asserted their rights to be identified as the authors of this work in accordance with the Copyright, Designs and Patents Act 1988.

First published 2010 by
PALGRAVE MACMILLAN

Palgrave Macmillan in the UK is an imprint of Macmillan Publishers Limited, registered in England, company number 785998, of Houndmills, Basingstoke, Hampshire RG21 6XS.

Palgrave Macmillan in the US is a division of St Martin's Press LLC, 175 Fifth Avenue, New York, NY 10010.

Palgrave Macmillan is the global academic imprint of the above companies and has companies and representatives throughout the world.

Palgrave® and Macmillan® are registered trademarks in the United States, the United Kingdom, Europe and other countries.

ISBN 978–0–230–55073–5 hardback
ISBN 978–0–230–55074–2 paperback

This book is printed on paper suitable for recycling and made from fully managed and sustained forest sources. Logging, pulping and manufacturing processes are expected to conform to the environmental regulations of the country of origin.

A catalogue record for this book is available from the British Library.

A catalog record for this book is available from the Library of Congress.

10 9 8 7 6 5 4 3 2
19 18 17 16 15 14 13 12 11

Printed and bound in China

# Contents

| | |
|---|---|
| List of Figures, Tables and Boxes | ix |
| Preface | xiii |
| Acknowledgments | xv |
| About the Authors | xvii |
| List of Abbreviations | xix |

### PART I  INTRODUCTION

| | | |
|---|---|---|
| | Introduction | 2 |
| 1 | **What Is Institutional Economics About?** | 5 |
| | Introduction: a world of transactions | 5 |
| | Coordinating transactions in a complex world | 8 |
| | Institutional Economics | 13 |
| | Institutions matter | 36 |
| | A brief outline of the book | 38 |
| | Review questions | 42 |
| | Appendix A: Neoclassical analysis of market structures | 44 |
| | Appendix B: Deviations from the perfect competition model | 50 |

### PART II  THEORY

| | | |
|---|---|---|
| | Introduction | 54 |
| 2 | **Theoretical Framework** | 55 |
| | Introduction | 55 |
| | On theory | 56 |
| | Two schools in Institutional Economics: NIE and OIE | 64 |
| | On the relevance of institutional theories | 78 |
| | A closer look at economic systems | 82 |
| | Concluding remarks | 85 |
| | Review questions | 85 |
| | Appendix A: Veblen and Commons, the founding fathers of Institutional Economics | 87 |
| | Appendix B: Douglass North | 88 |

## 3 Static Approaches to Institutions — 91
Introduction — 91
Property rights theory — 93
Contract theories — 106
Transaction cost theory of governance structures — 118
The vested interest approach — 129
Concluding remarks — 132
Review questions — 133

## 4 The Dynamics of Institutions — 135
Introduction — 135
Drivers of institutional change — 136
The evolutionary approach toward the dynamics of institutions — 141
The design approach toward the dynamics of institutions — 150
Dynamics of economic systems — 155
Concluding remarks — 157
Review questions — 158

## PART III PRIVATE GOVERNANCE STRUCTURES
Introduction — 160

## 5 Markets — 167
Introduction — 167
The static efficiency approach to markets — 170
The static vested interest approach to markets — 183
The dynamic efficiency approach to markets — 185
The dynamic vested interests approach to markets — 192
Concluding remarks — 196
Review questions — 197
Appendix: Different types of auctions — 198

## 6 Firms — 201
Introduction — 201
The static efficiency approach to firms — 203
The static vested interest approach to firms — 211
The dynamic efficiency approach to firms — 221
The dynamic vested interest approach to firms — 226
Concluding remarks — 232
Review questions — 233

## 7 Cooperation between Firms — 235
Introduction — 235
Cooperation between firms in theory and practice — 236
The static efficiency approach to hybrids — 245
The static vested interest approach to hybrids — 250
The dynamic efficiency approach to hybrids — 251

|  |  |  |
|---|---|---:|
| | The dynamic vested interest approach to hybrids | 254 |
| | Concluding remarks | 258 |
| | Review questions | 259 |
| **PART IV** | **PUBLIC GOVERNANCE STRUCTURES** | |
| | Introduction | 262 |
| **8** | **State Intervention to Protect the Public Interest** | 271 |
| | Introduction | 271 |
| | The static approach to state intervention | 272 |
| | The dynamic approach to state intervention | 305 |
| | Concluding remarks | 319 |
| | Review questions | 319 |
| | Appendix A: Elaboration of the fixed costs argument and returns to scale | 321 |
| | Appendix B: Graphical illustration of the difficulties of regulating a natural monopoly | 323 |
| | Appendix C: Graphical illustration of a corrective tax in case of a negative externality | 324 |
| **9** | **Government Failures** | 325 |
| | Introduction | 325 |
| | The static approach to government failures | 328 |
| | The dynamic approach to government failures | 348 |
| | Concluding remarks | 362 |
| | Review questions | 363 |
| | Appendix A: Arrow's impossibility theorem | 364 |
| | Appendix B: Graphical elaboration of the bureaucracy theory | 366 |
| | *Epilog* | 367 |
| | *Glossary* | 369 |
| | *References* | 379 |
| | *Index* | 385 |

# List of Figures, Tables and Boxes

## Figures

| | | |
|---|---|---|
| 1.1 | Hierarchical institutional scheme | 33 |
| 1.2 | Market equilibrium in perfect competition | 46 |
| 1.3 | Deadweight loss in a monopoly situation | 50 |
| 1.4 | Remedying market inefficiencies | 51 |
| 2.1 | The relationship between actor and structure | 59 |
| 2.2 | Endogenous and exogenous variables in NCE | 61 |
| 2.3 | Institutions matter | 62 |
| 2.4 | The NIE model of institutions | 66 |
| 2.5 | The OIE model of institutions | 69 |
| 2.6 | The economy as part of the societal system | 70 |
| 3.1 | Agency costs | 114 |
| 3.2 | A contracting scheme | 124 |
| 4.1 | Institutional reproduction | 137 |
| 4.2 | Exogenous drivers of institutional change | 138 |
| 4.3 | An endogenous description of the dynamics of institutions | 142 |
| 4.4 | Institutional dynamics as artificial selection | 156 |
| III.1 | Transaction costs as a function of asset specificity | 164 |
| 5.1 | The domain of the market | 174 |
| 6.1 | The domain of the firm | 207 |
| 6.2 | The Anglo-Saxon model | 216 |
| 6.3 | The Continental European model | 217 |
| 6.4 | The product life cycle | 223 |
| 6.5 | The unitary (U-form) organization | 224 |
| 6.6 | The multidivisional (M-form) organization | 225 |
| 7.1 | The domain of the hybrid | 246 |

| 7.2 | Porter's five forces | 255 |
| 8.1 | Natural monopoly | 323 |
| 8.2 | Internalization of a negative externality | 324 |
| 9.1 | Costs and benefits resulting from government intervention | 326 |
| 9.2 | The different goals of politicians and bureaucrats | 366 |

## Tables

| | | |
|---|---|---|
| 1.1 | Explanation of governance structures: the four approaches combined | 36 |
| 1.2 | Capital shares of total wealth | 38 |
| 2.1 | Comparison of New and Original Institutional Economics | 77 |
| 3.1 | Division of goods according to their characteristics | 96 |
| III.1 | Attributes of governance structures | 163 |
| 5.1 | Static and dynamic efficiency and vested interest approaches to the market | 169 |
| 5.2 | The market and the characteristics of its main institutional conditions | 177 |
| 5.3 | The influence of institutions on running a business | 182 |
| 5.4 | The domain of the labor market within the Continental European and Anglo-Saxon models | 195 |
| 5.5 | Characteristics of different types of auction | 199 |
| 6.1 | The static and dynamic efficiency and vested interest approaches to firms | 203 |
| 6.2 | The hierarchy and the characteristics of its main institutional conditions | 211 |
| 6.3 | The domain of the firm in the Continental European and Anglo-Saxon models | 231 |
| 6.4 | Characteristics of the firm | 232 |
| 7.1 | The static and dynamic efficiency and vested interest approaches to hybrids | 236 |
| 7.2 | The hybrid and the characteristics of its main institutional conditions | 249 |
| 7.3 | Sources of reliability | 253 |
| IV.1 | Different forms of state intervention to serve public interests | 267 |
| IV.2 | The static and dynamic efficiency and vested interest approaches to government interference | 268 |
| 8.1 | Progressive government intervention | 304 |
| 8.2 | Input–output table of a central plan | 307 |
| 8.3 | Corporate tax rates in thirty OECD countries, 1996–2008 | 318 |
| 9.1 | Amounts spent on lobbying in the USA, 1998–2008 | 353 |
| 9.2 | Corruption Perception Index 2008: the ten best and ten worst scoring countries | 357 |
| 9.3 | Preference ordering leading to the Arrow paradox | 365 |

## Boxes

| | | |
|---|---|---|
| 1.1 | How large are transaction costs? | 23 |
| 1.2 | Coordination of transactions in a supply chain | 30 |

| | | |
|---|---|---|
| 2.1 | Culture and the art of machine maintenance: a cautionary tale | 63 |
| 2.2 | Elites and power: just not letting go | 63 |
| 2.3 | The weather: endogenous or exogenous? | 72 |
| 2.4 | Associations and journals in Institutional Economics | 78 |
| 2.5 | General equilibrium: Walras, Arrow and Debreu | 81 |
| 3.1 | Tragedy of the commons in numbers | 97 |
| 3.2 | Private property rights in communist regimes: the Soviet Union and China | 101 |
| 3.3 | The Coase theorem in numbers | 103 |
| 3.4 | Risk aversion | 108 |
| 3.5 | Adverse selection in the insurance market | 110 |
| 3.6 | Moral hazard in the insurance market | 113 |
| 3.7 | The formal theory of implicit contracts | 117 |
| 3.8 | Hold-up in the gas sector | 120 |
| 4.1 | Money: a self-enforcing institution | 143 |
| 4.2 | Path-dependent sequence of economic changes: QWERTY | 146 |
| 4.3 | The video wars | 147 |
| 4.4 | Cumulative causation and working women | 149 |
| 4.5 | An Inconvenient Truth | 153 |
| 5.1 | The spot market for dairy products | 171 |
| 5.2 | The futures market for milk | 172 |
| 5.3 | Reputation and the diamond industry | 176 |
| 5.4 | Cradle to Cradle | 178 |
| 5.5 | The Fulton Fish Market | 178 |
| 5.6 | The market for used automobiles under asymmetric information | 180 |
| 5.7 | The Fisher Body case | 181 |
| 5.8 | Institutional entrepreneurs in emerging market economies | 191 |
| 5.9 | The effect of consumer boycotts | 194 |
| 6.1 | The pin factory | 204 |
| 6.2 | McDonald's and the *Oxford English Dictionary* | 210 |
| 6.3 | Stork | 215 |
| 6.4 | The case of Google and DoubleClick | 218 |
| 6.5 | Three firms, one dominant position? The Airtours/First Choice case | 219 |
| 6.6 | Dragon's Den | 222 |
| 6.7 | Historical examples of U-form and M-form organizations | 226 |
| 6.8 | The Constant Gardener | 230 |
| 7.1 | The prisoner's dilemma illustrates the need for cooperation | 237 |
| 7.2 | Cartels and cheating | 238 |
| 7.3 | Cartel or warranted cooperation? | 240 |
| 7.4 | Cooperatives affect economies of scale and save on transaction costs | 243 |
| 7.5 | Walt Disney: made in China? | 244 |
| 7.6 | Tit-for-tat as a self-enforcing equilibrium strategy | 254 |
| IV.1 | Trias politica, government, state and public administration | 262 |
| 8.1 | Energy labels in the EU and Japan | 275 |
| 8.2 | Different liability systems | 277 |
| 8.3 | The chinese food and drug inspection service | 279 |

| | | |
|---|---|---|
| 8.4 | Regulation in the US financial sector | 280 |
| 8.5 | Saving big banks | 281 |
| 8.6 | Dominance and abuse in European and American law | 285 |
| 8.7 | Leniency policy for cartel involvement | 287 |
| 8.8 | Sustainability of natural monopolies | 289 |
| 8.9 | Two-part tariff | 290 |
| 8.10 | A Swedish beauty contest | 291 |
| 8.11 | Emissions trading | 296 |
| 8.12 | Fighting deforestation | 297 |
| 8.13 | Ban on tobacco smoking: an application of property rights theory | 298 |
| 8.14 | North American ban on unsafe products | 300 |
| 8.15 | Protection of World Heritage sites | 303 |
| 9.1 | Compliance costs: a time for tax | 327 |
| 9.2 | The risks of bank nationalization | 332 |
| 9.3 | Excessive use of national health care | 334 |
| 9.4 | Excessive costs of social security: the German and Dutch cases | 338 |
| 9.5 | The adventures of Shell and BP in Russia | 350 |
| 9.6 | Lobbying in the eco industry | 352 |
| 9.7 | Lobbying for or against the low-energy light bulb | 354 |
| 9.8 | Lobbying in the tobacco industry | 356 |
| 9.9 | The Californian experience | 359 |

# Preface

Institutions are a pervasive part of economic life and receive attention from different subdisciplines in economics. As we shall explain in this book, institutions include all kinds of social rules and accompanying sanctions that make economic interactions less risky and more predictable, to smooth transactions and increase welfare.

Institutions have always played a role in economic theory and economic policy; for example, to correct market imperfections such as externalities and the abuse of market power through the introduction by governments of laws and regulations. Traditionally, the involvement with institutions was restricted to the rules that make the market function well, but with the arrival of Institutional Economics that changed. Institutional Economics introduced a broad conceptualization of institutions including values and norms, laws and regulations, as well as all kinds of modes of organization, such as market contracts and firms. The central task of Institutional Economics is to explain the emergence of institutions, how they change, and how they affect economic behavior.

Within Institutional Economics, two different schools of thought have developed: Original Institutional Economics (OIE) and New Institutional Economics (NIE). Compared to Neoclassical Economics (NCE), OIE works on very different assumptions about economic behavior and how the relationship with institutions should be modeled, whereas NIE is related much more closely to the principles of NCE. In this book we discuss both schools of Institutional Economics, in an attempt to show how both approaches can contribute to a better understanding of institutions in a complementary way.

Institutional Economics has now found its place in many curricula at universities all over the world, but a textbook in which both the insights of New Institutional and Original Institutional Economics are treated in a balanced way is hard to find. This is why we have taken on the challenge of writing this book. It has been a challenge indeed, because presenting both schools of Institutional Economics to students in an introductory textbook forced us to go back to the fundamentals of both approaches, and to present them in the simplest way possible. In doing so, we have not always been able to focus on all the nuances that exist within both OIE and NIE. We are aware of the many points of overlap between NIE and OIE, and of developments that have taken place in both schools. However, our aim is to make the fundamentals of Institutional Economics as clear as possible to students who have only a basic knowledge of the principles of Neoclassical Economics. It was not our aim to discuss the histories of the approaches, or the many disputes that have arisen between them over the years. Certainly, it was not our aim to classify institutional economists as either strict followers of NIE or of OIE, nor to demonstrate to students who might be right, and who wrong. On the contrary; we aim to show that both approaches have their pros and cons, and that, depending on the research question at hand, it is sometimes preferable to use the ideas of NIE, while on other occasions the OIE perspective may be more suitable.

To avoid the reader getting lost between the differences of opinion that exist among – and even within – the two schools of thought, we have decided to make use of a simple dichotomy, in which the static view is set against the dynamic view on institutions, as can be inferred from both the NIE and OIE approaches.

The book consists of four parts: the introduction; theory; applications to private governance structures; and applications to public governance structures. In Part I we introduce the basic concepts of Institutional Economics, making the reader familiar with its body of thought in an uncomplicated way. In Part II we elaborate on our theoretical framework, which incorporates both the static and dynamic approaches of Institutional Economics, following the insights of NIE and OIE. As transactions are placed central stage in Institutional Economics, much attention is devoted to the different mechanisms through which transactions between actors take place, called governance structures. Hence, we apply the theoretical approaches to private governance structures in Part III, and to public governance structures in Part IV.

JOHN GROENEWEGEN
ANTOON SPITHOVEN
ANNETTE VAN DEN BERG

# Acknowledgments

This book has been created with the help of many people.

In the first place, and foremost, we are very much indebted to the invaluable support given by Jan Kees Winters and Max Heywood, who both devoted much of their free time to help us improve the content of the whole manuscript.

We are also very grateful for the valuable comments given by seven anonymous referees and several of our colleagues. In particular, we want to thank Paul D. Bush, Bas van Groezen, Gerwin van der Laan, Tim Legierse, Katrin Muehlfeld, Peter van Santen, Erwin van Sas, Anna van der Schors and Arild Vatn. All their comments have contributed to the improvement of our text.

We have furthermore benefited from the questions raised by our students while using the draft version of this manuscript in our course at the Utrecht University School of Economics (USE).

Our text has been improved tremendously by the work of Keith Povey Editorial Services Limited. The layout of the book was influenced by Hanneke Mouelhi-Van Nijkerken and Juana Sanchez, while our figures have been redrawn in a professional way with the help of Yolanda Grift, Imre Kaposi and in particular, Malka de Castro Campos. You all did great work!

Words of thanks are in order as well for Jaime Marshall and Neha Sharma of Palgrave publishers, who have been very patient and encouraging throughout.

Finally, we are grateful to the following organizations for permission to reproduce copyright material:

The Center for Responsive Politics/OpenSecrets.org for using their Lobbying database; and

Transparency International for allowing us to use their Corruption Perceptions Index 2008 and Global Corruption Barometer 2007.

# About the Authors

**John Groenewegen** is Professor of the Economics of Infrastructures at Delft University of Technology. His research interests are in economic organization and the relation between institutions and technology.

**Antoon Spithoven** is an Assistant Professor at the Utrecht University School of Economics, where he is a member of the Department of Institutional Economics. His current research interests centre on issues of the ageing of population and health care.

**Annette van den Berg** is an Assistant Professor at the Utrecht University School of Economics, where she is a member of the Department of Institutional Economics. Her main research interests concern corporate governance issues, notably the role of worker participation.

# List of Abbreviations

| | |
|---|---|
| CEO | chief executive officer |
| EC | European Commission |
| ENEPRI | European Network of Economic Policy Research Institutes |
| EU | European Union |
| FDA | Food and Drug Administration |
| GAO | Government Accountability Office (USA) |
| GDP | gross domestic product |
| GM | General Motors |
| ICT | information and communication technologies |
| IMF | International Monetary Fund |
| INSEE | Institut National de la Statistique et des Études Économiques (France) |
| KPCS | Kimberly Process Certification Scheme |
| LCD | liquid crystal display |
| NATO | North Atlantic Treaty Organization |
| NCE | Neoclassical Economics |
| NHS | National Health Service (UK) |
| NIE | New Institutional Economics |
| OECD | Organisation for Economic Co-operation and Development |
| OIE | Original Institutional Economics |
| OPEC | Organization of the Petroleum Exporting Countries |
| RAPEX | Rapid Alert System for non-food consumer products (EU) |
| R&D | research and development |
| SEC | Securities and Exchange Commission |
| SEZ | Special Economic Zones (China) |
| TCE | Transaction Cost Economics |
| UN | United Nations |
| UNESCO | United Nations Educational, Scientific and Cultural Organization |
| WHO | World Health Organization |
| WTO | World Trade Organization |

# PART I

# Introduction

Chapter 1  What Is Institutional Economics About?

# INTRODUCTION

In this first part of the book you will become acquainted with the basic notions of Institutional Economics. We shall show how these elementary concepts can be applied to a range of real-life examples, to underline the relevance of this field of study.

If you are a student of economics, your first courses will probably have dealt with the principles of Macroeconomics and Microeconomics, and with an introduction to Business Economics. Most probably you will have learned about the ways that consumers maximize utility and how managers aim to maximize profits, and you might have been taught how to calculate these profits. You have possibly also been introduced to the way in which firms keep their books and report annual results to the shareholders.

In all probability, these introductory economics courses have focused on running a business in a somewhat idealized world, in which managers do their utmost to reach the highest possible profits, and in which they allocate workers and machines in an optimal way. In such an idealized representation of the working of an economy, consumers are also well-off, since they are pictured as individuals who know exactly where they can buy high quality products at the best prices. People and the world around them are rather abstract in the sense that much of the real life context is left out. They are modeled with a specific type of rationality, they receive information through prices, and are positioned in precisely defined market structures. No attention is paid to the question of how transactions are coordinated, or what costs are involved in concluding transactions.

In Part I of this book you will learn that Institutional Economics focuses explicitly on transactions in the economy, and how these transactions are coordinated. You will learn that the type of coordination has everything to do with the transaction costs involved and how institutions can reduce those costs. You will also learn, by means of examples, what underlies the fact that transactions are not costless, and how this gives rise to the creation and evolution of institutions that can make the coordination of transactions less costly. Broadly speaking, institutions are rules that facilitate transactions. One thing you will come to realize is that, if institutions are meant to facilitate transactions and improve efficiency, this does not mean that they always succeed in doing so. In the economy, vested interests may exist; that is, people seek to maintain and control institutions because they derive specific private benefits from them. The actions of vested interests may lead to institutions that fail to facilitate transactions that are welfare-enhancing to society at large and only serve the interests of specific groups. In addition, you will learn that institutions may sometimes prove to be ineffective when individuals show opportunistic behavior and evade the rules successfully.

People try to correct such opportunism by changing the institutions. You will learn in Part I that institutions change over time, and that such changes are the result partly of purposeful actions of people, and partly of an unintended spontaneous process. Institutions may be adhered to voluntarily or they may have to be enforced.

You will see that the world of institutions is rather complex. In order to make complexities understandable, the theories in Institutional Economics make abstractions of the complex world and often present institutions in a static way. In Part I you will become acquainted with both the static and the dynamic perspectives on institutions. Moreover, you will learn about two approaches through which institutions are understood – from an efficiency perspective and from a vested interest perspective.

Finally, you will be able to infer from Part I how managers of firms and governmental policy-makers can use the insights of Institutional Economics to improve the performance of both their firms and their national economies. However, before we discuss real-life policy issues, you need to know about the subject matter of Institutional Economics.

# 1 What Is Institutional Economics About?

## CONTENTS

- **Introduction: a world of transactions**
- **Coordinating transactions in a complex world**
  - Problematic transactions in real life
- **Institutional Economics**
  - Transactions
  - Optimizing behavior and opportunism
  - Risks and uncertainties
  - Perfect competition and efficiency
  - Market imperfections
  - Transaction costs
  - Institutions
  - Economic systems and governance structures
  - The subject matter of Institutional Economics
- **Institutions matter**
  - Institutions and development
- **A brief outline of the book**
  - Pirate economics: a preview of what you will find in this book
- **Review questions**
- **Appendixes**

## INTRODUCTION: A WORLD OF TRANSACTIONS

Loosely speaking, institutions are rules that facilitate transactions. So, what are transactions and why would special rules be needed to facilitate them?

All over the world, people do business with each other by transacting products such as goods, money, information and services. In other words, they come to an agreement and coordinate transactions. They could be self-employed, producing and selling products themselves; they could employ others; or they could be earning a salary working for someone else. Or perhaps they are not able to work for whatever reason and depend on family, the local community or the state for income. The creation of products and incomes enables people to trade money for goods and services, and vice versa.

All this would not be necessary if individuals could produce everything they needed themselves, but that is hardly ever the case. It has been known for a long time that specialization can increase overall productivity, and hence the economic growth of a society. If there is a focus on the production of just one or a few items, this can be done more efficiently and will, for example, increase workers' experience, which in turn can speed up and increase production.

Of course, specialization is only possible if people can transact their surplus production. So, along with specialization, places for transactions, 'market places' developed. Through the ages, the network of markets and firms has increased tremendously through the development of technology, which has enlarged transport and communication possibilities. As a result, there are now numerous ways of exchanging products. These range from small shops and local banks to shopping malls and electronic banking for consumers; from local investment projects to international stock exchanges for investors; and from local suppliers to large auctions for tradesmen, to name just a few. Transactions can take place between private individuals or organizations, but often also involve the (inter) national government, which can act both as a producer and a consumer of products. We shall use the term *actor* to describe any decision-maker in an economic activity (production, distribution, consumption), be they an individual, a group of individuals, an organization, a firm or a government.

Historically, people traded mainly on a local scale, but reduction in transport and communication costs down the centuries has meant that over time the world has became 'smaller' so that these days people are able to transact their products worldwide. We often buy goods or services without knowing the sellers personally, and without being able to estimate the true quality of what we are purchasing before buying. We lend or borrow money without always being able to gauge the trustworthiness of the other party or parties involved. In other words, transactions take place in a world that is characterized by incomplete information.

The question is, in what circumstances do these transactions run smoothly, and how can the successes and failures of transactions be explained? We shall see that sometimes different actors in the market place could potentially benefit from a transaction, but they are not able to reach an agreement because they might mistrust each other too much, or they are not able to reduce uncertainty sufficiently. We shall explain in this book that in some cases private organizations (such as a firm, or a joint venture) and in other cases public organizations (such as a ministry, or a regulator) can help to facilitate the transactions.

At this point it is convenient to define for the remainder of this book the word *product* as the catch-all term for any entity that can be transacted; namely, goods, services, resources, capital, labor, assets, money or (intellectual) property rights. An innumerable number of products are produced with the aim of selling them on the market. In order to start producing, investment is usually needed first. If people do not have enough capital for the investment themselves, they have to convince others that it is worthwhile to invest money in their business. On the basis sometimes of trust alone, but more often on the basis of a sound business plan, capital can be raised to start a business venture. Individuals may entrust their savings to a venture and become shareholders, or a bank may entrust its money to a venture by providing a loan. Once the business is in operation, it must convince potential customers that it is worthwhile to buy its products.

Several protection devices (safeguards) need to be in place to enhance the trust of (prospective) creditors and customers. On the one hand, creditors will need to be reasonably sure that they will get their investment back and earn a profit on it as well. And on the other hand, consumers will need to be reasonably sure that they are getting value for money. These safeguards can be private or public. Private safeguards include collateral, or the threat of fines or higher interest rates in the case of increased risk of debtor default. For consumers, warranties and guarantee funds can contribute to trust. Another quite effective method to incite businesses to be trustworthy can be the presence of critical consumer associations that inform the public about good and bad business practices. Public safeguards include governmental regulations, such as contract law, that may serve as legal backup in case of problems between the company and its creditors, or between the company and its customers. The latter could, for example, be dissatisfied with the quality of the products they have acquired and turn to a court to have a judge decide the issue.

Despite the presence of safeguards, transactions often run into difficulties and end in conflict. Disagreements can sometimes be resolved by the private parties themselves, but quite frequently a public authority has to settle the dispute. These events may lead to new safeguards being introduced. It can also happen that no solutions are found at all, in which case the transaction fails altogether.

Transactions can be accompanied by all kinds of complications. Sometimes people do not live up to an agreement because they think they can get away with it. They may take advantage of the fact that others cannot always observe their actions. Employees may work less hard than they are supposed to if they can pull it off. Shopkeepers may profitably sell poor quality products if consumers can only discover the quality after they have bought the product. This applies to new technical gadgets of which consumers have no experience; or a used auto that might look perfect on the outside but turns out to have hidden defects which only become obvious some time after it is driven. Or managers who have been entrusted with other people's money may spend it rashly or for their own benefit, as was the case in 2008 with former Nasdaq manager, Bernard Madoff. He offered an investment scheme with a guaranteed high profitability, but these high profits were provided by new investors and not by productive activities, so that in the end the system could no longer be sustained and his clients jointly lost over 50 billion dollars. This kind of fraud is also known as a Ponzi scheme, after Charles Ponzi, who first introduced it.

Alternatively, people take advantage of the fact that others are dependent on them. For example, the sole supplier of an indispensable product may be able to raise its price because there is no competition. Or one of the few employers in a region may be able to succeed in forcing employees to accept less advantageous terms of employment. It could also be that certain individuals form a powerful interest group that is able to manipulate the government so that rules are made or maintained in their favor, to the disadvantage of the majority.

Next we look at some interesting real-life examples of problems worldwide involving transactions, and the steps that people have taken to deal with such problems by creating institutions.

## COORDINATING TRANSACTIONS IN A COMPLEX WORLD

Earlier we raised the question of under what circumstances transactions either run smoothly or not, and how this can be explained. This refers to the coordination of transactions: how does the transaction between actors take place? Despite the fact that we exchange products in a modern society that is characterized by its complexity, there are several ways to make sure that all parties involved in a contract keep their promises and deliver what they have agreed to do. Often these transactions are beneficial for both sides, because both know that usually it is in the other party's best interest to comply with their part of the deal, and that if they do not, there are written and unwritten rules and mechanisms at the injured party's disposal to enforce compliance. These rules we call *institutions* and can – for the moment – be described loosely as rules and accompanying sanctions that can make interactions less risky and more predictable; in that way, institutions are meant to provide certain safeguards before entering into a transaction. Consequently, transactions may run smoothly.

The examples below will show that we can distinguish several different circumstances in which transactions do (or did) not run smoothly, at least not in first instance, and give (or gave) rise to the introduction of institutions. We shall start by presenting these illustrations without much interpretation. After this overview, we shall attempt to interpret these coordination difficulties with the aid of Institutional Economics. We shall also be ready to provide a more elaborate definition of institutions.

## Problematic transactions in real life

### *Enron and Parmalat*

In most developed countries there are heated debates about good corporate governance. In a nutshell, this refers to the way in which firms are run, not only for the benefit of shareholders but also for the benefit of all other stakeholders, such as employees, suppliers, banks and people living in the vicinity of the firm. These debates caught the attention of the public as a result of several large business scandals in the beginning of the twenty-first century, of which the Enron case in the USA, and the accounting scandal of Parmalat in Italy are just two infamous examples.

What these scandals have in common is that several of their top managers misinformed the public about the profitability of the business. By deliberately creating the impression that they were making high profits, these executives made investors believe it was a good idea to supply capital to the firm. It is unclear to what degree the top management of these firms also misled the outside auditors who were supposed to monitor them in order to publish reliable accounts of the annual returns, or whether in fact management and auditors were in collusion. But the bottom line was that, when the fraud became known, it caused a sharp fall in the share prices of these firms, bringing serious harm not only to shareholders but also to employees and suppliers. Enron and its auditor became bankrupt and many people lost their jobs as a result. Parmalat also filed for bankruptcy because of huge debts, but it was saved by the efforts of its own personnel, the trade unions and the national government. Despite the subsequent recovery of Parmalat, several creditors and many small savers lost a large amount of money. As a reaction to these and other scandals, public rules with respect to corporate governance became stricter all over the world, in order to restore investor confidence.

## *The financial crisis*

An even more infamous example of failing corporate governance is the worldwide financial crisis that came to the fore in 2008. In the USA, high mortgages were sold to people who would never be able to repay them because of a lack of income and assets, while the houses purchased were not valuable enough to redeem the mortgages. These mortgages were bundled with other mortgages and formed the basis (collateral) for other types of financial products, in such a way that it was completely unclear as to the real value of the products. These packages were sold to banks and private investors worldwide for a much higher price than the factual underlying risks warranted.

As a result of the improper assessment of risks, banking assets were valued too highly. As a consequence, once this was discovered, the ratio between debts and assets worsened. Since no one knew, not even the banks themselves, the extent of this valuation problem, the banks were unable to estimate the true value of their assets. This led to problems of confidence among the general public; the fear rose that if, the public no longer trusted the banks, individuals would try to withdraw their savings and investments, which would lead to a collapse of one bank after another, as banks are connected financially via interbank lending. This lending came to an almost stop. Some banks indeed became bankrupt, some were saved by the government – hence by the taxpayers, and this financial crisis affected the real economy in that reduced lending and lowered confidence had a negative influence on investments and consumption, with the consequence of reduced growth, or even depression and increasing unemployment.

Expert observers argue that the unsound business deals that underlay the crisis came about as a result of the incentive pay systems in the whole commercial sector. In a nutshell, the argument runs as follows. Incentive or performance-based pay systems were introduced originally as a way of aligning the interests of managers with those of the owners (see also Chapter 6). Reaching certain growth targets benefited both the shareholders in terms of higher stock values and dividends, and the managers in terms of much higher salaries. But eventually these performance-based pay systems incited many executives in charge to take great risks in providing financial products (the risks being virtually unknown to almost everybody). In Part IV you can read more about the way governments have intervened to deal with these problems.

## *Watchdogs and boycotts*

Businesses that do not transact honorably do not always need to be set straight by means of public, legally-enforced mechanisms. Sometimes private intervention may work just as well, if facts about the company are revealed. Many multinational companies are permanently monitored by special interest groups and the media ('watchdogs'), which inform the public if the companies are found to be violating ethical or legal norms. Familiar examples include watchdogs that uncovered firms using child labor in developing countries, mainly in Africa and Asia, or firms that were cooperating with authoritarian regimes that suppress their citizens.

Because of the great advance of the internet in particular, people all over the world can now learn more easily about corporate abuses. As a consequence, action groups are able to launch consumer boycotts, hoping that businesses not complying with ethical norms can be forced to adjust their strategies if their income is affected. Boycotts have been launched against firms such as PepsiCo, Heineken and Austrian Airlines because they were doing business with the military government of Burma (Myanmar). These boycotts turned out to be very effective, since these companies all left the country shortly afterwards. In other instances, after being targeted, firms stopped using child labor (such as firms in the sportswear industry) or developed better working conditions overall (for example, firms in the fast-food industry were responsive to a campaign that promoted 'fair food').

## *Microsoft*

The examples presented so far refer to situations of incomplete information, where customers were at first unaware of social wrongs and/or which firms were deliberately trying to mislead the public. It could also be the case, however, that organizations or even individuals may openly cause harm to investors or consumers, simply because they are powerful enough to do so. As soon as a party has control over a highly desired product or resource for which few or no substitutes are available, it will have the power to increase the price of the product. A well-known case in point is the company Microsoft, the world's market leader in software thanks to the Windows operating system for personal computers. Because of this supremacy, Microsoft seems to have been able to obstruct attempts by producers of competing software to enter the market successfully.

Two cases stand out. In the last decade of the twentieth century, Microsoft included the browser Internet Explorer in Windows without charge, and forced computer suppliers to install Windows including this browser. This reduced the browser sales of its competitor Netscape tremendously, and led to a long-lasting antitrust trial in the USA. Eventually, a settlement was reached in which it was determined that Microsoft had to make its server protocols publicly known, so that its competitors would be able to develop compatible software. In a second trial in 2007, the European Commission had Microsoft convicted for abusing its market power in several ways. Among other things, it was accused of a similar offence as in the Netscape case, because it had bundled the program Media Player with Windows, again making it virtually impossible for other suppliers to compete effectively. Microsoft was also convicted for not making known to competitors, Sun being one of them, the information necessary to build Windows-compatible (or interoperable) work group server systems.

## *Gazprom*

Not only firms can have dominant market positions; nation states can have them as well if they have access to an important resource, such as oil or gas, say. This was illustrated vividly by the gas conflicts in Europe since 2004, initiated by the Russian state enterprise Gazprom. This company delivers natural gas through pipelines to both Western and Eastern European countries, which have hardly any alternative suppliers. As from 2004, Gazprom gradually started to demand higher prices for its gas from the former Soviet republics that used to pay a low, subsidized price. After becoming independent, these countries were faced with price increases to double or more than double the old price, leading to much protest. Countries such as the Ukraine and Belarus first refused to agree and started negotiations to prevent the price increase, claiming that Gazprom had no legal right to unilaterally change the terms of the contract, and that this would jeopardize their competitiveness. Gazprom, in turn, refused to give in and threatened to cut off the gas supply to these countries, which it did in fact, in early 2004 in the case of Belarus and early 2006 in the case of the Ukraine. Shortly afterwards, negotiations resumed, leading to some concessions on both sides, though Gazprom gained the most. Early in 2009 the story repeated itself once again, affecting several European countries; Bulgaria in particular was hit very hard by Gazprom's behavior.

These conflicts made clear the European Union's high dependence on Russian gas. On the other hand, Russia is also highly dependent on European gas payments as a source of income. This interdependence means in fact that neither side can abuse its position for very long, because this will create ultimately an unwanted boomerang effect. If one of the parties puts its reputation as a reliable business partner at stake, the other party will start to look for substitutes. In fact, in Europe, these events have stimulated the search for alternative sources of energy.

## *Protectionism*

Transactions can also be hampered by the protectionist behavior of nation states. At present, more than 140 nations, including the USA, China and all the member countries of the European Union (EU countries) are members of the World Trade Organization (WTO), which promotes free trade worldwide. All the WTO member states have signed a set of multilateral rules governing international trade, obliging them to treat their trading partners equally based on the principle of nondiscrimination. In addition, WTO members have committed themselves to reduce import tariffs and unfair subsidies. The aim is to ensure that trade can flow everywhere, ultimately benefiting all parties concerned.

Despite their WTO membership, some of the main proponents of free trade, namely the USA and the EU, have recently taken several protectionist measures. The reasons are diverse but perhaps the main one is the mounting threat from so-called 'low-wage countries' (most notably Asian nations such as China and India) to the competitiveness of (American and European) industrial sectors, and consequently to domestic employment. Interest groups such as national industries and trade unions have urged the EU and the US government to take protectionist measures – for example, by restricting the import of Chinese products such as textiles, chemicals and steel. However, the gains for these beneficiaries of protectionism generally will not compensate for the costs of the losers: because of the restrictions, American and European consumers will pay more for these products than would have been the case under free trade. Moreover, producers and workers in the low-wage countries could have earned more, and used their increased purchasing power to buy more from the USA and the EU.

Many observers question whether, in practice, the World Trade Organization has the power to force its own members to adhere to the rules they have jointly formulated.

## *Global warming*

Sometimes transactions lead to side effects, which can be harmful to third parties not involved in those transactions at all. One of the most significant examples of such side effects in the world today is carbon dioxide, released into the air by factories, autos and airplanes. This gas has the property of trapping the sun's heat within the atmosphere. A little carbon dioxide is good; without it, life would not have developed. The problem is that there is overwhelming evidence that excessive emissions are causing the Earth to overheat, according to the United Nations' Intergovernmental Panel on Climate Change. The Earth's average temperature is said to have risen by 0.75° C during the past century, and is likely to continue rising. This is already causing problems, such as the melting of the polar icecaps. As these melt, the level of the oceans will rise, leading to flooding in many areas of the world, and potentially massive changes in the weather.

So why is it so difficult to combat global warming? The main issue is that carbon dioxide is a by-product of economic activity. This means that in the absence of technological breakthroughs, countries may have to reduce their economic growth in order to cut carbon emissions. Very few countries are willing to do this unilaterally, sacrificing their growth while allowing others to benefit from this reduction; curbing emissions will require coordinated action. And coordinating action is very difficult, as was seen at the Bali global warming conference in December 2007, where essentially many of the major players said that others should act first before they themselves begin to make serious reductions.

## *Hurricane Katrina*

These examples show that, when a large group of people have a common goal, some in the group tend to try to get other group members to make a greater effort than they do themselves. This may lead to neglect and to a situation in which a specific desirable transaction does not come about at all, or at least not in sufficient quantities. The drastic consequences of such a situation are illustrated by a famous example of a failing defense system against flooding. In late August 2005, the city of New Orleans was devastated as a result of Hurricane Katrina. The severe storm and tidal surge caused so many breaches in the local dikes (known as 'levées') that most of the town was flooded, leading to about thousand casualties and leaving hundreds of thousands of people homeless. The rebuilding process was, and still is, very costly and will take many years.

Shortly after this catastrophe occurred, many observers made a comparison with the Dutch flooding disaster of 1953. Here too, the neglected dikes burst as a result of a big storm, causing major damage to a large area and the loss of more than 1,800 lives. Immediately after that terrible event, the Dutch government quickly revived plans to defend low-lying land against new flooding. By means of public funds, the so-called Delta Works were built: a series of dams and barriers able to withstand the ultimate storm. In the case of New Orleans, it was also known that the levées were not sufficiently strong, yet despite several warnings not enough was done about it. This inaction was largely because of the problem of generating enough funds to finance this huge project. For the – largely poor – inhabitants of the area, it would have been too expensive to pay for it all themselves. Furthermore, they knew that the National Congress had approved a large construction budget, specifically to support costly projects like theirs. These two reasons may explain why, a few years before the disaster, the local residents rejected a proposed tax increase to fund further improvements in the levees.

After several years of debate about who or what was to blame for the damage, in early 2008 a federal judge produced his verdict. He found that the US Army Corps of Engineers, the agency that was established in 1965 as a result of prior flooding, had neglected to provide flood protection for the citizens of New Orleans. The crucial failure was that, at a federal level, large funds had been made available for water projects nationwide, but that in the end the money was allocated on the basis of political power and lobbying, and not on the basis of the greatest urgency.

With this we round off our exposé of real-life examples of problematic transactions. Next, we shall show that the discipline of Institutional Economics focuses on the explanation of the different ways in which transactions take place.

## INSTITUTIONAL ECONOMICS

Institutional Economics concerns itself with explaining the different ways in which individuals transact; in other words, how do they coordinate their transactions? Institutions assist in coordinating transactions smoothly at low cost. But institutions are not only about efficiency. They also distribute rights and duties with implications for who reaps the benefits and who meets the costs. As with any other scientific discipline, Institutional Economics starts from several assumptions and uses particular definitions, which we shall address below.

### Transactions

A central concept in Institutional Economics is *transactions*. Several definitions of transactions exist in the literature, and the following description summarizes the most important features. It is vital to stress that a transaction comprises a (legal) transfer of ownership and therefore includes an exchange of rights and duties, which have been determined by the transaction parties or society involved. Transactions are not just the 'exchange of commodities, but the alienation and acquisition, between individuals, of the rights of property and liberty created by society, which must therefore be negotiated between the parties concerned before labor can produce, or consumers can consume, or commodities can be physically exchanged.' (Commons, 1931, p. 652).

The implication of this broad meaning of a transaction will become clearer after having introduced the three types of transactions that can be distinguished (based on Commons, 1931; and Furubotn and Richter, 1998):

- *The market transaction*, which takes place in the market between individual buyers and sellers, resulting in a voluntary transfer of property to customers and a transfer of money to suppliers. Market transactions, also referred to as 'bargaining transactions' (Commons, 1931), concern the exchange of ownership between actors who are legal equals. However, legal equality is compatible with economic inequality: bargaining power determines what the price will be.

- *The managerial transaction* is characterized by the relationship between a legal superior and a legal inferior within an organization. This type of transaction is between one person in control (the manager, employer or master) and one being managed or ordered (the employee).
- *The political transaction* is agreed on by decision-makers, who have the legal authority to determine how wealth in society should be distributed. When a country produces goods and services, then all kinds of laws, regulations and organizations decide about how the costs and benefits of the national wealth are distributed among the members of society. It can be that the distribution of property rights determines the distribution of wealth, but it can also very well be that a collective decision is taken in society to redistribute wealth through taxes and social allowances. Political transactions are about the rules that distribute costs and benefits. Clearly those transactions are decided by government, but it could also be a private consultative body such as an employers' association and trade unions that jointly settle on the terms of employment (think about minimum wages or working hours, for example); in this context, the term 'rationing transactions' is also used (Commons, 1931).

From this it follows that the question of whether a transaction can take place and under what conditions, is determined not only by competition and scarcity, but also by the institutional setting of laws and rules reflecting economic and political power. In Institutional Economics, much attention is paid to the distribution of power between interest groups in society. From the daily headlines in the news we know that much of political debate is about the distribution of wealth: who should get what, and who is to meet the costs? In Institutional Economics, the answer to that question is not that 'the market will take care of it'. No, every allocation mechanism in the economy is part of a wider environment in which laws, rules and organizations determine the outcomes of markets. It is the role of this environment and its influence on the behavior of the economic actors that Institutional Economics places central stage.

## Optimizing behavior and opportunism

The examples above show that transactions are not coordinated in a vacuum. In order to make people exchange their surpluses they need to have enough certainty that such a transaction will make them better off. In standard economic theory it is assumed that people strive after self-interest, which means that they want to improve their own welfare. In economic terms, welfare is denoted by 'profit' or 'utility'. Individuals are supposed to maximize their utility or their profits, which at the same time implies that they are minimizing costs. In other words, people are assumed to show *optimizing behavior*. If they show this intentional behavior aimed at the realization of clear objectives, then economists say people are showing *rational behavior*. In Appendix A to this chapter we shall elaborate briefly on this concept of rationality.

On many occasions, optimizing behavior leads to an outcome that benefits others, intentionally or unintentionally. An example of the former is an altruistic person who derives personal utility from helping others. However, the more common case is when private transactions unintentionally promote the well-being of third parties: this is often referred to as the *invisible hand*. The invisible hand metaphor basically states that while every individual is motivated by his own interests, he also serves the interests of other people and of society at large as well. This expression was introduced by the great philosopher and economist, Adam Smith. In the context of the invisible hand, he wrote: 'It is not from the benevolence of the butcher, the brewer or the baker that we expect our dinner, but from their regard to their own self-interest. We address ourselves, not to their humanity, but to their self-love, and never talk to them of our own necessities but of their advantages.' (Smith, 1776, p. 14).

The benevolent invisible hand presupposes that the parties involved behave according to the assumptions as described in Appendix A to this chapter. If they do not do so, if the assumptions are changed, individual optimizing behavior can lead to an outcome that harms others; we have already seen some examples of this earlier in the chapter. When two actors have signed a contract and the supplier of the goods decides that it is in her own interest not to deliver, then she can decide to break the contract. A selfish person can calculate whether the utility of following or breaking the contract pays the most. Institutional Economics pays much attention to selfish behavior. In Chapter 3 of this book you will learn about problems around contracting, and how people include clauses to protect themselves against the consequences of the selfish behavior of others. In Chapter 4 we ask the question of how institutions can evolve spontaneously when selfish individuals are driven by an invisible hand.

In reality you not only have to deal with people that are selfish, but also with actors that in the pursuit of self-interest deliberately take advantage of information asymmetries at the expense of other people. In Institutional Economics this behavior is called *opportunistic behavior*. It is often described by institutional economists as 'self-interest seeking with guile' (this expression was coined by the well-known institutional economist and 2009 Nobel Laureate, Oliver Williamson) referring to the fact that one may try to achieve one's goals through lying and cheating.

Institutional Economics teaches under what set of conditions you can expect opportunistic behavior, when you should protect yourself, and which instruments are available to you. Institutional Economics also teaches you that opportunism depends on the wider environment of norms and values. You will learn that in one society, or market, people are inclined to opportunism, but that in another environment they tend to trust each other.

## Risks and uncertainties

Ideally, people should always take into account that optimizing behavior may lead to undesirable outcomes, even if this was not the intention of any of the transaction parties involved. As has already been mentioned, the wise thing to do is to build in safeguards to that effect before a business deal is concluded. Protective measures are needed to save people from making a loss as a result of economic risks and uncertainties.

We define *risk* as a situation in which it is known what the probability is of a set of given (known) possible outcomes. As an example, throwing a dice has six possible outcomes; and each outcome has a probability (generally speaking) of one in six. Or, the risk (probability) that you will lose your luggage during a flight with a US airline has been estimated to amount to, let's say, 0.8 percent.

We define *uncertainty* as a situation in which it is not known what (exactly) is the set of all possible outcomes and/or a situation in which it is not known what is the probability of a possible outcome. For example, it is uncertain how much oil an oil company will have in reserve in the longer run; moreover, it is uncertain how future technological developments might lower the costs of supplying alternative sources of energy. Because of these uncertainties, oil companies may be reluctant to make large investments in oil exploration, even if the price of oil is high at a given moment, which theoretically should provide an incentive to invest.

Risks and uncertainties may also result from the behavior of business partners, or more broadly, from any form of market imperfections, which we shall deal with below.

## Perfect competition and efficiency

The benchmark for market imperfections is the neoclassical market model of *perfect competition*, which is characterized by its efficient outcome. In Appendix A to this chapter you will find more background information about the underlying assumptions and graphical analysis of markets in Neoclassical Economics, and their relationship with efficiency. Here we confine ourselves to the essential aspects of the standard model of perfect competition. This model assumes that transactions are conducted in a fully transparent world by many buyers and sellers, so that nobody can individually influence the price to her own advantage. In equilibrium, the competitive price will equal the marginal costs of production. Perfectly competitive markets are said to result in an optimal allocation: with all relevant information being available, rational individuals will arrive at the best possible trading conditions (among other things, with respect to price and quality of both products and production factors). Economic welfare is then maximized for society at large.

Two types of efficiency are relevant here: productive (or technical) efficiency, and allocative efficiency. The former simply means that any amount of a product is produced at the lowest possible costs given a specific technology. The latter type of efficiency includes the preferences of the consumers and the efficient allocation of resources (including inputs): it is one thing to produce at the lowest costs possible, but it is another thing to produce something consumers prefer to consume, so that resources (inputs and outputs) are allocated in the most efficient way. In economics, the concept of Pareto efficiency is often encountered: this is similar to allocative efficiency and stresses in its definition the role of the given preferences of individuals. *Pareto efficiency* is reached if it is not possible to improve anybody's welfare without decreasing the welfare of another person. This is also known as the 'first best solution' (see Appendix B to this chapter). The attainment of such an allocative efficient outcome is what Adam Smith meant by the invisible hand mechanism.

Economists draw attention to the fact that a Pareto efficient solution holds under a specific given distribution of resources among the members of society. If this distribution is changed (through political transactions) then the preferences expressed via the market change, and consequently the allocation of resources changes too.

Both productive and allocative efficiency are forms of *static efficiency*, as opposed to the third type of efficiency that can be distinguished, namely *dynamic efficiency*. This latter type occurs if, as a result of technological developments (innovation), production or distribution techniques are improved; for example, as a reaction to real or potential pressure from competitors. Institutional Economics is very interested in the conditions that facilitate innovations, in the role of entrepreneurs who take risks and enter markets with new products, in exactly how the process of innovation works, what role governments can play, and so on. You will learn in later chapters that some societies are more efficient in the dynamic sense than others. Institutional economists argue that these differences have a lot to do with the institutional environment in which entrepreneurs operate.

## Market imperfections

We continue our discussion on efficiency by staying close to our benchmark of the standard model of perfect competition, which is characterized by allocative efficiency. From that perspective we speak of a market imperfection when the market does not correspond with the basic assumptions of the standard model of perfect competition, so that inefficiencies are generated. In real markets you may encounter several types of market imperfections, leading to efficiency losses to a lesser or greater degree. In succession, we shall elaborate on the following market imperfections:

- imperfect information;
- market power;
- pure public goods;
- externalities and (de)merit goods; and
- natural monopolies.

We shall show in Chapters 5 to 7 when and how private actors deal with these problems by making additional institutional arrangements. In several situations, however, they will not be able to come up with solutions themselves. Therefore, you will see in Chapter 8 that an important aim of government policy in a market economy is about dealing with the imperfections so that the market can function as well as possible. In Figure 1.4 in Appendix B we present a diagram that roughly indicates in which circumstances market imperfections could be counteracted, and in the preferred way of doing so. This scheme is elaborated throughout Parts III and IV of this book.

### *Imperfect information*

Contrary to what is assumed under perfect competition, in reality people are usually not fully informed. This is denoted by the term *imperfect information*. Roughly speaking, information can either be unequally distributed among the different actors, or knowledge can be imperfect for all the actors involved in a transaction. Both situations cause risks and uncertainty, and will be illustrated below.

The first type of imperfect information occurs when some economic actors have more knowledge than others, which they could use to their advantage. This is referred to as *asymmetric information*. Insiders in the security markets (where shares and bonds are traded) may have information that outsiders do not have; and some people with connections to a certain company may know that it is about to publish bad results and gain by selling their shares just before the announcement. When other investors find out about this, they may lose confidence in the stock market and perhaps stop trading. If this abuse of foreknowledge (also known as insider trading) occurs frequently, it will lead to a downward spiral in which ever-fewer people are willing to buy shares, making it more difficult for entrepreneurs to acquire capital for their businesses. In the end, this process will have a negative effect on economic growth. That is why, in most countries, authorities try to prevent insider trading by declaring it illegal.

The corporate governance scandals of Enron and Parmalat also show how certain individuals (in this case the top managers) acted opportunistically by abusing information asymmetries to their own advantage, thereby causing serious harm to other stakeholders of the firms.

The second instance of imperfect information is a situation in which there is a fundamental lack of information for all actors involved. One interesting illustration of this is a phenomenon that often occurs at auctions and leads to the *winner's curse*. Imagine that during an auction several actors can bid for a product, but none of them knows its exact value. The original example refers to the oil industry in which a number of oil companies search for new oil fields and compete for drilling rights. Because the true value of the oil field is unknown and must be estimated, it can be assumed that the various companies obtain different assessments of this value from their experts. The auction will be won by the highest bidder, and the chances are that the experts advising the winner will have made too high an estimation of the true value of the oil field, in which case the winner turns out be a loser: he is 'cursed' (Thaler, 1988, p. 192).

Both types of imperfect information lead to an inefficient market outcome. Even though transactions may take place, insufficient information about the true value of the product being traded results in prices that are too high and/or quality that is too low. Consequently, the total number of transactions is not optimal, compared to the perfectly competitive outcome.

## *Market power*

Contrary to conditions of perfect competition in which none of the profit maximizing market parties influences the price (leading to equality between price and marginal costs), *market power* is the ability of a single seller or a group of sellers to set the price above the level of marginal costs. Market types that involve market power are monopoly, oligopoly and monopolistic competition. In all these market structures, suppliers are able to set prices and possibly to make a profit higher than the profit would have been in a perfectly competitive world.

A market imperfection can also be caused by the demand side of the market. This is the case in a monopsony, in which a single buyer has the power to pay a price that is below the competitive level. There is more (technical) background information about these different forms of imperfect competition in Appendix A to this chapter. Here it suffices to stress that: when either on the supply side or on the demand side of the market only one or a few firms are active, and they are able to deter others from entering the same market, then powerful suppliers will have the opportunity to set a higher price than if they had experienced more pressure from competitors, while powerful buyers are able to set a lower price than there would be in the presence of other rivals.

Competition can be curbed by private actors in several ways. A barrier to entering an industry occurs when an actor has (almost) sole access to an important resource. Think back to the Gazprom example earlier in the chapter; this state-owned company is the only supplier of gas to many countries, which puts it in a very powerful position. This was demonstrated by the huge price increases Gazprom demanded for continuing to deliver gas to the former Soviet republics. A decrease in competition can also occur if a group of firms agree to reduce mutual rivalry by jointly reducing the supply to the market, which will have an upward effect on the price. A well-known example of this is the OPEC (Organization of the Petroleum Exporting Countries) cartel in the oil industry (see also Chapter 7). Entrance to the industry may also be blocked by legal rules, which we shall discuss in Part IV.

## *Externalities*

The decisions of the consumers or producers of a good or a service sometimes have direct costs or benefits for others who are not involved in the transaction. These effects are called *externalities*. An externality is an economic side effect not addressed by the market, and consequently not reflected in the prices. The effects may be positive (benefits) or negative (costs). Some classic examples of positive externalities include: people making improvements to their real estate, thus increasing the quality of life of a neighborhood, which then raises prices of other real estate in that area; a beekeeper whose bees yield honey and at the same time pollinate nearby orchards, thereby contributing to the crop of the fruit growers; and a creamery that increases demand for milk by advertising, which all creameries benefit from freely. Examples of negative externalities include: people playing loud music and annoying their neighbors, people throwing down trash in public places, and production processes causing environmental problems, such as air or water pollution. These actions may be convenient for the individual directly concerned in the transaction, but they reduce the welfare of others without having to pay for it.

If externalities occur, there is a discrepancy between private and social costs or benefits, which means that an efficient outcome is not possible. Positive externalities may result in an under-allocation of resources, because the consumer or producer of the product cannot charge the benefiting third party for their gains; consequently, the traded quantity falls short of what is optimal. Negative externalities may result in an over-allocation of resources, because the consumer or producer of the product is not charged for the costs she imposes on others; consequently, the traded quantity on the market is too high. The example of global warming at the beginning of this chapter illustrates the high costs for third parties that can be the result of a negative externality, in this case in the form of carbon emissions causing an imminent threat to the natural environment and the health of the population.

A special subcategory of externalities concerns so-called *merit goods* and *demerit goods*. Merit goods are products that (supposedly) are good for the consumers themselves, and in addition have positive external effects, while demerit goods are products that (supposedly) are bad for the direct users and in addition have negative external effects. The idea is that individual consumers are not always aware of the benefits generated by merit goods or the disadvantages of demerit goods. A (paternalistic) government may then take steps to actively promote the consumption of the former, while discouraging consumption of the latter.

Examples of merit goods are visits to museums, libraries, health care and sport facilities and education. It is reasoned that being (culturally) educated raises the overall civilization level of the population, stimulating broad-mindedness and contributing to social peace, and that a healthy and fit population reduces medical costs that are borne by the whole society. If greater numbers of people have access to higher levels of education, the more knowledge is spread in society, which fosters economic growth. Individuals may underestimate the advantages of these types of goods; for example, teenagers sometimes dislike to go to school because their time-horizon is rather short. Chapter 8 elaborates on the positive external effects of education and the activities undertaken by governments to encourage involvement.

Similarly, in the case of a demerit good, a government may feel the need to discourage consumption by intervening in the market; for example, by increasing the price through extra taxation. High-fat foods, tobacco products and alcohol have a negative effect on the person consuming these products, as well as everyone else who is confronted with the consequences. For example, people who are overweight, smoke tobacco or drink too much alcohol may suffer from obesity, lung cancer or brain damage, and are likely to produce less as citizens in comparison to what they might produce if they had healthier habits; moreover, these bad habits can lead to diseases that increase the costs of health care for all. These negative costs are not always taken into account by firms and consumers when they provide or consume these goods. Hence state intervention may be called for.

The people affected in a negative way by these goods can potentially negotiate compensation with the producers for their reduction in well-being, but often the intervention of the government is needed, frequently by taxing the product that is causing the externality. Because of this levy the selling price rises, thus lowering the number of sales and consequently the size of the damage to third parties. But on other occasions private parties may be able to reach this outcome. For example, all suppliers of drinks may agree on the introduction of a deposit on each unit sold, to encourage the buyers to return the empty bottles. This can be a cost-neutral solution to the problem of littering. In this case, the market is well able to coordinate the transaction via a contract.

However, when many actors are involved, or when the externality is very complex, then the costs of coordinating the transaction may be prohibitive and the additional damage cannot be internalized. In that case, we say that the market fails because the externalities that influence the costs and benefits to society cannot be internalized. This is considered a failure, because prices in markets should reflect the right scarcities. In other words, the price of the traded product should reflect the costs involved in compensating for the noise, smell or pollution. As was mentioned earlier, the negative side effects of carbon dioxide have not been combated successfully until now, precisely because of its complexity, the large number of interested parties involved and the enormous financial consequences of dealing with the problem.

## *Pure public goods*

There are certain products, from the benefits of which people cannot be excluded, such as street lighting or the defense of a country, as opposed to so-called private goods, which are characterized by the possibility of exclusion (see Chapter 3 for a further elaboration). In the case of so-called pure public goods, the market is not able to coordinate demand and supply, because any potential supplier is aware of the fact that as soon as the product exists he cannot exclude others who have not paid for it. This is related to the specific nature of the good in question: the moment a street light is installed, all passers-by enjoy the safety and comfort that comes with it. It is in general impossible for the supplier of the street light to exclude those who have not paid for the consumption of the benefit of the light. In economics, this feature is referred to as nonexclusiveness and the behavior of those who enjoy consumption uninvited without paying is called 'free riding'.

Knowing the problems of nonexclusiveness and free riding, no one in the market will produce this pure public good, and no consumer will demand it through the market mechanism. In Chapter 3 we shall elaborate on this phenomenon. The example about the poor flood defenses in New Orleans, discussed above, is a case in point. Dikes typically have the characteristic of nonexclusiveness. While the inhabitants of the city badly wanted an upgrading of the levée system, this upgrade did not happen. Aside from the question of whether or not the individuals directly involved and most in need of better dikes could have afforded the costs, the fact that some would be able to enjoy the benefits of the dikes without paying for them was sufficient for construction not to begin.

## *Natural monopoly*

A final type of market imperfection is caused by the specific characteristics of the production process: production technology leads to continuously decreasing average costs. In other words, the efficient scale of production, as compared to the total demand in the market, does not allow for two or more firms in the market, resulting in a so-called *natural monopoly*. This monopoly is 'naturally' a result of the production technology. To have one firm in the market is then the best way to produce the good or service because it minimizes production costs; in other words, a monopoly is the most efficient from the point of view of costs. Examples of natural monopolies are typically utilities such as water and electricity. Once the costly infrastructure for these products has been implemented, the supply of an increasing quantity of water or electricity spreads the fixed costs over higher levels of output, thereby lowering the average costs constantly.

The market functions imperfectly because this monopoly has the ability to set prices above marginal costs, in order to maximize profits. If the supplier of this product were forced to set his price at the competitive level (equal to marginal costs), he would suffer losses and decide to stop production. So, here is a dilemma: cost efficiency calls for one supplier, but allocative efficiency calls for price regulation in order to prevent monopoly pricing, while marginal cost pricing will lead to losses. In Chapter 8 you will learn more about this dilemma of a natural monopoly, and about how governments can regulate such monopolies.

## Transaction costs

We continue our discussion on efficiency with the question of how actors in the economy can coordinate their transactions efficiently. This question is not addressed in Neoclassical Economics, but is at the core of Institutional Economics. We are not only interested in minimizing production costs, but in minimizing transaction costs as well.

From the above you have learned that actors in the real economy face all kinds of imperfections and uncertainties. Market power and dependencies may force consumers to pay too much for a product, as might have been the result of the behavior of the Microsoft and Gazprom management, for example. Not every detail about (future) transactions is known, as the uncertainty about (and the value of) the available oil reserves has shown. Information is not complete and is quite often not evenly distributed among the different participants of a transaction, which may result in opportunistic behavior, as was the case in the Enron and Parmalat scandals. The occurrence of pure public goods and externalities may lead to free riding behavior; this appears to be the case in the examples with respect to the failing flood defenses in New Orleans, and the ongoing negotiations about reducing carbon emissions. In short, people do not have the expertise to judge whether what is being considered is good value for their money, neither from a private nor from a societal perspective. It would be very costly – even if it were possible – to gather and evaluate all the information necessary to make an optimal decision. But, assuming optimizing behavior, actors do try to make the most profitable transactions possible.

In order to be able to transact at all and to transact safely, actors have to incur costs to find out how and where transaction opportunities occur, and about the possible risks and uncertainties involved. These expenses are called *transaction costs*. The resources that have to be used to carry out the transaction diminish the welfare gain derived from the exchange itself. These transaction costs have to be added to production costs and comprise all costs incurred when preparing, concluding and enforcing market, managerial and political transactions. In the following, we shall discuss briefly the accompanying costs connected with the three types of transaction.

With respect to market transactions, the costs consist of several aspects:

1 *Search and information costs.* These are related to the effort required to get answers to questions such as: Who offers the product? Is the seller the owner? What are the conditions? What is the quality of the product? Time is required to acquire this information, and sometimes one is also confronted with expenses for advice or traveling.
2 *Costs to draft, to negotiate and to conclude the contract.* The time factor is also involved here, but there may be other costs, such as mediation costs, judicial advice or the services of an estate agent.
3 *Monitoring costs and enforcement costs.* These are costs that are incurred to make sure that the other party commits to an agreement, whether this is of a private nature (concluding a business contract) or of a public nature (complying with the law). The buyer has to inspect the quality of the product and the seller has to monitor the payment; the seller has to verify that a credit card is valid, for example. In addition, costs are incurred when one party finds out that the other has not kept to the agreement: an attorney may need to be hired to defend the parties' interests in court.

The costs listed under points 1 and 2 above are called *ex-ante* costs, while the ones mentioned under point 3 are *ex-post* costs. *Ex ante* means 'beforehand', and *ex post* means 'afterwards'. When decisions are being made about a future undertaking – for example, about a contract, parties base their expectations on the incomplete information they have at the moment of deciding, before the event has taken place. After the signing of the contract people may behave differently from what others expected beforehand, which leads to additional costs in order to prevent or combat cheating. Consequently, before a final decision is made about the contract, transaction partners should anticipate likely problems that might occur. *Ex-ante* costs are incurred to reduce *ex-post* costs as much as possible. In Chapter 5 in particular we return to the topic of market transaction costs.

With respect to managerial transactions, the transaction costs refer to the costs that a superior, a manager, makes in directing and supervising an inferior, an employee. A variety of costs are also incurred in this situation, such as search and information costs (with respect to the application procedure), costs to negotiate, to make contracts and agreements, and costs to monitor and sanction, in order to prevent and tackle opportunistic behavior within the organization. We return to the topic of managerial transaction costs in Chapters 6 and 7.

With respect to political transactions, the collective decision-making process to formulate laws and regulations, or to change them, involves transaction costs of searching, producing and disseminating information, of organizing the consultation process, of drafting the laws, and the like. Also, governmental agencies must check whether or not the law has been broken (enforcement costs). So, political transaction costs refer to all costs associated with setting up, maintaining and adapting a system's formal and informal political organization, and all ensuing executive costs. This entails not only costs related to governmental organizations such as the judiciary, the military, the ministries and the educational system, but also the expenditures made by political parties and pressure groups that try to participate in the political decision-making process. We return to this topic in Chapters 8 and 9.

Box 1.1 gives an idea of the magnitude of transaction costs in modern societies.

---

### BOX 1.1   HOW LARGE ARE TRANSACTION COSTS?

How important are transaction costs in practice? According to Wallis and North (1986), the share of transaction costs in US gross domestic product (GDP) has been rising steadily since 1870, and by 1970 the 'transaction costs sector' represented 54.7 percent of GDP.

*Transaction costs in the US economy*

| Year | Transaction costs from private sector (%) | Transaction costs from public sector (%) | Total transaction cost sector as % of US GDP |
|------|-------------------------------------------|------------------------------------------|----------------------------------------------|
| 1870 | 22.5 | 3.6  | 26.1 |
| 1890 | 29.1 | 3.6  | 32.7 |
| 1910 | 31.5 | 3.7  | 35.2 |
| 1930 | 38.2 | 8.2  | 46.3 |
| 1950 | 40.3 | 10.9 | 51.2 |
| 1970 | 40.8 | 13.9 | 54.7 |

*Source*: Wallis and North (1986, p. 121).

> A more recent attempt to calculate total transaction costs is by Furubotn and Richter (1998, p. 51n), who estimate that these costs may amount to over 60 percent of GDP in developed economies.
>
> These estimates suggest that transaction costs are equally or more important than production costs in a modern economy. Traditionally, economists associated transaction costs with wasteful bureaucratic activity, and ignored them in favor of production costs. But without contracts, and without the secretaries to type them, attorneys to enforce them, and accountants to keep track of their results, today's complex world would simply not be possible.

Much attention is paid to the question of where transaction costs come from. What are the sources and are there efficient ways of minimizing these costs? Next we shall discuss in more detail how Institutional Economics addresses the question of coordinating transactions and the role of institutions.

## Institutions

In English, the word 'institution' has several meanings depending on the context, including:

- an established organization;
- the building in which an organization is housed; or
- a custom, practice or rule.

In the press, the first meaning is the most common; for example, banks are often referred to as 'financial institutions', and the United Nations and NATO are 'international institutions'. An institution can also be a place where a disabled or impoverished person is sent (becoming 'institutionalized'). Or a person who has worked within an organization for many years and has an important (usually social) role is considered to be an institution: 'She is more than a colleague; she's an institution!'

However, in Institutional Economics the word 'institution' has been assigned a specific connotation. What we mean is closer to the third meaning listed above. As already mentioned briefly, institutions are rules that influence behavior, and which are meant to provide certain safeguards before we enter into a transaction. Over the course of time societies have introduced many kinds of safeguards, by developing rules and sanction mechanisms. In this context, institutions are man-made rules and their accompanying sanctions that are intended to make interactions less risky and more predictable.

Institutions can take many different forms, ranging from very implicit beliefs among people about how to treat each other, to practical (trading) rules about the use of currencies and quality standards. They also range from implicit understandings and contractual agreements between business partners or between employer and employee, to clearly defined rules enacted by the government. Language, customs, norms, etiquette, legal rules and standards, such as systems of weights and measures, are thus all considered to be institutions. Organizations such as firms, schools and courts, to name just a few, can also be viewed as institutions.

In the literature, institutions are described in a variety of ways (see, for example, Vatn, 2005 and Hodgson, 2006). In this book we define *institutions* as systems of hierarchical man-made rules that structure behavior and social interaction. They consist of established, durable and stable rules, and vary from social values through norms to laws with ensuing specific rules. Institutions are systems, in which the rules are positioned in a hierarchical way: the more general rules set the boundaries for the more specific ones. Rules are only part of the system when they are durable and structure behavior. Below we shall further explore the characteristics of different types of institutions.

## *Formal and informal institutions*

First, we make a distinction between formal and informal institutions, even though it is often hard to draw a clear dividing line. Also, a distinction can be made between public and private institutions.

We define *formal institutions* as *public* rules of behavior that are designed by a public authority with legislative power (parliament or senate) and enforced by (i) a public authority with executive power (the administration or government, making use of police, regulatory agencies and other enforcement agencies); and (ii) a judiciary power (judges) that has the right and the power to penalize an individual or organization for breaking the rule. Typical examples of formal institutions are laws and governmental regulations aiming at the realization of specific policy objectives. The introduction of stricter rules after the Enron case and the judicial verdicts in the Microsoft case all fall under the heading of formal institutions. In addition, many *private* rules, such as stipulations in contracts with respect to the delivery of goods or services or labor agreements, are backed by the law (such as contract law) and hence can also be legally enforced.

We define *informal institutions* as *private* rules of behavior that have been developed gradually and spontaneously and do not need any legal enforcement because the rules are sanctioned by the private parties themselves or because it is in the self-interest of the actors to follow the rules of their own accord. The first subcategory contains *self-regulating mechanisms*; that is, standards and possible sanctions are agreed on by the private actors involved. The second subcategory refers to *self-enforcing mechanisms*, implying that the rules will be complied with spontaneously. The example discussed earlier concerning the rules formulated by the supranational WTO can be seen as an illustration of a self-regulating mechanism, while the boycott examples showed that the fear of loss of reputation can be considered as an illustration of a self-enforcing mechanism. Thus the first type refers to informal institutions and sanctions that have been mutually agreed upon, whereas the second type refers to informal institutions and sanctions that will be respected spontaneously.

It should be clear that 'formal' and 'public' are not interchangeable terms, and neither are 'informal' and 'private'. What also should be stressed is that the motives behind these formal rules can either be found in the intention to improve efficiency overall or in the intention to protect certain vested interests. In the latter case, efficiency (in terms of economic welfare) often suffers. We come back to this important topic shortly.

## Institutional environment

People do business in an *institutional environment*, which consists of all rules, formal and informal, that have an impact on behavior in economic transactions. Because of differences in institutions worldwide, each society, be it on a local or a national scale, has its own specific institutional environment consisting of a hierarchy of different kinds of institutions: values, norms, conventions, laws and specific rules, whether formal or informal (Williamson, 2000; North, 1990).

*Values* are embedded in a society's culture (all aspects of human behavior and society that are shared by all, or almost all, members of some social group), are generally-held preferences about pursuable goals, and embody what most citizens in a certain society consider to be 'good'. Values represent beliefs about what are considered to be the most important things in life. Important values in a large part of the world are, among other things, individual freedom, justice, security, peace, prosperity and a civilized environment. Because values in general give directions with respect to how people behave, they can be interpreted as general coordinating institutions (Ayres, 1961; Hodgson, 1998).

*Norms* are generally-held opinions about how to achieve the values. They define agreed ways in which people should behave, according to the members of a group, so that the values of society are realized, or at least not violated. Examples of norms include: solidarity (to achieve justice), competition (to achieve prosperity), and the 'polluter pays' principle (to achieve a tolerable environment). Individual members of the society have sometimes internalized the norms into their own way of thinking in such a way that the norm has become part of their conscience. Then people adhere to them if only to avoid a guilty feeling. On other occasions, people are persuaded to follow the norms because of external (social) pressure and the fear of becoming an outcast.

*Conventions* are practical rules that structure behavior in complex situations. Conventions reduce coordination problems, which is particularly important in an increasingly complex world. Examples of conventions are the use of a common scale to measure lengths, weights and time with the aid of the same units, and rules on how to behave in social interaction and in traffic. So if the norm is that people should drive safely in order to contribute to the value of security in general, the convention is driving either on the right-hand side, or the left-hand side of the road.

When actors in society agree about the values, norms and conventions and they all consider these institutions as functioning in their own interest, each of them will spontaneously support the values, norms and conventions. They have internalized them into their own values and behavior and expect that the other members of the society have done the same. However, that is not always the case. In society, different values can exist, supported by different interest groups. It can very well be that, in the interests of society as a whole, a specific norm of behavior is necessary, but that a large part of the population considers the norm not to be in their interest. Similarly, different groups in society can also disagree and have conflicts about conventions. In such cases, institutions do not automatically structure the behavior of people in the right direction. Then formal laws and formal sanctions are needed to further structure the behavior of the members of society.

*Laws* (and regulations) are formalized rules enacted by the government, in the shape of codified norms and conventions. Sometimes people are tempted to break the existing rules when they think this will be to their advantage. For these situations, third-party sanctioning through legal enforcement is necessary. Laws result in all kinds of specific stipulations that either enable or constrain actors' actions so as to comply with norms and conventions, in order to avoid or deal with conflicts. Examples include the tax laws of a country (to comply with the norm of solidarity); the legal obligation of firms with limited liability to give information to the public about their profits or losses, thus allowing (prospective) investors to make a correct judgment (to comply with the norm of competition); and the moral or even legal duty to throw rubbish in waste bins (to comply with the norm not to pollute). People generally adhere to laws because breaking these rules could lead to a sanction by the government (such as a fine or a jail sentence).

Values, norms, conventions and laws are interrelated hierarchically. From the above you can discern a hierarchy from more general to more specific, and from spontaneous adherence to formal sanctions. Values are the basis for norms, and norms are the basis for conventions, laws and the resulting specific rules. In other words, going from values to laws with specific stipulations is a matter of a decreasing level of generality. However, norms, conventions and laws are not unilaterally connected to values. For example, individual freedom is one of the fundamental values of many societies, but this value is underpinned by different norms, conventions and regulations in different countries, though the value may be the same. To achieve freedom of religion, freedom of assembly and freedom of the press, democratic principles may be the norm. But democracy works in different ways around the world. In the USA and the UK, elections are organized by district and the 'winner takes all', while most countries in continental Europe have a rule of proportional representation. Similarly, countries may differ in their opinion of how to maintain peace: one norm may be through building trust relations with as many other nations as possible, but another may be through building a large arsenal to accomplish a deterrent effect, with a possible arms race as result.

## *Institutionalization as a process*

In Institutional Economics, attention is paid to the different types of institutions, how they relate to each other, how they influence behavior, how they can be designed or how they spontaneously evolve, and how they influence ideas about central concepts such as competition and efficiency. When values, norms, conventions and laws are mutually conflicting, the society must develop ways to solve, or at least deal with, the conflicts. In Institutional Economics there is an important school of thought inspired by the work of John R. Commons in which institutions are analyzed as being conflict-solving mechanisms (see Chapter 2). Conflicts may arise because people differ about the ranking between values. In an emergency, the fundamental value of justice (the right of all individuals to be treated equally) may be subordinate to the fundamental value of security; freedom of speech can conflict with religious freedom; laws of succession can conflict with laws on land consolidation, and rules that arrange safe working conditions (rough floors that prevent workers from losing their footing, for example) may conflict with hygiene rules (smooth floors are easy to keep clean).

Not only are there problems concerning the ranking of different values and norms; the definition may also differ. Take the value of individual freedom. There are people who value individual freedom highly and therefore strongly support private property and the market mechanism. But there are others who lobby ardently for a strong intervention in the market mechanism and the redistribution of income in order to offer the poor the possibility of developing and educating themselves.

According to institutional economists, values, norms, conventions and laws should be considered as products of a continuing dialogue between groups in society. Institutions are part of an ongoing process of change. People do not always stick to one opinion; they will reconsider their aims if circumstances change, and as a result of this institutions will also change. What is desirable in terms of economic performance is a matter of values and choices of the community. Values, norms and laws are the result of social and political processes. These processes are never value-free; the ideas and interests of groups and individuals are always involved.

It is the task of social science in general and of Institutional Economics in particular to explain how the values in a specific society and at a specific period of time are selected. Is it the result of a democratic process in which different interest groups can participate, or is it the result of a decision-making process controlled by a powerful elite? Is it, for example, the result of a process controlled by powerful labor unions who wish to protect the labor market from unwanted immigrants? Is the outcome the result of a lobby by powerful multinationals that threatened to outsource their production to cheap labor countries unless their interests were protected by policy-makers?

It is the task of Institutional Economics to show when the outcome is the result of an efficiently working market in which the different interests are in balance, or that the outcome serves specific vested interests. It is also the task of social science in general, and of Institutional Economics in particular, that, if other values should be served, what an effective institutional structure would be. So, if the community wants to change the allocation and distribution of resources, it is the task of social science to show how such a change can be accomplished. If behavior needs to change so that global warming will diminish, what then is an institutional setting that influences behavior in the right direction?

Changes may have their origins not only in the shifting attitudes and preferences of citizens but also in the changing attitudes of politicians (resulting from new insights based on scientific studies, say). Recent developments in the beliefs commonly held about the aging population may highlight this dynamic process: because of the increase in the number of people above the age of sixty-five, the concept of retirement is changing in order to deal with the imminent labor shortages in many Western economies, which is a reversal of the trend toward earlier retirement that was seen in the 1980s and 1990s. Workplace institutions, such as the number of hours that the elderly work per day, must as a consequence also change (Spithoven, 2008).

Not only the ranking of values and the definition of values may differ in different countries or may change within a country, but also ideas about how to achieve these values may differ. One example is the value of prosperity. Ideas about how to achieve prosperity for all inhabitants vary widely from country to country; in certain countries, the government aims to increase welfare by intervening as little as possible, promoting rules of free competition. But in other countries the majority of people are of the opinion that welfare is best served by more government intervention, among other things to correct for market imperfections and to improve the position of the weak in society, or to protect the competitiveness of the own national industries, as in the example of the WTO discussed earlier.

Institutional economists underline the importance of studying different institutional environments, because in that way the differing behavior of the economic actors can be understood and anticipated. Moreover, the institutional environment is not static but subject to an ongoing process of change. Different drivers of institutional change exist, and we shall discuss this further in Chapter 4.

## *Effectiveness of institutions*

When are institutions effective? Under what conditions will the objectives of the institutions be realized? When norms in society exist, but nobody adheres to them, then the norms are ineffective and do not structure behavior sufficiently. For an institution to be effective, two conditions must hold (Kasper and Streit, 1999). On the one hand, a sufficient percentage share of individuals must subscribe to the institution for it to become accepted; but on the other hand, even if the majority of people accept the rules and behave accordingly, there must be credible (enforceable) sanctions to prevent the rest of the population from acting against the norm. We shall discuss both conditions below.

For all rules to be broadly accepted, they need to satisfy three requirements: they must be *general, certain* and *open*. General means that rules must be nondiscriminatory; that is, they must apply equally to all people and in all circumstances. Class justice (different laws for different types of people) should not apply, and people must be sure that the rulers themselves are also subject to the law. The condition that rules must be certain refers to the requirement that rules be transparent and reliable, so that all citizens know what the rules imply and what will happen if the rules are not observed. The third criterion of openness means that rules should be flexible, in the sense that they permit actors to proceed in response to new circumstances. There is a certain tension between, in particular, the second and third criteria, because the more open (flexible) the rules, the less certain (fixed) they become.

With respect to the second condition for institutions to be effective, institutional economists stress that sanctions must be credible to prevent part of the population from acting opportunistically. Therefore, all effective institutions must be complemented by *enforceable sanctions,* which may be informal and based on self-enforcing or self-regulating mechanisms, or be based on formal laws. The presence of credible sanctions is important. If people can simply break a rule with no consequences, other individuals may start to do the same, leading to a downward spiral and a complete undermining of the institution.

Sanctions may be negative or positive. *Negative sanctions* are instruments for dealing with norm-violating behavior, while *positive sanctions* are rewards or encouragements to behave in a certain fashion. An example of a positive sanction for students is an honors degree (cum laude) to raise student achievements. Another example of a positive sanction is performance-based pay (replacing seniority-based salaries) to stimulate workers' productivity.

## *Institutions enable and constrain*

Institutions structure behavior and in that sense institutions increase the predictability of behavior. Uncertainty about the actions and reactions of others in the market is reduced, which enables actors to prepare contracts and coordinate transactions. Institutions *enable* economic transactions to take place – both nationally and internationally. For example, two basic institutions are language and money. A language is a means of communication that depends on linguistic rules and on the shared interpretation of meanings. Without a proper mutual understanding based on a common language, communication errors can have serious detrimental effects. Similarly, a common currency is necessary to transact goods and services. Products are traded in the market generally using money as the standard currency, as it has proved to be an effective institution for trade: using money makes it easier to compare different products and to sell or buy products. Also, a trustworthy financial system to support transactions is essential. If people lose trust in the system, they might panic and all withdraw their savings from banks at the same time, leading to a (possibly worldwide) crisis.

Many things that people do are unthinkable without institutions – such as, for example, the international specialization of labor for the production of a specific component of a product (see Box 1.2).

---

### BOX 1.2 COORDINATION OF TRANSACTIONS IN A SUPPLY CHAIN

Nowadays much of the work in the electronics industry is modularized. Memory cards, keyboard, hard drives, wireless cards, graphic controllers and microprocessors for computers are not only produced in different firms but also in different countries.

This implies that the different producers must interact closely to coordinate design, manufacture and distribution of computers. All these production stages simply cannot be planned separately. The planning and design of the different modules must be synchronized. For the system to work smoothly it is necessary that workers in, say, Taiwan, Malaysia or Thailand, speak the same language and employ the same standards as workers in the USA. Additionally, in industries with a rapid pace of technological change, the continuous training of workers is essential: without a common language, coordination failures are highly likely.

One striking example of a failure in coordinating different teams working on the same project was the loss of the Mars Climate Orbiter in 1999. One engineering team used metric units while another team at NASA used imperial units for a key spacecraft operation. The failed information transfer scrambled commands for maneuvering the spacecraft to place it safely in orbit around Mars. Consequently, it smashed into the planet.

As well as enabling transactions, institutions also impose *constraints* on human behavior. A considerable part of all rules refer to limitations and bans, to prevent actors from behaving in ways that might harm others. The smooth coordination of transactions is based on people following the rules. For example, in supply-chain production, it is very important that every component is delivered on time. A delay in the delivery of one component can create friction throughout the whole chain, and the gains of specialization may diminish or be lost completely if workers in the successive steps of the chain cannot do their jobs. Enforceable rules and deterrent sanctions must discourage people from delaying delivery. Payment must also be timely, or suppliers will lose money, or in the worst case become bankrupt.

In conclusion, owing to both their enabling and constraining functions, institutions enhance the predictability of behavior, which is why a society is unthinkable without them.

## Economic systems and governance structures

The concept of the institutional environment is closely linked to the concept of an *economic system* – a framework of interrelated institutions that influence the ways in which people organize production, consumption and distribution of goods and services in a particular society. An economic system can be viewed from different perspectives.

On the one hand, we can look at it from a macro perspective: in this approach the economic system can be of two extreme forms ('ideal types'): (i) a *pure market economy* (pure capitalist system) with private property and markets as central characteristics; or (ii) a *centrally planned economy* in which products are owned by the state or the community at large. On the other hand, the economic system can also be understood from a micro perspective: from the point of view of the market, with firms and households as the individual actors.

Institutional Economics as a discipline studies how these economic systems work, at both macro and micro levels. The central question is how institutions enable and constrain behavior, and how the coordination of transactions is made possible. This is what we call 'the subject matter' of Institutional Economics. What are the mechanisms at work in different economic systems that result in a specific performance in terms of macroeconomic growth? Let us take a closer look at the two perspectives from which economic systems can be observed, starting with the macro view.

In a pure market economy, the people themselves decide how to make the best use of economic opportunities. The government confines itself to establishing, monitoring and enforcing the rules that provide the conditions under which the available resources may be used by private actors. In contrast, in a centrally planned economy the government tries to satisfy the needs of the people. Because planners cannot know individual supply and demand functions, the government has to decide what different actors need, but this may falter because of a lack of information. In Chapter 8 you will read more about this.

These two ideal types are merely theoretical and do not exist in real life. Every economic system is a *mixed form* of a completely free market economy and a planned economy. In some countries the economic system is characterized mainly by elements of the market with only a modest role being played by the government, while in others there is some economic freedom but the influence of the state is large. Most countries are placed somewhere between the two: in principle, all citizens have a good deal of liberty to transact as they see fit, but at the same time governments may want to interfere in the process of free trading, either to protect the public interest (to improve efficiency) or to promote the interests of certain lobby groups. Even though state intervention in the economy usually cannot raise economic welfare for all citizens at the same time, most governments intervene all the same: a trade-off between economic goals and other goals (for example, equity) is made for political reasons. Part IV of our book is devoted to this topic.

In the micro perspective of economic systems we focus on the mechanisms at work within the economy, such as the functioning of individual markets and organizations. In this context a *governance structure* is defined as an institutional framework within which economic actors coordinate their transactions. Examples of governance structures include market contracts, private firms and state-owned enterprises, regulatory public agencies and ministries. A governance structure describes, among other things, which parties are involved in the transaction, who owns what, and who is allowed to make decisions. Because a governance structure in itself is a system of rules, it can itself be viewed as an institution.

As will be explained in detail in Chapter 3 and in Part III of this book, private actors choose the optimal governance structure, given specific economic circumstances. In a fairly secure market environment, transactions are more often organized by contracting in the market place, which then is the most efficient way of transacting. In a more complex and insecure situation, however, people often choose to organize activities within a firm to save on transaction costs. They give decision-making power to a central authority, such as a CEO (chief executive officer), to coordinate these activities. Both market contracts and firms are examples of private governance structures. In other situations the government may decide to take an active part in transactions, either by defining strict rules for private parties (via public regulations) or by organizing the transaction itself by means of state-owned enterprises. Regulation and state-owned enterprises are examples of public governance structures, which occupy center stage in Part IV.

We have defined institutions as systems of hierarchical, man-made rules that structure behavior and social interaction. By way of a summary, the hierarchy of institutions is sketched in Figure 1.1. At the top are the general institutions in the form of values. These have an impact on norms, which for their part have an impact on public and private rules, both formal and informal. The lower down the scheme, the more specific the rules become. Since governance structures are also considered to be particular forms of institutions, they appear in this scheme in the lowest layer.

## The subject matter of Institutional Economics

As we already noted above, Institutional Economics analyzes how economic systems work (a description of what 'is'). In addition, it is about how the system should work in order to realize the goals the community has set for itself (a normative what 'ought to be'). Institutional Economics is about designing effective and efficient institutions to structure behavior in such a way that the system performs well. The desirable outcomes are set in a political process and can be about production in the agricultural sector, the level of innovation in the chemical industry, the productivity of labor in manufacturing,

**Figure 1.1** *Hierarchical institutional scheme*

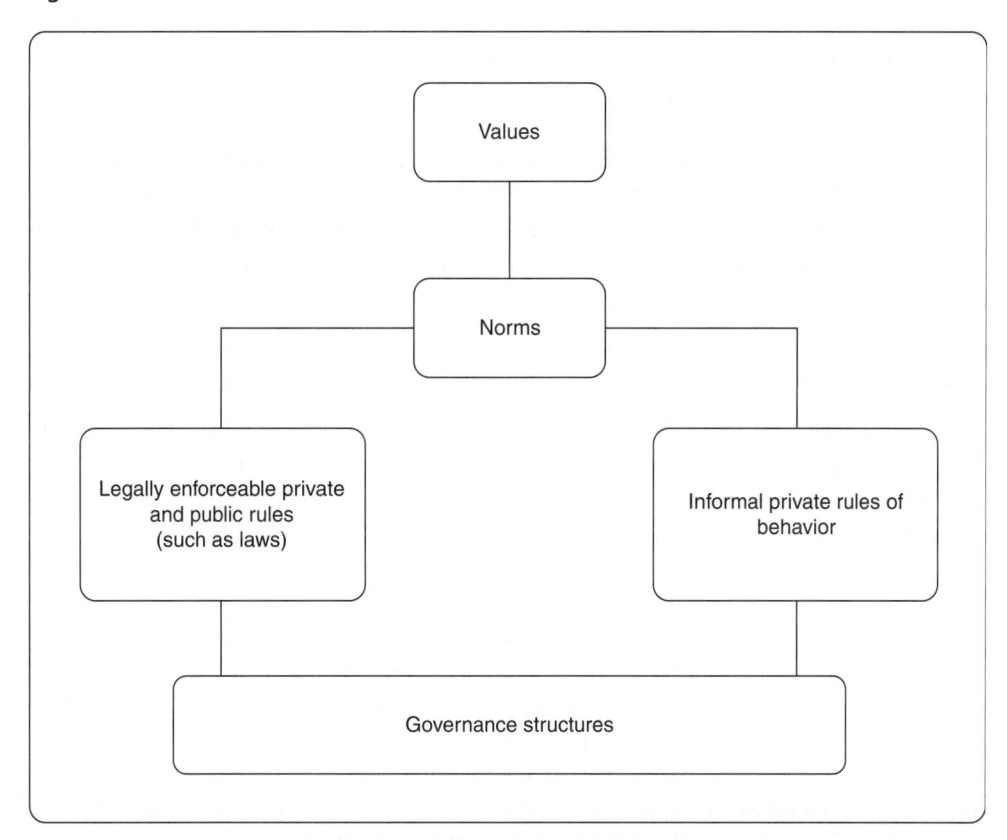

```
                    ┌─────────┐
                    │ Values  │
                    └────┬────┘
                         │
                    ┌────┴────┐
                    │  Norms  │
                    └────┬────┘
           ┌─────────────┴─────────────┐
┌──────────────────────┐      ┌──────────────────────┐
│ Legally enforceable  │      │ Informal private     │
│ private and public   │      │ rules of behavior    │
│ rules (such as laws) │      │                      │
└──────────┬───────────┘      └──────────┬───────────┘
           │                              │
           └──────────────┬───────────────┘
                   ┌──────┴──────────┐
                   │ Governance      │
                   │ structures      │
                   └─────────────────┘
```

the worldwide reduction of pollution, the distribution of benefits and costs over different income groups in society, and so on.

The subject matter of Institutional Economics is rather complicated. It involves different layers of institutions that are interrelated and can change over time. Moreover, striving for efficiency can be a reason for institutions to exist and to change, but equally important is the role of vested interests. In addition to that, valuation plays a crucial role: if the value of a clean environment and the norm of 'the polluter pays' are central, then the outcome of markets depends largely on the laws that constrain the behavior of producers and consumers, on the existence of markets for emission rights, on the attitudes and norms of individual consumers, and the like. If, on the contrary, polluters form a powerful lobby group, the chances are that their particular interests will be given precedence over those of the general public. This specific distribution of rights determines the market outcome (Vatn, 2005).

Now that we have a better understanding of the relationships between the different layers of institutions, and understand that institutions change over time and are subject to processes of valuation, we can also better understand that people think and behave differently, depending on the (institutional) environment in which they are operating. What generates an efficient outcome in an American context may not work in a Chinese one. And even within a single society, what was efficient in the year 2000 can become inefficient by 2010. Why? Because values and norms with which economic actors evaluate and take decisions are different in the American and Chinese societies, and because institutions change over time. In Chapter 2 we shall elaborate further on the influence of the institutional environment.

For analytical and didactical reasons we have decided to deal with the complex subject matter of Institutional Economics in two different ways: from a comparative static viewpoint; and from a dynamic one. Moreover, in both viewpoints, we shall allow for both the efficiency approach and the vested interest approach, as will now be explained in more detail.

## *Static efficiency and static vested interest approaches*

In the *static approach* toward the working of economic systems the focus is on explaining which governance structure is chosen by optimizing actors given a number of environmental factors like technology (this is standard know-how to produce the good), natural resources, laws and public regulations (concerning for instance competition), and the preferences of the producers and consumers (maximizing profits, minimizing transaction costs, maximizing utility). This optimizing behavior may or may not lead to static (allocative and/or productive) efficiency, depending on whether the goal is to serve everybody's welfare or just the interests of a particular group in society, at the expense of other groups.

In the static approach, the focus is on optimizing under given constraints. When optimizing decisions are taken on, for example, the type of governance structure, this situation remains until a change takes place in one of the constraints. For example, an innovation can lead to a change in the technology that forces optimizing firms to alter the scale of production or the governance structure. Similarly, a change in the power structure changes the constraints of vested interests and consequently leads to a change in the governance structure. The two situations, namely before and after the change in the environmental factor, can be compared with each other. What is the governance structure chosen before the change, and what is the one chosen after it? If this comparison is done we speak of comparative statics: that is, two static situations are compared. You will learn more about the static approach in Chapter 2.

To improve efficiency in a static sense would imply, on the one hand, the minimization of production costs, while on the other hand, it concerns the minimization of transaction costs (are the costs of the coordination of transaction minimized?), which is a central issue in the static approach of Institutional Economics. In that part of Institutional Economics institutions are understood as the result of optimizing behavior in the economic system under the constraints of technology, laws and so on. Politicians make efficient laws and regulations, and actors at the micro level choose efficient governance structures. Because this analysis is made in a given static environment of technology, values, norms and preferences, we call this the *static efficiency approach* toward institutions.

As already indicated, however, next to the efficiency perspective there is another important perspective explaining the existence of governance structures, which we call the *static vested interest approach*. The actors in the economic system will constantly try to protect their own interests. Suppose they have private property rights, and they are free to do what they want with the property to maximize their private profits. These actors might oppose any attempt to create institutions that constrain these possibilities.

Actors in the economic system will create opportunities to maximize their profits and utility, and they will use their power to protect their vested interests. They have their own objectives and use all kinds of instruments to realize these objectives, which do not always conform to fair competition. In many cases, some people have more power than others, and can manipulate the way transactions are governed. If a firm can prevent competitors that have to make use of its integrated network (what we may see in parts of the energy sector) from doing so, then the explanation of the existing governance structure has little to do with efficiency goals but much more with power play and the protection of vested interests. There are plenty of real-life examples of this: we have already mentioned the abuse of power by Microsoft and Gazprom, and the negative role that vested interests played in the poor flood defenses of New Orleans.

Institutional economists will investigate in their research both the reasons for efficiency and the reasons for vested interests to explain the existence of institutions.

## *Dynamic efficiency and dynamic vested interest approach*

In the *dynamic efficiency approach* the question is about how the process of institutional change develops over time. The researcher explores the drivers of institutional change and how the causal mechanisms of change in an economic system work. In the case of efficiency, the researcher is interested in the question of existing information: how do firms in the market know about the most efficient scale of production, and how do they know about the most efficient governance structure? Is information available through the price system, so that actors know *ex ante* about the most efficient solutions? Do they learn over time in a process of trial and error? Are they able to imitate their most efficient competitors?

Analyzing the process of institutional change informs the researcher about the flexibility of institutions, their inertia, and of the reasons why actors might stick to old routines. The dynamic perspective questions the assumptions that the static perspective makes about the flexibility of actors to adopt more efficient alternatives. Sometimes the circumstances indeed allow for smooth changes to more efficient alternatives, but very often this is not the case. This is not only because of inertia, but also because of the protection of vested interests, so we then have to make use of the *dynamic vested interest approach*. Institutional change always implies a redistribution of costs and benefits: some actors are better off after the change and some worse. So, in the dynamic approach, the explanation of the change or the rigidity of the institutions can also be found in the strategies of powerful interest groups which protect their long-standing interests.

Both static and dynamic approaches have their merits (see Chapters 2 and 4). Depending on the exact issue to be studied, sometimes the static approach is more appropriate and at other times the dynamic approach is to be preferred. Whereas Chapter 3 will focus solely on the static approach and Chapter 4 solely on the dynamic approach, in all subsequent chapters of Parts III and IV we shall apply the theoretical insights of Part II from both a static and a dynamic perspective, and within these two perspectives we shall pay attention to both the efficiency approach and the vested interest approach. For each of these application chapters we shall set up a convenient scheme, similar to the one shown in Table 1.1.

**Table 1.1** *Explanation of governance structures: the four approaches combined*

|  | Static approach | Dynamic approach |
|---|---|---|
| Efficiency | Given the institutional environment and the characteristics of actors, which governance structure minimizes transaction costs? | How do institutional changes come about when actors operate out of an efficiency perspective? |
| Vested interest | Given the institutional environment and the characteristics of actors, which governance structure is chosen when powerful interest groups protect their vested interests? | How do institutional changes come about when actors operate out of a vested interest perspective? |

Whatever the perspective focused upon, they all stress the importance of institutions in structuring economic behavior and social interaction, which will be underlined below.

## INSTITUTIONS MATTER

Since the institutionalist, Douglass C. North, received the Nobel Prize in 1993, the saying 'Institutions matter' has become well-known. As North said when accepting this prize: 'When it is costly to transact, then institutions matter. And it is costly to transact' (1994, p. 360). Countless empirical studies by numerous economists have followed to substantiate this proposition. They all demonstrate that when societies that are similar with respect to several indicators such as size of the population, size of the country, climate and natural endowments are compared there remain large disparities in economic prosperity that can only be explained by pointing toward differences in the institutional environment.

The informal and formal rules in a society have a large impact on whether or not economic transactions are performed with low contracting costs. Trust plays an important role here. Is there a reliable government and an objective judiciary to protect the rights of all individual actors? Is the community characterized by high ethical values that promote respect and create opportunities for all members? If people live in such circumstances, they have more incentives to engage in an economic activity, which in turn favors the development of society at large. We shall concentrate on this argument below.

### Institutions and development

Simple, everyday transactions, such as going to the bank, and buying or selling goods, can be very different experiences in developing countries. For even the simplest deals, there are barriers to be overcome: corruption, red tape and distrust, for example. Other transactions, such as raising capital for a new business, can be almost impossible. There are fewer available ways of enforcing an agreement if the other party does not comply with it; the judicial system is slow and inefficient, and believable safeguards are rare.

These difficulties are a fundamental reason why certain countries have developed less than others over time. Fewer transactions imply fewer business opportunities and lower growth. The worse these problems are, the more both local and foreign investors will decide to try their luck elsewhere. Since the pioneering work of North (see, for example, North, 1981) showing how institutions have been linked to economic growth throughout history, there has been a large body of literature showing how intangible concepts such as trust play a large part in development. Citing North (1994, p. 359), 'Institutions form the incentive structure of a society, and the political and economic institutions, in consequence, are the underlying determinants of economic performance.'

The benefits of specialization can only be fully appropriated if the institutional framework is correct. For example, the Industrial Revolution in the eighteenth and nineteenth centuries depended on the enforcement of property rights. Adam Smith was already aware of this, when he said that 'Commerce and manufactures can seldom flourish long in any state...in which the people do not feel themselves secure in the possession of their property' (Smith, 1776, p. 862). In the increasingly knowledge-based economy in which we live today, factors such as trust and justice are becoming more and more important.

Down the centuries, the wealth of a nation has been linked to many things: resources such as gold or oil (what the World Bank (2006) calls 'natural capital') or heavy industry and machinery ('produced capital'). Yet it is easy to find oil-rich countries that are underdeveloped, and on the other hand rich countries with few natural resources (such as Switzerland). Countries like India or Argentina, which chose to promote and protect their heavy industry during the mid-twentieth century, discovered that long-term growth was elusive. Other authors have emphasized the importance of education and technological progress in creating national wealth.

However, an influential paper by Rodrik *et al.* (2004) looks at the 'deep' determinants of growth. Referring to the fact that the per capita income of Luxembourg is over a hundred times that of Sierra Leone, they say 'it is harder to think of any question in economics that is of greater intellectual significance, or of greater relevance to the vast majority of the world's population' (2004, p. 132). The authors attempt to answer the question of why some countries are able to innovate and accumulate more than others over time. They find three candidates to be deep determinants of this: geography, trade and institutions. Their main result is that institutions, in particular property rights and the rule of law, are the single most important factor in explaining the differences in development across countries.

Their findings are supported by the World Bank (2006, p. xiv), which finds that 'the preponderant form of wealth worldwide is intangible capital – human capital and the quality of formal and informal institutions'. Intangible capital captures everything that is not physical, or in other words not included in the estimates of produced and natural capital. It includes skills (human capital), the degree to which there is trust and cooperation in a society (social capital), and the way in which societies are governed, such as the degree to which institutions such as a fair judicial system and an encouraging, protective government are present. As Table 1.2 shows, in high-income countries, natural capital represents only 2 percent of the total wealth, while 80 percent is intangible capital. On the other hand, natural capital continues to be relevant for low-income countries (26 percent of total wealth).

This does not mean that all that developing countries need to do is to mimic the institutions of developed ones. Europe, the USA and Japan are all highly developed, and yet have different institutions. North (1994) warns that transferring the political and economic rules of Western economies to Third-World countries will not guarantee their growth. But there is a consensus that what developed countries have in common is the necessary respect for property rights and the rule of law. The development of, for

**Table 1.2** *Capital shares of total wealth (percentages)*

|  | Natural capital (%) | Produced capital (%) | Intangible capital (%) |
|---|---|---|---|
| Low-income countries | 26 | 16 | 59 |
| Middle-income countries | 13 | 19 | 68 |
| High-income OECD countries | 2 | 17 | 80 |
| **World** | 4 | 18 | 78 |

*Source:* World Bank (2006, p. 4).

example, South Korea since the 1960s, Singapore since the 1970s, and Spain and Ireland since the 1980s, shows that policies providing the correct incentives can potentially set a country on the right track within a couple of decades.

## A BRIEF OUTLINE OF THE BOOK

This book consists of four parts. After this first introductory part (Chapter 1) we move on to the theoretical part (Chapters 2, 3 and 4). Our point of departure will be the presentation of a theoretical framework that incorporates both the static and the dynamic approaches of Institutional Economics. You will learn that theory can help you to study the complex institutional environment in which people make their transactions. Using theories and models can also help you to explain how and why changes occur in this environment. Throughout the book, we shall link theory to real-world examples. Just as in the preceding example about institutions and development, we will make clear throughout this book that 'institutions matter', in the sense that economic behavior (in the sense of coordinating transactions) is always influenced by the formal and informal institutions that are present in society.

At the same time, we shall make clear that those involved in transactions may try to influence (alter) the institutions themselves to serve their own interests, possibly at the expense of others. In the third part (Chapters 5, 6 and 7) we shall focus on the different ways in which transactions are coordinated in the private sector, while the fourth part (Chapters 8 and 9) deals with transactions that are regulated or even completely coordinated by public authorities. Also, throughout the book we shall show that the workings of economic systems can be both the result of actors striving to improve efficiency and of others striving to protect their vested interests.

In order to emphasize the importance of institutions, we round off this chapter with one more example, inspired by the work of Leeson (2007a, 2007b), which illustrates some of the key notions that will be expanded in the rest of the book.

### Pirate economics: a preview of what you will find in this book

When the film *Pirates of the Caribbean: At World's End* was released in May 2007, several critics noted that long sections of the film were dedicated to meetings and discussions, including a climactic scene where, following the rules set down in a large, dusty pirate constitution, an international gathering of pirates elected a pirate king. One critic wrote: 'For free and reckless rogues of the high seas, these pirates sure seem to love their bureaucracy ... these could be Lawyers of the Caribbean' (Rose, 2007, p. 8).

And yet it would seem that the filmmakers had actually done their homework. Historians have shown that rules were essential for pirates to prosper, and without them they 'could no more subsist than a structure without a foundation' (Rediker 1987, p. 287, quoted in Leeson, 2007a).

During the golden age of piracy (usually set by historians as between 1630 and 1730), pirates ran an extraordinarily successful and well-organized enterprise. They coordinated attacks using fleets of ships, sometimes involving several thousand pirates at a time, and carried off millions of pounds in loot. And all this was achieved within organizations which for the most part were composed of volunteers, and which, being outside the law, had to make up their own rules as they went along. As we shall see in Chapter 2, this arrangement fits quite nicely into the analytical framework in which actors determine their *governance structure*, given a certain *institutional environment*.

## *Pirates as rational agents*

According to several sources mentioned by Leeson (2007a), the pirates had a very well-organized society. The rules of pirates can be explained as the actions of rational beings who were seeking to maximize their profit. Despite their image as debauched, rum-drinking rascals leading adventurous lives and dying violent deaths, most pirates probably died of old age, in many cases as wealthy men, and the risks they ran were no greater than those of other merchant seamen.

*Formal and informal institutions* both played an important part in the pirates' lives. Although piracy was illegal, and would often be punished by death (which evidently was a *public regulation* with a formal, *negative sanction*), there were clear *incentives* to join the pirates. For a seaman, becoming a pirate was often a perfectly rational decision. Captains of (legal) merchant ships had unrestricted powers on board, and they tended to abuse these powers and mistreat seamen. Officers were well-fed, while seamen went hungry. Pirate captains, on the other hand, had good reasons to treat their crews well. They had no formal legal framework to support them in case of mutiny, and a pirate captain who persistently mistreated his crew had a high chance of ending up overboard. This way of dealing with a cruel commander was an informal institution with an effective *self-regulating mechanism*. Therefore, pirates usually enjoyed more freedom and better living conditions than ordinary seamen.

Of course, the money wasn't bad either. An ordinary merchant sailor in the period 1700–50 would make about £1.6 a month on average, approximately £200 pounds sterling at current values. Even a captain would be paid no more than £6 a month. A pirate, on the other hand, could potentially make enough money to retire after a single successful raid. There are documented cases of pirates receiving £500,000 each, such as in 1720 for the Flying Dragon's crew. Considering that at the time £500 meant being set for life, these takings were considerable, to say the least.

The role of *incentives* is crucial in economics. Institutional Economics in particular looks at how best to design an organization so that its members have the correct motivation to work toward a shared goal. Incentives are dealt with in many places throughout this book: Chapter 3, for example, includes an analysis of incentives in the context of property rights theory, contract theories, and transaction costs economics, after which Parts III and IV look at incentives in the *different governance structures* that we distinguish.

## *Decision time*

Before boarding the ship, pirates convened in a council to decide where to sail first to get provisions. Once this was arranged, a second council determined where they would go next to steal treasure. This second council also agreed written articles, specifying clearly how much money each pirate would make from the voyage, usually expressed in shares of the loot, on a 'no prey, no pay' principle. These specific rules established the payments for all crew members, including the carpenter and surgeon, as well as a crude form of health insurance in the form of compensation for loss of diverse body parts. For example, loss of a right arm: 600 pieces of eight, or five slaves; and loss of an eye: 100 pieces of eight, or one slave ('pieces of eight' were the Spanish coins used at the time). Sometimes incentives were also established in the form of positive sanctions, such as bonuses for courage or spotting targets.

The articles set down in the pirate constitutions had to be agreed unanimously and are an example of a *contract*. As time went on, crews copied the most useful provisions from other constitutions, and dropped unsuccessful ones, leading to a relatively unified law system within this community. One advantage of democratic proceedings in the pirate councils was that the *effectiveness* of institutions dramatically increased. Given that the pirates had agreed the articles themselves, there were far fewer discipline problems than if they had been imposed by the captain or quartermaster. In other words, the contract tended to become *self-enforcing*, reducing the need for *sanctions*. We could look upon this law system as a sort of *convention*, to which everybody would adhere because it had proved its usefulness over the years. The shaping of this system was in fact the result of a *dynamic process*, which in general terms will be elaborated on in Chapter 4.

Additionally, the fact that pirates had some sort of health insurance reduced the *incentive to shirk* when attacking merchant ships. Shirking is an often-used term in economics and denotes the behavior of someone who (tries to) avoid an assigned task. There is a large literature on incentives and the reduction of shirking in organizations; you can find more on this topic in Chapters 3 and 6.

Other rules were equally clear. Any pirate keeping a piece of loot for himself was severely punished, or at the very least cast out of the society. There were random searches, to check that nobody was hiding treasure somewhere on the ship; pirates were very serious about *enforcing* their *property rights* (see Chapter 3).

## *Resistance is futile*

But pirates faced several obstacles to their 'transactions', chief among them the violent means by which they took over other ships ('prizes'). Crew members could die in battle, or be maimed, which meant additional resources would be spent on compensation. Also, there could be material damage to both the pirate ship and the prize, which in the worst case would mean either or both sinking, and the treasure being lost. Despite being known as bloodthirsty murderers who loved a good fight, in fact pirates sought to minimize these *transaction costs*. As we shall see in Chapter 3, *transaction costs* are not only crucial to understanding the private governance structures of 'market contracts', 'hierarchies' and 'hybrid structures' (all three will be elaborated in Part III), but also the public governance structures 'regulation' and 'state-owned enterprise' (see Part IV).

This does not mean to say that pirates were nice people: when they had to torture or kill captives to obtain information or punish them for resistance, they could be extremely creative in their methods. See Leeson (2007b) for details of their gory practices, which include graphic descriptions of intestines on deck, and niceties involving knives, fire, rope and the like. So how could pirates take over a ship without using force? One of the ways in which they tried to avoid bloodshed was to emphasize their status as violent men who would give no quarter; in this way, they hoped to frighten opponents into immediate surrender. We deal in Part III with the importance of *reputation* in reducing transaction costs.

At a time when the only way to identify other ships at sea was by means of flags, the famous Jolly Roger with the skull and crossbones was an emblem that seamen of all nationalities came to know and fear. Other pirates used a red flag, meaning that they would give no quarter if resisted. Both flags had the same intention: to try to convince the captains (or crew) of merchant ships to surrender peacefully. The rule of quarter to those who surrendered was strictly observed by pirates. Unfortunately for those who did try to resist, pirates were also very strict in enforcing the no quarter rule, and both crew and captain were usually killed if they proved to be uncooperative. In any case, there is evidence that the Jolly Roger and the red flag worked extremely well, and conflict was often avoided. These symbols in the form of flags can in fact be looked upon as an *effective informal institution* that aimed to *constrain* certain behavior.

## *The quartermaster*

While they were usually treated well, pirates were well aware of the risks of being exploited by captains, and sought to limit their powers. To do this, pirates created the position of quartermaster, a person who was in charge of the distribution of food, and the selection and distribution of loot. The captain was mainly in charge during battles. This separation of powers helped to limit abuses of power. Both captain and quartermaster were elected democratically, and if the pirate crew was unsatisfied with their performance, they could be discharged (and sometimes marooned on a desert island).

The relationship between captain, quartermaster and crew on board pirate ships can be analyzed using the principal–agent theory, which is presented in Chapter 3. The principal–agent theory, in short, deals with the problems of delegating decision power to other people, whose actions are difficult to observe. This theory has multiple applications in the analysis of governments, businesses and nonprofit organizations, which we shall see in the application parts of this book.

## *The role of government*

Not all pirates were outside the law, and the relationship between nation-states and pirates was often complex. 'Privateers' were pirates specially commissioned by national governments to attack the ships of enemy countries, and the goods stolen in this way were split between government and privateer. Unfortunately, privateers would sometimes forget that they were only supposed to attack enemy ships, and revert to their traditional practice of stealing from everyone.

Other government policies had an indirect influence on pirate activities. After the War of Spanish Succession ended in 1713, many naval seamen faced unemployment. At the same time, the mercantilist policies favored by governments put in place many restrictions on shipping, which limited the options for seamen to find lawful employment. For example, English seamen were not allowed to work on foreign ships. Inevitably, these restrictions on trade led to the rise of black markets and smuggling, thus providing an attractive alternative for out-of-work seamen.

## *Modern piracy*

Today, pirates continue to operate, particularly in locations such as Indonesia, the coast of Somalia and the north of Brazil. According to the International Maritime Bureau, the high-risk areas in 2007 were Indonesia, Nigeria, Somalia, Bangladesh and Tanzania. Instead of knives and pistols, pirates now use automatic weapons and rocket-propelled grenades. They also have new methods, including holding the crew and ship to ransom rather than merely stealing the cargo.

Pirates are also attracted by the cash kept in a safe on most ships, which is used to pay port fees and seamen's wages, and to buy supplies. A major problem in combating modern piracy is that, if an attack occurs in international waters, there is a legal vacuum as to which country should defend the cargo ships and/or should take responsibility for investigating and punishing the attackers. This is connected to the phenomenon of *free riding behavior*, which will be encountered several times in this book. In fact, attacking a largely unarmed crew at sea, where it can take days for backup to arrive, is easy work for criminals. The shipping companies often do not report incidents, as they fear both the bad press and losing their insurance.

A report in the *National Geographic* magazine (Gwin, 2007) featured pirates boasting of their ability to make entire cargoes 'disappear'. Interestingly, they also claimed that the expensive training required to obtain a license as a seaman pushes many into piracy. It would seem that, given a particular *institutional environment*, a certain brand of seaman continues to evaluate rationally the benefits of working legally compared to piracy. As long as their economic analysis favors robbing ships, there will be pirates.

---

## REVIEW QUESTIONS

1 What is meant by institutions?
  (a) First explain in general terms;
  (b) Elaborate with the aid of the institutional scheme (see Figure 1.1);
  (c) Discuss the relevance of studying institutions.
2 What is the difference between formal and informal institutions?
3 Why do societies usually have both formal and informal institutions?

4. Can you think of institutions that exist in your own country, but not in others?
5. What is the link between market imperfections and institutions?
6. Explain in your own words the difference between the 'efficiency approach' and the 'vested interest approach' of Institutional Economics.
7. A well-known phrase is 'institutions matter'. Elaborate on this giving your own example, and connect this to the enabling and constraining function of institutions.
8. Describe free riding behavior.
9. Select your own real-life case (or research topic) and apply at least three of the Institutional Economics concepts of this chapter to that case.

# Appendixes to Chapter 1

## APPENDIX A: NEOCLASSICAL ANALYSIS OF MARKET STRUCTURES

Institutional Economics focuses on the way that actors organize their transactions in an imperfect world. The basic neoclassical model describes the perfect world, and therefore serves as a reference. Moreover, modern Neoclassical Economics (NCE) also analyzes market imperfections, but does not focus on institutional solutions. Appendix A is in particular intended for the reader who is not yet familiar with the basics of NCE. The assumptions made about the characteristics of the actors will be described first, followed by those about the characteristics of the markets in which the actors operate.

### Neoclassical assumptions with respect to the actors

In NCE, actors are seen as fully rational, optimizing individuals with given preferences, whose transactions result in equilibrium outcomes. We shall elaborate briefly on this. Actors (persons or firms) act *(fully) rationally* if they maximize their total utility (or profit) subject to certain constraints. This is called *optimizing behavior*.

Fully rational actors have a clear picture of the objectives they want to realize. They also know precisely which instruments are available to them that make it possible to realize the objective; they know which combination of production factors minimizes costs, or which combination of products maximizes utility. Their behavior is *preference driven*. A rational preference is, to put it simply, a statement that one product or one package of products is favored over another in a consistent way. Preferences are assumed to be given.

Neoclassical theory deals exclusively with *individual* behavior. This implies that individual actors are the units of analysis, irrespective of whether they are a producer or a firm on the one hand, or a consumer or household on the other. In a perfectly competitive market, *equilibrium* is defined as equality of aggregate demand of individual consumers and aggregate supply of individual suppliers. The fully rational individuals receive through prices the information they need to make the right decisions (in terms of optimizing behavior).

### Neoclassical assumptions with respect to the markets

To give the reader a greater understanding of the functioning of markets in neoclassical theory, in this part we shall briefly present the basic ideas behind models of perfect and imperfect competition.

## Perfect competition

The basic model of NCE assumes equilibrium in a market, whereby all consumers maximize their utility and producers maximize profits. Consumers take their preferences (utility) as a given, and producers take the production technologies as a given. If certain technical conditions are met with respect to preferences and technologies (which will not be discussed in this book), then an equilibrium in the neoclassical model of perfect competition can be described on the basis of the following five important conditions:

1 Products are *homogeneous* and perfectly substitutable for each other. This implies that suppliers do not compete on the basis of differences in quality but only on the basis of price.
2 The *number of buyers and sellers* is large enough to ensure that nobody has market power; in other words, no one can individually influence the price of either the resources used in production or the final product.
3 Everybody has all relevant *information* about price and quality, as a result of which only one price results (given homogeneity).
4 There are *no barriers of entry or exit* into any type of market (with respect to goods and services, labor, capital and natural resources). This implies that entrepreneurs can move freely into markets that are profitable and out of markets that are loss-making.
5 *Public goods* and *externalities* do not exist.

When all these conditions apply, the price mechanism will ensure that a competitive equilibrium outcome will be reached such that individuals' utility and firms' profits are maximized. This is explained in more detail below.

### Partial equilibrium

In a *partial* equilibrium analysis the conditions of equilibrium in a market for one specific product are examined. Simplified to one supply curve and one demand curve, the diagram is as shown in Figure 1.2. Prices (P) are on the vertical axis and quantity (Q) is on the horizontal axis. The demand curve D indicates the maximum price individuals would be willing to pay for a certain quantity of a product, given their income, the prices of all other goods and their preferences. In other words, the demand curve represents *the marginal benefits* that buyers derive from consuming one more unit. The supply curve S indicates the minimum price at which sellers would be willing to supply a certain quantity of a product, given the number of suppliers, the level of technology and the prices of the production factors. Or in other words, the supply curve represents the *marginal costs* (MC) that suppliers must incur to produce one more unit.

At price $P^e$ and quantity $Q^e$ the price that consumers are willing to pay equals marginal costs (P = MC) and the market will clear: the market is in equilibrium. In the case of perfect competition, in which all markets are in the above-mentioned equilibrium, economic welfare is maximized. This is referred to as an efficient outcome.

### General equilibrium

The disadvantage of partial equilibrium analysis is that individual markets are studied in isolation, while in reality all markets are connected to one another: if the

**Figure 1.2** *Market equilibrium in perfect competition*

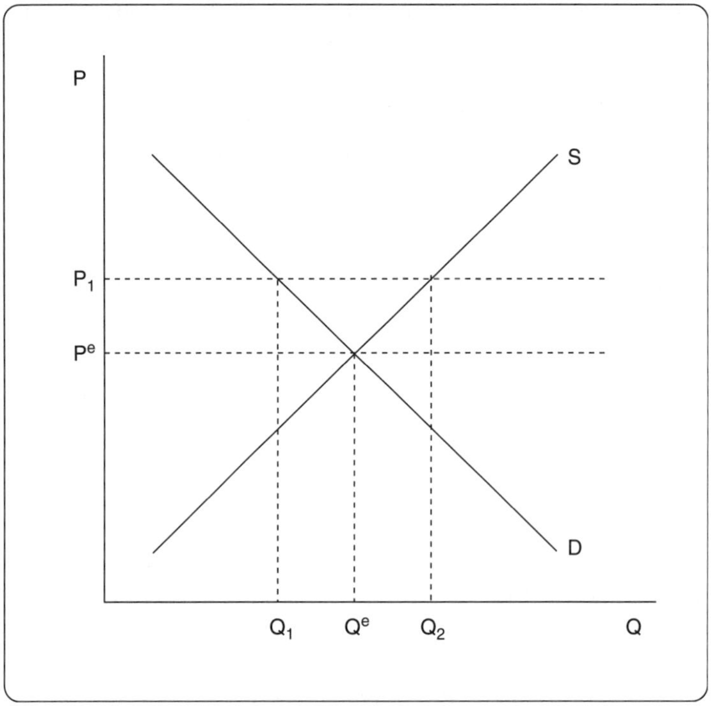

equilibrium in the labor market for apple pickers changes – for example, because wages go up – this increases the production costs for apple suppliers and consequently drives up the equilibrium price in the market for apples. If consumers suddenly become aware that eating apples is much healthier than eating hamburgers, this will affect the equilibrium in other markets – such as, for example, the markets for oranges and French fries – if these two products are considered to be substitutes for apples and hamburgers, respectively.

Therefore, in *general* equilibrium analysis, all markets are taken into account simultaneously. The influential economist Léon Walras described a general equilibrium in the sense that all markets characterized by perfect competition are in equilibrium at the same time, given that they are interconnected via the budget constraint (income earned on input markets is equal to the value of goods and services consumed on product markets). As a consequence, all markets reach an efficient outcome.

Because all markets are interdependent, all prices and all quantities demanded and supplied must be balanced simultaneously. However, if the economy is in disequilibrium, market parties must try to find out what the equilibrium prices and quantities are by way of repeated experiments. Prices will be adjusted through trial and error until equilibrium is reached. Walras called this process of achieving equilibrium a process of *tâtonnement*, or groping. To adjust prices, Walras introduced a hypothetical entity in the form of an auctioneer. The auctioneer facilitates market adjustment in disequilibrium by announcing prices and then modifying these until equilibrium is achieved. Trade only takes place in equilibrium.

In terms of the partial equilibrium model shown in Figure 1.2, the role of the auctioneer can be illustrated quite easily. Suppose that the auctioneer starts the bidding process by announcing price level $P_1$. Producers will thereupon announce that they want to supply the amount $Q_2$, while consumers announce that they only want to buy amount $Q_1$. The auctioneer will then conclude that this results in disequilibrium and hence no trade comes about. Consequently, the auctioneer will lower the price until equilibrium is reached at price level $P^e$.

The role of the auctioneer in equilibrating the economy shows that institutions are not completely neglected by Walras.

The outcome of the general equilibrium model (prices and quantities and a corresponding distribution of products over individuals, hence of income) maximizes total economic welfare (the total of consumer and producer surplus), and is therefore also called a 'first best solution'. This implies that all production factors are used in the best available way, and that those products are produced that are valued most, both in terms of profits and in terms of utilities. Therefore, this outcome is also called *allocative efficient*. Yet another way to look at this outcome is to realize that it also implies that no actor can be made better off (higher utility or higher profits) without making someone else worse off. This situation is also called *Pareto efficient*. This is easy to see: if someone could be made better off without someone else being worse off, total utility or total profits could be increased (called a *Pareto improvement*), but this implies that total welfare was not maximized in the first place.

## *Endogenous and exogenous variables*

The perfect competition model is very convenient to illustrate the concepts of endogenous and exogenous variables, which we shall discuss in more detail in Chapter 2. An endogenous variable is a variable that is explained within a model in which it appears. An exogenous variable is also part of a model, but is not explained within this model: it is predetermined with respect to the model.

Note that the actors in the model of perfect competition take prices as a given, so that demand and supply can be defined. Demand and supply together determine prices; these prices (in equilibrium) are exactly those that are assumed to be given for individual actors. This happens simultaneously, as the example of the Walrasian auctioneer showed: only when prices are in equilibrium will trade take place. Hence, prices are given for individuals, but they are endogenous variables in the model.

The following description illustrates the endogenous and exogenous variables in the partial equilibrium model. Each individual consumer maximizes his utility with respect to the amount of products to be bought, given income and prices. The utility function (preferences) of each individual and his income are exogenous, in the sense that they are not explained by the model; prices are also given to the individual consumer, but they are to be determined by the model in the following way. Utility maximization leads to a relation between the amount of products to be bought individually as a function of the given prices, income and preferences: this defines an individual demand curve for each product. All individual demand curves for each product are added to one market demand curve. Given a market supply curve for each good, we can determine the market price (an endogenous variable) for each good and the market quantity (also an endogenous variable).

One of the assumptions in this model is that the number of firms is given and not determined by the model (only price and quantities are endogenous variables). We can extend the model and make the number of firms also endogenous. For example, if the market prices are such that profits are made, this will attract new firms. Hence, supply will change (more of the goods will be produced), so that prices will decrease, thereby increasing the quantities demanded. Also, the larger amount of goods implies an increasing demand for inputs, hence (generally speaking) higher input prices. These higher input prices will increase costs for the firms, which will have an additional effect on the supply curve. When there are no more profits to be gained by entry, the model determines what is the (equilibrium) number of firms. A model that focuses on the short-run determination of market prices will take the environment (such as the number of firms) as an exogenous variable. A model that focuses on the long-run determination of prices must take into account the effects of entry and input prices. So, what endogenous or exogenous variables are depends on the research question one wants to answer. As noted earlier, there is more on this in Chapter 2.

## *Imperfect competition*

Contrary to conditions of perfect competition, in which none of the market parties influences the price, *market power* is the ability of one or more sellers to control the price of a product to some extent, by setting the price above the marginal cost level. We distinguish monopoly, oligopoly and monopolistic competition. In addition, there is the case of monopsony, in which a single buyer has the power to pay a price that is below the competitive level. We shall elaborate briefly on all four terms:

1. A *monopoly* is a market structure in which there is only one seller on the market. This situation can only endure if entry into the industry is blocked. Monopoly power might arise through location effects: a local store may be able to demand higher prices because its customers would have to incur high transport costs to buy from distant competitors. Another kind of barrier to entering the industry occurs when economies of scale are so prominent that competition is impractical. We refer to this as a *natural monopoly*. Economies of scale of this kind can be found in, for example, activities in which capital costs are predominant such as gas, water and electricity networks. Finally, the entrance to the industry may be blocked through legal rules, with the reservation of production rights being offered to licensees or patent holders only.
2. A market in which only a few suppliers are active is called an *oligopoly*. Each producer in this type of market has a substantive market share such that he can influence the price to a certain degree. Since there are only a few rivals, all suppliers realize that they are interdependent: an action by one supplier will cause a reaction with the competitors in order to defend (or win) market share. In some cases, oligopolistic firms form a *cartel*. This is a market structure in which firms collude: an agreement among firms in an industry to remove competition. Adam Smith warned in his book, *The Wealth of Nations*, that businessmen are inclined to collude to defraud the consumer: 'People

of the same trade seldom meet together, even for merriment and diversion, but the conversation ends in a conspiracy against the public, or in some contrivance to raise prices' (Smith, 1776, p. 128). A well-known current example of a cartel is the OPEC. In many countries, cartels are illegal.

3 A *monopsony* is a market structure with only one buyer. It is the mirror image of a monopoly. A sole supplier with market power can set the price above the level of marginal costs, while a sole buyer with market power can set the price below the level of marginal factor costs. An example of an almost pure monopsony is a government that is the buyer of almost all road construction, or a factory that is the only employer in a certain region, and hence the only one demanding labor.

4 *Monopolistic competition* is prevalent in markets in which there are several sellers of products that are all in some way unique, but at the same time close substitutes for one another. These types of products are found in the clothing and food industries, and in services such as hairdressers, restaurants and so on. While each supplier has his own variety of a certain product he does not have much influence over his price because of the close similarity between his product and those of the competition. Therefore, every seller has to differentiate her product in order to acquire a larger share of the market. This results in a wide range of products, styles and brands from which the consumer may choose.

The less competitive the market becomes, the more prices can be set above marginal costs, with the result that economic welfare is not maximized. This is a 'deadweight loss' to society, which is illustrated below.

### Deadweight loss in case of imperfect competition

*Deadweight loss* is an economic inefficiency. It is the reduction in *social surplus* or *economic welfare* (the sum of consumer surplus and producer surplus) caused by market power: prices are higher than the level of marginal costs. The magnitude of the deadweight loss is illustrated in Figure 1.3, in which $P_m$ = the monopoly price; $P_c$ = the perfect competition price; $Q_m$ = quantity supplied and demanded under monopoly; and $Q_c$ = quantity supplied and demanded under perfect competition. The monopoly maximizes its profits by setting MC not equal to price but to marginal revenue (MR). Consequently, the equilibrium quantity is reduced and the market price is increased. The shaded triangle shows the size of the reduced social surplus.

Although the higher market price on balance increases the producer surplus, because of the smaller quantity that is traded, economic welfare has diminished because of a relatively larger loss in consumer surplus.

To recapitulate: in the case of market power, price will be higher than marginal costs, which implies that consumers are willing to pay more for an additional unit than it costs to produce that extra output. So, this is an inefficient outcome; in a sense, there is too little output on the market and, consequently, too little use of resources (labor, capital and so on). The higher the degree of market power, the more serious this problem: higher market power implies a greater difference between price and marginal costs, hence a higher deadweight loss. For any given level of marginal costs, a higher price is determined by a (relatively) steeper demand curve, hence the steeper the demand curve, the higher the deadweight loss.

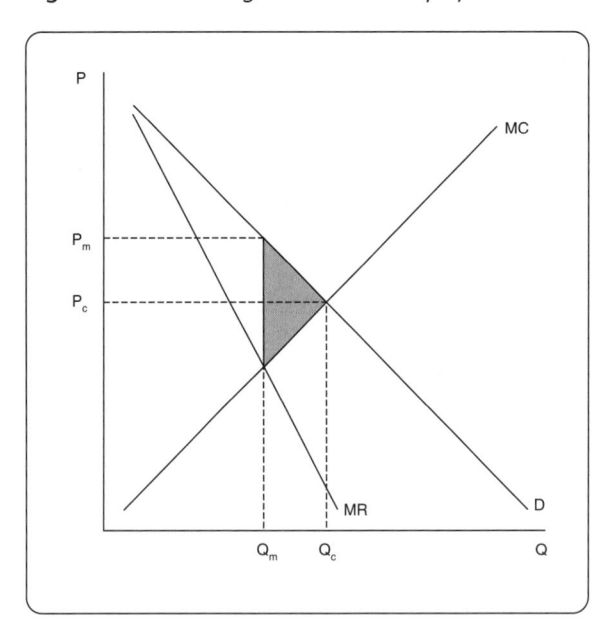

**Figure 1.3** *Deadweight loss in a monopoly situation*

## APPENDIX B: DEVIATIONS FROM THE PERFECT COMPETITION MODEL

As was made clear in Appendix A above, at least five conditions must hold in order to speak of perfect competition. If one or more conditions do not hold, the situation immediately becomes an instance of *market imperfections*. This is the case with respect to any of the market structures described in Appendix A (other than perfect competition). A deviation of the perfect competition model may also be the result of the existence of pure public goods, imperfect information and externalities. These issues are dealt with elsewhere in the book.

For now, the question is whether or not additional institutional arrangements are able to repair the inefficiencies. If they *can* be repaired in the technical sense, then another question arises: *should* the inefficiencies be repaired? To see why this is an important question, consider the following situation. If a monopoly, hence an inefficiency (deadweight loss), exists: how can this inefficiency be repaired? A simple answer would be to regulate the price. This calls for an enforcing agency or regulator (see also Chapter 8). But the fact that the inefficiency *can* be repaired does not mean that it *should* be. This depends whether the institutional arrangement itself is efficient. Suppose that the costs of having the regulator are higher than the deadweight loss that is being avoided. Clearly, this would be inefficient.

A slightly different way of looking at the monopoly situation is to answer the question of whether free entry is possible with sufficient speed: if so, the monopoly position will be temporary and, generally speaking, might not call for regulation.

Another example is the market structure 'monopolistic competition': the heterogeneity of the product does enable each single seller to charge a price above marginal

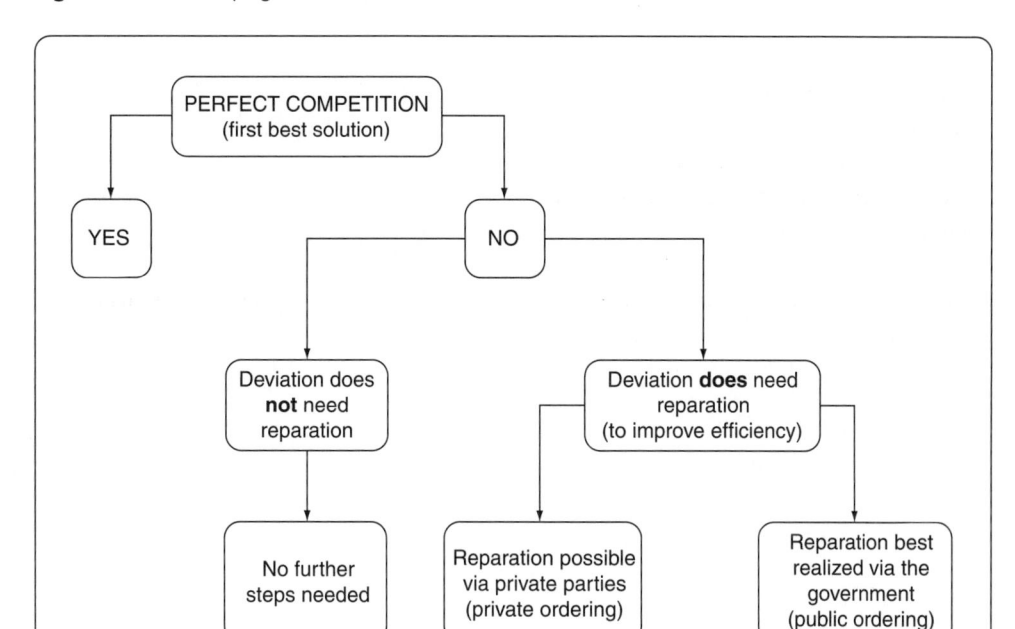

**Figure 1.4** *Remedying market inefficiencies*

```
                    PERFECT COMPETITION
                    (first best solution)
                    /                   \
                  YES                    NO
                                        /  \
                    Deviation does          Deviation does need
                    not need                reparation
                    reparation              (to improve efficiency)
                         |                   /              \
                    No further      Reparation possible    Reparation best
                    steps needed    via private parties    realized via the
                                    (private ordering)     government
                                                           (public ordering)
```

costs, but not that much more because of the existence of a large number of suppliers of similar products; and at the same time, consumers enjoy a wide choice of products. So, interference in this type of market cannot remedy inefficiency, since that would imply that the products should be made homogeneous. This, generally speaking, is not possible. But, even if it could be done, it would not be what consumers and producers would want. But even if consumers and producers would not really mind, it would be very hard to see how an institutional arrangement would be able to remedy the inefficiencies in an efficient way (if at all). So, even if it could be remedied, it should not be done.

We sum up these questions in Figure 1.4. If there are deviations from the perfect competition model, can and should these deviations be remedied by an additional institutional arrangement? If they cannot be remedied, or if they can, but should not (from the efficiency perspective), then the deviations need not be repaired. If they both can and should, they need to be repaired. Of course, Figure 1.4 does not inform us when and how the remedy should take place: that will be discussed elsewhere in the book.

The reparation of an efficiency loss will generally involve additional (transaction) costs. Economic welfare may then be optimized, albeit at extra cost compared to the 'first best solution' (corresponding to a perfectly competitive general equilibrium); this optimal welfare level is therefore called a 'second best solution'.

For all forms of market imperfections, it depends on the gravity of the efficiency loss and the cost of the available solutions, whether institutional solutions can best (at the lowest possible transaction costs) be realized by private parties or by the government. This applies to:

- Imperfect information;
- Abuse of market power;
- Natural monopolies;
- Externalities and (de)merit goods; and
- Pure public goods.

In Part III, and in particular in Chapter 8, in Part IV we shall discuss this central topic in more detail.

# PART II

# Theory

Chapter 2    Theoretical Framework
Chapter 3    Static Approaches to Institutions
Chapter 4    The Dynamics of Institutions

# INTRODUCTION

In this part of the book we introduce the main institutional economic theories. Before we do so in Chapters 3 and 4, we shall first set out in general terms in Chapter 2 what a theory entails. In short, in a theory, facts are analyzed in relation to one another. A theory of the price of oil, for example, would relate the price (the variable the theory wants to explain) to one or more variables the scientist considers important for that explanation (such as the demand and supply of oil, and the technology to produce and distribute it).

A theory aims at explaining a phenomenon – for example, an institution – and in doing so the scientist makes an abstraction, a model of reality. In this abstract, theoretical world the scientist aims to reduce the complexities observed in reality to a limited number of explanatory variables and relationships. In other words, the purpose of theory is first of all to understand and explain causalities in the real world by reducing complexities to the smallest possible number of 'fundamentals'. When the explanation is tested and the scientific community agrees that a phenomenon is caused by a specific set of variables, our knowledge of the real world has grown. We better understand how 'the world works', and that knowledge can be used for making predictions. Furthermore, when we understand causalities we are able to design effective policies for both managers of firms and politicians in government.

You will learn in this part of the book that different theories exist within one discipline (such as economics) and even within one part of the discipline (such as Institutional Economics). You will discover that scientists disagree, and that several rival theories can exist, each claiming to explain the same phenomenon. You will also learn that different theories exist within the domain of Institutional Economics, addressing different questions and working with different abstractions and models. However, these diverse theories can be complementary and together provide a better understanding of the complex real world than each of them could do separately. In Chapter 2 we shall introduce you to two different schools of Institutional Economics: New Institutional Economics (NIE) and Original Institutional Economics (OIE). The details of these schools will be spelled out in Chapters 3 and 4.

Following the classification used in Chapter 1, you will make acquaintance with both institutional theories that are designed for answering questions of a comparative static nature and with theories that are better equipped for dynamic issues. Similarly, some institutional theories work from an efficiency approach, while others use a vested interest perspective.

# 2 Theoretical Framework

## CONTENTS

- **Introduction**
- **On theory**
  - Theory is abstraction
  - Agency and structures
  - Methodological individualism, collectivism and interactionism
  - Endogenous and exogenous variables
  - Institutions matter
- **Two schools in Institutional Economics: NIE and OIE**
  - New Institutional Economics (NIE)
  - Original Institutional Economics (OIE)
  - Comparing the NIE and OIE approaches
- **On the relevance of institutional theories**
  - Is the theory relevant to the question being asked?
  - Is the theory relevant to the conditions at hand?
- **A closer look at economic systems**
  - The Anglo-Saxon model
  - The Continental European model
  - The Asian model
- **Concluding remarks**
- **Review questions**
- **Appendixes**

## INTRODUCTION

In Chapter 1 we introduced the characteristics of institutions and their role in economic life. We have applied a broad definition of institutions and consider them to be durable systems of rules that structure social interactions. Institutions both constrain the behavior of economic actors and enable their activities. Norms and legal rules, for example, constrain the possibilities of actors choosing governance structures to co-ordinate their transactions, and at the same time institutions reduce uncertainties and align the expectations of actors, which make planning for the future possible.

We indicated how efficiency can play a part in the creation of institutions, but also that the role of vested interests is important for understanding the existence of specific institutions. We pointed out the role of values and norms, and the interaction between legal rules and organizational structures resulting in a dynamic process of change of institutions. In Chapter 1 we also touched on the importance of technology in the economy: as a static variable it determines the optimal scale of production, and as a dynamic factor it largely influences the competitiveness of firms and countries. This way of looking at the subject matter of Institutional Economics means that, by definition, we are dealing with complex systems in which different elements interact. Moreover, economics is a social science, implying that we are dealing with human beings, who can choose and who have the free will to make decisions. People differ with respect to motivation, use of power, respect for the welfare of others and so on.

In this chapter we present theoretical models designed to study institutional structures and their dynamics. How can we understand, explain and predict institutions in a complex world? Institutional Economics tries to deal with these complexities by making abstractions and models, in which the complex world is reduced to a limited number of fundamentals. As social scientists, we make assumptions about behavior, about the environment and about the relationship between actors and their environment. You will learn that, in different theories, different assumptions are made about the actors, and that different structures in the environment are part of the theory.

In the first section of this chapter we shall discuss in general terms what is the purpose of theory, how models and theoretical frameworks can be constructed, and how these models can be applied. In the second section, we introduce two schools in Institutional Economics and explain how they are structured. In the third section, we further explore what kinds of problems are relevant to the two schools. In the fourth section, we round off with an illustration on economic systems.

## ON THEORY

### Theory is abstraction

Every scientific discipline, be it history, sociology, physics or economics, makes abstractions about reality with the purpose of understanding the basic causal mechanisms of a phenomenon. A central question in Institutional Economics is about the existence and dynamics of firms. Why would the firm exist as an organization when we have markets and contracts to co-ordinate transactions? And when a firm has been created, why would it change over time; for example, why would it merge with a supplier or a customer to become a vertically integrated firm (see Chapters 5, 6 and 7 for more details)? Institutional Economics can explain these and many other questions.

When a scientist is able to explain a phenomenon, she can also make predictions. When technology changes in a specific direction (such as towards a mode of production that is less labor-intensive), it can be predicted how firms will change their combination of production factors and their scale of production. Based on these predictions, a scientist can be consulted about effective management and policy instruments to realize specific outcomes. If policy-makers want to increase the competitiveness of a specific region and for that purpose would like to have more investments by firms in innovative projects, how could government then stimulate such investments (see Chapter 8 for more details)?

You can imagine that a detailed description of the phenomenon shows you all the actors involved, each with their own specific characteristics, as well as all the elements of the environment and all possible relationships that might influence behavior. Such detailed research would provide a rich picture of the phenomenon. The downside of rich pictures is that they may tell you about every detail, but that they do not provide a clear oversight and insight into the basic structures and causalities. For that purpose, scientists make *models*, which are representations of a phenomenon. These models can be physical, such as a scale model of a house; mathematical (perhaps a set of equations in an economic model); or logical, when a prediction is logically derived from a set of assumptions. A model is not a precise description of reality, but rather a representation. But a correct representation is important, because when predictions and policies are based on models that do not represent reality correctly, all kinds of unexpected and unintended outcomes of the policy instruments occur.

In this book, a theory is used as a plausible general principle, or body of principles, offered to explain a phenomenon and supported by facts. In economics, for example, the theory of demand and supply can help to explain changes in the price of a product. In Institutional Economics you will encounter theories that explain institutions based on the general principle of cost-minimizing behavior in relation to specific structures in which the actors operate. In these theories you will find abstractions of actors, the structures in their environment and the relationship between the actors and those structures. These three elements of every economic theory will be discussed in the next section.

## Agency and structures

Suppose you are about to buy a new bicycle and there are many more consumers like you, who also plan to buy a bicycle in the near future. These plans are, generally speaking, unknown to producers of bicycles. Suppose these producers want to reduce their uncertainty about (future) market demand and would like to have an idea of the demand for bicycles – say, in the coming five years. In order to estimate future demand, each bicycle producer tries to guess what the preferences of his (future) customers are, how they will react to price changes, how they evaluate product innovations, to what extent they will imitate the behavior of others, to what extent their behavior is based on habits, and so on. The producer would also like to know about the behavior of his competitors. How will they react when a new type of bicycle is offered in the market? Can they quickly imitate it, or are they tied to existing products and production techniques? How do they react to a price change among any of the other producers?

The situation described in the example can be rephrased in terms of agency and structures:

- The term *agency* is often used in social sciences, and refers to the capacity of individual actors to act freely and without constraints.
- The term *structure* refers to the environment of the actor, which may have an impact on his behavior to a lesser or greater extent. That environment consists of different

types of structures, such as market structures, the structure of (in)formal institutions, governance structures, technology, the natural environment, and finally, the structure of power in society. We shall discuss these various structures in Parts III and IV of this book.

The discussion about agency and structures is also in fact a discussion about actors and structures. To put it simply: how do structures determine an actor's capacity to act freely, and how does an actor's capacity to act freely determine structures? In order to economize on terminology, we shall continue here to discuss agency and structure in terms of actors. This is to avoid confusion about the different ways that 'agency' is also used; this will be examined in Chapters 3, 8 and 9.

In our bicycle example, one way to know more about the behavior of the other actors in the market is to analyze the environment in which these actors operate. In Chapter 1, we discussed several parts of the actors' environment. First is the *market structure*. Different types of market structure can be distinguished, such as perfect competition, oligopoly, monopolistic competition and monopoly. In a theory, the role of the structure can be modeled in such a way that the structure constrains, or even determines, the behavior of the actor. In the micro theories detailed in the Appendixes to Chapter 1 you saw that, in neoclassical theory, actors face a given structure and then determine their optimal output level. However, in real markets situations will often be encountered in which market structures not only constrain behavior, but also leave several options open to individual producers. In Chapter 5 we shall discuss in more detail the role of market structures in relation to the behavior of consumers and producers. Here it suffices to point to the role of market structures in constraining the behavior of actors, and hence making their actions more predictable.

The same holds for the other elements of the environment of economic actors: the *structure of informal and formal institutions* and the *governance structures,* such as firms. You saw in Chapter 1 that institutions such as values, norms, laws and organizations enable and constrain behavior and make predictions about behavior possible. In Chapter 1 we also pointed to the role of power in protecting vested interests. The power structure of society is reflected in the distribution of property rights and the rights conferred by political decisions that structure to a large extent the behavior of the actors in the economic system.

The degree to which structure determines behavior can be different: sometimes a market structure will leave the actors with almost no options, but at other times they will have more room to maneuver and to follow their own strategies. In the case of the latter situation, we say that actors have 'discretionary space', or that there is 'latitude of choice'. In these situations, our producers of bicycles would want to know more about the characteristics of the actors in order to evaluate future developments in the market. The less constraining the structures, the more important our knowledge about the motivations and habits of the actors becomes.

In Institutional Economics, as well as the constraining and enabling role of institutional structures being emphasized, there is also the possibility that actors can create and influence these structures. For example, bicycle producers can merge, making the market structure more concentrated; or producers can create a branch organization that negotiates with government about laws and regulations. The branch organization can promote the use of bicycles because it is an environmentally friendly means of transportation, which, they might argue, deserves lower taxes. Eventually, actors are not only able to influence laws and regulations, but also norms about the 'right' means of transportation. In other words: actors and structures interact.

## Methodological individualism, collectivism and interactionism

The discussion on the relationship between actors and structure is closely related to the question of the methodology of the theory. Is the basic building block the individual, and are all structures explained by the behavior of individual actors? Or, on the contrary, is the structure the point of departure, and does the structure determine behavior? When all social phenomena, such as institutions, are only explained in terms of the characteristics of the individuals involved, then the theory is *methodologically individualistic*. And, in contrast, when all social phenomena are explained fin terms of social structures, then the theory is *methodologically collectivistic*, also called methodologically holistic.

In the case of methodological individualism, the characteristics of individual actors are known and constant; that is, the characteristics of the individual do not change during the analysis as a result of the influence of other actors or because of changes in structures. In Figure 2.1 this is indicated by the one-sided arrow that only points from the individual to the structure and not the other way round. In other words, preferences and characteristics are not explained by the structure of the system.

In the case of methodological collectivism, social structures have their own specific characteristics, which cannot be reduced to the characteristics of individuals. Moreover, structures have their own dynamics, which determine the behavior of the individual. Individual actors are fully captured by the structures, and in the extreme their behavior is determined completely by the structure. This view is summarized in the second column of Figure 2.1. According to critics, the reduction of the explanation of the behavior of individuals to structures alone is untenable, because structures cannot exist without individuals. Similarly, again according to critics, the reduction of

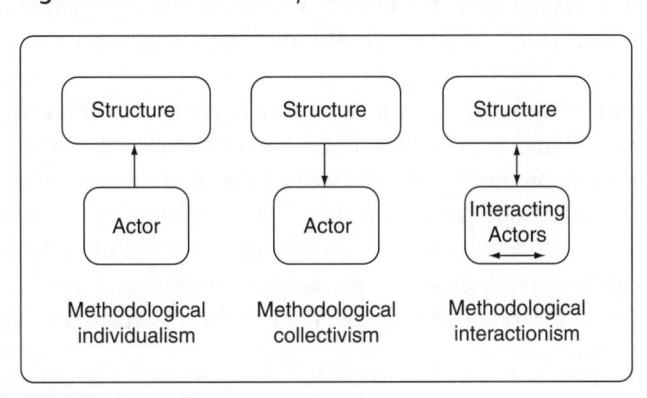

**Figure 2.1** *The relationship between actor and structure*

the explanation of structures to individuals alone is also untenable, because individual actors cannot communicate and interact without structures, such as institutions (Hodgson, 2007).

Methodological individualism and methodological collectivism have been criticized for presenting one-sided pictures of the relationship between actors and structures. As shown above in the example of the bicycle producers, there will often be simultaneous interaction between individuals among themselves as well as simultaneous interaction between individuals and structures. *Methodological interactionism* (see Nooteboom, 2007) is the explanation of social phenomena by the simultaneous interaction(s) between actors and structures such as social phenomena, and among actors. The interactions are shown in the third column of Figure 2.1 by means of the bi-directional arrows, both among the actors and between the actors and structures.

The environment itself has an influence on individuals and modifies their way of thinking, their norms and their values, and these in turn influence the environment (for example, the types of institutions that actors design). You can imagine that firms in the Japanese environment, with a specific structure of values and norms, create a network type of governance structure (called a *keiretsu*; see Chapters 3 and 7), and that, in return, these governance structures influence the values and norms of Japanese society. Similarly, the structure of the *keiretsu* influences the behavior of the firms that belong to the network, which again has an influence on the interaction between members of the *keiretsu*. So structure not only interacts with actors but also influences interaction among actors. Actors simultaneously influence society through both their intentional and unintentional behavior, and give direction to institutional dynamics. In doing so, the individual actors interact with one another, creating shared visions and perceptions. In Chapter 4 we discuss the dynamics of institutions and will give further details of the interactive relationship between actors and structure.

## Endogenous and exogenous variables

When building a theory, a scientist should first be explicit about what she wants to explain. What is the variable to be explained *(endogenous variable,* also called the *dependent variable)* and what are the potential explanatory variables *(exogenous variables,* also called the *independent variables)*? Exogenous means literally 'outside' and refers to the fact that this variable is not explained by the model. Endogenous (inside) means that the phenomenon *is* explained by the model. An example of endogenous and exogenous variables in the neoclassical context has already been presented in the Appendixes to Chapter 1.

The next important step the scientist has to take concerns the distinction between the potential key explanatory variables (to be part of the model) and the ones that are less relevant and therefore need not to be part of the model ('omitted by assumption'). Distinguishing between important and unimportant explanatory variables makes it possible for the theory to concentrate on a limited set of a relevant variables, resulting in clear causalities of the type 'A (endogenous) happens because of B (exogenous)'. A theory should be made as simple as possible; that is, the number of explanatory variables should be kept to a minimum.

Often variables influence each other through complicated feedback. A rise in the price of oil, for example, will have an effect on the innovations in which oil producers and consumers invest, with consequences for future production capacity. Additionally, consumers of large quantities of oil have an incentive to make investments in alternative sources of energy, such as wind power or nuclear energy. This, in turn, will have an effect on the demand for oil. On the other hand, rising prices will make it attractive to exploit new oil reserves, which increases supply. In other words, several related variables explain the changes in the price of oil. The question then becomes how to deal with this feedback, and how to determine what are the exogenous and endogenous variables. When the process of price formation is analyzed in historical time, taking all interdependencies into account, then we typically apply the dynamic approach as described in Chapter 1. We now briefly discuss how Neoclassical Economics models the interdependencies. In this book we refer to the NCE model because it is a clear benchmark against which to compare the different schools of Institutional Economics.

In economics, the school of Neoclassical Economics (NCE) is known because of:

- its precise distinctions between endogenous and exogenous variables;
- the precise descriptions of the actors (their characteristics and the rules of behavior);
- the clear description of the environment in which they operate (market structures, such as perfect competition or monopoly); and
- the precisely formulated relationship between the environment and the actors in the model.

Figure 2.2 shows a simplified representation of the endogenous and exogenous variables of neoclassical theory. In this approach, institutions are omitted, and technology and preferences are important explanatory variables. Typically, the research questions are formulated in terms of 'optimal end states'; for example, what is the least-cost combination of labor and capital to produce 10,000 automobiles at the least cost per auto? Endogenous variables are the quantities of labor and capital, and exogenous variables are the prices of labor and capital, the technologically given relationship between output on the one hand and labor and capital on the other (the *production function*) and the level of output (10,000 in the example). The optimal combination (the outcome of the model) is

**Figure 2.2** *Endogenous and exogenous variables in NCE*

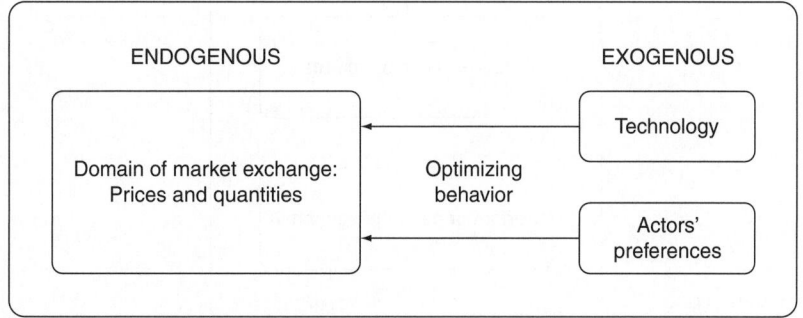

determined as the least-cost combination, hence the model relates the exogenous variables and the endogenous variables in terms of cost minimization.

The actors in NCE models typically operate in an institutional vacuum; institutions are not an exogenous variable; they are just absent, or implicitly assumed to exist and to function perfectly. So, in NCE the structures are given to the actors. In that sense, Figure 2.2 represents the methodological individualistic approach.

In the following section we shall show that in Institutional Economics actors do not operate in an institutional vacuum, but that, on the contrary, 'institutions matter'.

## Institutions matter

Institutions matter as explanatory variables. In Figure 2.3, as we shall explain, the arrows between the variables illustrate that the institutional environment influences behavior, and consequently has an impact on the performance of the economy in terms of economic growth, level of innovation, level of transaction costs and so on.

Economic historians (North, 1990; Greif, 2006) have demonstrated the effects of the institutional context of laws, regulations and informal rules on the investments that actors make, and the consequences of these for economic growth. The general conclusion is that well-defined property rights and well-functioning, objective public courts reduce uncertainties for economic actors and facilitate *efficient* decision-making. Countries with such an institutional structure experience faster economic growth than those without. More specifically, economic growth in China in the 1950s differs from its growth in the 1990s because of the changed institutional context. Economic growth since the 1990s in China has been based on changes in laws and regulations, which provide incentives for producers (also from abroad) to make investments that contribute to economic growth. In the same way, in 2008, economic growth in Japan differed from growth in the USA partly because of differing institutions. Box 2.1 provides an example that institutions matter.

**Figure 2.3** *Institutions matter*

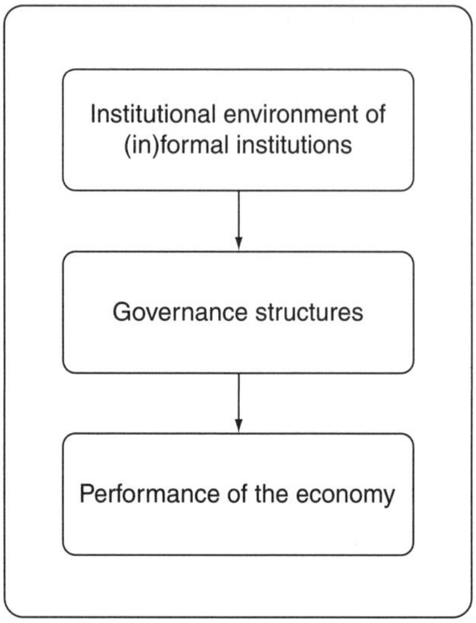

```
┌─────────────────────────────────┐
│  Institutional environment of   │
│    (in)formal institutions      │
└─────────────────┬───────────────┘
                  │
                  ▼
┌─────────────────────────────────┐
│     Governance structures       │
└─────────────────┬───────────────┘
                  │
                  ▼
┌─────────────────────────────────┐
│   Performance of the economy    │
└─────────────────────────────────┘
```

## BOX 2.1  CULTURE AND THE ART OF MACHINE MAINTENANCE: A CAUTIONARY TALE

The idea that culture has an influence on economic outcomes is widespread in popular perception: the Japanese are hardworking, the Germans are great at building quality autos, and Italians rely extensively on personal contacts in business. But the immediate question for the researcher is: what is the impact of culture? If we cannot explain the role of culture, we run the risk of using it as a vague 'catch all' variable to which we refer when all else fails.

Gertler (1997) looked at the interactions between Canadian companies and the German firms that supply them with machines. He found that there were often communication problems between parties: the Canadians complained that the Germans made everything too complicated, while the Germans complained that the Canadians did not look after the machines properly.

However, the author went beyond simply ascribing these problems to culture. According to Gertler, each country's culture is a result of a certain regulatory regime at the national level. The German labor market is characterized by the strong presence of labor unions, leading to low wage competition and low employee turnover. Additionally, union representatives have an active presence on the boards of companies. As a result, workers tend to have a strong feeling of attachment to their company, often as a result of a long-term relationship; and the company, in turn, has an incentive to invest in training for its employees.

On the other hand, in Canada, with its more flexible labor markets, both employees and companies have a more short-term view of the labor relationship, resulting in lower incentives to invest in training and maintenance. From this example, Gertler warns that an over-emphasis on culture may ignore more important factors such as laws and regulations at the national level.

In the explanation of differences in economic growth, an institutional analysis can also point to the existence of institutional structures that provide power to specific interest groups. When in an industry or country a specific group controls the resources of the economy and at the same time has the political power to enact laws, it can be argued that power and vested interests influence economic development in such a way that growth is limited and wealth is distributed unequally (see Box 2.2).

## BOX 2.2  ELITES AND POWER: JUST NOT LETTING GO

In a paper entitled 'De Facto Political Power and Institutional Persistence', Acemoglu and Robinson (2006) introduce a model which explains how, in many cases, power can be remarkably resilient, even when specific institutions, such as constitutions or electoral systems, change. In particular, they present a case in

> which a small elite succeeds in retaining power to the detriment of the majority of the population.
>
> Given its smaller numbers and experience with power, the elite finds it much easier to organize itself to reach its goals, and the rest of the people cannot compete politically. When there is a change in *de jure* (on paper) rules to limit the power of elites, they simply use lobbying, bribery or force to return to their previous position.
>
> Before the American Civil War, the Southern states of the USA were relatively poor. The economy was labor-intensive and based on slavery. After the Civil War, and despite the fact that slavery had been abolished, the Southern elites managed to retain their power by blocking further reforms that would, for example, have helped former slaves to educate themselves. As a result, until the 1940s, the South was still much poorer than the US average, and it took large-scale intervention from the federal government and the Civil Rights movement in the 1950s and 1960s to help overcome the status quo.

In the examples given in Boxes 2.1 and 2.2, institutions are included in the analysis as exogenous, explanatory variables. Institutions are a given variable in the analysis and explain the differences between countries in their levels of investments, types of innovations, distribution of power, level of economic growth and so on. Insights from this type of institutional analysis have been influential in policy circles of the World Bank and the International Monetary Fund. The idea is that 'institutions matter': specific institutions promote economic growth, and developing countries should copy these 'benchmark' institutions. See also pages 36–8 for an example of the relationship between economic growth and the institutions of a country.

## TWO SCHOOLS IN INSTITUTIONAL ECONOMICS: NIE AND OIE

In the USA at the end of the nineteenth century, Thorstein Veblen was a well-known institutional economist, who was highly critical of NCE. In his opinion, NCE was too formal and abstract, too static and wrongly based on individual actors that were disconnected from their institutional environment. Until around 1945 an influential group of institutional economists dominated the development of the discipline in the USA. Clarence Ayres, Wesley Mitchell and John R. Commons joined Veblen in his criticism of NCE and underlined the importance of including institutions in the economic explanation (see Gruchy, 1972 for details).

Modeling actors as maximizing machines operating in an institutional vacuum was not considered to be an adequate model of economic reality. In the opinion of these American institutionalists, the economy was first of all a matter of the dynamics of changing institutions that influenced economic behavior. In that process, technology, values and laws interact, and economic models and theories should capture that aspect of reality. Economic actors operate in specific institutional environments and markets are institutionalized structures, in which power is as important as efficiency in understanding their performance (see Chapter 5). In Veblen's renowned analysis of the business world he described how big business dominated markets and politics, and how business was able to manipulate political decision-making in favor of its vested interests (Veblen, 1904). In Appendix A at the end of this chapter you can read more about Veblen and Commons.

In this book, the school of Institutional Economics that is built on the insights of authors such as Veblen and Commons is called the Original Institutional Economics (OIE). In the literature you might also encounter the terms Old Institutional Economics, American institutionalism, Neo-institutionalism or classical institutionalism (Rutherford, 1994; Vatn, 2005).

From the mid-1970s, the New Institutional Economics (NIE) began to attract increasing attention within the discipline of economics. In 1975, Oliver E. Williamson published his groundbreaking book, *Markets and Hierarchies*, and called his approach 'New Institutional Economics'. He explained that, in contrast to NCE, his NIE addressed questions about institutions. Why do firms exist? Why are transactions sometimes coordinated through contracts in markets and sometimes through hierarchies such as firms? These questions were not addressed in NCE, in which firms and markets, consumers and producers already exist and are taken as given points of departure for the solving of optimization problems. In NCE, firms are modeled as production functions and markets are 'signaling devices', providing actors with the relevant information via changes in relative prices (see Chapter 5 for more details). Williamson's point of departure is the transaction itself, and his question is: How can transactions best (that is, most efficiently) be coordinated? Different governance structures are available to the actors, and the one that is most efficient will be selected. Sometimes this can be a market contract, while in other cases it is a firm, or some intermediate form (see Chapter 3 and Part III for more details).

Because Williamson's theory explains firms and contracts, which are institutions, he called his theoretical approach 'Institutional Economics' to differentiate it from NCE. However, his methodology was very similar to the one used by the NCE (largely of a methodological, individualistic nature) and because the methodology used by the OIE was very different (largely of a methodological interactionistic nature; see Chapter 4), Williamson did not want to be associated with OIE. That is why he added 'new' to his type of Institutional Economics. In Chapter 3 you will learn about other theories that belong to the NIE, such as the theory of property rights and agency theory. In the following subsections we shall explain the basic mechanisms of how NIE and OIE explain institutions (see also Groenewegen, 1996).

## New Institutional Economics (NIE)

In Figure 2.4 we present the basic building blocks of NIE based on the transaction cost economics of Oliver Williamson: what are the characteristics of the actors, what is the environment in which they operate (structures), and how do actors interact with their environment? We present the foundations of the model here; details are discussed in Chapter 3.

**Figure 2.4** *The NIE model of institutions*

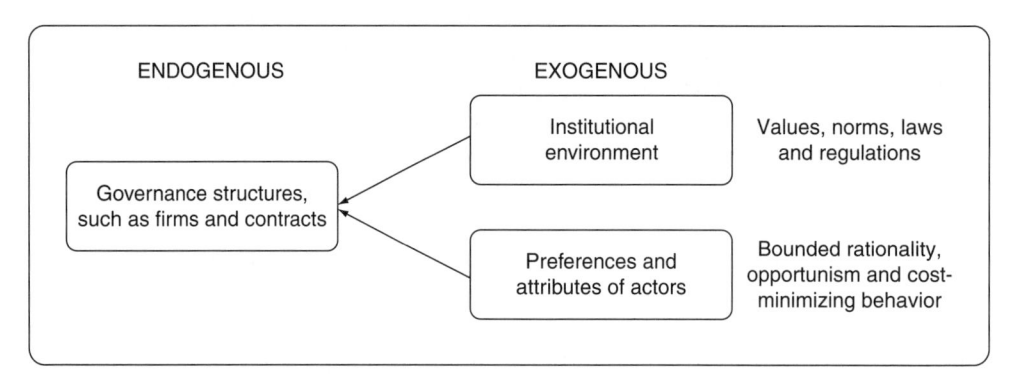

```
ENDOGENOUS                    EXOGENOUS

                          ┌──────────────┐
                          │ Institutional│    Values, norms, laws
                          │ environment  │    and regulations
                          └──────┬───────┘
┌──────────────────────┐         │
│ Governance structures,│◄───────┤
│ such as firms and    │◄───────┐
│ contracts            │        │
└──────────────────────┘        │
                          ┌─────┴────────┐
                          │ Preferences and│  Bounded rationality,
                          │ attributes of  │  opportunism and cost-
                          │ actors         │  minimizing behavior
                          └────────────────┘
```

## Endogenous and exogenous

In the NIE, a distinction is made between governance structures and the institutional environment. Governance structures, such as firms and contracts, are the endogenous variables, whereas the institutional environment of (in)formal institutions is exogenous. The preferences and characteristics of the actors are also exogenous. In other words, the theory aims at explaining why different governance structures exist, and why transactions are coordinated through contracts or through organizations, while the exogenous institutional environment of values, norms, conventions, laws and regulations is taken as a given.

## The actors in the model

Williamson considers his NIE to be complementary to NCE: it addresses other issues, but uses the same methodology. Both NIE and NCE assume that actors display optimizing behavior (under specific constraints), such as cost minimization given a specific production function, or choosing a governance structure that minimizes transaction costs. The difference between the two is that the actors in NIE are characterized by different 'attributes'. More specifically, they may show opportunistic behavior and are bounded in their rationality. We shall now explain both concepts more fully.

Opportunistic behavior was introduced in Chapter 1, and refers to the possibility that actors may deliberately provide false information and abuse nontransparent situations. In economic transactions, actors can cheat. This does not mean that economists such as Williamson claim that all actors are constantly trying to cheat one another. The issue is rather that actors in the market do not know what kind of behavior the counterpart will adopt during the negotiation of a contract and after the contract is signed. Will the counterpart turn out to be an honest person who complies with the conditions of the contract, or will he turn out to be dishonest and behave opportunistically every time he can? The crucial point is that actors in the market do not have this kind of information before they start their negotiations. More specifically, opportunism can be considered a permanent part of human nature, but need not always be displayed: whether someone shows opportunistic behavior depends on the circumstances. This means that actors have to find out what kind of behavior they can expect from others, and how they can safeguard themselves against opportunism. Both the search costs and the cost of safeguarding add to the costs of the contract.

*Bounded rationality* means that the capacity of human beings to formulate and solve complex problems is limited. A good example is the game of chess. A chess player has all the information he needs to make decisions: the rules of the game are known as well as the position of the pieces. In order to make a specific move, the player needs to evaluate all possible moves that the opponent can possibly make. The problem is that the number of possible sequences of moves and countermoves is too great for a single human mind to analyze fully. In other words, every player would like to make fully rational decisions, but his capacity to do so is limited. Similarly, bounded rationality is still marked by optimizing behavior, but under the twin restrictions of incomplete information and limited human capacity to process all available information. You will learn that the difference between the full rationality of the NCE and the bounded rationality of the NIE has far-reaching implications for the types of contracts the actors can conclude. In the NIE model it is possible for contracts to be incomplete and to leave uncertainties.

The arrow in Figure 2.4 going from the actors to the governance structure indicates that actors with specific characteristics and rules of behavior choose the most efficient governance structure. The model is similar to the NCE model in the sense that there is no feedback from the governance structure to the actors, which implies that the attributes of the actors are given and cannot be explained by the model. If, say, a producer who wants to coordinate a transaction of capital with a shareholder behaves opportunistically and provides misleading information to the shareholder about potential profits, then the unidirectional arrow in Figure 2.4 shows that the attributes of the actor are not influenced over time by the choice of the governance structure.

This is a bit of an oversimplification. Generally, some feedback exists by way of simultaneity, or in the sense that (depending on what one wants to model) it can be imagined that a change must result from an outcome of the model. The opportunistic outcome described above may well make the shareholders more cautious next time. This does not change their attributes in the sense of their preference structure, but it will give rise to, for example, a more careful appreciation of the next producer who wants to raise money. This, however, is not really what we mean by the unidirectional arrows in Figures 2.3 and 2.4. Basically, they are meant to imply that some very fundamental characteristics, like the preference structures, are generally taken to be exogenous under all types of modeling.

As discussed above, this way of building theory is called methodological individualism, meaning that the central building block of the theory is an individual actor with exogenous preferences, specific 'attributes' such as bounded rationality and opportunistic behavior, and a specific decision-making rule. Of course, this is an abstraction and the scientist is well aware of that (see, for example, Bowles, 1998). In the real world, actors can and do change their characteristics. It is clear that, in reality, the governance structure of a firm such as McDonald's or Toyota has an impact on the preferences and attitudes of its employees. In other words, in reality, preferences are endogenous. However, in the model shown in Figure 2.4 that feedback is omitted.

## *Structures*

As you can see from Figure 2.4, the institutional environment plays an important role in 'structuring' behavior. The NIE models the environment of the actors as 'complex and uncertain'. This environment and bounded rationality imply that actors are not fully informed and have to face situations in which there is uncertainty. If they can also be opportunistic this means that they will attempt to set up governance structures that protect them against opportunism in uncertain situations.

In Chapter 3 you will learn more about how property rights theory, principal–agent theory and transaction cost economics (TCE) analyze these issues, and how institutions can coordinate behavior in uncertain environments.

### Comparative statics

The NIE as presented in Figure 2.4 is basically a static analysis (as is NCE, by the way). Given the institutional context of values and legal rules, actors choose the most efficient governance structure to coordinate a specific type of transaction. When that choice is made, none of the actors in the system has an incentive to adjust his or her position; this is called an *equilibrium*. However, if an exogenous variable changes (also called an exogenous shock – resulting from a change in the law or in individuals' preferences, say) the theory predicts what the new efficient governance structure will be: the cost-minimizing governance structure given the new value of the exogenous variable.

This approach is of a comparative static equilibrium nature: the characteristics of the old equilibrium are compared with those in the new one, without studying exactly how the change has come about. The dynamic issue of how the process from one equilibrium to the other takes place is not analyzed. It is assumed that actors will get the right information in time, and that they will make the right decisions. In Part III you will find out more about the role that competition plays in the selection process of the most efficient governance structures.

### Dynamics

In Chapter 3 you will learn more about the design of efficient institutions in NIE, and in Chapter 4 you will learn that the efficient design of institutions can be interpreted as 'dynamic'. When actors adapt the governance structure after an exogenous shock then the governance structure is changed, and in that sense the theory informs you about 'dynamics'. However, as will become clearer after reading Chapter 3, the dynamics of institutions is not really the focus of NIE. In the analysis it is assumed that actors are forced to adapt as a result of competitive pressures: if they do not change the governance structure to the more efficient one, they will not survive the competition in the market. However, how actors get the right information in time, and how the process of selection takes place, is not analyzed in NIE (see Chapter 4 for details).

Later in this chapter we discuss the work of Douglass North and explain how his focus is more on explaining the dynamics of institutions, in contrast to what we have seen of Oliver Williamson's work, discussed above. In order to get a better idea of what we mean by the dynamics of institutions, we now turn to Original Institutional Economics.

## Original Institutional Economics (OIE)

Figure 2.5 represents the OIE institutional model. The OIE has always considered the dynamics of institutions to be the central question of economics. How do institutions evolve over time? How are revolutionary changes in institutions, such as laws and regulations, or

**Figure 2.5** *The OIE model of institutions*

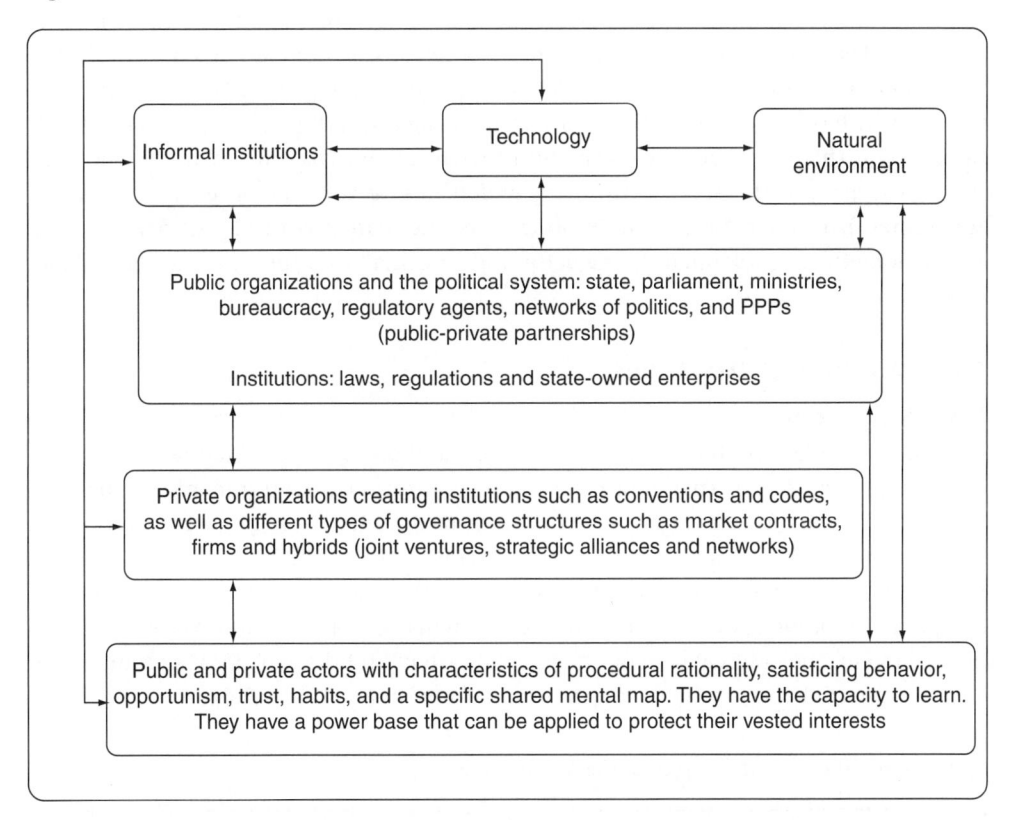

[Diagram: Top row shows three connected boxes — "Informal institutions", "Technology", "Natural environment" — with bidirectional arrows between them. Below, a box labeled: "Public organizations and the political system: state, parliament, ministries, bureaucracy, regulatory agents, networks of politics, and PPPs (public-private partnerships) / Institutions: laws, regulations and state-owned enterprises". Below that: "Private organizations creating institutions such as conventions and codes, as well as different types of governance structures such as market contracts, firms and hybrids (joint ventures, strategic alliances and networks)". Bottom box: "Public and private actors with characteristics of procedural rationality, satisficing behavior, opportunism, trust, habits, and a specific shared mental map. They have the capacity to learn. They have a power base that can be applied to protect their vested interests". Arrows connect all levels.]

structures of firms, to be explained? Why did, for example, competition and corporate laws change relatively gradually in China from the 1980s onwards, and why was there a different, more radical type of process in Russia? Did firms in France in the twentieth century evolve along a similar or dissimilar path of development to firms in Germany? We discuss below how the models of the actors and structures in OIE differ from the NIE.

You can see from Figure 2.5 that in the OIE approach more explanatory variables, such as technology and the natural environment, are included. It is an encompassing model in which all possible explanatory variables are included, showing that interactions may take place between all of these variables. This is not to say that all original institutional economists deal with all these interacting variables in all their research. Depending on the research question at hand, the scientist will perhaps focus on the relationship between technology and the natural environment, or on that between laws and private governance structures. If you are interested in the interaction between technology and governance structures (which types of firms stimulate innovation, say) then from an analytical point of view it may be useful to take the natural environment as being exogenous. Similarly, if you are interested in the consequences of global warming for both the technology of firms and the environment of specific markets such as the market for tradable emissions rights, then you should make both technology and the natural environment endogenous, while considering the institutional environment of (in)formal institutions as being exogenous; see Box 2.3 on global warming.

## 70 Theory

Figure 2.5 aims to show that in OIE no explanatory variables are excluded beforehand and that no interaction is excluded in advance. In the figure, the potential interactions between all variables results in a large number of reciprocal (double-sided) arrows. In the remainder of this discussion we shall elaborate on the elements of this figure. Note that the actor in terms of the decision unit can be located at different levels of Figure 2.5. At first sight this might be confusing, but in what follows you will learn that the location of the actor as the decision unit largely depends on the type of research question. Sometimes firms are actors, while in other cases the managers inside the firms are the actors. Sometimes, parliament is the actor and in other cases the actors are individual politicians.

### *Endogenous and exogenous*

#### System approach

OIE aims to explain both (in)formal institutions and governance structures in a system approach, which means that all aspects of the institutional environment are analyzed as a whole. The focus can very well be on a part of the whole system – on the economic or the political system, say – but when the dynamics of an individual part is studied, it is analyzed in relation to its interaction with the other parts of the system (Wilber and Harrison, 1978). We distinguish different subsystems such as the value system, the economic system, the political system, the judicial system and the ecological system, which are all connected and together form the societal system (see Figure 2.6).

**Figure 2.6** *The economy as part of the societal system*

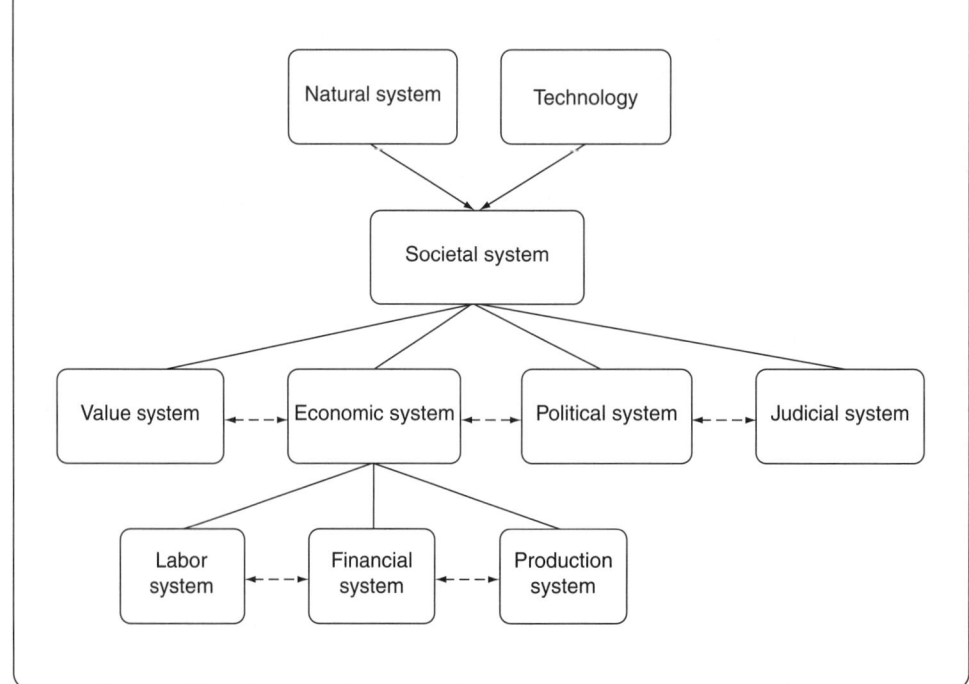

The economic system, the economy, is a system of social rules that structures individual behavior and coordinates interactions with respect to the production, consumption and distribution of goods and services. The economic institutions that coordinate transactions include organizations such as firms, trade organizations and consumer organizations, but also the 'rules of the game' as determined by the judicial system. Competition, contract and corporate law, laws on the quality of products and services, and the rules on property rights, are important examples of the judicial system that structure behavior with respect to production, distribution or consumption transactions. The judicial system consists of all the legal rules that regulate behavior of actors in society. The value system is about the culture and the values and norms of society. The political system concerns the institutions that coordinate the political process, such as parliament. Of course, these systems all interact with one another.

The economic system as such is connected to the value system (values, norms and conventions), the judicial system (laws and regulations) and the political system (among which are the government, parliament and public agencies). In Figure 2.6 the technology and the natural resources are presented as exogenous variables influencing the societal system as a whole.

Figure 2.6 illustrates that the economic system can be divided into subsystems, such as the labor system, the financial system, the production system, and so on. Each economic subsystem is again characterized by a specific set of institutions that structure behavior and coordinate transactions with respect to specific economic functions, like production, consumption, innovation, finance. Within the economic system coordination among its subsystems is needed in order to produce a desirable performance at the level of the economic system as a whole. When, for example, the government of a country decides that the economic system should be more innovative, but the financial system would not be able to supply risk capital to innovating entrepreneurs, then the coordination between the subsystems fails, and consequently either (possibly costly) measures must be taken (the government provides the capital itself, which happened during the economic recession of 2008–9) or not enough innovation will take place. On pages 82–5 we take a closer look at economic systems.

OIE aims to explain the dynamics of the economic system in relation to the other parts of the societal system. The researcher neither includes nor excludes explanatory variables beforehand. The destruction of the natural environment may lead to the creation of new laws and regulations, and these institutions may lead to innovations in products and processes. Technological development may play a key role in understanding the emergence of a specific law or a specific way of organizing production (think about robots producing automobiles). An innovation such as genetic manipulation may raise ethical questions, which in turn demand new laws. Over time these developments can change our norms and values about food and health.

When we discuss the dynamics of institutions and economic systems in more detail in Chapter 4 you will learn that some theories focus on the relations between the social system and the economy (so-called socio-economic system), some also include the political system (socio-economic–political system), whereas other theories address questions about the relationship between the economy and natural resources (so-called economic–ecological systems). Where the boundaries of the system are drawn, what is taken to be endogenous and exogenous depends first of all on the research question that is being asked. We shall come back to that on pages 78–82 but you can see one example in Box 2.3.

---

**BOX 2.3   THE WEATHER: ENDOGENOUS OR EXOGENOUS?**

In Chapter 1 we referred briefly to the well-known problem of global warming. Traditionally, the weather has been viewed as exogenous (local superstitions notwithstanding); does global warming mean that weather can now be considered as an endogenous variable?

It depends on who is doing the research, and what is their objective. For a farmer, or the owner of a beachside restaurant, the weather remains a completely exogenous variable. On the other hand, for the representatives of countries involved in the negotiations leading up to the Kyoto protocol, who were essentially trying to reduce overall carbon emissions while not cutting down on their own economic growth, global temperatures are an endogenous variable, or at least one over which they have some influence.

Also in the context of large, worldwide scale models, such as the one used by Nicholas Stern in the Stern Report (2006) to estimate the economic costs of global warming, temperature growth is viewed as an endogenous variable.

Industries can also trade their carbon emissions on the carbon market, and in this way internalize some of the externalities they produce. As we shall explain in more detail in Chapter 8, this means that firms can only produce more if they own more emission rights. Since these can only be bought from other firms, the firms with the highest expected profits (hence the most efficient ones) will buy these rights from less efficient firms. In this way, at least part of the negative externality gets a price (it is internalized and becomes a cost to the firms themselves rather than to third parties), and total production is more efficient overall.

And even for individual consumers buying a plane ticket, for example, it is now often possible to offset carbon emissions. While the direct impact of an individual actor on the weather is infinitesimally small, as is his individual impact on countering carbon emission effects; the point is that the sum of these impacts is a problem, but also part of the solution, since the sum impact of carbon trading and offsetting helps in itself and leads to increased awareness.

---

## *The actors in the model*

We have explained that actors do not take decisions in a vacuum, but in an institutional environment. The way they do business, how they react to one another, what they take into account when they decide about an investment or a purchase depends on their own private objectives and the institutions in their environment that constrain and enable them in their decision-making. Also, their private objectives, their preferences, are determined endogenously within the societal system. Moreover, rationality is influenced by the dynamic process of interaction of the different elements of the societal system. What actors consider rational differs from society to society, from region to region, and from organization to organization.

Rationality is also defined by uncertainty. In an uncertain world actors use a search process, with procedures to get better information that keeps options open, creating flexibility so that adjustments are possible when more information becomes available or when actors have learned from past experiences. In this context, rationality is more about the process of finding the right solution 'along the way' than about defining optimal solutions concerning final objectives. During the process the actor relies strongly on what she has learned in the past, and what has proved to work in the community to which she belongs and with whom she shares knowledge and experience. This is called *procedural rationality*, in which concepts such as satisficing, trust, habits, mental maps and learning play important roles. In the words of the 1978 Nobel Laureate, Herbert Simon (1976, p. 130): 'Behavior is procedurally rational when it is the outcome of appropriate deliberation. Its procedural rationality depends on the process that generates it.' Simon explains that habits, rules of thumb and problem-solving repertoires are all part of procedural rationality. Actors make extensive use of such procedures when they face uncertainties.

## Satisficing behavior

The concept of satisficing behavior (Simon, 1976) is not the same as maximizing behavior. In the latter, the actor evaluates all possibilities simultaneously with respect to her objective of utility or profit, given some restraints. A maximizing actor is able the select the option that will bring the highest return, or that will minimize the costs. In the case of satisficing behavior, the actor has formulated for her objective or objectives so-called *aspiration* levels – that is, levels of profit, market share, wage increases, dividend and so on – with which the actor is satisfied. When that level is reached she takes the decision. The concept of satisficing behavior is appropriate in a dynamic analysis of institutions in which there is uncertainty and change, hence it can be seen as an optimal way of deciding under such circumstances.

## Opportunism versus trust

Perhaps you were surprised to see in Figure 2.4 that actors are modeled as being opportunistic, because in real life you encounter many situations where people trust one another and where taking advantage of an information asymmetry is 'not done'. That is certainly the case, and you will discover that also in Institutional Economics *trust* is an important attribute of actors. We define trust, very generally, as 'A trusts B when A expects B not to exploit a vulnerability of A by behaving opportunistically'.

For an economic analysis, the existence of opportunism or trust is very important, because it has implications for the costs involved in transactions. You can imagine that in situations where contracting partners trust one another they do not need very complicated contracts to exclude opportunistic behavior. Contracts can thus be very simple and entail low transaction costs; substantial deals can be agreed with a simple handshake.

## Habits

You may also have been rather surprised to read about the rational way that actors are modeled in NCE and NIE. They are assumed always to behave intentionally and purposefully, aiming at the realization of clear objectives. From your own experience you may have noticed that behavior is often based on *habits* that people have. Habits involve automatic behavior that is repeated regularly, often 'without thinking'. The habits of actors are an important element in their capability to make choices, especially in complex situations. In Chapter 4 we shall explain how institutions influence habits, and how behavior based on habits also reinforces the institutions.

## Mental maps and learning

In the OIE model of Institutional Economics, creativity and learning are central characteristics of actors. Actors do not make decisions in a vacuum; they are embedded in a specific institutional context. They are rooted in an environment of values and norms that structure their 'mental maps', or model against which they perceive the world around them. At birth, human beings are highly malleable, but over time, individuals become culturally conditioned and this determines their view of reality. People share their mental maps with others, with whom they form a community, and through interaction with each other these shared mental maps are shaped and adjusted.

The group with which individuals share their perceptions can be a division in a firm, an industrial group, a community or a country. These shared mental models guide the actors as to what they perceive as desirable objectives, what they perceive as problems that need to be solved, and which instruments are available to them. They also determine what actors consider 'rational' and 'efficient'.

Individual actors get information about society, nature and technology from the results of past experiences. Language and communication channels provide the actors with information and assist in the process of convergence of the individual mental models into shared mental models of the community.

In this context, it is of interest to quote North (1993, pp. 3–4):

> As tribes evolved in different physical environments they developed different languages and, with different experiences, different mental models to explain the world around them. To the extent that experiences were common to different tribes the mental models provided common explanations. The language and mental models formed the informal constraints that defined the institutional framework of the tribe and were passed down intergenerationally as customs, taboos, myths that provided the continuity that we call culture...
>
> With growing specialization and division of labor the tribes evolved into polities and economies; the diversity of experiences and learning produced increasingly different societies and civilizations with very different degrees of success in solving the fundamental economic problems of scarcity...The complexity of the environment increased as human beings became increasingly interdependent, and more complex institutional structures were necessary to capture the potential gains from trade. Such evolution required that the society develop institutions that will permit

anonymous, impersonal exchange across time and space. But to the extent that 'local experience' had produced diverse mental models and institutions with respect to the gains from such cooperation, the likelihood of creating the necessary institutions to capture the gains from trade of more complex contracting varied. The key to this story is the kind of learning that organizations acquired to survive. If the institutional framework made the highest pay-offs for organizations piracy, then organizational success and survival dictated that learning would take the form of being better pirates. If on the other hand productivity raising activities had the highest pay-off then the economy would grow.

### Power and vested interests

In OIE, much attention is paid to the power of individuals and interest groups in society. Property rights are not distributed equally, and the laws and regulations made by the political system reflect the power structures in society. Markets are not neutral allocation mechanisms, but are institutionalized arenas where conflicts are solved between opposing parties. Understanding the behavior of economic actors demands an analysis of their power base, as well as their objectives and conflicts.

## *Structures*

### The socio-economic–political system

The public and private governance structures are shown in Figure 2.5. The political system develops policies and makes laws and regulations. These institutions influence the behavior of both private and public actors. Figure 2.5 also shows the influence of actors on the public institutions. We shall explain in Part III how large businesses or large labor unions are able to influence the political system and to 'capture' policies. We shall also explain in Part IV that democratic systems serve the purpose of balancing the influence of different interest groups in order to prevent the interests of specific groups from being dominant. The political system is often dominated by economic powers, and the laws made by legislators often protect the vested interests of specific groups in society.

Figure 2.5 shows that, according to OIE, the explanation of institutions and their dynamics demands an integrated system approach in which values, technology and private governance structures interact. In Chapter 8 we shall discuss details of how the political system can improve efficiency in markets and society in general; and in Chapter 9 we shall pay attention to the dangers that threaten the effectiveness of the political system. You will learn that the conceptualization of the role of government in a market economy differs substantially between the NIE and the OIE. The NIE considers the market first of all as a neutral allocation mechanism that is isolated from the political system. While government can improve the functioning of markets by defining clear property rights and by creating public courts to solve conflicts, essentially the political system is separated from the economy. In contrast, the OIE perceives the economy to be an integral part of the political system and vice versa. Markets are embedded and reflect power structures that aim to manipulate prices, say, or may block innovations that would increase general welfare but harm private benefits. OIE aims to understand the dynamics of institutions and the dynamics of the system as a whole.

### Technology

Technology is an important variable in the analysis of OIE. Technologies such as the steam engine in the past, and electricity, oil and information and communication technologies (ICT) nowadays, are drivers of economic development. Where do innovations come from, and what are the conditions that stimulate technological development? In Chapters 5 and 6, the role of the entrepreneur will be discussed and you will learn how institutional structures influence innovations and technological development. We shall discuss the fact that technology does not develop in an isolated way. On the contrary: values, public and private governance structures are interwoven with technologies.

### The natural environment

Socio-economic–political systems interact with nature. Nature supplies the resources to be employed in economic production and consumption. As mentioned at the beginning of this chapter, in economic theory, nature is mainly an exogenous variable. However, after the emergence of the subdiscipline 'Environmental Economics' with a focus on the economic–ecological system, nature can be considered endogenous. Then the interaction between the different elements in Figure 2.5 is modeled in such a way that the use and depletion of nature is endogenous and explained inside the model. Nature is strongly influenced not only by environmental laws and regulations, but also by changing values in society. A real-life example showing the endogeneity of nature comes from the 2008 Olympic Games in China: before the Games, the Chinese authorities experimented with rockets loaded with dry ice, which they fired into clouds to try to reduce rainfall on the sports venues.

## Comparing the NIE and OIE approaches

We have discussed the OIE approach as being quite different from that of NIE. We have underlined the basic characteristics of the two approaches and tried to stay close to underlying models of methodological individualism, collectivism and interactionism. We tried to be explicit and precise about the distinctions between endogenous and exogenous variables. In general, one could say that the main difference consists in the following: OIE always puts the emphasis on dynamics and change from a broad descriptive perspective, whereas NIE puts the emphasis on an efficiency analysis of the origins and working of institutions as well an efficiency analysis of changes in institutions. The differences between NIE and OIE are summarized in Table 2.1.

At the end of this section we would like to point to some important nuances in the schools of Institutional Economics. As Rutherford (1994) clearly shows, the characterizations we have presented here are the basics elements of the two approaches, but within the two schools there are nuances and developments which make the boundaries much less clear. Because this is an introductory textbook we cannot discuss all the nuances and differences, so we have concentrated on the general principles.

**Table 2.1** *Comparison of New and Original Institutional Economics*

|  | **New Institutional Economics (NIE)** | **Original Institutional Economics (OIE)** |
|---|---|---|
| Research question | What are the efficient governance structures, given the institutional environment? What are efficiency reasons for the origins of and changes in institutions? | What explains the dynamics of institutions including (in)formal institutions and organizations from a broad perspective (not necessarily efficiency)? |
| Actors | Bounded rationality and opportunism; rule of behavior to minimize transaction costs | Procedural rationality; shared mental maps, habits and defense of vested interests |
| Structures | Technology, culture and formal institutions are given; limited number of explanatory variables | All structures are constituted in an interactive process; wide range of interdependent explanatory variables |
|  | Role of government is first of all 'getting the formal institutions right' | Role of government is pro-active in formulating societal objectives based on a broad participation of the population |
|  | Markets are efficient allocation mechanism under the conditions of adequate institutional environments | Markets are no neutral mechanism but reflect societal power structures |

Nevertheless, it is important to note that in NIE many authors also deal with issues that traditionally belong to the domain of OIE. Both in *New Institutional Economics: A Guidebook*, edited by Brousseau and Glachant (2008) and in the *Handbook of New Institutional Economics*, edited by Ménard and Shirley (2005) a number of contributions may be found by NIE economists in the fields of political institutions, legal institutions, regulation, development economics and transition economics. Many institutional economists nowadays use a pluralistic approach: their theoretical framework is interdisciplinary and they apply both theories of the NIE and OIE. North (2005), Greif (2006) and Vatn (2005) are good examples of such integrated approaches.

In Appendix B in this chapter we pay special attention to the contributions of North because he can be considered an institutional economist who has made important contributions in the domains of both OIE and NIE. From his work you will discover that over time he adapted his theoretical framework to the questions in which he was interested.

If you are interested in further exploring contributions in Institutional Economics and related fields, we suggest that you have a look at the websites of the (nonexhaustive) list of organizations and journals shown in Box 2.4.

> **BOX 2.4   ASSOCIATIONS AND JOURNALS IN INSTITUTIONAL ECONOMICS**
>
> **Associations**
> Association for Evolutionary Economics (AFEE)
> Association for Institutional Thought (AFIT)
> Association for Social Economics (ASE)
> European Association of Evolutionary Political Economy (EAEPE)
> European Group of Organization Studies (EGOS)
> International Confederation of Associations for Pluralism in Economics (ICAPE)
> International Society for New Institutional Economics (ISNIE)
> Society for the Advancement of Behavioral Economics (SABE)
> Society for the Advancement of Socio-Economics (SASE)
>
> **Journals**
> *Cambridge Journal of Economics*
> *Evolutionary and Institutional Economics Review*
> *Journal of Economic Behavior and Organization*
> *Journal of Economic Issues*
> *Journal of Economic Methodology*
> *Journal of Economic Psychology*
> *Journal of Evolutionary Economics*
> *Journal of Institutional Economics*
> *Journal of Institutional and Theoretical Economics*
> *Journal of Law and Economics*
> *Journal of Post Keynesian Economics*
> *Journal of Socio-Economics*
> *New Institutional Economics Abstracting Journal*
> *Organization Studies*
> *Review of International Political Economy*
> *Review of Social Economy*
> *Socio-Economic Review*

# ON THE RELEVANCE OF INSTITUTIONAL THEORIES

NIE and OIE put different emphasis on what they want to model and how. Generally, this means that they model actors differently, include different variables in the exogenous environment, and model the relationship between the actors and their environment differently. Sometimes the insights from NIE are more appropriate, and sometimes those from OIE are more so, if they have different insights to offer in the first place. So, in this book, we have chosen to show you how both the OIE and NIE can contribute to a better understanding of institutions.

Some theories in institutional economics are rather abstract and make use of somewhat strong assumptions about the rationality of actors. Other theories remain closer to the complexities of the real world in their assumptions, try to take all potential explanatory variables on board and try to reflect the interdependencies between the variables over time. Such theories are certainly more realistic and provide models that can describe reality in more detail, but these more complicated models are less appropriate for making precise predictions.

In this book we discuss different institutional theories ranging from the highly abstract to those that try to capture the complexity of the real world 'as it is'. From the point of view of method, we distinguish four categories of static and dynamic analysis of institutions:

1  A static analysis, which focuses on the determination of endogenous variables by use of other exogenous variables, in accordance with the principle that using fewer variables to explain a phenomenon is preferred. In the Appendixes to Chapter 1 we discussed endogenous variables and exogenous variables in more depth with respect to NCE. In New Institutional Economics, the static analysis in terms of endogenous and exogenous variables could be described as: the endogenous variable 'governance structure' (G) is a function of 'asset specificity' (A), 'uncertainty' (U), and 'frequency' of transactions (F). Given the values of A, U and F, the optimal (cost minimizing, or equilibrium) value of G is either market (M), firm (C) or hybrid (H). All other aspects of reality have given values: technology, culture, formal institutions and so on. The analysis is timeless in the sense that the current values of the exogenous variables determine the current equilibrium value of the endogenous variables instantaneously; the process towards the outcome of the model is not part of the research question.

2  A comparative static analysis, which compares two equilibrium outcomes. A change in the value(s) of the exogenous variables (generally) leads to an immediate change in the equilibrium outcome of the endogenous variable. The differences between the equilibrium outcomes are explained by the change in (one of) the exogenous variables. At values $A^1$, $U^1$ and $F^1$ the optimal governance structure is, for example, M. If $U^1$ changes to $U^2$, the optimal governance structure changes to, for example, H. The change in the governance structure is explained by the change in the value of U. The process towards the new equilibrium is not part of the research question.

3  A mathematical dynamic analysis, in which time becomes an essential variable. The outcome of the model is a description of the endogenous variable as a function of time: it describes what the equilibrium value(s) of the endogenous variable(s) is (are) and whether the path over time converges to that equilibrium value. Typically, this description concerns (linear or nonlinear) difference equations or differential equations. In addition, game theory is able to explain why cooperation (or 'altruism') can be an equilibrium strategy in the dynamic setting of a game that is played an indeterminate number of times (see Chapter 7). Evolutionary stable strategies in game theory are able to explain how strategies can be stable against alternative strategies.

4  A dynamic analysis using historical time, which unfolds the process of change in such a way that the causalities between historical events are analyzed. The interaction between structures and actors, as well as interactions between actors, are the focus

of the analysis, showing the role of efficiency and how it is interpreted by the actors. It also shows how rationality and preferences are constituted over historical time in interaction with other actors. Such an analysis reveals when vested interests play a role, and how these interests influence the course of historical events. The inclusion of historical time implies that mathematical modeling is less useful, and that detailed case studies are a more appropriate method of research.

We present the different institutional theories in a *pluralistic* way. We consider different theories relevant to different types of questions and in different sets of circumstances. We consider the institutional theories we discuss to be complementary, and that together they can potentially cover all the important aspects of the subject matter. It does not make much sense to criticize theory for being abstract in modeling actors and their environment in an unrealistic way, or to accuse a theory of being too encompassing. The point is that the assumptions and structure of the theory should be relevant. In other words, the theory should be 'useful' or 'appropriate' for the issues raised and for the conditions that prevail in the reality studied. We distinguish between two types of relevance:

- is the theory relevant for the questions being asked; and
- is the theory relevant for the conditions present in the situation at hand?

## Is the theory relevant to the question being asked?

Certain theories are more relevant for answering specific questions than others. When the researcher is interested in the question of how the incentives for managers of firms can be changed so they better serve the interest of the shareholders, then this question can be analyzed in a static setting of given laws, preferences, rights of shareholders and so on. In Chapter 3, you will meet principal–agent theory, which is designed to address these types of incentive questions. The theory can be constructed in such a way that it has universal explanatory power. In other words, the theory is not only applicable to the case of the manager and the shareholder, but also to all cases in which there is a principal (the commissioner of a task) and an agent (the actor who is commissioned to execute a task). Think about your relationship as a principal with your dentist (the agent), or the relationship between the Ministry of Economic Affairs (principal) with a state-owned electricity firm (the agent).

Contrast this example with the case of a researcher interested in the question of why firms changed their structure in the USA at the beginning of the twentieth century. This type of question could be analyzed in a dynamic setting in which changes in technology, growth in consumer markets, changes in transportation facilities, changes in corporate law, and the role of the entrepreneurial spirit are all part of the analytical framework. In Chapter 4 we shall discuss theories of institutional change that are designed to capture this variety of interacting variables. Again, the theory can be constructed in such a way that it is applicable to a range of issues concerning institutional change and not only to the case of American firms.

In short, theories are designed to analyze specific research questions. The issue of interest determines the relevance of the theory. This type of relevance is summed up by the phrase 'different theories for different issues'.

## Is the theory relevant to the conditions at hand?

The relevance of theory is not only related to the questions asked, but is also determined by the assumptions made and the conditions that hold in the 'reality' that is being analyzed. Do the assumptions align with the conditions? This is called 'different theories for different conditions'. If a theory assumes a competitive market, forcing firms to choose the most efficient scale of production or the most efficient governance structure, then such a theory is only relevant for analyzing real world situations where this type of competitive market exists. If the theory assumes complete price flexibility and in reality the market has all kinds of institutions that hinder flexibility, then researchers are better off not applying insights from that theory, but rather looking for theories that are better equipped to tackle the problem.

### *Procedure of diminishing abstraction*

The question about the relevance of theory can also be presented in terms of the right level of abstraction. Some issues are formulated in very abstract terms and should therefore be addressed with theoretical concepts that are also of a high level of abstraction. For very general, abstract questions – such as questions about the existence of a stable equilibrium in a theoretical market model – a very abstract theory which omits many variables may be appropriate. A good example is the general equilibrium model of Arrow and Debreu, who asked themselves the question 'Does a general equilibrium exist for all (contingent) goods and services in a market system where independent actors receive only price signals?' (see Box 2.5).

---

**BOX 2.5   GENERAL EQUILIBRIUM: WALRAS, ARROW AND DEBREU**

In the nineteenth century, the French economist Léon Walras was the first to attempt a mathematical formulation of a general equilibrium model (see also the Appendixes to Chapter 1), in which utility and profit-maximizing individuals reach equilibrium in every market for every product in the economy, with their behavior being guided only by relative prices. Essentially, this was a formalized expression of Adam Smith's invisible hand metaphor, which was mentioned in Chapter 1.

In the twentieth century, Kenneth Arrow (Nobel Prize for Economics in 1972) and Gerard Debreu (Nobel Prize for Economics in 1983) developed a rigorous mathematical model, by which they were able to prove the assumptions under which a general equilibrium exists.

---

However, if one asks a question about the dynamics of firms in China in a specific time period, then the theory needs to be more specific. The theory should include specific laws and regulations in China at the time; cultural traits are important and political aspects play a role.

In the example given in Box 2.5, the theory works at a highly abstract level, whereas in the example of China the theory specifies concepts in a detailed way. In other words, when a specific issue is analyzed and specific details of place and time are needed, then the theory needs to specify general concepts such as the laws, markets, motivations of actors, the role of politics and values. Put differently, to answer specific questions, the theory moves from the general to the specific, which is called the *procedure of diminishing abstraction*. Note that, in this way of presenting theories, one theory can be considered a specification of the other.

## A CLOSER LOOK AT ECONOMIC SYSTEMS

In relation to the financial crisis that started in 2008, politicians and economists often talk about the crisis in the 'capitalist system', or more specifically about the failure of the 'Anglo-Saxon type of market economy'. In this section we introduce different types of capitalist systems – that is, systems in which markets and private property play a central role in the allocation of scarce resources. In doing so, we follow the system approach outlined in this chapter and make explicit the different types of institutions we discussed in Chapter 1. In Chapter 1 we discussed two 'ideal types' of economic system: the pure market economy (also called the pure capitalist system), and the centrally planned economy. In this section we focus on different forms of capitalist market economies. Here we shall distinguish successively three models of market economies: the Anglo-Saxon; the Continental European; and the Asian model (see Whitley, 1999; Dore, 2000). Again, we shall describe them as 'ideal types' in order to emphasize the main differences.

### The Anglo-Saxon model

We start our description of different types of market economies with the Anglo-Saxon system, found in countries such as the United States of America, the United Kingdom, Canada, New Zealand and Australia. Each of these countries has its own specific configuration of institutions, but they also have much in common, especially with respect to the dominating role of markets and contracts and a role of government at 'arm's length'.

In market economies the value, economic, judicial and political systems form a consistent whole (see Figure 2.6). A general characteristic of a market economy is the dominant role of private property, of decentralized decision-making, and of competition in markets. In the Anglo-Saxon perception, markets are expressions of the individualistic values of freedom, personal responsibility and accountability. The norm of competition relates to these values as the 'right' mechanism to allocate scarce resources. Generally speaking, competitive markets are considered to be the adequate governance structure to coordinate transactions. When competition works well, prices reflect the scarcities, which make efficient decision-making possible at the micro level. Connected to the individualistic values the norm is that decisions ought to be taken at a decentralized level, that the costs should be paid at the decentralized level of the micro unit, and that benefits should be collected at that level. Then the actors will be optimally motivated to search for the most efficient solutions for the allocation questions around production, distribution and consumption. In the value system that supports the decentralized allocation in markets it is believed that those efficient private decisions will add up to the best possible public benefits.

The formal institutions and governance structures of the Anglo-Saxon model correspond with the values and norms: in this model, the government is at a distance but plays an important role in the introduction and enforcement of laws. Crucial in this regard are the clear allocation of property rights and strict competition law that basically forbids any type of collusion among firms. The rationale here is based on the idea that markets produce competitive pressures that compel all actors to be efficient. This means that markets should be perfectly transparent (so that all actors have all the information necessary to make choices for their own benefit) as well as perfectly flexible (when a new technology offers a more efficient allocation of labor, such a change in the combination of production factors should be adopted without delay).

The government in the Anglo-Saxon model should be strong and active to safeguard the correct functioning of the market, yet always at arm's length; that is, the government does not interfere in the market process to realize certain outcomes in terms of industrial structure or sizes of firms. An Anglo-Saxon government does not intervene to orchestrate a merger between 'national champions', or to prevent a takeover by a foreign firm. As long as the rules of the game are clearly set and enforced, individual actors can coordinate their transactions in contracts and organizations as they please. Employers and employees stipulate in contracts the conditions they consider relevant and reasonable. Firms merge, or are subjected to hostile takeovers, when efficiency so dictates. To create the necessary certainty for the private actors, a neutral and efficient public court is essential. In the judicial system the laws and regulations must be specified clearly and an independent public court watches over the correct application of the formal rules.

The political decision-making about the laws and regulations in which markets are embedded (such as the law of competition, corporate governance law, codes for the behavior of shareholders), is in every market system preferably coordinated by a democratic system. In the Anglo-Saxon model, the 'one man, one vote' system offers the individual actors equal access to the political decision-making process.

## The Continental European model

The characteristics of the Continental European model, which Sweden, Denmark, Germany and the Netherlands follow, are more or less the opposite of the Anglo-Saxon model. In the latter, the role and responsibilities of the individual are highly valued, whereas in the former, collectivistic values dominate. In the Continental European model, mechanisms of decision-making exist in which the objectives of the collectivity of the firm, the industry, the region or the nation are taken into account. The consequences for the system as a whole, and in particular with respect to long-term stability, are an important part of the value system. In the Continental European model, these collectivistic values are translated into laws and regulations that recognize the interests of collectivity and allow individuals to act in cooperation in order to optimize the performance of the larger unit. With respect to the contracts and organizational structures, the model allows and stimulates long-term contracting and organizational forms that create stability for individual actors.

An important role is, for example, reserved for labor unions and employers' associations as representatives of the collectivity of 'labor' and 'capital'. The organized participation of groups in the economy reflects a fundamentally different value attached to the capabilities of 'free markets' to serve the interests of all members of society. Consultation is considered to be crucial for both the production and dissemination of information, and for establishing (macroeconomic) objectives, which the government specifies explicitly in plans at both industry and regional level. The consultation process, in which a variety of stakeholders participate, is such a central characteristic of the Continental European model that it has also been labeled 'the consultation model'.

With respect to laws and regulations, the Continental European model offers more opportunities to the market parties to 'organize' the market. Often, at the national level, the representatives of labor unions and employers' associations negotiate with the government (tripartite negotiation) on the development of macroeconomic indicators such as the general wage level, inflation, investments, employment and so on. The results are formulated in a National Plan or National Agreement, which serves as a guideline for the negotiations at lower levels in the system. An important feature of the consultation process is the establishment of a common vision regarding future developments, which facilitates a long-term perspective for the different actors in the economy. Because the results of the consultations and negotiations at the macro level are formalized in contracts between representatives of the different societal groups, the Continental European model creates a certain degree of stability for the actors at the micro level.

In short, the Anglo-Saxon model places the market center stage and regulates the socio-economic system in such a way that competition among independent individual actors results, whereas the Continental European model places consultation and agreement between different groups in the economy, including government, at center stage.

## The Asian model

The Asian model has more similarities with the Continental European model than with the Anglo-Saxon one. However, here the state plays a greater part in initiating and directing the development of the economic structure than is the case with the Continental European model. Examples for our presentation of the Asian model are Japan (especially in the period 1960–2000) and the so-called Four Tigers (Republic of South Korea, Taiwan, Singapore and Hong Kong).

In the Asian model, collectivistic values and 'group-orientation' are central. Government is assigned a central coordinating role. National agreements are concluded between the three parties: labor unions, employer associations and government. Compared to the Continental European model, the government in the Asian model is much more in the driver's seat, initiating the formulation of long-term objectives in a National Plan, in which the desired development of the structure of the economy is listed:

- What should the role of agriculture, manufacturing industry and services be over a period of, say, five years?
- What should the level of investments be in an industry such as ICT?
- How can it be guaranteed that sufficient qualified labor will be available during that time?

In the Asian model, the government is strong. It is recognized that the market and private actors play a central role at the micro level, but their activities are embedded in a state vision of the future. Consequently, the government has effective instruments in the Asian model to direct investments, and the bureaucracy that guides the process is well-informed and very highly qualified.

## *Ideal types and real economic systems*

We have now introduced the basic characteristics of three ideal types of market economies. You have learned about the institutions in the economic system and how these are embedded in the value system, political system and judicial system. Bear in mind that we described ideal types: the models are abstractions of reality. These models are based on real economies, but never perfectly reflect them; Lee (2006), for example, applies the relevance of these different types to the Korean economy. In the real world you will find many more varieties and combinations of elements from different ideal types. Moreover, you will discover that systems change over time; this will be subject of our discussion in Chapter 4.

# CONCLUDING REMARKS

In this chapter we have introduced you to two perspectives on Institutional Economics: NIE and OIE. We have shown you the main characteristics of the approaches and explained how the insights of the different perspectives may be used.

We stated that, in this book, we do not aim to favor either NIE or OIE. On the contrary, we shall present insights from both approaches to discuss the relevance of institutions, their origins and the changes in or development of them. This means that when you read about different theories of Institutional Economics in this book you will encounter rather abstract, narrowly focused theories that are good for making general predictions, but are useful only in a limited set of specific real world situations. But you will also find broad theories that attempt to include many possible explanatory variables and are good at describing specific real world situations, but are not good at predicting. Try to evaluate the different theories with the criteria discussed above:

- What do they contribute to the understanding of the issues in which I am interested?
- How do their assumptions correspond with the world I am studying?

Overall, this book examines different theories about institutions in a broad sense. In order to maintain focus, we distinguish between static and dynamic theories, both from an efficiency point of view and from the point of view of vested interests. In this way, many insights from OIE and NIE will be presented as instruments to help in understanding the (economic) world around you.

## REVIEW QUESTIONS

1 What is the purpose of a theory?
2 Describe the trade-off a scientist makes in building a theory between description on the one hand and simplicity on the other.
3 How does a market structure determine the behavior of an economic actor?
4 How is the power structure of society reflected in economic institutions?

5 Explain the terms New Institutional Economics and Original Institutional Economics.
6 What are the characteristics of the actors in the NIE and OIE models, respectively?
7 How would you describe the relationship between the (institutional) environment and the actors in the NIE and OIE, respectively?
8 What are the similarities between the models of the NCE and the NIE, and what are the differences?
9 What are the four categories distinguished in this book of static and dynamic approaches towards institutions?
10 Compare trust to opportunism in an example.
11 Explain the importance of habitual behavior in an economy.

# Appendixes to Chapter 2

## APPENDIX A: VEBLEN AND COMMONS, THE FOUNDING FATHERS OF INSTITUTIONAL ECONOMICS

To Thorstein Veblen (1857–1929), the heart of the economy is its evolution. In his analysis of institutional change he was inspired by the work of Charles Darwin (see Chapter 4), but also by insights from anthropology, sociology and psychology. Veblen saw the economy as a process of evolution driven by social and cultural forces, but individuals, with their habits and 'instincts', also play an important role in his analysis. He strongly criticizes NCE and in particular the 'economic man' as a rational optimizer. Utility and profit maximization are caricatures of the economic reality.

In contrast, Veblen sees consumption mainly as a way for people to show their status (which he coins 'conspicuous consumption'), and business people are primarily protectors of their vested interests and manipulate market prices in order to increase their income. Important concepts in Veblen's theory refer to a dichotomy between so-called 'instrumental values' and 'ceremonial values'. The former refer to the 'real' economy of industrial production, technology and progress, and the latter to the 'pecuniary' economy, in which activities serve the monetary interests of a small, powerful elite.

Some of his most important publications are: *Theory of the Leisure Class: An Economic Study of Institutions; Theory of Business Enterprise* (1899) and the article 'Why Is Economics Not an Evolutionary Science?', in the *Quarterly Journal of Economics* (1898),

John R. Commons (1862–1945) paid much attention in his writing to the role of law in a capitalist society. In his view, the introduction of new laws and changes in existing ones, is the way to settle conflicts between interest groups and to guide individual behavior in such a way that a better outcome results for the whole of society. He defined institutions such as laws as a collective action in control, restraint and liberalization of individual action. By this he meant that institutions force individuals to act in a specific way (institutions constrain), but they also liberate individuals (because laws make actions possible) and educate individuals (because institutions offer individuals the possibility of acquiring education and force public institutions to offer schooling to all citizens). The change of institutions in the world of Commons is primarily a matter of actors aiming to resolve conflicts.

His most important publications are: *Legal Foundations of Capitalism* (1924) and *Institutional Economics: Its Place in Political Economy* (1934).

## APPENDIX B: DOUGLASS NORTH

Douglass C. North (born in 1920) published a number of important books on Institutional Economics. Quotes from his own website demonstrate how his ideas developed over the years (Groenewegen *et al.*, 1995).

First, it is important that North explicitly introduced the existence of 'inefficient' institutions:

> In *Structure and Change in Economic History* (1981) I abandoned the notion that institutions were efficient and attempted to explain why 'inefficient' rules would tend to exist and be perpetuated. This was tied to a very simple and still neo-classical theory of the state which could explain why the state could produce rules that did not encourage economic growth. I was still dissatisfied with our understanding of the political process, and indeed searched for colleagues who were interested in developing political-economic models.

North's second important insight concerns the concept of rationality:

> The development of a political-economic framework to explore long-run institutional change occupied me during all of the 1980s and led to the publication of *Institutions, Institutional Change and Economic Performance* in 1990. In that book I began to puzzle seriously about the rationality postulate. It is clear that we had to have an explanation for why people make the choices they do; why ideologies such as communism or Muslim fundamentalism can shape the choices people make and direct the way economies evolve through long periods of time. One simply cannot get at ideologies without digging deeply into cognitive science in attempting to understand the way in which the mind acquires learning and makes choices. Since 1990, my research has been directed toward dealing with this issue. I still have a long way to go, but I believe that an understanding of how people make choices; under what conditions the rationality postulate is a useful tool; and how individuals make choices under conditions of uncertainty and ambiguity are fundamental questions that we must address in order to make further progress in the social sciences.

The third important insight was published in 2005 with his book *Understanding the Process of Economic Change*, and concerned the need for a pluralistic, interdisciplinary approach:

> Since receiving the Nobel Prize in 1993 I have continued my research trying to develop an analytical framework that would make more sense out of long-run economic, social and political change. With that objective in mind, I have gone much more deeply into cognitive science and attempted to understand the way in which the mind and brain work and how that relates to the way in which people make choices and the belief systems that they have. Clearly these underlie institutional

change and therefore are a necessary prerequisite to being able to develop a theory about institutional change. I have also attempted to integrate political, economic and social theory since, obviously, a useful theory of economic change cannot confine itself purely to economics but must try to integrate the social sciences and integrate them also with cognitive science.

# 3 Static Approaches to Institutions

## CONTENTS

- **Introduction**
- **Property rights theory**
  - Assigning property rights
  - Enforcing property rights
- **Contract theories**
  - Agency theory
  - Implicit contract theory
- **Transaction cost theory of governance structures**
  - Transaction costs economics
  - Governance structures
- **The vested interest approach**
  - Property rights
  - Agency
  - Governance structures
- **Concluding remarks**
- **Review questions**

## INTRODUCTION

As discussed in the preceding chapters, in real life economic actors usually do not have perfect information when they trade. On the one hand, this is the result of market imperfections, and on the other, people cannot foresee everything and do not have the capacity to always make optimal decisions. Uncertainty exists for the economic actors, both with respect to the behavior of others in the market and with respect to demand and supply, and consequently (future) prices.

Additionally, individuals may have a tendency to behave opportunistically. Moreover, there are areas of environmental uncertainty, such as developments in technology, climate change, natural and economic crises, and so on. In order to deal with these market characteristics and aspects of human behavior, different institutions, both formal and informal, have developed to support economic action. The static approach of Institutional Economics focuses on these issues: it studies the ways in which a given institutional environment has an impact on economic decision-making. Phrased in the terminology of the preceding chapter, this means that institutions are the exogenous variables that explain the choices made by individual actors, who are characterized by a set of given attributes. Within this static approach, the dominant school of thought is the New Institutional Economics.

In this chapter, three closely connected NIE theories will be introduced that will shed light on how people perform transactions. These three theories are property rights theory, contract (agency) theory, and the theory of transaction cost economics. In the world of NIE, actors are assumed to be driven entirely by optimizing behavior, whether this is described as profit maximization or as minimization of (transaction) costs. The key concept and ultimate goal is, therefore, *efficiency*.

Optimal institutions with respect to property rights will be explained below: how property rights (or the lack of them) influence transactions. The type of property (private, shared or public) and the degree of exclusiveness of a product determine whether or not the owner will have sufficient incentives to make efficient use of his resources.

We then elaborate on this by showing that the exchange of property rights can entail contracts that involve many kinds of transaction costs: search and negotiation costs; the costs of formulating the contract; the monitoring costs to check whether the terms of the agreement are complied with; and finally the costs of enforcing the observance of the contract. Several contract theories will be discussed. A frequently encountered problem in these circumstances is the principal–agent problem, which occurs if one party to the agreement acts opportunistically and uses information asymmetries to the disadvantage of the other party. Agency theory explains optimal contracts and monitoring.

The discussion on transaction costs also leads to the central issue of transaction cost economics. This concerns the question as to which governance structure is best suited to coordinate transactions. Given specific circumstances, the best option can sometimes be to coordinate a transaction with the help of your own organization ('to make') and at other times by working through the market ('to buy'). The question concerning the 'make or buy' decision will be worked out in more detail below, with the aid of a 'contracting scheme' by Williamson (1985, 1998). In short, this scheme assumes that the degree of asset specificity and the degree of built-in safeguards determine whether people will transact through the market or through organizations. Ultimately, it will be shown that, in certain circumstances, transactions cannot (easily) take place through the market or by means of a private organization, in which case the government creates governance structures such as forms of regulation or state-owned organizations.

Despite the emphasis on the efficiency approach, later we shall look at aspects of *vested interests*. The static approach to institutions entails more than just the efficiency perspective, which we touched on earlier. We have argued that institutions matter, not only with respect to whether institutions enable actors to reach an overall efficient outcome – in other words, a situation of optimal economic welfare. In addition, we argued that given institutions can provide *power* to specific interest groups, which consequently are able to reach an optimal outcome for themselves that does not necessarily coincide with maximum economic welfare.

We conclude by discussing briefly the connections between the different theories explained in this chapter.

# PROPERTY RIGHTS THEORY

People usually treat goods more carefully when they own them, because then the returns generated by the possession of these goods accrue to them and not to others. In other words, private property leads to responsible guardianship and motivates the owner to make use of it in such a way that it renders maximum utility. This applies to all goods where a person has the exclusive right

  (i) to make use of the good;
 (ii) to earn income from it; and
(iii) to manage the good and to transfer control of it (or to sell it) to another party.

This is what we mean by a *bundle of property rights* (Hart, 1998; Furubotn and Richter, 1998). The holder of all three property rights is called the owner of a good. So, the owner is the only one able to legally transfer control of the good to someone else (also referred to as the *right of disposal*). However, he can allow other people to use the good for a stated period of time in exchange for compensation. The owner (lessor) of goods may then transfer part of his bundle of rights temporarily to another person (the lessee). The property rights the lessee acquires are the right to use the good and to earn income from it. He does not acquire the right to sell or to destroy it. Hence, a lessee owns only part of the property rights. From this it follows that the owner of a property right does not necessarily have to be the owner of the good itself; for example, a lawyer's office can be rented from a real estate developer, a piece of farm land can be rented from a landowner, and an employee can be hired by a firm. In all these examples, at least two parties exercise property rights with respect to the same good. For that reason it is better to speak of *holders* rather than owners of property rights. The holder of a private property right is legally entitled to exclude others from using this right without permission. This is called *full excludability*.

In a market economy with scarce resources, property rights will be transferred to the party who is prepared to pay the highest price. It is important to note that the holder of the property right not only has rights but also obligations: the holder is accountable for possible inconvenience or damage that the use of the good may cause for others; for example, the operator of a fairground attraction may be held responsible if a visitor is injured during a ride.

Basically, there are two types of problems involving property rights. First, there is the issue of designing and assigning property rights, because in the absence of property rights there is the problem of excludability; anything not privately owned tends to be considered common property, which may lead to inefficiencies. If, for example, in the absence of property rights a person decides to exploit a piece of land to grow fruit, the produce could be taken by anyone else, which will either undermine the incentive to continue growing fruit or lead to high protection costs. In such circumstances, the need to define property rights may arise. In a broader sense, this relates to the choice of a property rights system: are the rights held by individuals (private property) or by agencies of the state or the community (public property or shared property)? As will be shown below, the different systems lead to different incentives.

Second, there is the issue of exercising property rights. The exercise and transactions of property rights do not always occur without problems. Sometimes it is not clear who is the holder of a property right. For example, somebody who is selling a bicycle does not necessarily have to be the owner. He may have stolen it. If it is not clear precisely to whom the property rights belong, costs must be incurred to establish the ownership. Another problem relates to enforcing property rights – as in the case of possible externalities. It often happens that the holder of a property right causes negative externalities such as air or water pollution, the costs of which are borne by others. Finally, even when the questions of ownership and responsibility have been solved, a transaction can fail because the parties to the contractual agreement may not comply with it.

In all these cases, institutions are in place to influence behavior in the desired way (to improve efficiency). It is the institutional environment that defines who has which property rights in the first place. In any society at any moment in time, a wide range of formal and informal rules determine how people may transact goods and services (North, 1990). Below we shall deal with problems of assigning and enforcing property rights. The problem of contracting will be dealt with separately.

## Assigning property rights

How and why did property rights arise? In early and small societies, it was often sufficient to make use of informal institutions (conventions) whenever a conflict arose about property:

> When the father died tradition often dictated that the family business go entirely to the eldest son (the convention of primogeniture). Two persons aspiring the same office or the same advantage, such as the better plot of land, might find that some code of chivalry would award the prize to the older or the weaker... In the simplest societies such conventions might have worked: A person would not want to break a convention if it would cost him the esteem of the community or it would jeopardize his prospect of being treated chivalrously himself in the future.
> (Phelps, 1985, p. 68)

As societies increase in size, and contacts become less personal, such conventions no longer work (North, 1990). People may be brought up with different values and norms. They start to do business with people they do not know and whom they may not trust. They might speculate that cheating on someone they do not know will have no consequences because there is no reputation at stake. This increases the risk of conflicts between (groups of) people who are contesting the use or possession of products. If, for example, two farmers are arguing about the ownership of a piece of land, they will have less time to bring produce to the market, to the detriment of consumers as well as themselves. A system of formal property rights can deal with this problem. When it is clear to the people involved who is entitled to what, disputes about ownership will decrease, provided that some form of legal enforcement exists. Such a *system of property rights* can be advantageous to all members of society, because conflicts are usually unproductive or disruptive.

Whereas informal sanctions could suffice in smaller communities, in larger populations a system of property rights must be established and enforced by a central authority, such as a ruler or government. When a democratically chosen and controlled authority is given the exclusive right to intervene in case of conflicts, if necessary by means of force (the police, the military), citizens can be reassured that their property rights will be protected. In Chapter 8 you can read more about the role of government.

A system of property rights could imply that all resources are in the possession of private owners, who receive all the benefits and bear all the costs associated with the ownership. This is the case with *privately owned goods* accompanied by full excludability: no one else may use the goods without the consent of the owner or holder of the property right. So, if, for example, someone has a piece of farmland on lease, in principle he holds the exclusive right of use and the exclusive right to earn income from it: the landowner cannot lease out the same piece of land to someone else at the same time without the permission of the lessee. At the other end of the spectrum, a system could exist in which all resources (land, raw materials and the products derived from them) belong to the public at large. This is the case of *shared (common) and public property*, and exploitation is not restricted to a single party.

These two extremes follow the distinction that was made in Chapter 1 between a pure market economy and a centrally planned economy. In reality, different forms of property coexist in societies, not only depending on whether people live in a market economy or in a socialist state, but also on whether particular products are easily excludable or whether they are scarce or not. Below, several existing types of property will be described.

Before we discuss each type of property separately, however, we shall start by elaborating on the general features that characterize the different types of goods in the economy. Each type of good can be characterized as being *exclusive or nonexclusive* on the one hand, and *rival or nonrival* on the other. A good is said to be exclusive when other people can effectively be prevented from using it. Rivalness refers to a good whose consumption reduces the amount of the good available to others. A so-called *private good* – such as bread – is both exclusive and rival: its consumption makes it unavailable to others (rival) and its consumer can prevent others from sharing it (exclusive). A so-called *pure public good* is both nonexclusive and nonrival. We have already touched on the problems involved with pure public goods in Chapter 1. A classic example of a pure public good is a lighthouse, because using it does not hinder the amount consumed by others (nonrival) while no one can be barred from using it, even if they do not pay for its use (nonexclusive).

Table 3.1 shows that, next to private goods and pure public goods, two more categories can be distinguished: *common property resources* and *club goods*. The former is defined as products that are nonexclusive yet at the same time rival, such as fish in the ocean, while the latter are products that are nonrival yet at the same time exclusive, such as cable television or golf courses.

All four types of goods are discussed in more detail below, in relation to the different types of property that can be distinguished. In succession, we shall consider (i) private property; (ii) free goods; (iii) shared property; and (iv) public property. We shall show

**Table 3.1** *Division of goods according to their characteristics*

|  |  | Exclusive | |
|---|---|---|---|
|  |  | YES | NO |
| Rival | YES | Private good | Common property resource |
|  | NO | Club good | Pure public good |

that the specific intrinsic characteristics of a certain product may have an impact on the degree of excludability and hence on the property's status.

## *Private property*

Given the characteristics mentioned above, this short discussion of private property must start by stressing that a *private* good is not necessarily the same as a *privately owned* good, and vice versa. When someone is riding a bicycle, this product has all the attributes of a private good, but it may be that this person has never been assigned the property rights to that bicycle. Alternatively, someone may possess a privately owned good that has all the attributes of a pure public good, such as information (often referred to as *intellectual property*). Think, for example, of a story or a poem: as soon as it is published, in a newspaper, say, it becomes nonrival and nonexclusive: in principle, the author cannot prevent anyone from using (reading) the text. Still, it may be important that property rights are formally allocated (and protected), so that others can be prevented from using (printing) the text without authorization: an incentive is then provided for the holder of the property right to continue exploiting it (in this case, to write more poems). This can be realized by giving someone the unique legal right of utilization: and the nonexclusive good then becomes *excludable*.

From the above it becomes clear that there is an important distinction between the concepts of exclusiveness and excludability. And it also becomes clear that there is a distinction between *tangible* and so-called *intangible goods*: the latter are products that cannot be physically touched. Property rights can be assigned to both types of goods.

As noted earlier, privately owned goods create incentives for the owner to maintain these products and to put them (now or in the future) to profitable use. To quote Milgrom and Roberts (1992, p. 288): 'On a more familiar level, people tend to take better care of their own cars than they do of cars they rent from Hertz or Avis. Similarly, since Avis was purchased by its employees, the employees reportedly work harder and use more ingenuity in their jobs than they did before.' If this observation holds true for all cases of private ownership, the economy at large will benefit. All holders of private property rights will be encouraged to use their resources as efficiently as possible and the consequent productivity increase will stimulate overall economic growth as well. But this positive effect is only possible if people believe that their property rights are ensured.

When shielded by effective laws and a trustworthy court system and police force, among other things, the holder of a property right need not incur very high *exclusion costs*: expenses to prevent others from making use of his property without permission.

## Free goods

A special category of property that is not shown in Table 3.1 is so-called free goods. This occurs when goods are not at all scarce; that is, when supply exceeds demand at all price levels. Hence the equilibrium price is zero. In this case, property rights do not need to be allocated to (groups of) individuals, because no conflicts can arise about the use of these goods: they are available to everybody so no one has to be excluded. Nowadays free goods are very rare; 'air' is a typical example.

## Shared (or common) property

In modern times, hardly any free goods exist any more – population growth, accompanied by increasing production and consumption, has led to air pollution and overexploitation of land and waters. Formerly free goods – such as clean water, meadows and fishing grounds – are therefore becoming scarcer. In other words, these free goods have (often) turned into common property resources: because property rights have not been established or assigned to specific individuals, these goods are still characterized by nonexclusiveness (everybody has free access to them) but they have become rival because of their scarcity. If managed carefully by the community – that is, if the resource is protected and maintained – continuous exploitation might be possible. If not, the stock is bound to be exhausted and may well finally disappear. This phenomenon has become known as the *tragedy of the commons*.

Garrett Hardin (1968) introduced the term 'tragedy of the commons' with the classic example of the herders who bring their livestock to the pasture that is open to all herdsmen or women. If an individual herder brings more cattle to this meadow, the benefit for him will be the extra proceeds from the additional animals. The accompanying cost of increasing his herd size is the additional grazing needed, and this will affect all users of the land. So, the gains are private, but the costs are distributed over all herders. This may imply that the individual gains exceed the distributed costs, hence each rational individual herder will increase his own herd size as long as the private gains exceed the costs. Because all herdsmen and women will act in a similar manner, tragedy is inevitable: 'Each man is locked into a system that compels him to increase his herd without limit – in a world that is limited. Ruin is the destination toward which all men rush, each pursuing his own best interest in a society that believes in the freedom of the commons. Freedom in a commons brings ruin to all' (Hardin, 1968, p. 1244). See Box 3.1 for a small numerical example.

---

### BOX 3.1 TRAGEDY OF THE COMMONS IN NUMBERS

Suppose that local farmers bring a number of (privately owned) cows to the commons. In the beginning, the number of cows is not large, so there is no rivalry. Assume that each cow delivers 1,000 liters of milk per year and that after deduction of costs the milk can be sold for €0.10 per liter. When the total number of cows reaches 100, a further expansion of the livestock will lead to rivalry in the use of the meadow, and to a decrease in milk production by 10 liters per year per cow, as can be seen from the table below:

*Example of the tragedy of the commons*

| Number of cows | Net benefit per cow | Total net benefit |
| --- | --- | --- |
| 1 | 100 | 100 |
| 2 | 100 | 200 |
| .. | | |
| 10 | 100 | 1,000 |
| .. | | |
| 100 | 100 | 10,000 |
| 101 | 99 | 9,999 |
| 102 | 98 | 9,996 |
| .. | | |

It follows that increasing the total livestock is profitable for all farmers collectively as long as there are no more than 100 cows grazing; after that, the total net benefit starts to decrease. However, at that stage, each individual farmer still has an incentive to bring more cows to the meadow, as his private net benefit is still increasing; suppose he had 10 cows, implying a net benefit of 1,000; then an increase to 11 cows would raise his total net benefits to $11 \times 99 = 1,089$.

According to Hardin (1968, p. 1248) there was only one way to solve to this tragedy: 'The commons, if justifiable at all, is justifiable only under conditions of low-population density. As the human population has increased, the commons has had to be abandoned in one aspect after another.'

Modern variants of commons that are in danger of facing the same kind of tragedy include fish in the ocean, open public spaces that suffer from littering, and global climate problems created by the burning of fossil fuels. In fact, what is happening in all these cases is that increasing rivalry leads to a negative externality: an action by one or more producers or consumers that affects third parties adversely, while the aggrieved parties are not reimbursed. Possible institutional solutions for this problem will be dealt with more extensively later in the book (see pages 102–6).

In order to manage and ration its scarce utilization, former free goods and (open-access) common property resources need to have a different property status, to prevent conflicts and depletion. Either these goods can be sold to individuals, thus turning them into private property, or the property rights of these goods can be acquired by a group of people, in that way turning them into club goods with appropriate rules. Alternatively, they can be confiscated by the state and turned into some form of public property.

The second form of shared property to be discussed here are products that have the characteristics of club goods (see Buchanan, 1965). A group of people can voluntarily form a club whose members are entitled to use a certain resource in return for a (monetary or physical) contribution, while nonmembers are excluded. Examples include recreation areas, private golf courses, health clubs, libraries, universities and trade unions.

Where there are a fairly small number of members there is no rivalry in consumption; the consumption of one member does not hinder that of another. The advantage of this form of property is that the members can share the costs, knowing that the gains accrue only to themselves and not to outsiders. Of course, people will only join if they anticipate that the total benefits will be higher than the costs. As long as the size of the club is relatively small, members can see whether all are contributing to the maintenance of the club good; if someone is found not to be abiding by the rules he will be sanctioned or lose his membership, and thereby the benefits of using the club good. In this situation informal institutions and sanctions can be very effective.

From this it follows that when the number of members increases, problems may arise regarding the preservation of the club good, which will start to become rival, leading to some kind of rationing to deal with these 'crowding costs'. At the same time, it will become more difficult to monitor and control each member's behavior. The more people who are involved, the greater the risk that individuals will show *free riding behavior* – in this case meaning that members of the group who do not contribute (enough) to the maintenance of the common go unnoticed, because the group is large. In the extreme, abuse (or mismanagement) of the club good may lead to a 'tragedy of the commons' as well.

One way to prevent this problem is to introduce a so-called *two-part tariff*. All members must pay a flat (entrance) fee in advance, which should be enough to cover the maintenance costs of the club good. In addition, members must pay a per-unit fee, the level of which is determined by the degree of scarcity. Think, for example, of a fitness or sports club, which often not only charges a fixed membership fee but also demands an additional contribution from all members who use the club at the busiest time of the day; that is, after work. Another example is a video rental outlet, which may set a fixed annual membership fee and then charges a certain amount for each video or DVD borrowed: this amount may vary according to the day of the week – renting a film at the weekend is usually more expensive, reflecting greater demand.

A related problem with respect to disincentives with shared property can be found in *egalitarian societies* or cooperative enterprises that become too big: a community based on the principle that all members share equally in the productive returns will create the wrong incentives as soon as the yield of someone's effort must be shared with a group of increasing size (Phelps, 1985). Equal rewards will have perverse effects: first, people would tend to opt for the pleasant tasks only, which could lead to lower productivity; and second, no one would be inclined to work any harder than necessary, since the extra return from their efforts mostly accrues to others. This ultimately could also lead to free riding behavior: why should a person work at all if he can get part of the total returns in any case?

Another difficulty with club goods appears if imperfect information makes it hard to distinguish members from nonmembers. People dodging fares on public transport are a prime example; deterrence mechanisms to solve this problem include monitoring and penalties when caught (Sandler and Tschirhart, 1997).

## Public property

The final category of property is public property, which can be divided into pure public goods and other forms of public goods.

Given the two characteristics of a pure public good, nonrivalness and nonexclusiveness, it follows that once a pure public good exists, everyone can consume it freely without lowering the consumption possibilities of others and without paying for its use. As well as the famous example of the lighthouse, other typical examples include dikes, national defense and public firework displays. Take, for example, public firework displays: as soon as the (costly) fireworks are displayed, all spectators can view and enjoy this without payment. In this case, we speak of *positive externalities*: an action by one or more producers or consumers that benefits third parties, without any compensation taking place for the party that incurs the costs.

Because pure public goods are always accompanied by positive externalities, the question becomes: Who will finance them? If too many people decide to free ride, it may very well turn out to be too expensive to produce this particular good at all. In many cases, this is undesirable, because many pure public goods are important to maintain. Dikes are a good example. As soon as a dike has been built, no one can be excluded from its protective power, so everyone has a private incentive not to contribute to the building costs. If the construction of the dike was funded by private contributions alone, not enough people would be prepared to pay for it, and consequently the dike would not be built at all, or would not be maintained properly; think back to the New Orleans example in Chapter 1. That is why pure public goods are often supplied by the government: payment is extracted from all citizens via a levy to avoid this free riding problem.

It is important to note that some goods can be publicly owned even though they do not have the characteristics of pure public goods. Governments may have several motives to want to have control over certain goods and these can be related to reasons of improving efficiency (economic welfare) and to power motives. We shall discuss these briefly below.

There can be good (welfare enhancing) reasons to protect civilians against abuse by powerful organizations such as natural monopolies and the military, by bringing these structures under state control (see Chapter 8). First, natural monopolies can mean that consumers have to pay too high a price for goods that are *not contestable* (potential competitors cannot enter the market profitably because of the sizeable scale economies that the incumbent monopolist has achieved). Second, the government needs to be in command of institutions such as the police, law courts and the military, to assure private citizens that they can expect fair treatment from these institutions. A third reason why a government may want to take control of production is to promote the consumption of merit goods (see Chapter 1) or to aid weaker members of society (social policy) by providing free education or social housing and health care at low cost, for example.

From the perspective of property rights theory, public property contains the risk that individuals do not feel responsible for maintaining products that have shared ownership. Box 3.2 illustrates with two historical examples why private property rights are (often) preferred because they motivate people to become more productive.

## BOX 3.2 PRIVATE PROPERTY RIGHTS IN COMMUNIST REGIMES: THE SOVIET UNION AND CHINA

When the communists seized power in Russia in 1917 and formed the Soviet Union after a civil war, all private property was nationalized and private associations such as the Church and political parties were suppressed. Many Russian people resisted these reforms, so the state's policies had to be enforced.

As a consequence of coordination failures and a complete lack of trust in the new institutions, total output declined rapidly and hyperinflation occurred. Millions of Russians fell into poverty and starved to death. In order to revive (agricultural) production, V. I. Lenin introduced the New Economic Policy in 1921 in which private property was reintroduced on a small scale: farmers were allowed to sell their surpluses on the market, inducing them to produce more. As a result, harvests increased again.

In 1929, the new ruler, Joseph Stalin, decided to collectivize all arable land and penalized private trading one year later. Central planning with a strong focus on industrialization became the main feature of the Soviet economic system. Overall, these measures turned out to be very harmful for the development of economic growth in the Soviet Union.

When Mikhail Gorbachev introduced *perestroika* in 1987, the socialist system became liberalized along capitalist lines. After this collapse of Stalin-style communism, it soon became clear that Soviet industry was profoundly backward compared with the West, and there were (and still are) huge problems in adapting to a capitalist system, not least of which was that workers were not used to taking decisions and had little personal motivation.

From the autumn of 2003, Western newspapers began to cite Chinese state-run media as stating that in China the Communist Party had begun formally to accept private property rights, in order to create a more capitalist economy. This move has been interpreted as an acknowledgment by the communist state that the protection of private property rights fosters economic growth, by keeping the fast-growing middle class satisfied. At the same time, the Party wants to remain in power.

Although the following comment by E. S. Phelps was written almost two decades before the changes in China began, it is highly appropriate:

Because equality is recognized to be counterproductive, and quite destructive in large groups, every country of which we have any knowledge makes it a rule to permit a person to keep more when more is earned – not all of any additional income, but at least a fraction. Not to do so would appear to be an act of spite, for it would be hard to understand what else but sheer spitefulness could motivate a national policy that by withdrawing an incentive to earn operates to pull everyone down. (Phelps, 1985, p. 142)

## Enforcing property rights

It was mentioned earlier that property rights can sometimes be protected effectively by members of the group, with the aid of informal institutions. In smaller communities in particular, the influence of social (or religious) norms can be quite successful. We also saw that in larger, more complex societies, private property rights can be protected effectively by the government.

Over time, extensive judicial systems have appeared and been refined in modern societies. In many cases when a conflict arises, formal institutions may serve to enforce property rights. In addition, societies have developed many kinds of informal institutions that from time to time have proved to function just as well in preventing or resolving disputes concerning the use of property rights. The advantage of informal institutions is often that it is much less costly to enforce them, as long as the majority of the people support these unofficial rules. Unfortunately, modern societies cannot function smoothly with the aid of informal institutions alone, and the implementation of formal state-enacted rules implies higher costs because of the employment of bureaucrats, police, lawyers and judges.

Another problem is related to enforcing property rights in the case of possible externalities. It often happens that the holder of a property right causes negative externalities, the costs of which are borne by others. The 1991 Nobel Laureate, Ronald Coase, showed in the *Coase theorem* that a solution consists of assigning property rights to these negative externalities – for example, 'the right to clean air' or 'the right to pollute'. Coase wrote about this feature in his famous article 'The Problem of Social Cost' (1960). He showed that parties will be able to reach an optimal solution to a problem without state intervention, given three conditions:

(i) it must be clear who possesses the property rights;
(ii) negotiations about solving the problem must be costless (implying that there are no transaction costs involved); and
(iii) wealth effects are not allowed to occur.

His argument will be described below.

Coase used a historical example to demonstrate how two parties can solve the problem in private that emerges as a result of a (negative) externality. He presented a railway company, whose steam locomotives emit sparks that could set fire to land owned by farmers. Legally, if the railway company was entitled to run its operation without any consideration for nearby farmland, the result would be a great deal of damage. Alternatively, if the farmers were given the right to compensation for any losses caused by the railway, the latter would have to take costly measures to prevent the damage by sparks.

Regardless of which of the two parties has in fact been granted the property right, Coase showed that both sides could gain by trading legal entitlements (that is, the transaction of property rights). If, for example, the railway held the right to use the railway lines with no restrictions, the farmers might decide to pay a certain amount of money to the company in exchange for a reduction in the damage; as long as this compensation is smaller than the money value of the total damage caused by the sparks, and as long as this compensation covers the costs incurred by the railway in reducing the emission of sparks, this makes both parties better off. The same argument holds if we start with the assumption that the farmers have the right to apply for an injunction against the railway. The trading process continues until an efficient allocation of resources has taken place and neither side can improve its position further unless the other side loses. At this point, the negative externality has become completely *internalized*, which implies that all social costs inflicted on third parties are now being taken into consideration when determining the level of production (or consumption). We show a numerical example in Box 3.3.

Unfortunately, in real life, many circumstances obstruct this efficient outcome. The three conditions mentioned earlier (unambiguousness about the ownership of property rights; absence of transaction costs; and absence of wealth or income effects) often do not apply. To begin with, it may not be entirely clear who is the holder of a property right, and hence who is responsible for possible damages. And even when it is perfectly obvious who owns the entitlement, negotiations about another distribution can still fail, either because of high transaction costs or because of an unequal division of power between the negotiators.

The first situation occurs if, for example, the farmers with land adjoining the railway form a large, disjointed group that has divergent interests and in which some try to free ride on the efforts of others. The second situation would occur if, in contrast, the farmers were all rather poor and unable to collect the funds needed for the trade of entitlements. In other words, in those circumstances, wealth effects are not absent but instead play a decisive off-putting role.

### BOX 3.3   THE COASE THEOREM IN NUMBERS

Suppose a smoker and a nonsmoker have to work together in the same room. The nonsmoker would much prefer the smoker not to smoke, but in the absence of a 'right' to clean air, the smoker can smoke as much as he likes. Suppose the smoker has a utility (in monetary terms) of 10 in case he smokes 1 cigarette, an additional utility of 9.5 for the second cigarette, 9 for the third and so on: each additional cigarette adds utility that is 0.5 less than the previous one. The smoker will smoke 21 cigarettes a day.

The nonsmoker has utility for the first cigarette of –8 (a disutility), –9 for the second and so on: each cigarette adds one more unit of disutility.

Joint additional utility is 2 (10 – 8) for the first cigarette, 0.5 (9.5 – 9) for the second, and from the third cigarette onwards, joint additional utility becomes negative. Obviously, it would be 'optimal' to let the smoker have two cigarettes instead of the privately optimal 21 cigarettes.

Now suppose that the nonsmoker *does* have the right to 'clean air'. A smoking ban forbids the smoker to smoke. But what he can do is to 'bribe' (persuade) the non-smoker into letting him smoke two cigarettes: it is privately and socially optimal for the smoker to smoke two cigarettes and pay the nonsmoker for the disutility. This disutility is –17 in the case of the two cigarettes, but the smoker's utility is 19.5.

> This will also be the solution when the smoker has the right to smoke: he will let himself be persuaded by the nonsmoker to cut his consumption to only two cigarettes. Each additional cigarette would add more disutility to the nonsmoker than utility to the smoker; hence the nonsmoker will pay the smoker for not-smoking more than two.
>
> Of course, an alternative (informal) institution could have developed: even in the absence of property rights, the nonsmoker might have an incentive to pay the smoker for not-smoking. In that case, a 'contract' would have resulted between the smoker and the nonsmoker.
>
> However, this might lead to the following problem: the smoker might collect the money and still smoke more than two cigarettes. The nonsmoker finds herself in a dilemma: pay and not get what she wants (or 'go to court' to enforce the contract, which in itself is a costly solution), or not pay and tolerate the smoke. In general, this would imply an inefficient solution. Besides, the opportunistic behavior of the smoker might also arise in the case of the right to smoke. Moreover, the possible problem remains that the nonsmoker may not have the financial means to pay the 'bribe'.

Because the Coase theorem in its pure form can very rarely be applied in practice, Coase has underlined the importance of defining and assigning property rights, and the significance of the need to curtail transaction costs by creating proper institutions, formal or informal.

## *Incentives: problems and solutions*

What should become clear from the description of the different property right systems is that these generate different kinds of *incentives*. While in general, private property rights stimulate people's productivity and efficiency the most, several situations can justify the existence of another system, in which property is shared among groups, as we saw above. But one of the greatest problems that can occur with collective ownership is free riding, which generates social costs and enforcement problems.

Hardin (1968) was pessimistic about the chances of survival of common property systems. But later authors have argued convincingly that solutions to prevent a tragedy of the commons are possible, without abolishing the commons as a form of property. In particular, the 2009 Nobel Laureate Eleanor Ostrom (1990) provided empirical evidence of where a local community manages property resources effectively, because the people involved realize that their total net benefits are larger if the resource in question remains as shared property. In such a *common property regime*, a large number of community rules and sanctions are defined, which work very well because the system functions at a local level and monitoring is easy.

In the case of pure public goods or club goods, free riding may cause financing problems if people (or nonmembers) cannot be excluded from utilization. Sometimes the solution lies simply in charging the whole community by means of government *taxation*, but the drawback of this is that nonusers are also forced to pay. At times, nonusers can be convinced to pay, as a form of solidarity if the good in question is too expensive for the target group and is considered to be of high importance (dikes and systems of national health care are typical examples).

At other times, it would be preferable if only the actual users were charged. This can sometimes be achieved by technological improvements that make it possible to reduce or eliminate free riding. Think of electronic entrance gates at train and subway stations, or technology that makes it possible to monitor how much use automobile drivers make of certain roads, as happens in the city of London.

A special case already mentioned briefly is the case of information goods, which are also (intrinsically) characterized by nonrivalness and nonexclusiveness – such as, say, intellectual property or inventions. To prevent third parties from taking this information without any compensation, both formal and informal institutions exist. An informal solution to protect valuable information is secrecy (think of the famous recipe for Coca-Cola). Typical legal solutions include *copyrights and patent rights*, which protect the producers of information goods and stimulate others also to become innovative (dynamic efficiency), knowing that the law will protect the results of their efforts. In fact, as a result of these different solutions, the public good character of the information good has turned into an excludable private good.

The downside of effective protection is that it may, but need not, create a monopoly position for the holder of the property right, but the fact that legislators generally do create patent rights, suggests that on balance the positive effects on economic growth are considered to be more important than the possible negative effects of temporary market power: after all, copyrights and patents expire after a number of years. We shall return to this issue in later chapters.

It is worth mentioning that government intervention is not always necessary when problems associated with property rights occur. If the circumstances are right, and a sufficient number of people share a value system that respects the upholding of public property, informal institutions (such as the value of 'good citizenship'), together with informal sanctions (losing one's position in society), may be quite effective.

One last solution to incentive problems that can be found in the property rights literature relates to the so-called *residual rights of control* (see Hart, 1998). Remember that different property rights may apply to the same good: in many cases, the owner of a good grants the right to retain income from that good to another party, in return for compensation. Examples include a landowner who leases his land to a farmer or to the operator of a campsite; an owner of real estate who rents out his building to firms or to private tenants; or the owners of a firm (shareholders) who authorize managers to operate the firm on their behalf.

In all these cases, the lessees have been granted the right to make use of the good and to earn income from it, but the ultimate right of disposal (the right to sell the good to another party), remains with the owner. In other words, the owner always has the so-called residual rights of control and income: in principle, all decisions, revenues and costs not specified in the contract between the owner and the lessee fall to the owner.

However, there is an argument that the automatic allocation of residual control rights to the owners might not always be optimal. Think, for example, about a firm renting a certain plot of land, on which it has built a factory; the operator of the firm does not have any incentive to treat the surroundings of the factory with care, which could lead to abuses such as accumulations of waste, pollution, or deterioration of the road. The owner of the industrial estate will have then more difficulty in leasing out other parts of the estate. Clearly, something needs to be done to prevent this from happening: the lessees need to be given the right environmental incentives in the contract.

Another example is the *employment relationship*. In the traditional view on the hiring of labor the following transfer of property rights takes place: the employee offers his working power in exchange for a wage, which gives the owner of the firm the right to exercise control over the use of this labor. Moreover, the owner is entitled to the entire profit (residual) that results from the use of the labor, making her the *'residual claimant'* (Alchian and Demsetz, 1972). In this situation, the owner has the incentive to maximize the firm's profits, but the employees do not have any incentive to perform well. As long as they receive their wage for a certain number of working hours, they might be inclined to behave opportunistically (for example, by shirking).

For that reason, the residual claimant must incur additional costs to monitor workers and to prompt them to apply greater effort. This led to the realization that it might be worthwhile for the owner to share the residual with other stakeholders in the firm, to motivate all parties to dedicate themselves to improving the firm's performance. As a consequence, the specifications of the labor contract will change: to prevent (*ex post*) opportunistic behavior, it becomes essential to support the contract (*ex ante*) with specific arrangements (Furubotn and Richter, 1998).

This brings us to the subject of contracts, which will be dealt with next.

## CONTRACT THEORIES

All transactions are concluded with some form of contract. A *contract* is an oral or written agreement between two parties who consent in advance to exchange goods or services (property rights), whether or not in return for a certain payment. To increase the possibility that both parties will keep to their side of the agreement, contracts often contain some kind of sanction on nonobservance, or are governed by formal rules of liability. *Formal contracts* are legally enforceable promises. However, not all contracts are formal; there are also *informal, implicit contracts* that inherently facilitate compliance with the agreement.

Freedom of contract is assumed, which implies that the owner of a good is allowed to transfer property rights to whomever he wishes under the conditions he chooses, as long as the contractual agreement does not conflict with the law or with the rights of third parties.

Contracts are concluded primarily because the parties to the transaction think that they can all benefit from them. It is convenient to make a distinction between more complex or long-term transactions and spot transactions. Particularly in the first case, the parties involved realize that, in order to draw up a contract, there will be transaction costs. Moreover, anticipated problems involving uncertainty and opportunistic behavior must be dealt with as fully as possible: the degree to which these issues are handled determines the degree of completeness of the contract.

In an ideal world in which parties act entirely rationally and are fully informed, individuals can transfer property rights and record their agreements in *complete contracts*. This implies that any agreement can be monitored and enforced free of charge. In a perfect market, full information and competition would force all parties to meet their contractual obligations. In reality, however, incomplete information and bounded rationality (limited cognitive competence) lead unavoidably to *incomplete contracting*, because it is too costly to specify all contingencies. Nevertheless, contracting takes place as soon as the parties involved have enough confidence that agreements will be met, thanks to a wide range of possible institutions, both formal and informal.

Contracts come in many forms and can apply to many sorts of transactions, both in the market place and within organizations, as we shall see below. Contracts can apply to just two people (one buyer and one seller) but also to groups of people (think of individual and collective labor contracts). Additionally, contracts can apply both to nonrecurring and recurring transactions.

There is a difference between a *one-off, simultaneous contract* (*spot transaction*) and a *nonsimultaneous contract*. The former involves an immediate exchange of property rights, so by and large both parties comply straight away with the (unwritten) agreement, and the contractual relationship ends immediately. Still, this does not imply that no complications are involved. For example, the (spot) exchange may also include a future promise such as a warranty on the product sold. Or it may turn out that the product is of poor quality and there is no warranty; in this case the seller did not meet the – implicit – expectations of the buyer, which lowers welfare. In Chapter 5 we shall analyze the famous example of the 'market for lemons'. Welfare in this case can be improved formally by, for example, rules of liability, which we shall deal with below. Other solutions in the case of 'lemons' will be presented in Chapter 5, in so far as private parties have found ways of dealing with this problem. In Chapter 8 we shall elaborate ways in which the government can tackle this problem.

Nonsimultaneous contracts are more complicated, because the agreement will only be fulfilled at a stipulated point in time in the future, which increases the risks of noncompliance. As a consequence, there is a greater need to write down the terms of the agreement.

Many different contract theories can be distinguished in the economic literature. See, for example, Furubotn and Richter (1998) for an extensive overview. We shall restrict ourselves here to the distinction that Furubotn and Richter make between agency theory on the one hand and implicit contract theory on the other. The first type of contract theory refers to formal contracts that are legally enforceable agreements. The second type refers to self-enforcing contracts.

## Agency theory

Basically, contracts can be understood as the need of parties to insure themselves against risk. Contracts are then said to be the result of the degree of risk aversion (or risk neutrality) of the parties involved. The term *risk aversion* means that a person prefers a secure outcome to an insecure one, given that the insecure outcome generates the same expected (monetary) value as the secure outcome. *Risk neutrality* means that the person is indifferent between a sure and an unsure outcome, where again the (expected) outcomes have the same monetary value. A simple example may clarify these concepts; see Box 3.4.

> ### BOX 3.4   RISK AVERSION
>
> Suppose we have the following uncertain outcome (of a lottery in this case, but it can also be any other risky event): a person has a probability 1/4 of winning €40 and a 3/4 probability of winning €0. Hence, the expected monetary value of this lottery is €10. If this person is risk neutral she will be indifferent between playing the lottery or getting €10 in cash. In other words, both outcomes give her the same utility. If the person is risk averse, however, she will strictly prefer a fixed amount of €10 instead of playing the lottery with an expected value of €10. This also implies that the risk averse person will strictly prefer a slightly lower amount than €10 (say, as low as €9) over playing the lottery. In other words, receiving an amount of cash of anywhere between €9 and €10 gives the risk averse actor a higher utility than playing the lottery.
>
> Now suppose that the risk averse individual has a probability of 3/4 that she receives nothing and a probability of 1/4 that €40 will be won, we can have a simple *welfare improving contract* of the following nature: the risk neutral actor 'insures' the risk averse actor by taking over the lottery and paying €9.50 for it. Since the risk averse actor strictly prefers the €9.50 to the lottery and the risk neutral actor is willing to pay the €9.50 because he is even prepared to pay at most €10, both individuals gain and hence welfare has increased.
>
> Many risky (economic) outcomes can be interpreted as a lottery; think, for example, of workers in jobs where there is a high risk of disability (and consequently a high risk of losing a regular income), or the risk of being robbed or losing your possessions in a fire. In all these instances, a risk averse person can search for a risk neutral person (or a less risk averse actor) or organization to 'take over' the risk, insurance companies being logical examples.

Not only contracts between insurance companies and their insurants are characterized by this (optimal) allocation of risks. All economic contracts have similar features. For example, a labor contract typically involves an agreement between an employer and an employee in which the latter is generally more risk averse and prefers a fixed moderate wage to a wage that fluctuates as a direct result of the business cycle. But, as another example, the customers of a restaurant or of a cinema usually prefer to pay a fixed, known price for their meal or film rather than a fluctuating price that is influenced by the number of customers that want to buy this product at the same time (as a result of a price that is influenced by the demand and supply conditions at that very moment).

Even though this 'insurance' contract forms a solid basis for a welfare-enhancing agreement that could make all parties involved better off, this will often still not be the case because not everyone involved in the contract has the same information and may be tempted to abuse this information asymmetry. *Agency theory* deals with the question of how to incorporate the right incentives into a contract in order to prevent this opportunistic behavior and reach an efficient outcome, as we shall see below.

The most important formal institutions that act as safeguards against a breach of contract stem from the existing contract law of a country. In a well-developed law system, many uncertainties that remain after concluding an incomplete contract can be dealt with. First, legal sanctions can be formulated in such a way that they serve as good deterrents. And second, even if a contract is breached, people can go to court in order to either enforce the contract or to obtain compensation. However, monitoring the observance of the contract on the one hand, and going to court on the other, are costly activities, which is why parties to the agreement also try to build in other incentives and sanctions that should restrain both sides from breaching the contract.

In agency theory, a distinction is made between the party who gives an assignment and delegates part of her decision-making powers, and the party who has the responsibility of carrying out the assignment, together with the ability to make certain decisions (this party receives *discretionary powers*). The party that commissions the task is called the *principal*; and the party that receives the task is called the *agent*. That is why the terms agency theory and *principal–agent theory* are used interchangeably.

The principal–agent *relationship* (in this case, an act of delegation) only becomes a principal–agent *problem* when two conditions hold:

(i) The principal and the agent have different, *conflicting interests*. The principal wants to maximize her own welfare, for which she needs the agent to make his best effort, which need not be the agent's objective: he might prefer to shirk, for example.
(ii) There is *asymmetric information*. One of the parties, usually the principal, has less knowledge about what the other one, generally the agent, is able to do (hidden characteristics, hidden information) before the contract is concluded, or what the agent does (hidden action, hidden decisions) after the contract has been signed. So, one of the actors has an informational advantage.

When the above two conditions both hold, this will give rise to either *ex ante* opportunism or *ex post* opportunism (Milgrom and Roberts, 1992). On the one hand, one of the parties to a contract may conceal certain facts (for example, about his true capabilities to meet his obligations) without the other side finding out prior to the signing of the contract. This shortage of information before the contract has been signed (*ex ante*) could lead to what is termed *adverse selection*. On the other hand, one of the parties may not do what is expected of him after the contract has been signed (*ex post*), without the other side finding out. This is called *moral hazard* behavior and will be explained further below.

## Adverse selection

A core problem of insurance companies when offering insurance is to distinguish between people with differing risks; for example, between those who will often make claims and those who will hardly ever do so. The following case will illustrate why this may cause problems.

Suppose an insurance company decides to start offering auto insurance; first, it has to determine the level of the insurance rate for its prospective clients. As long as the company knows nothing about these clients, it could begin with setting one and the same insurance premium for everyone, say €2,000 per year, based on current statistics. Since these statistics are determined by all people – those who are accident-prone and those who are not – what will happen is that drivers who seldom or never make a claim will find this premium too high so they will not buy the insurance, whereas accident-prone people all rush to sign the contract because the premium is relatively low for them. So, it is not the average risk that the insurance company will cover, but a higher one.

As a result, the insurance company will incur losses and will decide to increase the premium for the following year, which in turn will deter those clients for whom this new insurance rate is just too high. See the numerical example in Box 3.5.

---

### BOX 3.5   ADVERSE SELECTION IN THE INSURANCE MARKET

Assume that there are three risk averse people (A, B and C) who each may incur damages of €3,000 with differing probabilities: A has a probability of 1/6, B of 2/6 and C of 3/6. Average damages are therefore €3,000.

Suppose that an insurance company would like to offer a premium of €1,050, expecting these three people to buy this insurance, so that the company will earn €3,150: enough to cover expected damages of €3,000 and its own costs, including a profit. Since A has expected damages of €500, because of risk aversion she may want to pay a little more than this amount of €500 in order to be insured (see Box 3.4). Assume that she is prepared to pay at most €600 in order to be insured. Then obviously she will not buy the insurance.

So only B and C will buy the insurance: B is prepared to pay a little more than his expected damages, which are €1,000, and C is prepared to pay a little more than her expected damages of €1,500. Thus the insurance company effectively earns €2,100, while its expected damages increase to €2,500.

If the company tries to raise the premium to €1,300 in order to make up for the increased damages, B will no longer want to buy the insurance (assuming that his risk aversion is such that he wants to buy insurance only up to a premium of €1,200), hence the insurance company will eventually insure only C at a premium of slightly more than €1,500.

This mechanism involves a welfare loss: both A and B, because of risk aversion, would prefer to have insurance, but cannot obtain any that is based on average risk. If the insurance company was able to distinguish between the different risk types, it would offer three different premiums and welfare would be increased.

If, additionally, we assume that C is unable to pay €1,500, the insurance will not come about at all.

---

As illustrated in Box 3.5, adverse selection poses problems that may lead to welfare losses. Luckily, insurance companies can prevent this adverse selection problem from happening. Even if they do not know the prospective clients personally, they have several tools at their disposal to distinguish between lower and higher risks. For example, they are able to predict people's likely claim behavior based on general information such as age and gender. Statistics show (worldwide) evidence that, on average, younger people (and particularly men) are more accident-prone, while older people have higher health costs. It then becomes possible to *differentiate* between clients, offering them different premiums. Another possibility would be to offer at least two kinds of package: one consisting of a relatively low premium but with a very high additional *own risk*, and one with a relatively high premium but with low additional own risk. The term 'own risk' is also known as 'excess risk' and means, for example, that the first €100 of the damage has to be paid by the insurant herself. It is to be expected that, via a process of *self-selection*, low-risk people will opt for the first package, while high-risk ones will opt for the second.

Finally, the possibility remains that these measures will not be sufficient to induce companies to offer insurances that everyone can afford. In these cases, a solution could be found that makes insurance *mandatory*. One example of this can be seen in the Netherlands, where the government has introduced a national health care system in which every citizen is obliged to take out basic health insurance, while insurance companies are not allowed to refuse any client. If companies should suffer losses as a direct result of this obligation, they receive compensation from a special fund.

Instances of principal–agent problems in the form of adverse selection cannot only be found in the insurance market, but also in any market in which the transaction of a certain product involves asymmetric information with respect to higher and lower risks, or with respect to higher or lower quality of the product involved in the transaction.

The problem of differing product qualities, that are unknown by consumers, is akin to the insurance problem (as we shall show in Chapter 5); effectively only low-quality products will be offered on the market. This problem can be solved by a system of *liability*. Suppose that a customer is thinking of buying a product that might have a defect, but she cannot observe whether it is defective before its purchase. If she found out afterwards, and took the case to court, the court might rule that the seller has to compensate for the loss of value: this means that the supplier is liable for the damages incurred by the customer. As soon as this damage payment exceeds the costs of improving the quality of the product, he will have an incentive to deliver a product of good quality from the start. Hence, the system of liability may enhance the functioning of markets.

However, if the supplier was found not to be liable, then obviously the damage would have to be borne by the customer. Consequently, two effects would occur. One, the customer would consider the expected damages to be part of the product's price and therefore would buy less than in the case of a good quality product. Two, because the supplier cannot signal the quality of his products, he has no incentive to supply products of good quality. In this case, a nonoptimal outcome results.

Of course, the question of who is liable is determined by law. In this example, it is clearly optimal to correct market outcomes by assigning liability to suppliers. If this type of formal rule was not in place, then (by default) the consumer would be liable.

## *Moral hazard*

So far, we have described problems resulting from an *ex ante* perspective. Now we turn to *ex post* problems. After a contract has been signed and some decision-making power is delegated from the principal to the agent, the latter might take advantage of the fact that he has more information than his principal about his efforts. It is likely that the agent will try to maximize his own welfare instead of the principal's. Because his actions may go unnoticed, the agent might avoid being punished. This kind of opportunistic behavior has been termed 'moral hazard'.

Many principal–agent relationships that could potentially lead to moral hazard problems can be distinguished in real life. One that is observed very frequently in business is the relationship between an employer and his subordinate. In a large organization, an employer cannot supervise everything that an employee does or does not do. Especially when team work is involved, the degree of effort of the individual may go unobserved, which could lead to shirking, because the agent can speculate that he will not be dismissed.

But there are many more examples of principal–agent relationships, not only within companies. In the market, an individual or firm may contract another party and give him an assignment to act in their best interest. Think, for example, of a client who hires an attorney, or a patient who wants to be treated by a doctor. Agency problems are possible, because often a client cannot know whether an attorney really spent the amount of time claimed on the case; and a patient cannot know whether a doctor is prescribing the most effective as well as the cheapest medicine. In Part III of this book you will find more examples and applications.

Examples can also be found in the public sector, ranging from the citizen voting for a politician with the expectation that the elected representative will fulfill the promises made before the election, to delegates in parliament issuing laws with the expectation that ministers will carry them out accordingly; and to the minister himself, who is dependent on his civil servants to enforce the law. We shall elaborate on this in Part IV of this book.

In all these cases there is a risk that agents may act opportunistically, giving rise to efficiency losses, which have to be prevented by different types of institutions. Because principals often do not have all the available information about the people with whom they are dealing, there is a risk that, after the signing of the contract, an agent may start to behave differently from before. Moral hazard may occur as soon as one party has more information than the other party and exploits the situation.

The term originates from insurance literature, in which moral hazard is a very common phenomenon. This post-contractual opportunism may take different forms. On the one hand, insurance takers may be temped to claim more (and more often) against the service they are insured with than they would if they did not have insurance. For example, if a person is insured against paying doctors' fees, he would consult the doctor more often than if he had to pay a fee every time. On the other hand, the insurants may become more careless, thus increasing the risk that they will in fact need to make a claim against the insurance. Moral hazard behavior is not only costly for the insurance companies, which have to pay out insurance claims and hire lawyers to prove that their clients have been imprudent; ultimately, society at large will be worse off, because moral hazard will lead to higher insurance premiums. See the numerical example in Box 3.6.

## BOX 3.6   MORAL HAZARD IN THE INSURANCE MARKET

Suppose we have an insurance company and two risk-averse people, D and E. Before having insurance, each person has a probability of 1/6 of incurring damages of €3,000. Average damages are therefore €1,000 (€500 for each individual). A premium of €550 will cover these damages, including costs and profits for the insurance company.

Since D and E are risk averse we may assume that they are prepared to pay the €550. Given the insurance, they might be likely to incur more losses – for example, claiming more than €3,000 damages, or by becoming more careless so that, apart from possible higher claims for damages, the probability of more frequent damages is also increased. D and E might incur losses of €3,600, say, and create a higher probability of 2/6. The insurance company will effectively face expected damages of €2,400. Adjusting the premium to slightly more than €1,200 will mean that both D and E, having the choice of becoming more prudent again at average damages of €500 each, will not buy the insurance.

Countless real-life examples of moral hazard exist. It is not uncommon for people to try to declare the loss of expensive items when on holiday, when in fact the items are still in their possession. Or perhaps they do lose the items, but only because they were not careful enough. And, in the same vein, it may well be that people visit their doctor more frequently once their health insurance covers the visit. The insurer cannot observe this opportunistic behavior, but can try to discourage it by building in institutional devices such as the introduction of an 'own risk', as discussed above, or setting up a system in which the insurants pay lower annual premiums in a given year if they have not made a claim in the preceding year.

The efficiency losses resulting from moral hazard behavior are better known by the term *'agency costs'*, of which there are three categories (Jensen and Meckling, 1976, p. 308):

(i) monitoring expenditures; (ii) bonding expenditures; and (iii) residual loss.

(i) *Monitoring expenditures*. Given the possible divergence of interests, the principal will try to steer the agent in the desired direction by establishing appropriate incentives for the agent and by incurring monitoring costs. There are many devices by which to observe the behavior of agents, which could either discourage the agent from misbehaving, by means of strict supervision and appropriate punishment such as lay-off or demotion (negative incentives), or stimulate the agent to behaving as desired by means of merit pay, offering career promotions or even small gestures such as compliments (positive incentives). A more extensive treatment of these so-called *disciplinary mechanisms* can be found in Chapter 6.

(ii) *Bonding expenditures*. It sometimes pays for the agent to spend resources (bonding costs) aimed at signaling to the principal that he does serve the interests of the principal. He might be willing to pay these extra costs if he has much to lose if the contract is terminated; for example, in a situation in which the agent has made *transaction-specific investments* (see more on this subject below).

In principle, monitoring costs and bonding costs are two sides of the same coin: if the agent has signaled successfully that he can be trusted, the principal may have less need to monitor the agent's actions intensively. Conversely, if the agent has not made much effort to convince the principal that his intentions are good, the latter may feel inclined to increase the level of monitoring. Hence, a rise in bonding costs coincides with a decline in monitoring costs and vice versa.

(iii) *Residual loss*. This is the monetary value of the principal's welfare loss that may still remain even if optimal levels for monitoring and bonding are taken into account.

Figure 3.1 illustrates that total agency costs are the sum of monitoring costs, bonding costs and residual loss. For easy reference, residual loss and bonding costs are presented in one curve. In the figure it is assumed that with a rising level of monitoring, both bonding costs and residual loss (the costs of the agent's suboptimal decisions) will decline.

In Figure 3.1, agency costs can be minimized if the principal chooses a monitoring value of L*. From this it follows that the optimum level of monitoring does not coincide with zero agency costs. Particularly in large organizations, monitoring may be so costly that residual loss is likely to persist.

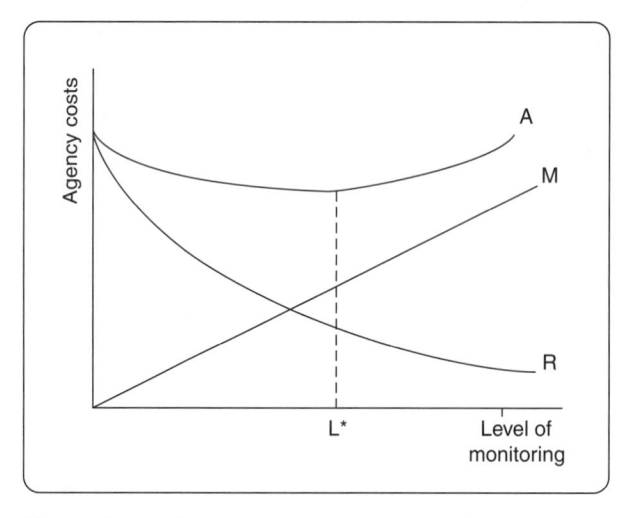

**Figure 3.1** *Agency costs*

*Notes*: A = total agency costs; M = monitoring costs; R = balance of residual loss and bonding costs.

In agency theory as described above, the main incentives for parties to a contract to keep their side of the bargain are rewards and punishments. If necessary, these formal contracts can be legally enforced. But not all contracts can be imposed with the aid of the law. The judicial system may be imperfect or courts may be unable to pass judgment because they lack the necessary information about the question of whether the contracting parties have lived up to the agreement. The more incomplete the contracts, the more difficult it becomes for outsiders to determine whether and to what degree the terms of a contract have been violated. This brings us to the subject of implicit contracts, which will be dealt with next. At the outset, however, it should be noted that there is a certain overlap between agency contracts as described above and implicit contracts as described below, because agency relationships may also be characterized by implicit contracting.

## Implicit contract theory

If parties are considering a transaction even though they know it will be hard to enforce the contract legally, there are still several ways to reach an agreement. It is possible to design a so-called *self-enforcing agreement* with which agents comply because it is in their best interests to do so. Such an agreement is closely related to the self-enforcing and self-regulating mechanisms we introduced in Chapter 1. It is an informal institution that is not legally enforced and that, because of built-in norms of behavior, unwritten institutions or other private rules determined by the social group, will be complied with voluntarily, because the benefits of adhering to the agreement are higher than the benefits of defaulting on the (often implicit) terms of the contract. In other words, the contract is designed so that violating the agreement leads to such high costs that people will spontaneously refrain from doing so (see also Rosen, 1985).

### Self-enforcing and self-regulating mechanisms

In the literature, the terms implicit contracts and self-enforcing agreements are often used synonymously. Several self-enforcing mechanisms and self-regulating mechanisms are distinguished, and below we point out briefly the most important ones. Part III will elaborate on several of these issues.

1 The threat of losing one's *reputation*. Fear of loss of reputation is very much a reality in business life. Others will know that you have cheated on your contract partner, so your reputation will be damaged and your business or career will suffer. From this it follows that business people and, for that matter, other professionals (including politicians), may be reluctant to breach a contract.
2 *Tit for tat*. Deceiving your business partner may cause him to retaliate in the same way. This prospect may help to prevent contracting parties from breaking their promises, because the costs of doing so will greatly exceed the benefits, especially in the case of employment contracts, which usually involve a great amount of mutual dependency. This is also related to the so-called iterated prisoner's dilemma, which is part of game theory; we shall discuss this further in Chapter 7.
3 Installing *third parties* to resolve disputes and to evaluate performance. These independent parties can act as a mediator with nonbinding judgment, or even as an arbitrator who has the right to give a binding verdict. The independent mediator or arbitrator is usually an expert in the specific area or trade, which makes him much more knowledgeable than a judge in court might be. This third party could also be a branch association. All tradespeople who are qualified can be affiliated to such an organization, which has the advantage that it signals a certain quality or expertise for the affiliated

member. If someone concludes a contract with such a business person, she can be more certain that she is dealing with a trustworthy party, and if she later finds that the business person does not live up to his promises, she knows that she can complain successfully to the branch association. At the same time, the business person has an incentive not to cheat because he runs the risk of losing his membership of the branch association, and therefore also losing the quality mark.

4 Presence of (mutual) *commitments*. If contracting partners have invested in each other in various ways, this leads to bonding effects. This may vary from symbolic, intrinsic investments such as small gifts and friendship, to much more expensive investments such as brand-name capital. This may lead to feelings of solidarity or loyalty (whether or not mixed with self-interested motivations) that help people to meet their side of a contract.

An even stronger form of bonding is the use of so-called *hostages* as a credible commitment (Williamson, 1983). If parties are about to transact a high value product, the party that stands to lose the most may demand extra security to support the contract. This security often takes the form of a down-payment that is forfeited in the case that not all obligations are met. An illustration is the lease of an apartment for which the tenant must pay a deposit, which he loses if he does not leave the building in its original condition. Another example of a security is a mortgage: to buy a house, people often take out a large, long-term loan, where the house serves as collateral. In the event that the borrower is unable to continue to pay the regular mortgage repayment, the bank retains the right to evict him from the house and to sell it.

5 *Unification* of parties. Furubotn and Richter (1998, p. 163) call this 'perhaps the strongest form of protection against ex post opportunism'. If parties to a contract decide to merge (*vertical or horizontal integration*), the advantage is that arrangements that previously existed between the independent companies are now dealt with internally. This can save a great deal on transaction costs, but on the other hand it might also introduce new costs, as we shall see in Chapter 6.

## *Relational contracts*

A prevalent contract type that contains several implicit mutual understandings and self-enforcing mechanisms is the so-called *open-ended* or *relational contract*, referring to an agreement over an indeterminate period, which is often found in working relationships in a firm. While a relational contract can be partly specified and subject to contract law and labor law, not all eventualities for the future can be specified. Therefore, parties involved need informal institutions able to inspire confidence that everyone will live up to the agreement in case of unforeseen events. Especially for open-ended contracts, over the course of time transaction partners may develop unilateral or bilateral dependence, because they have invested in this contractual relationship and therefore need certain safeguards to be built into the agreement.

A labor contract is a good example of an implicit relational contract, because it would be far too costly and perhaps even impossible to specify exactly all the services that an employee should perform in exchange for a salary – as soon as conditions in or around the company changed, there would have to be a (costly) adjustment of the contract.

In general, it is chosen to leave the contract somewhat open, stipulating only that the employer has the right to give directions to the employee, who in turn has the right to receive a certain monetary compensation. This makes the contract much more flexible, which is cost efficient.

All the same, several underlying implicit agreements concerning the rights and duties of both parties are in force. These obligations are usually characterized by the fact that they cannot (easily) be enforced by courts or third parties because it is difficult to assess them correctly by outsiders; for example, the employee has the duty to perform to the best of her ability in the interest of the organization (she should not shirk) and in return has the right to be rewarded or promoted accordingly, if circumstances allow. If she failed to meet these tacit agreements, she would put her position at risk.

At the same time, the employer has the right to expect good work from the employee and has a duty to reward her accordingly. If the employer failed to meet these implicit obligations, he would jeopardize his reputation as a good boss. This in turn could lead to dissatisfied personnel and a higher turnover rate, as well as to more difficulties with hiring new employees.

Hence, as long as the benefits of complying with the implicit agreements are beneficial to both parties (or, alternatively, if both parties have much to lose by cheating), self-enforcement mechanisms will be effective. This 'invisible handshake' (Okun, 1981, p. 89) from the employer fuels trust and commitment in the organization, which contributes to favorable job expectations. Chapter 6 will expand on this topic of reputation effects within firms.

As well as the interpretation of implicit contracts given above, which emphasizes the effects of norms of behavior on the efforts of workers and employers, there is a more formal elaboration of implicit contracts that makes use of mathematical models and emphasizes the need to share risks. While the focus in this book is on the informal theory of implicit contracts, the formal methodology is so widespread that we would like to give some attention to it here. In Box 3.7 there is a verbal interpretation of this approach, which often applies to labor contracts. In Chapter 7 you will find another example of an implicit contract: implicit collusion.

### BOX 3.7 THE FORMAL THEORY OF IMPLICIT CONTRACTS

In the eighteenth century, Adam Smith noted that labor contracts in some sectors included much higher wages than elsewhere and attributed this to the occupational hazards of certain professions. Individuals who run a greater risk of becoming unemployed, such as seasonal workers, need to be compensated by means of higher wages:

> A mason or a bricklayer...can work neither in hard frost nor in foul weather, and his employment depends upon the occasional calls of his customers...What he earns, therefore, while he is employed, must not only maintain him while he is idle, but make him some compensation for those desponding

> moments which the thought of so precarious a situation must sometimes occasion... The high wages of those workmen, therefore, are not so much the recompense of their skill, as the compensation for the inconstancy of their employment. (Smith, 1776, p. 103)
>
> In the twentieth century this observation has been worked out in further detail (Furubotn and Richter, 1998). Unlike the owners of large firms (shareholders), who can diversify their risks by investing their capital in several enterprises, employees are not able to diversify, because their possession is usually limited to human capital that is invested in one trade only. If workers are supposed to be risk averse while employers are supposed to be risk neutral, workers who enter a labor contract would like to eliminate uncertainties as much as possible.
>
> It appears that workers prefer a contract with a fixed wage, with the small risk that they may be laid off temporarily, to a contract with a variable wage (meanwhile keeping their job) that fluctuates all the time, following the conditions in the market. For risk-neutral employers, on average the total wage bill will be about the same for both types of contract, so they are willing to offer fixed payment. Hence, contract wages implicitly contain some form of insurance against employment risks.

It can be concluded, then, that contract theories have a strong link with property rights theory. Holders of private property rights aim to achieve the best possible trading results. To avoid agency costs as much as possible, all contracts need to be specified in such a way that property (control) rights are allocated optimally, and that the correct incentives to follow up on the agreement are incorporated. In order to realize this, a specific governance structure must be chosen to minimize transaction costs.

## TRANSACTION COST THEORY OF GOVERNANCE STRUCTURES

Transaction cost economics (often simply denoted as TCE) originates from the seminal work by Coase (1937), while Williamson has elaborated and extended this theory from 1975 onwards. According to Coase, firms (organizations) emerge as an alternative to the market, if people can save on costs in that way. By contracting the suppliers of production factors within a firm (also called a hierarchy in TCE), the entrepreneur can circumvent several of the uncertainties of using the price mechanism (Coase, 1937). In the literature, the term 'contracting costs' is sometimes used instead of market transaction costs, while the term 'organizational costs' is sometimes used instead of managerial transaction costs.

As was noted in Chapter 1, institutions influence behavior, which may reduce transaction costs. We now discuss this in more detail, first by explaining the basic theory of

TCE. From this, it follows that transaction costs may differ substantially, depending on the specific circumstances. Therefore, the way in which economic activities are organized will also show large variations, leading to different governance structures.

## Transaction cost economics

On concluding a contract, property rights are transferred. To recap: all costs that arise from the specification of a contract and monitoring compliance with the agreement are called transaction costs. This implies that property rights theory, contract theories and transaction cost economics are closely connected. In property rights theory, the emphasis is placed on the optimal allocation of property rights and their ensuing *ex-ante* incentives, while transaction cost economics stresses the *ex-post* costs that result from the contracting and searches for the most efficient governance structure (Williamson, 2000).

Searching for an efficient governance structure implies that, in TCE, actors are assumed to be optimizing: they aim to minimize transaction costs, even if they are not completely informed and have to deal with uncertainties. Take, for example, the transaction of intermediary goods. Should a producer make the components himself or buy them in the market place? Or take over the transaction of labor, capital, or information? Whatever the available choices and decisions, there are always costs involved in the coordination of an economic transaction.

On the one hand, there are uncertainties with respect to organizing the production process; in order to deliver goods or services of high quality, contracts have to be signed with the owners of the production factors needed to create these goods and services. This involves search costs, negotiation costs, monitoring costs and enforcement costs, because the people contracted may behave opportunistically.

On the other hand, and at the same time, there are uncertainties with respect to the sale of the final product; the entrepreneur has to find out whether there is a market for his products, while both seller and buyer have to take into account that the other party may be cheating in a transaction – for example, by not delivering the promised quality. The features of some products are well-known or can easily be observed before making a purchase. These goods are called *search goods*. In other cases it is much more difficult to search for the desired quality – for example, when experience is needed to acquire information about the quality of the product; and services such as education and health care. Here the consumer can ascertain the quality only on consumption (at least in the first instance – as soon as people have used a certain product they can share their acquired knowledge about this product with others). Products for which quality characteristics are difficult to observe in advance are called *experience goods*.

In TCE it is assumed that human behavior can be characterized by bounded rationality (the capacity of people to formulate and solve complex problems is limited) and opportunism. Williamson (1985) further distinguishes three main dimensions with respect to which transactions differ, namely:

 (i) asset specificity;
 (ii) uncertainty; and
(iii) frequency.

Depending on the degree to which these dimensions play a role, and in combination with the presence or absence of bounded rationality problems or opportunism, actors choose to coordinate economic transactions via the governance structure that best applies under the given circumstances, and that economizes on their transaction costs.

## *Asset specificity*

This is considered to be the most important dimension; if one of the contracting parties has made transaction-specific investments, this results in high dependence, which may be abused by the other party.

Asset specificity can best be introduced by means of the following example (Milgrom and Roberts, 1992): suppose a coal mine uses a railway to transport coal to a coal-burning electrical plant. Since coal is heavy, and has a low value per unit of weight, no other means of transport can be economically viable, hence without the railway the mine could not be run efficiently. At the same time, the electrical plant could not function without the delivery of the coal. These investments (in the mine and the plant, respectively) are characterized by the fact that it is impossible to switch them to alternative uses, or this switch is only possible at high cost. This implies that the investments consist of a large amount of *sunk costs:* expenses that cannot be retrieved once incurred.

In a contractual agreement, the counterparty may abuse the inflexibility of the party who has made the most transaction-specific investments. This is known as a *hold-up problem*: because the holder of the transaction-specific property right has no substitution possibilities his contracting partner, who holds complementary property rights, may act opportunistically and exploit this situation by (re)formulating the provisions of the contract in his own favor. In the case of the coal mine, its only customer, the plant, could offer a lower price per ton for the coal; the plant could speculate that the mine will accept this offer, because the latter cannot sell the coal anywhere else unless by investing in highly costly additional means of transporting the coal to alternative customers. Alternatively, it could be that the mine is the sole supplier of coal to the plant, and in that case the plant may become dependent on the mine, giving the mine the opportunity to create a hold-up in the form of a forced increase in the price of coal. See also Box 3.8 for a real-life example of a hold-up.

---

### BOX 3.8   HOLD-UP IN THE GAS SECTOR

In early 2006, Western Europe was suddenly confronted by a shortage of gas as a result of a conflict between Ukraine and its gas supplier, the Russian company Gazprom. The latter had announced that, as from 1 January 2006 it would drastically raise the gas price that it used to charge Ukraine. As a former republic of the Soviet Union, Ukraine for a long time had had to pay much less for gas than did the Western European customers of Gazprom.

Now, as the case in many other countries, Ukraine was very dependent on the gas being delivered. It is safe to conclude that Gazprom had hold-up power over Ukraine, because the latter could not easily switch to other sources of energy, nor to another supplier of gas: their gas is transported through special pipelines owned by Gazprom. A new supplier of gas would first have to build and install new pipelines, which would probably take several years.

At the same time, however, Ukraine also had a powerful weapon to hold up Gazprom, because the gas that Gazprom supplies to the majority of its West European customers is transported through the pipelines that run through Ukraine. From the moment that Gazprom decided to cut Ukraine off from its gas supply, Ukraine started using the gas that was meant for Western Europe.

Now, Gazprom had to deal not only with one angry customer (Ukraine) but with many concerned customers elsewhere as well. In Western Europe it caused a fierce debate about the need to be less dependent on just a few energy suppliers that apparently could not be trusted completely.

Different types of asset specificity can be distinguished (Joskow, 1998):

- site specificity;
- physical asset specificity;
- human asset specificity;
- dedicated asset specificity; and
- intangible asset specificity.

The case of the mine and the railway is an example of *site specificity*, because, after being put into operation, the resources are highly immobile.

The case of the mine and the plant can also be an example of *physical asset specificity*, if it involves investments in equipment that is designed for a very specific purpose (such as a boiler that can burn only a particular type of coal).

*Human asset specificity* refers to the firm-specific knowledge (human capital) that workers may accumulate. It could be the case that an employee's know-how is so specialized that it is only valuable within one company; in these circumstances, he would have difficulty in finding employment elsewhere, which would make him dependent on his employer.

*Dedicated asset specificity* is described as a general investment (as contrasted with a special purpose investment) that is made specifically with the objective of selling a large amount of product to one particular customer; if the customer changed his mind, the seller would be left with high excess capacity.

Finally, *intangible asset specificity* refers to immaterial valuables such as brand name capital. Think, for example, of franchise holders who have obtained the right to sell products of companies such as, say, Heineken or McDonald's, but have to invest heavily in equipment and accessories that lose their value if they are not allowed to sell the brand name any more.

## Uncertainty

Transactions often involve *uncertainties*, both with respect to the behavior of the contracting parties and with respect to (market) developments. Suppose that an automobile manufacturer faces a make or buy decision: either she makes the intermediary good inside her own hierarchy, or she can buy it in the market. When the component is technologically simple and the competitive market is clear and stable, then uncertainties about prices, quality, delivery dates and so on can easily be taken care of in a simple market contract.

The situation is completely different if the auto maker is considering ordering the development of a complex engine that has to fit into a new model. Now the uncertainties about the transaction can be such that the capacity to include all future events in a contract is too limited. Consequently, the contract will contain open ends that could be abused by one of the contracting partners. A good solution to this problem could be a merger between the two trading partners into one firm (see Chapter 6 for more details).

## *Frequency*

The costs of transactions may also depend on the *frequency* with which parties interact; if they have regular dealings this implies that they will develop certain routines and implicit mutual understandings that will reduce the need for formal enforcement mechanisms. This may lead to substantial investments in transaction-specific resources, because the costs will be easier to recover in the course of a long-term relationship.

These specific investments will lead to mutual commitment and dependence, and will rule out competition by other market parties. The reason is that contracting parties have invested in their collaboration, which makes it more expensive to look for another trading partner, and thus harder for rivals to take over that position. Williamson (1985, pp. 61–3) calls this process 'the fundamental transformation': while there may have been competitive bidding over a trading contract at the outset (*ex ante*), in the end (*ex post*) the consecutive specialized investments in each other lead to a bilateral supply relationship.

When a supplier is awarded a contract to deliver an intermediate good for a period of, say, five years, then he has an advantage compared to the competitors he defeated. He can continue to develop his expertise and specific technological know-how in the years to come. Only competitors that have this kind of contract with other customers can also develop and improve their knowledge and become equal competitors when contract renewal is negotiated after the five years period.

The actor who has won the contract not only develops technological knowledge during the contract period, but often also establishes a specific relationship with the customer. Buyer and supplier learn about each other's habits and norms, and learn how to solve conflicts in an efficient way. This can give the supplier a more-or-less monopolistic position after the contract period: and this market power may be abused, to the disadvantage of the customer. Anticipating this, the customer should protect himself by means of long-term contracting.

## *The determinants of a governance structure*

The choice of whether to transact through a market or through a certain type of organization (either private or public) will depend on the degree to which the three dimensions mentioned above (asset specificity, uncertainty and frequency) matter, and on the degree to which bounded rationality and opportunism are present. In TCE, it is assumed that economic actors are *far-sighted* in the sense that they will look ahead and try to anticipate contractual hazards by building safeguards into the agreement, notwithstanding bounded rationality.

If actors operate in a transparent environment that allows parties to specify all terms of the market contract, opportunism can easily be prevented. Also, if the business environment is not transparent but asset specificity does not play a role either, opportunistic behavior can be combated, because an actor can easily switch to other contracting parties. In this way, there is no risk of a hold-up situation, so actors may choose a *market contract* as the most suitable governance structure.

On the other hand, the more that people work in a very complex and insecure environment in which not all eventualities can be foreseen and in which transaction-specific investments form a major part of the business, the more often people choose to establish a *firm* as the most suitable governance structure, because in these circumstances the transaction costs of a hierarchy with an internal organization can be lower than when external market contracts are concluded. In this way, the production process is under much better control, so it may support the goal of minimizing transaction costs. However, we must keep in mind that transaction costs are still present within a firm, in which imperfect, asymmetrical information between the principal and the agent can play an important part, as we saw above.

Next, we shall elaborate further on the different governance structures that are distinguished. Part III of this book discusses governance structures in the private sector in much more detail, while Part IV deals similarly with governance structures in the public sector.

## Governance structures

Here we explore the governance structures from which actors may choose when coordinating transactions efficiently. A *governance structure* deals with all the necessary steps to coordinate the transaction. The market is a governance structure that actors can use to negotiate around the items upon which they want to agree. One of the main characteristics of a market is the autonomy of the actors. Another governance structure is the firm: an organization with internal rules that also has the capability of coordinating and executing transactions efficiently. Contrary to the market, the firm is a hierarchy in which the actors are no longer autonomous. As explained in Chapter 1, a governance structure is an institution, as it contains both rules and sanctions.

The government also plays a role; and sometimes even a dominating one. In such circumstances, *private ordering* is replaced by *public ordering*. This can be the case in sectors of the economy where competition needs careful regulation in order to prevent firms from abusing a dominant position, or to prevent unwarranted collusion between firms. In other sectors such as energy, telecommunications, public transport and health services, the government creates governance structures to assure a specific performance of the market. For example, the provision of energy at reasonable prices to all citizens is an objective of public interest that needs specific governance.

We shall now provide an overview of a range of governance structures from the ideal market to the state-owned enterprise, which can be considered the extremes on a continuum of governance structures (see Figure 3.2). This figure is called a 'contracting scheme' (after Williamson, 1985, 1998), because it describes the variety of contractual arrangements from which actors may choose.

**Figure 3.2** *A contracting scheme*

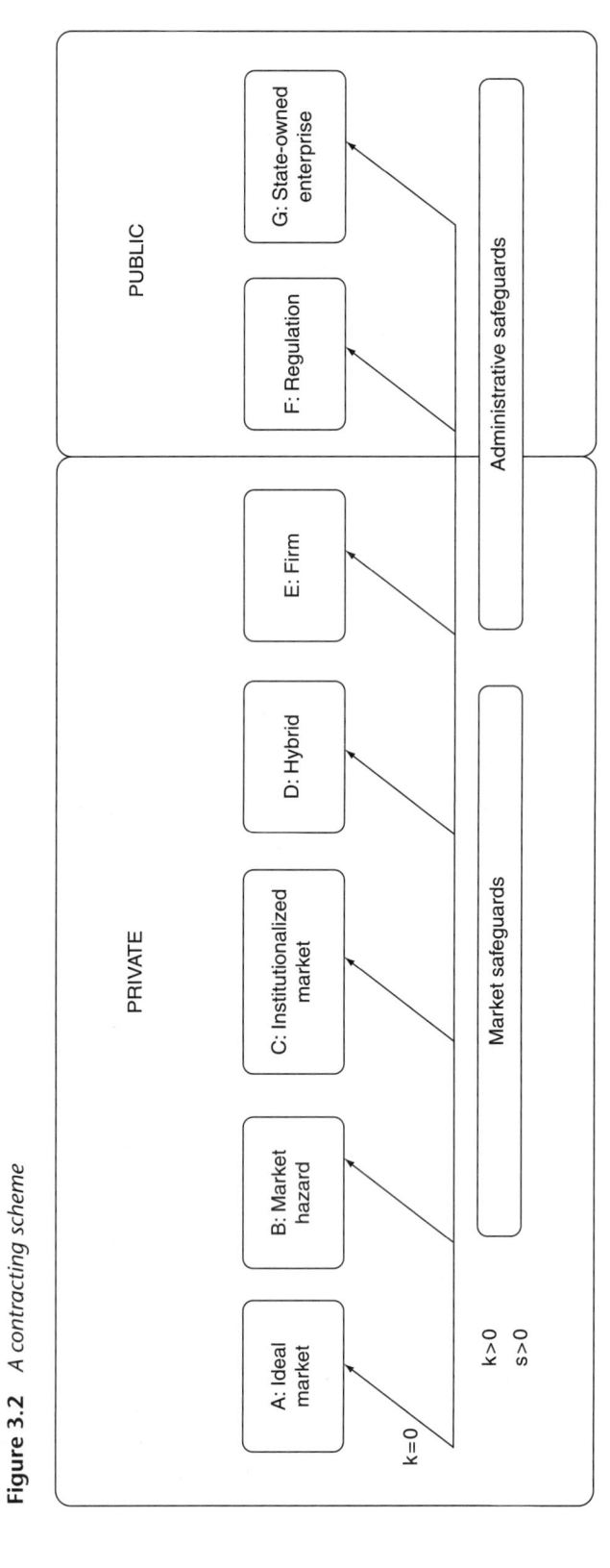

```
PRIVATE                                                    │ PUBLIC
                                                           │
┌─────────┐  ┌─────────┐  ┌──────────────┐  ┌────────┐  ┌────────┐  ┌──────────────┐
│A: Ideal │  │B: Market│  │C: Institutio-│  │D: Hybrid│  │E: Firm │  │F: Regulation │  │G: State-owned│
│ market  │  │ hazard  │  │nalized market│  │         │  │        │  │              │  │  enterprise  │
└────┬────┘  └────┬────┘  └──────┬───────┘  └────┬────┘  └────┬───┘  └──────┬───────┘  └──────┬───────┘
     │            │               │               │            │             │                  │
     ↓            ↓               ↓               ↓            ↓             ↓                  ↓
┌──────────────────────────────────────────────────────────┐  ┌───────────────────────────────────┐
│               Market safeguards                          │  │     Administrative safeguards     │
└──────────────────────────────────────────────────────────┘  └───────────────────────────────────┘

k=0     k>0
        s>0
```

*Notes:* k = level of asset specificity; s = level of safeguards.
*Source:* Based on Williamson (1998), p. 47.

The continuum in Figure 3.2 shows types of governance structures related to the degree of asset specificity (k). The influence of all other possibly relevant factors such as frequency and uncertainty (discussed above) will be ignored for the moment and will be taken into account later. So, for this graphical exposition, these and other possible factors that influence the decision on a governance structure are taken as given; this is known as the *ceteris paribus clause* (*ceteris paribus* is a Latin term meaning 'all other things being equal', or 'everything else remaining the same'). We follow the lines of reasoning explained earlier, when it was mentioned that in cases of high asset specificity, transaction costs will be minimized in hierarchical institutions. To recap: asset specificity concerns the types of investments actors make in order to have a good or service transacted. When the investments are very specific, then the investment is worthless if the transaction is terminated. The degree of asset specificity has implications for the possibility of opportunistic behavior and therefore for the need for safeguards.

In Figure 3.2, the asset specificity increases from left to right. To the left, the situation of the *ideal market* (referred to as node A) is pictured, in which there is no asset specificity (k = 0) and there is no need for safeguards because perfect competition rules out opportunistic behavior. In node B (*market hazard*) there is some asset specificity (k > 0) but the parties to the market contract have not incorporated any safeguards (s = 0) to protect themselves against possible hazards of opportunistic behavior.

Moving further to the right, with increasing transaction-specific investments, we see that safeguards are being built in (s > 0). As long as asset specificity is still not very high, actors may prefer a market contract with built-in safeguards: then we speak of an *institutionalized market* (node C). With asset specificity increasing further, actors in the market could opt for some form of cooperation with others and share decision-making on certain joint activities, thereby relinquishing their autonomy. That is why this governance structure is called a *hybrid* (node D): it combines features of the market and the firm. The parties to the contract protect their interests by means of market safeguards, which take the form of additional contractual clauses.

Still further to the right, a very high degree of asset specificity may incite actors to organize transactions completely within a *firm* or hierarchy (node E), and then safeguards take the form of so-called administrative safeguards. If private ordering is replaced by public ordering, we subsequently encounter government *regulation* of private actors in node F, and the *state-owned enterprise* in node G. Safeguards in this context are also called administrative safeguards. We shall now pay more attention to these different governance structures, explaining the hybrid structure after the market and firm structures, since the hybrid is a combination of both market and firm.

## *Ideal market*

The first governance structure is the ideal market, which coincides with so-called classical contracts. As the name indicates, this coordinating mechanism will rarely (if at all) be observed in reality; it depicts the ideal situation and forms the benchmark for the more realistic governance structures. The typical case of a complete market contract is efficient in a very competitive environment when no asset specificity exists and the uncertainties can be formulated in generally accepted standardized terminology. In that case, the investments made are of such a general-purpose nature that actors can always and instantaneously switch to other suppliers, or use the investments for alternative purposes. No misunderstandings can arise about the timing, quantity or quality of the goods and services involved, because the transaction is standardized according to publicly accepted classifications.

The competitive environment ensures the availability of alternative buyers and suppliers. The situation resembles the typical case of perfect competition. The price mechanism, the pressure of competition, and the search for utility or profit maximization provide *high-powered market incentives*. In other words, if someone modifies his efforts this will have an immediate effect on his earnings. If the contract is ended, or the other party abuses her position, no lengthy renegotiations begin, and no complicated procedures in court follow. Instead, the classical contract lists all rights and duties of actors should something go wrong during the execution of the transaction. The contract determines such things as the fine a supplier must pay if the good or service is not delivered on time, or if the quality is of a lower standard than specified. Should parties have a disagreement about the interpretation of the wording of the contract, public courts can make a decision at low cost about who is right and who wrong. The contract does not leave any room for different interpretations.

## *Market hazard*

With rising asset specificity, the danger of hold-ups increases and it becomes ever more difficult to include all contingencies and corresponding actions of the actors within a watertight contract: the contract becomes incomplete. Of course, parties have the option not to create safeguards and accept the possibility that the contracting partner may fail to perform. In that case, no countermeasures are taken and the market hazard is accepted as incidental risk. These so-called 'fly-by-night actions' will be discussed further in Chapter 5. It is unusual to run high risks without safeguards: in economic exchanges, actors will normally protect themselves against the dangers of potential hold-up situations by means of additional institutional arrangements.

## *Institutionalized market*

Incomplete contracts demand 'assisting institutions'. Safeguards need to be built into the contract to such an extent that people feel secure enough to accept the risk of the remaining incompleteness. As we shall see at length in Chapter 5, most real-life market contracts are accompanied by supplementary protection devices, among which are all kinds of self-regulating mechanisms. Typical of these are the initiatives taken by private parties involved in a certain industry, such as the introduction of quality marks and the installation of professional associations to watch over the activities of their members.

## *Private firm*

When asset specificity increases even more, the *hierarchy* (vertically integrated firm) will be the most efficient from a transaction cost point of view. The private firm that has internalized transactions, with respect to intermediate goods, labor and capital, replaces the market contract. The hierarchy can have a number of advantages over the market contract when dealing with highly specific transactions. Because of the risk of losing a great deal of money if asset specific investments go astray, safeguards in market contracts may not be sufficient. Hold-up risks may become too large to enter a market contract safely. Instead, within a firm, property rights are transacted under so-called *unified ownership*: in return for a specified level of compensation, owners of property rights (especially labor and capital) offer their products to be put in productive use under the control of some *authority* (for example, a CEO and a management hierarchy) to whom discretionary decision powers have been given. The motivation to perform at the service of the firm is referred to as *low-powered incentives*: if someone changes his amount of effort within the firm environment this will usually not have an immediate effect on his earnings (Williamson, 1991).

So the capacity of the management to use authoritative command (also referred to as *fiat*) determines the degree to which the factors of production (in possession of the owners of the property rights) are optimally motivated and hence deployed efficiently in the firm, compared to the situation with market contracts. Ménard (2005) discusses several advantages of the use of fiat (or administrative safeguard) as a coordinating device, among other things in circumstances in which adaptation to changes in the economic environment is needed. First, it gives some flexibility to supervisors to decide on a reallocation of tasks without the need to renegotiate the terms of the (labor) contract. Second, it may effectively curtail opportunistic behavior – provided that the right incentives and sanctions are enforced. And third, it makes it possible to deal with conflicts without the costly use of legal arbitrage; internal control such as auditing is much more capable of judging the relevant information, compared to a court. In addition, within an organization specific implicit codes of behavior are developed which are accompanied by self-enforcing and self-regulating mechanisms, such as the risk of losing long-term promotion prospects if someone defects from the spirit of the agreement (Williamson, 1991).

Transaction cost economics not only explains why firms exist, but also why different types of hierarchies coordinate transactions with high asset specificity. For example, economic historians such as Alfred Chandler (1962, 1977) explain the existence of the multidivisional enterprise as the result of transaction costs minimizing behavior. The change from a *unitary organization* (the *U-form*) to a *multidivisional organization* (the *M-form*) can be understood as a separation between strategic and operational decisions that allows the top management of a multidivisional firm to reduce the information and command flows to lower management levels. In the multidivisional firm, each separate division performs the functions of the unitary firm.

The advantages of this are twofold: one, it enables the top management to concentrate on long-term decision-making while delegating short-run operational activities to the officers who lead the divisions, thereby reducing problems connected to bounded rationality. Two, it reduces the responsibility of managers to specific tasks, which increases the probability that they will be more committed to their task, thereby reducing problems connected to opportunistic behavior. You will read more about this in Chapter 6.

## *Hybrid*

To distinguish private governance structures in markets on the one hand and hierarchies on the other, is too limited a reflection of reality. The market is the governance structure, in which parties negotiate in a setting of equal rights about the content of a contract. In the hierarchy, superiors give commands to agents at lower levels of the organization. However, this simple division cannot cover the variety of governance structures that exist in reality. The hybrid is the concept between the market and the hierarchy that is able to accommodate the range of mixed forms – such as networks, franchising or strategic alliances.

A *hybrid* is based on a contract that is the result of negotiations between equal parties, aimed at some form of collaboration. Depending on the specific form of the hybrid and the goals of the contracting parties, the degree of cooperation may vary widely, but what all hybrid forms have in common is that they partly 'pool their resources'. This means that the contracting parties share part of their assets; for example, personnel (know-how) or machines. In the contract, the private actors create organizational structures that can direct the actors hierarchically into specific directions (branch organizations), or prescribe certain solutions in case of conflicts (arbitrage committees). These private hybrids are generally based on long-term contracts. Because a hybrid is a form of cooperation between independent private firms, the applicable contractual protection devices may be regarded as market safeguards rather than administrative safeguards, as is the case within hierarchies.

The Japanese *keiretsu* is a famous example of a hybrid (also referred to as a *network firm*). In the *keiretsu*, independent, autonomous organizations coordinate their behavior without any of them being the central player. Because there is a common interest among the organizations that form the network, each of them is willing to invest in coordination between them, which helps to realize the common objectives. Coordination can take the form of creating interdependencies through cross-stockholding, or interlocking directorates. Financial, economic and personal relations create and strengthen mutual dependence among the members of a network, and the willingness of each member to coordinate the transactions inside the network. In the literature on networks, the phenomenon of trust plays an important role. Actors are then not opportunistic, but trustworthy. More information about the *keiretsu* and other types of hybrids can be found in Chapter 7.

## *Regulation*

So far we have discussed the ways in which private actors in the economic system create institutions that assist either the market contract or the firm as the optimal governance structure. In this case, we have a *'privately ordered market system'*, meaning that the institutions are created privately. However, public actors, such as the government, also create governance structures that coordinate transactions.

*Corporate law* sets the constraints within which people create firms and defines the roles of the different actors within the firm (think about the roles of shareholders, and management); and *competition law* is an example of a set of rules that actors have to consider when setting prices, or when they plan a merger or a takeover of a firm. Competition law regulates the behavior of firms in order to realize a 'healthy' degree of competition in the market. The responsible authority has instruments to forbid collusive agreements between firms, or behavior of firms that is considered an 'abuse of market power' (think back to the public trials of Microsoft, which were mentioned in Chapter 1).

Also, sector-specific public institutions can be created by law, and regulate the behavior of firms in sectors such as telecommunications, electricity supply or public transport. Here, the government assists the market in achieving a specific market performance, with or without a certain degree of competition. Different instruments are provided to the regulator by law. In some cases the regulator can apply a rule that sets a maximum price, or the regulator can set standards about the quality of the service, stating how frequently the service should be delivered in all regions of the country. The public ordering assists the privately ordered market in order to secure a specific market performance. Part IV will elaborate on this topic.

### State-owned enterprise

The provision of certain goods and services can be considered so crucial to the economy or society at large that the government decides not to leave their production, maintenance or distribution in the hands of private actors. This is the case with pure public goods such as infrastructures, or defense systems that would be underprovided as a result of the inherent characteristics of nonrivalness and nonexclusiveness. The public interest could also be at stake in cases that do not necessarily concern pure public goods, such as the health service, public transport and electricity, for example, in which the government wants to ensure that all citizens are able to obtain these products and services.

Economists would advise that property is kept in private hands as long as possible, because then the 'right incentives' will be in place. But, as transaction cost economics shows, regulating private actors can be so costly because of information asymmetries that the transaction can be coordinated more efficiently in a state-owned enterprise. Of course, when the production is organized in a state-owned enterprise there will be bureaucratic costs and incentive problems. Monitoring by the principal can become costly, but the point is that, according to the state, the policy objectives must be realized: in this case, effectiveness has priority over efficiency. You will be able to read more about this topic in Part IV of the book.

All governance structures on the continuum have pros and cons. From a TCE point of view, the choice between the governance structures is, and should be, based on the motivation to minimize both production and transaction costs. If, for that reason, a market contract is chosen, the structures will provide high-powered market incentives. If a firm is chosen, the cost will be the loss of market incentives, but with a gain by fiat that may deal more effectively with problems associated with opportunistic behavior and bounded rationality. No governance structure can combine the best of all other structures; it is always a matter of selection and carefully balancing of the pros and cons in order to minimize the sum of the costs.

## THE VESTED INTEREST APPROACH

As we announced in the introduction to this chapter, the static approach to institutions is dominated by the efficiency approach of New Institutional Economics, but it does not provide a complete explanation of the ways in which actors transact. In principle, as was set out in Chapter 1, economists assume that people strive for their own self-interest. On many occasions, this optimizing behavior coincides with realizing optimal economic welfare, whether intentionally or not. On other occasions, however, selfish or opportunistic behavior benefits only a fraction of the population: in these circumstances, a powerful minority group succeeds in maximizing its own profits at the expense of others. From this it follows that economic welfare is thus not maximized, as a result of the protection of vested interests.

We shall now deal once again with property rights, agency and contracting, and governance structures, but now the focus will be on their relationship with the vested interest approach.

## Property rights

Institutional theory points out that the allocation of property rights is closely related to the distribution of power in society (Libecap, 1989). The groups that are in control, such as landowners, Church leaders, owners of capital, and so on, are in a position to define the 'rules of the game' and consequently have a large influence on the laws and regulations that distribute costs and benefits in society. An important part of such rules are property rights: the ones who own, have the right to benefit. In other words, the allocation of property rights reflects the power structure of society, and negotiation among the owners of the rights always takes place within that initial distribution of power.

It is one thing to say that the exchange of property rights should take place in the market so that the preferences of people are best served, but it is quite another to say that the initial distribution of property rights is such that the negotiation takes place among equals. When groups in society conclude that the distribution of property rights is not correct and should be changed, a discussion begins about the process of changing property rights, which belongs to the dynamic approach towards them (see Chapter 4).

As we saw above, property rights can be privately owned, shared with other private actors, or publicly owned. Obviously, the citizens with power may be in a position to influence the government in such a way that either the allocation of private property rights is to their advantage, or that they may benefit directly from the way in which goods are publicly owned.

With respect to the impact of power on private property: certain (groups of) citizens may receive preferential treatment when it comes to paying taxes, and receiving subsidies and special political favors. Chapter 9 will elaborate on this.

With respect to the impact of power on public property: in several instances there is no sound efficiency reason for rulers or governments to assign public property rights to certain goods, but instead this is done out of self-interest – which means, in fact, in the interest of those in power and those supporting the ruler or government. Examples are usually related to the revenues that can be extracted from state monopolies: state-run companies often exploit natural resources such as precious stones, gas or oil. While the revenues could be used for the benefit of the whole population, much of the resulting profits is often invested in objects such as large and richly decorated buildings for the rulers. In addition, geopolitical power motives may play a role, as countries do not want

## Agency

It must be said that, of all NIE theories, the agency theory already takes into account the possibilities of misuse by individuals or groups with power, as this theory prescribes how these problems may effectively be prevented by building in the proper incentives. The most widely applied topic in principal–agent theory refers to the question of how top managers can be induced to act in the interests of their principals – the shareholders. Broadly speaking, the chosen incentives can be found both in monitoring devices and in setting the right payment, so that the interests of management and shareholders become aligned.

However, there also exists a rival theory, called the *managerial power theory*, which argues that powerful executive officers are in a position to use their discretion and alone determine the level and type of their salary (Bebchuk and Fried, 2003). In particular, if the firm is owned by many different and dispersed shareholders, these people are often not able to control the behavior of the CEOs. In order not to arouse too much indignation among the investors and the general public, which would coincide with so-called 'outrage costs' (such as reputational harm and a drop in the share price) influential managers put much effort into covering up their payment schemes, leading to so-called 'camouflage costs'. From this it follows that these managers are indeed incited to perform according to the incentives generated by their contracts, but since these contracts have not been formulated by their principals (the shareholders) the outcome will be suboptimal for the latter. Indeed, as many observers claim, the financial crisis that started in the USA in 2008 and has spread across the world since then, could be attributed, at least in part, to this kind of opportunism and power display by top managers.

## Governance structures

In the standard theory of transaction costs economics, actors seek precisely that governance structure for their transactions, which minimizes transaction costs. This clearly fits the efficiency approach. However, governance structures often arise out of power motives, or are sustained for that reason. One of the most obvious examples refers to cartels, which do not exist to serve economic welfare but rather aim to serve the interests of powerful industrialists, at the expense of consumers who pay prices that are too high. The result of this is a deadweight loss for society. Cartels can be seen as a specific form of private governance structure hybrids, and as such will be discussed further in Chapter 7.

Another noticeable example refers to public governance structures that do not serve economic welfare. We mentioned earlier the example that certain state-owned enterprises do not operate for the purpose of increasing public welfare, but rather for the welfare of the ruler and his supporting factions in society. In Chapter 9, we shall deal extensively with the propensity of some rulers to provide wealth to certain individuals and elites in exchange for political power. We shall show that the quest for power may in the extreme lead to corruption, and is very detrimental to welfare.

## CONCLUDING REMARKS

Property rights theory, contract theories and transaction cost economics are closely connected. Being the three main representative theories of New Institutional Economics, they emphasize the importance of efficiency as the driver of economic behavior.

Generally, most goods and services cannot be obtained for free by everyone, and problems of scarcity can best be solved (in the sense of optimal welfare) by exchange transactions, so that those who value the products most also obtain them at the lowest possible cost. A necessary condition for such optimal transactions is the existence of enforceable property rights. These ensure that people may use and profit from resources that are either in their legal possession (in the case of full ownership) or are leased to them by the legal owner. In the absence of (enforceable) property rights, the 'strongest people' would be able to obtain all products, which of course would undermine any incentive to produce these items; generally speaking, such a society would not be able to optimize welfare.

The existence of enforceable property rights enables people to create, consume and exchange products. This will give (at least theoretically) the proper incentives to produce and exchange what is most valued by consumers. Hence, in this chapter, we have described how different property rights, such as common property and private property, give different behavioral incentives to people, and how this will lead to different outcomes for welfare. Still, the existence of enforceable property rights is only a necessary condition. It does not guarantee optimal welfare in the sense described. In practice, many problems are involved in realizing optimal transactions, because all kinds of transaction costs may lead to nonoptimal outcomes. What are the implications of transaction costs for incentives and welfare, and how can we reduce these costs? In short, how should transaction costs be dealt with optimally?

The central question in contract theories is whether the contract that underlies the transaction incorporates the proper incentives for all parties to the agreement to observe the terms of the contract. Because of imperfect information and bounded rationality, contracts cannot be specified completely. As a result of the potential risk that people may behave opportunistically – that is, abuse this contractual incompleteness to their own advantage and at the detriment of the other party – safeguards need to be built in. All costs that arise from the specification of a contract and monitoring the compliance with the agreement are examples of transaction costs.

Basically, contracts are needed to solve informational problems caused by information asymmetries and/or to solve hold-up problems. The first type of problem, known as a principal–agent problem, consists of moral hazard and adverse selection problems, while the second type, the hold-up problem, is related to asset specificity. Solving both types of problem will in general imply the need for enforceable contracts.

Contracts can be concluded within different organizational settings, referred to as governance structures: we distinguish between the market place (market contracts) on the one hand and organizations (private and public) on the other, with hybrids forming an intermediate structure. As we shall see in more detail in Part III, private actors will choose the specific governance structure that minimizes transaction costs, irrespective of whether this implies maximum welfare only for themselves (vested interest perspective) or for society at large (efficiency perspective). In cases in which the hazards of opportunism are rather low or not very costly to deal with, contracts will more often be concluded in the market place. At the other end of the (private) spectrum are cases in which contractual hazards are very high; most of the time this leads to the establishment of a hierarchy in which (relational) contracts are concluded.

In the economy, an important role is reserved for the government, which assigns property rights and formulates all kinds of laws on which private and public actors base their contracts. Moreover, a government may decide that an economy should not be run through private governance structures alone, but that, in addition, either regulation or state-owned enterprises (or both) are necessary. It may do so either because it is of the opinion that the public interest (and hence economic welfare) would not best be served by means of private ordering, or because it is under the influence of power groups that aim to protect their particular interests at the expense of others. In Part IV of this book we shall elaborate the role of the state, both from the perspective of efficiency and of vested interests.

## REVIEW QUESTIONS

1. What is the difference between private goods and pure public goods?
2. Explain the difference between exclusiveness and excludability. Illustrate how an exclusive good can be nonexcludable and how a nonexclusive good can be excludable.
3. Why are private property rights important? In which circumstances are shared property rights preferable?
4. Explain why it is so difficult to apply the Coase theorem in practice.
5. Explain the relationship between property rights, contracts and transactions.
6. What are the costs involved in designing contracts? Explain how enforcement and monitoring costs can sometimes be better dealt with through formal institutions and sometimes through informal institutions.
7. Explain the phenomena adverse selection and moral hazard by applying them to real-life examples.
8. Explain the hold-up phenomenon by applying it to a real-life example.
9. What is the relationship between transaction costs and governance structures?
10. Explain the contracting scheme (Figure 3.2) in your own words.
11. How does the vested interest approach shed a different light on transacting, contracting and governance structures?

# 4 The Dynamics of Institutions

## CONTENTS

- **Introduction**
- **Drivers of institutional change**
  - Exogenous drivers of change
  - Two motivations of change: efficiency and vested interests
- **The evolutionary approach toward the dynamics of institutions**
  - Institutions as an equilibrium
  - Cumulative causation
- **The design approach toward the dynamics of institutions**
  - Designing efficient institutions: the NIE approach
  - Designing effective institutions: the OIE approach
- **Dynamics of economic systems**
- **Concluding remarks**
- **Review questions**

## INTRODUCTION

In Chapter 2 we introduced several approaches to institutions: the static and dynamic approach, both from an efficiency and a vested interest point of view based on theories of NIE and OIE. In the static efficiency approach, Institutional Economics analyzes the optimal institutions under a set of constraining exogenous variables. We discussed how, in a comparative static analysis, the theory is able to predict the new optimal end state under a new set of values for the exogenous variables. In Chapter 3 we showed how, for example, transaction cost economics (TCE) is able to predict the new, efficient governance structure after a change of just one of the characteristics (dimensions) of the transaction.

We also showed that actors do not only make decisions based on efficiency considerations. The objective of realizing specific goals in the interests of particular individuals or groups turned out to be of equal importance in understanding why some governance structures are preferred over others: the static vested interest approach.

In this chapter we address the question of institutional change, implying that we analyze the process of change of the different types of institutions that were introduced in Chapter 1.

Next we discuss the exogenous drivers of institutional change (culture, technology and the state) and analyze how these influence the endogenous variables of governance structures. Here we are still using a comparative static analysis.

Following this we present the dynamic analysis of institutions, by distinguishing two perspectives: one the so-called *evolutionary* or 'spontaneous' perspective, and the other known as the *design perspective* (see Vatn, 2005). We first analyze the evolutionary change of institutions. By evolution we mean that the change is not the intended outcome of (a collective of) actors, but that the change emerges as the unintended outcome of behavior. We shall also show that such institutions are self-enforcing, so there is no need for a specific authority such as the state to apply any pressure. In other words, the actors in the systems spontaneously behave in accordance with the institution.

We shall then discuss the so-called design approach toward institutional change. Here the institution is the intended result of individual or collective choice. Laws and rules are designed by an authority (legislative powers) and enforced by a bureaucracy and judicial system. We shall close with a discussion on the role of both efficiency and vested interests in the process of designing institutions. On the one hand, regulations and governance structures are designed by intentional actors to reduce costs; hence efficiency is improved. Here, specifically, insights of the NIE will prove to be relevant. On the other hand, vested interests of groups in society play an important role in the design of institutions. Institutions also change because of powerful lobbying by groups of business people, nongovernmental organizations (NGOs), or labor unions attempt to change the balance between costs and benefits to their own advantage. Businesses want, for example, more flexible labor laws so that employees can be more easily dismissed, whereas unions want more rules concerning job security, safety, working hours, minimum wages and so on. Understanding institutional change is about understanding conflicts between interest groups, and how such processes develop over time. Here, specifically, insights of the OIE will prove to be relevant.

Toward the end of this chapter we shall move the analysis to the level of the economic system. In Chapter 2 we introduced you to three models of economic systems, which were presented in a static way. In this chapter we discuss the dynamics of economic systems. An important question concerns the convergence of the systems: will the systems become more similar over time, or will the 'varieties of capitalism' continue to exist and will there always be an Anglo-Saxon system alongside Asian and Continental European systems?

## DRIVERS OF INSTITUTIONAL CHANGE

We start our analysis with a model in which the interactions between institutions and actors are depicted as a process of reinforcing existing institutions. Actors make themselves familiar with institutions through a process of *enculturation* and they enforce existing institutions through a process of reproduction. This will be explained in more detail below. The system has a specific logic that is reinforced by the relationships between the different elements, such as the (in)formal institutions, the public and private governance structures and the shared mental maps. The institutional reproduction is shown in Figure 4.1.

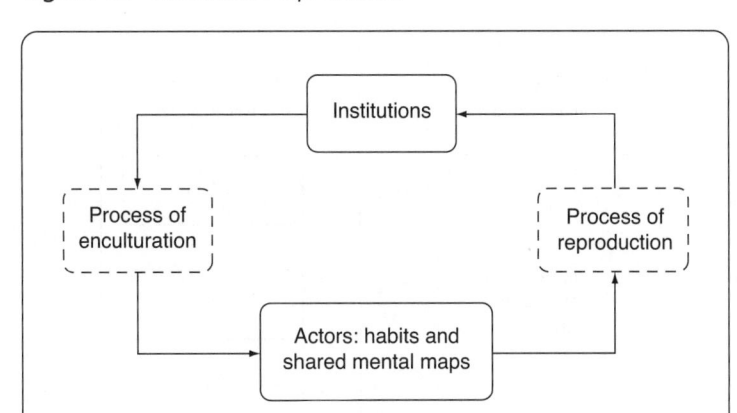

**Figure 4.1** *Institutional reproduction*

[Diagram: Institutions → Process of reproduction → Actors: habits and shared mental maps → Process of enculturation → Institutions]

But what would make the system change? And how does the process of change take place? In Chapter 2 we discussed endogenous and exogenous variables. A change in the exogenous variables leads to a change in the equilibrium choice, as was illustrated in Chapter 3 with respect to the choice of a governance structure (comparative static analysis). These changes took place within an institutional setting (the judicial system, values, norms, mental maps, preferences and so on) that was taken as given. Next we make these exogenous variables more explicit and show how exogenous changes can influence the choice of governance structures. The variables we shall focus on are three drivers of change: culture, technology and the state; and we identify two motives of actors: the desire to improve efficiency; and the wish to protect their own interests. After that, we shall discuss how the institutional dynamics can be analyzed as an endogenous process, in which the different variables are interdependent.

## Exogenous drivers of change

In Figure 4.2 we illustrate how a change in one of the three exogenous variables (culture, technology and the state) changes the private or public governance structures.

### *Culture*

In Institutional Economics, *culture* is conceived as the aspects of human behavior and society that are shared by all, or almost all, members of some social group. Culture includes material phenomena (buildings, paintings) and immaterial phenomena (values, norms, conventions, laws and governance structures). Culture is passed on by the older members of the group to the younger members because the group considers it to be valuable. Culture shapes behavior and structures one's perception of the world. The shared mental maps discussed in Chapter 2 are part of a group's culture. Enculturation refers to the process whereby the members of a group (be it a firm or a society) acquire a culture through formal or informal training. The culture of a country is reflected in its laws and regulations, in the corporate culture of business, and finally in the norms and attitudes at the level of individual actors (such as households).

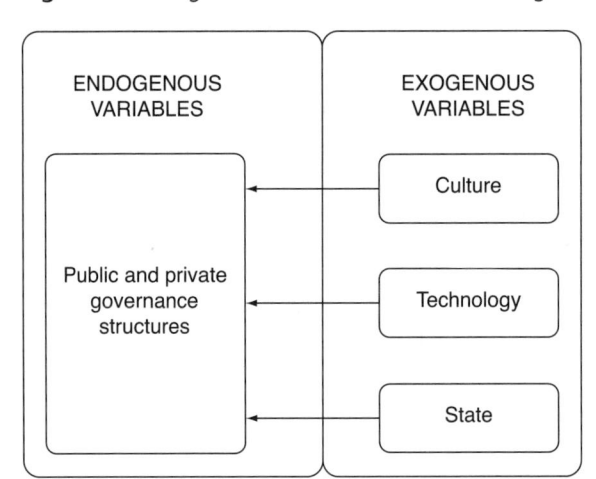

**Figure 4.2** *Exogenous drivers of institutional change*

In general, the culture of a group changes gradually. Over long periods of time the values of a society can change from, for example, collectivistic group values to more individualistic ones. In the former, the group as a collectivity is central: the behavior of individuals is evaluated from the perspective of what they contribute to the continuity of the system as a whole. In the latter, the society values highly the autonomy of the individual to pursue her own interests. In such a culture, the idea is that the collectivity should not constrain, but rather facilitate the individual to realize her own individual objectives.

When over a fairly long period of time the collectivistic values change into more individualistic ones, as seems to be the case in many Asian and Continental European countries, then a misalignment will emerge with the formal institutions. When, for example, the laws and regulations, role of the bureaucracy and structures of firms still align with collectivistic values, while most of the actors in society have adopted individualistic values, then the different parts of the culture become misaligned. Tensions in society arise and pressure builds up to change the public and private governance structures (North, 2005). In other words, the change in the formal institutions is driven by an exogenous change in the country's culture.

## *Technology*

How do technological developments drive the transformation of institutions? Economic historians such as Alfred Chandler have shown how technological revolutions in, for example, transportation (railroads) and communications (telegraph and telephone) as well as production techniques (assembly lines), gave an impetus to the introduction of mass production. Consequently, private governance structures changed to become larger, vertically integrated structures.

Chandler (1962) explains that the larger hierarchy is the governance structure that best accommodates large-scale production because economies of scale and reduction in transaction costs can be realized most efficiently in hierarchical organizations (see also Chapter 6). Chandler, who analyzes the history of private governance structures in relation to changes in their environments, describes how, in contrast to the assembly line, craft production technology gives rise to the creation of small hierarchies, subcontracting and networks (see Chapter 7). The point is that an exogenous change in the technology drives the institutional change in private governance structures, such as the size and structure of the firm.

Another example of technology driving the change in governance structures is provided by the role of ICT. The personal computer and the internet have made decentralization and looser, network types of structures both possible and efficient.

The influence of technology on governance structures can be more or less deterministic in the sense that the technology determines only one type of efficient governance structure. However, technology is often of a so-called 'unruly' nature: the technology drives a transformation toward new governance structures, but whether this happens and which governance structures will be selected out of a range of possibilities, is a matter of choice by the actors involved. In studies concerning the 'actors and structure' relationship (see Chapter 2) examples can be found in which the technology is rather deterministic, together with studies in which the technology is unruly and the actor is autonomous in her choices. Moreover, the selection process is influenced by the presence or absence of other conditions, such as the availability of finance, of human skills, of entrepreneurial talent, and so on.

## *State*

The state takes many decisions that drive other actors in the system to change their institutions. We shall address this topic in more detail in Part IV. When the political system, for example, changes the competition law in a country and forbids private governance structures that were allowed under the previous law, this will also change the private governance structures, most importantly the cooperation possibilities. Assume that cooperation between firms on certain investment plans was allowed, resulting in contracts between firms in which they coordinated their investment plans. Assume then that a new law forbids such cooperation: you can expect that firms that want to coordinate their investment plans will replace the contract with a merger, or will take over their competitor. In this way, the state drives the dynamics of the firm toward a larger integrated governance structure.

Another example: most European electricity firms have their own transmission and distribution network (grid). The EU has decided to introduce competition in the electricity sector, and new suppliers must be able to enter the market and deliver electricity to households and firms. Incumbent firms have ample means to behave opportunistically toward the new entrants, which depend on them for the use of the network. In the EU directive it is stipulated that incumbent electricity firms must unbundle their production and sales activities from their transmission activities (using the grid), to create a level playing field for all electricity suppliers.

The EU has chosen to unbundle these activities so that the vertically integrated incumbent is replaced by a set of market contracts in order to coordinate the transactions between the firms that handle the transmission and distribution of electricity on the one hand, and those that deliver the electricity to the end users on the other. So, the state as an exogenous variable drives the incumbent electricity firms to change their private governance structure.

## Two motivations of change: efficiency and vested interests

### Efficiency

Economists typically discuss the effects of exogenous changes in terms of changes in scarcity of resources, which are reflected in prices and signal to the actors that they should adapt to the changed circumstances. In the case of efficient behavior, one of the objectives is the minimization of the sum of production and transaction costs. In economic models, actors are stimulated to make institutional adaptations, because with a change in the technology or 'the rules of the game' it is efficient to adjust the governance structure. Firms adjust, for example, the scale of production by means of integration (larger scale) or splitting up(smaller scale). The examples above describing the changes in mass production and the electricity sector show how exogenous changes can drive firms to adapt their governance structures to minimize transaction costs.

An important question in understanding the dynamics of institutions is why and when actors are motivated to look for the most efficient solutions. In many economic theories it is assumed that actors are forced by competition in the market to search for the most efficient private governance structures. In Chapter 2 we presented these models as being 'static', because the process of adjustment to the new equilibrium is not analyzed. You may remember that we referred to the assumption often made in the static approach, that the competitive pressures of the market force the actors automatically to select the most efficient governance structures. However, when the research question is about understanding the process of institutional change and its outcome, then another type of analytical framework is needed.

In a dynamic approach toward institutions, the analysis should show how agents obtain the right information about the changed scarcities, how they know about the most efficient alternative governance structures, and how they are able to implement the necessary changes. You will learn that this selection of the most efficient institutions occurs only under certain specific circumstances.

Sometimes, the most efficient choice from a theoretical point of view is not always possible under existing law, or in the shared mental maps there is no room to implement that efficient solution. An example of the latter would be the efficiency of networks with loose relations based on trust that do not fit the mental maps of competitors used to cut-throat competition. Research on the American and Japanese auto industries has shown that the efficient type of Japanese supply network was at first considered to be impossible in the mental maps of the American CEOs, who were trained in a world of strict price competition and vertical integration (Dyer, 1996). Moreover, a dynamic analysis of institutions can show that the change towards a more efficient governance structure is sometimes blocked, because of economic lock-ins (high switching costs), technological lock-ins (the technology requires an integration of activities) or because of an institutional lock-in (changes in complementary institutions do not come about in the same way as an adaptation of the competition law that permits the new network-type of governance structure).

In a dynamic analysis of institutions, the emergence of new institutions and the development of existing ones can be understood from an efficiency point of view (under what conditions does the market select the most efficient ones?), but a dynamic analysis can also show why that efficient solution is not implemented.

## *Vested interests*

From a societal point of view, competition is considered as a positive force driving firms to search for the most efficient solutions. However, at the level of the individual firms and managers, competition may be considered a burden. Managerial strategies often aim at the control, or even the elimination, of competition in order to protect their vested interests. It is then no surprise that firms invest a lot in increasing their power and control over market developments, to reduce the pressure of competition. As we shall see in detail in Chapter 6, horizontal and vertical mergers, as well as acquisitions, are means of decreasing or eliminating competitive pressures. Networks (see Chapter 7), in which information is exchanged and actions are coordinated, can also be examples of governance structures through which firms try to increase their power. The effect of private governance structures can be to control the demand and supply sides of markets (see Chapter 5). To put it in a different way, firms change the modes of governance aiming at the control of the behavior of other actors in the market to create situations that serve them best, possibly at the cost of reduced welfare or efficiency for others.

Politicians, bureaucrats, labor unions, NGOs and the like also develop strategies to realize their objectives, even if the cost of this is reduced welfare for others. Like firms, they try to control resources, manipulate information and to influence the division of costs and benefits in their own interests alone. In Chapter 9 we shall come back to this behavior in more detail.

To sum up: in a dynamic analysis of institutions, the process of change itself is analyzed. The research is about whether efficiency plays a causal role and if so, how actors are able to make efficient decisions. Or, if vested interests play a role: what is the power base of actors, what are their motivations, and how does power change over time? A dynamic analysis really digs into the historical causalities of how the different events are related. Such an analysis is generally very context specific, focused on interdependencies between different parts of the system and consequently mainly of a broad, interdisciplinary nature. Unavoidably, the nature of the research then becomes more descriptive and less of a suitable object for rigorous mathematical models.

## THE EVOLUTIONARY APPROACH TOWARD THE DYNAMICS OF INSTITUTIONS

Above we discussed the drivers and the motives for change separately from each other. From an analytical point of view, such a separation is allowed. In a dynamic analysis the researcher will often meet all kinds of interdependencies between the variables. A number of possibilities is shown in Figure 4.3. The relationships between the variables and motives (efficiency and vested interests) can be conceptualized as interactive, which makes the explanation of the dynamics of institutions more endogenous than in Figure 4.2.

As already discussed in Chapter 2, the researcher has to choose which interactions she wants to include in her analysis; what is chosen will depend on the problems the researcher wants to solve, and the conditions encountered in the reality under investigation (see also the Appendix to Chapter 2, on Douglass North). Here you will learn how

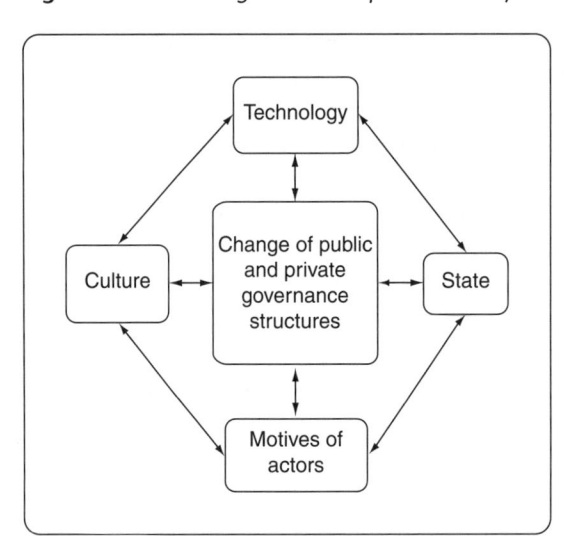

**Figure 4.3** *An endogenous description of the dynamics of institutions*

[Figure 4.3: A diagram showing four nodes — Technology (top), Culture (left), State (right), and Motives of actors (bottom) — each connected bidirectionally with a central box labeled "Change of public and private governance structures", and also connected to each other around the perimeter.]

the dynamics of institutions can be modeled when the researcher aims to understand the evolutionary process, and later you will see how the researcher can use modeling to understand the design of institutions.

In Institutional Economics, the famous quote by Adam Ferguson (1767, p. 187), 'establishments, which are indeed the result of human action, but not the execution of any human design', is often paraphrased as 'institutions are the result of human action, not of human design'. That is, the actors behave in a specific way because it is in their own interests to do so, and as an unintended outcome an institution such as a norm or convention emerges. Such behavior at the individual level may be intentional (aimed at minimizing costs) or habitual, but the institution as such is not intended by the individual actions.

The point in the evolutionary approach is that institutions can come about without individual or collective action being intended to create an institution or to change an existing one. The outcome of all the individual behaviors can be the emergence of an institution that, once in existence, is durable, and motivates and coordinates individual behaviors.

The 1974 Nobel Laureate, Friedrich Hayek, wrote many articles and books on this subject and once compared the emergence of an institution with the creation of a footpath (Hayek, 1979). A footpath comes into existence when individuals who travel through a forest, or walk alongside a river, follow the track of their predecessors. It is easier for an individual to follow a track than to explore the most suitable way for himself. Out of the behavior of all individual walkers over time a footpath is formed, which makes life easier for all future walkers. However, creating the footpath was not the intention of any of the walkers. All of them wanted, for selfish reasons, to walk alongside the river, or to travel through the forest. In doing so, a footpath was created unintentionally, but it was valued positively by all walkers. No authority was needed to create the path, and its maintenance is self-enforcing, because all walkers use the same path and keep it accessible to others simply by using it frequently. Next we discuss different approaches toward the evolution of institutions.

## Institutions as an equilibrium

The metaphor of the footpath is applied in Institutional Economics to the emergence of conventions, norms and markets. Under specific conditions, independent actors, who behave in their own interest, unintentionally create institutions that are durable and that coordinate the behavior of economic actors. All actors consider behavior in line with the emerging norm to be in their own interest, and would like to see others to behave in a similar way. Behavior according to the emerging norm reduces uncertainty, or information costs. For the individual actors, it is efficient to behave according to the emerging institution. It is possible that over time actors at the micro level create institutions spontaneously, which become equilibrium situations (for an example, see Box 4.1). In the process, three phases can be distinguished:

1. Externalization: the regularity in behavior must become visible to others. In other words, the behavior that was at first known only to the individuals themselves (internal) must become external (visible to outsiders).
2. Objectivization: the regularity in behavior must become a 'fact', a reality that others take into account.
3. Enculturation: the reality becomes part of the behavior of all the people in the community: the reality becomes internalized into each individual's mental map.

---

### BOX 4.1   MONEY: A SELF-ENFORCING INSTITUTION

Carl Menger (1892) explained the emergence of money as the result of an evolutionary process that started in a barter economy. When economic actors trade a good (say, a cow) for another good (say, a textile), then we speak of a barter economy: there is no intermediate good and the trade between the cow and the textile is a direct trade.

As you may imagine, it is not always easy to find people who want to trade a specific good for the good you want to trade: a barter economy has high costs of searching the traders for goods that match. Menger explained that actors learned over time about goods that most people wanted; in other words, goods that have a greater saleability than other goods. For traders, it became efficient to have those highly saleable goods in their possession, and to use them as intermediates. That saved a lot of the time previously spent searching for the people who wanted to obtain the product you wanted to trade. Both of you valued the intermediate product, which made trade much easier.

Over time, traders learned about gold being the most saleable good. According to the evolutionary perspective on money, the emergence of the standard for trading of all goods (money) was not the result of conscious design or based on an agreement or legislation, but came about spontaneously from the actions of the traders. When the good was generally accepted as a desirable intermediate good, then all actors appreciated having the good because they had learned that the other actors also appreciated it. It had become an institution that was durable and self-enforcing.

According to the *'institutions as an equilibrium'* approach, a regularity becomes an institution (a norm, or convention) when a large majority of the actors in the community internalize the regularity.

Institutions as an equilibrium is analyzed by game theorists such as Masahiko Aoki (2001, 2007). It can be shown that, under certain conditions, boundedly rational actors will be able to create stable institutions. The definition of an institution that corresponds to this approach is formulated by Aoki (2007, p.6) as follows: 'An institution is self-sustaining, salient patterns of social interactions, as represented by meaningful rules that every agent knows and are incorporated as agents' shared beliefs about how the game is played and to be played.'

In the literature, the institutions as an equilibrium approach is also called 'spontaneous', because it is a matter of self-enforcement: no external authority is needed to force actors to behave according to a specific institution. The process emerges spontaneously, based purely on the self-interest of the individuals. The point is that actors discover that cooperative behavior and compliance with the institution create mutual gains. In such a situation, they are all motivated to behave according to the institution: each actor realizes that it is costly to ignore the institution, and beneficial to comply with it.

The question can be raised as to whether the institution that evolves as an equilibrium is also the most efficient solution possible. Recall the footpath example. It can very well be that the footpath was originally made by walkers who just wanted to stroll around and did not intend to cross the forest in the fastest way possible. The footpath that was originally created was afterwards used by others, therefore has nothing to do with efficiency. Even if people become aware of a faster way to cross the forest, they are stuck with the existing footpath because it is more costly to create a new one. So, an equilibrium institution can be inefficient but still be maintained.

The example of the footpath can be reformulated in terms of so-called multiple equilibria. It seems possible that different equilibria can exist, depending on different initial conditions.

## *Multiple equilibria: history matters*

The existence of multiple equilibria can explain why institutions differ all over the world, even in countries or regions that are very much alike in terms of their economies and culture. The idea is that, depending on different initial historical conditions, different paths evolve that result in different equilibria. Think about the differences between American automobile manufactures and Japanese ones: a difference that can be described as being vertically integrated (American) as opposed to a small hierarchy with many networks relations with suppliers (Japanese). Or think about the differences between the role of public institutions in a country such as France compared to Germany, China compared to Japan, or the USA compared to Canada (see, on the latter comparison, also Spithoven, 2009). When we take different historical roots into account, different initial conditions such as the original reason for making a footpath, or establishing a production organization, we then understand that different paths of evolution might end in multiple equilibria.

If we want to understand the institutions as an equilibrium approach, we can make use of the insights of game theory as applied by Aoki, but we are also in need of the insights of the discipline of history to be able to describe the specificities of the institution, and to explain why institutions differ from country to country or over time. In the words of Aoki (2000, pp. 13–14):

> Game theory provides a useful tool for understanding the self-enforcing nature of institutions. However, it is unlikely to provide a complete closed theory of institutions. To understand why one equilibrium is chosen and not others, we are required to make use of comparative and historical information...I regard them (the institutions) as endogenously created through the interactions of agents in a relevant domain and thus self-enforcing.

Here, you see an example of interdisciplinary research, in which the insights of both game theory and history are combined. It is also an example that uses different methods of research: a pluralistic interdisciplinary approach (see also Chapter 2).

## *Darwinian evolution*

Charles Darwin's research question is not focused so much on equilibrium, but more on the selection process that takes place over time. Why is there variety out of which selection takes place? How does selection work? Much of the research on the evolutionary process of institutional change is inspired by Darwin's work on biological evolution. If one species or institution is selected, how are its characteristics transferred over time? Large differences exist between biological and institutional evolution, because of the creative power of human beings (see below, on designing institutions). However, there are interesting analogies between biological and institutional evolution. We mention three key elements of Darwin's theory: (i) mutation; (ii) selection; and (iii) inheritance and retention; we argue briefly below how these would compare to the evolution of institutions.

(i) A *mutation* (change in an existing situation) has to start somewhere. In Darwin's approach the mutation is incidental (blind, at random). The 'deviation' in the world of institutions can result from an error, or from an incident, but can also be the result of purposeful human behavior. The change in the institution can be a creative act by an entrepreneur or a politician. The new institution can also be the result of a long, gradual learning process.
(ii) The next element in Darwin's evolution of species is the concept of *selection*. Many of the mutations are not copied by others and do not survive. But when a new type fits better to (a changing) environment and it has a better possibility of surviving and prospering, then that variety will grow faster than the less fitting ones (the survival of the fittest, in the terminology of Darwin). In the world of institutions, the governance structures that fit best and have the highest potential to adapt to changes in the environment will survive and be imitated by others. In Institutional Economics, the concept of 'adaptation' refers to purposeful human action. When, for example, firms make profits and these are invested in innovative products or processes so they can better survive the competition, those firms fit the competitive environment better. These firms will grow at the cost of others, or will be imitated by their competitors.

Note that the concept of the 'fittest' is always related to a specific environment. Recall that we discussed in Chapter 2 that efficiency is 'context specific', and that the environment of (in)formal institutions and technology largely determines what is considered rational and what is considered efficient. In no way does survival of the fittest imply efficiency in some absolute sense.

(iii) When a mutation is successful it will increase by passing on its genes to future generations. In the world of nature, the concepts of *inheritance and retention* are applied, whereas in the world of Institutional Economics, the concepts of institutions and habits are relevant. Institutions that survive create habits, and individuals develop shared mental maps. In this way, the 'fittest institutions' are 'inherited' and 'retained' by future generations.

## *Path dependence*

The dynamic process of institutional change is essentially of a historical character. The decisions that people make today are strongly constrained by the past, and the decisions taken today will strongly influence the room to maneuver in the future. The linkages of the past to the present and the future are captured by the concept of *path dependence*. In the words of David (1985, p. 332): 'A path-dependent sequence of economic changes is one of which important influences upon the eventual outcome can be exerted by temporally remote events, including happen-stance dominated by chance elements rather than systematic forces.'

One could say that an outcome in the present is the result of a specific sequence of events in the past that led to a current limited set of possibilities from which to choose. This choice can be made optimally, given these possibilities, and thereby becomes part of the 'path'. Initial conditions and the sequence of events that sprang from it then form the path that was followed. Trivially, path dependence means that 'history matters'. From the point of view of Institutional Economics it means that the path of development is forced by technical or institutional factors. At a later point in time it is impossible or very costly to switch to another path (one is 'locked in'). A famous example of a lock-in is the case of QWERTY case (see Box 4.2).

---

### BOX 4.2   PATH-DEPENDENT SEQUENCE OF ECONOMIC CHANGES: QWERTY

David (1985) illustrated path dependency by means of the keyboard with the QWERTY layout. The characters of the first mechanical typewriters were arranged on the keyboard in a way that caused clashes and jams of the type bars when the operator was typing at high speed. The QWERTY keyboard was designed to prevent the bars from clashing too often. However, other, much faster, keyboards exist (such as the Dvorak simplified keyboard), but even in the age of electronic typing, the less efficient QWERTY keyboard has not been replaced by a more efficient one.

> The problem of mechanical clashes no longer exists, so in an efficiency approach one would argued that manufacturers would replace the QWERTY keyboard and we would all buy the faster one. But that has not happened, because also in the case of QWERTY, history matters. Among other things, the high switching costs caused a lock-in. A detailed historical analysis shows the technical and institutional relations that eventually account for the existence of a phenomenon such as the QWERTY keyboard.

Institutions can play an important role in establishing a path-dependent development. In Chapter 2 we discussed how, over time, individuals form a mental map, with which they perceive and interpret the world. People form habits that guide them in their behavior. Habits structure behavior, which makes it possible to predict the actions of others, and in that sense it reduces costs. Also, institutions in general (and habits in particular) can prevent actors switching to another technology or another governance structure. The switch might simply be impossible because the new governance structure is not part of the mental map of the actors, or because it is too costly to switch. See also Box 4.3.

### BOX 4.3   THE VIDEO WARS

In the 1970s, two home video systems appeared on the market: Sony's Betamax and JVC's VHS (Video Home System). The systems were not compatible, and consumers were unlikely to buy both a Betamax and a VHS player. Therefore, both companies were aware that it was crucial to quickly become dominant in the market, for their product to be considered the 'standard'. The more units of one format that were sold, the more likely it was that producers and distributors would choose that format as the carrier of their films, so that new purchasers of video players would also be inclined to choose the same format. This mechanism is called a positive network externality. With a slight advantage in the sales of one format, there is a large probability that the scale will tip in the direction of that format, so that it becomes the one and only standard type.

The battleground was not just in the video player market, but also the market for complementary products such as films and cassettes in each format. VHS finally beat Betamax in the 1980s as a result of the strategic decisions of the producers of these complementary products, rather than there being any clear technological or price advantage (Cusumano et al., 1992).

In the early twenty-first century, Sony was engaged in a similar format war in the market for high definition digital video, only this time with Toshiba (Kiss, 2008). Despite the fact that Toshiba's HD DVD had higher-quality image and sound, Sony's Blu-ray Disc technology eventually prevailed, and Toshiba announced in February of 2008 that it was retiring from the market.

> Again, complementary products played a crucial role. Sony's victory was based on the fact that its popular Playstation consoles were compatible with Blu-ray, whereas HD DVD required consumers to buy a dedicated player. Also, large film distributors, including Warner and Disney, chose Blu-ray, limiting the availability of film titles in HD DVD.

### *Gradual change and 'punctuated equilibria'*

So far, we have discussed evolutionary change as being slow and gradual. The actors can learn how to improve the allocation of resources, but that learning takes place within a specific setting of institutions and habits. It can be an evolution to an (in)efficient equilibrium, or a path-dependent succession of historical events. However, such a gradual evolution is not necessarily always the case; evolution can also sometimes lead to radical fundamental changes in the system.

When such a radical change takes place, the shared mental map of the actors is completely replaced, along with the corresponding institutions. The framework with which actors describe and understand the world is then completely 'redescribed'. In the literature, such a radical change after a long process of gradual change is called a *punctuated equilibrium*. In the words of Denzau and North (1994, p. 23): 'Punctuated equilibrium involves long periods of slow, gradual change punctuated by relatively short periods of dramatic changes, which we can presume to be periods of representational redescription.'

The Betamax and VHS story in Box 4.2 illustrates the 'sudden change' character. Originally, both systems competed with each other, each having part of the market. This 'suddenly' changed to a monopoly position for VHS, as described by the example. Some small changes in the environment led to a stable monopoly equilibrium, though beforehand one could not have predicted which technology would win.

## Cumulative causation

The dynamics of institutions and of economic systems as a whole can also be analyzed from the perspective of so-called cumulative causation. Veblen (1899), Kapp (1976), and in particular, Myrdal (1944, 1968) have made important contributions to the theory of cumulative causation. The basic idea refers to changes that reinforce developments in the same direction. In Macroeconomics we find this mechanism in the famous multiplier: if demand is stimulated (for example, by government expenditure) this leads to additional income for the recipients of the increased expenditure, which will in part be spent again, so that new and additional income is generated, and so on. Ultimately, the original government spending is multiplied to a larger national income.

There are also examples of investment in a specific region that attracts more investment, and in that way contribute to a process of agglomeration (see the discussion about Silicon Valley in Chapter 7). The reverse is also possible: when an important firm transfers production facilities abroad to low-wage countries, an accumulation of events can lead the region where the firm is situated into a state of recession.

A well-known example of what Gunnar Myrdal (1974 Nobel Laureate, together with Hayek) called 'circular and cumulative causation' is his study in 1944 on the position of African Americans. He asked why they did not break out of the vicious spiral of poverty and improve their position, but on the contrary became victims of an increasingly worse situation. In the case Myrdal studied it was shown that poor people react by having large families, because in their situation more children meant a larger possibility of parents surviving when they become old (children are a kind of insurance). The problem was that large families made the poor even poorer, leaving them without any means to invest in education or a business, which could have offered the possibility of breaking the vicious spiral. Myrdal (1968) is an important study about continuing poverty in Asia, and he also analyzed the 'Asian Drama' in terms of cumulative causation. One more applied example can be found in Box 4.4.

> ### BOX 4.4 CUMULATIVE CAUSATION AND WORKING WOMEN
>
> An example of cumulative causation is the labor market for women in Western countries. The shift from the norm that males are breadwinners stimulated the labor participation of women. Consequently, household income rose. This enabled households to afford more luxuries, such as eating out. Gradually, more and more people started to enjoy meals away from home more frequently. This boosted employment in restaurants, bars and canteens. Because most of the employees in restaurants, bars and canteens are female, this development implied that more women workers were needed, which led to more women participating in the labor market and so on.

## *Intentional and habitual behavior*

The focus in the standard evolutionary approach is on unintentional individual behavior. There is no purposeful relationship between individual behavior and emerging institutions. However, within the evolutionary approach we can also find some examples in which the initial act of an individual or group of individuals was a deliberate action to create an instrument or tool to solve a problem. If this was later followed spontaneously by others, it became an institution.

So, the spontaneous process can also start with an intentional act at the individual level, which is then spontaneously copied by others. Individuals with a creative will can deviate from existing methods of production or existing norms. Those (institutional) entrepreneurs (see also Chapter 5) can become an example to be followed by others. In this case, both intentional behavior and spontaneous processes are involved.

To use the metaphor of the footpath again: to cut a passage through the forest could very well have been the explicit goal of an individual or group of individuals. Because others later spontaneously followed the track and it thus became a 'self-enforcing' footpath (by habit), makes it an example of evolutionary development.

Next we shall elaborate on the approach in Institutional Economics in which the purposeful design of institutions is central.

# THE DESIGN APPROACH TOWARD THE DYNAMICS OF INSTITUTIONS

Actors can create and change institutions intentionally: firms can create a joint venture, politicians in parliament can adopt a new law, and consumers can decide to create a consumer organization to protect their interests.

In Chapter 1 we discussed how institutions can restrain, liberate and expand the range of human action. In the tradition of Commons (1934), we have asked how institutions can motivate actors and coordinate behavior in such a way that the processes result in a desirable performance. How can the 'ought to be' be realized when the 'is' differs from societal objectives? In the design approach we both look at purposeful design by actors who aim to realize their micro objectives, and at collective design that aims to realize societal objectives. After all, that is what designing institutions is all about: to change the structure in which the behavior of the actors is embedded in order to produce a more desirable outcome.

We first discuss the design of institutions from an efficiency point of view, and then have a closer look at designing from a vested interest point of view.

## Designing efficient institutions: the NIE approach

Our earlier description of dynamics can be interpreted in the sense of optimal choices, given a certain history. This history (path dependence) determines the set of choices one has at every point in time. In the NIE approach, the focus with respect to these choices is on the design of institutions from an efficiency perspective. Designing institutions takes place at two levels:

(i) the level of the formal public governance structures of laws and regulations; and
(ii) the level of private governance structures.

The NIE considers the design of formal public institutions as 'first order economizing' (Williamson, 1998). Actors in markets can only behave efficiently when the formal institutions are appropriate. The assumption of efficient markets prescribes the existence of a well functioning political system producing efficient public governance structures such as a transparent system of private property rights and a clear set of laws and regulations about competition. Only when these institutional conditions are fulfilled will the private actors be able to design efficient governance structures. In other words, when politics has designed and executed the efficient formal public institutions, then the private actors in the economy will design and execute the governance structures that minimize production and transaction costs. In the NIE this is called 'second order economizing'.

### Efficient public governance structures

Economists generally have rather straightforward ideas about what are appropriate public institutions. In a market economy, the formal institutions should be general, certain and open (see Chapter 1): the rules of the game should apply to all actors equally, and no interest group should be able to influence the decision-making process in order to create laws that are more favorable to them than to other groups.

When politics has decided about the rules, these should be clear in the sense that different interpretations are not possible. Moreover, the rules should be stable, so private actors in the market can also ground their decisions for the future on the existing system. As explained in Chapter 1, we encounter a dilemma here, because actors in the economic system prefer certainty about the formal institutions, whereas institutions should also be flexible so they can respond to changing circumstances.

In the process of designing public institutions we distinguish two steps: first, the formulation of the objectives (what is the desired outcome of the institutions?); and second, what should the set of public institutions look like? In NIE, both steps are relatively straightforward: the objective is a competitive market and the desired public institutions are about competition law and corporate law. In designing an efficient market economy, NIE advises governments first to 'get the institutions right' (first order economizing). You can read more about this in Chapter 8.

## Designing effective institutions: the OIE approach

### Institutions: a matter of valuation

In Chapter 1 we discussed the subject matter of Institutional Economics: to explain the working of the economic system. We pointed to the relationship between institutions, the motivation of actors, their behavior and the performance of the economy. It was explained that institutions both constrain and enable: they limit actors in their possible choices, but at the same time they offer actors the chance to make decisions and to act, because the existence of institutions allows for the prediction of the behavior of others. Moreover, one could say that to a certain extent institutions also construct individual behavior. What one considers rational and efficient depends on the institutional context in which they operate. In other words, what actors consider to be rational is in fact 'socially constructed' (Bromley, 2006; North, 2005).

In previous chapters we also pointed out the importance of vested interests and the power structure of society in helping to understand the institutional structure and its dynamics: who owns which resources; and who has which political rights? When only a small elite has the right to change laws and regulations, and rights to allocate property, it should be no surprise to discover that existing rights change only very slowly, or that institutions do not change at all when a redistribution of benefits would be at the expense of the elite (look back at Box 2.2). The allocation of rights, such as property and decision rights, is not a 'neutral' process, and the existing distribution of rights should not be considered as a kind of 'natural given'. Institutions are human constructions and as such are subject to evaluation and redesign.

### About 'is' and 'ought to be'

In Chapter 1 we explained that institutions such as values in society are subject to evaluation and change. In Chapter 2 you learned that such an approach is typical of OIE: both ends and means are subject to scientific inquiry, and individual and collective decision-making. In other words, both the societal ends and the values, being the standards of judgment, are subject to choice.

According to OIE, the first task of an economist is to describe 'how the system works' and to explain what drives the economy. Institutional economists explore the interdependencies in the economic system, and how the economy interacts with the value, political and judicial systems (Hayden, 2005). In short, the relationships shown in Figure 2.6 offer the analytical framework for an OIE analysis.

No doubt the NCE and NIE also aim to describe what 'is' and to explain causal relationships. As discussed in Chapter 2, the theoretical frameworks used by the different schools show the way in which the actors, the environment and the interaction between the two are modeled. However, central to OIE is the perspective that the nature of the economy is dynamic and that the economy should be explored in a holistic way as part of a societal system. In an OIE analysis, the division of power in society is a starting point to understand the existing institutional structure, and from there to understand the performance of the economy. The analysis includes the value system: namely, who in society is in control, who makes decisions about the standards of judgment, and on whose values the standards are based. The scope of OIE is wide compared to the NCE and the NIE, because more variables are taken into account, and because the analysis is of a dynamic and interdisciplinary nature.

When the 'is' is described in a holistic, interdisciplinary way, the next step in the research is of a normative nature. The different levels of the societal system should formulate what the performance of the system 'ought to be'. This would include the value judgment; that is, the choice of the value, and of the standard of judgment. What are the objectives the process should realize? Society, industry and the actors at micro level all formulate explicit objectives and all participate in choosing the values.

The following step should be a comparison of the 'is' and the 'ought to be', and where there is misalignment, what changes are needed? Changes in institutions are central in the OIE approach. Which institutions will provide the actors with the right motivation and incentives so that the outcome of the economic process corresponds to the objectives at the different levels of the system? This can be at the level of the firm (such as better control over management by shareholders or other stakeholders; see Chapter 6); at the level of industry and the market (better supervision by public agents, perhaps; see Chapter 8); at the regional or national level of the country (laws that coordinate investments so that regional or national objectives are fulfilled, for example; see Chapter 8); and at global level (such as standards to reduce carbon dioxide worldwide; again, see Chapter 8). The changes correspond to all levels of institutions. 'Ought to be' is about the desired change in the institutions so that these become instrumental to the societal objectives. Which values and norms, and which public and private governance structures are instrumental with respect to the societal objectives? OIE scientists speak in this context about the *'instrumental value theory'*. From the study of their work it is clear that these scientists place a high value on the fact that all members of society are able to participate in the political decision-making process. It is very important that all actors in society are educated and have the ability to 'reason' about the effectiveness and efficiency of institutions, to participate in the debate, and to convince others with solid arguments.

The societal objectives – the values that are considered to be the correct standards of judgment – are not absolute, but always relative and subject to (re)evaluation, change and improvement. In the OIE literature, this is called the process of *instrumental valuation*: which institutions are instrumental to societal objectives? As important as the values themselves is the democratic valuation process. In many economic theories the distribution and role of power is not addressed, or it is assumed that power is distributed equally among the actors in markets and among actors in the political system. According to OIE, in the selection process the values of groups are always involved, but the power to participate is not distributed equally.

In Chapters 8 and 9 we pay attention to the authority that should be in place to guide the process of collective decision-making and is responsible for the implementation and monitoring of the decisions. Many countries now have democratic institutions that are responsible for the process of collective decision-making.

One of the founding fathers of OIE, Thorstein Veblen, points in his work to the role of institutions in protecting vested interests (so-called 'ceremonial institutions'). These institutions protect the interests of specific groups based on distinctions of race, gender and religion. It is a matter of valuation whether such existing institutions need to be replaced or that existing institutions are considered to work properly. In particular, when we consider institutional changes as changes in the value system, we are dealing with long historical periods of time. We know from the history of the USA that it can take a long time from the abolishment of slavery to the election of a colored president, as the country now has in Barack Obama. It takes many years of political struggle, debate and institutional change to solve problems step by step. In society, a 'collective commitment' can gradually emerge about correct societal values and desirable objectives.

What is desirable in economic terms is also a matter of valuation: goods can be produced using child labor, by paying women less than men, by spending less on safety measures to protect personnel, or by polluting the atmosphere more than the level the community has agreed upon. It is a matter of valuation about what is considered 'right', what is considered rational and what is considered efficient. Again, changing the institutions in society is a long and complicated process. To build a fresh 'collective commitment' to a new value system needs purposeful action by many members of society. In this process, 'institutional change agents' are crucial. An example is the worldwide impact of Al Gore's documentary movie, *An Inconvenient Truth* (see Box 4.5).

### BOX 4.5   AN INCONVENIENT TRUTH

In the movie *An Inconvenient Truth* (2005), American former vice-president and presidential candidate Al Gore looks at the problem of global warming, presenting scientific evidence in an entertaining and compelling manner.

The movie has been credited with helping to boost public awareness of global warming, and has been particularly popular in schools. However, it has not been without controversy. Climate change skeptics and conservative commentators claimed to find flaws in the movie's science, and some school boards and teachers' unions in the USA refused to promote it. Gore was also accused of hypocrisy because he lived in a large home which consumed much more energy than the average citizen's.

> This did not stop *An Inconvenient Truth* from becoming one of the highest-grossing documentaries of all time, as well as winning an Oscar in 2006 for the best documentary.

When we analyze institutional change in these cases, we discover that we often deal with a long process of slowly-changing value judgments, of private initiatives that fight for specific societal interests, of opposition by vested interests, who consider a change in institutions threatening to their position, and of public intervention by governments. When studying institutional change from the OIE perspective we discover that changes in laws, or changes in the power to make decisions in firms and society, are processes in which many conflicts have to be solved. In analyzing these processes we discover processes of cumulative causation, and of the emergence of collective commitment.

## *'Settled beliefs'*

Another important concept in OIE when attempting to understand the dynamics of institutions is that of *settled belief* (Bromley, 2006). When, in a process of collective decision-making, society discusses several options, experts in the different disciplines play an important role. To solve ecological problems, society demands the views of ecological experts; to deal with financial crises, the expertise of financial economists are called on, and so on. As discussed in Chapter 2, experts in the different disciplines can have different views, different 'beliefs' of how the systems work, and what kinds of institutional changes are needed. In general, a belief is something on which we are prepared to act. A settled belief means that the (scientific) community has no doubt about a claim that, say, the financial market works according to a specific theory 'in the fullness of time and in repeated cases'. In other words, a belief is 'settled' in the community if there is no doubt on the part of citizens that the belief represents reality, and that policies and institutional changes should be based on that belief. Nevertheless, the belief is always tentative and in every case its relevance depends on the conditions at hand. A settled belief is not the Truth with a capital 'T', but always refers to several small truths with a lower case 't', indicating that our models and theories about complex systems are relative and never absolute (Tool and Bush, 2003).

The settled belief largely determines the choices scientists make with respect to the problems they consider to be part of their domain, with respect to the endogenous and exogenous variables. It also largely determines which mechanisms make the system work as it does, which causalities are crucial, and which public and private institutions should be redesigned. We know from our discussion in Chapter 2 that among economists there is no single, settled belief. Several theories can exist within one discipline and within one school of thought. Added to this, the beliefs among scientists about 'how the world works' change over time, and we can distinguish periods in which belief in the efficient functioning of markets is replaced by periods in which a more interventionist government is warranted. These differences are rooted in different values, norms, habits and mental maps, which influence all actors in the system: scientists, consumers, businessmen and politicians alike.

## *Ongoing process of artificial selection*

At any point in time the institutional structure is inherited from the past. The existing institutions, habits and division of costs and benefits, the values against which judgments are made, and societal objectives are all challenged continuously by individuals and groups in society.

When what 'ought to be' differs from what 'is' there is a task for science to explain and to make suggestions for improvements. Actors at different levels in society with different objectives and powers take part in the selection process of the desired institutions. This view on the dynamics of institutions portrays actors as purposeful designers realizing that a new institutional setting will distribute the costs and benefits differently, and will affect the power relations in society.

Designing institutions is then a matter of evaluation, political decision-making, argumentation and procedures to solve conflicts, all in the spirit of Commons (1934). He labeled this process 'artificial selection', indicating the role of human will and design. This OIE viewpoint is summarized in Figure 4.4.

## DYNAMICS OF ECONOMIC SYSTEMS

We have already discussed three ideal types of market economies: the Anglo-Saxon, European Continental and Asian models. We indicated that economic systems are not static, but change over time. When the financial crisis began in 2008 we saw the US government playing a much more active and controlling role in the economy than it had in the years before the crisis. From the 1980s onwards, many elements of the Anglo-Saxon system were introduced into the Continental European and Asian systems (Whitley, 1999; Dore, 2000). We have also noticed the changing role of shareholders in European firms since the 1990s. In short, economic systems change, and we ask, why is this so?

In the evolutionary approach to economic systems, decisions at the decentralized level result in the evolution of the system as a whole even though there is no intentional design at the centralized level. Where the efficiency driver is central, the system finds a new equilibrium after an exogenous shock because independent individual actors search for new and efficient institutions. In a competitive environment, actors are motivated to search for and adopt the most efficient solutions. In the evolutionary efficiency approach it is assumed that decentralized decisions will result in the necessary changes at system level. When the need for more flexibility in the labor market calls for changes in the judicial system, or changed economic circumstances call for a less important role for employees (and a more influential role for other stakeholders), these judicial adaptations happen. When, as a result of these changes, amendments to the value system are also required (values regarding the role of collectivity, or about the dismissal of employees), then that value system will also adapt. In such a process of adaptation, its historical roots can play a very important role in the evolutionary path of a system.

From the information about multiple equilibria and the role of historical initial conditions you know that the different economic systems, such as the Anglo-Saxon, the Continental European and the Asian ones, will evolve along their own paths and need not converge. In other words, the differences between the systems may be reinforced rather than reduced.

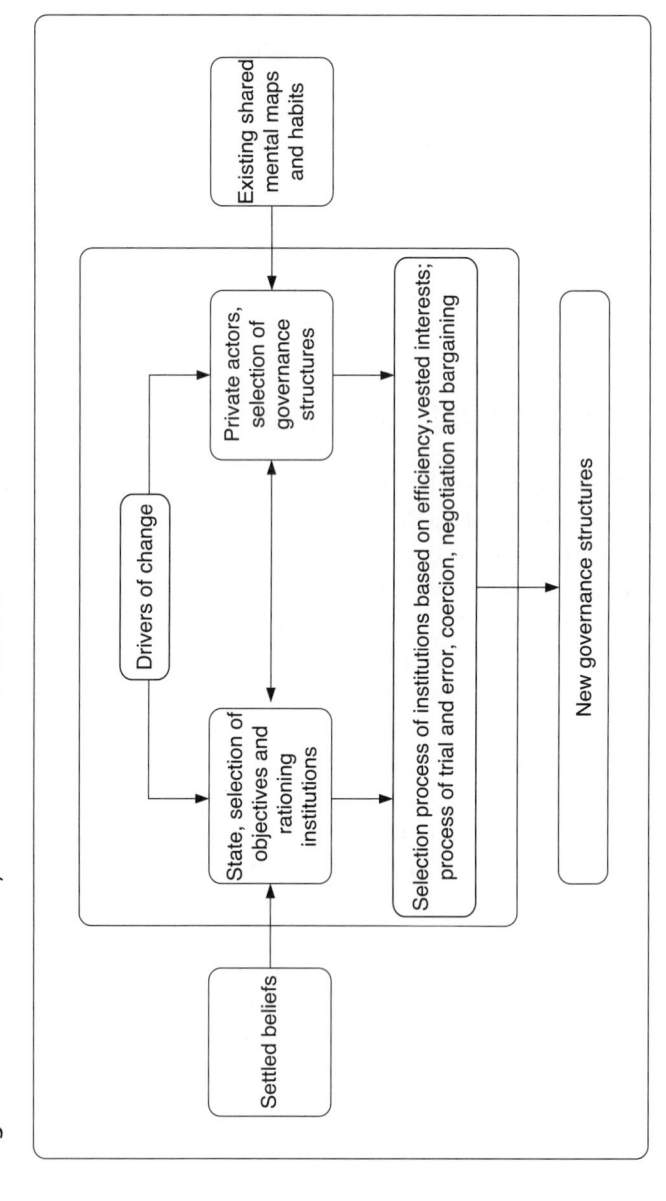

**Figure 4.4** *Institutional dynamics as artificial selection*

When we study the dynamics of economic systems we often encounter changes that are not the result of an evolutionary process, but the result of design at the system level. The changes in the centrally planned economies of the Eastern European countries such as Poland, the Czech Republic, Hungary and Russia are well known. These examples show how difficult it is to design and implement changes to complete systems. In these circumstances, the political, judicial and economic institutions all have to be redesigned at the same time, so that a new and coherent system may emerge.

As you can see from the complexity of institutions and the interrelationships between the different parts of the societal system, the designing of economic systems as such is a very complex task. When you study specific cases you will find out that often the political designers concentrated on a part of the whole system (for example, the introduction of competition on markets and the privatization of firms) and did not always pay sufficient attention to the necessary complementary changes to the political, judicial and value systems.

When studying the (re)design of economic systems, the approach can be taken in which the government, at the central level, designs and implements what is considered best for society. The government is then considered as the institution that takes decisions in the interests of the system as a whole (see Chapter 8).

It is also possible to take another approach, and to analyze the dynamics of economic systems as a process of redesigning institutions in which the interests of some specific groups are disregarded and those of others are served. The dynamics in this more OIE approach are then analyzed as a process of solving conflicts between different societal groups. Interest groups in society, such as labor unions, employers' associations, large firms, and representatives of small and medium-sized firms will try constantly to influence the dynamics of the economic system. This is done at the level of the market, but also through the political system and sometimes even through the value system. In Chapter 9 you will learn more about how interest groups campaign and manipulate information in their attempt to influence values and norms.

## CONCLUDING REMARKS

A static description of the world could be presented as an equilibrium that does not change over time. Such a description can be informative depending on the type of question one wants to answer. In this chapter we posed questions of change. One simple way of dealing with change is to use comparative static analysis: what happens with the equilibrium outcome of the model (the endogenous variables) if an exogenous variable changes or if any other given aspect in the model is changed?

In the dynamic approach, the analysis focuses on an explanation of the process, which implies a historical analysis in which real time is involved. Dynamic models are formulated and equilibrium solutions become functions of time rather than static values for endogenous variables. In terms of Institutional Economics, we have described how, under a given set of circumstances, (equilibrium) choices are made that will determine future (optimal) choices. The institutions (and changes in them) are the outcome of individual choices. These choices can be based on efficiencies or on vested interests.

We showed how, in evolutionary processes, institutions emerge from the (un)intentional behavior of actors and may result in an equilibrium, or may follow a specific path which can be either efficient or inefficient. We also showed that not all change is gradual, but that under specific conditions a radical change in the system is also possible. Finally. we discussed the process of artificial selection.

All these theories and insights may be relevant to researchers. Depending on the research question being posed, or depending on the conditions that prevail in the individual research domain, a decision is made about the relevance of the different approaches. In the following chapters you will see how the theoretical insights that have been discussed in these early chapters are applied to both private and public institutions. In the remainder of this book we shall apply the static and dynamic approach, as well as the efficiency and vested interest approaches to the choice and development of institutions, notably governance structures.

## REVIEW QUESTIONS

1. Does the phrase 'Ask not what your country can do for you. Ask what you can do for your country' concern a collectivistic group value or an individualistic value? Explain.
2. Discuss the three drivers of institutional change.
3. Do you think that technological change (such as ICT and the internet) has changed the governance of research and teaching at universities, and did this improve efficiency (think, for example, of plagiarism)?
4. Discuss the following: the institutions as an equilibrium approach can explain that different equilibria arise, but not which institution is chosen.
5. Do you think that evolution always results in a better society? Explain by use of the concept of selection.
6. Explain the phenomenon of path dependency by referring to an example of your own.
7. Discuss conditions for public institutions to be efficient.
8. Do you agree that distribution of income is not 'naturally given' but rather the outcome of human decisions that can be changed? Explain.
9. What type of dynamics might result from vested interests?
10. During the economic crisis of 2008–9, the US government intervened much more in the private sector than previously, compelled by the serious circumstances. Could you apply Figure 4.4 to this real-life case?

# PART III

# Private Governance Structures

Chapter 5   Markets
Chapter 6   Firms
Chapter 7   Cooperation between Firms

## INTRODUCTION

Historically, there are different ways of allocating goods: they may be allocated by brute force, tradition, authority or by market exchange. An example of allocation by *brute force* is the recent outbreak of piracy off the coast of Somalia, where it is able to flourish because there is no national government that can maintain law and order effectively. Allocation by *tradition* is, for example, found in the form of gifts at ceremonies. This was practiced by tribes in India before they came into contact with Europeans; they would exchange goods as gifts at family ceremonies such as weddings and funerals. The Toda tribe provided the Kota tribe with butter made from buffalo milk as well as with buffalos to sacrifice at funerals. In return, the Kota provided the Toda with utilities they could use in their everyday life and also played music at Toda ceremonies. Allocation by *authority* is found in government, in firms and in organizations such as churches. For example, a manager may decide which resources are to be allocated to individual departments. And finally, allocation through *markets* makes use of the price mechanism.

Exchange by tradition or by authority are both types of relational exchange: exchange within a family is confined to the members of that family, and exchange within a firm is restricted to the employer and employees. Both types of allocation of goods differ from market exchange. Within markets, the exchange of goods and services is via market prices. Since the Industrial Revolution, price-making markets have applied not only to the exchange of consumables but also to labor and capital.

In Part III we focus exclusively on the allocation of goods by authority or prices. Neither brute force nor tradition are explained in detail, as these are no longer dominant mechanisms for the distribution of resources in modern capitalist societies. We focus on the static and dynamic approaches of markets, firms and cooperation between firms, mainly in developed countries.

In the Institutional Economics literature, the different mechanisms for the allocation of resources are labeled governance structures; these were introduced in Chapter 3. Private governance structures have three basic forms:

1 The price mechanism is structured by what is called the *market*.
2 The structure of alignment of allocation of resources through authority in the firm is called the *hierarchy*.
3 The structure of governance of cooperation between firms is called a *hybrid*: this structure combines the sharing of decision rights related to pooled material or immaterial resources (for example, machines or know-how), while preserving some degree of autonomy for those actions that are unrelated to the pooled resources. So, the hybrid comprises both the market and hierarchical allocations of resources.

Theories about governance structures provide concepts explaining both their existence and their dynamics.

As discussed in Chapter 3, one of the approaches that is well equipped to explain the existence of different governance structures is the transaction cost approach. In the static version of this approach we focus not only on efficiency but also on inefficiencies generated by vested interests, and in the dynamic approach the focus is on the efficiency enhancing role of the entrepreneur and the influence of technology on the development of governance structures. Because of entrepreneurial activities, the market is continuously mobile, and the development of technology influences the form of governance structures. From the perspective of vested interests, we explain how countervailing powers challenge the authority of large firms and/or the position of management (and their policy advisers).

In Part III we shall deal with markets, firms and hybrids – in Chapters 5, 6 and 7, respectively. We have chosen this arrangement because a hybrid is a governance structure that covers features of both markets and firms. To understand the governance structure of hybrids it is first necessary to understand the governance structures of both market and firm.

The remainder of this introduction to Part III briefly reintroduces the governance structures discussed in Chapter 3, plus an outline of the topics to be dealt with more fully in later chapters.

## The static approach

It was a long time before social scientists acquired an understanding of the price mechanism. In 1776, Adam Smith laid down the basis of our modern understanding of the market: in the ideal, perfectly competitive market, prices provide sufficient information to optimize behavior. But it was many years before a theory of firms was developed: for a long time the firm was approached as if it were a 'black box'. As recently as the 1930s, Ronald Coase observed that the exchange of property rights through the market is in general not costless because of search costs, and because of the costs of negotiating and concluding separate contracts for each transaction on the market. The occurrence of transaction costs is the basis of Coase's explanation of the existence of a firm.

The Coasian approach was developed in greater detail by transaction costs economists. As already mentioned in Chapter 3, the level of transaction costs is mainly a function of the asset specificity (the degree to which an asset is useful for only a few purposes) of an investment. However, the frequency of trade between trading partners, and uncertainty concerning market developments and the behavior of a transaction partner all affect the choice of governance structure.

Because Coase and his followers identify uncertainty with risk, when we discuss the static approach to private governance structures we shall also ignore the distinction between the two concepts, as introduced by Knight (1921). According to Knight, risk means that people can assign probabilities to different outcomes, while uncertainty means that determining probabilities is not possible (see also Chapter 1). Unless explicitly stated otherwise, the two concepts will be used interchangeably here, since in general this will not lead to a fundamental misunderstanding of the theories involved.

## The static efficiency approach: transaction cost economics

In Chapter 3 we introduced the three dimensions of transactions according to transaction cost economics (TCE): asset specificity, risk (or uncertainty), and frequency. We shall now focus mainly on the first two dimensions (given any level of frequency) and formulate two hypotheses with regard to the relationship between these first two dimensions and governance structures:

(i) the higher the specificity of an investment, the higher the value of investment that will be lost in its next best use (when it is used in any alternative way), so the more likely it is that either a hybrid or a firm is the preferred (least cost) governance structure, rather than the market; and
(ii) the higher the risk involved in a transaction, the higher the incentive to build in safeguards, which may lead to a choice of any of the three governance structures, depending on the total transaction costs involved.

Given the frequency of transactions and the degree of risk, the degree of asset specificity determines which governance structure generates the lowest transaction costs, and it is the market that usually generates the lowest transaction costs when asset specificity is low. If there is neither asset specificity nor any risk involved, we call this an ideal market – one that does not need any institution (apart from the existence of property rights) to safeguard the investment. However, enforcement of institutions may be appropriate if some asset specificity or considerable risks are involved in the transaction. In these cases, we are facing institutionalized markets (see below).

Under circumstances of high asset specificity, precautionary measures are necessary to safeguard investments. It may be obvious that the higher the risk, the more precautionary measures that have to be taken in realizing transactions.

In the ideal type of market, incentives are high because of strict individual property rights. This is most effective when asset specificity is zero. The ideal market type concentrates on the transaction at the time it is made, and individual contracts are approached as discrete entities; that is, they stand on their own. These types of contracts are called classical contracts (see Chapter 3). However, markets may deviate from the ideal type, and may require additional institutions to enable them to work properly. This market assisted by institutions is known as an institutionalized market. In general, because of a strong reliance on allocation through the market mechanism – that is, through prices – administrative controls are low in comparison to other governance structures.

As introduced in Chapter 3, in hierarchies, high-powered incentives are uncommon, because workers are expected to perform the tasks managers assign to them. Another characteristic of the hierarchy is that, because of the allocation of resources and adaptation to disturbances by fiat, a high degree of administrative control is required. Decisions taken by management have to be communicated to employees and their implementation has to be monitored.

It is no surprise, then, that the attributes of hybrids are somewhere between those of markets and hierarchies, as hybrids comprise aspects of both the market and the hierarchical allocation of resources. Consequently, they are characterized by less high-powered incentives than are found in the market, but by more high-powered incentives than in the firm, and have rather more administrative support than the market but less than the firm. Finally, the hybrid relies in particular on different kinds of credible commitment supports (such as penalties against premature termination of the contract, and specialized dispute

**Table III.1** *Attributes of governance structures*

|  | Asset specificity | | |
|---|---|---|---|
|  | General to semi-specific | Semi-specific to highly specific | Highly specific |
|  | Governance structure | | |
| Attributes | Market | Hybrid | Hierarchy |
| Incentive intensity | Strong | Medium | Weak |
| Administrative controls | Weak | Medium | Strong |
| Contractual enforcement | Strong | Medium | Weak |

settlement mechanisms; see also Chapter 3). The different attributes of governance structures as they are shown in Table III.1 are discussed in Chapter 5, 6 and 7.

In a simplified model, transaction costs can be seen as a function of asset specificity. Different governance structures have different transaction cost functions, because each governance structure employs specific devices to coordinate transactions. In other words, different types of governance structures are associated with different types of contracts, different arrangements of property rights, different reputation effects and different risks.

To explain this more clearly, let us focus for a moment on the influence of asset specificity on transaction costs for the different governance structures. The influence of all other possibly relevant factors, such as frequency and risk, will be ignored for the moment but will be taken into account later (think back to the *ceteris paribus* clause, introduced in Chapter 3).

The situation is as shown in Figure III.1. In the case of 'markets', transaction costs will, *ceteris paribus*, be low for low asset specificity, but increase rapidly for higher levels of asset specificity; hence, this function has a rather low intercept with the vertical axis, but a rather steep slope.

In the case of 'hierarchies', transaction costs will, *ceteris paribus*, be higher (compared to markets) with low asset specificity, but the impact of rising asset specificity on transaction costs will be relatively low (compared to their impact in the case of markets).

Finally, in the case of 'hybrids', transaction costs will, *ceteris paribus*, be somewhere between the previous two cases.

Figure III.1 shows that the transaction cost functions of the three different governance structures intersect. A shift from one governance structure to another occurs at these intersection points in order to achieve the lowest transaction costs possible. As long as asset specificity has values of between $k_0$ (zero) and $k_1$ (these values imply that asset specificity is either absent, as in the case of a generic investment, or rather low, as in case of a semi-specific investment), 'markets' are the preferred choice. If asset specificity is between the values $k_1$ and $k_2$ (the level of highly specific investment), 'hybrids' will be preferred. If asset specificity is higher than $k_2$, then 'hierarchy' will be chosen.

**Figure III.1** *Transaction costs as a function of asset specificity*

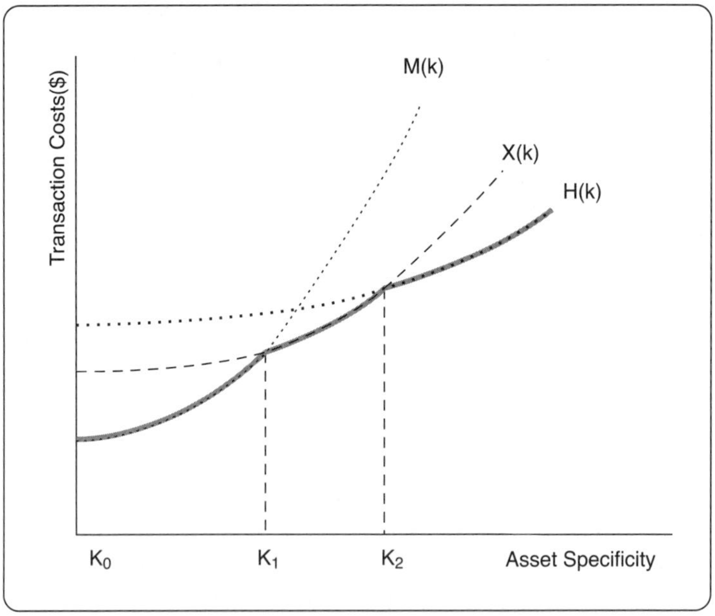

*Notes:* K = asset specificity ($K_0$ = generic investment, $K_1$ = semi-specific investment, $K_2$ = highly specific investment); M = market transaction costs; X = hybrid transaction costs; H = hierarchy transaction costs.
*Sources:* Based on Williamson (1996, p. 108) and Ménard (2004, p. 369).

The market transaction cost curve shown in Figure III.1 does not cross the vertical axis at the lowest point, because market transactions require institutions such as property rights. Without clearly assigned property rights, markets cannot allocate resources efficiently. Market exchange requires that individuals have secure property rights, not only for their material possessions but also covering the fruits of their labor. People must be sure that contracts will be enforced, and that the income from their efforts is protected. If this is not the case, incentives to produce are weakened. The protection of property rights is essential for the efficient allocation of resources. This requires diverse expenditure for the establishment, operation and maintenance of judicial independence, impartial courts and the integrity of the legal system, as well as for the protection of property rights and legal enforcement of contracts.

It is now quite easy to analyze the effects of other relevant determinants, such as, for example, risk. The different transaction cost functions shift with every change in the institutional conditions involved. For example, if risk increases, all three functions will shift upward: transaction costs will be higher because of a higher risk for all governance structures. How each specific function will change cannot be determined, but in general it is expected that the intersection points will change. It might be, for example, that an increase in risk will make 'markets' a relatively worse governance structure, in the sense that the intersection point with the 'hybrid' will be lower than $k_1$.

In circumstances of no asset specificity – meaning that the product is supplied by using a *general purpose technology* and consequently investment can be transferred without any loss in value, transactions will occur in the market at competitive prices. If there is a dispute between parties – about the quality of the product delivered, say – a court can determine which party is in the right and award damages if necessary. The more that *specific purpose technology* is used in supplying a product, the higher are the risks of opportunistic behavior during the implementation and (re)negotiation of the contract. The degree of risk of opportunistic behavior creates incentives to safeguard the specific investment, for which both parties will be prepared to spend money.

A shift in governance structure from market coordination to alternative governance structures such as hierarchy or hybrids may become profitable because of lower transaction costs. Transaction costs in markets include search and information costs, among other things. Transaction costs in hierarchies include items such as the costs of internal and external auditing, as well as expenses associated with meeting statutory requirements. In circumstances where asset specificity is high, these costs may be lower than transaction costs in the market. Transaction costs in hybrid forms of production organization, including inter-firm agreements, can be classified as an intermediate position, because control mechanisms can be implemented more easily than in firms, as illustrated in Figure III.1. In Chapters 5–7 we shall develop the different transaction cost functions in more detail.

## The static vested interest approach

Actors, whether individuals, single firms or cooperating firms, are price takers in the neoclassical, principal–agent and transaction cost approach. Actors cannot deviate from the price that the market generates. However, firms or alliances of firms may become large enough to have the power to set the price above the competitive level. Another source of price setting comes from monopoly positions established by patents or registered trademarks. Whatever the source of the price setting power, however, the key fact is that firms or alliances of firms may deviate from the competitive price. In these cases, the choice of the best governance structure is possibly not driven by efficiency motives, but rather by motives of vested interest. Society may then face a suboptimal outcome as a result of this power play.

## The dynamic approach: efficiency versus vested interests

Technology and preferences are exogenous variables in the static approach. This results in neat models that may predict market outcomes in the short run. However, in the long run, technology, preferences and other factors such as a growing awareness of environmental problems or the emancipation of certain social groups – which are taken as given in the short run – may change or be influenced by the economic system itself. For example, an economic system that focuses mainly on private consumption may disregard public consumption, neglecting the maintenance of parks and other public spaces. This could increase the feeling of insecurity in society and lead to a growth in demand for safety provisions. Or unregulated production may result in severe environmental problems, inducing institutional change and creating new economic opportunities.

*Entrepreneurs* who own and/or manage firms are continually searching for opportunities in the market. They not only decide what to produce, but also how they want to combine factors of production, whether as an individual producer, as part of a firm, or in combination with other firms. However, when the prevailing institutions do not allow them to exploit new opportunities, they may try to change existing rules or to introduce new ones. These types of entrepreneur are known as an *institutional entrepreneurs*. The ongoing process of entrepreneurial search for new opportunities results in perpetual *innovation* in products and governance structures. An innovation in governance structures could be a firm entering an agreement with others to pool specific resources and achieve mutual gains. This strategic alliance may be motivated by the need to survive competition or by a desire to avoid cut-throat competition.

This kind of behavior is not analyzed within the TCE approach, which focuses only on the efficient choice of governance structures. In the dynamic approach, strategies aim at changing governance structures. Furthermore, while the change of governance structures is a deliberate choice of firms, the organization of the hybrid can also evolve over time. Firms may learn from cooperation. They may find that they can trust each other, so will then abstain from opportunistic behavior, realizing that they do not have to arrange their cooperation in detail, because of the self enforcing mechanisms of implicit contracts.

Another dynamic force of governance structures was introduced by John Kenneth Galbraith in many of his works. He challenged the static assumption of given preferences with his theory of *revised sequence*. In his view, large firms may create a demand for the goods they (are planning to) produce, through marketing and salesmanship. As long as marketing and salesmanship are confined strictly to informing customers about a particular product, this may contribute to higher wealth in society. However, if it influences customers by informing them tendentiously or manipulating them, this maximization of private welfare (serving vested interests) comes at the cost of overall economic welfare.

Consumers or other stakeholders may organize themselves to gain sufficient power to counterbalance that of large firms. This competition between organized powers is one of the dynamic forces of modern economies, which is why a restriction of the organization of consumers or other stakeholders may be harmful to progress. The organization of stakeholders determines the character of the social and economic system. In Anglo-Saxon countries *laissez-faire* principles are dominant and production is focused on generating shareholder value. In Continental European countries, in contrast, the state intervenes more actively in economic activities, but the opinions of all stakeholders are taken into account; for example, there is mutual consultation between employers and employees. Both approaches are explained in broad terms in the following chapters.

# 5 Markets

## CONTENTS

- **Introduction**
- **The static efficiency approach to markets**
    - Neoclassical approach to markets
    - TCE approach to markets
    - Different competitive market governance structures
    - Opportunism and externalities
- **The static vested interest approach to markets**
    - Market power
- **The dynamic efficiency approach to markets**
    - Market process theory
    - Institutional entrepreneurs
- **The dynamic vested interest approach to markets**
    - Change implies a redistribution of costs and benefits
    - Two ideal types of labor market: Continental European versus Anglo-Saxon
- **Concluding remarks**
- **Review questions**
- **Appendix**

## INTRODUCTION

Competitive markets can be found all over the world, but their welfare enhancing function should not be taken for granted, and will, generally speaking, not arise spontaneously: some form of design will be necessary.

This can be illustrated by the transition from a planned economy to a market economy in Russia after the fall of communism. The Russian economy lacked the necessary institutions for the market to operate properly, and the result was very high levels of unemployment. Neither employees nor managers had any first hand experience of decision-making in a market economy. Markets could not function well because managers lacked the driving values of profitability and efficiency. Unable to compete with foreign companies, the result was the closure of many of the large firms that had operated under the Soviet regime. Employees too lacked the skills to function properly in a market economy. This caused particular problems for older workers: if they lost their jobs they often did not know how to 'sell' themselves on the labor market.

Eventually, this inability to deal with the market economy led to severe economic decline and social decay, because under the Soviet regime large organizations had been responsible for a broad range of social arrangements (housing, education, health and so on). With the dissolution of the Soviet Union in 1991 and the attempted transformation of Russia into a market-oriented economy, economic welfare suffered severely, since these large organizations could not compete internationally. The transition in China from a planned economy into a market economy also illustrates how markets have to be designed in order to function properly.

The transition of the Russian planned economy into a market economy shows that the market is preceded by institutions. Exchanges themselves involve property rights and take place in a legal framework. The market requires clearly defined property rights in order to perform its task of allocating resources. This implies that it must be clear as to who has which rights, and this in turn involves political decision-making. For a long time in Russia under the tsars many people worked as serfs and did not have the right to earn an income. This right was acquired only with the introduction of wage labor; that is, with the abolition of serfdom.

Not only property rights but other institutions are often involved as well, to optimize the task of the market. The choice of specific market institutions may be explained by the minimization of transaction costs. This is related to (i) imperfect information; (ii) asymmetric information; and (iii) externalities. The market may try to reduce imperfect information by increasing entrepreneurial alertness, which will be discussed in greater depth later in this chapter, or by generating information as a product in itself that can also be sold on the market. In order to reduce a possible asymmetry in information, the market can be assisted by guarantee certificates. This occurs, as noted in Chapter 1, in the market for used autos, where it is difficult to assess hidden damage or problems a vehicle might have. In markets where quality is easy to assess, the situation is different. For vegetables, say, a guarantee certificate is not necessary, because the quality of vegetables can usually be assessed at face value. However, with the growing popularity of organic food, quality signaling has also appeared in the market for vegetables.

Finally, there are also market solutions to externalities. When negotiation is costless, conflicts about externalities may be settled efficiently (see Chapter 3). However, when transaction costs *are* involved, then additional institutions may be required to generate an efficient outcome.

The reason for choosing different market institutions is that they reduce transaction costs. Without a guarantee certificate, the market for used automobiles would not exist, or would be accompanied by the high cost of solving disagreements about the quality of the auto. The choice of particular institutions is therefore explained by efficiency.

Neither the neoclassical nor the transaction cost approach tells us anything about how the market moves from one equilibrium to another. This gap is covered by *market process theory*, which aims 'to understand how the decisions of individual market participants interact to generate the market forces which compel *changes* in prices, in outputs, and in methods of production and the allocation of resources' (Kirzner, 1973, p. 6). In this approach, the entrepreneur performs a pivotal role as the source of innovation, which leads not only to changes in economic structure but also to economic fluctuations – because each product has its own life cycle, as will be explained later in this chapter.

As well as the efficiency approach to markets, there is the vested interest approach. The static variant of this approach explains power play – for example, anti-competitive behavior by powerful firms, such as predatory pricing (selling a product or service at a very low price) that leads to market imperfections. The dynamic variant of the vested interest approach highlights the interplay between interest groups: not only the anti-competitive behavior of large companies but also their ability to influence consumers' preferences may encourage cooperation between interest groups to provide a counterbalance to the power of large companies.

The structure of this chapter is as follows. First, we describe the market from a static perspective. This takes two forms: the static efficiency approach, and the static vested interest approach. We start with the efficiency approach, by analyzing the ideal cases of the spot market and the contingency market. Next, we look at the four conditions of the market as given by TCE. A change in each of these conditions causes shifts in the comparative costs of governance and may therefore influence the choice of governance structure. We continue with a discussion of different market structures; that is, differences in institutions that make up different markets.

Later in the chapter we describe the market as a process. This approach puts the spotlight on entrepreneurs, who are constantly searching for business opportunities. Entrepreneurs identify market imperfections as business opportunities. By coordinating resources to exploit these opportunities, they may restore balance in the market. We also describe the interaction between interest groups, such as consumers, and the power of large companies to set prices and to influence consumer preferences. In the economic literature, the latter phenomenon is known as *revised sequence*. The possibilities of stakeholders organizing a counteracting force may differ between countries. Institutions reflect a country-specific and cultural climate that cannot be separated from the society's history. The culture of Continental European countries differs from that of Anglo-Saxon countries, and consequently the organization of stakeholders and their influence on economic outcomes also differ.

All these approaches are summed up in Table 5.1, where each quadrant shows the main topics that will be dealt with in this chapter.

**Table 5.1** *Static and dynamic efficiency and vested interest approaches to the market*

|  | **Static approach** | **Dynamic approach** |
|---|---|---|
| Efficiency | Different market structures:<br>■ spot market<br>■ contingent market<br>■ markets assisted by institutions (TCE) | Markets as a process:<br>■ entrepreneurial learning and innovation<br>■ institutional entrepreneurs |
| Vested interest | Inefficiencies through anti-competitive behavior of firms with market power:<br>■ power of management<br>■ predatory pricing | Power of management:<br>■ revised sequence<br>Countervailing power<br>Labor market: Rhineland versus Anglo-Saxon approach |

In this chapter we focus on markets in which both individuals and firms are active. We start with the analysis of the market from the neoclassical perspective, and continue with the analysis of markets that are assisted by institutions.

## THE STATIC EFFICIENCY APPROACH TO MARKETS

The ideal, perfectly competitive market is illustrated by *spot markets*, as will be examined below. *Contingent markets* are an extension of these. Contingent markets are not only limited to commodities that are characterized by physical properties and by place and time of availability, but also include a differentiation of products with (environmental) risks. However, even ideal markets cannot operate properly if certain institutional preconditions are not met. These conditions include the contract law regime, property rights, reputation effects and risk. When a market deviates from the ideal type, additional safeguards are needed; for example, because of bounded rationality, opportunistic behavior and limited competition.

### Neoclassical approach to markets

In Appendix A to Chapter 1, a short description of the NCE approach to markets was given as a reminder. This description of a market is of a highly abstract character. In reality, the specific functioning of the market, in particular the decision regarding an equilibrium price, will depend on the circumstances, such as the nature of the goods and the transactions. This can best be introduced by the simplest type of real-life markets: spot markets.

#### *Spot markets*

Sellers and buyers, who may be private individuals as well as firms, exchange property rights in the market by bidding and asking. In a simple perfect market, commodities or currencies can be traded for immediate delivery: on the *spot market*, a market made up of buyers and sellers whose relationship consists of a single exchange. The product is delivered at the moment of payment and the identities of the partners to the transaction are irrelevant, because transactions in spot markets have a one-off character. Spot markets are characterized by homogeneous products and the independence of all parties, and prices react immediately to changes in availability of the product.

The spot market is an archetypal example of an ideal market, with all the relevant information included in the prices. Alternative sources of supply are available, and therefore the identity of the supplier is of little importance. Transactions can be conducted anonymously within a legal framework: problems are solved by referring to the formal terms of the sales contract and the application of the rules of contract law. Spot markets exist in the oil trade, securities, grain, gold, RAM chips, dairy products and other commodities. Theoretically, institutions do not play any part in these, but in practice institutions are always involved in real markets, as will become clear in our description of the dairy spot market (see Box 5.1). In this case, the exchange between a buyer and a seller is mediated by brokers.

## BOX 5.1 THE SPOT MARKET FOR DAIRY PRODUCTS

Prices fluctuate sharply on the dairy spot market. Since autumn 2005 there have been shortages in supply. One of the reasons for these shortages is the rising demand for dairy products in China. As these shortages increased, the dairy spot market price rose accordingly. However, with the fall in demand resulting from the financial crisis, dairy spot market prices declined dramatically in the second half of 2008.

Most milk traded in Europe is still determined by long-term contracts. These contracts specify a certain cancellation period during which farmers commit themselves to supplying milk to milk factories. In turn, the factories are obliged to buy the milk and collect it from the farms. However, milk factories do not guarantee a price, nor is there a fixed pricing system. Consequently, fluctuations in world market prices affect prices paid to contracted firms, but often with a significant delay.

When world market prices for milk rise for longer periods, this system results in dissatisfaction among the farmers who have a contractual relationship with the milk processing industry: because of the delay in prices adjusting to market fluctuations, farmers get the feeling that they are constantly being paid less than world market prices.

For the milk brokers buying and selling on the world market, this represents a business opportunity. Brokers take excess milk from one party and sell it to another, taking a percentage from each deal for their services and paying farmers the market price, which fluctuates with (possibly worldwide) demand and supply.

The dairy spot market is a relatively small market in comparison to all the milk that is produced. Why don't all farmers deliver to the spot markets? First, many farmers are risk averse. They prefer lower but stable prices over spot market prices that may fluctuate heavily. In the figure below you can see the large price fluctuations in the first half of 2009).

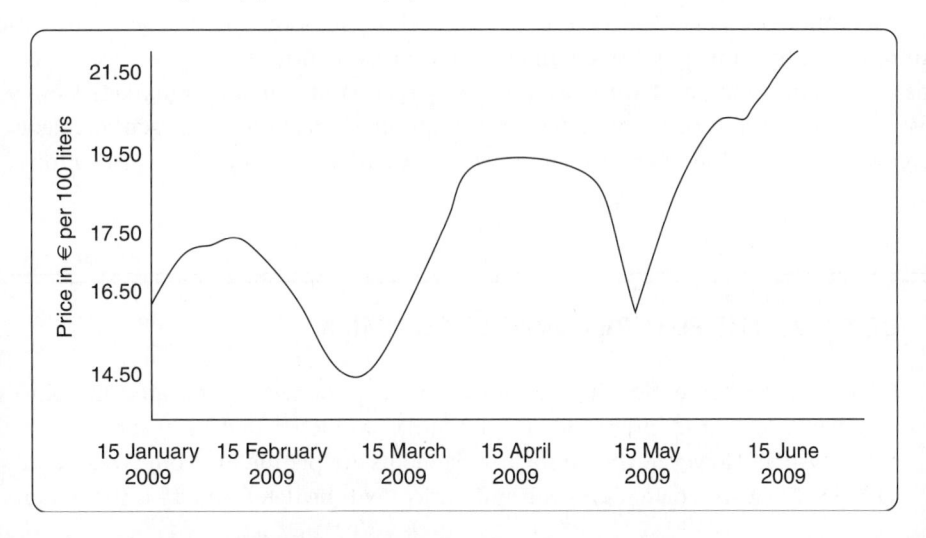

*Prices fluctuating sharply on the dairy spot market in the first six months of 2009*

*Source*: www.dca-markt.nl; accessed 1 August 2009.

> Second, farmers must have surplus capital available to be able to offset a sharp fall in prices. Third, banks are reluctant to lend money to invest if a person's or a firm's income is variable. Fourth, because the intermediaries are not obliged to buy the farm's product, farmers may be concerned that they will have to dump their milk if demand falls. Fifth, because transportation costs have to be paid by the producer and not by the broker, the farmer knows that he will not always make the highest profit. If a broker is able to sell Dutch milk for a marginally higher price in Germany than in the Netherlands, he would naturally want to sell the milk in Germany. But given the higher transportation costs, it would be in the interest of the farmer to sell the milk in the Netherlands.

## *Contingent markets*

We have assumed implicitly that products are defined with respect to their physical properties: an apple is an apple. But a physical product is not necessarily the same economic product: products can also be defined by the time, place and environment of their availability. An apple now and an apple a year from now are two distinct economic products. It is also possible to define products in relation to the aspect of risk: some products will not be viable if a certain state of the world does not materialize. To give an example of such a situation: if you are not going to be ill, you will not need a doctor's services; her services are contingent on you becoming ill. Another example is the service provided by an attorney. The fee he charges may be conditional on the results he can obtain. The contract between client and attorney may stipulate that the client will not be charged fees by the attorney if the case is lost.

For convenience, we shall define *contingent products* in this book as products that are not only defined by their physical properties, but also with respect to time, place, environment and contingency. In the case of the attorney introduced above, his payment is called a *contingent fee*; that is, a fee has to be paid only in the case of a favorable result. This definition diversifies the number of commodities substantially, and generates different prices for the same physical commodity. Of course, contingent markets are subject to the same equilibrium mechanism as the spot markets (and every other market). However, just as in our example of a spot market, a description of a real-life contingent market cannot avoid the inclusion of an institution. For the exchange of milk, these institutions are known as *clearing houses* (see Box 5.2).

> ### BOX 5.2   THE FUTURES MARKET FOR MILK
>
> Government intervention in the European dairy market has resulted in comparatively stable milk prices. Since 1983, milk production has been subject to a quota system. However, the quota arrangements are planned to come to an end in 2015. From that date, European milk prices will be determined on the world

market, which will lead to higher price volatility. Milk is a contingent commodity, because production, and consequently delivery, are at the mercy of weather conditions. Milk produced in the summer is subject to different conditions than milk produced in the winter. Furthermore, extreme weather changes can influence milk production – summers with a lot of rain may be succeeded by those with prolonged drought, so that more feed will have to be bought for the animals in the latter years. Higher farm inputs coupled with lower production cause problems for dairy farmers. On the world market, weather conditions may result in price volatility.

Such volatility of milk prices may induce dairy farmers to use the futures market for milk in order to stabilize their income. Since August 2008, European dairy farmers have been able to sell their production on the European Milk Exchange (Eumix) via a futures contract.

Dairy factories may also use the Eumix to guarantee the delivery of milk in the near future. Futures contracts are binding obligations to buy or sell a certain amount of milk at a specified future date that meets a preset grade and standard, at a price agreed in advance. The milk does not have to be delivered before the expiration day of the contract. In the meantime, the contracts may be traded on the stock market. The payment is guaranteed by the clearing house and its clearing members. The clearing house provides clearing and settlement services for transactions in milk futures.

A futures milk contract provides price certainty but no guarantee of a profit. For example, farmer John sells a 10,000 liter future at €30 per 100 liter. If the milk price changes to €25 per 100 liter, farmer John will have a €5 profit per 100 liter in his futures account. But he also has to consider the transaction costs. The future contracts are traded on the stock exchange, and all traders have to pay a margin that depends on the amount of traded futures. So broker fees will lower the guaranteed price John may expect. Additionally, if for some reason he cannot provide the milk when the time comes, he will have to buy in milk on the spot market in order to comply with the requirements of the contract.

## TCE approach to markets

Based on Figure III.1 in the Part III Introduction, we argued that, *ceteris paribus*, the choice of governance structure is determined by the degree to which transaction-specific investments are involved. But other conditions play a part as well. According to Williamson (1991), generally speaking, the market is the most efficient governance structure if asset specificity is low (see Figure 5.1). Low asset specificity generates the lowest possible transaction costs when contracts are standard, property rights are clear, information about reputation is easily generated, and risk is limited to contingencies. These conditions will be explained in more detail below.

**Figure 5.1** *The domain of the market*

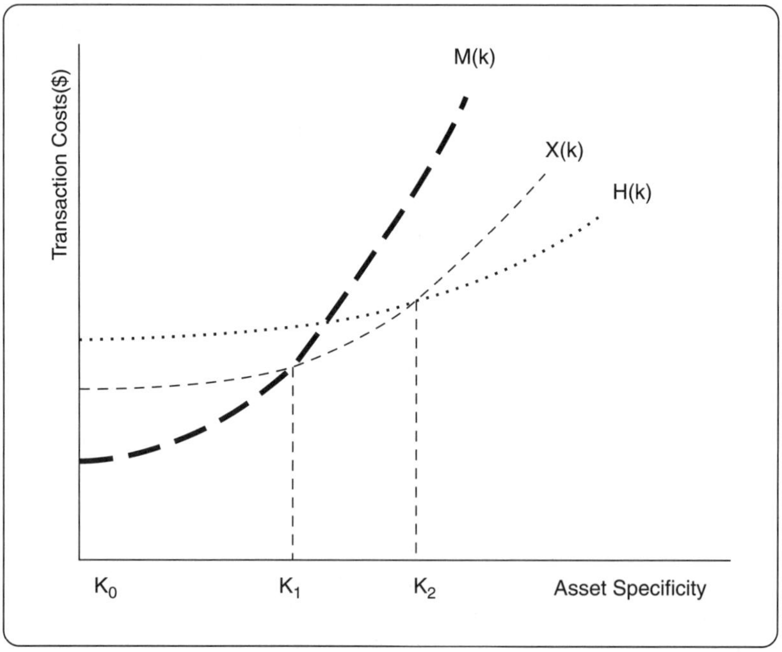

*Notes*: K = asset specificity ($K_0$ = generic investment, $K_1$ = semi-specific investment, $K_2$ = highly specific investment); M = market transaction costs; X = hybrid transaction costs; H = hierarchy transaction costs.
*Sources*: Based on Williamson (1996, p. 108) and Ménard (2004, p. 369).

## *Contract law regime*

Standard types of contract are also known in institutional theory as *classical contracts*. This classical contract law regime applies only to transactions that meet certain criteria.

First, the identity of the partners is irrelevant. Otherwise, one would have to take into account the particular characteristics of the contracting parties. This greatly complicates contracting, and consequently the question arises as to whether the market would still be the most efficient solution.

Second, the nature of the transaction must be defined precisely. Problems can arise if the transaction is not specified exactly, and consequently the deal may lead to an undesirable result for one or both of the parties involved, and will make the preparation of the contract more complicated in order to solve those problems.

Third, because informal (often oral) agreements can easily be the subject of misunderstandings, more formal (generally written) agreements supersede informal agreements.

Fourth, it is not always necessary to specify all details. However, it is important that solutions to possible problems are organized in advance, in a way that makes clear what the consequences will be in case of problems with the exchanged property right.

Finally, classical contracts are supposed to be restricted to the contracting parties. These conditions of a classical contract constitute the so-called ideal market in which transaction partners are autonomous; that is, they are not interrelated. After the transaction, independent transaction partners can each go their own way without incurring significant costs.

## *Property rights*

Without a well-designed system of private property rights, a market would not be able to perform efficiently, if at all. This has been discussed already in Chapter 3. It is in their interest for individuals to do their utmost when the benefits of property rights accrue to them completely. In that case, workers will choose the highest-paying job they are able to perform, and entrepreneurs will produce the most profitable product they are able to bring to the market.

The resulting specialization (with respect to labor and capital as well as to specialization in production) and the possibilities of producing large surpluses imply a need for transactions so that each actor can gain from specialization, obtaining desired surplus goods produced by others.

As long as market alternatives protect each partner in a transaction against opportunistic behavior from their counterpart (buyers can easily move from one supplier to another, and suppliers can easily find an alternative buyer), knowledge about prices will be enough to communicate the relevant information. Economic actors adjust autonomously to changes in the market, which are mainly signaled by changes in prices.

## *Reputation effects*

Reputation does not play a role in the ideal market, where a market exchange takes place through 'anonymous actors'. However, the market structure may deviate from the ideal market. Reputation effects can be important in a competitive market in the case of asset specificity or sequential transactions. First, the lower the reputation of the transaction partner, the higher the need for costly bargaining and contracting. Second, we mentioned in Chapter 3 that reputation is an important institution to safeguard actors from any opportunistic behavior by the transaction partner. The need to uphold one's reputation is pressing in a competitive market environment in which homogeneous products are traded, because buyers can easily switch to another seller.

Reputation may help to ensure that transactions can be enforced without third-party monitoring. However, institutions may be required to help the market to function smoothly. Reputation can be enhanced through quality marks or certification (see Box 5.3), rating services or the experience of other buyers (or sellers) of an identical product that can easily be checked when occasional, nonspecific transactions are being considered. Rating services – as used by eBay and other websites (which ask people trading on the site to rate the performance of the other party), word-of-mouth advertising or tit-for-tat strategies (see Chapter 3) in repeated interactions will in theory at least provide incentives for the seller or the buyer not to behave opportunistically.

> **BOX 5.3  REPUTATION AND THE DIAMOND INDUSTRY**
>
> The diamond trade had been under pressure as a result of its alleged links with 'conflict diamonds', mined by rebel groups to finance wars in Africa; the problem was highlighted by the 2006 Hollywood movie *Blood Diamond*, starring Leonardo DiCaprio.
>
> In 2002, after two years of negotiations between governments, industry and NGOs, the Kimberly Process Certification Scheme (KPCS) was created, in an attempt to restrict the entry of illegitimate diamonds into the market. This certification scheme is an example of a quality mark. Participants must meet the requirements of the KPCS, and can only trade with partners who have also met certain minimum requirements.
>
> The participants in the KPCS claim to have reduced conflict diamonds to less than 0.2 percent of the world's total diamond production by volume (though a report by Amnesty International in 2006 claims that the KPCS has been 'too weak' to end the trade in conflict diamonds).

### Risk

Institutions assist markets to deal with contingencies. The risks of contingencies are many and varied, and can be related to issues of health, the state of the economy (related to the business cycle), safety, culture or weather. Individuals do not know in advance if they will be ill or become unemployed, get robbed, or be involved in an accident. But private actors will perceive these risky situations as business opportunities and may offer safeguards in a variety of forms. As we saw in Chapter 3, people deal with risks by taking out different types and levels of insurance, depending on their risk aversion. Specialized Companies specialize in providing health insurance, unemployment insurance, vehicle insurance, travel insurance and so on. Moreover, weather forecasting bureaus provide customers with probabilities of rainfall, sunshine and ranges of possible temperatures. And health care centers provide influenza vaccinations for people with higher than normal risks of serious complications. In all these examples, (optimizing) private actors in the market adapt unilaterally to risks: in order to enhance efficiency, people (independently) offer or seek safeguards against risks. It is simply a matter of supply and demand, resulting in an equilibrium price.

### Summary

Transactions can take place efficiently via the market when certain conditions are met. From the transaction cost perspective these characteristics are summarized in Table 5.2.

## Different competitive market governance structures

Markets differ in their safeguards, and safeguards do not have to be designed as long as there are no hazards. No interference by auctioneers or go-betweens is needed. However,

**Table 5.2** *The market and the characteristics of its main institutional conditions*

| Conditions / Asset specificity | General to semi-specific |
|---|---|
| Contract law regime | Strongly applicable (classical contract law) |
| Property rights | Individual |
| Reputation effects | Dependent on market structure (many actors) |
| Risk | Unilateral adaptation |

not all markets meet the requirements of the ideal type, but this does not imply that safeguards are created for all markets that do not meet the ideal type. There are market hazards for which no safeguard has been designed. These types of transactions are called *fly-by-night* transactions (see also Chapter 3). Fly-by-night describes businesses that appear and disappear rapidly, and has also been applied to individual traveling tradesmen. The expression implies that the quality of a service or a good sold is so inferior that the person responsible must leave town under cover of darkness to escape from angry customers who do not have the support of a legal authority.

Hazardous transactions without safeguards are embarked on when the costs of safeguarding are relatively high in comparison to the price (or benefits) of the transaction. In these cases, people decide to run the risk of being cheated.

In many other situations, risks may be high enough that it makes sense to take measures to safeguard the transaction. A necessary condition is, of course, that the benefits outweigh the costs. Our next topic is markets that are assisted by institutions to safeguard risks – for example, you may want to know who sold you a product as this information will allow you to return it if it is discovered to have hidden defects. There is often a period of time during which it is legally allowed to return a product if it does not meet the purchaser's expectations.

Free competitive markets can have different forms of organization. An example of a perfectly competitive market form can be found at fruit or flower auctions, where a 'clock' is used to organize the bidding. Buyers sit in a large hall watching a 'clock' that shows descending prices for the product moving in batches on trolleys across the front of the hall. The buyer who presses the button first sets the price and buys the batch. The opposite case is an art auction, based on the principle of raising bids. For more information on different types of auctions, see the Appendix to this Chapter.

Markets also differ based on the way that buyers are informed about the quality of the product. Products are often displayed in advance to give buyers the opportunity to inspect the quality. However, to inform the buyer about the quality of the product, additional information is often necessary. This information may be provided in the form of a label containing the ingredients of the product, a warning that the product is dangerous for the consumer (cigarettes, alcoholic beverages and drugs), a quality mark (organic food, energy rating and all kinds of other ratings) or information on how it is produced (without child labor, or following the concept of Cradle to Cradle, see Box 5.4).

## BOX 5.4  CRADLE TO CRADLE

Cradle to Cradle (C2C) is an innovative approach to the relationship between industry and the environment. It was developed by William McDonough and Michael Braungart (2002) and starts from the view that it is irrational to produce waste, proposing an eco-effective design of products; that is, the design of products has to make use of the intelligence of natural systems.

Nature flourishes in diversity and abundance, which is eventually returned to nature again in the form of nutrition. Applying this concept to industrial production requires products to be designed in such a way that they become available as inputs for the next generation of industrial products. This concept is being applied successfully by Ford and Nike, among others.

In general, prices are generated by supply and demand, assuming given preferences and optimizing utility under bounded rationality and possible opportunistic behavior. However, there is no uniform way in which supply and demand meet each other – the organization of a fish market differs from that of a supermarket or a stock exchange (see Box 5.5).

## BOX 5.5  THE FULTON FISH MARKET

Would you visit a fish market every day for research purposes? Kathryn Graddy of Oxford University did just that. For a month, she got up early and drove to the Fulton Fish Market in New York, observing the transactions of a particular seller and taking notes. She discovered that the Fulton market has several interesting institutional aspects. As prices are not advertised on boards, but are arranged individually with each buyer, there is not perfect information on the price of fish. The fact that fish is a highly differentiated product, with 100 to 300 varieties sold each day, and that prices can also vary according to freshness, makes pricing even more complicated. Additionally, sellers 'were discreet when naming a price. A particular price was for a particular customer' (Graddy, 2006, p. 212).

As a result, Graddy found that, of two customer groups, Asian and white, the Asian customers were getting lower prices. On average, white people paid 6.3 cents per pound more than Asians (for the same quality and type of fish). Why was this?

The first reason is related to the final consumer market: Asian customers tended to come from poor neighborhoods, and used the fish for products such as fish sandwiches. Therefore, they could not raise the price very far, and had to bargain hard at the Fulton market to increase their margins. Sellers in other neighborhoods had less price-sensitive customers, and could explain to their customers that prices were higher on a certain day because they had risen at Fulton.

> Second, Asian buyers seemed to be well organized, with an active retailers' association. This association had the option of buying direct from trawlers, and at one point even boycotted a seller; they claimed he was packing lower weight than stated in each box.
>
> In theory, the Asian buyers could 'arbitrage' the two markets: buying at low prices at the market and selling in the richer neighborhoods, undercutting white retailers. But, according to Graddy (2006, p. 214), 'it is very unlikely that either white buyers or Asian buyers actually knew this [the price differential] was happening'. As well as the sellers being discreet, Asians and whites rarely socialized at the market.

## Opportunism and externalities

Opportunistic behavior has already been addressed in several places in this book. *Ex-ante* opportunism or adverse selection is characterized by *hidden information*. Information that could influence a contract is deliberately not revealed at the moment of negotiation. This can result in, for example, hiring an employee who is not right for the job, or buying a defective product. In this case the counterparty has been misled by erroneous information, resulting in extra costs and unnecessary inefficiencies.

*Ex-post* opportunism or moral hazard refers especially to *hidden action*, which is understood to be undesirable behavior that contract partners develop after the contract has been agreed (see also Box 3.6). One specific form of *ex-post* opportunistic behavior is a hold-up situation, which can arise after a contract has been signed. This situation may occur if at least one of the transaction partners has made a transaction-specific investment that makes him vulnerable to possible abuses on the part of the other contracting party, who could exploit the situation by (re)formulating the provisions of the contract in his own favor. If all parties to an agreement anticipate this possible abuse they will attempt to build in safeguards in the contract to prevent opportunistic behavior. Normally, in business, people do not dare to put all their trust in informal self-enforcing sanction mechanisms such as reputation. They will try to specify a contract as much as possible to cope with future eventualities.

Not only *ex-ante* and *ex-post* opportunism are examples of market imperfections that may be addressed by the market itself, but also externalities. Below we discuss several institutions that have been created to deal with these three forms of market imperfection.

### Adverse selection: markets for lemons

The 2001 Nobel Laureate, George Akerlof, described a model of adverse selection in his seminal article about the market for lemons (Akerlof, 1970). In the USA a *lemon* is the general term for a bad used automobile, and refers to the sour feeling experienced after buying a poor quality article. The model assumes that the seller has more information than the buyer The example shows that, without appropriate institutions, this market will not survive (see Box 5.6).

> **BOX 5.6 THE MARKET FOR USED AUTOMOBILES UNDER ASYMMETRIC INFORMATION**
>
> Assume that the value of a used auto with no defects is $5,000 and the value of a used vehicle with a defect is $4,000. Also assume that there are just as many autos with as without defects. If the quality of the vehicle is not known, the buyer will expect an average quality worth $4,500. So, the buyer (unable to know whether a good or a bad auto is on offer) would certainly not pay more than $4,500. But the seller of a good vehicle would never accept a price lower than $5,000. Although she knows the automobile is good, she is the only partner in the transaction who possesses this information, but is unable to substantiate the claim because people selling bad automobiles would claim the same.
>
> Meanwhile, a seller offering a bad auto would gladly accept any offer larger than $4,000. Hence, in fact, the only option a buyer has is to offer a price no higher than $4,000, with the consequence that only bad autos will be on offer: thus, the market for good used automobiles fails.
>
> This is inefficient, because potentially profitable transactions (involving good autos) will not take place. If there are even more different qualities, the same line of reasoning would lead to the same conclusion: only the lowest-quality used automobiles will be on offer.

In general, the adverse selection problem arises when there are no built-in safeguards to protect the trading partner who has the inferior knowledge: in other words, when there are neither effective public quality assurances (by regulation) nor effective private guarantees. However, in modern societies, several institutions, both informal and formal, have been developed to tackle this problem. In small communities, the reputation mechanism could be quite effective. When trading takes place in more anonymous markets, different devices may assist the ignorant buyer. Think, for example, of a guarantee system backed up by a trustworthy *umbrella organization*, of which the seller has to be a member.

An example of an umbrella organization is the nonprofit Fairtrade Foundation, set up in 1992 by a group of charitable organizations including Oxfam and Christian Aid. It aims to improve the trading position of producers in developing countries, mainly by using a certification system of product labeling. A product displaying the Fairtrade Mark must meet international Fairtrade standards, set by an international body. Among the standards is a minimum price for producers, and social, economic and environmental criteria that must be met over time, such as, for example, increasing the role of women in decision-making.

In sum, when a consumer buys a product that is produced under the Fairtrade label, she knows that the product has been produced under good working conditions and with respect for the environment. Institutions contribute to more trustworthy behavior on the part of sellers because the accompanying sanctions serve as deterrents.

## Moral hazard: hold-up

The concept of hold-up was illustrated in Box 3.8, which described a contemporary hold-up situation between Gazprom and the Ukraine. In the economic literature there is a well-known hold-up case, which occurred in the first half of the twentieth century: the case of Fisher Body and General Motors.

While there has been considerable scientific debate about whether the central problem in this case could in fact be considered as a hold-up (see the series of articles about this controversy in the *Journal of Law and Economics* of 2000, among others by Coase and Klein), researchers agree that this case is a classic example of problems regarding the decision of whether to buy on the market, or to make the product oneself within a hierarchy, and what circumstances influence the decision. The Fisher Body case is presented in Box 5.7.

### BOX 5.7 THE FISHER BODY CASE

Fisher Body (FB) was an independent and very successful coachbuilder in the USA. Led by the two Fisher brothers, it delivered vehicle bodies to several large automobile producers, including General Motors (GM), with which it signed a long-term contract in 1919. GM had decided to buy these auto parts in the market place, instead of making them itself. Because both parties realized that their relationship would involve several transaction-specific investments and therefore could be susceptible to possible abuse, the contract contained a number of clauses as safeguards.

The first contractual provision was an exclusive dealing clause, stating that GM was obliged to buy metal bodies from FB for a period of as long as ten years. In this way, the parties prevented the possibility of GM creating a hold-up situation for FB, because FB would make considerable specialized investments tailored to GM's needs (which were useless or less useful for other companies).

This clause by itself, however, could have turned the tables in FB's favor: with this stipulation GM would be forced to purchase from FB even if the latter increased its prices or reduced its quality. Therefore a second and a third clause were also incorporated, establishing a specific price formula to ensure that FB would charge a competitive price (the price would equal variable cost plus a surcharge of 17.6 percent to cover anticipated capital cost) on the one hand, and a most-favored purchaser provision on the other, stating that FB had to charge the same price for similar bodies to all of its customers.

No contract can ever specify all future states of the world, so neither did the contract between GM and FB. However, because both parties were prominent and reputable companies, maintaining their reputations was an additional silent (self-enforcing) provision; the parties could consider this informal institution as an extra safeguard.

This contract worked very well until 1924. In these first five years, FB invested heavily in assembly plants located in the vicinity of GM factories. However, from 1925 the market situation started to change rapidly, because the demand for 'closed automobiles' (made of metal instead of wood) increased substantially, as a result of which GM needed many more bodies produced by FB; in just two years, sales from FB to GM grew by around 200 percent. By refusing to locate a body-producing plant near a large GM facility, the Fisher brothers were able to put pressure on GM. For FB, the possible gains of renegotiating the terms of the contract had become bigger than the possible costs resulting from loss of reputation. As Klein *et al.* (1988, p. 202) put it, 'the large increase in demand placed Fisher's short-run hold-up potential of General Motors...outside the self-enforcing range'.

In the course of 1925, GM started to experience body shortages and had to reduce production. This over-dependence on one supplier made the board of directors of GM decide in 1926 that it was best to take complete control of FB. GM bought all FB's shares, completing the vertical integration of the two firms; and the buy-decision was replaced by the make-decision.

*Sources:* Klein *et al.* (1988); Klein (2000); Roider (2006).

## *Externalities*

An externality occurs when someone's actions affect another party without compensation. If the person is affected negatively by the action, then one would expect the action in question to be regulated by law. However, this is not necessarily the case when negotiations are costless. Coase argued that, when there are no transaction costs, a dispute with regard to externalities results in an efficient outcome, regardless of how the law assigns responsibility for damages (see Chapter 3).

When negotiations are not costless, then we no longer get the most efficient outcome, irrespective of the attribution of responsibilities or, alternatively, property rights. An example is given with the aid of Table 5.3. Suppose that the noise of the operation of a confectioner's business disturbs a doctor, and that the gain to the doctor in a noise-free environment is £400 and the gain to the confectioner operating his business is £600. Furthermore, suppose that a soundproofing device costs £200, and that transaction costs for a private agreement are £250.

If the confectioner is not liable for the noise damage, the doctor will have to abandon his practice at the current location. It does not make sense for him to install a soundproofing device at his own cost: if he does, his total cost will be £450 (namely £250

Table 5.3  *The influence of institutions on running a business*

| Legal regime | Outcome | Net benefit | | |
| --- | --- | --- | --- | --- |
| | | Doctor | Confectioner | Total |
| Confectioner is liable | Confectioner installs soundproofing | £400 | £600 minus £200 | £800 |
| Confectioner is not liable | Doctor abandons practice | £0 | £600 | £600 |

transaction costs and £200 for the soundproofing system). If the confectioner is made liable for noise damage, then the efficient outcome is for the confectioner to install a soundproofing device for the doctor.

## THE STATIC VESTED INTEREST APPROACH TO MARKETS

Earlier we described spot markets, contingent markets and markets that are assisted by institutions. Spot markets and contingent markets are assumed to result in theoretical efficient outcomes, as defined by the model of *perfect competition* (see below). Efficiency is also improved if the benefits of institutions outweigh costs. However, efficiency cannot be taken for granted. Oligopolies and monopolies also operate in markets, and may exhibit their power in different forms, one of them being that market inefficiencies occur because of anti-competitive behavior.

### Market power

Perfect competition is the market situation in which each individual producer has no market power, with market power being defined as a situation with a price higher than marginal costs. In general terms, a monopoly has the most extreme form of market power: monopoly power. But there are many market situations with two or more producers who compete with each other, though they each may have some market power in the sense described above: price higher than marginal costs. So, almost any situation of imperfect competition will imply (some) market power for individual producers.

Hence, market power comes by degrees. There may be very little market power if there are many producers who each produce slightly different products (very little heterogeneity, but without reaching homogeneity): there will be some market power because heterogeneity implies that each producer has her own group of customers, but these customers will be able to move to a competing, but slightly different, product very easily. One can also imagine a situation with only two producers and conclude that each might have a lot of market power. However, two competitors in a market may compete so intensely that prices are driven down to marginal costs, therefore in practice their degree of market power may be low or even absent.

Even in a monopoly situation, the conclusion that there is monopoly power (the highest degree of market power) could be mistaken. Suppose that it is very easy to enter the market. Then potential competition could put very high competitive pressure on the monopolist, to the extent that she is forced to charge a price equal to marginal costs. Therefore, in general, there is no direct, straightforward relationship between the degree of market power and the number of producers. Still, it is safe to say that in a situation where there are many producers with slightly differentiated products (or a homogeneous product), market power is low. On the other hand, it would be wrong to link a high degree of market power automatically to a low number of firms in the market.

In reality, it can prove to be impossible, unrealistic or undesirable to determine marginal costs, and therefore to determine the profit maximizing price level exactly. In such cases, prices will be determined differently; they are called *administered prices,* and can be found in sectors that are planned by the state, such as the public health system or energy networks (we shall deal with topic of state intervention in Part IV of this book), or sectors that are operated by large corporations, such as automobiles and pharmaceuticals. Prices are set by administrators whose main concern is, for example, to maintain a certain market share over the long run rather than to encourage short-run profit maximization. Manufacturers set prices in order to cover all costs and to provide a profit margin. This phenomenon is called *mark-up pricing*.

In addition to mark-up pricing, oligopolies and monopolies have the option of applying price discrimination in order to reap higher profits. *Price discrimination* requires firms to be able to distinguish between buyers, and arbitrage is not possible (arbitrage means that an individual buys a product cheaply from one group of sellers and resells it to a group buying at a higher price; in the end this will equalize the price level). The more easily buyers can be distinguished, the higher the discriminatory power of monopolies. They can then charge different (groups of individual) buyers different prices: students might be offered discount subscriptions on magazines; membership fees of several scientific organizations such as the American Economic Association vary according to members' income; commuters outside rush hours may often travel at a discount rate; tourists may pay a higher price for public transport than locals; and people flying in the same airplane will generally have paid widely differing prices. Many other examples can easily be brought to mind.

The creation of market power through product differentiation, innovation and superior products or production processes is intrinsic to the competitive process. But market power can also be created by eliminating competition. In the case of existing market power, this can also be used anti-competitively.

To start with existing market power, let us assume that we have a monopolist (the highest degree of market power) – for example, because she is offering a superior product. As already noted, this in itself may provide incentives for others to enter the market. However, the monopolist uses different means to hinder potential entrants. In some cases it might be possible for the monopolist to lobby the government to obtain a position as exclusive provider, so that entry would be impossible or difficult for other companies.

Another possibility to hinder entrants is to engage in long-term exclusive contracting with customers. Of course, this would only be logical in the case of intermediate production, and not for a monopolist who supplies consumers. With long-term exclusive contracting, entry may be delayed for at least the period of the contracts.

Yet another possibility is to engage in or threaten competitors with 'predatory pricing'. Predatory pricing implies (in general) a short-term pricing policy that is loss-leading and therefore so unattractive to a (potential) competitor that he will leave the market (or not enter at all), so that afterwards, high profits can be reaped by the monopolist (*recoupment*). Such a policy can be seen as an investment in prolonging the monopoly position.

Note that such forms of behavior are not restricted to monopolists. A large firm facing a small number of competitors may also engage in this type of behavior. Generally speaking, this behavior of hindering competition is related to so-called dominant firms. *Dominance* is not a well-defined concept, but involves at least the criteria that the firm must be large (in terms of market share), competitors must be small (also in terms of market share), and there are entry barriers to the market.

We have seen earlier that a monopolist need not necessarily be able to exercise monopoly power because of potential competition in the case of very low entry barriers. It would be very difficult for such a monopolist to engage in anticompetitive behavior, unless this would lead to the creation of high entry barriers. Long-term exclusive contracts could be such a barrier, but customers are unlikely to agree to this type of deal if they know that better options can or will be available in the near future. Still, under some circumstances, the monopolist might be able to 'bribe' his customers into long-term contracting.

Predatory pricing in the case of easy entry cannot be effective: a potential competitor will definitely not enter the market, but prices will still be low for consumers, while the monopolist will not be able to profit from the fact that no entry occurs. If the monopolist started charging a much higher price, the potential competitor would simply enter the market in any case. Therefore, the monopolist might just as well not predate.

So, in general, market power will not pose a problem if firms are small. But if firms are large, further and specific investigation is needed, especially with regard to entry barriers, in order to determine whether a specific form of behavior is hampering competition.

### Creation of market power

Dominance can itself be created by anticompetitive means. To see this, let us illustrate the concept of a competitor. A competitor of firm A is a firm (or are the firms) that most customers will turn to in the case of a price rise by A, so that this price rise will be unprofitable (if the firms are in equilibrium). By raising prices simultaneously by mutual consent, therefore, competitors can restrict competition.

In practice, there are three ways of eliminating competition in this context. The first is to merge: two (or more) competing firms become one. This topic will be discussed in Chapter 6. The second way to eliminate competition is if each of the rivals, A and B, knows that if A raises his price, then so can B, and vice versa. Clearly, such a situation is unlikely if there are many firms. This situation is restricted to (small) oligopolies; a relatively small number of firms, where each of them has to take the other firms' behavior into account. With a large number of firms it would be impossible (or at least very costly) to take into account the behavior of many firms. The third way is to make an explicit agreement with rivals to raise prices together. We shall discuss the second and third methods in Chapter 7.

## THE DYNAMIC EFFICIENCY APPROACH TO MARKETS

Above we looked only at market outcomes, *ceteris paribus*, for technology, institutions and preferences. Here we focus on the process of coordination of individual decisions under two conditions: first, there are gaps in our knowledge that need to be filled; and second, preferences change.

If there are gaps in our knowledge, these may be filled by knowledge resulting from market interaction; that is, from the selling and buying of commodities. By trial and error, one may learn what is profitable and what is not. This trial and error process is set in motion by entrepreneurs, whose main characteristic is being alert to new market opportunities; through their alertness, entrepreneurs keep the market in motion.

## Market process theory

According to Hayek's metaphor of the footpath (see Chapter 4), markets are self-regulating devices that promote prosperity. In a perfectly competitive market, people decide for themselves how best to make use of economic opportunities, and the government confines itself to establishing and monitoring the rules that provide the conditions under which available resources may be used. However, it is important to note that these rules are important for the pursuit of people's individual aims. Knowledge about the market is distributed over a huge number of individuals and no single actor or group of experts knows everything, nor can deal with all available information. In a sense, everybody is handicapped by not having enough information to decide what is the best overall use of available resources.

In theory, this problem is solved via the perfectly competitive market that leads to allocative efficiency. Under perfect competition, prices act as communication signals, reflecting not only information about the particular circumstances of place and time, but also about changes in conditions. One example is the aging of the population, which may have far-reaching consequences related to consumer requirements, leading to an increase in demand for wheelchair-accessible vans, wheelchair ramps, elevators and so on. It also may increase the demand for clothing for older people, or lead to a greater choice of ready meals offered by supermarkets. A rise in demand for elevators will result in a price increase, *ceteris paribus*, and this increase will signal to a producer the need to produce more elevators. In a perfect market, this is easily coordinated through the price system.

However, because sell and buy decisions are widely dispersed in reality, finding the market clearing price is a discovery process, with disequilibrium prices along the way. Of course, disequilibrium prices also coordinate market decisions about offers and bids. Both sellers and buyers will learn from suboptimal results. But disequilibrium prices do not clear the market, and sellers will be disappointed if they are not able to sell all their products, and find themselves with an involuntary surplus stock. They will also be disappointed if they realize that demand is much larger than expected, so they are short of products to sell. Buyers will also be disappointed when they discover that they cannot buy as many products as they wish, or that they could have paid a lower price because of an excess of products.

Disequilibrium prices generate flows of information that result in a revision of initially uncoordinated decisions and result in a better coordination of market decisions. They coordinate market decisions because they reveal to buyers as well as to sellers how different decisions result in an outcome that comes closer to their desires. Prices that are too high will signal to sellers who were unable to sell as much as they wanted, to lower their prices.

Entrepreneurs may learn from profit or loss opportunities embedded in prevailing prices. Imagine that people who have an insurance contract that covers new spectacles decide to buy four new pairs per year, perhaps because they want to have a frame for every season. After some time, the insurance company will discover that it has underestimated the risk of insured shortsighted people demanding new spectacles. The insurer has underestimated the moral hazard behavior of the insured. As a result either the terms of the contract will be changed or the price will be increased, or both.

The market coordinates sellers' and buyers' decisions, not only at equilibrium prices, as is shown in the static partial analysis of the market, but also at disequilibrium prices, through the process of discovery. Because of the process of discovery, the best use of resources can be achieved only when the market is viewed as a process that generates information that can be used by those that are most able to do so.

## *The role of entrepreneurs*

Alert entrepreneurs are the driving force behind the process of acquiring more knowledge of potential demand and supply attitudes. Entrepreneurship is human action in a world of uncertainty, as in the thinking of Knight; that is, a world in which outcomes are uncertain in the sense that they cannot be expressed in terms of probability. In a world of uncertainty, it is the function of entrepreneurs to decide what to do and how to do it. Entrepreneurs are prepared to bear the costs of uncertainty (Knight, 1921). In other words, entrepreneurship can be viewed as an institutional answer to the problem of uncertainty. Entrepreneurship is an important institution in modern Western societies (see, for example, Brandl and Bullinger, 2009). Stories about heroic and successful entrepreneurs, educational programs and access to venture capital can all stimulate entrepreneurial skills.

An entrepreneur acts on changes in prices and output that occur in the market. He also sometimes acts when he does not know the prices at all. His world does not consist only of given prices and output data, though – boldness, imagination and drive are the main sources of his decision-making, because he needs to discover unknown market opportunities. In this case, an entrepreneur is not necessarily somebody who (also) manages a firm (see Chapter 6).

A good entrepreneur is continuously alert to market opportunities. These are not only the result of imperfect information but also of unknown ignorance. Imperfect information refers to information that is known to be available but which is costly to acquire. Unknown ignorance is previously undiscovered knowledge – ignorance that can only be reduced through a surprise discovery; that is, one is not aware of one's ignorance until the moment of surprise (Kirzner, 1997).

Entrepreneurial boldness and imagination are not always translated into profits; they may also lead to losses. Entrepreneurial misreading of the market may manifest itself in shortages, overproduction or misallocated resources. This, though, is the price entrepreneurs pay for being successful too; generally speaking, the value of the successes will outweigh the losses resulting from entrepreneurial failure. In competitive markets, entrepreneurial errors are corrected through the responses of alert entrepreneurs to the opportunities that are revealed as a result of the errors. By being alert to market opportunities, entrepreneurs compete continuously for their market share.

The profits that emerge from entrepreneurial activities are the reward for the discovery of the market opportunity. Most of the time, this will involve *incremental innovations*; that is, innovations that fit the market and involve low uncertainty. These kinds of innovation contrast with *radical innovation*, which involves the discovery of something valuable that was not known before. This type of discovery may include the discovery of unknown natural resources, product innovation or process innovation. *Product innovation* means developing a new or 'renewed' product or service, while *process innovation* is a change in the way that products or services are produced. Both may affect the structure of the market and can involve high risks.

Entrepreneurship is embedded in societal institutions. First, the social context of entrepreneurial activities influences their level in a society. Social support includes perceptions about the role of monetary profit and the *stigma of failure*; that is, how the market treats entrepreneurial failures. When monetary profits are regarded highly in society, this will support entrepreneurial activities. As to the stigma of failure, if entrepreneurial failure is considered shameful in a certain society, individuals will be more reluctant to become involved in such activities. Entrepreneurship will flourish in countries where entrepreneurial failure is seen as proof that somebody has been daring enough to exploit a possible market opportunity.

Second, formal institutions, such as financial institutions and property rights, are also essential for entrepreneurial activity. As we shall describe in greater depth in Chapter 9, formal institutions will not be conducive to entrepreneurship if laws often change and the legislative process is susceptible to influence from pressure groups. Influence from these groups may redirect entrepreneurial incentives from productive activities towards unproductive ones to obtain privileges from the state, for example. And informal institutions, such as the custom of bribing officials to obtain permits and licenses also hamper productive entrepreneurship. The topic of pressure groups and bribes is beyond the efficiency approach and comes closer to the vested interest approach (see Chapter 9).

## *The entrepreneur as a dynamic force*

The concept of equilibrium loses its significance from the point of view of entrepreneurship. An equilibrium, if it exists, is likely to be fleeting, because existing market conditions are changed by every entrepreneurial decision to exploit a new market opportunity. For example, the discovery of the internet created a whole range of market opportunities, some of which compete with traditional market opportunities and challenge entrepreneurs to discover new ones.

## *Creative destruction*

The introduction of new products or processes may have a destabilizing effect on the development of firms, and consequently on the economy. This can be a result of the process of *creative destruction* (Schumpeter, 1942), in which new capital and production processes replace existing ones. Creative destruction also includes the destruction of existing institutional settings to organize new combinations of economic resources or to make new products.

When innovations occur in clusters this may have dramatic effects for employment. Huge amounts of capital may be depreciated for economic reasons, despite the fact that 'old' capital could still be technically productive. In other words, the 'old' capital may no longer be profitable enough to beat the competition of entrepreneurs who produce a new design or cheaper products using new equipment, new sources of labor or raw materials, new methods of organization and management, new methods of transportation, new methods of communication, new methods of advertising, and so on.

The consequence of an early economic depreciation of capital is that workers employed in these 'old' industries become unemployed, while the 'new' industries urgently need employees who are able to work with the new methods. This often results in *frictional unemployment*; that is, a mismatch between the supply of and demand for labor, and requires the unemployed to be retrained.

The consequences of creative destruction are not limited to changes in economic structure. It also results in new institutions, as the following two examples illustrate:

- The internet is at the heart of the recent wave of ICT. With the operation of computers becoming increasingly fast, they are able to handle more and more information. This encourages increasing numbers of new services and opportunities. But this also calls for new institutions. For example, issues such as intellectual property in the context of the internet, safety for users of the internet and the (ab)use of information on it must be dealt with.
- Innovations clustered around genetic manipulation will probably prove to be another example. These innovations may concern the production of food, development of drugs, prenatal testing and the treatment of patients, with many resulting problems of safety and liability, being obvious examples.

In sum, changes in the economic structure through innovation not only result in structural change in the economy but also in new institutions. Just as old capital and old products become outdated and are replaced, so institutions have to adapt.

### *New products require a change in preferences*

New products or new features must first become known to consumers or customers. When people are ignorant of new products or new features they cannot buy them. That is why commercial advertisements may be seen as a source of information. However, because of opportunistic behavior, they may be deceptive as well.

As discussed earlier, the static approach to markets takes institutions and individuals as given. It is not denied that individual wishes and preferences are influenced by circumstances, but these changes are not integrated into static economic analysis. Given preferences, property rights, legally enforceable contracts and other parameters, the most efficient institutional setting is chosen for the different markets. Because not every transaction requires the same institutional safeguard, different transactions may be embedded in different institutions. The market is a relatively heterogeneous and differentiated entity, where different mechanisms operate.

In the dynamic approach to markets, prices are not the result of demand and supply in a context where institutions and characteristics of individuals are taken as given. Cultural settings, pricing procedures and tacit knowledge affect market outcomes and are influenced by the market outcomes themselves. Bowles (1998) describes how allocation rules in different cultural settings based on such things as kinship, grants, negotiation or market exchange affect personality, habits, tastes and values, and consequently also preferences. In other words, preferences are 'endogenous'; that is, they are not a given, but at least partly created. The view that preferences are also socially determined and that they may change according to social conditions implies that prices are not simply the outcome of supply and demand but also of social constructs (conventions), as discussed in Chapter 4.

All institutions involved in the process of price formation are relevant to understanding prices, but distribution and promotion decisions also have to be taken into account. Information about (potential) consumers (what is the elasticity of demand?) and competing suppliers is essential. It is important to know how competitors will respond to your pricing. If you set your prices too low it may result in a price war, but if too high it may attract other competitors. If you collude with other suppliers, this is usually a violation of the law worldwide. Generally, if you discriminate in pricing, this is not seen as a violation of the law, but in the USA individual states may formulate their own laws in this respect – in Missouri, for example, it might fall under the state's Anti Price Discrimination Laws.

Furthermore, you have to decide what your pricing objectives are. And what price strategy you will use. Will you attempt to aim for the qualitative top of the market, or do you want to sell as much as possible? Or do you pursue both aims? These questions illustrate that pricing does not just mean simple equilibrium price taking.

## Institutional entrepreneurs

Previously we stated that entrepreneurs are constantly seeking new market opportunities, and that they combine resources in order to exploit these. However, this is not only what they do. Entrepreneurs who want to start a new line of production or who want to expand their businesses also often have to cope with existing institutional barriers. Entry restrictions are common kinds of institutional barriers, and there are regulations that restrict businesses as soon as they are established, such as labor and safety regulations.

Entrepreneurs who help to set up market institutions are called institutional entrepreneurs. They not only have to integrate resources, as they are supposed to do in the traditional concept of an entrepreneur, but may also have to overcome institutional restraints. They may develop a new governance structure (such as a new type of contract, or a new network) in order to overcome such institutional barriers. For example, rules that give a worker a right of tenure may be avoided by hiring employees through temporary employment agencies. Which strategies may be applied by an institutional entrepreneur to overcome institutional restrictions?

Every entrepreneur has four possible strategies to change the rules. First, he may campaign openly for a change in prevailing institutions, using the media, or attending public forums or conferences. Second, he may lobby privately for a change in the rules. Third, he can argue to be exempted from prevailing rules because he is a special case. Finally, he can start his business without complying with existing rules. If he becomes successful, he could use this fact to justify the business and persuade the authorities to legitimize his investment (see Box 5.8).

Institutional changes initiated by entrepreneurs who want to make the most of new market opportunities may open new paths for other entrepreneurs to begin or expand their business activities. In other words, institutional entrepreneurs create positive externalities and as a result may enhance economic wealth. For the role of institutional entrepreneurs, see the work of Nathan Rosenberg (2009) on the importance of institutions for innovation, Rodrik (2004, 2008), Rodrik et al. (2004) on the right institutions, and Hausmann and Rodrik (2003, 2005) on cost discovery and externalities.

> **BOX 5.8 INSTITUTIONAL ENTREPRENEURS IN EMERGING MARKET ECONOMIES**
>
> In 1998, Li Shufu decided to expand his motorcycle business in China to include the private production of automobiles. Initially, the auto he made was a crudely built hatchback, but through learning and imitation it eventually developed into a range of sedans and sports cars with an international demand.
>
> At the beginning, Li Shufu did not have an official permit for his business. At that time, vehicle manufacturing was a state affair. However, from the early 1990s the political climate in China began to change. Incomes were rising and Li Shufu believed that people would soon be able to afford autos. Once he became convinced of the market potential of his Geely automobile he took the risk of starting up as a private auto manufacturer. To enable him to sell his vehicles in China, he lobbied local and central authorities, and in 2001 was given government approval to do so. Following Geely, other auto manufacturers also entered the market. Thanks to Li Shufu's path-breaking activities, licensing was no longer a barrier for private auto manufacturers wishing to enter the market (Li *et al.*, 2006).

## *Cumulative causation*

Economic forces interact in such a way that every change brings other supporting changes. This idea lies at the center of the concept of cumulative causation, introduced in Chapter 4. An example is the development of Silicon Valley in California. The concentration of high-tech businesses started here with the development of the electronics industry in the early twentieth century. The first radio station in the USA was set up in San Jose in 1909. Its development was supported by Stanford University and its affiliates. In the 1920s, because of a lack of jobs in the area, Stanford University encouraged graduates to start their own companies near the university, in the northern part of Santa Clara Valley. This initiative was followed up in the 1950s with the development of Stanford Industrial Park, which was designed to be a center of high technology that cooperated closely with Stanford University. Eventually, with the development of computer technology and programming companies, the area became known as Silicon Valley and was dominated by computer-based businesses. The location of Stanford University in the Valley, the development of the radio industry, the decision to establish an Industry Park for high-tech firms, and cooperation with military bases in Northern California were mutually enforcing developments.

The idea of cumulative causation is that expanding domestic markets result in increasing production possibilities in a specific location, which in turn attracts new companies. This expands production even further, and the whole ongoing process results in economic growth. The theory of cumulative causation thus helps to explain why development is unequal across regions. It suggests that an initial expansion can lead to a continuous expansion of industries and regions. On the other hand, an initial decline may result in a continuous decline. However, the degree of interrelatedness increases as cumulative causation develops. A higher degree of relatedness implies that components of the production process become more and more interconnected. Consequently, adjustment to marginal changes in techniques will become more complex, because a marginal change in one component may need changes in all related components.

## THE DYNAMIC VESTED INTERESTS APPROACH TO MARKETS

It is undeniable that technological change has an enormous impact on society and the economy. Through technological development we have been able to produce more than any generation before us. Living standards have improved in the industrialized world for almost everybody. Yet this development has also had unwanted consequences, a few of which we shall discuss here from the point of view of dynamic vested interests.

## Change implies a redistribution of costs and benefits

As introduced in Chapter 1, bargaining occurs between parties who are equal before the law but who are not necessarily equal in social and economic power. This raises the question of how much disparity in power is acceptable between contracting parties. When power is distributed too unequally, bargaining may result in conflict, and outcomes may be perceived as being unfair. Institutional arrangements can provide a framework for these bargains. For example, the unequal distribution of power between the unemployed and potential employers can be balanced by such means as implementing the institution of a minimum wage and unemployment payments to protect the unemployed from being exploited. Another example is the institution of alimony, which was introduced to prevent divorced and jobless women from becoming dependent on social security or charity. However, not all institutional arrangements are designed to solve problems for society as a whole, as we shall discuss below.

### *Changing power balances*

One of the largest economic impacts of technological development has been the division and subdivision of practical tasks into multiple components. For example, personal computers consist of several components that are produced in different countries. Some are produced in China, Thailand or India, and the final assembly may be in yet another country.

The traditional entrepreneur who both owned and managed a company has given way increasingly to owners who hire professionals such as executive officers and policy advisers (leading administrators, scientists and lawyers) to cope with the important aspect of the organization of knowledge, thus ensuring the success of a business. With the replacement of the individual owner/manager of a firm by this group of professionals, new information and reporting systems have come into existence in order to guide, control and assess the performance of these professionals.

Together with the rise of new information and reporting systems, such as cost accounting, a wide range of new financial arrangements were developed in order to meet the rising demand for finance for big business. Bond markets and stock markets expanded, along with the rise of bank syndicates and insurance industries. Eventually, banks and insurance firms became the largest corporations in modern economies. Some banks are classified as *system banks*, which means that these banks are too big to allow them to become bankrupt. Bankruptcy of a system bank would lead to a complete collapse of the economy, because not only would pension funds and shareholders lose a lot of money, but mainly because all trust in the financial system might disappear. Examples of system banks are the Bank of America and Citigroup.

The advancement of technology requires increasing investment in time, money and specialized personnel. In order to protect these investments from fluctuations in demand, it is in the vested interest of the executive officers and policy advisers (referred to below as executives) to control the market for the products they supply; this is also known as the *privately planned economy*. As long as they are able to control the market for the products they produce, to a certain extent they are not subject to the risks inherent to market competition. A sharp downturn of the market endangers profits. This may be evaded by influencing consumer preferences, and by creating barriers to prevent competitors from entering the market. In Chapter 1 we mentioned how Microsoft blocked other producers from entering the software market successfully. The abuse of its dominant position was punished by the European Commission in 2007 in order to open market opportunities for competitors.

Consumers' preferences are influenced by advertisements and other activities such as sponsoring or organizing events. First, buyers need to learn about the existence of the new product. Second, because innovation goes beyond buyers' routine-based decision-making, they will usually not be convinced automatically about the usefulness of the new product, and will need to be persuaded to change their preferences. Marketing employees have several instruments at their disposal to accomplish this. Among other things, they may influence buyers by giving (small) presents in combination with the purchase. They may refer in their advertisements to the positive experiences of other consumers. They also may employ physically attractive and/or familiar retail employees in order to increase sales. Or they may make use of psychological insights to display goods in an attractive fashion.

With the analysis of the influence of producers on consumer behavior, the relationship between producer and consumer is reversed. In the conventional market analysis, consumers are sovereign and their decisions govern economic life: the customer is always right. In the privately planned approach, however, large firms do not satisfy consumers' demands; it is the executives who try to persuade the consumer to buy by spending money on advertisements. The concept of *revised sequence* (Galbraith, 1974) between consumer and producer suggests producer sovereignty over consumer sovereignty.

## *Private affluence, public poverty*

The efforts of executives to control the market have created a consumer society, by promoting consumption through several marketing channels such as television commercials. They also influence consumers by sponsoring mass media and big events ranging from pop concerts to sport. And finally, they influence consumers through politics by lobbying, sponsoring political events and so on.

These executives try to persuade the electorate and politicians that what serves the purpose of technologically highly advanced business also serves the public interest.

Where the executives are powerful, the state responds strongly to their needs. This will be discussed in greater detail in Chapter 9 under the heading of regulatory capture.

## *Countervailing power*

In the modern world, and in case of few sellers in a certain market, private economic power is sometimes held in check by power from the opposite side of the market (Galbraith, 1952). Hence the term *countervailing power*. Individuals may organize themselves in order to improve their negotiation position. For example, workers may form trade unions to provide a counter power to large firms, and consumer organizations may try to influence firms to produce goods that conform to ethical principles. Consumers may require a guarantee that there is no child labor involved in the production process.

If consumers demand products and services that do not have a negative impact on the environment, on animals or on workers, it pays to provide these goods and services (see also Box 5.9). From this point of view, ethical business may also be profitable for shareholders. A corporate code of conduct and quality marks help to communicate the ethical principles of the business.

---

### BOX 5.9  THE EFFECT OF CONSUMER BOYCOTTS

Media reports can have a strong influence on a company's fortunes. Critical newspapers and television programs watch closely whether organizations are behaving responsibly and, if not, these organizations may get 'bad press'. Unfavorable reports lead in turn to a decline in sales, or in the worst case (for the company, at least) to a complete consumer boycott.

History shows many examples of effective consumer bans. In the 1970s and 1980s, consumers worldwide demanded that Shell, Kellogg's and Coca-Cola (among others) withdraw from South Africa. By not buying the products of these companies any longer, people aimed to convince the shareholders to put pressure on managers to stop doing business with the apartheid regime. Eventually, this strategy contributed to the fall of the regime.

In the 1990s, Shell again was the object of consumer protests when it tried to dump a large oil rig (the Brent Spar) in the Atlantic Ocean. The spectacular protest actions by environmental organization Greenpeace were reported in newspapers all over the world and inspired many consumers to stop buying fuel from Shell; in Germany, the sale of Shell fuel declined by 50 percent in just a few weeks. Additionally, several European governments turned against Shell's decision, after which the plan was quickly abandoned.

Many more examples exist. Today, adverse publicity reaches consumers through television, radio, newspapers and, increasingly, through the internet. Try typing 'consumer boycott' in Google; you will find numerous organizations that publish news about objectionable practices carried out by firms in many different sectors and countries.

## Two ideal types of labor market: Continental European versus Anglo-Saxon

Organized groups might not only have an influence on output decisions of large firms on product markets, but also the functioning of labor markets. Their actual influence may be dependent on the overarching culture of the society, which may be divided roughly into a Continental European culture and an Anglo-Saxon one. Bearing in mind that the two corresponding models are ideal types that do not fully correspond to reality, labor markets in the two models can be broadly characterized as follows. The main features of the Continental European approach are income security and the protection of collective interests, while the Anglo-Saxon approach features labor market flexibility and the protection of individual interests.

Some of the stylized differences between the Continental European and Anglo-Saxon models with regard to the labor market are summarized in Table 5.4.

In the countries that conform to the Continental European model, the approach to the labor market is based on institutionalized mutual consultation between employers

Table 5.4 *The domain of the labor market within the Continental European and Anglo-Saxon models*

| Aspects | Continental European model | Anglo-Saxon model |
|---|---|---|
| Position of workers within the firm | Management not only has to take into account the interests of shareholders but also the interests of employees, who have codetermination rights and sizable employment protection | Employees work in a very competitive environment, they are considered to be production factors and can be hired and dismissed at will |
| Type of contract | Stable; employees live in the vicinity of the firm and employers invest in the education of employees | Dual labor market: alongside a group of tenured workers there are fringe workers with flexible contracts |
| Labor productivity | Often high because of the investment in schooling and commitment of employees, and because strikes are rare | Sometimes low because of the relatively low commitment of employees. Sometimes high as a result of high-powered incentives in the form of profit-sharing schemes |
| Payment of employees | Payment is according to one's position. It is laid down in a collective labor agreement, offers stability of income and decreases managerial discretion | Scarcity determines payment. Payment varies according to the skills and performance of the employee. The payment level is negotiated individually or via company unions |

and employees. Wages are negotiated most often at sector level by collective labor agreements that are concluded by representatives of the national unions and national employers' organizations. Furthermore, employees are predominantly remunerated according to their position. This system of payment avoids permanent negotiations and offers income security. Depending on the labor market situation, sometimes the employees have more bargaining power (such as in prosperous times, when there are many vacancies) and sometimes the employers are in a position to leave their mark on the outcome of the collective agreement (as during a slump).

The government usually applies the sector-level agreement to all firms and employees in an industry, whether or not they were represented during the negotiations. The idea behind this institutional arrangement is that it prevents underbidding by nonorganized employers, thus reducing wage competition. At the same time, it means that nonunion members are also entitled to the wage increases that have been negotiated by the unions. Hence, in countries conforming to the Continental European model, the outcome of the wage bargaining is usually not the result of individual demand and supply but rather the result of a cooperative bargaining process that subsequently holds also for the collective.

Within the countries following the Anglo-Saxon model, the approach to the labor market is based on the *laissez-faire* principle, which assumes that individuals know best what is the most important aspect for them. Even though, in these countries, there are national union confederations and national employers' organizations, the focus of wage negotiations is at the company level, where trade unions do their utmost to represent their members, if necessary by means of strikes. Because of the focus on the protection of the interests of individual members, this bargaining system is also referred to as the *insider–outsider model*. This implies that a powerful union can enforce a relatively high pay for its members within the firm (the insiders), at great expense for the employer. This high cost of meeting these wages in turn causes the employer to hire fewer workers, which is to the detriment of people looking for a job (the outsiders).

## CONCLUDING REMARKS

Markets can be highly efficient means of transacting goods and services, as is pointed out by neoclassical economic theory. However, the benefits claimed by that model are dependent on a number of highly specific assumptions, and these benefits diminish or disappear when the assumptions are not fulfilled. Both in theory and in practice, the consequences of alternative, more realistic, assumptions have drastic consequences for the functioning of markets, – in terms of the types of institutions that are generated, and the choice of the market as the preferred governance structure.

Generally speaking, in spot markets, equilibrium prices are determined more or less instantaneously. In modern economies, the provision of different commodities does not always fulfill all requirements for equilibrium prices all the time. Commodities may be far from homogeneous, and new commodities and production processes enter the market continuously.

This has consequences for the models: different types of models result, with different consequences for welfare. These are described in various static market models of the neoclassical theory. Another consequence is that different institutional arrangements are generated in order to deal with problems that arise in markets, such as external effects or market power. These different institutions have different costs. TCE is able to explain how and why transaction costs determine the nature of chosen institutions.

From the dynamic point of view, the economy is in a constant state of flux. All this implies is that a state of disequilibrium seems to better reflect modern economies than does equilibrium. The implication of this observation is not that prices are inadequate to coordinate markets. On the contrary; disequilibrium prices may also coordinate the market.

The entrepreneur plays a central role in this coordination process. Entrepreneurs are central figures in the promotion of economic growth. They are capable of discovering new market opportunities thanks to their alertness. The higher the rate of entrepreneurship in society, the higher the chance of economic progress. Regardless of the fact that everybody has the capacity to be alert and look out for new market opportunities, not everyone becomes an entrepreneur. The probability of individuals choosing to make a livelihood as entrepreneurs is influenced by the prevailing institutions of a society.

## REVIEW QUESTIONS

1 What are the differences between spot markets and institutionalized markets?
2 In what sense are the NCE and TCE approach to markets compatible with each other?
3 The market for lemons often refers to used automobiles. Explain some problems and solutions by referring to an example of your own.
4 Explain how some forms of market power are intrinsic to the competitive process.
5 Abuse of market power is combated mainly by means of public institutions. Can you think of any effective private institutions able to curb abuse of market power?
6 Describe the role of entrepreneurs in the dynamics of an economy.
7 Why is entrepreneurship an institution?
8 Do you think that creative destruction and cumulative causation are compatible or incompatible? Explain your reasons.
9 You may probably be aware of a change in your preferences over time. Discuss (a) how this change came about; and (b) its consequences for economic analysis.
10 In the Continental European model, first order and second order economizing are both seen as a social responsibility, while in the Anglo-Saxon model, social responsibility concerns only first order economizing. Discuss the consequences of both approaches if they apply to the country in which you live.

# Appendix to Chapter 5

## DIFFERENT TYPES OF AUCTIONS

Suppose one wishes to 'sell an object' through an auction. This may be an art object, but may also be a plan to build a complex, or the sale of radio or television frequencies or any other means of communication via airwaves.

The seller wants to obtain at least some price $p(s)$, otherwise she will not sell. Buyers have some maximum price $p(b)$ they are willing to pay. The auction brings buyers and seller together, so that the object will be sold at some price in between $p(s)$ and $p(b)$, as long as there is at least one buyer that wants to buy at a price higher than $p(s)$. But what if there is more than one buyer willing to pay at least $p(s)$? Who will get the object, and at what price?

The following simple example will show the basics of the auction. Suppose we have two buyers (A and B) and one seller (with one object to sell). The seller wants to obtain at least 10, A wants to pay at most 15, and B at most 20. It is easy to see that, in general, B will get the object. Even if A obtains it, she could resell the object to B, since B is willing to pay more than A; hence a profitable transaction between A and B can take place. One feature of an auction is that it guarantees that the buyer who wants to pay the most will obtain the object.

There are a couple of mechanisms that will generate the price to be paid. We shall describe three of them: a Dutch auction, an English auction, and a 'sealed bid auction'.

## Dutch auction

At this type of auction, the auctioneer starts at some (high) price level and as long as no one bids, will lower the price progressively until someone wants to buy at the latest price called. For example, the auctioneer might start at price 25. Neither buyer of our previous example wants to pay that price, so the auctioneer will lower the price to 24 and so on. So what happens if the price goes down to 20? Now B has to decide either to buy the object and pay the maximum he is willing to pay, or to wait for a slightly lower price to make his bid. If he knew what A was willing to pay, he would wait until the price reduced to 16. Otherwise he has to take a risk. Generally speaking, if there are a lot of other buyers, B will buy at 20, because the risk of losing the object would otherwise be too high. Note also that, even if A was able to obtain the object, B might still offer a higher price to A. For example, if B waited until price 15, when A would bid for the object, B knows that he could offer A a price of 16 after the auction. So, with a small number of players, tactical considerations are important.

## English auction

Here, the reverse procedure is followed: the auctioneer starts at some low price (say 10) and will put the price up by discrete amounts until one buyer remains. At price 10, both buyers will want to buy. So the auctioneer might raise the price by one unit. It is clear that, at price 16, A will no longer want to buy, therefore B will obtain the object at price 16. Again, when there are many buyers with a different 'willingness to pay', the price would go up to the maximum level of the buyer willing to pay the most. So, generally, if there are many buyers, both English and Dutch auctions will generate the same price.

## Sealed bid auction

In this type of auction, both buyers have to deliver a price to the auctioneer simultaneously and independently. Here, each buyer has to decide what price to offer. Basically, there are two mechanisms to determine the price: a 'first bid' or a 'second bid'. The first bid means that the price offered (if the highest) will have to be paid, while the 'second

**Table 5.5** *Characteristics of different types of auction*

|  | Dutch auction | English auction | Sealed bid auction |
|---|---|---|---|
| Start | Auctioneer starts by asking a maximum price | Auctioneer starts by asking a minimum price | Buyers inform the auctioneer what they want to pay |
| Mechanism to determine the price | Auctioneer lowers the price until a buyer decides that he wants to pay the price | Auctioneer raises the price until one buyer remains | 'First bid' or 'second bid' |
| Condition (1) | Not many buyers (each with a different willingness to pay) | Not many buyers (each with a different willingness to pay) | Not many buyers |
| Outcome (1) | A deal at the highest price | A deal at the next highest price | The item will be sold to the highest bidder. What has to be paid depends on the mechanism applied; in 'second bid', the next highest price |
| Condition (2) | Many buyers (each with a slightly different willingness to pay) | Many buyers (each with a slightly different willingness to pay) | Many buyers (each with a slightly different willingness to pay) |
| Outcome (2) | A deal at the highest price | A deal at the highest price | A deal at the highest price |

bid' means that the buyer with the highest offer will obtain the object at the second-highest price.

It should be clear that the second bid mechanism implies that the best any player can do is to reveal his preferences honestly, so that A will offer price 15 and B will offer 20. B will gain the object, but pays 15 and not 20.

To see this: why should any buyer risk losing the object by not offering the maximum she is willing to pay? But she will not offer more than that, because if she did, she would run the risk that she would obtain the object at a second bid that is higher than the maximum she is willing to pay. For example; if A offered 21, she would obtain the object at 20, given that B had offered 20, which is in fact much higher than A was initially willing to pay. So offering more than the maximum is not a smart thing to do. The same is true for offering a lower price: that would increase the risk that the object goes to another buyer, or that the price to be paid will be lower, to no avail. For example, if A offered price 14, while B offered 20, B would still get the object, but at price 14 instead of 20, so there is no reason why A would offer a lower price. This example is summarized in Table 5.5.

Generally speaking, an auction leads to an efficient outcome under proper circumstances. Not all objects can be sold efficiently by means of an auction, however, as can easily be seen if one thinks about selling bread, for example, in that manner. Transaction costs should be taken into account in determining whether or not an auction is an efficient device.

# 6 Firms

## CONTENTS

- **Introduction**
- **The static efficiency approach to firms**
  - The neoclassical theory of firms: the firm as a black box
  - The classical firm: the firm as a contractual organization of inputs
  - A nexus of contracts: the firm as a legal fiction
  - The TCE approach to firms
- **The static vested interest approach to firms**
  - Separation of ownership and control
  - Mergers
- **The dynamic efficiency approach to firms**
  - The entrepreneurial firm
  - From unitary (U-form) to multidivisional (M-form) organization
- **The dynamic vested interest approach to firms**
  - The power of the executives
  - Countervailing power
- **Concluding remarks**
- **Review questions**

## INTRODUCTION

It may seem a waste of time to ask why firms exist. Most people probably take their existence for granted. However, if the market was the only efficient governance structure there would be no need for another. But markets are not always the most efficient mechanism to allocate resources: that depends on transaction costs. Nevertheless, it is not self-evident why firms should exist. As is the case with so many questions, economists also disagree with regard to this one. There are different approaches to firms, and these will be the topic of this chapter.

Neoclassical economists see firms as the profit maximizing market actor we described in Chapter 5: the firm acquires inputs and produces output that is sold on the market. How and why the inputs are transformed into output is described simply by a production function (the technological relationship between labor and capital on the one hand and output on the other).

This neoclassical approach was challenged by Ronald Coase in the 1930s, with his argument that firms exist because they save on transaction costs. In the Coasian approach, the entrepreneur is modeled as the central authority within the firm who organizes the firm's activities by means other than market transactions. This is summarized in the term *power of fiat* (orders and decisions taken by a central authority), that presupposes a power structure, hence a hierarchy. Eventually, in the 1970s, this idea became the starting point in the search for an explanation for the existence of firms.

Economists working in the neoclassical tradition are not convinced by Coase's arguments, however. They do not think that the power of fiat differs from market contracting. At the same time, the neoclassical view recognizes that approaching the firm as just a profit maximizing market actor is not satisfactory either. The application of marginal analysis – that is, rewarding production factors according to their marginal productivity (the output produced by one more unit of input) – becomes much more complicated if it is acknowledged that *team production* may raise productivity. Team production requires not only that an employer is able to monitor the contribution of each employee, but also an agreement concerning who does what and how much will be paid for each person's contribution. This agency approach analyzes the firm as a contractual organization of inputs. This was then extended to include a broad range of stakeholders with reciprocal arrangements or contracts, and has become known as the *nexus of contract approach* of the firm.

This nexus of contract approach focuses on reciprocal contracts and ignores the power of fiat, hence it does not explain the existence of hierarchy. This was accomplished by TCE, which reintroduces management as a hierarchical power that can settle issues of resource allocation by its authority. It provides a theory about the conditions under which a firm as a way of organizing transactions is preferred to market transactions or other governance structures. Authority allocates resources within firms, while prices allocate resources in the market. Consequently, transaction costs differ, which may be a reason to decide to make a good oneself instead of buying it in the market.

All these approaches to firms may be associated with efficiency and vested interest perspectives on firms. Firms may be seen as efficient solutions to the allocation of resources, especially when asset specificity is high. This approach is provided by the TCE. However, firms may also be seen as organizations within which vested interests defend their existing position. In relation to this approach, in this chapter we shall discuss the separation between ownership and control, and how firms acquire price-setting power through mergers.

Neoclassical analysis is of limited use when analyzing the dynamics of firms, because of its (comparatively) static nature. Therefore TCE is somewhat better equipped to analyze the dynamics of the firm. When firms are of a certain size it is argued that it may be more efficient to organize a firm along multidivisional lines rather than organizing it according to a strict top-down management concept. But this view ignores the fact that such decisions about the organizational structure of the firm may be the result of decisions taken to satisfy vested interests.

The power of the different stakeholders of a firm is not only a matter of structure; it is also embedded in a society's culture, and changes in that culture may result in a shift in relative powers. With the rise of the shareholder model since the early 1980s, the

**Table 6.1** *The static and dynamic efficiency and vested interest approaches to firms*

|  | Static approach | Dynamic approach |
|---|---|---|
| Efficiency | Production function | Entrepreneurship |
|  | The classical firm | Product life cycles and reorganization |
|  | Nexus of contracts | New forms of organization |
|  | Transaction costs |  |
| Vested interest | Separation of ownership and control | Power of the management |
|  | Systems of corporate governance | Convergence between stakeholder and shareholder models? |
|  | Mergers |  |

Anglo-Saxon culture challenged the Continental European culture of mutual consultation between stakeholders.

The different approaches to firms discussed above are summarized in Table 6.1, where each quadrant contains the main topics that will be dealt with in this chapter.

## THE STATIC EFFICIENCY APPROACH TO FIRMS

In this section we deal successively with the traditional neoclassical analysis of the firm, the analysis of the firm as a contractual organization of inputs, the nexus of contracts approach, and the TCE approach.

### The neoclassical theory of firms: the firm as a black box

In this framework, a firm is described as a production function that responds directly to changes in costs and market demand. What the firm does is simply to buy inputs on the market and transform them into output that is sold again on the market. The neoclassical theory of firms focuses on the efficient allocation of resources (see Appendix A to Chapter 1). There is no need for analyzing processes within the firm itself. In other words, the neoclassical firm is like a *black box,* of which only the input and output characteristics are known, but not its internal functioning.

### The classical firm: the firm as a contractual organization of inputs

Resource owners may increase productivity by cooperative specialization. This cooperation could be organized through the market but also within firms. Both types of coordination involve contracts. The difference between both types of economic organization of cooperation is that the latter includes team production, which is assumed to generate a value that exceeds the value produced by the total number of workers operating individually. Adam Smith illustrated the production enhancing power of team production in his *Wealth of Nations,* with his famous example of the pin factory (see Box 6.1).

> **BOX 6.1   THE PIN FACTORY**
>
> Smith uses the simple example of a pin factory to show how specialization leads to a rise in productivity (Smith, 1776, pp. 4–9). He begins by noting that if each worker performs all the tasks required to produce a pin, output per worker is relatively low. But if production is divided into separate operations, with each worker specializing in one of these operations (such as drawing out the wire, or straightening, cutting, pointing or grinding it at the top to receive the head), there is a large increase in output per worker.
>
> First, a worker who specializes in one simple activity becomes more experienced and consequently improves his skill at doing this type of work compared to a worker who has to devote his attention to several operations.
>
> Second, if every worker has to perform all the separate operations himself he wastes time when switching from one operation to another, especially if operations are carried out in different locations and with different tools. Drawing out a wire requires quite different tools than cutting it, and shifting from one operation to another requires not only that the worker has to move to another location, but also that he has to put down one set of tools and pick up another.
>
> The third, and probably most important, factor is that specialization facilitates the use of machinery. Workers whose attention is directed toward a single object are likely to discover faster and more efficient methods of performing their task.
>
> Because not all workers are equally capable of performing all the tasks required to produce a pin – some may be most skilled at drawing out the wire, while others are much more adept at straightening, cutting, pointing or grinding the top – overall the highest level of prosperity is achieved if everybody is free to specialize in that what he is most able to do.

Team production requires an organizational structure that is different from buying on the market. First, the productivity of workers who are cooperating may be much higher than would be generated without cooperation. Second, tasks may be performed that are impossible without cooperation. So, cooperation must be arranged. Third, with team production, some workers may try to shirk. So this requires an overseer to observe the behavior of workers and to estimate each one's contribution to total output.

Two conditions must be fulfilled before deciding to organize cooperation through the firm. The first condition that arises for firms is that team production must generate value that exceeds the sum of the value produced by individual workers. The second requirement is that it must be possible at reasonable cost to estimate the individual contribution to the total output.

To start a firm one needs to own inputs or resources: capital, for example. This may be acquired in several ways. A firm may acquire capital in advance from consumers in exchange for promises of future delivery (construction workers may ask for payment in advance before they start building, say). Firms may also borrow money from banks to finance their investments. Big businesses also often obtain capital in the form of stocks; that is, many investors contribute towards their capital. These investors tend to buy bonds if they are risk averse and shares if they are more daring. When approaching shareholders as investors and not as joint owners, the entrepreneur can best be visualized as an organizer of capital.

As noted above, to reduce shirking, someone has to check the behavior of team members. This may be the entrepreneur/organizer herself. If she has the rights to residual income (as in the principal–agent situation), she will have a powerful incentive to perform her task properly. But it may not always be feasible (from an organizational perspective) for the entrepreneur to perform this task as efficiently as someone else. In such situations the entrepreneur may choose to hire a 'monitor'. Of course, all this will depend on transaction costs, as we shall see later.

## A nexus of contracts: the firm as a legal fiction

Viewing the firm as a contractual organization of joint inputs in team production is a rather limited approach. There are many more stakeholders involved than the investor and the employees who must be monitored by the entrepreneur/organizer. Stakeholders include banks, bondholders, shareholders, chief executive officers, other executives, employees, customers, suppliers and creditors. All these groups of people have different stakes in the firm: every stakeholder in the firm has an arrangement or, as economists tend to call it, a contract with another stakeholder. Therefore, a firm does not consist of just one maximizing actor but rather of a whole range of them. Consequently, agency costs, such as the monitoring expenditure of the principal, bonding expenditure of the agent and a residual loss (see Chapter 3), not only exist with regard to the contract between the investor and employee, but also with regard to the contracts with other stakeholders.

The *nexus of contracts* approach sees private firms as being composed of a group of stakeholders with reciprocal arrangements or contracts (Jensen and Meckling, 1976). Also, the firm itself, despite it not being a 'real' person, can enter into contracts. In corporate law, the firm is treated as a legal entity.

In approaching the firm as a nexus of contracts, shareholders are viewed as having a contract with CEOs. The latter are supposed to represent the interests of the former. This means that shareholders are assumed to have only contractual claims against the firm. Consequently, according to the nexus of contracts approach, shareholders are not full owners of a firm. If shareholders were considered to be full owners of the firm, they would have the right to manage it and to earn an income from it. In the nexus of contract approach, shareholders have only a partial property right: they may enforce their residual claim only in the form of dividends. Note that, when firms make investments, several financial sources are available, and one of them is to issue shares; shares pay out dividends, but only when profits are made and after all other claims on the firm's funds have been paid. So, in that sense, dividends are the 'residual claim': only what is left over from profits will be paid to shareholders.

What is the implication of approaching firms as a nexus of contracts? First, it implies that shareholders who have a residual claim have the best incentives to monitor the firm. Because they do not have a fixed claim, they have an appropriate incentive to take decisions that maximize the creation of wealth of the firm. Second, it implies that a firm does not have duties that go beyond the obligations stipulated in the separate contracts. For example, a person may deposit confidence, good faith, reliance and trust in somebody else, but he cannot refer to this in disputes about compliance with the contract. Consequently, all obligations of a firm should be interpreted in terms of separate contracts. Therefore, the firm as a single system does not exist as such: it is made up of various subsystems – that is, contracts between different stakeholders. It is designed to minimize contracting costs. In other words, a firm is an artificial construct under corporate law. That is why the nexus of contracts approach sees the firm as a legal fiction.

## The TCE approach to firms

According to Coase, the (high) costs of using the price mechanism to organize the production of output efficiently is why the price mechanism is superseded by carrying out transactions in a firm. The costs of using the price mechanism are transaction costs: 'The most obvious cost of "organising" production through the price mechanism is that of discovering what the relevant prices are ... The costs of negotiating and concluding a separate contract for each exchange transaction which takes place on a market must also be taken into account' (Coase, 1937, pp. 390, 391).

Transaction costs caused by using the price mechanism may be high when a whole series of contracts is involved. For many repeated tasks it is much cheaper to offer one long-term contract rather than a series of contracts covering each task separately. An example of such a long-term contract is an employment contract, which is expressed in unspecified terms (Simon, 1991, p. 31):

> Employees agree to do, over the life of the contract, what they are ordered to do ... [One argument] for the existence of incomplete contracts is that in a world of uncertainty actions will have to be taken as the situation calls for them, without time for negotiation. The employee is rewarded, in the level of the wage, for his willingness to bear the brunt of this uncertainty as to what actions will be chosen, and to do so, when the time comes, whatever the employer thinks the situation calls for.

The rationale behind the choice to embed workers in a firm is that it is cheaper to allocate workers to tasks by command rather than by price (that is, the market). Contracting labor saves not only on search and contracting costs but also on wage costs, because workers tend to accept lower money wages in exchange for job security (see Box 3.7 on page 117).

While contracts are involved, in this approach a firm is much more than a nexus of contracts. What is truly distinctive about the hierarchical governance structure is that adaptation to changes is effected through fiat. Fiat as a control mechanism implies that authority is decisive in allocating resources. According to the TCE approach, markets cannot replace the firm efficiently, because of the higher transaction costs of contracting via the market rather than by hierarchical relations and authority.

Allocation of resources by authority is most efficient when asset specificity is high, and this is the case when a product is supplied by highly specialized production factors (see Chapter 3). The higher the asset specificity of a product, the greater the chance that the product will be made within a firm rather than bought on the market, because this may require additional measures to secure investment. However, as we also saw in Chapter 5, high asset specificity may lead to a hold-up situation. Protecting oneself against this behavior involves transaction costs. In cases like this, a substitution of vertical integration (a hierarchy) for market-mediated exchange often happens, as we saw, for example, in the famous Fisher Body case described in Box 5.7 (see page 181). The administrative costs of running a firm are offset by the benefits of the reduced opportunism resulting from fiat. In Figure 6.1, this occurs for transactions in which asset specificity amounts to more than $k_2$.

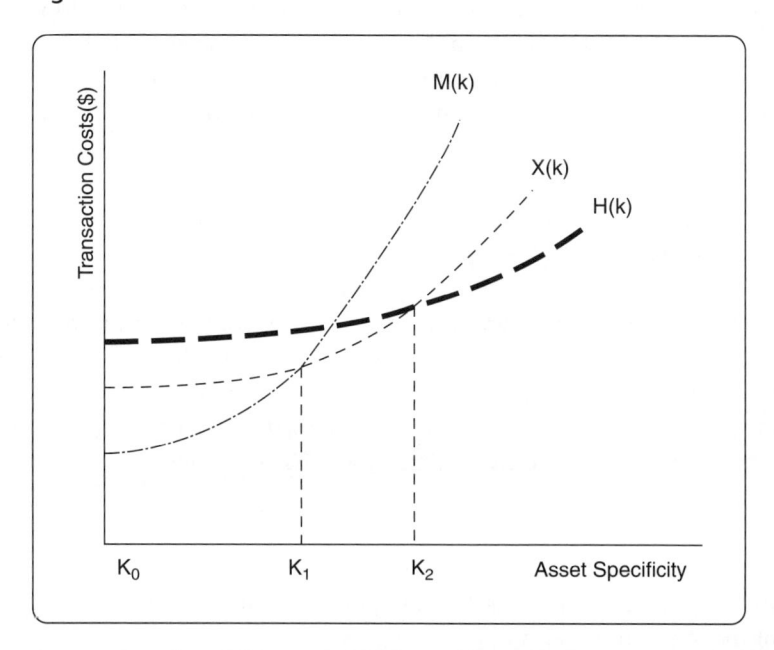

**Figure 6.1** *The domain of the firm*

*Sources:* Based on Williamson (1996, p. 108) and Ménard (2004, p. 369).

The level of asset specificity is one of the determinants of transaction costs. The frequency of transactions is another. Even with high asset specificity, a firm is not an efficient (cost minimizing) way of dealing with occasional transactions only; in these circumstances, the market may meet the optimal transaction needs. It is only appropriate to integrate transactions into a firm when the frequency of a transaction with the same partner is high, and integration may save on, in particular, safeguarding and other costs of concluding the contract. As in Chapter 5, we shall take a closer look at four institutional conditions that influence the choice of governance structure: the contract law regime; property rights; reputation effects; and risk. As we shall explain below, transaction costs in firms can be lower:

- because of the power of fiat: the implicit character of employment contracts means that not everything is decided on in detail *ex ante*, so giving authority to the top

executives in the hierarchy can be used efficiently where adjustments are necessary as a result of changing circumstances;
- if property rights are safeguarded more efficiently by administrative controls (monitoring, career awards, and penalties) instead of by market transactions;
- as a result of the reputation of managers: if this is positive, it reduces the costs of monitoring; and
- because a hierarchy is better equipped to deal with certain risks than the market. For example, through producing certain inputs itself, a firm may avoid the risk of fluctuations in market supply.

## Contract law regime

In Chapter 3 we introduced relational contracts that are dominant within the firm. Inside a firm, contracts can be incomplete because the management has been given the discretionary power to decide on how to adapt the terms of the labor agreement if circumstances warrant this. This saves on costs, because internal conflicts can to a large extent be solved within the firm without the need for going to court. The form of contract law that dominates in hierarchies is called *forbearance*, which means that judges usually abstain from giving verdicts and leave most of the decisions (in case of conflict) to the actors (managers) within the firm:

> Thus, whereas courts routinely grant standing to firms should there be disputes over prices, the damages to be ascribed to delays, features of quality, and the like, courts will refuse to hear disputes between one internal division and another over identical technical issues. Access to the courts being denied, the parties must resolve their differences internally. Accordingly, hierarchy is its own court of ultimate appeal. (Williamson, 1991, p. 274)

Of course, not all disagreements within a firm are technical. However, even in the case of personnel disagreements there is a presumption that these differences of opinion can in principle be solved internally.

## Property rights

Different property rights are united in firms not only because of productivity gains from specialization and team production, but also because of economizing on transaction costs (Alchian, 1991). In firms, the joining of property rights is facilitated by limited liability. In contrast to full liability, in which a shareholder (generally the shareholder/owner) is personally liable for the firm's debts with all of his wealth and property, the concept of *limited liability* implies that shareholders in a corporation cannot lose more money than the value of their shares if the corporation runs into debt. In this case, the owners of property rights are not dependent on the wealth of other owners of property; nor will they be ruined by the mistakes made by co-owners or executive officers. Therefore, they will be less hesitant to invest in such a venture, even if they do not know the other shareholders.

## Reputation effects

When an employer and employee enter into a labor contract, the question for both sides is whether or not to invest in this employment relationship. Okun (1981) points out the distinction between firms that attach great value to investing in workers' commitment, and firms that do not have this incentive. Both types of firm optimize their personnel management, but in very different ways. Firms that are not interested in their workers' commitment opt for the 'casual labor strategy', in which low-skilled workers are hired without costly screening efforts to perform routine tasks, they are paid low wages and can easily be replaced. Firms that do care about their workers' commitment, however, opt for the 'career strategy' in which the employer invests in (skilled) employees. They are offered the opportunity to specialize in return for a high wage and the prospect of a long-lasting relationship. According to Williamson (1991, p. 291): 'If internal reputation effects improve, then managerial opportunism will be reduced and the costs of hierarchical governance will fall.'

Depending (partly) on the alternatives in the external labor market, it can be either the employer or the employee who stands to lose the most by breaching the labor contract. This can be explained in terms of asset specificity and the risk of a hold-up situation. It is possible that the employer has a hold over the employee if the latter has made a large amount of transaction-specific investments in the firm and cannot easily find a job elsewhere. It is also conceivable that the employee can put her employer 'on the spot' by threatening to resign, if it is the firm that has invested in the worker.

The way to solve this potential hold-up problem is by building safeguards into the contract, either explicitly or implicitly. As long as an employer has not yet built up a reputation, he will need to write down the terms of employment in detail, to be able to attract highly qualified personnel. The more aspects that need to be specified explicitly in the contract, the more transaction costs are involved. The next question is, then, whether the employer will find it worthwhile to invest in his reputation. Reputation effects are not significant for 'fly-by-night' firms; that is, for businesses that appear and disappear rapidly, perhaps because they do not provide steady jobs or because they do not operate in a permanent location. But also for more 'respectable' firms, it may not always be worthwhile to invest in reputation since this also comes at a cost.

As already mentioned in Chapter 3, implicit agreements between employer and employee assume that both sides will act in the spirit of the (incomplete) employment contract because they both benefit from doing so. If they fail to live up to these implicit agreements, the employee will put his career opportunities at risk, while the employer will put his good reputation at risk and will have more difficulty in retaining current employees and hiring new personnel. Hence, the company can 'build a reputation that will both enhance the supply of willing applicants and hold down quit rates' (Okun, 1981, p. 81).

In addition to the availability of qualified personnel, an employer with a good reputation might also have highly motivated workers who can contribute to raising productivity. Moreover, a firm with a good reputation in the labor market also gives a signal to (potential) shareholders that the firm is a reliable investment, and a signal to (potential) customers that the firm delivers high quality products. An illustration of the importance of a good reputation is presented in Box 6.2.

## BOX 6.2  MCDONALD'S AND THE *OXFORD ENGLISH DICTIONARY*

In March 2007, fast-food giant McDonald's was in the news for attempting to remove the definition of the word 'McJob' from the prestigious *Oxford English Dictionary*. The dictionary defines McJob as a job characterized by low pay and low prestige, and with no prospects. This interpretation of the word has by now become widely accepted, much to the dismay of McDonald's, who had introduced the term themselves in the 1980s to describe their well-intended personnel policy for disabled employees.

To fight back, McDonald's was planning an advertising campaign in the UK to stress all the benefits of working for the firm, with the aim of changing the public's perception of the brand: 'McJob' should become 'McProspect' (Lamont, 2007). It seems that McDonald's attaches great value to upholding its reputation, not only with its employees but also with all other stakeholders in the company.

### *Risk*

Being dependent on markets involves risks. These may originate from a number of sources: perhaps from the actions of competitors, or be demand or input risks.

The actions of other competitive firms influence a company's market share and profits, and may be countered by competitive measures such as adjusting prices, increase marketing expenditure, cutting down on costs, attempting to innovate and so on. It may also be dealt with by an increase in market concentration – that is, by merging with or acquiring other firms. An acquisition is a takeover of another firm by purchasing the majority of the outstanding shares of the company. The firm that is taken over is 'swallowed'. An acquisition differs from a merger, in the sense that a merger is between equals. Mergers usually occur by mutual consent and result in a new firm.

Another type of risk is demand risk (fluctuations in demand). This type of risk is difficult to manage. It may lead to an increase in marketing and sales activities.

Also, there is the risk of input (cost). Prices and supply of inputs may fluctuate heavily. This type of risk is also difficult to manage because firms often have little influence over their suppliers. This may lead to firm deciding to start producing the inputs itself.

All these environmental risks have to be added to the unique risks a firm faces when running its business. Firm-specific risks may arise from internal changes such as entering a new market, acquiring another firm, or making changes in top management. Firms also take risks when implementing changes in production techniques or organizational form. These types of risks may be mitigated through research and the provision of information.

So risks can affect specific firms or products (depending on the competitive circumstances, firm-specific demand, firm-specific input prices, and so on), or it can affect a number of firms/products, or even all firms/products, at the same time. An example of the latter is a downturn (or upswing) in the business cycle, that has a negative (or positive) effect on demand for almost all products. Another illustration is the weather: this will influence almost all agricultural products at the same time and in the same place.

In all these cases, firms adapt to risk by letting the management decide about what is the best way to deal with the situation at hand. Not everyone working in the firm will be asked to participate in the decision-making process, as this would be very time-consuming (inefficient) and not very effective. Thanks to the power of fiat, the top management can respond to disturbances swiftly.

### *Summary*

From the transaction cost perspective, the characteristics of the hierarchy are summarized in Table 6.2.

**Table 6.2** *The hierarchy and the characteristics of its main institutional conditions*

| Conditions / Asset specificity | General to semi-specific |
|---|---|
| Contract law regime | Forbearance (relational contracting) |
| Property rights | Shared ownership and limited liability |
| Reputation effects | Reduction of managerial opportunistic behavior |
| Risk | Adaptation by fiat |

## THE STATIC VESTED INTEREST APPROACH TO FIRMS

The neoclassical, nexus of contracts and transaction costs approaches to firms all focus on efficiency. However, the presence of vested interests limits the usefulness of these 'ideal' types of analysis. When a firm grows in size, perhaps as a result of mergers that allow for economies of scale, ownership and control of the firm become separated. This separation causes several agency problems. We focus on these problems below. They are not dealt with sufficiently by TCE, because here it is assumed that hierarchy allocates resources efficiently within a firm. The agency costs created by the separation of ownership and control of capital are different in different corporate governance structures. The Anglo-Saxon model and the Continental European model are addressed in this context.

Another limitation for efficiency approaches is the concentration of firms that appears through merging. The creation of a dominant position in the market and the associated costs are described below.

### Separation of ownership and control

As far back as 1776, Adam Smith foresaw the agency problems that might appear in firms characterized by a separation of ownership and management (control):

> The directors of…[stock] companies, however, being the managers rather of other people's money than of their own, it cannot well be expected that they should watch over it with the same anxious vigilance with which the partners in a private copartnery frequently watch over their own. Like the stewards of a rich man, they are apt to

consider attention to small matters as not for their master's honour, and very easily give themselves a dispensation from having it. Negligence and profusion, therefore, must always prevail, more or less, in the management of the affairs of such a company. (Smith, 1776, p. 700)

In addition to the separation of ownership and control, the ownership of modern companies has become anonymous, leading to agency problems. For example, how can many shareholders coordinate their actions in order to impose profit maximization on the (often much better informed) management? Shareholders generally form a very large, dispersed group. This can give rise to a free rider problem: individual efforts to monitor the actions of the management (the firm's decision-makers), if possible at all, benefit all other shareholders, so that individuals have an incentive to refrain from monitoring. In that case, the shareholders as a group will not be able to monitor the firm's decisions properly. This will lead to the possibility that shareholders only receive a return on their capital that is sufficient to satisfy them, while the additional profits go to the management. The coordination problem between the shareholders will make it difficult or impossible to counter this situation.

In their original well-known study in 1932, Berle and Means (1947) found that the separation of ownership and control might induce one of three possible outcomes:

1 Managers might become trustees who are scrupulously monitored on behalf of the passive shareholders. This may have a negative effect on initiative.
2 Managers might operate the company in their own interests. When the controlling group is granted free rein, this can lead to 'a corporate oligarchy coupled with the probability of an era of corporate plundering' (Berle and Means, 1947, p. 355).
3 The modern corporation serves exclusively neither the sole interest of the passive owner, nor the sole interest of the active managers in control. This implies, for example, a type of capitalistic corporation that might fit into what is called the Continental European model of capitalism.

The first two alternatives are the theoretical possible outcomes of the separation of ownership and control within a capitalist society. The third alternative requires that the controllers take into account the interest of all the other stakeholders of the firm, whether they are employees, shareholders or consumers. How the interests of different groups can be taken into account successfully is the topic we shall address next.

## *Incentives*

In larger companies, where the owners no longer run the business but have become shareholders at a distance, the issue is not only how to ensure that the workers' actions are to the owner's benefit, but also how to make sure that the appointed managers will do the same. In a firm with limited liability, the shareholders can be regarded as the principal, and the top managers (who form the *board of directors* that runs the firm) as the agents. At a lower level, the management can be regarded as the principal (acting on behalf of the owners) and the employees as the agents. The shareholders sign contracts with management, who take charge of many high-level discretionary decisions. In turn, managers delegate discretion (giving autonomous decision power) to other employees at lower levels in the firm. The question is how can all different agents in the firm be motivated not to abuse information asymmetries to their own advantage, and to the detriment of the firm's principals?

As mentioned in Chapter 3, the firm is characterized by its low-powered incentives to encourage agents to act in the interests of the principal, which in theory can be achieved by monitoring and enforcement activities, or by rewarding the agent when he acts in accordance with the firm's goals. If the costs of monitoring and enforcement are higher than the costs of rewarding the agents, obviously reward is the appropriate choice.

*Positive incentives* include financial bonuses, promotion, or recognition. *Negative incentives* may include demotion or dismissal. In general, it is cheaper to give the agent an incentive for good behavior than to monitor him. However, incentives are not always as effective as management would like. Agents may be in a position where they have the power to pursue a self-interested strategy. If, for example, they provide the information necessary to enable monitoring, they may in fact manipulate the auditors.

## Managers

The first category of agents that might damage the value of the owners' property rights are the managers: how do managers attain appropriate incentives to maximize the owners' (shareholders') wealth? In order to deal with this risk, several *disciplinary mechanisms* to control managers' behavior exist, varying from positive to negative sanctions (Shleifer and Vishny, 1997). We shall mention three of them briefly: incentive pay; monitoring devices; and outside pressures.

*Incentive contracts* are often used. This implies the sharing of residual control rights (see Chapter 3). By giving stock options or share ownership to the managers, it is hoped that they will be motivated to serve the interests of the shareholders, because they will then share in the benefits. It should be noted, however, that there are many real-life examples in which managers acted opportunistically even with such benefits. In recent years, the CEOs of Enron (USA), Ahold (the Netherlands) and Parmalat (Italy) all had contracts that included one or more forms of merit pay, but they were still tempted to increase their earnings even more by means of essentially illegal methods, leading in each case to large accounting scandals. If, on the other hand, incentive pay is implemented successfully, the interests of owners and managers can be aligned, and the former can save on monitoring costs.

However, especially in large joint stock companies, monitoring will remain necessary, and for that reason many kinds of supervision (*monitoring devices*) can be introduced, ranging from internal audits and obligatory reporting at shareholder meetings to legally mandatory external audits and other legal forms of protection of shareholders' privileges (such as voting rights, or right to appeal to a court). Shareholders may decide that it is desirable for one of their representatives to become a (nonexecutive) member of the management board. This saves on monitoring costs and may contribute to maximization of shareholder value. Supervisory boards are another disciplinary mechanism (see also page 216 – *Stakeholders inside firms*–and Figure 6.3). The members of these boards (at least in Continental Europe) act from a greater distance from the firm than the managers, which could either be a disadvantage (monitoring might be more difficult for outsiders) or an advantage (they could be more objective).

Managers can also be disciplined by *outside pressures*. As long as a company is well run, this will be reflected by steady or rising share prices on the stock market, and by steady or rising market shares in the goods markets. In addition, professional analysts publish critical reports on company performance. If these indicators deteriorate, this signals that a management team is under-performing. Consequently, managers may lose their jobs. The owners or supervisors of the firm could decide to replace the managers (if there is a competitive labor market for senior managers) or they may be replaced as a result of a merger or acquisition (if there is an effective market for corporate control).

That the measures do not need to be effective is proved by a series of scandals and the recent ongoing financial crisis. Large companies often have a code of conduct in order to promote ethical behavior, apply internal auditing and accounting principles, and grant stock options to CEOs. The large corporate frauds that became public as the twenty-first century began, such as Enron, WorldCom and Tyco, and the banking crisis that started in 2008, made clear that internal control had not been as effective as investors and stakeholders would have liked. Bank managers received huge bonuses even as their banks were failing during the financial crisis. Managers had become a dominant power within the banking system and could exploit their position of power in their own interest despite this meaning a loss for shareholders. Just as markets are not able to operate efficiently without institutions to support the full enjoyment of property rights, additional institutions proved to be necessary to restore public confidence in, for example, the stock market. However, implementing and enforcing these institutions proved to be beyond the scope of these firms. Public intervention was required, which is the main subject of Part IV of this book.

### Employees

The second category of agents that may have a negative effect on the value of the property rights of the owners are all other employees who are directed by management. Again, the level of damage depends on the effectiveness of the incentive schemes or disciplinary mechanisms for personnel in general.

Employees may receive a *fixed wage*, a *variable payment* or a mixture of these. Most people in employment agree to accept a fixed wage, but in many countries elements of variable pay have been introduced, and proved to be increasingly popular. The idea is that individuals will be encouraged to work harder if their salary depends to some extent on their own efforts. As noted above in discussion on property rights, the problem is often that it is difficult to find out exactly how much an individual has contributed to the total (team) effort. In consequence, neither the worker nor his manager can be certain that the correct reward will be paid, which could lead directly to shirking or reduce the worker's motivation if his direct supervisor does not reward his efforts sufficiently well (which again could also fuel shirking).

A *nonpecuniary incentive* to align the interests of employees with those of the other stakeholders in the firm is to give personnel a say in company policies. This is known as the granting of *participation or codetermination rights*. In many Continental European countries, codetermination by so-called *works councils* is legally mandatory, though the degree of comprehensiveness differs significantly between countries. In the Netherlands and Germany, works councils have the most far-reaching rights: managers are obliged to ask the council for advice or even for consent before decisions can be made on diverse social-economic matters, especially those that will affect the working conditions of the workers.

The idea is that if employees are consulted on matters concerning their working environment or working conditions, and are taken seriously, this will increase their commitment to the firm, and hence they will become more productive (Freeman and Lazear, 1995). Enhanced trust will make workers more willing to invest their human capital in the firm, thereby increasing their asset specificity. Because of their participation rights, they can be more certain that they will not fall victim to a hold-up situation. At the same time, codetermination can be considered as an additional device for monitoring the management (by the employees), because of managerial obligations towards the workers: in that sense, it forms an additional disciplinary mechanism, which is also beneficial for the shareholders (Van den Berg, 2004).

Benefits for shareholders may be at risk not only as a consequence of opportunistic behavior by managers or employees, as discussed above, but also as a result of diverging interests among the different shareholders. The interests of investors depend very much on whether they have acquired shares for speculative reasons or if they have a long-term goal. Hedge funds that aim to earn a profit by taking advantage of market volatilities are of the first type (see Box 6.3), as their tactics include, for example, acquiring a substantial share in a company in order to split the company into separate divisions and sell their shares again at a profit. This may be undesirable for employees, as it could lead to unemployment. Other hedge fund tactics include making the company take on a large amount of debt, which can make the firm a riskier business. This tactic would not necessarily be to the advantage of the other stakeholders of the firm, such as the employees (including management) and long-term investors such as pension funds, all of whom are much more interested in preserving the continuity and stability of a firm.

### BOX 6.3 STORK

Shareholders in the Dutch engineering company Stork voted in October 2006 in favor of a plan created jointly by two major investors (hedge funds) to break up the company. These shareholders wanted Stork to focus on aerospace operations and to sell the less profitable divisions not directly related to this core business. The management of Stork attempted to fight off the proposal; they felt that Dutch corporate law supported them, in that the law gives managers the authority to determine strategy. According to Continental European law, firms are required to consider the interests of all stakeholders when making decisions. The court's verdict was that it was not the shareholders but the board of directors that has the final say in strategic issues. This is in contrast to US and British corporate law, in which much greater influence is given to shareholders, and shows the importance of the prevailing institutional environment on economic outcomes.

## Stakeholders inside firms: systems of corporate governance to control the abuse of power

The set of institutions put in place to overcome agency costs resulting from the separation of ownership and control constitutes a specific system of *corporate governance*. This refers to how a company is managed and monitored, and comprises: corporate principles and guidelines; the system of internal and external audits; and the supervision to which the activities of the company are subjected. Below we shall address the corporate governance systems that are associated with the Anglo-Saxon model and Continental European model, respectively.

In the Anglo-Saxon ideal type, the focus is mainly on shareholder value. Assuming that there is a positive correlation between the value of shares and the efficiency of corporate management, this system of corporate governance not only disciplines the managers but also guides shareholders in their decision to buy or sell the shares of a specific company. This approach to corporate control aligns management strategies with the interests of the investors.

The shareholder value model of corporate governance is the prevalent system in, for example, the USA (see Figure 6.2 for a graphical representation of this model).

Here, the board acts as an intermediary between the owners and the managers of the company. Notwithstanding the fact that shareholders elect the board of directors at their annual meetings, shareholders may see themselves as investors in, rather than owners of, the company: ownership of the company is so dispersed that individual shareholders think their influence is too small to steer decisions in their direction of choice.

However, other systems of corporate governance may allow for the interests of other stakeholders to be considered. As mentioned earlier, in Germany and several other European countries workers participate in company policies. The workers have a say

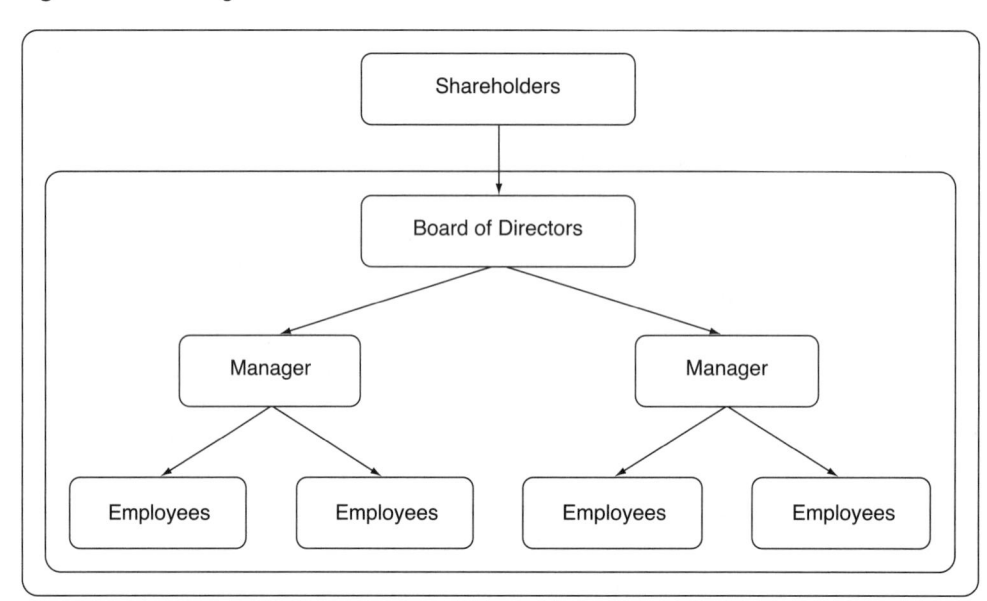

**Figure 6.2** *The Anglo-Saxon model*

in decision-making on the shop floor through works councils, and are also allowed to choose representatives on the supervisory board (see Figure 6.3 for a representation of this model).

## Mergers

Here we shall use the word 'merger' to describe any amalgamation of firms; therefore, it also includes acquisitions. Mergers can be horizontal (between competitors); vertical (between a supplier and a customer, see also Chapter 7); or conglomerate/diagonal (any other merger).

In Chapter 5 we mentioned how mergers between competitors can enhance market power; by eliminating mutual competitive pressure, prices will go up (this will be discussed in more depth in Chapter 7). However, there are many good reasons for firms to merge that may be described as efficiency enhancing. The most important one is that merging firms may create synergy (two or more forces working together so that their combined effect is greater than their individual efforts would be), and hence will be able to produce on a larger scale at lower cost. Merging also ensures cooperation between the merging partners; may lower overhead costs; makes it easier for firms to borrow money at lower interest rates; and enables firms to broaden supply and to grow faster.

Because mergers can have both positive and negative effects on welfare, depending on the amount of market power a merger creates, most countries introduced government agencies that have to authorize mergers (also called *merger control*), which will be dealt with in Chapter 8. We shall now discuss the negative effects of mergers in greater depth.

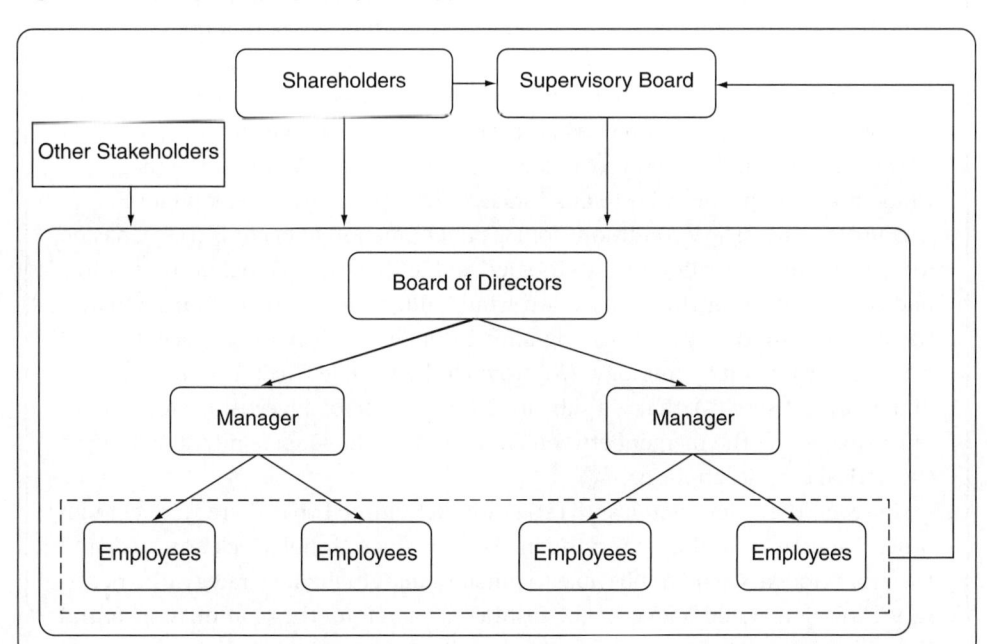

**Figure 6.3** *The Continental European model*

## Market power

Merging may create or increase market power, both in the sense of eliminating competition and in the sense of being able to abuse that position. Therefore, firms that merge do not need to be competitors in order to create market power. Vertical mergers, for example, may lead to foreclosure of competitors on either an upstream or downstream market. An upstream market is a market for an input to a product. A downstream market is the market for a product that uses the input(s) of upstream markets. For example, the market for bread is a downstream market because it uses flour, which is bought (as an input) on the upstream market for flour. Flour itself is produced by using the input grain, which is traded on yet another upstream market. So, an upstream market is a market higher up the vertical supply chain; the higher upstream, the closer to the basic inputs; the lower downstream, the closer to the final (consumer) product. Even 'diagonal' mergers may lead to price increases. An application of competition theory is illustrated in Box 6.4. The European Commission used theory in the case of the Google–Double Click amalgamation and found that the merger, though theoretically able to raise prices, could not do so in practice, because of the absence of the necessary conditions in this specific case.

### BOX 6.4   THE CASE OF GOOGLE AND DOUBLECLICK

In March 2008, the European Commission (EC) approved the takeover of online advertising technology provider DoubleClick by Google, the search-engine behemoth. The EC's decisions are based on economic reasoning and empirical analysis (RBB Economics, 2008).

Theoretically, the point is as follows. Suppose there are two complementary inputs, X and Y, needed to produce A. A is a substitute for product B, that does not need either X or Y in order to be produced. Still, a merger between B and X, say, might raise prices: if X were to raise prices after the merger, product A would become more expensive, and some demand would increase for product B (the merging partner of X), hence the merger would profit from X's price increase. Without the merger, X would not have the incentive to raise prices in order to increase demand for B.

One of the necessary conditions for this phenomenon to occur is that X has no (or almost no) substitutes. In the Google/DoubleClick case, Google's competitors had complained that this transaction would allow the company to marginalize them by raising the cost of placing advertisements. 'Advertising space' (Y) and 'advertising serving technology' (X, provided by Double Click) lead to a specific kind of advertising (A), that is a substitute for the kind of advertising Google provides (B). Hence, the merger between Double Click and Google might just fit the theoretical case description.

However, the Commission's investigation determined that there were enough other competitors in the 'ad serving' market in which DoubleClick operated, and therefore Google would not be able to pursue a marginalizing strategy (the necessary condition stated above is not fulfilled). Therefore, the Commission found that the third parties' worries about competition were unjustified.

If firms are competitors, there still not need be a problem of enhanced market power. Suppose there are many firms producing identical, or only slightly different, products. Competitive pressure for each individual firm does not come from one of the other firms, but from all of them. Merging with one competitor may not (radically) change this situation if enough competitive pressure remains. This is the same as stating that no dominant position is created where no dominant position existed before, as some competition is eliminated but not to the extent that no, or significantly less, competitive pressure remains.

An illustration of this is the contemplated acquisition in the autumn of 2008 of IKON Office Solutions by Ricoh, two office equipment companies active in the European Union. This purchase was allowed by the European Commission after it had concluded that the wholesale distribution market for photocopiers (one of the main products of these companies) was competitive, and that there would still be strong and effective competitors in the market for office equipment after the acquisition.

We have seen earlier that a situation may exist in which each firm knows that the other knows that a price rise would be profitable for both. It is possible that such a situation does not exist before a merger, but would be created by the merger. Such a situation is called the creation of a *collectively dominant situation*.

Generally, one can think of a situation when there are a small number of firms, so that a subgroup of them would be able to increase prices together, but only in the absence of competition from firms outside the subgroup. To make it simple, suppose that there are three firms, and two of them (A and B) come to an understanding and decide to raise prices together. Firm C, though, competes vigorously, trying to steal the other firms' customers in order to be profitable and gain market share. So, competition is generated mainly from C. This makes C a valuable asset for A and B. If C were to merge with either A or B, C would profit because of the additional profits the other two would make, while the other two would profit through raising their prices. Hence, a merger between C and either A or B will make customers worse off. An example of an investigation into such a merger can be found in Box 6.5.

---

### BOX 6.5   THREE FIRMS, ONE DOMINANT POSITION? THE AIRTOURS/FIRST CHOICE CASE

The European Commission's decision to block the acquisition of First Choice by Airtours in September 1999 was interesting for at least two reasons.

Normally, the Commission is concerned that mergers reducing three parties to two might create either a dominant position for the merged party or a dominant position between the two remaining firms on the market (also called a situation of 'tacit collusion', 'implicit collusion' or 'coordinated behavior' between the two remaining firms: we shall discuss these concepts in more depth in Chapter 7). In this case, however, it was the first time the Commission attempted to block a merger because it would have created a dominant position with three remaining firms rather than two: next to the merged parties, First Choice and Airtours, the

> other two parties on the market were Thompson Travel Group and Thomas Cook Group (the merged entity itself would not have had sufficient market power to raise prices, as Airtours' market share had previously been estimated at just 3 percent. The remaining firms on the market would still be large enough to compete with Airtours and First Choice).
>
> Even more importantly, the Commission's decision was later overturned by the Court of First Instance (the European court of appeal). Contrary to the decision of the Commission, the Court found that while coordinated behavior was possible in theory, the complexity of the short-haul package holiday market in which the firms operate made it highly unlikely in practice, because of, among other factors, the unpredictable evolution of demand from one year to the next, making coordinated behavior between the three remaining firms very difficult.

## *Costs associated with expanding vested interests*

The gains of expanding and of integrating with other firms may be surpassed by the costs resulting from the impairment of incentives. These costs – which are all associated with the expansion of vested interests – have different sources, as detailed below. The first category of extra costs applies to all expanding firms, while the remaining categories deal specifically with additional costs as a result of mergers between firms.

If firm size increases, *administration and organization costs* also rise. Administration becomes more complicated because of the necessity to monitor more (possibly opportunistic) agents. Organization costs increase because a larger firm implies, among other things, that more efforts are needed in order to inform agents about developments and decisions concerning the firm.

A merger of firms leads to different kinds of additional costs. First, it involves a change in property rights assignments to the agents within the affected firms. An example could be a former owner-manager becoming the manager of a division. A change in property rights affects incentives, and consequently economic behavior changes. A division manager may not have the same incentive to allocate resources carefully as the owner-manager, if as a result of a change in property rights he is exempted from full responsibility for possible losses (in the long run). As a result, procedures have to be installed in order to monitor the division. So integration of firms causes rising monitoring and enforcement costs.

Second, when innovation is involved, the manager of a division will be less motivated if she has to share the gains of a successful innovation with other divisions of the firms. As a result, the number of innovations declines.

Finally, there are adjustment costs because the organization has to be restructured. Workers may demand information or extra training if their jobs are affected by the merger or if the culture of the firm is affected. Several methods exist to classify different *organizational cultures.* Handy (1985) distinguishes a power culture, a role culture, a task culture and a person culture:

- in a power culture, one individual or one group forms the power base of the organization;
- in a role culture, individuals are controlled by procedures, role descriptions and authority descriptions;
- in a task culture, the emphasis is on results, and individuals are empowered with discretion and control over their work; and
- in a person culture, the organization serves the individual; organizations with highly trained professionals are an example.

An organization can be characterized by one or more of these types of culture. The mix of culture types determines how the members of an organization behave.

## THE DYNAMIC EFFICIENCY APPROACH TO FIRMS

In Chapter 5 we focused on entrepreneurs operating in markets. Here we focus on entrepreneurs who own a firm and whose entrepreneurial activities have consequences for the development of the firm.

Entrepreneurship and technology are two drivers of the dynamic development of firms. Entrepreneurial firms are constantly searching for new market opportunities. These may be found in new products or new production processes. Together with the development of products and/or the development of new production processes, the organizational structure of the firm may also change. For example, the development of a new product may induce vertical integration within the firm, as will be explained below. It also may encourage cooperation with other firms, which is the subject of Chapter 7.

## The entrepreneurial firm

The entrepreneurial imagination that lies at the root of the establishment of firms cannot be interpreted in terms of transaction costs, so that a TCE explanation of the entrepreneurial element is missing. Neoclassical theory has no room for entrepreneurs either. So, basically, the static approach deals with business people rather than entrepreneurs. Business people are managers who organize production. This is not the case with entrepreneurs, whose role we discussed in Chapter 5. Entrepreneurs are the driving force behind the competitive process. To put it simply: they are the ones looking for the business opportunities. That does not make them good managers, or even managers at all: that, in general, demands other qualities.

What defines an entrepreneur is that when he sees a business opportunity and decides to start a new firm, he can convince others to join his conception of that opportunity. This requires more than formal communication alone. It also requires skills such as eloquence, persuasiveness, patience and persistence, the capacity to gain sympathy, and confidence (Witt, 1999); see Box 6.6.

> **BOX 6.6 DRAGON'S DEN**
>
> The BBC television show *Dragon's Den* follows an international format that began in Japan. In *Dragon's Den*, entrepreneurs pitch for investment from multimillionaires who are willing to invest their own money in exchange for equity in a business. The game is subject to eight rules. The first rule states that the entrepreneur has three minutes to explain the investment he is proposing and the equity he will give in return, among other things. He also has to provide supporting information to convince the investors.
>
> The show reveals that a creative person with a good idea is not necessarily also a good business person. Being a business person depends on qualities such as confidence, flexibility, strength of mind and leadership. To convince potential investors, the entrepreneur has to consider the long-term aims of the business, how the business will achieve these aims, and how the business is performing at the moment. Failing to provide the necessary business information will probably make the multimillionaires decide that they will not invest in the plan.

Entrepreneurs are essential for the development of companies. A dynamic analysis of the firm is essential to do justice to the entrepreneurial element in economic progress. However, modern corporations also need to initiate production plans, organize access to finance, organize and plan the production process, and determine the marketing and pricing policy. Because all these tasks have to be performed correctly and in time, increasingly they become coordinated by written rules. Consequently, big companies have become large bureaucracies. The bureaucratized power of the executives within the firm is a dominant feature of some modern corporations.

The vested interests of the bureaucracy within the company on the one hand, and its essential role as an entrepreneur, make a dynamic analysis of the firm a very intricate one. We therefore use a highly stylized but intelligible depiction of these interactions below.

## *Product life cycles and the reorganization of firms*

Despite the fact that modern companies plan their production process, they also face fluctuations and uncertainties and have to adjust their plans accordingly. For example, through reorganizations within the firm: the division that is responsible for a new product, say, may expand rapidly after the launch of the product. However, when the product reaches a mature stage and competitors enter the market, cost reduction becomes the main goal of production, possibly with consequences for the division responsible for the product, which may then be reduced in size.

The dynamic theory of markets assumes an interaction between the structure of markets and the market behavior of entrepreneurs (Jacquemin and De Jong, 1976). In this theoretical approach, the market structure is determined by the concentration of firms, entry barriers to markets, and the degree of product differentiation. The market behavior of entrepreneurs is related to the different stages of the *product life cycle* (see Figure 6.4). Different characteristics and bottlenecks are attributed to these different stages, therefore different strategies are necessary and consequently behavior changes over time.

**Figure 6.4** *The product life cycle*

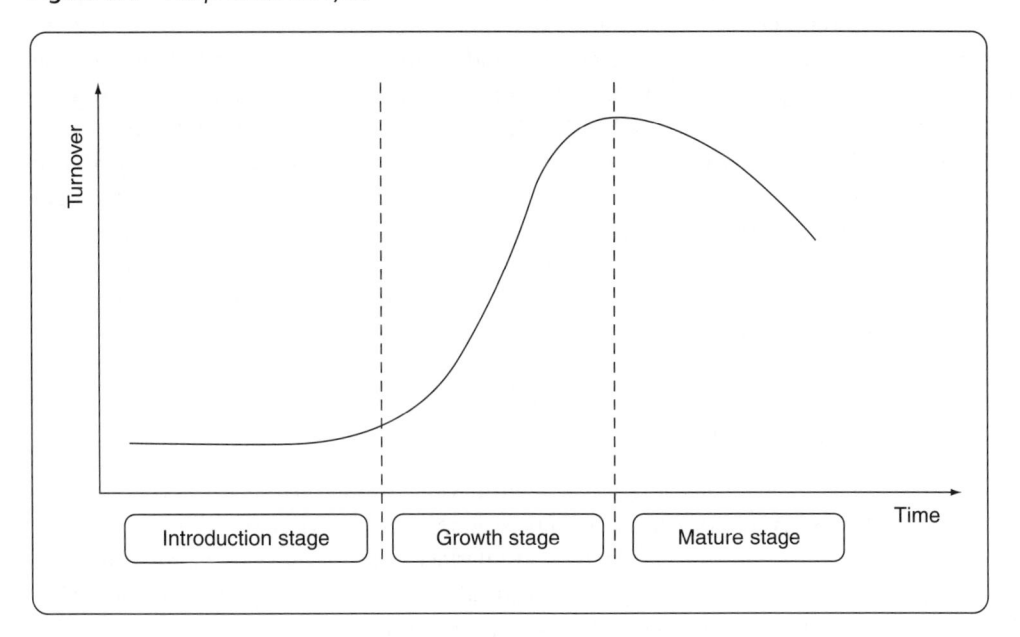

[Figure: A graph with Turnover on the vertical axis and Time on the horizontal axis, showing an S-shaped curve that rises through the Introduction stage, peaks during/after the Growth stage, and declines in the Mature stage.]

The product life cycle can be described briefly as follows. The *introduction stage* of a product follows its *invention stage*. During this stage, there is not yet a proper market for the product; the cost of production and prices are high, while the number of buyers is still small. The market has yet to be created and a production process that makes production profitable has still to be developed. At this stage, the market structure is usually monopolistic in the sense that there is just one producer of the product. The period over which an innovator may be a monopolist depends on the power of the innovating firm, the height of the entry barriers and the capability of other potential competitors to enter the market in question. During the introduction stage, comprising a testing stage and an initial commercial production stage, bottlenecks in the supply of input or in the commercialization of the end product may induce vertical integration of firms.

After the introduction stage comes the *growth stage*. More people become aware of the product. Possible price cuts forced by imitation products lead to growth in demand. New applications of the product may also be found, leading to further growth. The larger market will enable firms to apply new production techniques that fit the expanding market. Consequently, they will achieve economies of scale, which improves returns on investment. These higher profits will attract new competitors. Entering the market need not be difficult, as long as the product is not protected by a watertight patent, because imitators do not face the initial costs incurred by the innovating firm to develop the product, the production techniques and the market. New competitors will use the newest production techniques. Increasing competition during this expansion stage may induce horizontal specialization (more specialized products by different firms) and vertical differentiation (specialized firms for final products on the one hand, and intermediate products on the other). So, the growth stage is characterized by a process of de-concentration.

At the transition from the growth stage of a product to the *mature (and decline) stage*, which is characterized by a fall in the growth rate of demand, firms start cut-throat price competition, in order to keep up the growth rate as much as possible. The least efficient firms will fail and the surviving firms may tend to integrate the product chain (vertical integration) through mergers or may enter into a legal or illegal strategic alliance (such as a cartel, which will be discussed in Chapter 7). At the end of the life cycle, fewer (but the most efficient) firms will remain on the market. The market may possibly almost disappear, and only for nostalgic reasons will people carry on buying the product. For example, some consumers (continue to) buy long-playing vinyl discs (LPs) and record players to play them on, even though online streaming and downloads have become the most common method of supplying music. The surviving firms will be mainly specialist ones, sometimes with a monopolistic position, and operating in a niche market.

## From unitary (U-form) to multidivisional (M-form) organization

Within the firm, specialization requires coordination. Similar tasks such as the purchasing of inputs, acquisition of personnel and development of particular skills, planning of the production process, and marketing and sales activities have to be coordinated. The coordination of tasks may be organized centrally according to functional lines. That implies that the top management of a firm has to oversee all tasks that are performed within a particular branch of production. Such an organization is called a *unitary organization form (U-form)*; see the illustration in Figure 6.5.

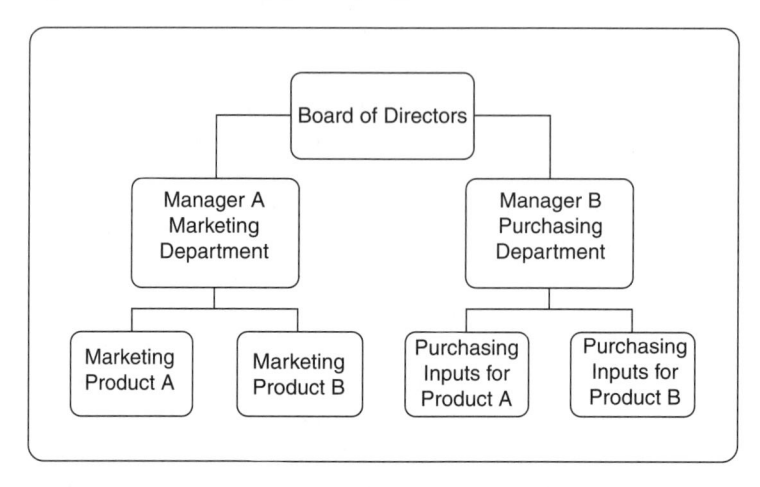

**Figure 6.5** *The unitary (U-form) organization*

*Notes*: 'Marketing' or 'Purchasing of inputs' may be substituted for 'Acquisition of personnel' or 'Planning of the production process'; the number of products may also be extended, with 'Product C', 'Product D', and so on.
*Source*: Based on Qian et al. (2006, p. 374).

The U-form is generally inefficient at providing a tailor-made approach to the marketing of different products. Because of the divisional structure according to functional lines, the marketing department makes all marketing decisions for all the products, which probably rules out a tailor-made approach for the market needs of any specific product. It is also inefficient in identifying each business division's contributions to the overall profit of the corporation: the functional division obscures how profitable a specific product is. When the profit contribution of different businesses is not clear, not only control of these businesses but also the optimal allocation of resources becomes more difficult. Moreover, because information about the performance of different business units is not available, management is unable to react effectively to changes in the external environment.

As a consequence, larger firms with this structure are forced to add additional layers of management or change the organizational structure, because not all decisions can be taken by the CEO and his board of directors. We mentioned earlier that this is one of the reasons for the existence of the *multidivisional organization (M-form)*, which structures its business along product, brand or geographical lines. Decisions can then be assigned to the most appropriate decision-making level (see Figure 6.6).

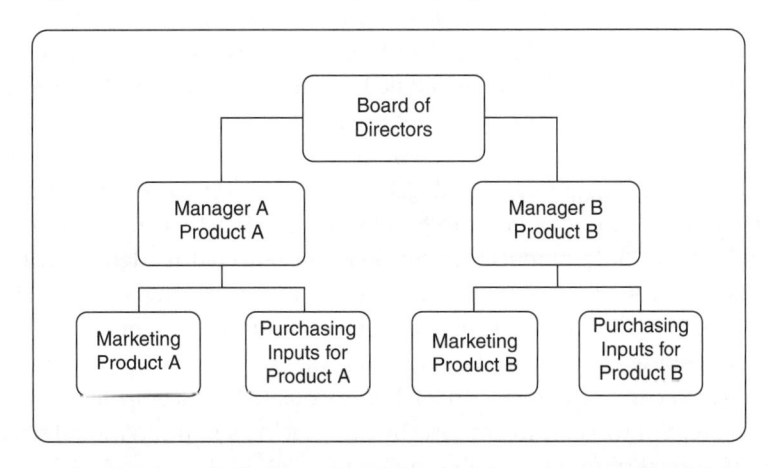

**Figure 6.6** *The multidivisional (M-form) organization*

*Notes*: 'Product A', 'Product B' or 'Product X' may replace 'Brand A, B, X' or 'Region A, B, X' and so on.
*Source*: Based on Qian *et al.* (2006, p. 374).

The driver that moves a company from the U-form to the M-form is efficiency. Because local policy advisers have access to local information they can solve coordination problems more easily under a decentralized regime than under a centralized one. While the local policy advisers focus on day-to-day matters, the executive officers may focus on strategic planning – that is, on the one hand the process of defining the direction of the company for the coming years, and on the other, the process of allocating resources to pursue the chosen direction.

The M-form structure generates information about the financial contribution of each division to the overall profit of the firm. This has far-reaching consequences for the management of the firm. First, it enables CEOs to monitor the performance of each division more precisely, and consequently makes control of each division easier. Second, it enables CEOs to compare the relative yield of different divisions. This facilitates decisions concerning the allocation of scarce financial resources. Third, it may put pressure on the managers of poorly performing divisions to do better. For a historical example of both forms of organization see Box 6.7.

---

### BOX 6.7 HISTORICAL EXAMPLES OF U-FORM AND M-FORM ORGANIZATIONS

The functionally centralized form of firm organization was applied in the 1920s in the American corporation DuPont, which mainly produced weapons. DuPont, which had expanded during the First World War, was looking for an alternative use for its unused production capacity after the war and found this alternative in the production of chemical fertilizers. However, the marketing of fertilizers is a very different business than the selling of explosives. Unlike governments at war who sorely needed explosives, farmers had to be educated about chemical fertilizers and to be convinced that these fertilizers would raise their income. Eventually, DuPont decided to establish a separate division, which was allowed to run its business without receiving detailed directions from central management.

Another well-known change in the 1920s from a U-form structure to an M-form one happened at General Motors (GM). At that time, the automobile manufacturer Ford had the biggest share in the automobile market. When the demand for autos fell in the 1920s, GM ran into problems. The Model T-Ford was immensely popular, but was only produced in black, a fact reflected in Henry Ford's famous comment 'You can have whatever color you want as long as it's black'. GM was able to grab some of Ford's market share by introducing product diversity. Consumer choice was increased by offering automobiles that were more luxurious or less expensive than the Model T, or available in colors other than black. Furthermore, GM was able to cut costs by introducing a multidivisional structure with professional staff in the central office.

---

## THE DYNAMIC VESTED INTEREST APPROACH TO FIRMS

We have already discussed the separation between ownership and control of the firm, and noted that it is difficult for shareholders to direct a firm's managers. Because some modern companies have become very large and operate internationally, they require a diversified group of executives to run the business. The executives form a powerful group who are able to set their own goals, and whose activities are often very hard to monitor. The power of the executives in large firms has extended beyond what is seen traditionally as the domain of the firm. They are able to influence the preferences of consumers through the application of modern marketing techniques and sales expertise (revised sequence; see also Chapter 5) and to influence politicians through lobbying and donations in the hope that they will receive political favors in return. Lobbying and donations are dealt with in Chapter 9.

What is important here is that the influence of large firms on consumer preferences and politicians' decisions has resulted in a society that is oriented towards private consumption, sometimes at the cost of public interest, such as negative environmental effects. As a result, countervailing power has appeared that challenges the policies of large firms. On the one hand, all kinds of pressure groups (such as environmental groups) have been able not only to put their own interests on the agenda of executive officers, but also to influence consumer preferences – for example, by promoting organic food. On the other hand, shareholders have been able to leave their mark on the policies of companies as well. This occurred not only in Anglo-Saxon countries, but in Continental European ones as well. However, because of the culture of mutual consultation in the Continental European countries, shareholder value never became as dominant as it did in the Anglo-Saxon countries.

## The power of the executives

Executives have become more and more powerful *vis-à-vis* shareholders. Along with the development of new production techniques and methods, increasingly specialists have become involved in the (mass) production of goods. The need of organizations for different specialists is based on three main factors.

First, with the division of labor, different branches of science, engineering and design (of products or advertisements) are involved in the development and provision of technologically advanced products. Because of bounded rationality, one individual cannot cope with all the aspects of the different interrelated specialized tasks that are necessary for doing business. The diffusion of knowledge requires combining the information dispersed over a variety of technical and scientific specialists.

Second, technologically advanced production methods require large investments, and consequently the development of a business plan. Investors demand a business plan before they are prepared to get involved. Private planning encompasses not only ensuring the availability of the requirements for a specialized plant, specialized workers, specific materials and components, but also a price and selling strategy. In short, technologically advanced production demands not only the organization of technical and scientific specialists involved in the production of a commodity but also the organization of specialists involved in planning.

Third, technologically advanced production requires the coordination of this variety of specialists. A specific specialist may have a clear idea about her contribution to the production process, but this must be aligned with the ideas of other specialists. Information must be exchanged between specialists, and tested for reliability and relevance.

The individual entrepreneur has been replaced by a group of managers encompassing the chairman, president, vice-president, occupants of major staff positions and perhaps even division and department heads. The joint taking of decisions attempts to bring all relevant and dispersed specialized knowledge to bear on the decision. At the same time, it provides a safeguard against individual self-interested activities. Group control curbs behavior in the sense that it becomes harder for one individual to enrich himself personally at the cost of the organization.

## Technology and executives

The ongoing division and subdivision of tasks into their component parts has not only enhanced efficiency but has also allocated influential power to executives. They have become one of the important carriers of technological development. Scientists are not only employed to produce highly advanced technological products but also to develop new products and production processes. Many large companies have a research and development (R&D) department. Consequently, technology is an integral part of the planning mechanism. This has far-reaching consequences for the organization of firms:

- This way of producing takes a lot of time: the specialized production of components has become an exacting process, and specifications prepared by designers proceed through orders to the component producers, delivery, testing and so on.
- The increased time between the initiation and completion of a product, and the increased investment in goods in process is expensive. And specialization in the components of products reduces the flexibility of the production process.
- When production equipment is designed to serve a specialized task, a change in the final product has important consequences for investment. A change in the specifications of the product or in some of its components may require an adaptation or replacement of the production equipment. However, with the increasing use of computer-aided production equipment this problem may become less urgent.
- Large-scale component production requires specialized and often highly qualified skills. This applies not only to the designers of the products but also to the planners of the production process.
- All components have to be combined so that the efforts of highly specialized workers lead to a coherent result: this organization of the production process must be financed.
- The investment in time and money adds to the need to control intervening events. For example, investment may be at risk because of the danger that technological development will supersede a product or method of production. However, through its R&D resources, the executives attempt to stay abreast of technological developments.

## Goals of executives

While the market dictates the economic behavior of owners of small firms who actively manage their businesses, the executives determine the economic behavior of large industrial companies where ownership and control of capital are separated. Even though profits are necessary for the owners of capital to invest in a product, the goals of the executives may differ from profit maximization for several reasons (Galbraith, 1974):

- Profit maximization within modern large industrial corporations is detached from individual decision-making and manifests itself on behalf of unknown, anonymous and individually powerless persons (the shareholders), hence profit maximization need not be a high-powered incentive.
- Individual power is curbed by interrelated decision-makers, and hence it is not guaranteed that profit maximization will be the firm's only goal.

- As long as salaries do not rise or fall with profits, profit maximization may not coincide with the goals of the executives. Consequently, in modern companies the incentive of maximizing one's own return by increasing that of the shareholders vanishes.

Instead of profit maximization, the executives are likely to strive for goals and strategies that lead to their own survival and well-being. Like the owner who controls the firm himself, they must secure their position, which may be threatened by shareholders, creditors, workers, consumers or the government. The executives can improve and protect their position by making the firm grow, but this growth requires uninterrupted earnings.

Why are uninterrupted earnings essential to protect the position of the executives? Shareholders and creditors may be satisfied by ensuring a certain level of earnings. As long as profits are above a certain minimum the executives have little to fear from the shareholders. And a basic level of earnings also provides the executives with a source of capital that is completely under their control. This protects decision-making from interference by creditors. A basic and continuous level of earnings can be achieved through price stabilization, cost control, demand management and lobbying to implement government policies that stabilize demand.

The position of the executives will also improve as long as the firm is growing. Growth of the firm not only enables the executives to earn more money to satisfy shareholders and creditors but also to secure their own jobs, payment, promotion and fringe benefits. In a growing firm, more jobs are created, enabling workers to achieve promotion without others being demoted. Salaries and privileges may also increase, to reflect added responsibilities resulting from the growth of the firm.

### A retreat from business diversification

The M-form of business structure has become the dominant organizational form in modern industrialized countries. However, the efficiency argument of the M-form structure has not gone unchallenged. Agency theory asserts that the executives have a utility function that includes their status, power, security and income as the main components. This behavior may be expressed in a tendency toward inefficient *empire building*. Shareholders have come increasingly aware of this and this is possibly one of the reasons for the reversal of the business diversification trend in the late twentieth century, when corporations in a wide range of industries such as finance, pharmaceuticals and chemicals, began increasingly to sell off 'noncore' divisions (Schuster, 2000).

## Countervailing power

The executives are not immune from criticism. This criticism may focus on the one-sided emphasis on private consumption and the neglect of the environment or working conditions, especially in low-income countries. However, when criticism stems from just a few individuals it may easily be ignored. It is more likely to be acknowledged seriously when it is supported by social pressure groups. These pressure groups – for example, organizations of workers, students or consumers – can be critical of an economic system in which large firms have a dominant say in social and environmental policy. These criticisms may not only undermine the authority of the executives in society but may also put the reputation of the firm at risk.

Examples are pressure groups that ask for improvements in medical care, protection of the environment or better working conditions in developing countries. Changes in these rules will not necessarily affect the members of the executive staff personally; the executives may be able to pass the costs on to customers or shareholders. That is why criticism by pressure groups may generate distrust among both the shareholders and customers, since they know that they will have to pay. Shareholders dislike lower profits and higher costs, while customers dislike higher prices. Consequently, the executives must find a compromise between criticism by pressure groups on the one hand and the aversion of shareholders and customers to changing working rules on the other.

Because the executives have to make money to secure their position, it goes without saying that they will direct R&D activities toward the reduction of production costs and the creation of profitable new products. Consequently, it is unlikely that R&D will be directed to the development of products that are needed by poor people in developing countries. These people have little money to buy medicines, and often neither do their governments. This can explain why most new drugs are for the treatment of so-called 'lifestyle diseases' and only a small number are for the treatment of tropical diseases. The executives may decide to direct R&D activities to the development of new tropical drugs if they succeed in convincing governments to guarantee the funding of the development of the new drugs, or payment for them. However, the executives may also decide to develop new tropical drugs if they expect to generate a positive image for the company that will eventually finance the costs of development.

Because the conditions of the Coase theorem are not always met, external effects may occur and not be dealt with. The testing of new drugs is an example. Medicines are tested on humans before they are allowed to be put on the market. Laws to protect participants in tests are less developed in developing countries. Consequently, pharmaceutical industries may test new drugs on patients in poor countries at lower cost, and with a lower risk of being sued for any damage caused by the new products, with possibly dramatic consequences – see the novel and movie allegedly based on truth described in Box 6.8. Of course, criticism may result in the strengthening of testing rules, or companies looking for alternative testing methods.

### BOX 6.8   THE CONSTANT GARDENER

The British movie, *The Constant Gardener*, based on the novel of the same name by John le Carré, is about the testing of medicinal drugs on poor people in Kenya. The unsavory practices of the pharmaceutical industry are not only undertaken with the knowledge of bribed local officials but also with the knowledge of the British High Commission in Kenya. These practices were possible because of Kenya's poorly developed law system.

## Continental European versus Anglo-Saxon model

In Chapter 5, the Anglo-Saxon and Continental European models were used to illustrate the different institutional choices that can be made with respect to markets. In this chapter both models are developed, detailing the different institutional choices that can be made by firms (De Jong, 1997). The main differences are summarized in Table 6.3.

**Table 6.3** *The domain of the firm in the Continental European and Anglo-Saxon models*

| Aspects | Continental European model | Anglo-Saxon model |
| --- | --- | --- |
| Policy | Profit-making with rendering account to stakeholders (banks, employees and consumers) | Value creation for shareholders |
| Decision-making | Consultative structure: policy is decided on *ex ante* in agreement with representatives of stakeholders in the supervisory board or the works council | Vertical ownership and authority structure; policy is assessed *ex post* on the basis of the net return to capital |
| Financing | High concentration of shareholders; firms are the most important shareholders in France and Germany | Low concentration of shareholders; private households own the biggest share of firms in the USA; institutional investors own the biggest share of firms in the UK |
| Time-horizon | Long-term profits for the continuity of the firm | Short-term profits to keep shareholders satisfied |

The most important difference between firms operating under a Continental European regime and those that follow the Anglo-Saxon model is the difference in the decision-making process. Under the Continental European model, a firm is an organizational unit that is also oriented to social problems and solidarity, so workers have a much stronger influence on management decisions compared to the Anglo-Saxon regime, because of the emphasis on shareholders' value in the latter rather than on all stakeholders.

The difference in the process of decision-making is accompanied by a different composition of shareholder groups. Under both Anglo-Saxon and Continental European regimes, firms are financed by outside capital. As shown in Table 6.3, in Germany and France, this capital is provided mainly by other companies; in the USA mainly by private households; and in the UK by institutional investors. In the UK, the share of private households in the financing of firms is at a level somewhere between France/Germany and the USA. Furthermore, within the Continental European model, the control structure of firms, the influential role of commercial banks and the modest role of stock markets enable firms and the whole society to focus on long-term goals and mutual interests. Within the Anglo-Saxon model, the firm is a commodity of which the owner (shareholder) can make free use.

In the 1980s, much more emphasis was placed on free market capitalism under President Ronald Reagan in the USA (1981–9) and Prime Minister Margaret Thatcher in the UK (1979–90). Accordingly, shareholders gradually achieved a greater say in company policy. To maximize profits, firms cut expenses and exported manual or simple tasks to foreign countries, where wage costs were much lower. At the same time, the rise in wages slowed, while the salaries of top executives grew at an increasing pace. Top executives were paid according to an incentive pay system, which encouraged a one-sided focus on profits.

However, this mechanism seemed to be less pronounced in the Continental European countries than in those following the Anglo-Saxon model. In the former group of countries, shareholder value also rose in importance and the directors of firms also received higher bonuses, but in general not as high as in the latter countries. The institutional framework in the Continental European countries usually does not allow shareholder value to become the dominant goal for firms.

The trend towards organizing firms according to the Anglo-Saxon model resulted in the worldwide growth of countervailing power, with protest groups criticizing, among other things, environmental problems caused by a perceived excessive focus on shareholder value. This criticism resulted in the development of ethical business concepts. In recent years, large firms have become eager to improve their reputation concerning all kinds of ethical issues.

## CONCLUDING REMARKS

Table 6.4 summarizes the main characteristics of the firm as seen from the different theories and perspectives.

**Table 6.4** *Characteristics of the firm*

| Theory | Main characteristics of the firm |
| --- | --- |
| Neoclassical Economics | Production function |
| Property rights | Nexus of contracts |
| Transaction Cost Economics | Efficient (transaction-cost minimizing) governance structure |
| Agency theory | Separation of ownership and control |

In neoclassical theory, the firm is essentially the production function that relates input to output. Since inputs are bought in markets and outputs sold in other markets, the firm, which is assumed to maximize profits, is also an actor in markets: a buyer in the input markets and a seller in the output markets. By modeling the production function as the firm's specific task, neoclassical theory implicitly assumes that a firm is efficient in transforming inputs into output.

However, this does not explain why the firm is efficient, or why it should exist from an efficiency point of view. One reason is labor specialization, which requires an organizational structure. In addition, TCE explains the existence and size of firms in terms of minimizing transaction costs. Transacting within the firm is efficient when it can solve problems related to search and contracting costs better than by transacting via markets only. Transactions within the firm take the form of the power of fiat: a hierarchy exists that determines the allocation of resources. To put it simply: one does what the boss says, because that is what one gets paid for.

That being said, new problems arise when transactions occur within a firm – chiefly agency and/or organizational problems. Theoretically, as long as the costs of having a firm are lower than of transacting via the market, the former will be the preferred choice. This will generally be the case with high asset specificity. How other government structures apart from the market or the firm (cooperation and the role of government) fit in with these views will be discussed in Chapters 7–9.

The existence of hierarchies and the consequent agency problems within the firm will lead to vested interests being pursued. We focused on the effect of the separation of ownership and control that can easily lead to high agency costs; for example, because management is able to serve its own interests much more efficiently than the (possibly) widely dispersed shareholders are able to monitor management. In a dynamic sense, serving one's own interests within a firm can go unchallenged for a long time, but will in the end be checked, though possibly at a high cost. The financial crisis which spread in 2008 and the subsequent recession in the real economy is a painful example of such a process.

## REVIEW QUESTIONS

1. Discuss the main differences in explanations of the existence of the firm as given by standard Neoclassical Economics, contract theory and transaction cost economics.
2. Explain why transaction costs also arise within firms.
3. Which types of incentives do you think are more effective in disciplining employees: positive or negative types? Explain your reasons.
4. Transaction costs economists used to advise the introduction of large bonuses within firms in order to establish strong incentives among employees to act in the interests of the principals. Do you think this instrument is still adequate to cope with the dangers arising from the ownership of management and capital? What other instruments can be used to discipline managers of a firm?
5. Explain why a self-interest seeking manager may support a merger, even when this may cost him his job.
6. Discuss the costs related to the protection of vested interests that are associated with expanding a firm.
7. Explain why it can be in the interests of executive officers to satisfy the interests of workers at the expense of shareholders. Do you think this is a type of opportunistic behavior?
8. Do you think that commercials are a device to inform people about products, or merely devices to manipulate people into buying the products?
9. Do you know of any device other than commercials that can influence your preferences, or do you think that you are immune to attempts to influence your buying decisions?
10. Are the countervailing powers in your country welfare-enhancing or not? Provide arguments to support your opinion.

# 7 Cooperation between Firms

## CONTENTS

- **Introduction**
- **Cooperation between firms in theory and practice**
  - Different theoretical approaches to cooperation between firms
  - Real-life examples of hybrids
- **The static efficiency approach to hybrids**
  - The TCE approach to hybrids
  - Information problems and opportunistic behavior
- **The static vested interest approach to hybrids**
  - The green lobby
  - Cartels
- **The dynamic efficiency approach to hybrids**
  - Trust
  - Learning
- **The dynamic vested interest approach to hybrids**
  - Market power theory
  - The OPEC and the development of substitute products
- **Concluding remarks**
- **Review questions**

## INTRODUCTION

Nike, a famous brand of sport shoes, does not produce any footwear itself. Gallo, the largest family-owned winery in the USA, does not grow any grapes itself. And Boeing, a world leader in aircraft production, manufactures only some of the aircraft components itself. This may seem strange at first sight, but becomes logical if one looks more closely at how these companies work. Nike, Gallo and Boeing, like many other companies in the world, have strategic alliances. A strategic alliance is an agreement between firms to pool specific resources and effort to achieve mutual gains. Cooperation is a governance structure that in the transaction costs economics literature is dubbed a 'hybrid': since they are neither markets, nor hierarchies, hybrids are the governance structures of collaboration, combining elements of both market and hierarchy.

Hybrids are a very common governance structure in modern economies. In Chapter 3, hybrids were described as governance structures in which cooperating firms preserve their autonomy in many respects (strategic decision-making, daily business activities) but allow some hierarchical intervention in affairs concerning cooperation (with respect to coordinating joint activities, also known as pooled resources and efforts). This may be in the form of subcontracting, supply-chain systems, distribution networks, franchising, partnerships, alliances or cooperatives (Ménard, 2006). Several of these types will be discussed in this chapter.

A hybrid combines features of market contracts with features of the governance structure of a firm. Without hybrids, an economic system would comprise firms and markets only, which does not do justice to reality. In the words of Richardson (1972, p. 883): 'I was once in the habit of telling pupils that firms might be envisaged as islands of planned co-ordination in a sea of market relations. This now seems to me a highly misleading account of the way in which industry is in fact organised.'

The effects of hybrids on economic performance may be analyzed by taking the governance structure as given (the static approach), but hybrids may also be approached as a subject of change (the dynamic approach). In addition, trust plays an important role in the way that cooperation between firms is formally arranged. As well as the efficiency approaches, hybrids can also be explained by vested interests. This will result in reallocating resources to vested interests, but lead to social suboptimal outcomes (in which economic welfare is not maximized). However, through external developments or countervailing powers, the power derived from cooperation between firms may also be curbed. The different approaches are summarized in Table 7.1.

Table 7.1  *The static and dynamic efficiency and vested interest approaches to hybrids*

|  | **Static approach** | **Dynamic approach** |
|---|---|---|
| Efficiency | Competition law<br>TCE approach | Trust and formal contracts |
| Vested interest | Networks of firms<br>Cartels | Market power theory<br>OPEC |

In this chapter we shall discuss the concepts presented in Table 7.1. As a general background we shall start the first section with the different theoretical 'welfare enhancing' and 'welfare reducing' concepts of cooperation, followed by some real-life examples.

# COOPERATION BETWEEN FIRMS IN THEORY AND PRACTICE

## Different theoretical approaches to cooperation between firms

The necessity for cooperation is easily demonstrated with the aid of a *prisoner's dilemma* game. This game illustrates a case in which the optimal result cannot be achieved if there is no possibility of cooperation, and market transactions and hierarchy are not feasible or efficient alternatives. The prisoner's dilemma is a so-called *one-shot game* (nonrecurrent game) in which two players have the choice of cooperating or not. Assuming that each individual player is maximizing his own payoff without taking the other player's payoff into consideration, the result of this type of game will be that no optimal cooperative result is reached. To reach an optimal result, cooperation (see Box 7.1) or some degree of monitoring of behavior and institutional incentive mechanisms are necessary (see Box 7.2). If the game is played repetitively (recurrent game), a self-enforcing mechanism can result.

---

### BOX 7.1 THE PRISONER'S DILEMMA ILLUSTRATES THE NEED FOR COOPERATION

The classic example of the prisoner's game describes the choice faced by two criminals being interrogated in separate rooms (keeping their mouths shut or confessing), but the same type of game abounds in economics, so we shall present the game in an economic context.

Each of two firms (A and B), producing a homogenous good, has the option of advertising or not. If they both decide to advertise, they increase demand together and will both profit. If one of them advertises (say A), but the other does not, then B can free ride on A's advertising expenditure. If they do not advertise neither has any additional profits.

Suppose that advertising on one's own costs 4 (each firm's advertising budget); hence advertising together costs 8. Also suppose that advertising together leads to additional gains of 12 that are split evenly; in this case, each firm has a profit of (6 – 4) = 2. If both do nothing, additional profits are 0 for each, and if one only firm advertises, this costs 4, but will lead to additional demand that is split between the two firms: assume that each gets half of the additional gains of 6. So, if A invests 4, he only gets (3 – 4) = –1, while B will end up with profits of 3. The different possible outcomes are shown in a so-called *pay-off matrix* in the table below.

*Advertising*

|  | **Firm B advertises** | **Firm B does not advertise** |
| --- | --- | --- |
| Firm A advertises | A gets 2<br>B gets 2 | A gets –1<br>B gets 3 |
| Firm A does not advertise | A gets 3<br>B gets –1 | A gets 0<br>B gets 0 |

For each of the firms, the *dominant strategy* is not to advertise: whatever B does, A will have an incentive not to advertise. Suppose B advertises, then A will free ride on B's expenditure, hence A will not advertise. Suppose B does not advertise, then A is also better off by not advertising, because otherwise B will free ride on A's expenditure. Since this is true for the other party too, both will decide not to advertise, even though advertising together would benefit both.

> Therefore, in this example of the 'prisoner's dilemma' there is a need for cooperation in advertising if both are to benefit. As can easily be seen, a hierarchy – perhaps via a merger – could also solve this problem, but would not necessarily be an efficient way of dealing with an advertising problem. A market transaction would not be an efficient mechanism either. For example, if A and B had the right to claim compensation for free rider behavior, they would have to face large transaction costs in order to obtain this compensation after advertising. Negotiating compensation beforehand would also be inefficient, because joining forces and drawing up a contract to advertise together would clearly be an easier and more effective solution.

Of course, there are many more examples in which cooperation rather than hierarchy or market transactions are preferred ways of transacting, both from the point of view of society as well as of firms. Remembering what was discussed in Chapters 3, 5 and 6 and looking at the example in Box 7.1, it is clear that the free riding problem may encourage welfare enhancing solutions such as contracts in the market, monitoring within firms or cooperation. Similar arguments can be made about R&D, perhaps, or cooperation aimed at diminishing transaction costs – such as establishing trust via a brand name.

On the other hand, we have forms of cooperation that enhance the cooperating firms' welfare at the expense of consumers. A cartel is the clearest example of this: competition is eliminated between firms through an agreement to raise prices collectively. Consumers are worse off, even though the profits of the cartel members rise: these additional profits are lower than the decline in consumer welfare, leading to a deadweight loss.

This type of cartel has a couple of interesting features. One we shall discuss here is that, even if there is an agreement to cooperate, it does not mean that it will be *self-enforcing*. We shall again use the prisoner's dilemma to show this. Whereas the game described in Box 7.1 was used to point out the (possible) need for cooperation, it will be used in Box 7.2 to show that the agreement to cooperate is not self-enforcing.

> ### BOX 7.2 CARTELS AND CHEATING
>
> Suppose two independent consumer-goods businesses compete with each other, and they both earn zero profits. One day, they decide to form a cartel and raise prices together, to eliminate competition. Since this will be at the expense of the consumer, both firms gain by it: they will each have profits of, say, 10. But, if one firm sticks to the high price, the other has an incentive to cheat on the deal by offering a slightly lower price to gain additional market share (in the case of homogenous goods, all consumers will switch to the lowest-pricing firm). This will, of course, be at the expense of the other firm. The cheating firm might earn 12, while the other firm will have a loss of 2. The pay-off matrix then looks like this:

*Cartel agreement*

|  | **Firm B sticks to the cartel** | **Firm B cheats** |
|---|---|---|
| Firm A sticks to the cartel | A gets profits of 10<br>B gets profits of 10 | A gets −2<br>B gets 12 |
| Firm A cheats | A gets 12<br>B gets −2 | A gets 0<br>B gets 0 |

Again, we have a prisoner's dilemma: the equilibrium is the competitive because of the possibility of cheating: the cartel agreement is unstable.

In order to sustain the cartel, additional agreements on monitoring and punishment are needed. In this example, problems of enforcement persist even with cooperation.

A situation with the characteristics of a prisoner's dilemma can only be avoided if effective institutions have been developed to make agreements possible and enforceable (with credible sanctions if the agreement is ignored). Effective sanctions induce people to keep to agreements, and as a result make them possible and profitable for trading partners. As soon as the conditions of the original prisoner's dilemma setting are changed by introducing new rules and incentives, the pay-off matrix and the optimal strategy of the players also change, in which case it ceases to be a prisoner's dilemma game.

Players' confidence that cooperation will be successful could be supported, for example, by naming an independent authority (third party) that has been empowered by all involved to monitor the transactions and make decisions in cases of conflict. A more informal institution that can also work quite well is the *'tit-for-tat'* strategy, which was introduced briefly in Chapter 3, and to which we shall turn again later in the present chapter.

In general, cartels are seen as unacceptable governance structures because they diminish wealth in the short run. However, in contrast to this approach, in the first part of the twentieth century, several politicians and economists were in favor of contracting freedom and did not support anti-cartel laws. At the time, politicians in most countries (with the exception of the USA) were of the opinion that cartels could also play a positive role in the economy and society.

There is now a general consensus that cartels have a negative influence on consumer welfare, which is why they are prohibited by *competition laws*. In this way, the principle of contractual freedom has been restricted to cooperation that enhances (consumer) welfare and is no longer applicable to cooperation that restricts competition. Therefore competition law has to take this feature into account: there must be a difference between cooperation that is welfare enhancing and cooperation that is not. Competition law in the USA, the EU and many countries all over the world takes this into account by only forbidding agreements that have the goal or the effect of restricting competition, without creating additional welfare that is shared with customers.

If welfare is created and shared with customers and the only way to achieve this additional welfare is to restrict competition, then the gains may outweigh the costs and cooperation is allowed.

Note that this is economically sound. If we define restricting competition as the possibility of creating market power through cooperation, but additional gains are also created – for example, new R&D, new products or lower costs (perhaps a result of improvements in distribution or production), then, on balance, the cooperation may be allowed (notice that the same kind of argument is made with respect to merger control: see Chapter 6). Of course, if no market power has been gained in the first place and competition is not restricted, then competition law does not apply at all. You can read more about state intervention in cases of anti-competitive behavior in Chapter 8.

To summarize, we have three types of agreements to cooperate: noncompetition restricting agreements; competition restricting agreements that increase total welfare; and competition restricting agreements that decrease total welfare. In practice, it is sometimes very difficult to establish whether total welfare is increased or decreased; however, it is still necessary to do so to be able to distinguish bad agreements from good ones (in terms of welfare). A case in point is the Citibank example presented in Box 7.3. In the remainder of this chapter, we shall use the term *cartel* or *collusion* in the sense of welfare-decreasing, competition-restricting behavior.

### BOX 7.3 CARTEL OR WARRANTED COOPERATION?

As vice-chairman and a director of Citibank, part of Citigroup, Onno Ruding argued in favor of cooperation with other banks in order to regulate the payment of executive officers and traders. According to him, short-term bonuses are dangerous for the continuity of banks, because these types of bonuses result in decision-making that loses sight of risks. He supported bonuses that would only be paid after three or four years. Then it could be assessed whether unacceptable risks had been taken. This is a typical example of the prisoner's dilemma: Citibank could not introduce this type of bonus without the cooperation of the other banks, because Citibank's executive officers or traders would prefer positions with these other banks in that situation. Only by implementing the proposed bonus system at the same time could all banks help to solve the problem.

Other banks argued that entering into an agreement with competitors was not an option because of the antitrust laws. However, in the context of the subsequent financial crisis, it seems that antitrust laws may not always benefit society in the long run.

But would the agreement have violated antitrust laws, had it been made? The agreement could have led to lower short-run risks for banks and for the economy at large. So, on balance, the effect of cooperation could very well have resulted in decreased risks.

# Real-life examples of hybrids

Firms may want to share costs by pooling resources, to gain access to new markets. Think of airline companies: they may acquire rights to land in certain countries through collaboration with other companies that already have those rights. A common form of cooperation in professional service industries are partnerships based on proven professional knowledge. These types of partnerships may be found in accountancy, judicial advice and physics, among many others. Or firms seek cooperation in order to obtain economies of scale, to diversify risk, to develop new products, to acquire means of distribution or a new technology, or to restrict competition (through the formation of a cartel). In connection with restricting competition, predatory pricing has already been mentioned in Chapter 5, and mergers and acquisitions in Chapter 6.

Here we present some examples of the countless varieties of hybrids available. Below we shall discuss the Japanese *keiretsu*, elements of which have been copied worldwide; three other examples of hybrids found in several countries – namely, cooperatives, licenses and franchises; and finally, Islamic banks, which are a mix of cooperatives and franchises. Licenses and franchises are different from cooperatives in that the members of a cooperative own the enterprise, whereas a license or franchise involves only the property right to use a certain concept, such as a brand name.

## *Japanese supply networks*

In Chapter 3 we introduced the Japanese *keiretsu* as an example of a hybrid governance structure. The *keiretsu* developed after the Second World War, replacing the *zaibatsu* – conglomerates controlled by their founding families with centralized ownership. The *zaibatsu* governance structure can still be found in South Korea under the name *chaebol*. In contrast to the *zaibatsu* and *chaebol*, a *keiretsu* is characterized by a cluster of independent, autonomous organizations that coordinate their transactions without any one of them being the central player. The organizations work together to further the group's interest. Two basic forms of *keiretsu* can be distinguished: the vertical and the horizontal.

Horizontal business groups (for example, Mitsubishi, Mitsui and Sumitomo) consist of autonomous industrial enterprises centered around a major bank and a general trading company. These groups are formed via cross-shareholdings, interlocking directorates and through regular meetings of the presidents of the member firms, where information is exchanged about new technologies, new markets and all kinds of political issues. The two main characteristics of the relations between the member enterprises are equality and the freedom to borrow from other banks, or to use the trading services of firms from another *keiretsu*.

Vertical business groups are groups of enterprises of subcontractors and trading firms. Their relationship is characterized by inequality; that is, the leading enterprise dominates the other enterprises. The management of the firms in the vertical business groups (for example, Tokai Bank, the Industrial Bank of Japan, Nippon Steel, Hitachi, Nissan and Toyota) are controlled by a 'core' firm. The aim of this structure is that the parent enterprise can create subsidiaries each with its own decision power (though the top management of the 'parent' has considerable influence on its 'daughter enterprises').

Here we shall illustrate the significance of cooperation through the example of the automobile company, Toyota, which is both a member of a horizontal *keiretsu* and a parent enterprise in a vertical *keiretsu*. The Toyota Motor Company developed a system aimed at eliminating waste; that is, the use of resources for any goal other than creating value for the customer. This type of production has become known as *lean production*. Toyota owns a stake in its main supply companies. These equity stakes enable the company to make credible commitments (see Chapter 3) to these suppliers, and to cooperate with them in improving the quality of the product and reducing the costs of production. Both share in the benefits that result from working together. It also enables Toyota to exercise control not only over the prices that suppliers charge for the different components, but also over the quality. This system eventually became known as *just-in-time, or stockless production* and requires a strong commitment from suppliers.

Toyota combines the advantages of craft production (variety) and mass production (low prices). Craft production is based on highly skilled workers using flexible tools, who adapt the product to the requirements of each customer. On the other hand, mass production is based on low-skilled workers using expensive, pre-programmed machines to make a large volume of standardized products. Logically, when large numbers of units are being made, craft production tends to lead to higher costs than does mass production. Toyota's 'lean production' methods avoid this crucial drawback while maintaining a large degree of flexibility. By applying the lean production concept, the Toyota Company was able to produce automobiles much more efficiently than North American or European producers in the 1980s. They produced autos with less of everything: 'compared with mass production: half the human effort in the factory, half the manufacturing space, half the investment in tools, half the engineering hours to develop a new product. Also, it requires keeping far less than half the needed inventory on site, results in many fewer defects, and produces a greater and ever growing variety of products' (Womack *et al.*, 1991, p. 13).

Proponents of successful lean production in the automobile sector claim that it can be extended to other sectors of the economy. The essence of the management system is that employees develop a loyalty to the organization as a result of a commitment to lifetime employment and rising wages with age and tenure. In North America and Western Europe, firms selectively attempted to imitate Japanese methods by adopting the just-in-time system and flexible work rules, but without the employment guarantees and without offering continuous challenges. Instead, these firms only selected symbolic trappings from the new cultural paradigm, by introducing terms such as 'mission statement', 'total quality management' and 'multi-skilling' (Waters, 1995, pp. 85–6). In such an environment, 'workers may feel they have reached a dead end at an early point in their career.... [As a result] They hold back their know-how and commitment, and the main advantage of lean production disappears' (Womack *et al.*, 1991, p. 14).

## *Cooperatives*

A *cooperative* is an association of autonomous individuals or firms who seek their common goals through a jointly owned and democratically controlled enterprise. Cooperatives exist in many countries and in diverse economic sectors, such as in agriculture, the retail trade and banking. The members may be suppliers, as is the case with a cooperative dairy factory; or customers, as is the case with a cooperative bank. In the agricultural sector, numerous cooperatives have evolved that support autonomously operating farms; for example, cooperatives owned by several farmers to process the milk they produce; see Box 7.4.

> ### BOX 7.4 COOPERATIVES AFFECT ECONOMIES OF SCALE AND SAVE ON TRANSACTION COSTS
>
> Farms in Western Europe were traditionally family-owned and family-run businesses. Their optimal size was small. On the other hand, the optimal size for processing products such as milk rose remarkably in the nineteenth century because industrialization opened up the possibility of factory-based processing, resulting in economies of scale. To take advantage of this opportunity, farmers have to invest in a reorganization of their business, and entrepreneurs have to invest in a milk factory. This creates a mutual dependency or, in other words, hold-up problems.
>
> The milk factory entrepreneur does not invest because he cannot be sure that the farmers will supply him with milk at a reasonable price. The farmer does not invest in the reorganization of his business because he does not trust the entrepreneur to continue buying his product at a fair price. Consequently, neither the milk factory entrepreneur nor the farmer will pay for the investments necessary to enable the processing of milk in factories. The problem is solved by establishing a specific governance structure in the form of a cooperative milk factory.

## *Licensing and franchising*

A *license* involves the transfer of a property right; for example, the right to use a brand name, trademark or a type of know-how. In exchange for the use of this right, the licensee pays a fee to the licensor. A license contract addresses issues such as:

- the brand name or trademark the license covers;
- the quality standards;
- the period that the license will cover;
- the geographical area within which the licensee is allowed to sell;
- the minimum fees that have to be paid; and
- how the relationship will be concluded when the license ends.

The Body Shop and Walt Disney are examples of license agreements. Walt Disney grants licenses to independent firms that want to sell Disney items. These firms have to meet all kinds of specific requirements, one being that they must be able to prove that they already have sufficient relevant experience in manufacturing, distribution and/or retailing. The issuing of licenses is a way to assign and protect property rights. While one may assume that licensing is an efficient device, there are also some risks involved, as Box 7.5 shows.

---

### BOX 7.5   WALT DISNEY: MADE IN CHINA?

Licenses are one possible way to protect and exploit intellectual property rights. Without a license, actors are not allowed to bring a product to market that has been invented by another firm. If caught, the offender will be sued and will probably have to pay a fine or compensation. Many illegal copies of products originate from China, and they are quite hard to combat for foreign companies such as Walt Disney, especially when it is not clear who can be sued.

In May 2007, Walt Disney discovered that, in an amusement park near Beijing, employees were walking around in costumes that looked very much like Donald Duck, Mickey Mouse and other famous trademarked Disney characters.

Despite the clear resemblance, the park management denied any similarity and therefore claimed that they were not obliged to sign a license with Walt Disney. Instead of going to court and stirring up a political row, the Disney Company used another tactic: by making sure that the media worldwide publicized the amusement park's illegal practices, the park's owners were put under pressure and had to stop using Disney look-alikes.

---

A *franchise* is a specific, more restrictive form of license. Franchising is the licensing of a business concept of a franchisor to a franchisee – for example, the acquisition of the right to use a well-known brand name or trademark, specified procedures and marketing strategies. A franchise agreement includes, among other things:

- the fee that has to be paid;
- the name or trade mark it covers;
- audited financial statements of the franchisee;
- an estimate of the total investment of the franchisee;
- supply arrangements;
- the dress code of the employees;
- the training the franchisor will provide to the franchisee and his employees; and
- all other substantial assistance such as marketing plans, business methodologies and operating manuals.

The difference between licensing and franchising is that the latter is regulated much more stringently. A franchise agreement may include hundreds of rules. With a general license agreement, a business people retain more autonomy in running their businesses than they would with a franchise contract. Well-known examples of franchising companies are McDonald's and Coca-Cola. The production and distribution of Coca-Cola is organized according to the franchising model: Coca-Cola syrup is produced by the Coca-Cola Company itself, and then sold to various licensed Coca-Cola bottlers who hold a Coca-Cola franchise for a certain region.

The franchisor benefits because she saves on transaction costs when entering and exploiting (foreign) markets (among other things, the advertising and promotional support of the franchisee can strengthen the brand or trademark, and the franchisee has easy access to the local labor market). The franchisee benefits first because he gets substantive assistance in replicating the original business model, and second because the franchisor advertises the brand or trademark.

### *Islamic banking*

Islamic banks are growing rapidly (between 10 percent and 15 percent annually (Ilias, 2008). One of the organization forms is that of a Special Purpose Entity, that is, a limited partnership to fulfill a particular or temporary objective. The bank contributes financial assets and the firm contributes productive assets. This construction may give a bank a right to a share in the profits. This business concept complies with *Shariah* (Islamic law). The Koran prohibits lending and borrowing with interest.

The mechanism that replaces interest under Islamic law is profit sharing. Capital will be invested in those sectors that offer the highest profit-sharing ratio to the lenders. It is this system of profit sharing that represents one of the features of cooperatives. There are different ways of financing investment in which profit and loss are shared in a prearranged manner. Borrowers benefit from Islamic banks because it enables them to acquire assets without breaking Islamic law. The bank can buy an asset (land, a building or a machine, say) and sell it to a buyer at above the market price. The buyer is allowed to pay in installments, and is not required to pay interest because, formally, no money is being borrowed. Other systems of financing the acquisition of assets through a bank are leasing, hire-purchase agreements, sell-and-buy-back constructions and letters of credit from a bank to allow clients to buy an asset abroad (Abdul Gafoor, 2002).

## THE STATIC EFFICIENCY APPROACH TO HYBRIDS

The transaction cost approach stipulates that independent transaction partners may gain from cooperation if total transaction costs are lower than in the cases of noncooperation (market contract) or of complete merger (firm). In general, hybrids arise when transactions involve moderately specialized production factors, or semi-specific investments. In terms of Figure 7.1, asset specificity is between $k_1$ and $k_2$. We explain below, from a transaction cost perspective, why it can be suboptimal to organize semi-specific investment through the market or through the firm.

### The TCE approach to hybrids

In general, if investment is semi-specific to highly specific, the hybrid is more effective than other private governance structures. However, with rising asset specificity, hazards increase. Then it may become profitable to invest in a relationship, especially in the

**Figure 7.1** *The domain of the hybrid*

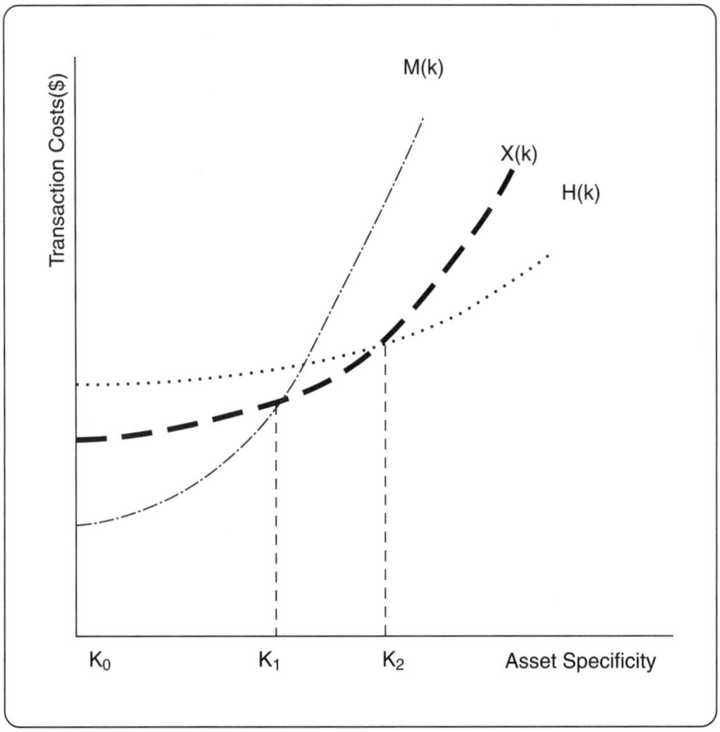

*Sources:* Based on Williamson (1996, p. 108) and Ménard (2004, p. 369).

case of recurrent transactions, in order to enforce compliance. As in Chapters 5 and 6, we shall once again take a close look at four institutional conditions that influence the choice of the governance structure: the contract law regime; property rights; reputation effects; and risk. We shall explain how the efficacy of a hybrid depends on these four conditions.

## Contract law regime

A hybrid is a mode of cooperation, with rules that establish monitoring and enforcement of the contract, which is set out as clearly and as completely as possible: not as complete as in the case of classical contracts in the ideal market (because that would be too costly), but also not as incomplete as in the case of relational contracts in a fully integrated firm. Hierarchical relational contracts, as in the firm, would be too hazardous because, in the hybrid, the contracting partners retain more autonomy compared to unified ownership in the firm. The parties preserve autonomy but are dependent on each other to a significant degree.

The contract regime that applies here is 'complex contract law'. This regime allows contracts to be mediated by a flexible enforcement mechanism (referred to by the term *arbitrage*) rather than by courts. It applies to those deviations from the contractual agreement (disturbances) that are serious (costly) enough to look for adjustments (adaptations). As long as disturbances do not occur too frequently, arbitration involves lower costs than going to court, because the appointed arbitrator can usually investigate and adjudicate in a much more informal way. Additionally, an arbitrator is usually an expert in the field. However, if disturbances become more frequent and costly to adjust to, the agreement may become subject to legal enforcement. Ultimately, an alternative governance structure, such as a merger, may be necessary.

## Property rights

Individuals and firms only invest with confidence if they consider that their property rights are protected. If hazards are present, incentives to invest will be weak. As far as the firm is concerned, opportunistic behavior can be curbed by designing contracts with the owners of different inputs to avoid the hold-up problem. However, in the case of hybrids, it is not always necessary to pool all assets. Actors may decide to pool only a proportion of their property rights in order to be more efficient, while retaining full autonomy over the remainder. Joint activities based on inter-firm coordination may be organized, to reap the benefits that accrue from cooperation, while at the same time avoiding bureaucratic costs and maintaining market incentives. In this way they can remain flexible and will be able to adapt to market developments in the way they see fit as autonomous owners/managers.

Depending on the degree to which the pooling of assets creates mutual dependencies, the signed agreements will be specified to a greater or lesser extent (hence have more or fewer built-in safeguards). For example, a dairy farmer who is a member of a cooperative has a share in the cooperative based on the quantity of milk she delivers, while two firms developing a new product together will require a much more tailor-made agreement. One real-life example is the development and market research necessary for the creation of the Senseo Coffee Maker, which created a ten-year interdependency between electronics producer Philips and coffee producer Sara Lee/Douwe Egberts.

The Senseo Coffee Maker would not have become a success without the right coffee 'pods'. During the development stage, both firms had to agree about the required specifications of the complementary products, and both companies had to decide how much money they would allocate to the development of this new product. At the launch of the new coffee maker, both firms had to agree a market price for the coffee pods as well as a price for the machine itself. Philips obtained a license for the design of the coffee maker and registered its coffee pod system. Douwe Egberts, on the other hand, did not succeed in patenting the concept of the coffee pod. As a result, several other coffee brands now produce similar pods, while other companies later introduced different types of coffee machine that were substitutes for the Senseo Coffee Maker, but for which Philips' patent offered no protection.

## Reputation effects

The more specific a mutual investment, the higher the risk of opportunistic behavior and the higher the need for safeguards. *Brand names* require the implementation of modes of control between partners to secure the reputation of the brand; McDonald's, for example, has specified the whole process of the just-in-time production of the food served in all its restaurants. The company's quality assurance process involves on-site inspections and training of restaurant personnel in the proper storage, handling and preparation of the food, among other requirements.

The reputation of a brand can be endangered if actors who are involved in selling it behave opportunistically – for example, by cutting costs and not delivering the required quality standards. The immediate gains of this short-term opportunistic behavior have to be weighed against future costs. Incentives to behave opportunistically are constrained in horizontal networks, because reputation effects are quickly communicated in nonhierarchical contracting relations, and because sanctions are available to the partners.

While reputation effects as such may be relatively small in comparison to total costs, they are significant in deciding which governance structure is optimal. An improvement in reputation weakens incentives to behave opportunistically and will therefore reduce the costs of contracting between firms. As a result, in Figure 7.1 the transaction cost function of the hybrid shifts downward and therefore the intersection point for choosing between a hybrid or a hierarchy governance structure shifts to the right. Asset specificity has to become even higher before a firm decides to produce the product completely on its own.

## *Risk*

In Chapter 6 we discuss some risks related to markets that might be good reasons for producing within a firm. However, in addition to the choice of allocating resources through prices (the market) or hierarchy (the firm), we now have an intermediate alternative: cooperation. Consequently, the risks mentioned in Chapter 6 that explain production within a firm have to be reassessed here: the risks involved in market allocation are a necessary condition for integrating transactions within a firm, but these risks are not a sufficient condition, because one first has to consider the risks of cooperation.

If there is not much market risk involved, there is no reason to cooperate. Actors (firms) may retain their autonomy and continue to deliver their output through the market. However, the higher the level of risk, the higher the need for cooperation. In such cases, firms realize that a mutual adaptation to risks is most efficient.

Risks that could induce cooperation include financial ones. The development of new products or technologies may require large investments, and the financial risk involved may be regarded as too high for a single firm to face. Firms therefore might decide to cooperate and thus spread the risk. Another example of the need for cooperation is the cost of preventing the risk of burglary. If the risk of burglary is low, firms located on the same industrial estate may decide to have their assets protected by a simple burglar alarm, but if the risk is high they may each decide that it is worth employing a security guard. If there is an 'intermediate risk' they may opt for a hybrid solution, jointly hiring an external security company to watch over the area.

Of course, cooperation itself also involves risk. When these risks are too high, firms may decide to produce completely under their own authority. Risks related to cooperation include:

- *A clash of cultures*, which can occur in the case of firms within the same country or when collaboration extends beyond national boundaries. International cooperation

not only has to face language barriers but also specific cultural situations; for example, if local workers do not want to be supervised by a foreign manager, or if politicians dislike foreign dominance of national firms. In Italy, the governor of the Bank of Italy allegedly tried (ultimately unsuccessfully) to keep ABN Amro (being a foreign bank) from acquiring Italy's Banca Antonveneta.
- *A lack of trust*, which may frustrate cooperation. Partners must trust each other's commitment, otherwise they will constantly run into disputes about one another's contribution to the cooperative effort. If one partner in particular contributes more than the other toward the success of an alliance, conflicts may arise about the sharing of gains. The less partners trust each other the more has to be stipulated in contracts.
- *Lack of coordination* of (middle) management groups, which may be expressed by managers pursuing goals that are not congruent with the goals of the CEOs.
- *Performance risk*, which refers to the danger that an alliance may fail despite the full commitment of the partners. This has to be faced by the collaborators before they enter an alliance. Performance risks include external forces such as the actions of competitors, demand risk and input risk; these were introduced in Chapter 6.

The risks involved in allocating resources through market contracts, together with the risks involved in cooperation, may reach a level where it becomes rational to internalize transactions within the firm. From the transaction cost perspective, the way these four conditions determine the efficiency of the hybrid as compared to alternative governance structures is summarized in Table 7.2.

**Table 7.2** *The hybrid and the characteristics of its main institutional conditions*

| Conditions / Asset specificity | Semi-specific to highly specific |
|---|---|
| Contract law regime | Average relevance (complex contract law) |
| Property rights | Mainly individual, with some pooled resources |
| Reputation effects | Reduce interfirm contracting costs |
| Risk | Mutual adaptation |

## *Summary*

### Information problems and opportunistic behavior

A hybrid is a governance structure in which parties remain legally autonomous, despite being mutually dependent for important decisions. The mutual dependency makes a hybrid sensitive to hazards that stem from information asymmetries. Measurement problems (when determining how much each individual participant has contributed to total output), weaknesses in the institutional environment, and changing conditions over time are also sources of hazards. To reduce these hazards it is self-evident that the partner(s) must be selected carefully. In practice, *selection* is based mainly on past experience and/or on reputation.

Hazards can also be reduced by including clauses in the contract that constrain opportunistic behavior efficiently. However, because it is too costly to design and implement comprehensive binding contracts, the contracts in use are almost always incomplete. Only some essential features can be covered by a contract, such as the duration of an agreement, the quality standards, and the tolerance zone for deviations from the benchmarks, which indicate acceptable deviations from the standard. Contracts in hybrid organizations are usually standardized, not customized to include features or incentives to meet the specific local circumstances of different partners. This is why bilateral or multilateral agreements are usually supplemented by safeguards. In this context, trust can be seen as an informal safeguard.

An essential question is: How to arrange the protection and distribution of the gains of the cooperation? Since partners mainly remain autonomous and may engage in other activities alongside the partnership, it is difficult to measure the individual contribution to the gains. While contracts in hybrid organizations deal explicitly with rules for sharing expected benefits from joint actions, *ex-post* opportunism is difficult to handle. One solution can be found in franchising, where fixed payments for the franchisee are combined with merit pay in the form of royalty rates based on the number of sales. However, determining the amount of the royalty rate is also a complex issue. One solution to induce partners to maximize their joint efforts is the *equity principle* (share everything equally) that dominates many partnerships (Ménard, 2004).

## THE STATIC VESTED INTEREST APPROACH TO HYBRIDS

Japanese supply chains, cooperatives, licensing and franchising, and Islamic banking are all examples of hybrids that can enhance efficiency. In several instances, however, cooperation between firms is not aimed at increasing overall economic welfare. Producers of final products, suppliers of intermediate products, but also buyers might strive after their own interest at the expense of others. Below we briefly highlight two illustrations: the first applies to the agricultural sector, and the second to cartels in general.

### The green lobby

To guarantee the supply of food and to stimulate productivity, governments are involved in the organization of agriculture. Higher productivity in farming implies that industrialization is stimulated: fewer workers are needed in the agricultural sector, new production techniques in agriculture imply more machines and so on. Consequently, this also stimulates industry. The growing involvement of governments in farming has been accompanied by lobbying by vested interests to benefit the agricultural sector (the phenomenon of lobbying is dealt with further in Chapter 9).

The agricultural sector in many industrial countries has significant power. Farmers are organized into cooperatives that process their products. Cooperative banks also operate in the agricultural sector. In several countries, the agricultural sector is supported by Ministries (or Departments) of Agriculture and Universities of Life Sciences, while other sectors have to rely on the Ministry of Economic Affairs and on specialized faculties within universities. Both in the USA and the EU, farmers receive subsidies or have their surplus produce purchased by the state, thus generating an inefficient outcome. Chapter 9 deals with this in more detail. Farmers might also enjoy certain tax benefits, especially with regard to family succession. If a farmer's daughter wants to continue the father's business, she might be allowed to buy the farm for its 'agricultural value', which could be (far) below the market value of the farm.

## Cartels

Different kinds of agreements between firms may lead to a cartel outcome. Firms may agree to raise prices jointly at the same time, but they may also agree to restrict output, or to divide up geographical areas. Basically, all these options amount to the same thing: prices will rise.

The only purpose of a cartel is to eliminate competition, as was discussed above. This implies that public policy is needed in this case. There are some practical problems, though. In practice, firms will realize that an overt cartel agreement is welfare decreasing. Since this behavior is usually forbidden, firms will try to conceal their agreements, or try to make agreements to eliminate competition indirectly.

In some situations, especially with a small number of firms, companies realize that a price rise is profitable because they each know it is also in the interest of the other firms to raise prices. The firms do not have to agree to raise prices simultaneously. This situation is normally called *implicit collusion*. This is in contrast to a cartel, which involves an agreement among firms to raise prices, also known as *explicit collusion*. Later in the chapter we shall discuss implicit collusion in more depth.

In terms of Institutional Economics, explicit collusion is typically a hybrid. It is not a market solution, but neither is it a hierarchy. Explicit collusion implies an agreement among firms that would normally be forbidden. Therefore this agreement is not enforceable by law. Hence, it must be enforceable by the firms involved. It therefore requires the involvement of not too many firms, a mutual monitoring and a disciplining device (as discussed earlier). A famous example of a cartel involving the OPEC will be discussed later in the chapter.

## THE DYNAMIC EFFICIENCY APPROACH TO HYBRIDS

The dynamic approach emphasizes corporate strategy as the reason for changing the structure of governance and institutions. This occurs, for example, when firms are confronted with an external shock in the form of a huge decline in demand resulting from an economic downturn, and consequently decide to develop a new governance structure because the existing one proves to be inadequate.

An example is the decision of the Italian firm Fiat to begin a close collaboration with the bankrupt American automobile firm Chrysler, to enable the latter to carry on in business. As of May 2009, the two firms formed an alliance in which the following deal is made: in exchange for, initially, 20 percent of Chrysler's shares, Fiat will deliver the technology and knowledge needed to make small and energy-saving autos. Moreover, the two firms will start to use each other's worldwide distribution network and will combine forces in purchasing components, to save on costs. One final advantage of this alliance is that both firms will acquire access to new markets (Vlasic and Schwartz, 2009).

The governance structure may also be changed deliberately by building on trust. Cooperation between firms may be based on contracts and/or trust. Contracts and trust are related. Consequently, it pays to invest in building trust if it saves on contracting costs. As noted earlier – the more one party trusts the other, the less do contracts need to be specified in detail.

## Trust

The TCE approach assumes that people may have a propensity to act opportunistically, and underlines the necessity to take precautionary measures with rising asset specificity. Sanctions from authorities (such as the law, churches, organizations and monarchs) and contractual obligations, as well as self-interest and reputation effects, are some reasons why people keep their side of an agreement (see Chapter 3). These control mechanisms limit opportunistic behavior.

Controlling behavior assumes that the controller knows *ex ante* what to control. In reality, this is not always the case. There is always the possibility that the parties do not have all the relevant data. Consequently, contracts will almost never be complete and monitoring will almost never be perfect. Trying to conclude more detailed contracts and to stipulate more detailed monitoring will add to costs, and hence form serious barriers for cooperation.

Sometimes uncertainty may be so high as to make it impossible to draw up a detailed contract or to monitor behavior effectively. This occurs in particular when innovation activities are involved. In the case of R&D, outcomes and rewards are largely unknown. Since it is often also highly expensive, R&D is a very risky investment, meaning that cooperation would be an effective way of dealing with this risk, as saw earlier in this chapter.

While it is not possible to assess propensities to opportunistic behavior perfectly *ex ante*, this may change with repeated transactions. Over time, parties learn more about the behavior of their business partners. If the transaction partner is trusted to refrain from opportunistic behavior, detailed contracting and monitoring become unnecessary. Instead of using formal contracts, cooperation may be arranged on the basis of informal agreements or trust. Trust lowers transaction costs and supports cooperation, and it therefore pays to invest in building trust.

Firms may strengthen their relationships with present partners or partners they know from the past. Trust is the belief that all aspects of a partnership that are not stipulated in a contract will be successful. In other words, it is the belief that partners will behave reliably. As we have seen in the case of the self-enforcing mechanism of repeated interaction, the future rewards of cooperation and the possibility of retaliation form a disciplining device that may enhance cooperation: this mechanism might also be the basis for trust.

While contracts and trust may thus be substitutes, they might also be complements in the sense that contracts are not always used and interpreted in a formal way. Trust may curb relational risks. It is enforced at a macro level by values, social norms of proper conduct and social obligations, and at a micro level by bonds of friendship, kinship, routines, habit and empathy. In less economic terms, one can characterize trust as being the result of egoistic, altruistic or reciprocal behavior, where the latter may be seen as an intermediate form between egoistic and altruistic. The egoistic part of reciprocity is based on an assessment of the future benefits of present cooperation. This may include reputation effects and expressions of appreciation, so a gift may be given in order to satisfy long-term self-interest. The altruistic part of reciprocity may be based on shared values and norms. Altruistic behavior is also endorsed by personal relationships (family, friendship or empathy).

Through reciprocal and altruistic behavior, managers of different teams may set up or strengthen a trusting relationship in such a way that they will exchange useful information. Cooperation between firms could also be strengthened by improving existing personal ties between members of the different management teams. However, people might also behave reliably because opportunistic behavior would undermine their reputation. The mechanisms that enforce cooperation under egoistic, reciprocal and altruistic behavior are summarized in Table 7.3.

**Table 7.3**   *Sources of reliability*

| Type of behavior | Macro level | Micro level |
| --- | --- | --- |
| Egoistic | Sanctions (the law, churches and monarchs) and contractual obligations | Self-interest, reputation |
| Reciprocal | Values and norms | Reputation, expressions of appreciation |
| Altruistic | Values, norms, sense of duty | Bonds of friendship, kinship |

*Source*: Based on Nooteboom (2002, pp. 64, 74).

## Learning

Trust is adaptive. It may be strengthened or weakened according to the experience with a partner's commitment to a relationship. If a person has proved to be disloyal in a former relationship, trust is weakened and one may wish to safeguard future relationships with this person through more detailed contracting and monitoring. However, in general, trust may be assumed to increase with the duration of a partnership. As the partnership progresses, the counterparty's commitment is increasingly taken for granted and similar loyalty expected in the future.

These personal experiences may be enforced by a reputation mechanism. An individual's reputation might reveal that other people have similar experiences with the transaction partner in question. This may influence a firm's decision to either reinforce existing networks or to expand to new network partners. The latter action bears a higher risk. When risk is high and big investments are at stake it is likely that firms will want to tighten their existing network ties rather than enter relations with potential partners they do not know.

Through experience one may learn about the trustworthiness of transaction partners. It may foster trust and make it cheaper for firms to conclude a contract or to make agreements without contracts. In terms of Figure 7.1, the transaction costs function of the hybrid shifts downward: and the intersection point for choosing between a hybrid and a hierarchy governance structure shifts to the right. Asset specificity has to become higher before a firm decides to produce the product completely on its own.

# THE DYNAMIC VESTED INTEREST APPROACH TO HYBRIDS

As already indicated at the start of this chapter, explaining the dynamics of cooperation between firms requires an analysis of the strategy of firms. With regard to the dynamics of their vested interests, it is essential to focus on the strategies of firms to strengthen their power.

The search for market power is a complicated process, as will be seen later in the chapter. Firms are constantly competing with each other either to keep their position (market share) or to improve it. Firms may try to strengthen their power through cooperation with other firms. This cooperation can sometimes be realized implicitly, as we shall illustrate. However, power formation by cooperation also has its limits, as will be shown by the case of the OPEC, discussed below, where we shall look at the threat of new entrants and new substitutes.

## Market power theory

At the start of the chapter we stated that the risk of cheating in prisoner's dilemma types of transactions can sometimes be overcome by a strategy of 'tit-for-tat'. This strategy is an example of a self-enforcing equilibrium: because parties can punish each other in the case of repeated interactions, complying with cooperation becomes a serious option. This is true regardless of the nature of the cooperation: it may or may not be welfare enhancing. If a cartel is self-enforcing in the sense of the repetitively played prisoner's dilemma game, then, as noted above, it is called an implicit cartel or implicit collusion. In Box 6.5 we illustrated that the occurrence of implicit collusion can be a reason to prohibit a merger, and in Box 7.6 we illustrate how implicit collusion comes about.

---

### BOX 7.6   TIT-FOR-TAT AS A SELF-ENFORCING EQUILIBRIUM STRATEGY

The prisoner's dilemma is a static game that is played once: a so-called 'one-shot game'. But in general many agreements cannot be characterized as one-shot games and may be played more than once. In this kind of recurrent setting, other strategies to enforce an agreement in the setting of a prisoner's dilemma situation are possible, among them 'tit-for-tat'.

This strategy must be seen from the following 'dynamic' perspective: in each period of time, the prisoner's dilemma game is played. If you cheat on your business partner in some way, you can very well expect her to retaliate in the next time period; so the gains of your opportunistic behavior are likely to be more than offset by the effects of her retaliation.

So, assume that one of the firms starts to charge the cooperative (highest) price. The other firm has the choice to also charge this price, or to undercut it. Now the tit-for-tat strategy is that, starting from the highest price, if the other firm undercuts, the punishment involves returning to the one-shot game (competitive) equilibrium outcome and not to return to high prices.

The following happens, if we take the example of Box 7.2 as our starting point. Each firm has the choice of charging the high price, so that profits of 10 are realized in each period, or to undercut, in which case a profit of 12 will be realized in one period, and zero profits ever after that. Each firm has to weigh the additional one-time profits of 12 against the profit loss of 10 for ever after. This may result in a stable outcome. Because of the specific assumptions of the model, it is not possible to state that 'tit-for-tat' automatically results in a stable dynamic equilibrium, but intuitively one can see in this specific example that such an equilibrium is plausible: either a profit of 12 once only as against profits of 10 for ever.

The model requires that the game will be played for ever, or alternatively ends at an unknown date. If the game ended on a predetermined and known date, at that moment the game would become 'one-shot' again, with no more cooperation. Since the game ends, there is no possibility of punishment in the following period. And if punishment is no longer possible on the last date, then the game in the time period before the last also becomes a 'one-shot game', with the same consequence: given that no punishment is possible, there is no deterrent effect, so self-enforcement is no longer a viable alternative.

In Chapter 4 we pointed out that in this type of model, many equilibria may exist. This is also the case with the tit-for-tat strategy: many prices can be equilibrium prices, and the model cannot predict which price will be chosen. This means that some additional mechanism is needed in order to determine which of the possible outcomes will result.

The question of how to determine market power in practice can be answered by using the model developed by Porter (1980). According to Porter, market power is determined by five fundamental forces:

1 The threat of new entrants.
2 The threat of substitute products.
3 The bargaining power of buyers.
4 The bargaining power of suppliers of intermediate products.
5 Rivalry among existing firms.

These are illustrated in Figure 7.2 and discussed below.

**Figure 7.2** *Porter's five forces*

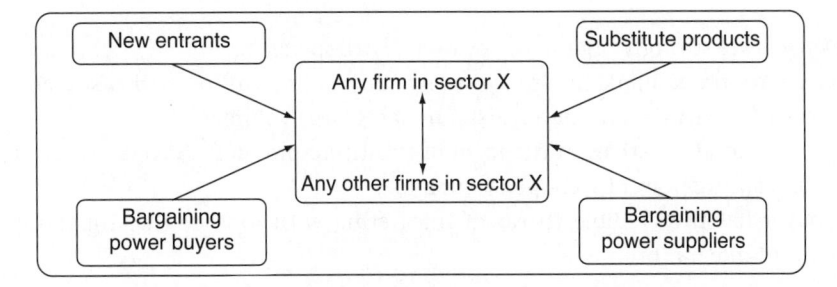

## Threat of entry

Entry barriers come from several sources. Major barriers include:

- economies of scale;
- product differentiation: design and brand image, technology, customer service, dealer network;
- capital requirements: entry may require large financial resources;
- switching costs: changing from one business to another involves costs such as employee training and sunk costs that are not recovered when leaving one market in exchange for another;
- access to distribution channels: costs to persuade dealers or retailers to stock a product;
- cost disadvantages independent of scale: new firms may lack rent-producing resources such as patents, technology know how or access to raw materials; and
- government policy: licensing requirements, limits to access to raw materials, water and air pollution standards, safety regulations and so on.

Through cooperation firms may secure distribution channels and exclude new entrants from the market. For example, an automobile manufacturer may give adealer the right to sell his vehicles. Through cooperation, firms also may achieve economies of scale.

## Threat of substitute products

For most if not all products, substitutes exist; common examples are the different music systems available, such as CDs and radios. These products compete with each other not only in price but also in quality. When buying CDs became relatively expensive in comparison with using new music systems such as MP3 players and digital radios, customers began to turn to these alternative products. For some consumers, however, choice is most importantly determined by quality: tube television sets are relatively cheap compared to flat screen liquid crystal display (LCD) and plasma TVs, but have a lower image quality, so the more expensive items are preferred. The existence of substitutes limits the power of firms to raise prices.

## Bargaining power of buyers

Buyers compete with suppliers by forcing down prices or by negotiating higher quality or more services. By doing this they may play firms off against one another. Buyer power is high if:

- the buyers are strongly organized (possibly by cooperating);
- it is a concentrated market (with a few large buyers in terms of market share);
- the buyer (or organization of buyers) purchases large volumes;
- the buyer has alternatives in the form of substitute products. Buyers also strengthen their bargaining power by cooperation; and
- the buyer has the credible threat of integrating with (one of the) supplying firms (backward integration).

Buyer power tends to be low if:

- the producer has a credible threat of integrating with (one of the) buyers (forward integration);
- buyers are small (in the sense of low market share); and
- buyers are locked-in (high asset specificity), hence have high switching costs.

## Bargaining power of suppliers of intermediate products

Suppliers of products and production factors may decide to raise prices or reduce quality. This policy may be pursued if the industry is dominated by only a few (cooperating) firms while buyers are dispersed, or the product is an essential input to the buyers' industry. Bargaining power is also high when the supplier does not have to fear substitute products.

Labor may also exercise power. The main explanatory variables for the power of labor supply are the degree of organization and the scarcity of the skills involved. The greater the percentage of workers organized into labor unions, or the greater the scarcity of their skills, the stronger the probability that workers will gain higher wages at the cost of profits. Furthermore, just like buyers, suppliers of intermediate products and of labor may form a countervailing power.

## Rivalry among existing firms

Firms not only face negotiations with buyers and suppliers of capital, labor and intermediate products, but also with other firms in the same industry. This competition may be simple price competition, but also marketing competition, new product launches or more and/or improved customer services. This multiple competition is the dynamic driver of economic development.

However, here also cooperation between firms may restrict competition and enhance the power of the cooperating firms. An example of cooperation between firms in order to constrain competition is the OPEC.

## The OPEC and the development of substitute products

The OPEC is a standard example of a cartel that decides on price and each partner's contribution to output. The OPEC countries regularly meet to decide on these issues, without always attracting particular attention. But in 1973 and 1979 the OPEC decided to cut oil production dramatically. This was repeated in December 2008 when once again it decided to cut the volume of oil production significantly in order to stop the fall in the price of oil as a consequence of the financial crisis of 2008. However, even cartels such as the OPEC face limits as to the price they may set. Six of these limits are:

1 If OPEC restricts production enough, higher prices may make it profitable to exploit small oil wells, or oil wells that are difficult to reach and had previously been unprofitable. So the OPEC always has to take into account potential rival oil producers.
2 OPEC can never be sure that every member will stick to the agreement to cut production.

3 Not all fossil-energy producing countries are a member of the OPEC: the supply of crude oil from the OPEC countries was 36 percent of the total world supply in 2008.
4 Not all of the buyers on the oil market are able to pay any price demanded. Businesses with high energy costs may become bankrupt if oil prices go too high, thus diminishing the demand for energy.
5 High oil prices provide incentives for the development of energy-saving products. Numerous energy-saving products are already on the market, including automobiles that need less fuel or no fuel at all (hybrid or solar-powered autos and so on), energy-conserving household appliances (such as highly efficient heating systems and refrigerators), and low-energy light bulbs.
6 High oil prices provide an incentive to search for alternative sources of energy. This will now be explained in more detail.

The alternatives may range from nuclear energy to other fossil-energy sources (such as gas or coal) or durable energy (such as solar energy, wind energy, earth warmth energy and bioenergy). Because of the dangers of nuclear energy (think of the Chernobyl disaster in 1986, or the fact that a good solution for the radioactive nuclear waste does not yet exist), this alternative may at present be considered at a disadvantage. Biofuel also has a disadvantage because it requires a relatively large amount of land, which may be needed for the production of food (on this, see also Chapter 9). Nevertheless, efforts to find solutions for these problems may eventually pay off.

At the beginning of the twenty-first century, solar and wind energy seem rather promising. Both require relatively small amounts of land. Solar energy may be produced on a small scale on existing roofs and on a mass scale in deserts. Wind energy may be produced on a small scale in the countryside and on a mass scale out at sea. Furthermore, production costs have fallen dramatically since the 1970s, and are likely to go down further with technological improvements.

Wind turbines already produce electric power in several countries, such as the USA. Solar energy is also being produced on a relatively large scale. Germany, India, the USA and Spain are investing in concentrated solar power plants. In Saudi Arabia there are sun islands operating out at sea.

In short, the vested interest of the OPEC countries is not secure, because they can never be sure that all the cartel members will stick to the agreements, and because alternative energy sources and energy saving devices are being developed at speed, whether stimulated by government subsidies or not. In fact, once alternative sources of energy become a large-scale threat to OPEC, its optimal strategy could be to invest in these energies. In that case, the cartel would be contributing to efficiency improvements.

## CONCLUDING REMARKS

The governance structure of cooperation between firms is conceptually between market and hierarchy, which is why this governance structure is called a hybrid. In a static approach, the hybrid may be chosen for reasons of efficiency, while from a dynamic perspective, cooperation may be explained through the strategic choices of firms that strive for long-term profits. Their strategic choices may focus on increasing labor productivity, expanding the market, or controlling resources and/or competitors. All these objectives may be attained more easily through cooperation. From this point of view, cooperation may be seen as an extension of the analysis of the dynamics of a firm, as described in Chapter 6.

The dynamics of private governance structures have consequences for government policies, not only with regard to competition law and corporate law but also with regard to income distribution and the production of public services and goods (which may be ignored in the case of a one-sided focus on private consumption). Government policy and its governance structures are the central theme of Part IV.

## REVIEW QUESTIONS

1 The combined allocation of resources by market contracts and by the power of fiat is called a hybrid. Analyze the market contract components and the hierarchy components of the different forms of hybrids described in this chapter.
2 Do you think that game theory as represented by the prisoner's dilemma gives a useful theory to solve real economic problems? Explain your reasons.
3 Why are collective labor agreements in Europe exempted from antitrust legislation?
4 Why do cooperatives exist in a competitive market economy?
5 Discuss the specific hazards of franchises.
6 Look in today's newspaper and find a good example of a hybrid. Discuss.
7 Give an example of how changes in transaction costs may result in changes in the optimal governance structure for a specific transaction.
8 Give an example of how a change in asset specificity over time impacts upon the optimal governance structure for a specific transaction.
9 Discuss the importance of trust for minimizing transaction costs in hybrids.
10 Discuss three sources of reliability and apply them to your own social environment.
11 Give your view on the following statement: the OPEC is a blessing for the world because it has accumulated enough capital to invest in durable energy.

# PART IV

# Public Governance Structures

Chapter 8  State Intervention to Protect the Public Interest
Chapter 9  Government Failures

## INTRODUCTION

In Part III we focused on transactions between private actors, and how these parties make use of all kinds of institutions to solve their contractual problems. As we have already made clear, transactions between private parties do not come about in a vacuum, but take place within a legal system of a nation or a supranational entity. At the national level, each country has a government, whether or not democratically chosen, and this government sets the rules that influence how people transact. In addition, at the international level, countries have concluded agreements that apply to a large region such as the European Union or North America, or sometimes even to the whole world: think, for example, of worldwide treaties in the field of protecting the natural environment or children's rights.

Governments not only set rules, but also engage in transactions themselves. In the first place, any government needs a public bureaucracy to implement its decisions, to offer goods and services to (groups of) citizens, and to monitor whether people live by the legal rules. Examples of this public bureaucracy are the ministries, judiciary, the army and the police, and councils at the provincial and/or local level. In addition, government agencies are involved in transactions with private parties, which can be either of a mandatory or a voluntary nature. Examples of the former include all kinds of levies and taxes (income taxes, import duties, anti-pollution taxes, sales taxes and so on), while examples of the latter include a wide range of subsidies and all kinds of services, such as public transportation, radio frequencies, infrastructure, and so on.

Depending on the country in which you are living, the political and legal system is shaped in a specific, often unique, way. In the same way, worldwide, many different types of bureaucratic systems can be distinguished. As a consequence, the terms 'state', 'government' and 'public administration' are often assigned divergent meanings that may vary across countries. For the sake of simplicity, in this book the terms 'state' and 'government' will be regarded as identical. Together with its parliament, the government represents the political system of a country, while the term 'bureaucracy' represents the supportive administrative system of a country. In order not to be too simplistic, though, Box IV.1 elaborates on the many different aspects of the organization of a state.

---

### BOX IV.1　TRIAS POLITICA, GOVERNMENT, STATE AND PUBLIC ADMINISTRATION

In daily life, the terms 'state', 'government' and 'public administration' are often used as synonyms, but just as much these expressions are used in different ways.

One way to make a distinction between the three terms is that a state may be regarded as the coordinating political system of a country, based on a set of institutions such as a constitution. In this system, we formally distinguish between three powers, namely the executive power (the government), the legislative power (the parliament or its equivalent) and judicial power (the courts), together denoted by the term *'trias politica'* (meaning 'the separation of three powers'). The purpose of this separation of powers is to ensure that a sufficient number of checks and balances have been built in to the system to prevent one group abusing its position of power at the expense of the others. Each power is independent, and has its own rights and responsibilities toward the others and toward the citizens. The legislative power has been assigned the decisive right to initiate and approve laws. The executive power also has the right to initiate laws but these are subject to the legislative power's approval. The approved laws are subsequently implemented and enforced by the executive power, with the aid of a public administration. The judicial power monitors the way in which the laws and regulations are put into practice.

Different countries have implemented the *trias politica* in different ways, which may sometimes make it difficult to define exactly what is meant by terms such as 'government', 'state' or 'public administration'.

In the USA or Australia, the concept of a 'state' refers in the first place to a political unit within the federation – Texas in the USA and Queensland in Australia are examples. These states are only partially sovereign and are subject to the authority of the national government. To complicate matters further, while many countries use the term 'government' to denote the executive power, the Americans use the term 'administration' (as in 'the Obama administration') for this.

To avoid confusion, for the purposes of this book, we shall use the terms 'executive power', 'government', 'state' and 'public administration' as synonyms, and this is intended to capture the government proper, therefore the ministers and/or the president that rule over a country. The legislative power is being captured by the term 'parliament', which generally consists of two parts: a senate (House of Lords, Upper House) and a house of representatives (Lower House). The seats in parliament are occupied by the delegates of political parties.

In this book, the executive power and legislative power together represent the political system of a country, while the term 'bureaucracy' represents the administrative system. Both systems also exist at different lower levels (provinces, counties, municipalities and so on); we shall not differentiate between the different levels though. The bureaucracy comprises the whole organization that supports the government, most notably the ministries (including all bodies related to the ministries – for example, executive agencies such as the police and regulatory bodies) and the judiciary.

From an institutional perspective, the role of the government and its ensuing laws and policies can be found in two different layers of the dynamic model that was presented in Chapter 2. Figure 2.5 (see page 69) distinguishes between formal public rules and public governance structures on the one hand, and the way that public actors operate on the other. By specifying separate layers, more attention can be paid to important issues such as: How have all the different (formal) rules come about; and how do these rules apply in practice? In the end, neither the government nor the bureaucracy can be treated solely as a holistic entity, but must be seen as a pluralistic, complex organization involving many participants with possibly conflicting interests. As we shall see, especially in Chapter 9, both formal and informal institutions enable and constrain the behavior of the actors in the political and administrative system.

The role of the government can be analyzed from perspectives of both efficiency and vested interests. The efficiency approach emphasizes a (holistic) government that seeks to improve overall economic welfare by eliminating welfare losses, while the vested interest approach focuses on a (pluralistic) government that is swayed by interest groups.

A government may be regarded as the sole authority that safeguards the interests of the public at large by setting the rules of behavior, monitoring compliance with these rules and acting as an arbitrator in case of conflict. In line with this, the government has been given the so-called 'monopoly of coercive power' within a certain geographical area, which implies that only the representatives of the government, notably the police and the army, are allowed to use force to enforce the rules (Weber, 1964).

Basically, a government could merely set the broad rules within which a market economy can flourish. This is what is often referred to as the *protective function* of the government. In such a society, the government:

- is responsible for clearly defined enforceable property rights;
- has created a reliable law and court system;
- has set up a central bank that controls the money supply;
- has a police force to maintain public order; and
- has an army to defend the country against intruders.

Such relatively limited tasks of the government fit the role of government in the standard neoclassical analysis of the model of free competition. This is often denoted by the terms 'libertarian state' or 'night watchman state'.

As discussed in Chapter 1, each country has its own specific economic system, in which the government has a smaller or larger impact on the economy. Depending on the specific society, we see that governments are often endowed with other functions than the basic protective one. The question then arises as to why these differences exist. The general answer is that in each separate society there are certain *'public interests'* that are best served and protected by some kind of state intervention. This subject has already been touched on in Chapter 3.

Public interests can be defined in different ways. In the efficiency approach, the concept of public interest is related to the welfare of the total population that cannot be achieved sufficiently by private initiatives alone. If we assume that private actors tend to strive for the maximization of their own particular well-being, this could be at the expense of others. In a lawless society, the strong always gain at the expense of the weak, and opportunistic people will always achieve their goals at the expense of honest citizens. More specifically in economic terms, public interest can be at stake in situations of market imperfections. In the vested interest approach, the public interest is defined by the actors in control. Consequently, the government seeks to protect public values that may be defined differently over time, depending on the question of which interest groups are in power at any given moment.

As became clear in Part III of the book, to a certain degree private actors can deal with problems related to market imperfections themselves. However, it can also be the case that the transaction costs of dealing with these problems through private ordering are too high for the citizens involved, and then the government needs to intervene. Different motives may prompt this intervention. The government may act from motives of efficiency (mainly a microeconomic perspective); for macroeconomic policy reasons; from geopolitical motives (vested interests); or for social reasons. We shall focus in Chapter 8 on state intervention that aims to improve efficiency (economic welfare).

In several parts of Part IV, however, we shall also touch on macroeconomic policy, geopolitics and social policy issues, since many institutionalists argue that economic performance should be judged not only by the efficiency outcome of an economy but also by the extent to which a society has attained welfare in a broader sense, including characteristics such as security and equity (Tool, 1993; Vatn, 2005).

At this stage it is good to introduce the concept of *social welfare*. This term is an extension to the concept of economic welfare. If a government strives to optimize social welfare this means that it does not only take the enhancement of efficiency into consideration, but also the question of whether the distribution of wealth can (or should) be improved. Here we arrive once more at the issue of societal objectives and the question raised in Chapter 4, regarding which values and norms determine the societal objectives in the first place. Hence, social welfare is a more complex concept, combining the objective term efficiency with the more subjective terms equity and redistribution.

We would also like to stress here that market imperfections are not only studied by institutional economists. Modern mainstream Neoclassical Economics (NCE) also focuses on these phenomena, as you may have found from reading a microeconomics textbook, for example. The main difference between the two approaches is that in NCE the emphasis is usually on the mere occurrence of market imperfections and their effects on economic welfare, whereas Institutional Economics extends this analysis by trying to explain what possible institutional solutions exist to solve these inefficiencies, and how these solutions have evolved.

We can see that, in each country, the different forms of market imperfections create smaller or larger problems. Consequently, divergent public interests receive different degrees of attention. It may be that similar public interests are at stake but that governments come up with different solutions. This depends, among other things, on the historically developed value system of a society: in one country, the protection of the underprivileged among the population may be considered much more important than it is in another. We do not aim to explain the existence of the different kinds of economic systems that can be distinguished all over the world and throughout history. Instead, we want to set out, in general terms, why and how different forms of private ordering, such as those discussed earlier in the book, are supplemented with diverse forms of public ordering, from both a static and a dynamic perspective.

Broadly speaking, as introduced in Chapter 3, we distinguish two categories of public ordering in a market economy: regulation and state-owned enterprise. By *'regulation'* we mean state intervention in the free play of market forces: as a result of governmental rules, taxation or subsidies the government aims to influence the economic behavior of private actors in such a way that the public interest is served. Government interference may be limited to merely setting the basic rules with which private actors must comply, while letting them make their own choices within such a basic regulatory framework. Intervention may also imply that private actors are heavily regulated and can hardly take any decisions themselves, or even none at all.

The second category of public ordering we refer to as *'state-owned enterprise'*. With a state-owned enterprise, government intervention goes even further than regulation, because the government has taken the provision of certain products (goods, services) into its own hands. In that way, the government takes or keeps control over these products. The consequence of this is that the ownership rights now lie with the state and, as we know from the insights of property rights theory, that this leads to specific incentives for the people involved. These people are both the workers employed by the government and the private actors who need to transact with publicly owned enterprises. These state enterprises can dominate or monopolize a complete sector of the economy, or in an extreme situation, even the whole economy. In the latter case, the market economy has been replaced by a planned economy.

In Chapter 8 we shall focus on economic systems that are a mixed form of pure market economies and planned economies. The reason for this choice is that mixed economies are predominant in a large part of the world, and that Institutional Economics can clarify why this is the case.

Depending on political motives, a market economy may choose to install a political system in which the government acts mainly as a so-called *'regulatory state'* or as a *'developmental state'* (Johnson, 1982). While in both systems the private actors remain autonomous, the difference lies in the way in which the government intervenes, and for what purpose. In the first case, the government only aims to influence the economic process by setting general rules, with which private actors must comply, while in the second case, the government aspires to influence economic activities by giving many more directives to private actors. In the former case, the public bureaucracy can remain relatively small (and 'at arm's length'), but in the latter case, the size of the public bureaucracy is usually much larger and hence more costly.

The regulatory state mainly pursues a policy with respect to competition and corporate law (getting the institutions right). Through this the way is paved for competition, which can improve efficiency. In that sense, the regulatory state fits within the static approach: given the institutional environment, private optimizing actors can choose their own preferred governance structure and make the most favorable transactions. In contrast, the developmental state actively pursues a policy in which it determines the (political) goals, and actively designs and guides the process towards those goals, notably in the fields of technology and industrial policy. In that sense, the developmental state clearly fits within the dynamic approach. In line with this active interventionist approach are the policies pursued by governments to attract investors, high-skilled workers and companies to their country; this is referred to as institutional competition and will be discussed in Chapter 8.

The degree to which the government has come to influence decision-making by private actors can be both constraining and enabling. People tend to associate government intervention with restrictive rules, but many state directives are in fact aimed at creating opportunities. More examples will follow in Chapter 8, but for now we shall give two brief illustrations. There are rules in the field of competition law aimed at curtailing collusive behavior or abuse by dominant firms. On the one hand, these laws constrain actors, by forbidding and punishing the abuse of market power; but on the other hand these same laws enable firms to compete in a fair way and allow consumers to pay a fair price. Another illustration concerns rules in the field of corporate law. On the one hand, these laws constrain firms in the sense that they are obliged to disclose relevant information about their economic performance; but on the other, the laws thereby help (potential) shareholders to make a sound investment decision.

In fact, state interference could be compared with a firm in which a central authority has been given the power to direct people within the organization. And just as in a private enterprise, the government should, from the perspective of efficiency, use this authority in such a way that all actors involved receive the appropriate incentives to ensure they are both dedicated and productive.

There are many different ways in which a government can intervene. In Chapter 8 we shall indicate in which situations of market imperfection a government is likely to opt for a mild version of regulation, or for the most far-reaching type of intervention (in the form of a state-owned enterprise), or anything in between. Schematically, in Table IV.1

Table IV.1 *Different forms of state intervention to serve public interests*

| A. Regulation of private actors | Examples |
|---|---|
| Rules, directives about quality | Liability system; license to establish a business; mandatory disclosure of relevant information |
| Rules, directives about price levels | Maximum prices with respect to medicines; public transport; ban on price cartels |
| | Minimum wages |
| Monitoring by regulators (stemming from both types of rules mentioned above) | Competition authority |
| | Sector-specific regulators (telecoms, energy) |
| | Health inspection; product safety inspection |
| Taxation | Anti-pollution taxes for producers |
| ▪ aimed at constraining behavior | Levles on products that are 'bad' for consumers (liquor, tobacco) |
| ▪ aimed at redistribution and financing public expenditure | Income taxes, road tax, value added tax |
| Subsidies | Support of target groups to help finance the |
| ▪ aimed at stimulating behavior | purchase of 'good' products (schooling, art visits, proper housing) |
| ▪ aimed at redistribution | Social security system, to provide an income for the sick, the elderly and the jobless |
| Legal monopolies (whether through concessions or not) | Postal services; gas, water and electricity networks; public transport |
| **B. State-owned enterprises** | **Examples** |
| Public provision (alongside private competitors) | Recovery of oil and other natural resources |
| Public monopolies | Health care; national broadcasting systems; state prisons; central banks |

we distinguish two main categories of state intervention, and indicate several examples of subcategories. The first main category entails the regulation of private actors, implying that they can still make autonomous decisions; their behavior is intended to be influenced by the specific form of the regulatory measure. The second category involves state-owned enterprises, which operate alone on the market (*public monopolies*).

Worldwide, there are so many different forms of state intervention that we do not pretend to provide an exhaustive list of subcategories here. Moreover, it should be noted that the above examples do not hold in all countries across the world. Where some states have chosen to take complete control by, for example, nationalizing a certain sector (such as the extraction of energy resources), other states have taken the opposite course by privatizing that same industry. So, as a result, in several countries business activities, such as health care or public transport, are not state-owned but owned privately, and run either by a number of independent firms or by a so-called *legal monopoly*. This refers to a private firm that has obtained the exclusive right to supply a certain good, albeit under strict conditions with respect to prices and quality. You will read more about this in Chapter 8.

As already indicated above, there are many different economic reasons why a government chooses to intervene, and why it intervenes by means of regulation only or by taking complete control. As noted above, there may be motives regarding the improvement of efficiency, and those regarding the protection of vested interests. As institutional economists, we are, above all, interested in the effect of (changing) institutions on the economic outcome, either at the (inter)national level or at sector level, and vice versa. In Chapter 8 we shall concentrate on the welfare-enhancing impact of government regulation and state-owned enterprises, while in Chapter 9 the focus will be on the drawbacks of state intervention and public bureaucracies.

As was the case in Part III, in this part too we shall start each chapter with the static institutional perspective and then deal with the dynamic institutional perspective. In the former, the government intervenes in a given environment of, for example, technology and social values, whereas in the latter the government operates in a changing environment. In other words, in the static approach we explain the decisions and interventions

**Table IV.2** *The static and dynamic efficiency and vested interest approaches to government interference*

|  | **Static approach** | **Dynamic approach** |
| --- | --- | --- |
| Efficiency | Regulatory state<br>Policies to combat market imperfections<br>TCE approach to government interventions<br>Unintended government failures | Developmental state<br>Institutional competition |
| Vested interest | Government failures caused by agency problems and rent-seeking behavior | Regulatory risks<br>Long-term effects of lobby groups |

of governments in different countries with certain given (though often different) cultural backgrounds; while in the dynamic approach we explain how all kinds of changes in a society with respect to, for example, technology and public opinion, influence the way in which governments interact with the economy.

The four approaches are summarized in Table IV.2, in which each quadrant shows some of the main topics that will be dealt with in Chapters 8 and 9.

# 8 State Intervention to Protect the Public Interest

## CONTENTS

- **Introduction**
- **The static approach to state intervention**
  - Imperfect information
  - Market power and natural monopolies
  - Externalities
  - Pure public goods
  - TCE approach to public ordering
- **The dynamic approach to state intervention**
  - Central planning and indicative planning
  - Industrial and technology policy
  - Institutional competitiveness
- **Concluding remarks**
- **Review questions**
- **Appendixes**

## INTRODUCTION

In this chapter, we shall deal with the static view and dynamic view of state intervention. Our focus will be on the efficiency-enhancing effects of public ordering. The failures of state intervention will be discussed in Chapter 9.

As indicated in the introduction to Part IV, state intervention is needed when public interests are at stake. From a static neoclassical efficiency point of view, public interest is defined by market imperfections that cannot be solved by private actors. Hence, also from a TCE point of view, we shall try to answer how and why state intervention is the preferred (most efficient) governance structure. In Chapter 1, we introduced the main manifestations of these problems. Here, we refresh your memory by giving a brief clarification for each of the different forms of market imperfection, which will be addressed below.

1 *Imperfect information* can become a public problem if private parties are unable to detect (from a consumer's point of view) or signal (from a producer's point of view) the

true quality of an asset at reasonable cost. As a consequence, fewer products are traded, and certainly fewer products of good quality. This may, among other things, frustrate innovative entrepreneurs; it may endanger the health or safety of the population; and may ultimately hamper economic growth. Below we shall show how the government can improve these situations.

2 *Market power* as well as *natural monopolies* noticeably threaten the public interest, because, for example, the existence of a sole supplier or a cartel may reduce economic competition to such a degree that consumers are forced to pay high prices. We shall deal below with the different ways in which governments apply competition policy or install specific regulators to combat this problem.

3 *Externalities*, and in particular negative externalities (economic side effects, which harm third parties without compensation), can hurt the public interest even when property rights are clearly defined. As we shall set out below, the government could act as an arbitrator or instructor to solve or prevent problems related to complex negative externalities, such as air pollution. But also in the case of certain positive externalities – in the field of health care, say – government assistance may be needed to promote welfare.

4 *Pure public goods* are assets that are characterized by nonexclusiveness and nonrivalness, which leads to the problem of free riding behavior, with the consequence that a private market for the asset in question will generally not arise. If the government thinks it is important that the asset should be available to the public at reasonable cost, it must take measures itself to realize the provision. This will also be discussed below.

The static part of this chapter will be rounded off by applying transaction costs economics to state intervention. In the later part of the chapter, dealing with the dynamic view of state intervention, we shall discuss how the government can intervene efficiently by coordinating the process of change. We shall show the roles of government in terms of being an information provider (indicative planning), as well as an initiator of change in the field of innovation (technology policy), and at times a driving force in restructuring the economy (industrial policy). In addition, we illustrate how jurisdictions compete with one another in order to attract foreign investors and specialized workers, through the establishment of attractive institutional constructions.

## THE STATIC APPROACH TO STATE INTERVENTION

In the static approach of institutional economics, one of the main questions to be answered is: Why are transactions coordinated through different governance structures? When is it best to choose to contract via the market, and when do people prefer to transact via a firm? Alternatively, when do we see transactions by means of private ordering (market, firm, hybrid), and when do transactions take place through public ordering?

The overall answer from this static efficiency point of view would be that, in any given institutional environment, actors look for the optimal coordination mechanism in which to do business. In other words, people aim to trade property rights with the lowest possible transaction costs (*ceteris paribus*). Ideally, these transactions take place within the sphere of private ordering, in an economic system in which the fundamental rights of the citizens are clearly defined and protected.

Often, it is clear that the basic protective function of the government is not sufficient. The 'invisible hand' that supposedly makes private optimizing actors act in such a way that the whole society benefits does not truly materialize in the real world. In many situations, privately ordered markets fail. Bounded rationality and market imperfections may lead to opportunism to such an extent that the general public needs to be protected by the government. In this section we shall therefore look at state intervention that is motivated and justified by reasons of efficiency (transaction costs). Where appropriate, we shall also pay some attention to government intervention resulting from social and paternalistic motives.

As already touched upon in the general introduction to Part IV, in real life, markets hardly ever function perfectly because of instances of imperfect information and market power on the one hand, and all kinds of externalities on the other. In these circumstances, the government could decide to intervene because the public interest may be at stake, and consequently welfare is not maximized. State interference may reduce or even eliminate the arising deadweight loss, and hence increase efficiency. In this chapter, we assume that the government will only intervene with the objective of enhancing welfare; it will then choose that specific form of intervention to serve the public interest, which minimizes total costs, including transaction costs.

In succession below we shall pay attention to state intervention as a reaction to imperfect information; market power and natural monopolies; externalities; and finally, pure public goods. After that, we shall use the insights of transaction costs economics to explain the government's choices regarding different forms of intervention, ranging from mild regulation to strict direction, or even state-owned enterprises.

## Imperfect information

As we explained in Chapter 1, we distinguish between two types of imperfect information. On the one hand, knowledge can be distributed unevenly among the different actors, so that some could use it to their advantage. These are situations of asymmetric information that coincide with opportunistic behavior. For example, for consumers, it is often difficult to obtain reliable information about the prices and quality of goods for sale, so they might find themselves buying a 'lemon' (see Chapter 5). On the other hand, knowledge can be imperfect for all the actors involved. In these situations, the problem does not concern opportunistic behavior but rather the incapacity of actors to obtain accurate information to the degree that is needed to undertake a transaction. This latter type of imperfect information might still imply that knowledge is unevenly distributed, but not in the sense that actors can take advantage of it for their own benefit.

So, both types of imperfect information match up with different kinds of problems, and then the question arises as to what can be done about these problems. As we saw in Part III of the book, private actors attempt to deal with both types of imperfect information themselves in a number of ways. On the one hand, alert and innovative entrepreneurs attempt to generate extra information that they subsequently sell on the market. On the other hand, we observe all kinds of private initiatives to combat conditions of asymmetric information.

To protect themselves against the purchase of 'a lemon', actors can try to build in sufficient safeguards in their contracts with other private parties. In addition, organizations such as consumer associations increasingly attempt to inform buyers about the quality and prices of assets – this has become easier as a result of the rapid development of the internet. Thanks to modern communication possibilities and a critical media (the press, radio and television companies) the reputation of sellers is now influenced more easily. Furthermore, instigated by competition, suppliers of goods and services may have the incentive to disclose relevant information about their products themselves. They may also try to signal to the buyers that they offer good products with an accurate correlation between quality and price – by means of, among other things, their membership of a trustworthy trade organization, offering warrants, and being able to show proof of professional competence.

However, private solutions for problems of imperfect information may falter because of very high transaction costs. This applies especially with respect to products of which the risks or intrinsic quality cannot be assessed by outsiders, or can only be assessed some time after the acquisition of the products. How can consumers find out whether (new) medicines are safe and effective, or whether the food sold in stores is healthy? What prices are they willing to pay for products and services of which they cannot know the real quality? How can insurance companies, having to deal with problems of adverse selection and moral hazard, calculate the risk that somebody will lose a job, or become sick or disabled? For multiple reasons, banks were very reluctant to lend money during the 2008–9 financial crisis, which in fact aggravated the economic situation worldwide; how could private parties solve this problem?

These are just a few examples to show that, for several goods and services, imperfect information can lead to failing markets: many people may feel too hesitant to make a risky transaction as a result of their limited capacity to oversee the consequences of their sale or purchase. The resulting inefficient outcome can manifest itself in two different ways. First, fewer transactions take place than would be the case if people had complete oversight, with respect to goods as well as to investments, referred to respectively as underconsumption and underinvestment. Second, transactions might disappear completely, when people are not willing to pay the market price that is based on averages. This implies that certain transactions fail to materialize through private governance structures, even though it is commonly recognized that it is in the public interest if these products were to be made available.

To combat problems of imperfect information that harm the public interest, a government may therefore decide to intervene by using generic measures, or by way of more specific arrangements. We shall explain both types of intervention in more detail below.

### *Generic state intervention in case of information imperfections*

A government might think that the economy in general would function better if people were more secure about their business deals: if people feel more secure, they would be more willing to buy, and this would increase the number and volume of transactions, hence stimulating employment and economic growth. Consequently, the government might introduce regulatory measures, such as the mandatory disclosure of information about craftsmanship, ingredients, and quality of products and services, and set up an inspection agency to monitor compliance with these regulations; and it could augment the basic protective laws with new rules such as an extensive liability system that aims to make producers and consumers more careful.

To aid private actors (notably consumers) in general, governments to a smaller or larger degree require that producers give sufficient information about the goods that they are selling to the public. By doing so, these goods can be valued correctly before the purchase instead of afterward; in that way, you could say that as a result of mandatory disclosure of information, experience goods can be turned into search goods (see Chapter 3).

A good example of this relates to electrical appliances. Consumers often lack knowledge about the amount of energy that such machines use, and often tend to buy a less expensive device that is, however, more wasteful of energy. If at the outset they had had the information about the amount of energy consumption, they could have saved on future electricity bills and at the same time made a contribution to protecting the natural environment. That is why, all over the world, governments have been employing several initiatives in this field, as is shown in Box 8.1.

### BOX 8.1   ENERGY LABELS IN THE EU AND JAPAN

In 1996, the European Union introduced the mandatory EU Energy Label, a sticker that in all EU member states must be attached to a wide range of electrical appliances such as washing machines, refrigerators, lamps and so on. This label tells prospective customers how wasteful or economical the appliance at issue is, and distinguishes seven levels of energy consumption. In Japan, a similar labeling program was launched in 2000, but this is a cleverer concept because it is dynamic.

In the EU, once a producer has reached the (predetermined and constant) highest level (standard), there is less incentive to improve the product any further. In Japan, however, the standards are set according to the level of the most efficient product on the market in each category of electrical appliances. The energy label not only indicates whether or not the standard has been reached, but also, if applicable, by what percentage rate a certain product exceeds the efficiency standard. In that way, producers are continually incited to introduce innovations.

There are several additional methods in use to legally enforce the provision of more information on the price and quality of products and services. In many countries, shops are obliged to put price tags on their complete stock, and the law may stipulate that consumers can never be required to pay more than is indicated on those price labels. In addition, producers are often obliged to indicate the price per unit (such as a kilo), thus making it easier for consumers to compare the true purchase costs of products. Further, manufacturers are required to give detailed information about the composition of consumer products, to enable the user to compare the quality and to see whether a product may contain elements to which a person is allergic, for example. On that topic, there is also an obligation for producers to enclose information leaflets with their products about the composition and (side) effects of medicines.

Furthermore, governments may also require that producers disclose more information about themselves – such as qualifications with regard to their crafts. Many businesses can only start up after the government has issued them with a permit to establish their business, which can be considered as a more far-reaching form of state intervention. Such a license can only be obtained when the applicant has been able to show enough evidence of her expertise by way of a diploma or other certificate. Or it could be that a permit is only granted (and renewed) if an entrepreneur is able to prove that she is operating in accordance with environmental regulations and the stipulations of labor laws. Subsequently, the producers that operate with a license can signal to consumers that they work according to certain minimum standards, and that they have a sufficient amount of knowledge which is of a high quality.

Mandatory disclosure of information may, however. still not be enough to guarantee that consumers will always be satisfied with their purchases. Precisely because of an uneven distribution of information about the products for sale, opportunism may drive producers to take advantage of that situation despite all. They will weigh the costs of supplying good quality products and the costs of giving sufficient information against the possible benefits of selling greater amounts. And then they may come to the conclusion that it is not worthwhile to pay these extra costs, despite being legally obliged to do so.

To combat this potential behavior, the government can take additional measures to create suitable incentives for producers. Obligatory disclosure of information and the introduction of inspection agencies are examples of state interference that fall under the heading of *public law*. In these cases, it is the government that imposes the rules and actively enforces them, and in which the government is the counterparty in court cases. Another way to discipline producers is through an extension of the *private law*, by means of a liability system.

The more actively governmental *inspection agencies* monitor the behavior of private suppliers on the market, the higher the probability that actors will not try to use their information lead to their own advantage. This effect will be enhanced even further if the price for getting caught is high, either by way of fines, by losing the permit to operate, or by a jail sentence. As well as this, being caught by a public authority also jeopardizes an individual's reputation in the private sector, which may increase the incentive to be a fair businessman or woman.

In case of a conflict about *liability*, the aggrieved party can sue the producer and a court will have to decide whether, and how much, compensation should be awarded. In this case, private parties are counterparties in court cases. If this damage payment exceeds the cost of improving the quality of the product, an incentive is created to deliver good quality. In the USA, laws exist to provide remedies to consumers for mechanical products that repeatedly fail to meet certain standards of quality and performance. These are nicknamed 'lemon laws'. The federal lemon law (the Magnuson–Moss Warranty Act) protects citizens of all states. State lemon laws vary by state, and the rights afforded to consumers may exceed the warranties expressed in the purchase contracts. The federal lemon law as well as most state lemon laws also determine that the warrantor may be obliged to pay a complainant's legal fees if he prevails in a law suit.

> ### BOX 8.2  DIFFERENT LIABILITY SYSTEMS
>
> It is not automatically the case that liability is always assigned completely to producers; consumers may also carry some liability. The reason for this is that consumers may have the incentive to behave opportunistically (or carelessly) as well. If all liability falls on the side of the supplier, this could very well induce moral hazard behavior on the part of the consumer.
>
> Consider the responsibility of airline companies to transport the luggage of their passengers with care. This accountability does have its limits, however, because an airline would only be able to guarantee no damage at all to suitcases by incurring excessive costs. Therefore, it is customary that if someone's belongings do get damaged, or even lost, the reimbursement is limited to an official maximum. The idea behind this is that the traveler also has the obligation not to expose truly valuable luggage to the risk of breakage or disappearance: in such a situation, the traveler should think of alternative (and more expensive) ways to carry the valuables – by taking out supplementary travel insurance perhaps. The traveler shouldering part of the risk is most probably cheaper than the alternative: if the airline company were to be held fully accountable it would have to undertake costly measures, which would be very likely to push up ticket prices.
>
> So, most of the time the law stipulates that both parties to a transaction carry part of the liability. A manufacturer has the obligation to deliver a good quality (and safe) product, but the consumer also has the obligation to use this purchase with due care, otherwise there would be no entitlement to a reimbursement in the case of damage. Hence, the whole idea behind any liability system is to create the right incentives for all actors, from the perspective of the public interest.

## *Sector-specific state intervention in case of information imperfections*

State intervention may also be aimed at specific professions or sectors, because the goods they supply are considered to be of great importance to the public at large – professions such as public notaries, lawyers and doctors; and sectors such as social and health insurances, the pharmaceutical industry and the financial sector. Because of information imperfections, products from these sectors may be underprovided or the markets for these products may not come in existence at all, while they are considered to be crucially important for the well-being of the population. With respect to the provision of such products, the government could either enforce this by making public provision mandatory, or the government could install sector-specific regulators to ensure sufficient protection of the public interest. We shall focus attention on both aspects.

First, we take a look at government interference with certain *professions*. What is notable about these specialists is the fact that on occasion citizens can become dependent on the services of such a practitioner while the information asymmetry is large. The services these professions offer are referred to as *credence goods,* which means that clients simply have to trust that the service offered is of good quality. Contrary to the situation with *experience goods* – which buyers can discover the quality of after they have bought the item, with credence goods this might not be the case. Principal–agent problems may lie ahead, for example, when someone needs to be represented by an attorney in a lawsuit, or to be treated by a doctor. Because the efforts of the agent that is hired to defend the person's interests in court or to treat the illness can be of vital importance, those practitioners have to meet all kinds of strict legal requirements before they are allowed to establish their businesses.

Monitoring of these professions can be organized by the state or self-regulatory. Inspection agencies can be installed by the private parties themselves, which has advantages and disadvantages compared to being monitored by state agencies (Philipsen and Maks, 2005).

The benefits of self-regulating agencies are that they have the specific knowledge needed to monitor in the most efficient way, they can react more swiftly to changing circumstances, and the monitoring costs are borne by the profession itself. The drawbacks, however, are that the members of the profession can act as a special interest group that may abuse its specific knowledge. If self-regulating agencies can determine the quality requirements themselves, they may effectively block entry for newcomers, thereby restricting competition and increasing their own incomes. They could also abuse the information asymmetry by creating unnecessary 'supplier-induced demand', by making their clients believe that they need to take out extra insurance or undergo additional medical treatment. And finally, they are able to pass on part of the costs of self-regulation to consumers, by charging higher prices for their services.

Given these shortcomings, in many instances state regulation can be found alongside, or instead of, self-regulation. The government has several instruments at its disposal. It can set minimum quality standards and install a specialized public monitoring agency that oversees the quality of the supplied services and guards against deceptive advertising. Moreover, it can issue licenses that can only be obtained by members of the profession after they have been able to show proof of their expertise by way of diplomas, practical experience and so on.

At the *sector level* we also see government interference in certain industries, and for similar reasons to those regulating certain professions. Some industries deliver important products that should not be left completely to free market forces, because imperfect information puts individuals at too great a disadvantage with regard to their physical condition or financial means. State regulation can take the form of installing supervisory bodies, while another option is the initiation of mandatory social insurances. Both aspects of state involvement will be considered in more detail below. The examples we shall describe comprise the pharmaceutical industry and the financial sector at large, hence all organizations that are active in financial markets, including banks, insurance companies and firms that issue stocks.

The main reason for government regulation in the *pharmaceutical industry* is to protect the health of the population, because that affects economic growth. This is the case because, among other things, a deterioration of the people's well-being coincides with a range of negative externalities such as higher premiums for health insurance, higher amounts of sick pay and a loss of labor productivity. This may affect a country's competitive power. For these different economic reasons, governments all over the world have installed inspection services to monitor the quality of medicines. In Box 8.3 we illustrate this with a specific example.

---

### BOX 8.3   THE CHINESE FOOD AND DRUG INSPECTION SERVICE

In China, the State Food and Drug Administration (FDA) takes its tasks very seriously, and there is much at stake, since all kinds of Chinese products, among them foods and medicines, are being exported at an increasing rate. To remain an important supplier, China must ensure that the public trusts Chinese merchandise, both at home and abroad; in particular, the inhabitants of Hong Kong have shown themselves to be very critical about the quality of products from elsewhere in China.

However, much to the concern of the Chinese authorities, the civil servants running the various inspection services can be susceptible to bribery, and this is what happened at the FDA in 2007. The director of the FDA was found guilty of corruption because he received gifts from pharmaceutical companies in exchange for leniency in approving inferior products. When this was discovered, the director was sentenced to death, not only as a deterrent example to other managers but also to reassure (prospective) buyers all over the country and across the world that the (often cheap) Chinese products do meet the international quality standards.

---

Mandatory social insurances have been introduced in most welfare states across the world to deal with adverse selection problems that generally hit the less privileged in society the hardest. Imperfect information may drive up premiums, making insurance covering unemployment and disability risks and so on unaffordable for the people most in need of them (see Box 3.5 for this mechanism). Making this insurance obligatory for a considerable proportion of all citizens transfers the risk from the individual to the community, and may thus increase the welfare of the community.

This obligation would apply to both the insurers and the insured: the insurers would be forced to offer social insurance to all eligible individuals. Both insurers and insured may be aided financially by the government if they are unable to bear all the costs themselves. The end result of this policy is that people who are not able to work, for whatever reason, are thus supplied with social security. Primarily, this policy tackles an economic problem: when all citizens retain a minimum level of buying power, social unrest may be prevented. In addition, the economy at large will profit from the continuing demand for products. The rationale is that this regular consumer demand can preserve the level of employment, thus preventing a downward spiral.

The main reason for government regulation in the *financial sector* is to stimulate economic growth, by increasing transparency and building in financial security. Monitoring agencies can be found in many countries, and their main task is to make sure that financial organizations disclose all relevant facts with regard to financial products, so people may safely bring their money to a bank, buy stocks and bonds, or take out an insurance policy. We expand on this in Box 8.4.

---

**BOX 8.4   REGULATION IN THE US FINANCIAL SECTOR**

Probably one of the most illustrious financial regulators across the world is the Securities and Exchange Commission (SEC) in the USA. On its webpage you can find the mission statement of the SEC, namely 'to protect investors, maintain fair, orderly, and efficient markets, and facilitate capital formation'. The SEC was instituted by the US government because transactions in stock markets are considered to be a risky business: financial assets (securities) may fall in value as well as rise. The SEC's duty is to supervise all means by which American citizens invest their savings, since their standard of living is at stake and if that drops steeply it might endanger economic growth nationwide.

Many well-known companies and top managers have been the subject of SEC investigations into false information about firms' performance, manipulating the market prices of securities, stealing from customers' funds and so on. The punishment for breaking the rules is very severe in the USA, including high fines and jail sentences. Hence this is an example of a formal institution that should constrain other managers from making similar mistakes.

The SEC monitors all actors that are active in any of the US stock markets, including foreign companies. This is why the international oil company Royal Dutch Shell was found guilty by the SEC for misleading the public with respect to its proven oil reserves, which were overstated by 20 percent. These proven reserves are a measure of an oil company's value, which is information upon which investors base their decision to buy or sell shares in the company in question. In 2004, Shell had to pay a fine of US$120 million to the SEC, and in addition Shell agreed to pay about US$350 million to private investors, thus turning the case into a costly affair.

---

The beginning and later development of the severe worldwide financial crisis during 2008 and 2009 have shown that governments have been forced to go further than just regulation; that is, further than merely setting the rules with which private firms must comply. In some cases, important private banks and insurers have been taken over by their national governments. The financial troubles of large banks and insurance companies in several countries, starting in the USA, had their origins in shady and complex financial transactions that lacked solid collateral (see Chapter 1 for a more elaborate discussion of this topic).

As a consequence, several governments have taken the drastic step of intervening directly in the management of these financial organizations in trouble in order to avoid bank runs that would threaten the functioning of the whole economy and lead to a deep, and possibly lengthy, depression. In fact, several of these private banks (see also

Chapter 5) have been turned (temporarily) into state-owned enterprises (implying that they have been nationalized) to protect the public interest, as will become clear from Box 8.5.

---

**BOX 8.5   SAVING BIG BANKS**

In September 2008, the US government decided to take direct control of the country's two largest mortgage lenders – Fannie Mae and Freddie Mac, which had been suffering heavy losses as a result of homeowners defaulting on their mortgages. In October of the same year, the Dutch government announced that it was nationalizing ABN-AMRO and the Dutch branch of Fortis, as clients were losing confidence in these banks and had begun to withdraw their deposits. Meanwhile, in the UK, the government was forced to buy large stakes in the Royal Bank of Scotland, HBOS (Halifax Bank of Scotland) and Lloyds TSB (Trustee Savings Bank) to help keep them afloat.

Why was it necessary to save these banks? In a word: contagion. If, as a result of individual banks becoming bankrupt, enough clients lost confidence in the banking system as a whole, it might have led to an unprecedented bank run. The large number of investors around the globe, including central banks, holding investments in these banks meant that there were fears of a catastrophic chain reaction in banks worldwide. At a press conference on 7 September 2008, US Secretary of the Treasury, Hank Paulson, said: 'a failure of either of them [referring to Fannie and Freddie] would cause great turmoil in our financial markets here at home and around the globe'.

The argument in all cases was essentially the same: this is not ideal, but doing nothing would be worse.

---

This concludes the discussion on state regulation and intervention aimed at dealing with different kinds of information imperfections that cannot be solved adequately by private ordering.

## Market power and natural monopolies

In most countries, governments now actively combat market power when it is believed to threaten the public interest. If consumers have few or no alternatives they are forced to pay high prices. In comparison, in a situation of perfect competition no market party has the power to influence the price, which is to the benefit of the consumers. Although in reality perfect competition hardly, if at all, exists, it is true that in practice strong rivalry (competition) among market players may exist. Therefore, we deal here with the different ways in which governments stimulate competition, among other things by applying antitrust policy and by appointing specific regulators to combat the problem of market power.

Another way in which the government may curb market power is by stimulating 'competition for the market' as opposed to stimulating 'competition in the market'. To illustrate this: theoretically it is possible to have different bus companies that compete with one another with respect to public transport. This situation would be characterized by competition 'in the market'. It may be inefficient, though, to have different bus companies operating services on the same route (two buses half full, compared to one bus that is completely full). In that case the government may opt for the following solution. All (potential) bus companies may compete for the position of being the only bus operator for a certain period of time. In that case, competition does not take place between firms 'in the market', but between firms in an attempt to gain a sole supplier function on the market; hence, competition 'for the market'. The winning bus company will have a sole supplier function for the period that is established beforehand (this is an example of a concession). After the expiration of this concession, the competition procedure starts all over again.

Generally, situations may exist in which competition in the market is not necessarily efficient, hence a monopoly may be the sole solution if there is to be any efficient production. These situations may be efficient from the cost perspective but, since a monopoly is involved, not from the allocative efficiency point of view (price equals marginal cost). This tension between efficiencies may therefore be solved by regulation.

Below, we shall first recall the definition of market power and discuss when it may constitute a problem that warrants government intervention. We shall then go on to discuss different ways for a government to intervene: competition policy, regulation in case of natural monopolies, and providing concessions.

## *Market power*

The different forms of imperfect competition and their ensuing welfare losses were introduced in Appendix A to Chapter 1. The highest degree of market power is monopoly power. In the absence of potential competition or easy entry, monopoly power can be exerted. In case of market power, there is the problem of 'deadweight loss' (allocative inefficiency). However, this does not imply that all market power is detrimental, so calling for public policies in every case would not be justified (see also Appendix B to Chapter 1). Consider the following explanations regarding monopolistic competition, monopoly and fixed costs.

### Monopolistic competition

Many suppliers of different but very similar products operate in this market structure. Think of the market for hairdressers, bars, shoes, groceries and so on. Because each seller offers a slightly different product, she is the sole supplier and hence a sort of monopolist, who can determine her own price. However, because her competitors offer a product that differs only slightly from hers, she cannot afford to set the price too high, since she would lose customers. Despite the small degree of market power, rivalry forces her to compete on quality, differentiation and price, which is good from the perspective of consumers: they have more choice and do not pay too much.

Hence, any differentiation will in general lead to some market power. This, however, is inherent to the competitive process. Interfering with this process in order to achieve allocative efficiency would be interfering with the competitive process itself with probably much higher social costs involved. If producers were not allowed to differentiate products, and were forced to price according to marginal cost, incentives to innovate, invest or to become an 'entrepreneur' would be undermined. If markets were not created or did not flourish, then the economy would incur a welfare loss that was likely to be much higher than the deadweight loss related to market power. To put it differently: fighting deadweight loss would replace this market imperfection with an even worse one as a result of public policy.

## Monopoly

So, even a monopoly can result from competition. Hence, interfering with a monopoly may also be interfering with the competitive process. This implies that even in the case of a monopoly there is in general no reason for government intervention to combat deadweight loss. To put this in a different way: a trade-off exists between 'fighting static deadweight loss' and 'dynamic incentives' regarding the competitive process. This trade-off is recognized by policy-makers. Generally speaking it is not forbidden to have a monopoly position (if it is created by superior competition), but it is not allowed to 'abuse' this position. We shall come back to competition policy later. First, we shall consider in more depth why market power, and even monopolies, need not in themselves be bad:

1 Monopoly power may be regarded as the reward for superior competition. By taking (high) risks, by being innovative, by competing fairly, a monopoly can be created that may exert monopoly power (a monopoly profit). If this was not allowed, for efficiency reasons, the incentives to take those risks, to be innovative or to compete are discouraged. Again, as is the case with product differentiation, this will probably lead to a much higher social cost, because the incentives to compete or to become an 'entrepreneur' are undermined, hence even less of the product would be produced or nothing at all. Also, the incentives to invent are weakened, which would lead to the underdevelopment of new, innovative products or processes.

2 Related to the first reason, is that a monopoly may involve *dynamic efficiencies*. As noted above, incentives to innovate are related to the possibility of obtaining a monopoly position. Note that this is also related to the *patent* system: a patent is an exclusive legal right to reap the benefits of an invention for a certain length of time (in most countries, twenty years). An invention, once made public, is nonrival in consumption, which entails the danger of free riding (see Chapter 3). A patent is therefore an institutional device to protect inventors from free riders. The inventor has made the initial investment and needs the possibility of at least earning this back. If, because of free riding, inventors were not able to regain the amounts invested, inventions would decrease or would be kept secret (if possible), with possibly higher costs involved. A patent itself, as an exclusive right to reap the benefits of an invention by the inventor, confers some market power on the inventor, and may even lead to a (temporary) monopoly. It would be very curious to interfere with this dynamic efficiency by combating deadweight losses, because a monopoly generates both consumer and producer surpluses. To fight this efficiency loss might take away the incentive to produce a product at all, or to invent new products. This would involve the loss of a consumer surplus of

these (new) products. To interfere with monopoly situations to the extent that products or inventions would not be developed, would probably involve a much higher reduction of welfare through a decrease in (future) consumer and producer surplus, than it would create welfare by reducing deadweight loss.

3 The monopoly price is an important incentive for others to enter the market, so competition might be created or encouraged by the monopoly situation. Consequently, a monopoly might be a temporary phenomenon in any case. Interfering with this process would again undermine incentives to compete, once again with the most likely consequence that the competitive process is hampered so much that the social costs involved are higher than the deadweight loss. Still, the monopolist would have an incentive to keep potential competitors out of the market; this will be discussed below.

### Fixed costs

Yet another important reason why market power in general does not necessarily have to lead to public intervention is that market power may be necessary to enable production at all. This is a basically similar argument to the one presented above. If there is a choice between no product at all (but also no market power), or to have the product but necessarily with market power, it is easy to see that, generally speaking, having the product is superior to not having the product, because of the consumer and producer surpluses involved. The kind of necessity that we mean embraces the *fixed costs argument*. The technicalities of this are explained in Appendix A to this chapter.

The fixed costs argument means that, if a firm has high fixed costs, expansion of its production will lead to decreasing average total costs, which implies automatically that marginal cost is lower than average total cost. The result of such a situation for a firm without market power is that, since the price is equal to marginal cost in the case of perfect competition, and marginal cost is below the average total cost, the price is below the average total cost. Hence, there will be a loss for this producer: his profit margin is too low to recoup his high fixed costs. As a consequence, markets with high fixed costs cannot be perfectly competitive. To be able to make up for high fixed costs, a sufficiently high margin over marginal cost is needed. Hence this implies by definition that the price must be higher than marginal cost: market power is necessary to be able to pay for high fixed costs. However, this market power can be of a lasting nature (a natural monopoly). There are other solutions, such as regulation (hence government intervention).

We conclude that market power is a phenomenon that in itself does not warrant public intervention, because it can be a (necessary) part of the competitive process, even if it involves deadweight losses.

From an economic point of view, public intervention is justified in only a few situations, namely those in which the competitive process itself is at stake, and of which a natural monopoly can be an example. With respect to market power, the core concepts of competition policy are therefore 'dominance' and 'abuse of dominance'. *Dominance* is market power that may give rise to concerns about anticompetitive behavior. As we noted in Chapter 5, a dominant position is not a very well defined concept. Legally different descriptions of dominance exist, even if the word itself is not being used: see Box 8.6.

## BOX 8.6  DOMINANCE AND ABUSE IN EUROPEAN AND AMERICAN LAW

A dominant position is defined by the European Court of Justice as 'a position of economic strength enjoyed by an undertaking which enables it to prevent effective competition from being maintained on the relevant market by giving it the power to behave to an appreciable extent independently of its competitors, customers and ultimately of its consumers'.

Two very important elements in the determination of a dominant position are, according to the European Court, the market share of a firm and the market share of the next largest firm on the market. If a market share reaches 40 percent or more, and the next largest firm (in terms of market share) is much smaller than that, a firm may be considered to have a dominant position. Economically speaking, market shares are not enough to determine dominance; one aspect that at least should be taken into account is the existence of entry barriers.

In the USA, Section 2 of the Sherman Act deals with abusive behavior, but the word dominance is not used: 'Every person who shall monopolize, or attempt to monopolize, or combine or conspire with any other person or persons, to monopolize any part of the trade or commerce among the several States, or with foreign nations, shall be deemed guilty of a felony...'.

In practice, though, Section 2 implies that substantial abuse of dominance in the European sense is meant: a firm (or person within the firm) will generally only be able to monopolize a market by anticompetitive means if the firm already has a considerable degree of market power, otherwise it is hard to see how monopolization or an attempt to monopolize could be possible in a anticompetitive way. Take predatory pricing: it is hard to see how a rather small firm (in terms of market share) will be able by extremely low pricing to capture and serve a large part of its competitors' demand, so that it will entail a sustainable monopoly position at high prices after the predatory phase.

## Competition policy

As we saw in Part III, dominant positions are created by mergers, (cartel) agreements or the competitive process. Government intervention is warranted only in case of existing dominant positions that abuse this position, or in cases of the creation of market power by anticompetitive means. This last aspect implies that government intervention should focus on the goals, reasons and effects of mergers and agreements that might have positive and negative effects from the economic welfare point of view.

Most countries have laws against cartel agreements, but leave open the possibility of agreements between competitors that do not hamper or restrict competition, or (if they do hamper or restrict competition) if they also involve efficiencies that may overcome the anticompetitive concerns. This will be the case, for example, if the efficiencies can only be realized by restricting competition and the efficiencies are shared with consumers.

Also, in most countries, mergers are subject to screening by the government and abuse of a dominant position is forbidden. Public intervention in these cases is normally called *'competition policy'*; in general, this policy is applied by a competition authority.

**Competition authority**

How can competition policy be applied to ban the creation of market power that might arise as a result of implicit collusion? As we explained in Chapter 7, implicit collusion occurs among a small number of firms, each of which understands that raising prices will be followed by the others because it is in their own interest to do so. As long as each firm's decision is taken unilaterally, and not by any explicit agreement among those firms, a competition authority would have a difficult job to win a case against firms that decide to raise their prices independently, because the circumstances of the market allow them to do so profitably.

So, generally speaking, a competition authority will only be able to intervene in the following three situations:

(i) when market power is abused by (existing) dominant firms;
(ii) in order to prevent the possible (future) abuse of a dominant position when a merger is announced; and
(iii) when market power is exerted as a result of explicit collusion by cartels.

We shall elaborate briefly on all three situations.

(i) In the case of an *existing dominant firm*, as we have already discussed, this position of dominance may be abused. Abuse can be defined loosely as behavior that is beneficial to the firm, but that adversely affects customers and suppliers of inputs, and ultimately consumers. One type of abusive behavior can be described as raising rivals' costs: making it difficult for (small) competitors or entrants to compete, so that the dominant firm, as an immediate consequence, may raise prices. Another type of behavior can be described as predatory. In such cases prices are too low (with respect to some cost measure) in order to exclude competitors from the market, but afterwards prices may be raised to a higher level as compared to a situation without predatory behavior. In fact, predatory behavior can be seen as an investment strategy with the intention of changing the market structure.

In Chapter 1 we briefly discussed the Microsoft cases. The abuse with respect to the server protocols can be seen as an example of raising rivals' costs, while the bundling of Windows with Media Player can be seen as a predatory strategy, because basically Media Player was offered for free.

A basic problem for competition authorities with respect to 'abuse' is that it may be hard to distinguish between fierce competition by the dominant firm and abusive behavior. We shall discuss this in more depth in Chapter 9.

(ii) The underlying criterion for any merger analysis by competition authorities is always driven by the question of whether or not at some horizontal level of competition involved by the merger (be it a horizontal, vertical, or any other kind of merger), market power can be created or increased (see also Chapter 6). In the case of a contemplated merger, a competition authority will try to assess whether this merger will change the market structure in such a way that competition may be substantially lessened. This can be the case because a merger may create a new firm that either is able to impose its terms on the markets in which it operates (unilateral conduct) or by creating a situation in which implicit collusion will be (more) likely (we discussed this extensively in Chapters 6 and 7).

In situations where there is a risk that competition will be significantly lessened, a merger can be blocked by the competition authority. Alternatively, the merger may be allowed, but with very specific conditions, called remedies. One option may be that the merging firms are forced to sell a part of their business, resulting in a smaller market share.

(iii) In the case of explicit collusion (cartels), firms will make agreements about, for example, higher prices, lower quantities sold, client groups that are assigned to the members of the cartel, or geographical areas that are allotted to the members of the cartel (see Chapter 7). This will always lead to higher prices, because these agreements are intended to create market power by not competing on prices, quantities or operating areas. These agreements may even be made in the presence of a competition authority, depending, for example, on the probability of being caught.

## Means of competition authorities

Most competition authorities have powers that enable them to search the premises of the firms for material that could prove collusion. This includes the investigation of all digital material. Sometimes they are even allowed to search individuals' houses if the individuals involved are likely to store proof away from the firm's premises. Also, firms and individuals are generally obliged to cooperate with the authorities, short of incriminating themselves. Competition authorities may sometimes fine the cartel members themselves, or they may have to take their proof to another government body in order to have the cartel members fined. In general, fines may be as high as 10 percent of yearly (worldwide) turnover. Sometimes also the firms' leading individuals who are involved in creating or sustaining the cartel can be fined or even imprisoned (as is the case in the USA, for example). Competition authorities may be using smart tactics to combat cartels: see Box 8.7.

---

### BOX 8.7 LENIENCY POLICY FOR CARTEL INVOLVEMENT

The impression exists that the risk of being caught is rising; hence firms might be more inclined to participate in a so-called leniency (or clemency) program. By means of such a policy, firms that engage(d) in illegal collusive behavior in a cartel are tempted to confess and cooperate with the competition authorities, to provide hard proof against the other cartel members. In return, the firm that is the first to confess and actively cooperate in collecting evidence, is handed a much lower fine or even granted an amnesty. You may notice that this situation encompasses all the elements of a prisoner's dilemma game (see Chapter 7).

> An interesting illustration of a leniency case is the conviction of the members of a European rubber cartel in late 2006, among which were the Italian company Eni and the British–Dutch concern, Shell. They were ordered to pay €272 million and €161 million, respectively, by the European Commission, which found them guilty of fixing the price of synthetic rubber used for tires. A third major cartel member, the German firm Bayer, gained immunity (and avoided a fine of no less than €240 million) because it implicated the other offenders after requesting leniency.

## *Natural monopolies*

A specific form of monopoly is the natural monopoly. It is specific because it is intrinsically good to have such a monopoly in terms of cost efficiency, yet its monopoly character also implies that monopoly pricing will lead to an allocative inefficient solution (deadweight loss). Hence, this usually implies that such monopolies are regulated.

Generally speaking, a natural monopoly has average costs that decline with output. A graphical representation of this can be found in Appendix B to this chapter. This phenomenon can apply for two reasons: high fixed costs, or a specific production technology.

In the discussion of market power, above, we mentioned high fixed costs. Where these apply, average (total) cost declines with output, at least over the relevant range, which is decided by each individual firm's demand. If the firm is large with respect to market demand and average costs decline, this means that it is cost efficient to have only one firm in the market. Suppose the situation arises where there is at least one additional firm, which also has high fixed costs. Since total output is produced by two firms, each firm produces only part of this total output. Let us assume that each firm produces half of the total output. If the total output is 100, each firm produces 50. Suppose fixed costs are 500 for each firm and there are no other costs. Each firm therefore has average costs of 500/50 = 10. If only one firm had produced the total output, average costs would be 500/100 = 5. So, it is therefore cost efficient to have one firm only. But, as noted earlier, since such a firm could behave as a monopolist, monopoly pricing would reduce total welfare because of a deadweight loss.

Not all large firms (in the sense of being able to produce total market demand) with high fixed costs will be a dominant firm. As we argued in Chapter 5, a monopolist can also be disciplined by potential entrants. So, a natural monopoly resulting from, for example, high fixed costs, will be a problem only if there are entry barriers. It is possible that high fixed costs constitute an entry barrier, especially when these costs are 'sunk'. *Sunk costs* are costs that cannot be recovered once made. Remember that costs are related to inputs. If an input (a machine, for example) is dedicated to a certain production process (say X) and cannot be used for any other production process, then it has value for X only. Its value will be gone once production ceases.

Now suppose that we have a monopolist with high fixed costs. Suppose that an alternative producer is able to enter the market with a similar kind of production process. This producer will have to incur the same fixed costs, which, once made, are sunk. So, the newcomer will only enter the market if he can produce the goods more efficiently, and only then will the second producer be able to take over the market from the original monopolist. Since it may well be the case that a more efficient technique is not feasible, entry is then unlikely and hence an entry barrier exists. Of course, if a completely new technology is possible, entry is more likely and hence market power for the monopolist is reduced. Box 8.8 expands on this topic.

---

### BOX 8.8   SUSTAINABILITY OF NATURAL MONOPOLIES

Examples of high fixed sunk costs are infrastructure network monopolies such as electricity grids, or gas and water pipelines. The companies involved can be considered as natural monopolies.

A railway network might also be a natural monopoly, but it is possible that it is disciplined by other means of transport. So, in this case, an alternative exists that is totally different technically, but may have an effect on pricing behavior.

In the case of telecommunications, mobile or fixed, or broadband internet, alternative techniques exist that may also exert competitive pressure: cable television networks can be used to provide television, but also broadband internet and (fixed) telephony in competition with the fixed copper network system. Mobile phone networks also involve high fixed costs, but do not involve natural monopolies, since they exert competitive pressure on one another, and may be competitors of fixed telephony and vice versa.

Also, a completely new and highly efficient network is under development to provide services such as television, internet and telephone services: the glass fiber network.

---

Average costs may also decline for other technical reasons. If a production process requires inputs that become more efficient when the scale of production (and with that the amount of these inputs) increases, the average cost of these inputs declines; this is a well-known phenomenon that is also called *'increasing returns to scale'*: see Appendix A to this chapter for details. As long as increasing returns can be realized (compared to the extent of market demand), the effect of increasing returns is similar to that of high fixed costs: it is efficient to have only one firm for cost efficiency reasons. Also, the question whether or not such a natural monopoly is bad depends on the competitive pressure that may be placed on it, hence on the degree of market power.

### Regulation of natural monopolies
From the point of view of cost efficiency, a natural monopoly is to be preferred to competition. But dominance will lead to monopoly pricing. So there are basically two methods of ensuring cost efficiency: one is to regulate the monopoly; and the other is to introduce competition for the market. The second way is described later; here we shall take a closer look at the first method.

From the point of view of allocative efficiency and cost efficiency, the government requires that a natural monopoly sets a price that is efficient (we shall discuss this goal of regulation in more depth in Chapter 9). Since the monopolist will not set such a price voluntarily, he must be forced by law to do so, and some agency is needed to enforce this legislation: namely, the regulator. Many countries have regulators for electricity and gas networks, because for economic and technical reasons it is inefficient for competing companies to install cables and pipelines side by side. It is better to have only one network, and for a regulator to determine which companies can provide services to consumers.

Theoretically, through regulation, the price must be set at an efficient level. As we saw earlier, allocative efficiency is reached when price is equal to marginal costs. But we have also seen that, with declining average costs, such a price implies losses. So, how can this problem be solved? One simple solution is that the loss could be compensated. One way of doing this is to subsidize the loss. Another way is to cover the loss with a fixed fee. This defines a so-called 'two-part tariff': a fixed fee to cover the loss, and a (variable) fee per unit of output at the efficient pricing level (see also Chapter 3). Generally, pricing for consumers by means of two-part tariffs can often be found in the energy (gas and electricity) sector worldwide. The numerical example given in Box 8.9 illustrates this principle.

---

**BOX 8.9   TWO-PART TARIFF**

Electricity is supplied via the electricity grid. Costs involved are basically the network costs and the cost of production of the electricity. Let us assume that network costs are fixed and equal 500, while costs of production of each unit of electricity are 2 (marginal costs equal average variable costs). Also suppose that 100 people each consume 30 units of electricity.

The efficient price is 2, hence total revenues are $2 \times 30$ units $\times 100$ persons $= 6,000$. Variable costs are also 6,000, but in addition there are additional transportation or network costs of 500, hence there is a loss of 500 as long as prices remain at the level of marginal costs. If, in addition to the price of 2, each individual consumer also pays a fixed fee of $500/100 = 5$, then obviously the fixed costs are also covered.

---

One of the main challenges that regulators face is how to stimulate investment and innovation. This is a challenge because regulation, if done in the way described, implies (very) low profits, hence very little incentive to innovate; why innovate or invest if prices will be adjusted accordingly in order to reduce profits? This can be solved by allowing the monopolist to reap some of the benefits of investing and innovating. For example, if an investment would reduce costs, prices will not be adjusted immediately but at a later date, so that the monopolist can keep the profits involved. In fact, some allocative inefficiency is tolerated in order to stimulate dynamic efficiency.

Of course, regulation has many more practical problems; for example, the problem of 'regulatory capture' (rent-seeking attempts by the regulated firms to receive favors from the regulator). We shall turn to some of these in the next chapter.

## *The creation of competition for the market*

Sometimes there is another way of solving the problem of a natural monopoly. In this case, not regulating the monopoly position, but rather creating competition, or to put it more generally: creating competition for the market. There are different ways of doing this, but conceptually it involves the following procedures. Different possible suppliers of a certain product approach the government regarding 'pricing' and the amount and quality of the product. The government decides which supplier (or sometimes a group of suppliers) has tendered successfully. If the government chooses to select the lowest possible price, then the competing firms might offer their lowest possible prices (see below for more on this topic). On the other hand, of course, if the government opts for the highest value for itself, the competing firms will offer monopoly prices and the firm with the lowest costs will be able to offer the highest value to the government (see also below).

Different concepts of competition for the market exist, but they all involve the principle that, among two or more competitors, one is chosen by the government to supply a product as the only one on the market, and is thus awarded a *concession*. A concession is a contract or license associated with a degree of exclusivity in business within a certain geographical area. This exclusive right to supply a certain product, according to specific requirements with respect to price setting and delivered quality and/or quantity, is called a *legal monopoly*.

While we have introduced competition for the market as a solution to the problem of natural monopoly, this does not imply that competition for the market is restricted to natural monopolies. Examples of this category include the exploitation of gas and oil, while concessions can also be seen in the mail services or public transport, which do not necessarily have the characteristics of a natural monopoly.

Competition for the market is usually realized through state-organized auctions – a specific institutional arrangement to obtain 'free market solutions'. There are a number of ways in which the government can organize this competition. As well as the Dutch, English and the sealed bid auctions (see the Appendix to Chapter 5), we also distinguish a so-called *beauty contest*, which is a special kind of auction. Basically, the difference between ordinary auctions and beauty contests is that in an auction one uses some quantitative criterion (such as 'price') to choose from a set of alternatives, while in a beauty contest qualitative criteria, and hence other (subjective) considerations, also play a role in determining which alternative is the best from a set of alternatives. The winner of the auction or beauty contest acquires the concession and can operate the business for a specified period of time. There is an example in Box 8.10.

---

### BOX 8.10   A SWEDISH BEAUTY CONTEST

At the start of the twenty-first century, the governments of several developed countries began to analyze the introduction of 3G mobile phone networks. These allowed the transmission of large amounts of data for the first time, opening up the possibility of sending videos to mobile phones. However, radio bandwidth for mobile phones is a scarce resource. How to choose which company was the best?

> Andersson *et al.* (2005) looked at the process by which Sweden decided to allocate its 3G bandwidth. In practice, government agencies have two options: an auction, in which bandwidth is sold to the highest bidder; or a beauty contest in which a government agency determines certain criteria that must be met by the prospective providers.
>
> At the time, the Swedish government was interested in a fast implementation of the 3G network, as the IT sector was seen as key to national development. Therefore the two main selection criteria were (i) rapid roll-out; and (ii) nationwide coverage. Other criteria were related to financial capacity, and technical and commercial feasibility.
>
> Ten participants submitted proposals. In the first selection round, four failed the technical feasibility requirements and one was found to lack financial capacity. Surprisingly, one of the contestants excluded at the first stage was Telia, the former public telecom monopoly. At later stages, the contestants were also evaluated based on the correct completion of the application forms and experience in the telecom sector.
>
> Eventually, it was decided to allocate the 3G license to four companies, most of which later created alliances to provide the mobile phone service. Despite some drawbacks, such as the fact that several of the losing parties (unsuccessfully) contested the decision in court, Andersson *et al.* are positive about the Swedish experience. They point out that there were a large number of advanced operators among the participants, that the time involved was not much longer than that of an auction, and that the process was in general transparent, as the selection criteria were published beforehand. Also, as a consequence, Sweden obtained a highly advanced 3G network, which was the main objective. Their main recommendation for future beauty contests is that all documentation, including the evaluations of external consultants, be published to further increase transparency.

Why might competition for the market lead to an efficient solution? Only under ideal circumstances will an efficient solution result, but in such a situation, the mechanism is as follows. All participants have to compete for the market in terms of prices, quantities and quality. For the sake of simplicity we shall assume that only price matters. All participants know that, if they win, they will have a monopoly position. But does this mean that a monopoly price can be charged?

If the government wants an efficient solution, it will choose the participant that will offer the lowest price to obtain the monopoly position, given some level of quantity and quality. So, each participant has to calculate at what costs the given levels of quantity and quality can be realized. Each participant also has to recognize that if he asks the monopoly price, then another participant might undercut it slightly in an attempt to gain the monopoly position. But this is true for all participants, so they each have an incentive to offer as low a price as possible in order to maximize their chance of winning. Theoretically, this would be the price equal to marginal costs. The participant with lowest marginal costs will win.

Since the concession might involve a natural monopoly, different pricing structures may be involved: prices equal to marginal costs will not be profitable, hence some 'discrimination' in pricing is necessary, or a two-part tariff might be offered, or price should equal average (total) costs, or the government could subsidize the losses. Ideally, the government should specify beforehand what kind of pricing system is to be employed, to make the bids comparable.

When the legal monopoly position is attained, the auction mechanism underlying it effectively serves as a regulator would have done: prices are equal to marginal cost, even in the case of a natural monopoly (with a two-part tariff system), because of the competition for the market. Hence, consumers benefit directly from such a system.

The government might also decide to offer a concession not on the basis of the pricing scheme (given quality and quantity), which would benefit consumers, but on the following basis. The government could try to realize the monopoly profits for itself, but not by operating the monopoly itself. Through a concession, a private party may obtain the monopoly position and price accordingly, but with one difference compared to the situation described above. Here, the government does not give the concession to the 'lowest bidder' in terms of price offered to the consumer, but rather to the highest bidder in terms of a lump sum amount of money to be paid to the government.

Again, this may involve an auction, and again the participant with the lowest marginal cost will win the concession. Why? Because, with the lowest marginal costs, the highest monopoly profit will be obtained. Since the participant has to offer a lump sum amount of money in order to gain this position, she is prepared to offer (at most) this amount of money. Might she do so? Yes, because, to win the auction, she has to maximize her chances of winning, which means that she might as well offer the largest amount of money she can afford, which is the monopoly profit. So, the government realizes the monopoly profit for itself, while guaranteeing at the same time that production takes place at the lowest marginal cost possible (of course, this is in an ideal situation). Such a solution will lead to cost efficiencies, but at monopoly prices, with the monopoly profits going to the state. Essentially, the state realizes a 100 percent profit tax at the efficient cost level (meaning that there are no productive inefficiencies).

As you can see, 'competition for the market' as a regulatory device must imply that the government opts for the lowest price to be paid by the consumer.

As noted above, only under ideal circumstances will the efficient solution result from auctions organized by the state. In Chapter 9 we shall show how auctions as an institutional device are not always efficient or effective, meaning that they do not always accomplish the goals of the auction's organizers.

A last remark with respect to market power concerns legal monopolies that may also need regulation along the same lines as natural monopolies, unless they are state-owned enterprises, in which case the government makes all the firm's decisions. In many countries, state-owned enterprises have been privatized and liberalized, or legal monopolies withdrawn. Often these processes have also been guided by regulators. Examples include former fixed telephone companies and postal services. We discuss this further in Chapter 9.

## Externalities

In Chapters 3 and 5 we showed, with the aid of the Coase theorem, that there are circumstances in which private actors can solve the problem of a negative externality via mutual negotiations. However, the presence of high transaction costs or an unequal division of power between the parties involved may well result in a situation in which private negotiations about reducing such a negative side effect falter. On a global scale, the most obvious example of a negative externality problem that cannot be solved by private actors alone concerns threats to the environment as a result of human activities. We shall discuss this more fully below, and examine as well the societal problems that may result from positive externalities. Negative externalities lead to overconsumption and overinvestment, while in contrast, positive externalities lead to underconsumption and underinvestment. So in both situations economic welfare is not optimized and, when the accompanying problems cannot be solved by private actors, government intervention could correct and improve the outcome. We shall call these type of externalities *complex externalities*.

### Negative externalities

With regard to negative externalities, the greatest problems for human society worldwide probably emanate from environmental pollution as a by-product of economic activities. This comprises contamination of the air, the soil or water, usually as a result of the production process (polluting factories, industrial farms and so on), but it may also be caused by consumer activities (such as people throwing garbage on the street, or producing a noise nuisance when playing music too loudly). In many cases, the person or people responsible cannot be called to order effectively by private actors, for a number of reasons, of which we mention some of the most important ones below.

1. The offenders may be large in number and located worldwide, all contributing to, for example, global warming by releasing carbon dioxide into the air. The fact that those responsible are so widespread and their actions often also go unnoticed undermines the possibility of tracking them down and attempting to change their behavior.
2. Polluting behavior is very difficult to combat when the people responsible are not aware of the damaging effect of their actions. Pollution may happen unintentionally, but it nevertheless causes serious damage to the environment. Consumers may not realize that some of their electrical appliances use too much energy, or that their use of airplanes adds to the problem of the greenhouse effect. Producers could hurt the environment by individually using too many resources over a short period, thereby running the risk of depletion that could affect the whole of society (think of problems resulting from a tragedy of the commons, such as overfishing).

3 Alternatively, the polluters may be very well aware of the problems they are causing but intend to continue their activities because they have the power to do so. An example of this are the big, powerful multinationals in Latin America that are active in the soya industry who cause a lot of damage to the environment by contributing to the rapid and large-scale deforestation of the Amazon region. The governments of the countries concerned, such as Uruguay and Brazil, do not appear to take any action against these adverse developments.
4 Facing influential offenders, we often see powerless victims, reflecting an unequal power balance. Third parties that are being harmed by negative side-effects often do not make up a well-organized, homogeneous interest group. Also, they frequently lack the knowledge and ability to negotiate on an equal footing with the opposing party about a reduction of the externality, and/or they lack the financial means to hire an expert to negotiate and monitor on their behalf.

In most jurisdictions (on both national and international levels) worldwide public authorities have intervened to protect the public interest. Pollution, first and foremost, has an adverse effect on the natural environment, which in turn seriously affects the well-being and welfare of the people. It can have implications for the population's health, and hence for their labor productivity, and in due course it has a negative effect on possibilities for economic growth. Ultimately, the welfare of future generations is put seriously at risk.

Depending on questions such as:

- 'Who are the instigators?' (producers, consumers or both)
- 'What is the nature of the negative externality?' (air, soil, water or noise pollution, depletion or health problems, among other things)
- 'How many people are harmed and to what extent?'
- 'What are the consequences of intervention for the instigators?'

governments are choosing different countermeasures. The most important ones are tradable pollution rights, awareness programs and financial (dis)incentives (such as taxes and subsidies), quotas and outright product bans. These policy measures will now be discussed in combination with the four categories of situations mentioned above, in which it is too difficult for private actors to tackle the externalities on their own. It should be stressed that most policy measures can be applied in many different situations and not just in the specific ones described below.

## Widespread pollution

When a complex negative externality involves causers and aggrieved parties on a worldwide scale, governments of different nations need to negotiate about international solutions. As the meetings of the United Nations and of the G8 ('Group of Eight' – the eight most influential countries of the world) or G20 show time and again, the international community does not make much progress in really tackling such problems, mainly because the protection of national economic interests has up to now appeared to be of greater importance than solving global problems.

Having said that, it does not mean that cross-border environmental problems cannot be dealt with at all by means of state interference. From Box 8.11 it can be seen that the EU has taken the initiative to combat the emission of pollutants. But the above comments demonstrate that it will depend, among other things, on the scale and magnitude of the problem, and to what extent conflicting interests can be reconciled or overcome. For this, political will and commitment need to emerge, which involves a very slow process of changing values.

---

### BOX 8.11   EMISSIONS TRADING

Each company is given a maximum 'emissions allowance' or cap. If companies want to emit more than their allowance, they can buy the excess emissions on an emissions trading market from a company that is emitting less than its allowance. In theory, emissions trading is an efficient solution for manmade global warming, but in practice there are problems of measurement and enforcement.

In addition, political problems are becoming increasingly apparent. When, in October 2008, it started to become clear to policy-makers that the world economy was heading towards a recession, the European Commission announced that it was considering a cash boost to high-energy-consuming companies, to help them buy carbon allowances and increase their production. Effectively, this meant putting the political imperative to provide jobs ahead of environmental interests. The measure was partly a reaction to lobbying by large British and French firms and illustrates a larger problem: countries and companies arguing that they are 'special cases' could eventually undermine the whole trading system.

---

### Polluting behavior

Governments can combat the ignorance of the causers of negative externalities by introducing awareness programs, financial incentives or product bans, among other things. We have already touched on energy labels, which signal to prospective consumers if a product they are about to buy is energy wasteful or energy saving. However, most of the time actors make their consumption or production decision on the basis of prices and costs, and not because of effects on the environment. Therefore, logical additional measures of many governments concern, among other things, intervention in traded quantities or in prices, which we shall discuss briefly.

Problems related to 'tragedy of the commons' phenomena include resource depletion of fossil fuels, the oceans, arable land, pastures and forests, therefore careful management is needed to prevent complete exhaustion. A well-known policy measure concerns EU fish quotas. It is argued that imposing sufficient cuts on fishing will help to protect endangered fish.

By subsidizing 'clean' or 'green' products and taxing 'bad' products, consumers are guided to choose supported products. For example, less tax is levied on energy-saving cars; public transport is often subsidized, and so are durable goods such as low-energy light bulbs and solar panels, to name just a few products and services. In Box 8.12 there is another example of pecuniary incentives.

---

### BOX 8.12  FIGHTING DEFORESTATION

At the world climate summit in Bali in 2007, the participants agreed to found a new fund to fight deforestation. The aim was to approach farmers in developing countries such as Indonesia and Brazil who have the incentive to cut down tropical rainforests in order to grow cacao, oil palm trees, soya and similar crops. These farmers would be offered an attractive compensation out of the climate fund to leave the forest intact. The money to compensate them would come from the revenues of the international market for emission rights.

Not cutting down one hectare of forest saves approximately 500 metric tons of carbon dioxide. Companies and governments can only emit as much carbon dioxide as their purchased emission rights allow. On the international market, the right to emit 500 metric tons of carbon dioxide will cost them between US$5,000 and US$10,000. These figures show that the farmers in the forest areas can easily be compensated from the climate fund. In the influential report *Stern Review on the Economics of Climate Change* (Stern, 2006), efforts to combat deforestation are therefore called one of the most efficient ways of combating climate change.

---

There is another much discussed topic related to the negative externalities caused by ignorant consumers. Too much smoking, drinking and using drugs is not only bad for the direct user because that person may ultimately die from these activities, but it also causes expenses to the whole of society. If too many people need to be treated for diseases related to these 'bad habits', more resources need to be allocated to the health sector and will result in a rise in health insurance premiums for all. Abuse of alcohol moreover often leads to road casualties, violent behavior and vandalism, the costs of which also have to be borne by society in general.

Governments try to fight these bad habits by means of public awareness campaigns and corrective taxes, but if their attempts fail they could then take a hard line and forbid the use of cigarettes, alcohol and drugs. One such enactment that has received much attention worldwide concerns the ban on smoking, first in all public buildings (all government buildings, schools, hospitals and so on) and later also in all places of entertainment (in restaurants, cafés, theatres and the like). The introduction of this specific form of state intervention was heavily protested against by smokers in many countries, but at the same time was warmly applauded by non-smokers. Box 8.13 provides background information on this topic.

### BOX 8.13   BAN ON TOBACCO SMOKING: AN APPLICATION OF PROPERTY RIGHTS THEORY

Governments began to fight smoking behavior by taxing tobacco heavily, but worldwide the elasticity of demand (the degree to which a percentage price change causes a percentage change in demand) for tobacco proved to be very small. This often negligible effect on the reduction of smoking is both caused by the fact that smoking can be addictive and because in many cultures and subcultures (such as among young people) the norm is to smoke, since 'everybody is doing it'.

As a result, smoking has been institutionalized and is hence hard to give up. Via state-initiated awareness programs in the media and by means of warnings on cigarette packs that smoking seriously endangers the health (and even life), governments try to change people's views. In addition, producers are restricted in advertising tobacco and, especially in the USA, large tobacco companies have been sued because they allegedly kept silent about the health risks while increasing the level of nicotine in their products, thus making tobacco more addictive.

Being in the vicinity of smokers also leads to so-called passive smoking. The most effective way to reduce this problem is by forbidding smoking completely (at least in public places). This is what has happened in many countries and can be explained in terms of property rights. Let us take a look at the situation in restaurants, where visitors and personnel alike may suffer from the air pollution generated by smokers.

Who is entitled to the use of clean air? In other words, who has which partial property rights? Remember, we can distinguish between the right to use a product, the right to earn an income from it and the right to sell it. Before the ban on smoking, in a privately owned restaurant it was the establishment owner who had all these rights. So she could decide whether or not (part of) the building would be smoke-free. However, after the ban, clients and personnel working in the restaurant have been given the right to clean air and thus the restaurant owner is forced to provide a fully smoke-free dining area. If she doesn't agree, she still has the right to sell the restaurant.

A holder of a particular property right derives certain incentives from this. In the case of a non-smoker, he is now more inclined to visit the restaurant, which is also beneficial for the restaurant owner. The advantage for the restaurant personnel is that they are no longer forced to work in a smoky, unhealthy environment all the time. In the case of a (stubborn) smoker, he may be less inclined to visit the restaurant, which will have a negative effect on the restaurant's revenues. The net effect of these two opposite incentives can only be determined empirically. However, research in British Columbia, New York, Ireland, Norway and New Zealand into the effects of the introduction of the smoking ban shows that, on average, revenues did not suffer (Smoke Free Partnership, 2006).

## Determined polluters

Some causers of negative side effects are too powerful and rich to be stopped by private sufferers. Countermeasures by a government may only succeed if this public authority itself is independent from the provoking party and is not susceptible to being bribed or pressed. In such circumstances, the most straightforward way to combat polluting behavior is by means of corrective taxes and regulatory limits, and if that fails, a polluter could be fined or some of his economic activities could be banned. An illustration of the latter is the ban on noisy or unsafe air companies at several airports, a measure that is becoming increasingly popular in the world.

Corrective taxes are widely used to reduce or even eliminate the negative externalities of many firms. In Appendix C to this chapter you will find the graphical analysis of the effect of such a tax. Because of this levy, the firm is confronted with extra costs that are added to total production costs. When balancing marginal costs and marginal revenue, the producer will take a new and lower output decision. Ideally, the new output level will coincide with maximum economic welfare. In economics, this resulting effect of corrective taxes is called the 'internalization of the negative externality'.

## Protecting the victims

Aggrieved private actors are too dispersed and often lack the financial and/or intellectual means to improve their position. They may not even be aware of the negative side effects in question. Again, governmental measures such as statutory obligations, corrective taxes and product bans help to protect the sufferers. We shall elaborate briefly on two of these aspects.

The state can support citizens by introducing statutory obligations whenever firms or local governments are contemplating development plans for all kinds of projects that might endanger the environment. These projects include the construction of infrastructure or buildings, and the installation of new plants and industrial areas. In countries all over the world, environmental impact assessments exist stipulating the requirements that need to be met before a project is allowed to proceed.

Other, often invisible, defects in products which, according to governments, should not be allowed, often hit the headlines worldwide when they are discovered – for example, unsafe toys, and cosmetics. Public health is at stake in such cases. Countries attempt to ensure that such products cannot be imported. At the EU level, the Consumer Affairs Department of the European Commission monitors product safety and has developed the Rapid Alert System for non-food consumer products (RAPEX). Whenever a dangerous product is detected, the competent national authority must undertake action to eliminate the risk. In addition, all items on the 'black list' are published on the internet, to warn the public. In North America, there is also a multilateral program that bans unsafe products, in which Canada, Mexico and the USA cooperate. The reason why these three countries have joined forces is described in Box 8.14.

> **BOX 8.14   NORTH AMERICAN BAN ON UNSAFE PRODUCTS**
>
> During the North American Security and Prosperity Partnership summit in 2007, Canada, the USA and Mexico made joint agreements to block the import of unsafe products. Two statements by the political leaders responsible stand out because they stress that externalities play a role.
>
> The Canadian Prime Minister Stephen Harper said: 'We agreed to work together on consumer protection; we have to identify and stop unsafe goods from entering our country, especially those designed for our children', while US President George W. Bush said: 'there's a good reason why our leaders should come together on a regular basis...to figure out ways to continue to enhance prosperity. It's in our interests that the Canadian lifestyle be as strong as it is, and it's in our interests that prosperity spread to Mexico. If you're a US citizen you want people that live close to you to be prosperous. The more prosperity there is in your neighborhood, the more hopeful your neighborhood is.'

## *Positive externalities*

Also in the case of certain positive externalities, government intervention may be required to reach a higher level of economic welfare. In many cases, the advantages of positive externalities are too small to render state interference necessary, though a public authority may nevertheless decide to intervene. But particular examples of warranted state intervention resulting from positive externalities are a well functioning health care system and educational system, because these coincide with wide positive effects for the whole population, both nationally and internationally.

The standard example with respect to health care concerns vaccination. The external benefits of this are obvious: if every person was to be vaccinated against widespread infectious deceases such as influenza, malaria or yellow fever, the risk of contagion would decline drastically. As a result, the whole population would be much healthier and hence more productive. Since the costs of prevention are usually much lower than the costs of treatment, the choice seems easy. Without government intervention, many people do not have themselves vaccinated, either out of ignorance and/or because they do not have the financial means or the facilities nearby, and because they do not consider the positive externality. Private choice therefore leads to underconsumption of vaccination.

In the particular case of poor countries that lack the means to provide sufficient medical aid to their citizens, other nations and private organizations may come to the rescue. While there are humanitarian reasons to do so, there is also an important economic motive for foreign governments to offer financial assistance and to provide medical staff. If an epidemic breaks out in a distant region of the world, the health risks are not confined to that area but may easily spread, ultimately harming the health situation of people all over the world. Productivity will decline and so will international trade. So, when the deadly SARS virus broke out in China, Hong Kong and Taiwan in 2003, and the Mexican 'swine flu' in 2009, the whole world was gripped with fear because the infections spread so quickly via air passengers. An infected traveler carried the SARS virus to Canada, and contaminated others, and people died there as an immediate result. The international community cooperated closely with the World Health Organization (WHO) and was eventually able to suppress the disease. The 2009 Mexican flu spread all over the world, from the USA to Europe to New Zealand, and some people died as a result. Again, collaborative measures were taken to suppress the disease.

In developed countries, governments also intervene in health care in a number of ways. The relatively poor among the population often get support to guarantee that they are medically well supported. Mandatory health insurance is common in most member states of the European Union, as well as in other countries. The British National Health Service (NHS) system, founded in 1948, is quite well known. In Britain, universal (state-owned) health care, financed by national taxation, is provided for all citizens.

The second example concerns the importance of a good education for the whole population. Public authorities stimulate learning both to create more chances for the people to whom it relates (reasoning that, after higher education, they will be able to find more satisfying and better-paid jobs), and to allow for positive externalities: at the macro level, a more highly educated population generates higher productivity and higher incomes. This leads to greater purchasing power, which in turn stimulates employment and business sales, thus contributing to a rise in the national product. All these arguments apply worldwide, and in poor countries in particular, more and better education is seen as one of the most important ways of fighting poverty.

How do governments stimulate this process? All member states of the United Nations (UN) have subscribed to the vision that education is a universal human right. In addition, according to the UN declaration, education should be offered without charge, but outside the Western world that is still often not the case (Tomasevski, 2006). In the countries that encourage learning among their citizens, it is notable that education is often mandatory for children up to the ages of 16 or 18, and this is often free of charge (up to a certain age) or is heavily subsidized. If there is a payment required, this is often income-related, so that the lower-income groups in particular do not experience a barrier to education. In this way, everybody has equal opportunities. For students, cheap loans or even grants are often made available. In many countries, private schools and state-owned schools coexist, the latter generally charging less (or nothing) for their services.

## Pure public goods

Pure public goods were introduced in Chapter 1, and defined and discussed in more detail in Chapter 3. We recap here that there can be a difference between publicly provided goods and (pure) public goods. Only the latter are by definition characterized by nonrivalness and nonexclusiveness, which often compel governments to intervene.

The key problem is that the consumption of a particular pure public good does not hinder the amount consumed by others (nonrival) and they cannot be prevented from using it (or only at a very high cost) even if they do not pay for its use (nonexclusive). So, private consumers will not be inclined to reveal their willingness to pay for the product (see the explanation below), therefore private producers will not be inclined to offer it on the market. The market fails to deliver the product, even if it clearly supplies a need.

Private consumers will not state their willingness to pay, for the following reason: think of an individual consumer (A) on the one hand, and all other consumers together on the other. If all the others state their willingness to pay, and this will lead to the production of the pure public good, it pays for A not to reveal his true willingness to pay: the good will therefore be produced on behalf of the others (because of nonexclusiveness) so A gets the good for free. Since all others are made up of individuals like A, however, no individual has the incentive to state his true willingness to pay.

Then the only way to ensure availability is by state-induced production. The government may either decide to take the production into its own hands, or it appoints or invites private manufacturers to produce the pure public good at a fairly contracted price. Irrespective of who makes the product, they will be paid by the public via imposed contributions – for example, via state-levied taxes.

It is also relevant to note that, in most examples of pure public goods (streetlights, dikes, lighthouses) almost all 'users' or 'consumers' value the product. But sometimes a significant proportion of the users or consumers may dislike the (amount of the) pure public good (hence they consider it a 'public bad'): well-known illustrations are the public defense of a country (pacifists in particular consider this a bad) or public firework displays (many people do not like the sound, smell or sight of these).

A final remark concerns the issue of who, or which agency, actually takes care of the provision of a pure public good. Private initiative to supply a pure public good is surely conceivable when it comes to information goods. On the one hand, in several cases, people want to share free information with as many others as possible, regardless of the cost. Think of evangelists or environmental action groups, or people who send open letters to newspapers. On the other hand, people who do want to earn money from their ideas and inventions offer their information on the market after securing their intellectual property rights through copyrights and patents. As explained in Chapter 3, introducing this legal protection makes the good fully excludable and in fact turns the pure public good into a private good.

The protection of public interests can also be the result of supranational initiatives. First, the pure public good may be of importance to two neighboring countries when it concerns cross-border problems such as the building of a large and costly dam across a boundary river, which affects the population on both sides. Second, more than two countries may have an interest. An example is the protection of an alliance of states by an organization such as NATO (the North Atlantic Treaty Organization), which deals with the military defense of North America and Europe. And third, even on a worldwide scale, examples of pure public goods can be found, such as the so-called 'world heritage' sites that need to be saved from deterioration or destruction. Box 8.15 discusses the latter topic.

> **BOX 8.15   PROTECTION OF WORLD HERITAGE SITES**
>
> In 1972, UNESCO (the United Nations Educational, Scientific and Cultural Organization) organized the World Heritage Convention during which 175 countries ratified the agreement to protect world heritage sites (natural landscapes as well as cultural monuments) that are considered to be of exceptional universal value. At the time of writing, 186 countries have ratified this Convention, while the list contains 890 sites.
>
> Once on this list, national governments have a legal duty to do their utmost to protect, restore and maintain these valuable properties, which clearly contain the characteristics of a pure public good. They are to a great extent nonrival, and often they are also nonexclusive. Sometimes one can put an enclosure around a monument, therefore making it excludable. But sites such as rainforests and reef systems that stretch across several countries are impossible to fence, and often have not been assigned clear property rights, hence they are nonexcludable. Note that this also complicates the question as to who has the duty and responsibility for their upkeep.

This concludes our overview of the different ways that governments can intervene in the various situations of market imperfections. Our next aim is to interpret these forms of state intervention in a more analytical way, with the aid of transaction costs economics (TCE).

## TCE approach to public ordering

As we have seen in previous chapters, in TCE the central question concerns which governance structure is the optimal choice in a given institutional environment. So, if a society encounters an incidence of a market imperfection, and hence with an inefficient outcome, what would be the best way to coordinate the transaction?

Let us first take a brief look again at the benchmark of perfect competition, in which economic welfare is maximal. Only when the market is characterized by perfect competition is complete information available to all actors, and thus transaction costs are zero. Government interference in this ideal situation will by definition lead to an efficiency loss. However, such a market situation hardly ever exists in the real world, and since individuals are hampered by bounded rationality and have to take possible opportunistic behavior into account, transactions in real life always involve costs and society is faced with a deadweight loss. The question then becomes how economic welfare can be optimized, given these restrictions.

In the case of transaction costs, in order to increase their welfare private actors choose from among the governance structures market, hybrid or firm the one that will maximize their welfare (and minimize transaction costs). This choice is influenced by the severity of the contractual hazards, which in turn are determined by the degree of asset specificity, the reputation of the transaction partners, the frequency with which actors have to transact, the nature of the uncertainties involved in the transaction, and the degree to which private property rights are protected by contract law.

As we have seen, when transaction costs become too high for individual solutions, state intervention may be needed. Ideally, this intervention should consist of choosing those instruments that minimize transaction costs again. So where does TCE place intervention by regulation or by state-owned enterprise? In this context, there is a well-known quote by Williamson, who calls the state-owned enterprise a *'public bureau'*: 'The public bureau, in this scheme of things, can be thought of as the organization of last resort: try spot markets, try incomplete long-term contracts, try firms, try regulation and reserve recourse to public bureaus when all else fails (comparatively)' (Williamson, 2000, p. 603).

For public intervention, Williamson (1999, p. 316) introduced the so-called *'remediableness criterion'*: if no feasible alternative for the chosen governance structure can be implemented with expected net gains, then this governance structure is 'presumed to be efficient'. This could therefore also apply to government regulation or to state-owned enterprises. We have distinguished three types of transaction costs: namely, market transaction costs; managerial transaction costs; and political transaction costs. The first two are linked to private governance structures, while the third is connected to public governance structures. To evaluate which is the preferred (least inefficient) governance structure, both market and managerial transaction costs must be weighed against political transaction costs.

Admittedly, there are large disadvantages to public ordering over private ordering. We shall deal with these aspects extensively in Chapter 9. But against the drawbacks, several important advantages of government intervention can be posed, as we saw earlier. In Table 8.1 we present a scheme in which the degree of public interference is increasing. We interpret this scheme with the use of insights from TCE.

**Table 8.1** *Progressive government intervention*

1 Indicative rules with respect to information disclosure
2 Monetary incentives
3 Constraining rules with respect to quantity and quality
4 Strict requirements (directives) with respect to legal monopolies
5 Complete state control through public monopolies (state-owned enterprise)

1 *Indicative rules* with respect to information disclosure are the mildest form of government intervention; the rules specify only how much information should be made available so that prospective transaction parties know better what they are getting involved in. So, these types of rules facilitates transactions, while for the remainder, private actors retain their autonomy to decide how (and when, and with whom) to transact.
2 *Monetary incentives* through taxes, subsidies, and minimum or maximum prices go one step further, as they steer the autonomous decisions by private actors in a desired direction. So, actors are still free to choose how to transact, but because of, for example, taxation or subsidies, they will take different steps than they would have done without this financial interference by the government. As a consequence, in the case of taxes, they will produce or consume less, and in the case of subsidies will produce or consume more.

3 The degree of maneuverability decreases even more for private actors as a result of *constraining rules* with respect to quantity and quality. These kinds of rules will limit the options that actors have at their disposal. For example, in order to deliver high quality, firms are only authorized to supply certain goods or services if they have an official permit, which can only be obtained after demonstrated expertise. In other cases, firms are only allowed to bring a maximum amount of product to the market, to prevent depletion or to suppress pollution.
4 By *strict requirements* towards legal monopolies, we mean that firms are now not even free to choose how much they want to produce and/or at what price, while at the same time stringent stipulations are formulated with respect to quality. In the case of a legal monopoly, a large part of the firm's autonomy is lost because of state directives on price setting, quantity and quality, in order to prevent the abuse of their market power.
5 When the government has taken *complete control* via state-owned enterprises, it has decided to take production into its own hands. In terms of the 'make or buy' decision, the government has chosen in favor of the former. In the TCE approach, the government would preferably want to leave production to the market whenever possible, because this generates more high-powered incentives. But the market supply of certain goods sometimes coincides with such high welfare losses that, on balance, the costs of government interference in the form of public monopolies turn out to be lower than the costs of the welfare losses connected to market delivery.

The static approach limits itself to assessing which actions a government should take in a given institutional environment, in which actors are expected to choose the optimal governance structure. Think back to the concept of the regulatory state, which we touched on in the Introduction to Part IV. In this perspective on the role of the state, the state should only establish the rules of the game and intervene in a 'reactive way' if economic welfare is being diminished.

Institutionalists who analyze the functioning of a society from a dynamic perspective focus more on the concept of the developmental state. From this perspective, the state should intervene in a 'proactive way' to guide actors to achieve a certain desired economic development. This topic will be taken up in the next section.

## THE DYNAMIC APPROACH TO STATE INTERVENTION

Up to now in this chapter we have discussed the role of government in a static environment: given the technology, or given the value system, what then is an efficient role of government? In this section we focus on the role of government as an actor who influences the environment with the aim of creating a specific outcome of the economic process. We describe the government as an active planner. You learned in Chapters 2 and 4 about different economic systems, and how governments play a different role in the Anglo-Saxon system compared to the Asian system, say. Below we discuss the idea of planning in a market economy: the system of so-called *indicative planning*.

In a system of indicative planning, the government guides the economic development in the direction of the objectives it has laid down in a plan. In the ideal type of indicative planning the objectives are formulated at different levels of aggregation:

- at the macro level, objectives are formulated concerning issues such as the growth of national income, the rate of inflation and the percentage of employment growth; and
- at the meso level of industries and micro level of firms, plans are devised to realize these macro objectives: a disaggregation of the macro objectives into the requirements concerning the growth of investments in specific sectors of the economy, the impact on the level of imports of specific materials, the implications for the quality of labor, and so on.

Below, we shall first compare the content of a plan in a centrally planned economy such as the former Soviet Union with the indicative plans found in market economies. The differences and complementarities will give an insight into the nature of planning in a market economy.

A central question about 'planning in a market economy' concerns the guidance of the behavior of the actors at the micro level. A fundamental characteristic of a market economy is the autonomy of producers and consumers. The sovereignty of entrepreneurs to take decisions about innovations, investments in plants and entering markets is the mainstay of a successful market economy. Similarly, the sovereignty of consumers to 'reveal their preferences' in full autonomy is another strength of the market economy. Only when these two sovereignties are respected can the competitive process result in a supply of goods and services on the market that consumers desire, and at the lowest possible prices.

We next go on to explore the different ways that governments can guide micro behavior in a market economy, and finally we draw attention to the policy of increasing a country's competitiveness by introducing superior institutions that serve both to exert a pull on foreign investors and workers, and to make domestic products more attractive abroad.

## Central planning and indicative planning

It is important to have a basic understanding of the characteristics of a centrally planned economy, because the motivation to organize the economy in a centralistic way and the difficulties that come with this have many similarities with indicative planning in market economies. In the middle of the twentieth century, most Eastern European countries had centrally planned economies. China has been, and to a large extent still is, another example of an economic system in which the government plays a central role in the country's economic development. In addition, the discussions in the USA and in the different member states of the EU following the financial crisis of 2008–9 show how important it is to have a good understanding of the mechanisms of centrally planned economies. When in Europe and the USA governments are nationalizing major banks and supporting large multinational firms (see Box 8.5) the question arises to what extent a government is able to guide the economy. The difficulties become clear when we look into the experiences of governments, firms and consumers in centrally planned economies.

## Politics first

In the eighteenth century, market economies resulted in a dire situation for large sections of the population: wages at subsistence level, child labor, and very poor safety, health and working conditions. The market performed well for a small elite, but very badly for the majority of the people. Many politicians in those days saw the misery as an outcome of the 'invisible hand' and favored a system of a 'visible hand' controlled by the government. In a centrally planned system, politics dominates the economy: the political system decides on the economic objectives, and the economic system is then organized so that decisions taken at industry and micro level fit the politically defined objectives.

## Central economic plans

Let us take a look at some historical facts about centrally planned economies. The societal objectives were laid out in a plan in which the relationships between all sectors of the economy were specified. In the former Soviet Union, the Central Planning Bureau (Gosplan) was the institution responsible for drawing up the plans, which generally covered periods of five years. So, when the objectives were set, the planning agency calculated the implications for each sector of the economy. When, for example, national income was planned to grow by 5 percent, what would the implication be for the steel sector, the production of fertilizers, the chemical sector, and so on?

The next step in the planning procedure concerned the linkages and fine-tuning between the sectors. In order to do so, Gosplan made use of so-called input–output tables, in which the connections between all the sectors were shown, and from which the aggregated outcomes for investment, labor demand and imports could also be calculated (see Table 8.2 for an example).

**Table 8.2** *Input–output table of a central plan*

| Economic activities | Inputs to agriculture | Inputs to manufacturing | Inputs to transport | Final demand | Total output |
|---|---|---|---|---|---|
| Agriculture | 5 | 15 | 2 | 68 | 90 |
| Manufacturing | 10 | 20 | 10 | 40 | 80 |
| Transportation | 10 | 15 | 5 | 0 | 30 |
| Services | 5 | 10 | 5 | 10 | 30 |

The final step in the planning procedure was the translation of the output objectives at sector level into the directives for the individual firms. Each production unit in the economy received a directive from Gosplan stating how much to produce over what period, and to whom it should be delivered. The firms in this centrally planned economy were not entrepreneurial institutions that explored new products or new ways of production. They were simply executors of the directives calculated by the planning bureau.

## Problems in centrally planned economies

What went wrong with the planned economies? Why were the Eastern European countries not able to realize the production levels of the Western market economies? Why were the firms less efficient and consumers less satisfied? We shall show that the problems are rooted in the information, motivation and coordination mechanisms of the system. These problems are of great interest to us now because issues of information, coordination and motivation are central in the present discussion on liberalization, privatization and deregulation in markets, as well as in the discussion on the increasing role of government – in particular in the financial sector of the economy.

Recall the earlier discussion on principal–agent relationships. When two parties have different objectives and an information asymmetry exists between them, the principal–agent theory predicts a coordination problem. The action of the agent must be aligned with the objectives of the principal by means of additional institutions, such as contracts and monitoring mechanisms (see Chapter 3). The problems in a centrally planned economy can be analyzed by using the instruments of principal–agent theory: the relationship between the central planning bureau and the firms is clearly one in which the objectives of the actors are different, and the agents have more information than the principal.

When the central planning bureau has determined the production objectives of, say, the steel industry, and the bureau wants to formulate the objectives for the individual firms in the sector, it also has to arrange for a sufficient input of production factors (labor and capital), raw materials (such as ore) and intermediate products (such as machinery); otherwise, the firms would not be able to realize the targets. To stimulate an efficient allocation of resources in the system, the central planner aims at allocating just enough inputs to enable the firms to realize their targets if they carry out production in the most efficient way. In order to stimulate the managers of the firm to allocate the resources efficiently, the principal rewards a bonus when the targets are met with the inputs supplied.

But how does the central planning bureau know about the production function of a firm? How does it know what is the most efficient production method? This information is in the hands of the managers of the firm and costly to obtain by the central planner. The manager has an incentive to supply the central planner with distorted information: he will ask for more inputs than necessary and will inform the planner that he can produce less with it than is in fact possible. In this way the manager can easily meet the targets and receive the bonus. Moreover, the manager has no incentive to make efficient use of the inputs allocated to him, because the supply in the next period is based on usage in the previous period. On the contrary, in fact: the manager is stimulated to use all the inputs, otherwise the planner gets the message that production can be realized with fewer inputs. And there are no incentives for the manager to innovate and invest in new products or in more efficient production processes, because all decisions regarding what to produce and methods of production are taken at the central level.

In the history of the centrally planned economies, governments made many attempts to reform the system to enable politicians to maintain control over the economy, while at the same time giving management an incentive to become more efficient. Experiments have been performed offering greater autonomy for managers to invest a part of their means into their own company. However, each time increased autonomy was given to the actors at the micro level their behavior became less controllable and less predictable. More autonomy at the micro level implies less control over the realization of the objectives in the plan. Most of the issues concerning the regulation of firms in market economies resemble the agency problems in centrally planned economies.

Recall also the theory of property rights (see Chapter 3), where the strong incentives related to private property were discussed. In the case of central planning and nationalized firms, the property rights theory predicts less efficiency. The incentives to behave efficiently are weakened in cases of collective and common property.

## *Complexity of open systems and complicated industrial structures*

In a simply structured closed economy a central planning bureau is able to calculate with the use of input–output tables what the directives for each individual firm have to be in order to realize the macro objectives. However, when economies become large and are open to imports and exports, complex principal–agent problems increase, central planning is no longer realistic and the system has to be adjusted, as we have seen with the Special Economic Zones (SEZs) in China. The SEZs are an interesting case, because they show how in a planned economy separate areas can be governed by a different, more market-oriented system. The SEZs, such as Shenzhen, Zhuhai, Shantou and Xiamen were introduced in 1980 as areas that would focus on the production of export goods and would be financed by foreign capital. Because the SEZs are separate from national planning very different rules could be allowed, such as foreign investors having full ownership.

You will see below that the effectiveness of the role of government in a market economy is also closely related to the openness and complexity of the economy. We now turn to the discussion of the role of planning in a market economy and first discuss the nature of indicative planning.

## *Indicative planning*

In the description of the characteristics of the system of indicative planning we use the central planning system as a kind of benchmark. The main difference between the two systems is related to the degree of autonomy of the decision-makers at the micro level. With indicative planning, the individual producers and consumers decide about their demand and supply needs. The market with autonomous actors is central. However, there are also similarities between a centrally planned and an indicatively planned economy.

In the early days of indicative planning (the 1960s) in countries such France and Japan, the original idea was to design a process of information exchange among all participants in the economy with the intention of producing *indicators* (from where the concept of indicative planning originates) that guide firms toward the objectives of the plan (Estrin and Holmes, 1983). The indicators are obtained by a detailed consultation procedure in which the actors in the different sectors of the economy exchange information about their plans over a period of, for example, five years: their future supply and demand needs, their investments and so on.

After this consultation, the planning bureau aggregates the plans and decides whether the economy will be in equilibrium if all the individual plans are implemented. If it will not, the information is fed back into the consultation process with the producers. At this point, a question such as: 'Now you know that an oversupply will emerge in the future, what is your new investment plan?' is asked of the producers. After necessary adjustments have been made and equilibrium is reached, all participants conclude contracts with the planning bureau, in which they agree to behave according to the final round of information exchange.

In practice these contracts will be incomplete, the more so when the economy is open and of a more complex structure. Nevertheless, also in cases of incomplete contracts, the type of indicative planning described above can result in equilibria. When all firms consider it to be in their own interests to obtain the equilibria that are indicated in the plan, one can expect them to behave spontaneously according to guidelines of the plan.

A final possibility in the system of indicative planning is the one in which the government takes control over crucial sectors or technologies in the economy. In this situation, the market still functions and private actors still take decisions based on their own private interests, but essential parts of the economy are placed under the control of the government. Through the nationalization of specific firms (as the French government did in 1981), large parts of the industrial and financial sector may be brought under government control

## *The coordination problem*

We now take a closer look at the type of information a government must provide in an indicative plan.

In a market economy, with market and environmental uncertainty, the question of how to realize future equilibria is basically about the coordination of the plans of individual firms, which are based on expected future prices. A producer of, for example, electric autos, makes his investment plans today on the basis of the expected price for electric autos in, say, a period of five years from now.

How can these plans be coordinated at the present time to ensure equilibrium in the future? The distinction between market and environmental uncertainty is important because the nature of information differs. In case of market uncertainty, the question hinges on what actors in the market will do under different future circumstances (contingencies). This type of information is generally available in the system. It can be assumed that actors know what they will do under specific future circumstances in order to maximize their utility or profit. This information can be gathered by a central agency and aggregated, so the central coordinator is able to identify the possibility of emerging equilibria.

This is different in the case of environmental uncertainty: nobody in the system has information about the future of the technology, or how preferences will develop. The best that can be done is the construction of possible future situations and let the market generate an equilibrium as if one of these possible situations indeed materializes. This sketch of 'possible futures' is known as *scenario planning*: governments, but also large multinationals, develop scenarios in consultation with experts about possible developments in a number of variables (climate change, the political power of countries in world politics, new technologies concerning energy and so on). These different developments of the variables are put into logical groupings (a scenario) and then the government, or the management of the large firm, design policies under the assumption that a specific scenario will come about.

In Economics, it is often assumed that the price mechanism provides the correct information at the right time, but in Chapter 5 you learned that such a role for the price system is problematic. The important question underlying that assumption is about how the necessary information and knowledge are acquired and communicated (Hayek, 1937, p. 45):

> It appears that the concept of equilibrium merely means that the foresight of the different members of the society is in a special sense correct. It must be correct in the sense that every person's plan is based on the expectation of just those actions of other people which those other people intend to perform, and that all these plans are based on the expectation of the same set of external events, so that under certain conditions nobody will have any reason to change his plans.

From Hayek's quote we learn that two issues are at stake. On the one hand, the actors need to have similar expectations about developments in the exogenous variables, such as the preferences of consumers, the technologies and the political institutions. On the other hand, the actors need to make their own individual plans for each of the possible states in the future. Hayek points out that these plans must be 'compatible' in order to have equilibrium.

In theoretical general equilibrium models (see, for example, Debreu, 1959) it is assumed that markets exist not only for all products to be consumed currently, but also for all products to be consumed in the future: these markets are all in equilibrium. A market in which contracts are concluded concerning the future production and consumption of products is called a 'futures market' – a future in this context being a contract to deliver a certain amount of the product at a certain future point in time. However, in reality, insufficient futures markets exist and insufficient information is supplied through the price system. Filling these gaps is exactly what indicative planning is all about. To make clear the role an indicative plan could play in relation to the information and coordination problem raised by Hayek, we put ourselves in the position of a firm that has to make plans for the future. What are the firm's sources of information, and how can an indicative plan provide relevant information? We mention three of these information sources below.

First, price changes indicate changes in scarcities and are an incentive for actors to change their behavior, either as a consumer or a producer. In this respect, the futures markets are an important institutional innovation. As discussed in Chapter 5, futures markets reduce uncertainty for the firms because they can conclude contracts about future prices and deliveries. Futures markets now exist in many sectors of the economy, and reduce uncertainty.

Another important source of information for the actors in the market is their own capability to produce information. Think about the market research that firms undertake in order to find out what the potential demand for their products or services might be. You know from your own experience that producing information is not costless. Search costs can be so high that you are often forced to make a decision on the basis of relatively little information. To fill the resulting information gap there are institutions that produce information for the private actors. Consulting firms, trade organizations and consumer organizations are examples of associations producing this information. The economic explanation behind the existence of these suppliers of information is related to economies of scale. Consulting firms or consumer associations have access to a large database and have highly trained employees who can find specific information quickly. The consultants produce information on a more efficient scale than the individual firm can.

But not all information that is important for making decisions is provided through prices or produced by actors in the market. Most people have experienced often crucial information being provided via network relations. Simply because people interact with others and over time trustworthy relationships are built up, information is received 'free of charge', which comprises the third source of information.

Considering all these sources of information, one might wonder whether there is any role for the government as a producer and disseminator of information in an indicative plan. We have now arrived at the core of indicative planning: providing information that is useful for the market parties, but that is not available to them. We have already shown in this chapter several situations in which government intervention can be of substantial importance in increasing transparency. Here we focus on the reason why information is 'underproduced', which is related to the peculiar characteristics of information as an economic good.

Consider the situation in which a consulting firm receives a rather specific request from an agro-food firm that specializes in new, genetically manipulated vegetables. The request is to produce information about the development of the technology in relation to the changes of preferences in different countries with respect to the production and consumption of genetically manipulated food. This seems to be such a specific request that the consulting firm has to make quite specific investments to be able to do the research and produce the desired information. From Chapter 3 you know that, in such types of situation, negotiations about the contract can become very complicated and extremely costly: it will often be very difficult to agree about the kind of information needed and to determine a reasonable price for this information, because it is very uncertain as to what type of information can be produced in any case. This situation is known as the *information paradox of Arrow*: the customer knows that information has value to him and what price he would be willing to offer, but only after the information has been revealed to him. But in this situation the supplier of information must be careful because the customer might show opportunistic behavior.

A specific issue for the producer of information is the possibility that the customer, once he has bought and used the information, might share or resell the information to others. In this situation the original producer may not be able to exploit his investment, and if it is too costly to create safeguards he will probably not make the investment at all. A well-known safeguard is inserting a clause in the contract stating that it is forbidden for the customer to resell the information on the market.

Finally, there is the problem of externalities that result from the pure public good character of information goods. When a firm has bought information in the market or has produced information itself it can simply reveal the information to others through its behavior. Suppose the agro-food firm has information about future consumption opportunities for genetically modified foods in different countries, then its strategy to invest in specific countries and disinvest in others reveals this knowledge. By monitoring the behavior and strategies of a competitor others can learn about the knowledge the competitor has. So, this is another reason why information is underproduced in the market.

We conclude that the 'market for information' does not necessarily of itself produce all the information that is of use to the market parties. This is where the government is important, to provide the additional useful information to the firms in the form of an indicative plan. In this plan the government provides information about macro variables, about developments at the meso level, about technologies, about political developments worldwide and so on – all of which are important indicators for actors at the micro level. To produce solid information in a consistent way, the government makes an investment in a planning bureau or statistical agency, which develops the expertise of producing information in a consistent, long-term manner. Examples can be found at the global level (World Bank, OECD, IMF, World Health Organization – WHO); at the regional level (EU – for example, Eurostat); and at the national level (for example, the French Institut National de la Statistique et des Études Économiques – INSEE).

## *Embeddedness of indicative planning*

From the above it emerges that different systems of indicative planning exist, ranging from pure information-providing plans, to more interventionist strategies executed by the developmental state (see below for further discussion on this). Which type of indicative planning is found in different market economies around the world largely depends on the type of (in)formal institutions that exists. In an Anglo-Saxon type of socioeconomic system there will be a different type of indicative plan than those found in Continental European and Asian countries.

In the case of a more interventionist plan, the ministries and other public agencies should be well supplied with information, expertise and authority to fulfill their role. The other actors in the economy should not only respect the guiding role of government, but the whole culture should be such that the other actors align their strategies with the ones indicated in government plans. This has clearly been the case in countries such as France, Japan, the Republic of South Korea, Hong Kong (before it became part of mainland China), Taiwan, Singapore, and to a certain extent in China today. In these countries, the initiating and intervening role of government has been embedded in the layers of (in)formal institutions. The formal laws and regulations as well as the governance structure 'firms' were in harmony with the culture of a 'strong state'.

In most countries, we can see a development in which the nature of the indicative planning changes gradually towards an information plan, in which government agencies provide macroeconomic projections and in which specific issues in particular sectors and countries are highlighted. This evolution has been in harmony with the gradually changing attitude towards and appreciation of the role of government in market economies. From the 1980s onward, the wave of liberalization has positioned government more in a guiding role than in the driver's seat. The ideology of the market was dominant before the financial and economic crisis erupted in 2008–9. The aspect of embeddedness and changes over time in different periods of history is also clear in the industrial and technology policies of the government, to which we shall turn next.

## Industrial and technology policies

When discussing government policies and how a government can increase efficiency in the economy, an important distinction should be made between the role of government concerning the cyclical development of the economy on the one hand and structural development on the other.

The former refers to the level of economic activity in the economy: aggregate demand of households, firms, government and exports. If aggregate demand and exports are not in equilibrium with supply (the national production and imports), inflation or unemployment results. In such circumstances a government can decide to stimulate the economy by increased government spending or by lowering taxes. With such policy instruments, governments in market economies can restore the imbalance by increasing, for example, the demand for military equipment, infrastructure, education or health services. With tax and subsidy instruments the government can influence the level of demand of the other actors such as households, firms and foreign customers.

Such cyclical policies should be distinguished from structural policies, which concern the composition of economic activities overall (Elsner and Groenewegen, 2000). The structure of the economy consists of different sectors such as agriculture and mining, industrial sectors (steel, shipbuilding) and service sectors (banking, insurance). Within sectors, further subdivisions are made, as in the distinction between the chemical, manufacturing and construction sectors within the industrial sector.

Changes in the composition of the structure of the economy are mainly the result of (dis)investment. In market economies, firms make investments in R&D leading to the introduction of new products to the market. Below we discuss different types of government structural policies in market economies following the stages of the industry life cycle (graphically, this is the equivalent of the product life cycle shown in Figure 6.1). We start with *technology policy* in the introduction stage and end with *industrial policy* in the stagnation stage.

### *The introduction stage: technology policy*

Technology policy focuses on the first stage of the life cycle, where inventions are translated into innovation. Innovations can refer to products, production processes, new forms of organization and new markets. In the following we focus on innovations in new products. We ask what information and coordination problems there are for innovating firms, how these issues can be resolved by the firms themselves, and what additional role the government can play.

In the introduction stage of the life cycle the problems for firms relate to several issues, most notably the financing of investments in R&D and insufficient knowledge. When firms are not able to address these issues adequately they will not invest in R&D, innovation will not come about, and consequently the competitiveness of the economy will be harmed. In this case it is considered to be the responsibility of the government to intervene and support firms by means of a technology policy. We look first at financial problems.

## Financing innovations

When firms make investments, several financial sources are available:

- to issue shares on the stock market (and pay dividends) – when a firm issues shares it receives money from the ones who buy the shares and the firm pays a dividend to those shareholders when a profit is made;
- to issue bonds on the bond market (and pay interest) – when a firm issues bonds it receives money from those who buy the bonds and the firm pays a fixed rate of interest to the bondholders irrespective profits or losses made;
- to borrow from a bank (and pay interest); or
- to draw on internal reserves (finance itself out of past profits).

Shares only pay dividends if a firm makes a profit. In that sense, for the person or organization that provides capital, shares are a riskier way of providing money to a firm than the other alternatives. Because R&D investments are risky and deal with large uncertainties, banks and private actors are generally hesitant to provide the necessary financial backing. The connection between the firm and the potential financer can be seen as a typical principal–agent relationship, in which the parties have different objectives and information asymmetries exist between them. The firm will try to convince the potential suppliers of capital about the potential success of the innovation. However, because of information asymmetries there are possibilities for opportunistic behavior. It is interesting to see that, on the side of the capital suppliers, specialists have emerged, who reduce the information asymmetry and try to 'pick the winners'; these specialists are known as *'venture capitalists'*. They develop an expertise in specific sectors and specific types of risks and are willing to step in to support new ventures. However, in return for taking the high risks involved they demand a high premium.

Capital transactions to finance innovations can take place in different ways. However, the costs of R&D can be such that it is impossible for one firm to make a large enough investment, or that one outside supplier of capital can bear the risk. In such cases, the private actors find solutions in hybrid governance structures such as consortia and strategic alliances (see Chapter 7).

You can imagine a situation where, despite private solutions, the market is still not able to raise enough capital for the needed investment in R&D. The costs and risks are sometimes simply too high. In such a situation a government might intervene. The technology policy of the government then consists of a plan with concrete objectives for innovations in specific sectors of the economy – for areas such as telecommunications, biotechnology or sustainable energy. When clear objectives are set, the government invites firms to participate, with finance, human capacity, or knowledge and networks. To create sufficient commitment, both private and public actors must invest. Examples are the technology programs of the EU, while the American space program fulfilled the role of a state technology program that opened the way for private firms to innovate. The government can also implement its technology policy by subsidizing the R&D expenditure only in a generic way. Examples can be found in the wage subsidies for personnel in R&D departments of firms.

### Lack of sufficient complementary knowledge

We close our discussion on the introduction stage of the industry life cycle by pointing to another problem that firms encounter. To innovate, often combinations of different technologies and domains of knowledge are needed. The robotics in automobile manufacture is a good example. Robots are combinations of machine tools and electronics, two completely different domains that had to be combined to produce the innovation. In other words, in order to be innovative, firms often need knowledge they do not already possess, which is costly for them to develop and is not available on the market.

In Chapter 7 you saw how all kinds of hybrid governance structures can solve such knowledge problems; in joint ventures between firms, the different types of expertise can be combined, thus providing a private solution to the innovation problem. Could the government also play a role in that respect? When it comes to taking the first steps at the fundamental research stage, when the possibility of a commercial innovation is not at all clear, public research institutes often play a central role. Both in initiating combinations of research domains and in diffusing knowledge as a public good, government support can be crucial. It is often in the framework of large technology programs that a government finances and organizes that part of the fundamental research combining different areas.

## *The expansion, maturity and stagnation stages: industrial policy*

After the successful introduction stage, a market enters the expansion stage. Demand grows, more firms enter the market and each of them invests in production capacity according to its own ideas about the future. Individual firms do not need each other during that stage of growth, and certainly do not need an intervening government. When the market is expanding and optimism about increasing market shares is growing, firms are eager to make more investments in larger production units (economies of scale).

However, when there is no central coordinator supervising individual investment plans, none of the individual actors knows what the levels of aggregate demand and supply will be. It is to be expected that the sector will experience overcapacity at some point. The maturity and stagnation stages of the industry life cycle then begin, in which firms are confronted by aggressive price competition that often ends in price wars. Firms will first try to protect their market share through product differentiation, but a process of capacity reduction is inevitable. Generally, the process of capacity reduction goes hand in hand with a process of concentration. During this stage of the life cycle a government can take responsibility for an 'orderly retreat' by means of industrial policy. In contrast to technology policy, which focuses on so-called 'sunrise industries', industrial policy focuses on 'sunset industries'.

Industrial policy can result in efficient solutions if there is a lack of coordination between autonomous firms with different objectives at the individual level, but a common aim at the industry level. The individual objectives are to maintain at least a market share, which involves competing the others out of the market. However, the best outcome at industry level would be a gradual reduction of the overcapacity. In this way the least efficient capacity is reduced first, and firms make sufficient profit to be able to invest in new directions and innovations. The result would then be that the most efficient firms in the sector survive, and capacity to supply is in harmony with demand.

Yet the core of the problem in the stagnation phase concerns the impossibility of individual firms coordinating their behavior to bring about the desired result at industry level. How can firms coordinate their behavior to reduce production capacity efficiently? Note that each individual firm will have an incentive to behave opportunistically and not to reduce capacity while benefiting from the reduction of the others.

The solution to this problem is for the government or competition authorities to allow 'crisis cartels'. These cartels may, with certain restrictions, be exempt from competition law. If firms agree to organize the orderly retreat from the sector while maintaining the possibility of investing in the future competitiveness of the economy, a government can decide to approve such a cartel for a limited period of time. Moreover, the government will monitor the behavior of the firms.

## Institutional competitiveness

The activist policies described above focus on stimulating domestic companies and industries, with little reference to the international competitiveness of these industrial sectors. Of course, by actively pursuing technology and industrial policies, the government also supports its domestic sector in the sense that, as a result, their position may be strengthened *vis-à-vis* foreign rivals. But, in addition, states also compete with each other by setting more or less attractive rules with respect to businesses, labor and capital. We are now touching on the phenomenon of *institutional competition*: policies that, among other things, concern a jurisdiction's fiscal regime and business licensing requirements, both for individual firms and for workers (Kasper and Streit, 1999).

Some countries charge high corporate and income tax rates, while others charge low rates. In some countries, foreign workers receive a residence permit for a limited period of time, while elsewhere they are received with open arms. These differences between nations change over time. This depends, among other things, on the need to attract more foreign capital and workers ('pull-factors') and the desire to leave a particular country – for example, because of unfavorable economic or political circumstances ('push-factors').

Institutional competition does not only occur between countries; it also happens between (partly) autonomous regions within a country, such as the states within the USA and the cantons within Switzerland, and at a city level. Nations, provinces, states and cities compete with other jurisdictions to attract large corporations to site their headquarters or set up a branch in a particular country, province or town. The main reason for this is usually related to creating more employment in the area concerned. In this way, more people will have jobs and generate more income tax, while at the same time fewer people will need to be paid a social security benefit. In addition, having more businesses in one's jurisdiction means more revenue from corporate taxes.

It was once again Adam Smith who, more than 200 years ago, wrote about the importance of tax revenue in a comparative perspective:

> The proprietor of stock is properly a citizen of the world, and is not necessarily attached to any particular country. He would be apt to abandon the country in which he was exposed to a...burdensome tax, and would remove his stock to some

other country where he could either carry on his business, or enjoy his fortune more at his ease. By removing his stock he would put an end to all the industry which it had maintained in the country which he left. Stock cultivates land; stock employs labour. A tax which tended to drive away stock from any particular country would so far tend to dry up every source of revenue both to the sovereign and to the society. Not only the profits of stock, but the rent of land and the wages of labour would necessarily be more or less diminished by its removal. (Smith, 1776, p. 800)

Table 8.3  *Corporate tax rates in thirty OECD countries, 1996–2008 (percentages)*

| Country | 1996 | 2000 | 2004 | 2008 | Rank 2008 |
|---|---|---|---|---|---|
| Japan | 50.0 | 40.9 | 39.5 | 39.5 | 1 |
| USA | 39.5 | 39.3 | 39.3 | 39.3 | 2 |
| France | 36.7 | 37.8 | 35.4 | 34.4 | 3 |
| Belgium | 40.2 | 40.2 | 34.0 | 34.0 | 4 |
| Canada | 44.6 | 43.6 | 36.1 | 33.5 | 5 |
| Luxembourg | n.a. | 37.5 | 30.4 | 30.4 | 6 |
| Germany | 55.9 | 52.0 | 38.9 | 30.2 | 7 |
| Australia | 36.0 | 34.0 | 30.0 | 30.0 | 8 |
| New Zealand | 33.0 | 33.0 | 33.0 | 30.0 | 9 |
| Spain | 35.0 | 35.0 | 35.0 | 30.0 | 10 |
| Mexico | 34.0 | 35.0 | 33.0 | 28.0 | 11 |
| Norway | 28.0 | 28.0 | 28.0 | 28.0 | 12 |
| Sweden | 28.0 | 28.0 | 28.0 | 28.0 | 13 |
| UK | 33.0 | 30.0 | 30.0 | 28.0 | 14 |
| Italy | 53.2 | 37.0 | 33.0 | 27.5 | 15 |
| Korea | n.a. | 30.8 | 29.7 | 27.5 | 16 |
| Portugal | 39.6 | 35.2 | 27.5 | 26.5 | 17 |
| Finland | 28.0 | 29.0 | 29.0 | 26.0 | 18 |
| Netherlands | 35.0 | 35.0 | 34.5 | 25.5 | 19 |
| Austria | 34.0 | 34.0 | 34.0 | 25.0 | 20 |
| Denmark | 34.0 | 32.0 | 30.0 | 25.0 | 21 |
| Greece | 35.0 | 40.0 | 35.0 | 25.0 | 22 |
| Switzerland | 28.5 | 24.9 | 24.1 | 21.2 | 23 |
| Czech Republic | 39.0 | 31.0 | 28.0 | 21.0 | 24 |
| Hungary | 18.0 | 18.0 | 16.0 | 20.0 | 25 |
| Turkey | n.a. | 33.0 | 33.0 | 20.0 | 26 |
| Poland | 40.0 | 30.0 | 19.0 | 19.0 | 27 |
| Slovak Republic | 40.0 | 29.0 | 19.0 | 19.0 | 28 |
| Iceland | n.a. | 30.0 | 18.0 | 15.0 | 29 |
| Ireland | 36.0 | 24.0 | 12.5 | 12.5 | 30 |
| OECD unweighted average | 35.6 | 33.6 | 29.8 | 26.6 | |

*Note*: n.a. = data not available.
*Source*: OECD (2009).

So, from far back in history, setting the right level of taxes has been one of the key aspects in institutional competition. To curb the flight of capital, countries compete, among other things, by means of an attractive corporate tax regime. In Table 8.3 we show the development of the corporate tax rates of thirty OECD countries between 1996 and 2008. Countries such as Germany, Ireland, the Slovak Republic and Italy have decreased their corporate tax rates tremendously, whereas others, such as France, the USA and Japan (as from 2000) have kept their rates pretty well constant and very high. You can see that the differences between the two highest-ranked nations, Japan and the USA, and the lowest-ranked nation, Ireland, is huge. A study by Devereux *et al.* (2008) shows that countries indeed compete with each other over corporate taxes – they estimated that a 10 percent corporate tax reduction by an EU member state can lead to a 60 percent rise in investments by US multinationals.

## CONCLUDING REMARKS

Problems that are complex from the point of view of coordinating individual behavior in order to create efficiencies can best be solved by governments. Private solutions will rarely come about to solve such coordination problems. The main examples in the static sense are the provision by the government of pure public goods, finding solutions for complex externalities, implementing competition policy and sector-specific regulators to curb market power, and creating laws that will solve information problems in the economy. These solutions are all examples of institutions.

Governments can also play an important role in initiating, guiding and steering the dynamics of institutions. This is clearly the case in centrally planned economies, where the government is responsible for economic development and performance. But the role of the government in a market economy can also be of an initiating and steering nature. Governments can lead the development of the economic structure. Indicative planning, industrial and technology policies are examples of how a government can be effective in implementing policies and in designing institutions to solve coordination problems from a dynamic perspective. Much of the effectiveness of such policies depends on the embeddedness in the complementary value, political and judicial systems. The intervening role of government should be supported by the other actors in the system, and the expertise of governmental institutions and civil servants should be generally recognized. Only then can one expect the role of government to be effective.

## REVIEW QUESTIONS

1 What different roles can a government have? Base your answer both on the efficiency approach and the vested interest approach.
2 Look back at Figure III.1 that shows the relationship between the three private governance structures and the degree of assset specificity.
   (a) Draw the two public transaction cost curves in this figure.
   (b) Discuss the two curves with regard to the influence of the contract law regime, property rights, reputation and risk.

3 Given that public governance structures have to face political transaction costs, explain how it is possible that their transaction costs may be lower than in private governance structures.
4 What kinds of economic problems cannot be solved by private actors? Why not? Provide some real-life examples from your own experience (or that of your country).
5 Discuss the difference between the regulatory and the development state. In which of the two categories would you place your own country's government?
6 Describe the relationship between economics and politics in a market economy and in a centrally planned economy.
7 How would you characterize the firms in a centrally planned economy?
8 Why did the centrally planned economies fail?
9 What is the role of the planning bureau in a system of indicative planning as compared to a centrally planned economy?
10 What is the role of the information provided in an indicative plan?
11 What is 'institutional competition'? How does your own country (or region) engage in this?

# Appendixes to Chapter 8

## APPENDIX A: ELABORATION OF THE FIXED COSTS ARGUMENT AND RETURNS TO SCALE

Suppose that a firm (not necessarily a monopolist) has high fixed costs compared to variable and marginal costs to the extent that *average* total costs decline with output. That is, the higher the output, the lower the average total costs will be. The mechanism behind this is that variable costs will rise with output and, at least at higher output levels, so will average variable costs. By definition, fixed costs do not change with output, so average fixed costs will always decline: the more units of the good produced, the more fixed costs can be spread over this number of units. Since average total costs are the sum of average fixed costs and average variable costs, average total costs will either decrease or increase at higher output levels, depending on the strength of the underlying increase of average variable costs or decrease in average fixed costs. It is easy to see that, in the case of sufficiently high fixed costs, the decrease in average fixed costs will be stronger than an increase in average variable costs.

Now suppose that a firm does not have market power – for example, as a result of perfect competition. The price of the firm's product would be given at the level of marginal cost. How does marginal costs behave in the case of decreasing average costs? To answer this question, we shall first state a general principle with respect to the 'behavior of averages'.

Suppose that we have any average figure – for example, an average grade of 8 on a scale of 0 to 10. How can this average grade be increased? Only if the next grade is higher than 8. And, of course, the average will decrease if the next grade is lower than 8. This principle is always true. Any average grade will increase if the next, or marginal, grade is higher than the average, and will decrease if the next, or marginal, grade is lower than the average.

Hence, average costs (to be compared with the average grade) will decrease if the next unit of output adds lower costs (the marginal costs) than the average costs. So, average costs can only decrease as long as marginal costs are lower than average costs.

### Example

Suppose variable costs are constant, and each product costs 10 to produce. So, average variable costs are 10. Fixed costs are 100. The firm produces 20 units, so total costs are 20 units $\times$ 10 variable production costs + 100 fixed costs, making 300. Average total costs are $300/20 = 15$. This average will only decline when the next unit is being produced at a lower costs than 15, which is the case, because each additional unit costs 10 to produce. So, for 21 units, costs are $21 \times 10 + 100 = 310$. An average of $310/21 = 14.76$.

An immediate consequence is that, in the case of fixed costs, average total costs will only rise if variable costs rise with production, in which case there are diminishing returns to the variable production factor(s).

Suppose variable production costs are denoted by C(q), which means that variable production costs are a function of output. The fixed production costs are denoted by F. Total costs are then C(q) + F. Average total costs are [C(q) + F]/q = F/q + C(q)/q. Higher output means that F/q declines, because F is fixed. So, average total costs will only rise if C(q)/q rises more than F/q declines. If C(q)/q is constant, then by definition, average total costs decline. A graphical representation can be found in Figure 8.1 in Appendix B.

## Returns to scale

In many cases, increasing returns to scale result from technical or organizational changes. Larger companies can afford to use heavy machinery, buy supplies in bulk at a discount, and have a better division of labor. As long as these advantages are realized with a larger scale of operations, we speak of increasing returns.

In general, though, there has to be a limit to these returns to scale (dependent on the extent of demand). If there was no limit, in principle a single factory could supply the whole world's demand for the product. This suggests that there is an 'optimum' size for a factory, depending on the existing technology and market conditions: the minimum optimal scale. Production beyond the minimum optimal scale is no longer characterized by increasing returns, but by constant or even decreasing returns.

In the automobile industry, increasing returns to scale are of great importance, which has meant that, over time, the number of automobile manufacturers has declined dramatically as a result of mergers and the bankruptcy of smaller companies. In France, the two major automobile firms are Peugeot and Renault. Could these two companies continue to supply increasing demand based on their current scale? An empirical paper by Truett and Truett (2007) found limits to the returns to scale in these companies at high levels of production, suggesting that they had already reached, or perhaps even surpassed, the minimum optimal scale.

From an economic point of view, it may be relevant to distinguish between the concepts of 'increasing returns to scale' and 'economies of scale'. Economies of scale may be considered the more general term. All advantages of producing on a larger scale that lead to lower average costs are captured by 'economies of scale'. Hence, 'economies of scale' do not only contain the advantages involved in 'increasing returns', but also additional (financial) advantages, such as the ability to finance investments more cheaply, or to attract inputs at lower costs.

To put it in more theoretical economic terms: increasing returns to scale are the advantages obtained by operating on a larger scale with more efficient use of inputs, given the prices of these inputs. Economies of scale are also the additional advantages that may be obtained by being able to pay lower prices for inputs – being able, for example, to gain discounts when buying the inputs in greater quantities.

As long as increasing returns can be realized (compared to the extent of market demand), the effect of increasing returns is the same as that of high fixed costs: it is efficient to have one firm only because of cost efficiency.

## APPENDIX B: GRAPHICAL ILLUSTRATION OF THE DIFFICULTIES OF REGULATING A NATURAL MONOPOLY

As is explained in the main text, a natural monopoly is characterized by continually decreasing average costs (AC). This is illustrated in Figure 8.1.

Now, the problem is that the government cannot impose a price that equals the marginal costs, because this would mean a price of $P_c$ and a quantity sold of $Q_c$, which would lead to a permanent loss for the producer. This is the case because the regulated market price lies below the level of the average costs, implying that the revenue per unit is lower than the costs per unit.

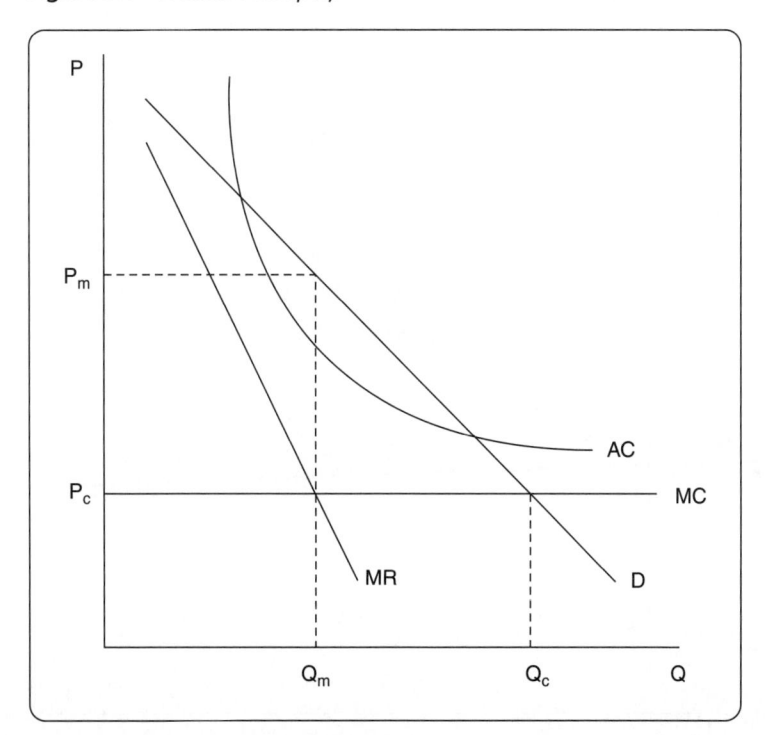

**Figure 8.1** *Natural monopoly*

## APPENDIX C: GRAPHICAL ILLUSTRATION OF A CORRECTIVE TAX IN CASE OF A NEGATIVE EXTERNALITY

Suppose that the market for a certain chemical product can be represented by Figure 8.2. The demand and supply curve (D and S) are drawn as straight lines. In the market equilibrium, an amount of $Q_p$ is sold at a unit price of $P_p$. The production causes air pollution as an unwanted by-product. This leads to costs for the population and the natural environment. Suppose, again for reasons of simplicity, that each extra unit produced by this industry increases the damage to both humans and nature by a fixed amount. Therefore, we can draw the MSC (marginal societal cost) curve parallel to the supply curve. The

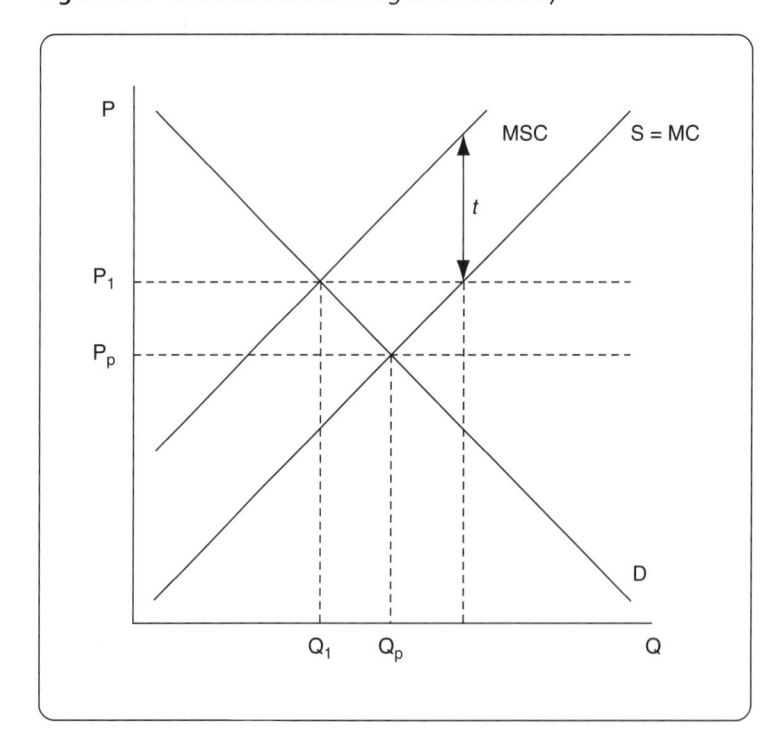

**Figure 8.2** *Internalization of a negative externality*

MSC curve represents the summation of the marginal production costs and the marginal costs of the air pollution.

In the figure you can see the effect of an environmental unit tax, $t$, that is exactly equal to the marginal costs of air pollution. Because of this tax, firms are faced with extra costs. The original supply curve S shows the minimum amount that firms want to receive for each output level, given their production costs. The unit tax raises these production costs, so that firms will then want to receive a higher price for each output level. When balancing the higher marginal costs with marginal revenue, producers will take a new and lower output decision. The new output level will coincide with $Q_1$, so that economic welfare is maximized. In economics, this resulting effect of corrective taxes is called the 'internalization of the negative externality'.

# 9 Government Failures

## CONTENTS

- **Introduction**
- **The static approach to government failures**
  - Government failures in situations of perfect information
  - Government failures in situations of imperfect information
- **The dynamic approach to government failures**
  - Regulatory risk
  - Interest groups
  - The process of liberalization, privatization and regulation
- **Concluding remarks**
- **Review questions**
- **Appendixes**

## INTRODUCTION

Almost every society needs a government that sets the rules within which its economy can flourish. This means that the state protects the people from foreign intrusion and crime, it enforces clearly defined property rights backed up by a reliable judicial system, and creates a basic financial system as a result of which people feel secure to transact. In such a 'night watchman state', problems related to all kinds of market imperfections may occur, which can be solved efficiently by means of private ordering. In the previous chapter we showed that several problematic situations remain that can only be solved by means of public ordering, and we focused on the welfare enhancing impact of government intervention.

However, public interference itself also has costs, so that on balance this intervention might not improve welfare. On some occasions this happens inadvertently, while the government strives to protect the public interest but fails to do so. On other occasions this is the result of purposeful behavior aimed at serving the vested interests of only a minority of the population. In this chapter we shall examine the negative aspects of government intervention, which, in one way or another, cause welfare losses: when this is the case, *government failure* occurs.

As we shall show in this chapter, running a government involves, among other things, monitoring costs and enforcement costs by the public administration, compliance costs by citizens and efficiency losses resulting from actions by civil servants and politicians who are not necessarily optimizing welfare. In typical institutional economics terminology, we can say that government interference also induces all kinds of transaction costs.

Figure 9.1 illustrates how state interference aimed at serving the public interest and/or particular interests may in general first decrease overall costs to the society at large but at some stage will increase overall costs. On the one hand, government policies and efforts to serve the public interest to the best of its ability would normally be beneficial for the population: regulation and intervention decrease welfare losses for citizens that result from market imperfections, as was noted in the previous chapter; this is represented by the downward sloping curve labeled 'Welfare loss'. These same efforts, on the other hand, lead to several kinds of political transaction costs that are represented by the upward sloping curve 'Policy costs', by which we mean the following, among other things.

Implementing state policies requires the involvement of the public administration, which leads to a range of expenses associated with running governmental bodies, from the salaries of the civil servants to expenditures on buildings and transactions on behalf of the state. Implementing state-enacted policies lead to both *enforcement costs* and *monitoring costs*. These costs are financed in the main out of taxes, so the *administration costs* of these taxes add to the policy costs of government. In addition, citizens incur *compliance costs* when they are subjected to public policies. These comprise all expenses incurred by private firms and individuals when acting in accordance with the rules set by the government, such as the paperwork needed to complete a tax declaration or to apply for a permit (remember, time is money). Box 9.1 elaborates on compliance costs. When people do not agree with certain rules or governmental decisions they could either try to evade the regulations or to start lobbying for political favors, which can benefit a small group but is usually disadvantageous for the majority of the population. To combat evasive or lobbying behavior, state agencies have to incur extra monitoring and enforcement costs,

**Figure 9.1** *Costs and benefits resulting from government intervention*

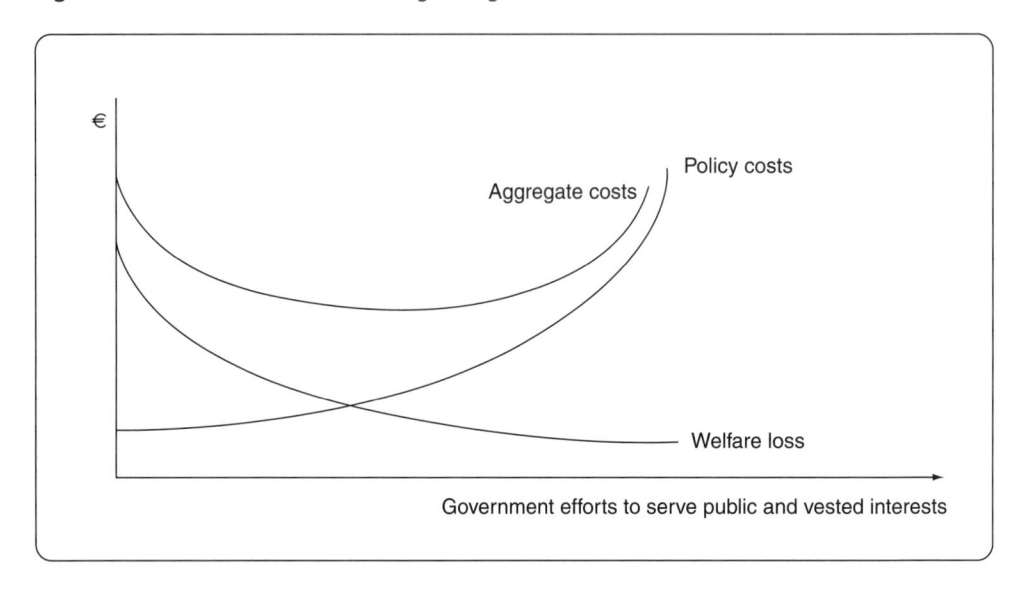

adding once again to the policy costs. Moreover, agents of the state can also make mistakes, which contribute to extra policy costs.

Ideally, the government should try to keep overall costs (the summation of Welfare loss and Policy costs), represented by the third curve 'Aggregate costs', as low as possible. The shape of the three curves will, however, be different for each particular situation. In one situation, the government may serve the interests of the whole population very effectively and efficiently, and then the costs to society may decline very rapidly in combination with only a modest growth in enforcement costs. In another situation, however, government policies may lead to great dissatisfaction among the majority of the population, which will lead to fast-increasing enforcement and monitoring costs. In yet another situation, the actions of the government (or one of its representatives) mainly benefit a minority group at the expense of the often ignorant majority, and as a result, net societal costs increase; note that this last situation cannot be seen from Figure 9.1, as this cannot capture all possible states of affairs.

---

### BOX 9.1   COMPLIANCE COSTS: A TIME FOR TAX

The average Dutch company needs 180 working hours a year to comply with tax regulations, as research by consultancy PricewaterhouseCoopers and the World Bank in 2008 shows. Despite government efforts to simplify the system, the Netherlands lagged behind sixty-one other countries in which the average company takes less time filling out tax forms. The top European 'easy tax' countries were Ireland, Denmark and Luxembourg.

However, the problem of time wasted because of regulations can be much worse in the developing world. As detailed in a bestselling book by the Peruvian economist Hernando de Soto (1989), in many developing countries entrepreneurs and small businesses have to spend a great deal of time and effort in complying with all kinds of red tape and assorted regulations: in Brazil, as one example, merely obtaining all the government permits to set up a new business there takes an average of 152 days.

This helps to explain why, in these countries, a large proportion of economic activity is driven 'underground' into the informal economy. These businesses mainly offer legal products and services, but choose to avoid the myriad complications involved in complying with regulations and paying taxes.

---

As in previous chapters, we shall start with a section that focuses on a static setting; in other words, the institutional, technological and natural environments are taken as a given. We shall observe how government intervention causes inefficiencies, and which additional institutional devices may possibly alleviate this negative effect. Later in the chapter we shall look at government failures in a dynamic setting and from the vested interest approach, also taking into account interaction processes and feedback mechanisms. Here we shall pay attention to the way in which all kinds of changes with regard to the condition of the economy or technology have an impact on public opinion and interest groups, which in turn influence the manner in which governments intervene in the economy.

## THE STATIC APPROACH TO GOVERNMENT FAILURES

In this section we shall make a distinction between problems and costs in government functioning in situations of perfect information, and in situations of imperfect information. This is a useful division, because failures in a transparent setting usually need to be treated differently from failures in a nontransparent one. When a government is aware of the harmful effects of its interventions it can attempt to introduce additional measures to combat these negative consequences in a straightforward way. In other words, if state intervention decreases social welfare, the government could neutralize this by introducing new institutions. In situations when it remains unclear or unnoticed that state interference is producing unwanted effects, the measures to tackle this become more difficult and society is more likely to be faced with a welfare loss. Nevertheless, we shall show that, even in situations of imperfect information, governments can introduce institutional solutions to prevent efficiency losses as much as possible.

### Government failures in situations of perfect information

As we know, even in situations of perfect information, market imperfections may occur, such as instances of market power and negative externalities. Likewise, a government may be perfectly informed about the adverse consequences of its own policy measures. In such circumstances, the best any government can do is to weigh the costs and benefits of its interference and attempt to make decisions that either create the highest possible overall welfare (taking an efficiency approach), or serve the welfare of specific groups in society in particular (taking a vested interest approach). In both cases, it could very well be that some groups are being made worse off than before by the government's intervention. Either way, the government can attempt to compensate the losers to the best of its ability.

Another negative aspect of government interference concerns the perverse incentives it sometimes generates. As we shall show below, the running of governmental agencies often leads to low-powered incentives not only among the civil servants, but also among citizens. Since the government is usually aware of these kinds of problems, several institutional solutions have been introduced.

We shall begin with a special case of government failure, dealing with fundamental problems related to majority voting, and then will go on to examine the topics mentioned above.

### *The Arrow paradox*

People often have to make choices jointly, and most often these choices are being made by majority voting. This seems an easy and 'right' way of deciding, but fundamental problems may arise. In a two-person household, for example, the choice might be made to go out together: either to have dinner, or to go to the movies. Now suppose that one of the two partners prefers having dinner to going to the movies, and the other prefers going to the movies. Also suppose that both prefer going out together to not going at all or to going out alone. It is easy to see that majority voting will not solve the tie. This problem is known as a game called 'the battle of the sexes'. Of course, this problem is easily solved by tossing a coin in order to decide which alternative to choose, and to agree that next time the other alternative will be chosen.

In relation to public choice, the people in a country generally make their preferences known by choosing among the manifestos of political parties. These concern many issues of both an economic and a non-economic nature. Politicians and their manifestos aim to represent the wishes of their voters by proposing solutions for perceived problems. This begs the question of how a government, or politics in general, is able to translate individual preferences for solutions into a 'social' preference. If we restrict ourselves to some general principles with respect to individual and social preferences, and if we rephrase the question as: 'Is it possible to have a social preference function that represents individuals' preference functions?', the answer is, in general, negative. This result is basically mathematical and is called *'Arrow's impossibility theorem'* or, popularly, the *Arrow paradox*, named after the 1972 Nobel Laureate Kenneth Arrow, who first proved this theorem. For more details see Appendix A to this chapter. Here it is important to realize that the problem can be solved in some way through making choices by majority voting.

## *Cost–benefit analysis and compensation*

Even if a government strives to serve the interests of the public at large and aims to intervene only on the grounds of combating market imperfections that cannot be dealt with by private actors, the subsequent effects of state-enacted policies may create new or additional efficiency losses. In so far as a government is able to oversee the possible negative side effects of its different types of intervention, it could weigh the costs of these against the benefits. Then, depending on the outcome of political decision-making, a choice is made about which action is preferred.

### Compensation: Pareto versus Hicks–Kaldor

When a government intervenes in the economy in the public interest this could nevertheless work out unfavorably for one or more groups in society. We start by giving some examples and then discuss possible solutions.

Counteracting negative externalities successfully (for example, by imposing specific levies or by introducing environmental laws) may not only reduce the amount of air pollution but will generally also reduce the amount of the product that caused the pollution. More specifically, it would make it more difficult for consumers to obtain this product (while paying a higher price), and would generate less revenue for the suppliers and a loss of jobs in this sector.

In the previous chapter we mentioned that in recent years in many countries a legal ban on tobacco smoking has been introduced in public places such as restaurants. Consumers and employees in these establishments can now spend their time without suffering the negative effects of smoke. However, in several European countries, it soon became clear that this prohibition was having drastic consequences, especially for owners of small cafés, who claimed that it has led to a substantial loss in clientele, as a result of which they have had to close down their businesses.

These examples illustrate that, in general, there are both winners and losers as a result of state intervention. In a reaction, the government could consider paying compensation to the losers. The government can do this itself, or it can make the winners compensate them.

Governments have to make choices to solve problems, as in the case of pure public goods (which public goods to generate and in what amounts), externalities and information problems (how to measure and how to solve them), and market power (how to regulate it). But governments also have to impose taxes in order to do their work, and in this and many other respects, usually want to redistribute income. For example, a tax system may be designed in such a way that higher incomes are taxed relatively highly compared to lower ones. In addition, some of the generated taxes may be redistributed to the 'poor'.

How can we say that choices made by a government are optimal – that is, the best of all possible choices (at least as seen from the perspective of the majority of people in society)? What criteria can be used to answer that question?

In Chapter 1 we described allocative efficiency. In economic welfare terms, this is also called a 'first best' solution or Pareto optimality. A first best solution need not be unique, so more than one Pareto-optimal solution may exist. Can these Pareto-optimal solutions be compared in such a way that one may be preferred to another?

A *Pareto-optimal situation* is one in which no individual can be made better off without someone else being made worse off. A *Pareto improvement* is a situation in which at least one individual can be made better off without someone else being made worse off. Now suppose that we have two Pareto optimal solutions. By definition, we cannot achieve a Pareto improvement by going from one of the solutions to the other. Hence, both solutions cannot be compared to each other in welfare terms. So, if a government tries to influence the outcome of the economic process, in the sense that it might be able to choose one of the two Pareto-optimal solutions, there is always at least one individual who would have been better off if the other solution had been chosen. So, in terms of Pareto improvement, no choice can be made socially.

Now consider a situation where there is no Pareto optimality as a result of any market failure. This implies that an improvement must be possible. In the case of negative externalities, in the absence of transaction costs the Coase theorem guarantees that a first best solution will be reached. With transaction costs, this is no longer true, so that a Pareto improvement is not guaranteed. Besides, in the case of other market imperfections, it may not be possible to solve them by way of Pareto improvements. This will make it very hard to use the Pareto improvement principle in practice.

A candidate for solving this issue is the principle of compensation: if welfare is improved, this must imply that on balance there are more gains than losses. A social cost–benefit analysis should, at least theoretically, be able to show that on balance a choice is optimal if this choice generates the highest overall profits. Subsequently, 'losers' could be compensated by 'winners' in such a way that in the end nobody is worse off. This criterion is also called the *Hicks–Kaldor criterion*, or a Hicks–Kaldor improvement.

In practice, governments frequently apply the Hicks–Kaldor criterion. An obvious example concerns the construction of a ring road to remove congestion from a town. At the same time this increases safety and air quality on and around the old road. Clearly, many people benefit from this new road, but others will suffer – such as the families whose houses are close to the new road, and those experiencing negative environmental effects caused by the increase in traffic. What authorities often do in such a situation, is to go ahead with the new construction because of the considerable economic benefits, while offering some form of compensation to those who have been inconvenienced – by building noise barriers, for example.

Still, in practice, the Hicks–Kaldor criterion cannot be used for making all decisions. A good illustration is a mandatory health insurance scheme to solve the adverse selection problem. In Box 3.5 we described this problem. In the context of this example, a mandatory insurance has the following consequences: three individuals (A, B and C) will each be insured at a premium of €1,050. Individual A only wants to pay €600, B is prepared to pay €1,200, and C is willing to pay €1,700. These figures imply that, on average, €350 welfare is created, with A being the loser (– €450), and with B and C being the winners (€150 and €650, respectively). From a general welfare point of view, the mandatory scheme is preferred to not having health insurance at all. Obviously, it would be impossible to find out each individual's willingness to pay; this would be much too costly. One of the problems is that none of the individuals has the incentive to reveal his true willingness to pay: A will overstate his, while B and C will understate their true valuations.

So, in this and many other cases, the Hicks–Kaldor criterion will fail in practice. Nevertheless, a proper evaluation of a project in terms of costs and (expected) benefits may be a useful tool even if it cannot be used to determine actual (expected) losses and gains for groups of individuals. Such an evaluation will generally be done in a qualitative way by political debate.

## *Property rights problems*

From property rights theory (see Chapter 3) it emerges that people tend to take good care of goods or assets when they actually own them, or when they have acquired the right to earn income from utilizing the asset in question. In other words, privately owned goods usually lead to optimizing behavior, and in Chapter 3 we introduced the term 'high-powered market incentives' to describe that, in the face of competition, when the holder of a private property right increases his efforts, this will have an immediate positive effect on his income. Therefore, in most cases, a competitive environment and private property are stimulated, as it will carry over to growth in the entire economy; in other words, there are positive externalities involved.

In the case of a public good, this can either be produced by private firms or by a state-owned enterprise. The risk of having a state-owned enterprise is that civil servants running the public firm have low-powered incentives. We have already encountered this phenomenon in Chapter 6, with respect to employees in (private) firms. In the public sector, however, this problem is even more serious, because competitive pressure is often absent. This, by the way, also holds true for firms in a centrally planned economy, which we discussed in Chapter 8.

In the public sector, lack of competition leads easily to efficiency losses, because managers cannot be punished as a result of a decline in sales or in the share price, as is the case in the market sector. In many cases, state-owned enterprises do not produce a good or service of which the price is determined by quantity supplied or quantity demanded. Either no prices are charged, as is most often true in the case of the services delivered by ministries, or products are subsidized because an ample supply of them is considered to be of more importance than obtaining the cost price. This holds true for several products with a pure public good character, or merit goods. State-owned enterprises are expected to deliver products in sufficient quantities to cater for the public need, and they often lack the urge to minimize costs. This means that the managers of these state-owned enterprises also feel less inclined to monitor or encourage their employees with the aim of making them work harder or more efficiently. Box 9.2 illustrates the risks by means of an example regarding the financial sector.

### BOX 9.2  THE RISKS OF BANK NATIONALIZATION

As we mentioned in Box 8.5, large banks in several countries had to be bailed out by national governments in order to avoid a domino effect worldwide, as a result of the financial crisis that erupted in 2008.

However, many economists are critical of this type of rescue operation, claiming that in the medium to long run it will have an adverse effect on the behavior of the management teams of these banks. After all, if the government acts as the ultimate guarantor of the banks, in the future the banks' executives will have no reason to be careful and may continue to make risky investments. These skeptical economists urged that, after the bailout, the banks should be returned to the private sector as quickly as possible. In this way, shareholders would be able to monitor the actions of the banks' management.

On the other hand, the financial operations of banks have become increasingly complex over the years. Do shareholders have enough information and the technical knowledge required to monitor the management? Naturally, the answer is no. Therefore, in all countries affected by the crisis, politicians and scientists are discussing the ways in which better regulation of the private financial sector could lead to more transparency.

In short, the absence of the right incentives in state-owned enterprises leads to efficiency losses, which ultimately implies that citizens will have to pay more tax to cover these expenses. Because governments are not blind to these shortcomings, several kinds of institutional solutions have been considered and implemented to generate the right incentives, which we shall expand on below. On the one hand, remedies could be found in the sphere of transferring public provision into private provision, or, on the other, governments may decide to keep provision completely in public hands but improve the situation with additional measures in the sphere of accountability and incentive remuneration for civil servants.

## Public versus private provision

With regard to the choice between the public and private provision of products, three dimensions are involved: decision-making, finance and production (Barr, 1998). For example, the government could finance and produce a product itself. Basically, what is meant by 'producing products itself' is that the asset is produced by civil servants, while all production decisions are taken by the government. Usually, 'financing itself' means that the funds needed to produce the asset in question are paid for with tax money, or sometimes with the revenues of state-owned natural resources such as oil or gas. National defense is an example of a (pure public) good that is produced and financed by governments in most countries. We call this the 'pure public provision' of goods, though of course some of the inputs (such as aircraft for the military) are produced by private firms.

Two other choices governments have for providing public goods are as follows. First, the government might finance a private firm with public money to enable this firm to produce a service or good, the specifications of which have been decided on by the state. One could think of universities in the UK, for example, or the inputs for public goods (see the example above with regard to aircraft for the military). Second, there is the situation in which private parties finance a public good. In this case, the production decisions are taken by the state, while the private firm finances and produces the good. An example is public transport in some of the EU countries, whereby private firms compete for the market, by, for example, a tendering procedure, involving different parameters such as the amount of public transport to be supplied and the price to be paid by the passengers.

Economically, it is an intricate matter to decide which public goods should be produced and financed entirely by the public sector, and which could be left partly or completely to the private sector. Different solutions may be efficient, depending on the time and place and the existing economic circumstances. Yet, it seems to be (at least for many Western countries) that in the past many products were both financed and produced by the government, while in the course of time, for efficiency reasons either finance or production, or both, moved from being in the public sector into the hands of private parties. When such a change occurs, we speak of privatization. Privatization is often followed by liberalization: we shall deal with these topics later in the chapter.

## Accountability

Even if the government decides that the provision of certain goods and services should remain under state control, for whatever reason, there are means by which civil servants can be disciplined to work efficiently, by making them more accountable for running the agency in a cost-minimizing way as much as possible. To that end, countries worldwide have installed 'national audit bodies' – independent public agencies tasked with monitoring and evaluating the effectiveness and efficiency of all public sector departments and agencies. An example is the Government Accountability Office (GAO) in the USA, known, according to its website, as 'the investigative arm of Congress' and 'the congressional watchdog'. National audit bodies generally report their findings to the members of Congress or countries' parliaments (the legislative power). Moreover, these findings are also published for the information of the general public. The work of national audit bodies forms a disciplining mechanism. These audit bodies can also often be found at the regional and even local level within countries. In addition, at EU level, a body has been established called the European Court of Auditors. This consists of independent professionals from all members states and checks whether EU funds have been spent according to the rules and with sound management.

## Remuneration

Another way to motivate (top) government officials to operate the civil service more efficiently is to build in positive incentives such as a pay increases or variable pay instead of a fixed salary. Merit pay for higher staff is commonplace in the private sector but can also sometimes be observed in the public sector, albeit to a much lesser extent. The idea behind merit pay is, of course, that it mimics high-powered market incentives. If certain performance targets (such as client satisfaction or an improvement in the level of service) have been met, civil servants may receive a bonus. Giving high-ranking public servants a bonus or a relatively high fixed salary is a delicate matter, however. Since the salaries of all workers in the public sector are financed by tax revenues, the population at large tends to object to high salaries for top civil servants.

## Incentives for citizens regarding public goods

Not only does state provision of public goods easily encounter efficiency losses resulting from insufficient incentives on the part of civil servants; citizens' behavior will also generally lead to efficiency losses. The basic economic argument runs as follows: if the price of a product is zero for consumers, demand increases, possibly enormously. In Chapters 3 and 8 we mentioned the adverse effects of collective property rights in communist systems. Another example can be found in Box 9.3.

---

### BOX 9.3   EXCESSIVE USE OF NATIONAL HEALTH CARE

Some countries have decided to provide equal access to health care for all citizens. In Chapter 8 we mentioned the British case, where all citizens are entitled to national health care, which is funded through taxes.

Governments sometimes deliberately choose not to charge for the use of (some parts of) national health care because it is feared that the poorer citizens will delay or even avoid seeking medical care, which may be both socially and economically undesirable. As a consequence, these systems of national health care easily run the risk of overconsumption (that is, consumption beyond one's needs) and hence also of efficiency losses, as they are open-ended. We have already shown (see Box 3.6) that this conduct is referred to as moral hazard. Given the circumstances, individuals tend to make more use of the service. This increases total national health costs unnecessarily, which in the end must be paid for by all citizens in the form of raised taxes or higher premiums. Therefore, political debates about the sustainability and design of the national health care system are a regular occurrence.

A related problem occurs when a public service is not free of charge but has a fixed price for everyone, irrespective of how much is consumed. In such circumstances, people also tend to make inefficient use of the service. A notable example is the processing of waste. If citizens pay a fixed fee for garbage collection, they will generally not be inclined to separate different types of garbage, even though the processing of waste would then become much more efficient and cheaper.

So, to combat improper and excessive use of any public good or service, additional institutional devices must be introduced by the government. A few common solutions to a range of problems are listed below:

- Analogous to the solution discussed earlier in the context of unjustified and/or excessive insurance claims, the state could set up an excess risk system in which the user is obliged to pay a stipulated sum of money for the first claim made.
- A quantity cap could be introduced – for health care, for example, when a certain amount of treatment would be offered free of charge (ten hourly sessions of physiotherapy, say), and additional consumption beyond that has to be paid for by the consumer.
- A city government could introduce a range of charges for collecting different sorts (or amounts) of garbage.

## Government failures in situations of imperfect information

The government will not be able to take suitable decisions for each and every citizen (that is, making them better off) at the same time. In addition to the problems described above, it is practically impossible (or extremely costly) to inquire about the preferences of all individual citizens. A government has also to take for granted that because of imperfect information its policy measures cannot benefit all. The government can also lean towards serving specific vested interests, in which case information asymmetry can be exploited.

Democratic representation cannot solve these problems either: delegates more or less know the preferences of their voters, but never completely. Besides, different voters have different preferences with regard to all sorts of (political) issues, but can only vote for one political party or person. Hence, preferences can and will be conflicting. Politicians have to weigh all these preferences, which, of course, cannot be done perfectly. This means that many political issues will have different losers and winners. A total of who has lost or gained and by how much is impossible to calculate.

We deal here with political decision-making in the face of imperfect information. First, even if representatives from both the executive power (president and/or ministers) and the legislative power (political parties in parliament) aim to enlarge the welfare of the public at large, they may still fail to do so because of unintended side effects. Second, several actors in the public sector may abuse their information lead to the detriment of the general public: the bureaucracy that is supposed to implement governmental policies may not always do so entirely according to the wishes of the politicians who made these decisions, and politicians themselves, who are supposed to act according to the wishes of their electorate, may do the opposite in order to protect their own vested interests.

## *Unintended side effects*

The economy is so complex and wide-ranging that the effects of newly introduced policies are very hard to predict. Therefore, below we shall examine several inadvertent side effects of government interference, by discussing briefly some unintended effects of (i) tenders; (ii) licensing; (iii) taxation and subsidies; and (iv) so-called 'false positives and false negatives'.

Unintended side effects can partly be prevented by making use of specialized agencies (policy research institutes) that try to assess the economic effects of any policy implementation. Some of these institutes are installed by national governments, while others are independent and can be hired by a government or a political party. In the USA, for example, the president has a Council of Economic Advisers. In addition, many 'think tanks' exist in the USA, such as the well-known RAND Corporation. In Europe, almost all of the EU member states have such bureaus that together are organized into the ENEPRI (European Network of Economic Policy Research Institutes). In addition, there are institutes such as the IMF (International Monetary Fund), the OECD and the World Bank that have been established by countries worldwide, which perform international comparative studies and often give unsolicited advice to governments.

### Tenders

As discussed in Chapter 8, in certain economic circumstances (for example, regarding natural monopolies or the provision of products with the characteristics of pure public goods) the government tries to stimulate competition for the market by organizing auctions to obtain 'free market solutions'. But auctions are also the basic mechanism underlying *tenders*: governments often invite construction and engineering companies to tender for large infrastructural projects, such as constructing roads, government buildings, social housing projects, dams, bridges and so on. Other governmental procurement projects such as installing computer networks also often use tendering. In terms of an auction, the government 'sells' a large project and the (construction) companies try to 'buy' the project.

With the aid of an example we shall now show that (state-organized) tenders or auctions as an institutional device are not always efficient, as they may lead to cartelization. Look back at the Appendix to Chapter 5 for the basic information on different kinds of auctions.

Assume that buyers A and B get together before the auction and determine the maximum that each of them is willing to pay. Suppose buyer B is willing to pay more than buyer A (say, 20 against 15), then B will obtain the object under all circumstances. What the two parties could do is to agree before the auction to both make lower bids than they would have done in competition. Buyer B might then obtain the object at a lower price, and share his additional profit with buyer A. For example, suppose both buyers know that the object will have to be sold for at least 10. By determining each other's preferences, they can simply decide the following:

- In a Dutch auction: buyer A will refrain from calling the price at 15 but will simply remain silent until the price reaches 10, in which case buyer B will claim the object as his.

- In an English auction: when the auctioneer starts at price 10, buyer A refrains from bidding for the object, so only buyer B will announce his willingness to pay 10.
- In the sealed bid (second price) auction: buyer B will state his willingness to pay 10, while buyer A will state any other higher price.

In all cases, the object will be obtained at price 10, and the difference between 15 and 10 can then be split between buyers A and B. This is a form of (illegal) collusion, also known as *bid rigging*. Bid rigging may take many forms, but can generally be summarized as follows (derived from the website of the US Department of Justice on bid rigging): with *bid suppression*, one or more competitors agree to refrain from bidding or withdraw a previously submitted bid so that the designated winning competitor's bid will be accepted; with *complementary bidding*, competitors agree to submit bids that either are too high to be accepted or contain special terms that will not be acceptable to the buyer (such bids being designed merely to give the appearance of genuine competitive bidding); and with *bid rotation*, all the conspirators submit bids, but take turns at being the lowest bidder. The terms of the rotation may vary: competitors may take turns on contracts according to the size of the contract, allocating equal amounts to each conspirator, or allocating volumes that correspond to the size of each conspirator's company. Many (government) tenders all over the world have been, or are still being, bid rigged.

## Licensing

In Chapter 8 we mentioned that governments may decide to grant licenses (permits) only to eligible firms and professions, to overcome a lack of information about trustworthy suppliers. However, there are some potential drawbacks to licensing.

One shortcoming occurs when a government is not completely informed about changed market conditions, and maintains the number of permits at too low or too high a level. As a result of this, a shortage or a surplus of certain professionals may arise that cannot be solved quickly. When there is a shortage of physicians or dentists, say, the government may raise the number of licenses to practice. So a school-leaver might decide to study dentistry. However, by the time this person finally finishes her studies, it may very well be that the labor market for dentists is already saturated and that there are no longer any licenses available. Both for the individual and for the government, it is hard to react in a flexible way to labor market developments.

Another shortcoming is that the assignment of licenses is usually quite restrictive, which inadvertently blocks the way for some high-quality suppliers who are not able to signal their quality with appropriate qualifications. A well-known example concerns highly educated refugees, whose qualifications are not accepted in their new home country. As a result of this, such people are often forced to take unskilled jobs, which economists would call an inefficient allocation of resources.

A related but different problem is that states may on purpose grant permits to serve only the interests of their own citizens. This is directed against an influx of foreign labor and is intended to protect domestic trade and jobs. A well-known example is the discussion in the EU regarding when to open the borders for workers from Eastern European countries such as Romania and Bulgaria after they became EU members. Early in 2009, almost half of all EU member states retained their restrictions regarding Romanian and Bulgarian workers. This will be forbidden after the year 2013, when full free movement of labor becomes the rule across the whole EU. As we indicated in Chapter 1, protectionism is bad for international economic growth and will also disadvantage domestic consumers.

### Taxation and subsidies

In addition to raising revenues for the government, the goal of many taxes is to lead to lower amounts of trade. Likewise, the goal of many subsidies is to lead to higher amounts being traded. In other words, taxes and subsidies can be institutional instruments providing financial incentives to steer actors in the desired direction. However, these instruments need careful balancing as they may lead to undesired or unexpected and inefficient behavior and outcomes. On the one hand, people may react opportunistically, and on the other, taxation and subsidies could displace superior alternatives or may be wrongly timed. We shall discuss these different aspects briefly below.

The existence of taxes and subsidies may spur opportunistic individual actors to try to find loopholes in the law or even to break the law to turn over as little of their money as possible to the government and to collect as much money as possible from the government. Citizens could make improper use of subsidies and social benefits by claiming too much, or by applying for a financial contribution to which they are not entitled. An example of the latter is that some people who receive an unemployment benefit work on the side at the same time. Another possible abuse of a social security system can be found with unemployed couples who falsely claim to be living alone because the unemployment benefit per person is larger for singles than for pairs. These kinds of inappropriate use can only be combated by strict monitoring, hence by enlarging the bureaucracy, which also comes at an additional cost.

In some cases, the increasing costs of social security are even taken for granted by the political decision-makers involved, out of selfish motives (see the section on rent-seeking behavior, below) or for reasons of solidarity. It can be a political choice that is supported by the majority of the population, to provide a relatively high minimum income level for citizens who are unable to work as a result of sickness or disability, for example. When such a society deliberately chooses to spend a great deal of (tax) money on the support of weaker fellow-citizens, equity may precede efficiency. The problem with these arrangements is, however, that they often tend to be open-ended, just like the systems of national health care (see Box 9.3). As a result, the costs of sustaining the system may get seriously out of hand. An illustration of this so-called 'law of unintended consequences' is presented in Box 9.4.

### BOX 9.4 EXCESSIVE COSTS OF SOCIAL SECURITY: THE GERMAN AND DUTCH CASES

For centuries, the German population has been preoccupied with their health. By the end of the nineteenth century, Bismarck had introduced mandatory health insurance, and today still around 90 percent of all German citizens are covered by this system. All employed people must pay a premium, the level of which

> is determined by individual personal income. This entitles them to all forms of health care, albeit with an obligatory contribution towards most treatments. Consequently, the social service sector is huge. To give a couple of illustrations: the number of pharmacies is exceptionally high; and all over the country there are health resorts that are visited frequently by the majority of the population. However, at the beginning of the twenty-first century, the system has become too expensive to sustain because of an increase in unemployment, and those without jobs do not have to pay premiums. The announcement by the government to cut back expenses in 2009 in subsidized health care and to increase substantially the individual contributions for treatment, for example, has given rise to a storm of protests.
>
> In the Netherlands, another part of the social security system has also led to excessive costs. As a result of rising unemployment in the 1970s, increasing numbers of people found themselves beneficiaries of the lucrative disability fund (with a permanent benefit payment of 70 percent of the last earned income) instead of the ordinary unemployment fund (with a short-term and lower benefit payment). At its height in 1994, about 15 percent of all workers were officially registered as being disabled, which was an unrealistically high percentage. In all probability, the real number of disabled people was much lower, but it was in everybody's interest to keep the number of unemployed as low as possible. Why? For employers, the Disability Law presented an easy way of getting rid of older, less productive workers. For the workers, they did not object because the benefit payment was good. For the government, it was good for the image of the country to have a relative low percentage of officially unemployed and it contributed to labor peace. However, because of the high costs involved, politicians began to realize that action needed to be taken, and since the 1990s the system has been drastically changed.

When it comes to taxation, there are plenty of examples to illustrate how actors try to evade paying taxes, but we shall confine ourselves to just a few. At the micro level, it may start with individuals who hire a 'moonlighter' – a person who works in the 'black economy' and does not pay tax. As a consequence, the services of a moonlighter are less costly and hence more attractive for consumers. Governments try to fight this, not only because they miss out on tax revenue but also because these illegal businesses cause unfair competition. There are many instances of this in the construction sector.

At the industry level, each country (and sometimes even each region within a country) has its own system of corporate taxes. As we showed in Chapter 8, this can lead to so-called 'institutional competition'. Firms may decide to transfer their business to another jurisdiction where a lower corporate tax rate is levied. The negative consequence of this, of course, is not only a drop in tax revenues but possibly also a rise in unemployment in this particular industry, which subsequently might raise the number of unemployment benefits, which in turn could put upward pressure on related insurance premiums for workers.

It could also be, however, that firms are unable or unwilling to move, as they often need or want to stay close to their resources (labor, land or raw materials) and/or to their selling areas. In these cases, firms try to find other methods to avoid paying too much tax. Numerous methods exist, for which fiscal experts are hired to find the optimal construction, given the specifics of the fiscal law in the state at issue. We shall mention two commonly used methods in the USA, both involving a change in the legal form of the firm. Varieties of this can be found in other countries as well.

The first scheme implies that a public limited company (C corporation, or C corp) is turned into a so-called S corporation (S corp) to avoid certain tax payments (Williams, 2006). The point is that a C corp is subject to double taxation; it is taxed both at the corporate level and again when the ultimate owners of the corporation receive dividends or make capital gains. The S corp structure means that all the firm's earnings pass through to the owners of the company and they report it on their regular income tax return. Given the fact that the US corporate tax rate has remained high while the US individual income tax decreased in 2003, ever more firms have changed their legal form, which on balance has yielded less tax revenue.

The second scheme is called the 'private equity solution', which implies that a public company has become private; publicly traded shares are withdrawn and the firm is subject to other, less restrictive, governmental rules and monitoring. What happens next is that such a firm is loaded with debts, the interest payments of which are tax deductible. Assuming that the firm is otherwise run profitably, the net effect is that it pays much less tax than a comparable firm that has not been privatized, hence creating a competitive advantage. If this method falters, however, and the debts cannot be repaid, the firm will become bankrupt and its employees will lose their jobs (and possibly their pension schemes as well). Nowadays and worldwide, private equity is on the rise and everywhere politicians have expressed their concern with respect to this danger, as the owners of such firms are usually only interested in short-term profits and seem to be less concerned with the continuity of the firm or the preservation of jobs.

We shall now turn to another aspect regarding unintended side effects of subsidies and taxation, which are not so much the result of selfish responses of private individual actors, but more related to failures at the macro (policy) level.

Subsidies are intended to improve a society's welfare, or at least to improve the welfare of the target group (the recipients of these grants). However, subsidizing always comes at a cost: this financial support not only needs to be paid for through taxes, but it could also lead to other market distortions, that have not been taken into account. Two real-life examples will illustrate this point, both with regard to agriculture but with different side effects.

The first example refers to the financial aid that for years has been given to farmers in the USA and Europe to ensure that their activities remain economically viable. On the one hand, this has led to artificially high supply levels that sometimes could not be sold at all and had to be bought by the government; in the EU, for example, we have witnessed the phenomena of 'butter mountains' and 'milk lakes'. On the other hand, these agricultural subsidies have made it very difficult, if not impossible, for outsiders to compete. Often, these outsiders are farmers from poor countries in Africa and South America, who are thus not allowed a level playing field.

The second example refers to a recent development, namely the subsidies for biofuels in a large number of countries, among which are Australia, the EU and the USA. The motivation for granting these subsidies is to reduce the dependency on energy imports from regimes in the Middle East and Russia and to exploit alternative energy sources. Nonetheless, the negative externalities are enormous, according to a critical OECD report (Doornbosch and Steenblik, 2007). In short, biofuels are generated as a by-product (in the form of ethanol) from growing agricultural crops such as maize and sugar. The generous subsidies for biofuels generate incentives to grow precisely those crops that create the highest overall revenue, thus creating shortages and high prices for other crops. Worldwide food and animal feed shortages may be the result. In addition, researchers have shown that the production of more biofuels and less conventional fuels on balance does not help the environment. On the contrary, it is argued that the production of biofuels endangers the biodiversity and coincides with soil erosion and a deterioration in water quality through the use of fertilizers and pesticides.

We now turn to some of the adverse effects of taxation. The basic idea is that government spending has a positive effect on the macro economy. In a simple version of this idea, the following happens. Even when all spending by the government is paid for by taxes, the effect is positive, which may seem counterintuitive: a dollar spent by the government that is paid for by a dollar of taxation might seem to imply that on balance, nothing changes.

At the macro level, government spending directly increases the national income (salaries to civil servants, for example), which means that the economy (in the sense of national income) will be directly stimulated. At the same time, taxes are increased to enable government spending to be financed. What happens is that the initial increase in national income resulting from government spending will itself lead to an additional stimulation of the economy in the sense of higher national income (civil servants buy more products and hence will stimulate private production). This additional income is taxed away, so that on balance the additional income is used to pay for the initial increase. The bottom line is therefore that it is just the initial increase by government spending that stimulates the economy, because additional income increases are used to finance the initial one.

There are some other more intricate mechanisms that also play a role, so that the stimulating effect we described above may not be realized.

- The first effect is denoted by the term *crowding out* and works along the following lines. It will always be the case that higher national income determines a higher demand for money on a macroeconomic scale. A higher demand for money means a higher price for money, hence a higher interest rate. This higher interest rate will affect private spending negatively and thus private investment will be reduced, with two possible consequences. One is that national income may be reduced, since lower investments imply less demand for the products involved (such as capital goods), and hence less income. The other is that, in the future, fewer goods may be produced: generally investments will lead to more future products, hence more future income ('growth'). So, the initial positive effect of government spending might result in a much less effective or even negative (future) effect by repressing ('crowding out') private investments.

- The second effect is related to the timing of fiscal measures. During an economic downturn, business activities in the private sector slow down and governments may try to stimulate the economy – for example, by lowering taxes (and/or raising subsidies). This is called *countercyclical* fiscal policy. However, given the fact that it is hard to know in what phase an economy really is, wrongly informed governments could by mistake boost the economy when it is already in the upswing phase. In that case, the fiscal policy has unintentionally turned *procyclical*, with the harmful result that it overheats the economy and increases inflation.
- Finally, government spending may stimulate private spending, but if this takes place in an open economy where many of the products are imported, then additional income leaks from the national economy to other countries.

### False positives and false negatives

A governmental decision that is designed to solve a certain economic problem might not solve the problem fully, with unintended side effects as a consequence. These side effects may constitute new problems and, hence, are costs of the decisions. Two particular instances of such costs are 'false positives' and 'false negatives'. Using some illustrations is probably the best way to describe these two cost categories.

Generally, the existence of a police force and some generally accepted criminal laws will not deter all crime, while the possibility also exists that innocent people might be wrongly accused and convicted. In this context, the criminals that get away with their crimes are 'false negatives': they are unjustly (falsely) found innocent. On the other hand, convicted innocent people constitute 'false positives': they are unjustly (falsely) found guilty.

Many of these false positives and false negatives may also exist in economic governmental decision-making. Most of these stem from the application of enforcing (economic) rules. Let us focus on the application of competition law. As in the case of criminal law, the application of competition law may lead to 'false positives' (the finding of a cartel, where in fact an agreement was not a cartel at all) or to 'false negatives' (not finding that an agreement is a cartel, when in fact it was).

Often, false positives and false negatives may be related to the eagerness of the enforcers and the consequent treatment of the cases by the courts, and can have far-reaching consequences. If, for example, a competition authority is likely to find that almost all agreements among competitors constitute a cartel and the courts are generally likely to sustain that decision, then the effect will be that firms are deterred from cooperation even if this welfare enhancing. Hence a vigorous application of competition law might result in negative welfare effects. On the other hand, a lenient competition authority and lenient courts will generate unnecessary cartels, which also has negative welfare consequences.

The problem of false negatives and false positives may also operate at different levels, as we shall see in more detail later in the chapter.

### *Agency problems in government*

In the public sector, many different individuals and groups of people are active who do not all share exactly the same interests, so the chances are that government policies will not be executed in the way they were intended, as a result of opportunistic behavior. As discussed in Chapter 3, agency theory deals with the optimal design of a contract between a principal and an agent, to fight the abuse of information asymmetries. Important principal–agent relations in political and administrative systems are between voters and their representatives in parliament, between the legislative and executive powers, and between ministers and their civil servants.

We explained that such a principal–agent relationship only becomes a problem in a situation of asymmetric information between contracting parties with diverging interests. This may result in residual loss, which the involved parties could try to prevent as much as possible via additional safeguards. However, this comes with extra transaction costs so that the overall agency costs will be positive, hence an inefficient outcome is the result. When this occurs in the public sector, it is a form of government failure. First, the civil servants work in one of the ministries or other government agencies, either at the national level or at regional or local levels. They are supposed to implement and monitor laws and regulations according to the wishes of the politicians, but may have their own ideas about how to carry out these policies. Second, the politicians themselves are supposed to take decisions in line with the wishes of the population (the voters) but they may have a hidden agenda. We shall address both types of principal–agent problem below.

## Principal–agent problems between politicians and the bureaucracy

Civil servants (or public officials) are expected to carry out the decisions made by politicians so that they serve the interests of the latter in the best way. However, the interests of politicians and bureaucrats may diverge. From the efficiency perspective, policy-makers are expected to strive after the improvement of the public interest. From the vested interest perspective, they might put their own personal interests first. This usually relates to the ambition to stay in power; hence, in this approach, they are assumed to strive after vote-maximization. Vote-maximization need not coincide (perfectly) with improving public interest, because many people will have different ideas about how and what public interests are served best. Either way, their goals will probably deviate from those of the civil servants, who usually have different priorities.

The role of bureaucracy can be described in several ways, ranging from rather simplistic to very detailed. Either one can depict this administrative system as a single entity and consequently focus on principal–agent problems between two unified, homogeneous groups: politicians and bureaucrats. Or one can take a pluralist approach towards the administrative system, in which the diversity of the different bureaus and the people working within them are also considered, which produces a much more complicated picture of all kinds of possible relationships within the bureaucracy on the one hand and between diverse public officials and politicians on the other. Given the scope of this book, we confine ourselves mainly to a basic discussion of principal–agent problems between politicians and civil servants, but we shall round this off with a brief excursion into the versatility of bureaucracy and some ensuing issues related to agency problems.

In a simple treatise of agency problems, an emphasis is placed on the conflict of interests between the whole group of policy-makers on the one hand and the whole group of civil servants on the other. Here we assume that politicians try to serve the public interest, taking into account the possible negative side effects of their involvement as much as possible. In other words, improving social welfare is their goal. On the other side, we picture the civil servants as having a wide range of goals, such as increasing their status, power, income, job security and enjoyable working conditions. Most of these objectives are supposed to be related to the size of their bureau, which in turn is dependent on the budget that is allocated to them. Hence, here we shall assume that civil servants strive after budget maximization. The corresponding *bureaucracy theory*, which we shall set out briefly below, was developed by the economist Niskanen (1971). The graphical analysis can be found in Appendix B to this chapter.

If civil servants in fact give priority to realizing their own goals, among which status and power (aspired to by the higher-ranked officials) and job security and pleasant working conditions (aspired to by the lower-ranked officials), these can best be secured by a sizeable department or bureau. To become and remain large, a bureau needs a high budget, allocated by the bureaucrats' superiors, the politicians. The latter need the bureau to execute and implement policy decisions. To realize this, they want the public officials to provide and extend services as long as the extra benefits of these exceed the extra costs; after all, the politicians wish to serve the public interests as efficiently as possible. In other words, ideally, the politicians want to allocate a budget that exactly covers this efficient level of services.

However, the civil servants would rather receive more resources to enable their bureau to expand, with all the private advantages of status and comfort that attach to this. In protecting these vested interests, they are more concerned with a budget where the total costs of the services equal total benefits, which is at a higher level of services than the politicians envisage (see also the Appendix). In practice, the policy-makers cannot fully oversee how much of a budget would truly be optimal. They require only a certain amount of output from the bureau and do not know exactly how much input is needed to achieve that. Hence, given an asymmetry of information, public officials will indeed receive a higher budget than is strictly necessary and thus cause an inefficiency. This is the core argument of the bureaucracy theory. Institutional solutions for this government failure have been mentioned already, under the heading of 'property rights problems', where we looked at the installation of an audit body and the creation of performance-related salaries.

While this is a simple depiction of the operation of contemporary bureaucracy, it does contain an element of truth if we look at countless developed countries, in which the share of the public sector has grown to enormous proportions. Of course, this development cannot only be ascribed to agency problems in government, but these have certainly played their part. In any case, the costs of many welfare states have risen so tremendously in recent decades that it has burdened the citizens with high rates of taxation and insurance contributions, and has forced several countries to try to cut back expenses incurred by the public sector.

We shall now briefly pay some attention to a more subtle approach to the way in which bureaucracies function. Following Dunleavy (1991), at least three aspects are relevant with respect to public bureaus:

(i) they do not consist of only one type of civil servant;
(ii) a distinction can be made between several types of budgets; and
(iii) a distinction can be made between several types of agency.

In succession, we shall comment briefly on these three aspects.

First, as in a private firm, within a public agency a hierarchy of employees also exists that could lead to additional principal–agent problems. There are higher-ranked and lower-ranked officials, white-collar workers (clerks) and blue-collar workers (for example, garbage collectors), all with quite different types of tasks and responsibilities, and hence with different goals and different information.

Second, any public agency has control of different types of budgets. All agencies have a *core budget* at their disposal, with which all their own (internal) activities are financed. By this we mean all expenses for salaries, accommodation, equipment and so on. In addition, most agencies have a so-called *bureau budget*, with which they settle the costs of public spending; that is, the payment of public transactions with private actors (individuals and firms). In addition , several (but not all) agencies might also receive a *program budget*; in this case the agency supervises funds that are transferred to other public agencies for implementation. Not only is it clear that having more types of budget increases the influence of a certain public agency, but in addition the size of the respective budgets at their disposal may also play a role in this. It is quite likely that the different agencies compete for parts of the overall budget, which can be viewed as unproductive activities contributing to a deadweight loss.

Third, and connected to the aspect of budget allocation, different public agencies fulfill many different kinds of tasks. Here we shall reduce the large number of different agency types to just a few main categories. One type is the *delivery agency* that provides products and services directly to citizens and firms, so it usually has a relatively large core budget to finance the often substantial personnel costs. Think, for example, of hospitals. A second type is the *transfer agency*, which ensures that flows of money (subsidies, taxation) flow between the government and private actors. Here the core budget is usually quite small compared to the bureau budget. An example could be the Ministry of Social Affairs. Another type is the *regulatory agency* (like a competition authority), which obviously has as its main task the monitoring and control of the behavior of individuals and organizations, and which usually operates on a relatively small budget, as most of the costs are borne by the people being regulated (compliance costs). A fourth type is the *contracts agency*, which engages in concluding contracts with private firms and commercial public sector firms. This usually leads to a high bureau budget. An example could be the Defense Ministry. Finally, the *control agency* has to ensure that all public agencies spend their budgets effectively and efficiently. This refers, for example, to the previously mentioned national audit bodies, or possibly the Finance Ministry.

This huge diversity in manifestations of public agencies – accommodating a great variety of different types of civil servants and managing different types of budgets that can either be relatively small or large – makes clear that Niskanen's bureaucracy theory is indeed too simplistic a reproduction of the actual working of governmental organizations. However, even though this basic theory does not do justice to all the different motivations that make public agencies and their civil servants perform in a certain manner, it still rightly stresses in a straightforward way that the occurrence of principal–agent problems in government is very plausible.

## Principal–agent problems between voters and politicians

From what we have seen already, politicians can be seen as the victims, because, in their roles of principal, their decisions are likely not to be implemented precisely by their agents, the civil servants. We could, however, also take a different view of the same politicians, namely in their role as agents *vis-à-vis* the citizens/voters, whereby the latter can be seen as the ultimate principals in a (democratic) society. And just as it is difficult for policy-makers to monitor and motivate civil servants adequately, it will be hard for citizens to oversee whether the politicians keep to their side of the agreement; that is, whether the latter will do as they have promised at election time.

Possible occasions of opportunistic behavior by politicians can occur both before and after elections. *Ex ante*, politicians need enough votes in order to be elected (or re-elected) so they must try to make a good impression on the voting public. The risk exists that opportunistic politicians are likely to make promises that sound good, but are unrealistic. Not all of the population will know or realize what are, or will prove to be, realistic or unrealistic promises. To gather such information, a great deal of political awareness is needed, and to invest in acquiring that knowledge might just not be worthwhile: people are then said to be *rationally ignorant* (Kasper and Streit, 1999).

*Ex post*, similar ignorance on the part of the electorate enables the politicians to act in ways that voters did not expect from them. For example, it is quite common for newly elected politicians to raise taxes when they previously promised not to do so. They produce a good explanation and speculate that they will not be removed from office. In the meantime, the extra tax money could, for example, have been spent discreetly on serving the interests of a certain minority group in return for special favors. We come back to this issue in the following section dealing with rent-seeking but it shows that the topics of principal–agent problems and rent-seeking behavior can overlap.

Just before elections, policy-makers tend to start doing good things for the whole population. As most ordinary citizens generally have a short memory and/or choose to be rationally ignorant, they will be pleased and may vote for these politicians again.

Politicians may carry out resolutions that on the surface appear to be beneficial for the electorate but in fact are reducing social welfare. For example, policy-makers may choose to finance a particular project that is inefficient (too costly) by increasing public debt. The direct, short-run effect of such a policy is that the people only notice the additional public provision of the project – some infrastructure, perhaps. They do not realize that the project is inefficient, because the actual price for the voter is going to be paid at a much later date. Sooner or later the citizens are faced with the consequences of the increased public debt, either through cutbacks in public expenditure or through tax increases. This phenomenon is called *fiscal illusion*. By the time the consequences appear, the politicians responsible are probably no longer in government, so cannot be punished. A similar manifestation of the short time horizon of politicians is that they may deliberately ignore complex future problems because of the election cycle. They are unwilling to support unpopular but necessary measures in the present for the sake of future generations.

Given the possibility that politicians do not act according to the social contract that they have with the voters, what can be done to prevent this? According to agency theory, the contract should consist of appropriate safeguards to steer the agents in the desired direction of the principals. In other words, the right incentives should be incorporated. There is a resemblance between the problems many shareholders face when trying to discipline top managers, and the problems the electorate faces when trying to discipline its political representatives. One thing that voters and owners of firms have in common is that they form a very large, dispersed group. This can give rise to a free rider problem: individual efforts to monitor the actions of the policy-makers, if possible at all, benefit all other voters, so that individuals have an incentive to refrain from monitoring.

If effective monitoring by the direct principals is not possible to solve the agency problem, according to the theory another standard option is to include positive incentives for the agents, usually in the sphere of variable pay and similar inducements. Unfortunately, this option does not work in politics, because policy-makers generally do not receive performance-based pay but rather a fixed salary, which moreover tends to be relatively low compared to the income of top managers in large commercial businesses. This pay system implies that no matter how well or badly a politician does his job, he will always receive the same compensation. In terms of our book, this is a low-powered incentive. There are no competitive forces or monetary reasons for a politician to serve the public interest to the best of his abilities. Instead, he could be more likely to opt for 'the easy life' and/or be more susceptible to pleas from vested interest groups, or even to bribes. We shall say more about this topic in the next section on rent-seeking and corruption.

Now, all of the above does not mean that policy-makers will everywhere and always strive after their own interests instead of advancing the public interest, because many leaders may be driven by the desire to serve the nation and its people. In fact, given the nature of the job and the nature and level of the salary, it is often claimed that people working for the government have reached that position through a process of what is called *self-selection*. This means that individuals with an intrinsic motivation to serve the public interest prefer to work in the public sector despite the possibly worse financial terms of employment; they get satisfaction out of nonmaterial issues.

However, a society should nevertheless always be cautious when giving power to politicians, because the possibility of power abuse in the face of asymmetric information cannot be ruled out. This brings us back to the question of what can be done to restrain potential opportunistic behavior by policy-makers? We shall show that countries do have several other means at their disposal to compensate for the weak influence of individual voters.

To begin with, all democracies have installed some variant of a '*trias politica*', an important institutional arrangement ensuring that various parts of the government monitor each other. In Box IV.1 in the introduction to Part IV of the book we have already briefly discussed the functions of the three powers: the executive power, the legislative power and the judicial power. In addition, modern countries have introduced several laws and devices to build in extra checks and balances. Here we shall mention two of these, namely the institution of the *ombudsman* and the *freedom of information legislation*.

Countries all over the world have installed an ombudsman, often not only in politics but also in private firms and other non-political organizations. Outside politics, an ombudsman functions as an intermediary between the organization on the one hand

and its employees and customers on the other, when one of the two latter groups has a grievance about or a conflict with the former. In the case of politics, an ombudsman is an independent official who can be approached by any citizen when she has a complaint against a governmental representative or public agency. Ombudsmen can be found at all political levels, from the central government to district or city councils. Even though the ombudsman usually does not have the power to prosecute the offending politician or public agency, he can still prove to be very effective. If the ombudsman has built up sufficient authority, the mere threat of being in the dock often proves a sufficient reason for accused politicians or agencies to change their behavior and/or to provide financial compensation to the aggrieved private party. Hence, also in government the reputation mechanism may work quite well.

Another worldwide device to discipline politicians and governments is the freedom of information legislation. The content of this legislation differs between countries, but the gist of it is that it gives all civilians the right to request and receive information from the government about the greater part of public decision-making. This usually excludes delicate policy documents containing information about personal particulars or information that could either harm a firm's competitiveness or jeopardize national security. Obligatory disclosure of information by the government is predominantly made use of by the media, so when they report about possible questionable decisions or actions by government officials and agencies, the reputation of the person or body named will be injured. If the freedom of press is guaranteed, this legislation can be very effective. An illustration of this effectiveness is the allowances scandal brought to light by the British press in May 2009, centering on the declaration behavior of British Members of Parliament (MPs). Journalists revealed that for a long time a large number of MPs had been claiming private expenses out of public funds, hence at a cost to British taxpayers. The publication of this information caused a public outrage and resulted in the resignation of a number of politicians.

## THE DYNAMIC APPROACH TO GOVERNMENT FAILURES

In this section we discuss examples of the process of interaction between private governance structures such as firms and lobby groups on the one hand, and public governance structures on the other. The outcome of these interaction processes is that they lead to a reduction in welfare.

We first pay attention to the phenomenon of 'regulatory risk'. It is important for private actors in the economic system to operate in a stable institutional environment so that they are able to anticipate the behavior of actors in the future. On the other hand, it is important that public governance rules can adapt to new situations caused by changes in technology, the internationalization of markets or in values in society. In this section we address the issue that a government can change regulations for opportunistic reasons, and consequently the other actors in the system run the risk that public governance rules will be different depending on the interests of politicians and bureaucrats.

These interests can be influenced by other vested interests, which will be discussed below when considering rent-seeking and interest groups. Politicians will sometimes come to a decision by being won over by lobby groups, or they can trade their votes for one issue with those of another political party on behalf on some other issue. We shall also pay attention to the phenomenon of corruption, considered to be the worst and ultimate form of rent-seeking behavior, which can be very obstructive to social welfare and economic growth.

The phenomenon of 'regulatory capture' will be analyzed in the later part of this section, as part of a dynamic process that started with the liberalization, deregulation and privatization in markets that were formerly planned by politicians and often controlled by vertically integrated state-owned enterprises: telecommunications, public transport and energy markets are examples of these.

## Regulatory risk

Once property rights are assigned to one or more individuals, this generates certain predictable incentives. Private property and optimizing behavior will enable economic growth, while collective property may lead to free riding behavior and will consequently constrain economic growth. For private property rights to function well it is important that the decision rights of the owners of private property are not changed by a government in an ad hoc and unpredictable way. If that were the situation, then private property rights would not provide stable expectations among actors about the behavior of the other actors in the economic system. However, in practice, because of action by the government, private property rights run the risk of *expropriation*, which will cause a change in individual behavior. We apply the concept of expropriation in a broad sense: not only do we mean the expropriation of rights by converting private rights into public rights (as in the case of the nationalization of a private firm), but also situations in which a government influences the costs and benefits related to the execution of private rights. Tax policy is an example of the latter.

Profits and wages are taxed by the government. Taxation rates affect the revenues that individuals or firms derive from acquiring and exchanging property rights. As long as a government does not alter its tax rules, private citizens know what to expect, and all their economic actions will be geared to that expectation. But if, on the other hand, a government often makes changes to its fiscal and redistributive policies, or has the power to impose rules that are unfavorable to trade, this will have a demoralizing effect on the entrepreneurial spirit and will change incentives, hence in general it will affect welfare negatively. The government's credibility is therefore a crucial factor when it comes to creating efficiencies.

### The international dimension

The concept of regulatory risk also has an international dimension. When governments change 'the rules of the game' unexpectedly in their own interest at the expense of (foreign) private firms, then such governments establish a bad reputation. This can range from the nationalization of foreign property and violating contracts with foreign firms to arbitrarily (dis)approving of mergers or acquisitions. Undoubtedly such regulatory risk has implications for the attractiveness of a country for foreign investment and for economic welfare. Box 9.5 provides an example.

> **BOX 9.5 THE ADVENTURES OF SHELL AND BP IN RUSSIA**
>
> While there is a mounting threat of worldwide shortages of fossil fuels, Russia still has a number of areas in which oil and gas are abundant. Several large international energy companies such as Exxon Mobil, Shell and British Petroleum (BP) have taken large shares in Russian energy projects in order to develop these natural gas and oil fields.
>
> In the Sakhalin-2 project, Shell initially had a 55 percent share, while two Japanese conglomerates (*keiretsu*) together owned 45 percent. The original contract stated that the developers had to share their revenues with the Russian government only after they had recovered all their investment costs. In the course of 2006, however, the Russian government started to put pressure on Shell and its two partners to break the agreement, on the pretext that their operation was harming the natural environment. By the end of the year, Shell had to give in because the government had simply withdrawn the environmental permits needed to exploit the gas and oil fields. In the new contract, the three developers sold part of their shares to the Russian state-owned company Gazprom, which thus acquired a majority share. In other words, the Russian state from then on had effective control over the project.
>
> A similar tale unfolded shortly afterwards: in January 2007 the joint venture of BP with Russian based TNK-BP was also targeted by the Russian government. BP had stepped into this strategic alliance in order to pool resources (see Chapter 7 on hybrids) concerning the large Kovytka gas field. The Russians need the multinationals because of their specialized knowledge, but also because of the accompanying capital investment. Still, the Russian government also wanted to control this project (via Gazprom again) and succeeded by once again threatening to withdraw the environmental permits. The government even had an additional hold on this joint venture, because the latter had not been able to deliver the level of production that was contractually agreed upon. The reason for this failure was in fact another strategic move by the Russian government: the required levels could only have been reached in case of export, but only Gazprom was legally allowed to export gas.
>
> The above two incidents have made it quite clear that the rules can be changed during the game. They represent a warning to private firms that even contracts backed up by legal safeguards do not form an absolute guarantee, at least not everywhere in the world, and if there is political involvement.

## Interest groups

Interest groups in society and how they lobby to influence the decision-makers in the political system (parliament, bureaucrats) are important features of economies. This influence is sometimes directed at creating rents: the phenomenon is therefore called rent-seeking. Here we shall discuss several aspects of rent-seeking, notably lobbying and corruption.

## Rent-seeking

*Rent-seeking behavior* when looked at in a negative way, can be described as a manipulative attempt to transfer resources in order to obtain favors without competitive effort; that is, without supplying any productive activity in exchange.

Rent-seeking does not only concern the lobbying activities of firms directed at politicians to gain certain privileges; it also extends to private actors. However, most often it is the state that creates the rents, because it has the power to allocate property rights by means of laws and regulations, taxes, levies and subsidies, or by awarding contracts and concessions. Consequently, rent-seekers will try to influence political decisions related to (re)distributing income to their advantage.

Considering the above description, rent-seeking is regarded as an inefficient outcome that is harmful for society as a whole. Not only firms that seek to by-pass their rivals engage in rent-seeking, but also nonprofit organizations such as Amnesty International or Greenpeace, to name just two, approach politicians to obtain certain favors. Even individuals may be involved in rent-seeking behavior, provided they have the (financial or political) power to do so. The pivot in all rent-seeking activities is in fact related to this aspect of power.

In his prominent book, *The Logic of Collective Action* (1965) Mancur Olson convincingly showed that the influence of a pressure group does not necessarily increase with its size, and that society has more to fear from powerful minority interest groups that can impose their will on the majority. There are several related reasons why relatively small groups can be more effective in reaching their goals than can larger groups:

- individuals who join any (large) group in order to strive collectively for certain benefits will have the incentive to let other group members do the work for them inconspicuously. Free riding is often easy when the group consists of many members, as we have seen before;
- this problem gets even worse if the desired outcome shows the characteristics of a pure public good, of which no one can be excluded once it has materialized;
- when a large number of people strive after a common goal, they must share the prospective success with many others. In anticipation of getting only a small share per person, individuals in large groups tend to show less effort;
- in a large group, the risk increases that not all members of the group have exactly the same goals, which will make collective action less effective; and
- when trying to cope with all these problems, the costs of organizing and monitoring the group's activities also rise with size.

It follows that small groups are easier to organize, because the gains are shared with only a few others, who are more likely to be aiming at the same target, while the individual members do not choose to free ride as this would easily be noticed and lead to loss of reputation. The incentive to organize a small collective also increases if the objective is not characterized by a pure collective good: if the outcome benefits the group members and no one else, people are much more inclined to make an effort. When their goal has been reached, they know that the costs of the provision sought (usually in the form of tax contributions) will be borne by all members of society and not by them alone. The chances of success increase not only because a small interest group usually has more cohesion and discipline, but also because the actions of a smaller group are often less visible to the general public, who as a result will not start protesting.

## Lobbying

In the NIE literature regarding the influencing of political decision-making via rent-seeking, sometimes a distinction is made between buying, lobbying and suing (Spiller and Liao, 2008). In the case of 'buying', the interest group uses financial means or other assets to make the political decision-makers pay attention to their cause. With 'lobbying', the interest group provides information in the hope of influencing the opinion of politicians. And in the case of 'suing', the issue is taken from the political scene to the court. Note that judicial action in itself can be so time-consuming that merely the threat of it can have an impact on the behavior of the actors in the political system. This aspect of interest groups will not be dealt with any further; our focus below will be on the combination of buying and lobbying.

In Box 9.6 you will find an example of lobbying practices from an environmental perspective. Similar cases exist in the automotive industry (pressure to relax pollution and safety standards) and the food industry (genetic manipulation).

---

### BOX 9.6  LOBBYING IN THE ECO INDUSTRY

Traditionally, academic analysis of environmental lobbying has centered on two groups: environmentalists and polluters. However, a third player, eco-industry, is taking an increasingly important role in the lobbying game. The eco-industry lobby will tend to support the position of the environmentalists, as it has an interest in more restrictive environmental policies which will boost demand for its products (Canton, 2008; Wang, 2009).

An early example from 1997 can be found in Germany, where the German Wind Energy Association successfully lobbied the government to retain a law subsidizing renewable electricity, thus allowing it to maintain its position in the wind power market.

Similar to what happens in other industries, the eco-industry in one country can lobby to gain an advantage over the eco-industry in another. In a contest between the German auto industry and French manufacturer Peugeot, each wanted the EU to adopt the emission reduction technology that was most convenient for them. In the end, the German auto industry gained a competitive advantage as it managed to get the regulation it wanted, which established its catalytic converters as the new European environmental technology.

Meanwhile, in the USA, the Obama administration has emphasized that it will provide support for 'green' jobs such as renovating buildings for energy efficiency.

> Even before the inauguration in January 2009, the renewable energy, biofuel and auto industries were queuing up with policy suggestions for the president elect. Among the numerous items on their wish list were a loans program for the development of solar energy, tax credits for companies installing 'smart' meters that reduce the use of electricity, and subsidies for the development of lithium-ion batteries to be used in electric cars.

A great deal of money is at stake when it comes to lobbying. With respect to the USA, for which we give some figures below, a distinction must be made between campaign money and lobbying expenditure. Campaign money can no longer be supplied directly from the funds of organizations such as corporations and trade groups as a result of the McCain–Feingold Campaign Finance Reform Act, so this money has to come from political action committees or individuals, among them employees of corporations and trade groups. Campaign money goes directly to a political candidate.

Lobbying expenses are incurred by corporations, trade groups and the like in their attempts to influence politicians and federal agencies, but do not flow directly to politicians. One can say that lobbying expenses are the costs incurred in producing lobbying activities.

From Table 9.1 you can infer that lobby activities in the USA are on the rise, both in terms of the number of lobbyists involved and with respect to the amount of money being spent in the process. Comparing 1998 with 2008: lobby spending per lobbyist has increased from roughly $135,000 to $214,000, and total lobby spending more than doubled between 1998 and 2008. As a fraction of GDP (according to the Bureau of Economic Analysis, US Department of Commerce), total lobby spending has increased from 0.016 percent to 0.023 percent, implying no less than a 44 percent increase.

**Table 9.1** *Amounts spent on lobbying in the USA, 1998–2008*

|      | Total lobby spending (billions US$) | Number of lobbyists |
| ---- | ----------------------------------- | ------------------- |
| 1998 | 1.44                                | 10,691              |
| 1999 | 1.44                                | 13,330              |
| 2000 | 1.54                                | 12,752              |
| 2001 | 1.63                                | 12,074              |
| 2002 | 1.81                                | 12,349              |
| 2003 | 2.04                                | 13,163              |
| 2004 | 2.17                                | 13,403              |
| 2005 | 2.42                                | 14,442              |
| 2006 | 2.60                                | 14,873              |
| 2007 | 2.84                                | 15,437              |
| 2008 | 3.23                                | 15,276              |

*Source*: Center for Responsive Politics (2009).

In the EU, lobbying is also important; there are about 15,000 lobbyists operating in the 'EU capital', Brussels. Based on a resolution of May 2008, all activists who want to influence members of the European Parliament, the European Commission or the Council of Ministers, have to register themselves as such. In addition, all lobbyists are required to state their goals, for whom they are working, and how much money is involved. This measure should contribute to transparency.

Critics immediately pointed out that registration is voluntary, so that lobbyists are not obliged to identify themselves, their clients or their goals (Phillips, 2008). This typically is a debate about whether formal or informal institutions are more effective. The proponents of the current system argue that making the registration mandatory would require a complex judicial process and hence would take much more time to implement. Moreover, they claim that informal incentives and sanctions may work just as well: only registered lobbyists will be supplied with information on developments related to their stated objectives, and when these activists do not comply with the code of conduct they will be dropped from the register and run the risk of being passed over by parliamentarians. However, the opponents do not give credit to these arguments, as they fear that the current informal sanctions will not impress lobbyists, especially not when large financial interests are at stake.

Successful rent-seeking means that the requested favors have been granted; hence this has led to *rent creation*. Why would politicians be willing to create these rents? One reason is that lobbying can in fact be welfare enhancing. Politicians may have an efficiency-driven motive to be receptive to lobby groups since the latter may provide the necessary information that is needed to reach careful decision-making. In this complex modern world, politicians cannot oversee everything, and gathering additional information is difficult and costly. In this respect, lobby groups contribute to efficiency.

However, lobbying is largely considered to be inefficient. When successful, the granting of favors must be paid for by the whole population, so taxes will rise and consequently deadweight loss also increases; these costs will generally not be taken into account by lobbyists (or their employers). As long as the private costs involved in realizing extra rents are lower than the expected private value of these rents it is profitable for the rent-seeking actors to stick to their behavior, even when this comes at the cost of general welfare. One real-life illustration can be found in Box 9.7.

### BOX 9.7 LOBBYING FOR OR AGAINST THE LOW-ENERGY LIGHT BULB

Despite the fact that low-energy light bulbs are claimed to be much better for the environment than old-fashioned incandescent bulbs, in the year 2000 the EU introduced an import tariff of no less than 66 percent on Chinese low-energy bulbs. This was done under pressure from powerful European light bulb producers, as they could not compete with the low Chinese prices. So, because of vested industrial interests, an artificially high price was maintained until October 2008.

> At that time, the so-called 'anti-dumping import duty' was abolished, with an acceptance of the former competitors. Why? Because all European light bulb producers had by then relocated their factories to China, so of course they were now against any import restrictions. No doubt for commercial reasons, they have concluded a pact with European politicians and environmental lobbyists such as Greenpeace to promote the energy-saving light bulbs.

So, if lobbying usually leads to a deadweight loss, why do policy-makers create rents? Below, we shall briefly discuss the (often interrelated) objectives of being re-elected, gaining and preserving power and status, and/or profiting financially as reasons for granting rents.

Once chosen, politicians will evaluate the costs and benefits for the electorate of each contemplated decision, and consequently whether implementing this policy will increase their chances of being re-elected. Political theorist Machiavelli observed in the early sixteenth century that the strategy of a ruler who wants to stay in power is to win the support of the right people and not the support of the majority *per se*. The following quote from Phelps (1985, p. 187) underlines this:

*Politician*: I will enact a general lowering of taxes and a general raising of the fight against disease and squalor, of which you and indeed all the other factions of society have complained, if in return you spurn my rivals, send your sons to the militia, and stop shooting at my tax inspectors.

*Pressure group*: Ruler, if you have any intention of doing those fine things you'll do them with or without the small help that the support you seek from us would provide you. So we will play the free rider. To win our support you must do for us something that we can see you would not have done anyway, except for our support. A special favor.

Politicians occupy a position that sometimes allows them to take decisions on their own, but on other occasions they need to form coalitions in order to introduce policy measures. When the latter is the case, a common practice is to trade votes. By this is meant that legislators mutually agree to vote in favor of a proposed law to which they are in fact rather indifferent, in exchange for support for another submitted proposal, by which they know they can please their own electorate and the rank and file of their party. This practice of trading votes is also known as *logrolling*. It is usually inefficient, because it often benefits only the inhabitants in a certain district or province, while the costs are spread over the entire population. This could, for example, refer to infrastructural projects or subsidies for a depressed area.

Strongly connected is *pork barrel politics*, which refers again to the phenomenon that politicians channel funds to particular subgroups in society in return for political support, perhaps by way of securing votes or by donations to their (re-)election campaign. Despite the fact that, in many countries, being in power does not coincide with a high income (compared to being, for example, a CEO in a large private firm), it does give status and consequently paves the way for a prospective highly paid job outside government. So, the financial benefit may lie in the future.

A final example of lobbying shows how vested interests are so strong as to be able to oppose both countervailing power actions and to preserve the power base (see Box 9.8).

---

### BOX 9.8   LOBBYING IN THE TOBACCO INDUSTRY

An internal Philip Morris memo quoted by Givel (2006, p. 410) bluntly states that the company 'will use direct lobbying, the media, and industry allies to minimize state and local tax increases... and preserve the industry's freedom to advertise and promote cigarettes to adult smokers'.

Until the 1960s, the tobacco lobby had managed to frame the debate in terms of jobs created and the livelihood of farmers, rather than as a health issue. But as the detrimental effects of smoking have become increasingly clear, its tactics have changed, and in public the tobacco industry argues that use of tobacco is a matter of personal choice.

Givel (2006) attempts to quantify the influence of the tobacco lobby on state tobacco policy legislation in the USA. The tobacco industry's primary approach has been to employ professional lobbyists, who have made a career out of working with state legislatures to advance or block regulations. Among other strategies, lobbyists made direct contributions to politicians' campaigns, and provided gifts to legislators. They also formed alliances with other interest groups, and funded public interest groups with names such as 'National Smokers Alliance'.

On the other hand, the anti-smoking lobby's methods are more direct than those of the smoking lobby, and include newspaper advertisements, media interviews, rallies and public demonstrations. According to Givel (2006), the evidence is that, during the 1990s, the tobacco industry was more effective than its opponents in its influence on policy, as among other things it managed to keep taxes on cigarettes low in most states. The author concludes that the industry was able to counter the increased activity by health advocates by using its much larger resources and political experience, and suggests that in future the 'health lobby' will need to review its tactics if it wants to increase its effectiveness.

---

### Corruption

Possibly the worst form of lobbying is related to outright corruption which, in the extreme, has devastating consequences for economies and their potential for growth. The practices of fraud, bribery and corruption in which government representatives are involved are phenomena that occur in many (if not all) countries to varying degrees. In nations where these practices are completely forbidden and considered highly improper they take place in secret, but in some countries politicians and other public officials engage in such activities quite openly and frequently. We shall focus here on *political corruption*, which is defined as the misuse of governmental power for private (financial) benefit. This abuse could be exercised by both politicians and bureaucrats, and presents a very serious problem as it hampers overall economic growth.

Numerous reports have been written by the World Bank about the problem of corruption, but it is omnipresent in many poor countries, which, partly as result, tend to remain poor. The NGO Transparency International publishes annually the Corruption Perceptions Index (CPI) and the Global Corruption Barometer. Both lists contain information about the ranking of all countries according to the degree of corruption. The former expresses the view of country experts on the severity of political corruption, while the latter measures the perceptions of the general public with respect to the level of overall corruption in their country. Table 9.2 shows which ten (out of 180) countries score the best and worst, respectively, according to the CPI 2008.

**Table 9.2** *Corruption Perception Index 2008: the ten best and ten worst scoring countries*

| Rank | Best performing countries | Worst performing countries |
|---|---|---|
| 1 | Denmark | Somalia |
| 2 | New Zealand | Myanmar |
| 3 | Sweden | Iraq |
| 4 | Singapore | Haiti |
| 5 | Finland | Afghanistan |
| 6 | Switzerland | Sudan |
| 7 | Iceland | Guinea |
| 8 | Netherlands | Chad |
| 9 | Australia | Equatorial Guinea |
| 10 | Canada | Congo |

*Source*: Transparency International (2008).

According to the Global Corruption Barometer (Transparency International, 2007), citizens worldwide perceive three types of public actors to be the most corrupt: political parties, parliament/congress members, and the police.

Political corruption can take many forms, which we, given the scope of this book, cannot deal with in detail. An elaborate study of numerous applications of Institutional Economics to issues of political corruption can be found in Lambsdorff (2007). It is sufficient to note that it involves public representatives who are either susceptible to bribes offered in return for political favors, or who even actively approach private actors and attempt to bribe or extort them. Examples of the former have already been touched upon in earlier discussions on rent-seeking, while typical examples of the latter are corrupt police officers who fine people on the spot for an offence they have not committed; or to customs officers who harass people, so that paying off those officers becomes the easiest thing to do. But it could also apply to the leader of a country himself, often in the person of a dictator, who oppresses the majority of the population while securing all the riches of the nation for himself and those who are loyal to him.

Countries characterized by a high degree of political corruption may experience a change of leadership, but quite often one repressive and corruptive regime is merely exchanged for another. This usually takes place in countries that lack a democratic tradition. What sometimes can be effective, however, is when the regime of a poor, corrupt country appeals for financial help to an organization such as the IMF. In these instances, the IMF will only give support under certain conditions, such as requiring that a regime changes its policies.

Another attempt to bring about changes in poor, corrupt regimes can be seen in the way in which rich countries and NGOs attach conditions to development aid. Examples are the direct financing of schools and education, and stimulating economic activities for individual inhabitants. Accommodating micro-credits, advocated by the 1998 Nobel Laureate Amartya Sen, has recently been gaining popularity. In the course of time, all these measures might make the population more knowledgeable, independent and hence more able to defy corruption.

## The process of liberalization, privatization and regulation

We have already discussed how governments can intervene to enhance welfare if natural monopolies are involved. Here we shall look more closely at the intricacies and problems involved in regulating state-owned natural monopolies, and more specifically at what happens if such a monopoly is privatized. *Privatization* means that collective property is transferred to private property, and this is frequently linked to *liberalization* – the process of making a former state-owned enterprise subject to competition (of which 'competition for the market' is an example). Often, the process of liberalization is guided by a sector-specific regulator. Below, we shall first briefly set out the nature of the problem, then deal with 'regulatory risk', 'regulatory capture', 'rent-seeking' and the 'commitment problem'.

### Natural monopolies

Some state-owned enterprises are natural monopolies as a result of transmission or transport networks (electricity grids and gas or water pipelines are important examples). These state-owned enterprises in the past used generally to be vertically integrated: they owned the network and provided the products to consumers.

Privatization of a vertically integrated natural monopoly implies that it becomes privately owned but otherwise remains the same. In such situations privatization is considered to be good in the sense that it gives higher power incentives with respect to cost efficiencies. Still, in order to avoid monopoly pricing, privatization implies regulation. Most often this is done by allowing competition for the product, so access to the network is regulated in order to stimulate this competition. If access to the network is guaranteed by allowing competitors to use the network indiscriminately at reasonable prices, then monopoly pricing can be avoided: at the network level, the price of access is regulated to be not too high, while the encouraging of rivalry at the product level will guarantee competitive prices for consumers.

However, rather than keeping this new entity intact as a privately-owned vertically integrated firm, privatization and liberalization can be better served by unbundling the vertical activities of the firm: the transmission or transport services are separated from the provision of the product as well as the ownership and two different firms are established (see also Chapter 4). The provision of the product is then privatized and liberalized as described in the case of the vertically integrated firm: the network firm is required to give access to competitors at the level of provision to consumers. Again, the access conditions need to be regulated.

One way of guaranteeing access on reasonable terms is to let the network firm remain state-owned, or (in order to give higher-powered cost efficiency incentives) make it privately owned, but regulated.

So, the main concern of a regulator is to induce competition at the level of the product by applying appropriate, non-discriminatory access conditions to the network at the right price. We shall discuss this below.

## Other types of state-owned enterprises

Other legal monopolies exist that are characterized by the fact that their activities (even if these monopolies possess a network) can be offered competitively by others through rival networks. Take postal services and telecommunication networks: before the early 1990s, fixed telecommunications network operators could be regarded as owning a natural monopoly, but competition from, for example, mobile telephone networks (and telecom services) and from cable television companies (which also own networks that are now able to provide telecom services) is increasing.

In these cases, a similar process of privatization and liberalization as described earlier can be followed, but now the main concern for a regulator is not only to induce competition at the level of the final product, but also to stimulate competition at the network level.

We have already explained the basics of regulating a natural monopoly with respect to price in a static setting. Here we explore the relationship between the process of liberalization, privatization and regulation in more detail. You will see that during the process unexpected and undesirable outcomes occur, partly because of attempts by regulated firms to manipulate the regulator, and this requires a re-regulation by the political system. A famous example of failed liberalization illustrates how intricate it can be to establish a proper process of privatization and liberalization (see Box 9.9).

### BOX 9.9 THE CALIFORNIAN EXPERIENCE

This is a highly simplified version of the much more intricate problems involved in this case. For our purposes, it suffices to focus on just some of the details.

In the late 1990s, California's electricity industry was liberalized. Legislation had the following effects: a maximum retail price for consumers was set; electricity production facilities became largely independent; California's electricity suppliers at the retail level were given incentives to make use of the California Power Exchange (the spot market for electricity); and wholesale prices (that is, the price for electricity paid by the electricity suppliers) were unregulated.

In the summer of 2000, very hot and dry weather increased demand for electricity but at the same time decreased the supply from California's electricity plants that used hydro energy. This forced electricity suppliers to increase demand on the spot market. On the supply side, electricity was produced by much more expensive gas-powered electricity plants (among other sources). Also, supply was manipulated by withholding (that is, keeping electricity supply opportunistically off the market). All these effects led to much higher wholesale prices, but these could not be passed on to consumers because of the maximum retail price. All the consequent losses and costs fell on the retail electricity suppliers and the State of California (the State was forced to take over the suppliers' role of buying electricity). The situation was so fragile that consumers even experienced power outages, and in the end retail prices had to be raised (Lee, 2004).

## *The transition from a state-owned to private natural monopoly*

Above we introduced the general tasks of a regulator: to guarantee access to the network on reasonable terms in order to induce competition at the level of the provision of the product to consumers, and (if possible) also to stimulate competition at the level of the network. In the following we shall describe at a simplified theoretical level what is essentially meant by regulation in the sense of guaranteeing access; the other type of regulation is beyond the scope of this book. By regulation, we mean here that the regulator determines what the level of prices must be, to maximize consumer surplus, but with the restriction that dynamic efficiencies (innovation) and investments must also be stimulated, as we saw in Chapter 8. After that, we shall explore somewhat more deeply the specific issues related to privatization and liberalization. This will include some of the problems resulting from imperfect information and imperfect institutions.

Competition for the product delivered to consumers using the network implies that the terms and conditions of access to the network must be regulated and include a (nondiscriminatory) access tariff. Think, for example, of transport companies who are allowed to use the railway system for goods or passengers, electricity traders that may use the grid to transport electricity and offer it to the consumer, and fixed telephone companies other than the former monopolist that are allowed to use the network to provide telecom services.

Suppose that access regulation is such that the price for access is not too high and induces competitors to make use of the network at the level of provision to consumers. This regulated price gives an (implicit) incentive to strive for cost efficiencies, given the regulated price, as lower costs imply greater profits for the network firm. Of course, it also suggests that consumers do not share these benefits; they would benefit from lower prices resulting from lower costs. However, if the network firm was forced to pass on the profits to consumers by lowering prices, the incentive to strive for cost efficiencies disappears. This poses a dilemma: how to deal with incentives for efficiency on the one hand and yet share the benefits involved with consumers on the other? The problem can be overcome by changing the regulation scheme slightly: the price is regulated for, say, three years, during which time cost efficiencies will increase profits for the firm; after three years, the regulated price will decrease in line with the cost efficiencies, to enable consumers to share in the benefits (but with a lag), and so on.

As you can see, taking into account these kinds of practical considerations will involve a large amount of information being available to initiate regulation. This implies that not only the total policy costs of this state intervention, such as the costs of the regulator's resource constraints, have to be taken into account, but also the costs of under- or overregulation (see below). Furthermore, in case of a large information asymmetry to the advantage of the regulated and if there are few or no alternatives for consumers, the regulated firm has sizeable opportunities to *capture the regulation*. The danger that this regulatory capture will occur must be considered, and will give rise to costs in preventing such capturing activities. Hence, regulation becomes more expensive depending on the effectiveness of the instruments available to the regulator. Costly investments in information, expertise, effective instruments, monitoring and sanctions are needed. These additional costs may be of great importance in deciding whether or not to regulate, how to regulate, or to liberalize the sector and how to do this. We shall now discuss two of the problems involved in more detail.

## Rent-seeking in public agencies: commitment and regulatory capture

We have seen the dilemma of how to keep prices as low as possible, while at the same time guaranteeing sufficient incentives for investment and innovation. Besides, the regulator has to guarantee access to the network and possibly to stimulate investments in alternative networks, thus the regulator must apply measures in such a way that the network owner (or the vertically integrated private monopolist) will not be able to hamper entrants (a long-term interest). In the meantime, the regulator also wants prices to be low, so that entry is not deterred, and at the same time customers will be able to benefit in the short run (a short-term interest).

So, the challenge of regulators is to align long-run and short-run interests, the short-run interests being that prices will be low enough to have consumer benefits. This will both lead to a 'commitment' problem and to regulatory capture (Armstrong and Sappington, 2006).

The *commitment problem* is a consequence of the possibility that short-term interests may be overemphasized by the regulator and/or by politicians and/or customers or other pressure groups. Consequently, prices may be forced to be so low as not to guarantee the future quality of the product, because (all) incentives to innovate or invest are being removed: why would the firm invest or innovate if the benefits go only to the consumers via lower prices? Notice that this is also an example of a false negative: unjustly, no investments take place.

To enable the regulator to commit itself also to safeguard the long-run interests, measures need to be taken. One can think of making the regulator independent from politics, or one can think of legislation that precisely defines the objectives and tasks of the regulator. In a sense these requirements are interdependent: the more independent the regulator, the more relevant will specific legislation on the goals and powers of the regulator have to become.

Another, yet related, problem is *regulatory capture*: the regulator becomes too involved with the regulated firm, and this dependence might imply that the regulator becomes a plaything of the firm. The regulator might then neglect its official duties: the firm's interests (especially the short-term interests of having high prices) will be served by the regulator at the expense of the public at large. The firm might use funds to influence the regulator's decisions in its favor, say – an example of rent-seeking.

Since the regulator is almost always dependent on the firm's provision of data (cost data, for example) to do its work, the data might easily be manipulated by the firm to its own benefit (compare Chapter 8 on the centrally planned economy). Also, the regulator might be persuaded to overemphasize the long-run interest, which, generally speaking, implies that prices are higher now in order to make investments and innovations profitable immediately: current consumers rather than future consumers pay for the investments, whereas normally (under competitive circumstances) investments are paid back by future rather than current consumers. The firm might expect that the regulator will not prune away all the benefits (profits) from the investment or innovation. Effectively, this will give too high-powered an incentive to innovate: prices cover costs now, so if the investment fails, the firm does not suffer. In this situation, there is a false positive: unjustly inefficient investment or innovation takes place. Consequently, the regulator might further the interests of the regulated firm, rather than the public interest.

In case of a liberalization process, regulatory capture may be curbed by a fierce application of the goal of stimulating entry. After all, it is competition that will break down the incumbent's dominant position. In case of a natural monopoly, it is also a matter of describing precisely the goals, both in the short and the long run, that society (and hence the regulator) wants to achieve. In this sense, regulatory capture and the commitment problem are related and may be solved by the same kinds of institutional arrangements.

## CONCLUDING REMARKS

Governments are not perfect. Many of the efficiencies we described in Chapter 8 may therefore not be realized through state intervention, or only imperfectly so. It is not even necessarily the case that government measures or institutions to solve problems (on balance) increase welfare.

Theoretically, it is not possible to guarantee that individual preferences are translated into a well-defined aggregate welfare function. Besides, aspects other than efficiency, such as equity, play a part in determining policy solutions. Hence, politicians will determine political outcomes, even if these are not really in the interest of all voters. Voters can choose to be rationally ignorant, which will leave much discretionary power to politicians and government. This also gives lobby groups the power and incentives to influence politicians.

Short-run and long-run interests will sometimes be in conflict with each other. This will lead to 'regulatory risks'; the government may prove to be an unreliable player in the economy. Private actors must take these costs into account, and this will lower their welfare. Besides, unintended side effects occur that cannot be foreseen. All problems involved with governmental interference lead to additional costs, and a search for (better) solutions.

## REVIEW QUESTIONS

1 What is meant by 'policy costs'? Give details of the different components.
2 What principal–agent problems arise in the context of the government?
3 Describe some unintended side effects of policy measures. Can you think of a few in your own surroundings?
4 Which instruments are used by governments to encourage civil servants to work efficiently? Do you think these instruments are effective in your country? Explain why/why not.
5 Explain how mandatory insurance may be Pareto suboptimal but Hicks–Kaldor optimal.
6 What are the differences and relationship between privatization, liberalization and regulation?
7 Describe the problems of regulatory risk and regulatory capture.
8 Do you agree with the statement that the German health care system has become too expensive to sustain, given the fact that in 2006 health care expenditure was 10.6 percent of GDP in Germany and 15.3 percent of GDP in the USA?
9 Do you think that rent-seeking behavior always results in a welfare loss? Give some examples to support your opinion.
10 Explain the relationship between (the presence or absence of) corruption and the institutional environment.
11 Do you think that government intervention in the economy is welfare enhancing? Explain your reasons.

# Appendixes to Chapter 9

## APPENDIX A: ARROW'S IMPOSSIBILITY THEOREM

To see why, in general, it is impossible to have a social preference function that represents all possible individual preferences by majority voting, we have to state the underlying assumptions (based on Mueller, 2003). An example will then illustrate why the answer is negative, since a general mathematical proof is beyond the scope of this book.

The first assumption refers to the individuals' preferences; it is assumed that they are complete and transitive with respect to the choices that have to be made. For example, any individual 'i' is able to rank *all* alternatives he has according to his preferences (*completeness*), so that if alternative A is preferred to alternative B, and B is preferred to C, then A must also be preferred to C (*transitivity*).

Assume also that society is made up of at least three individuals, and choices always consist of three or more alternatives. In the following we assume that we have three individuals (1, 2 and 3) and three alternatives (A, B and C) that may be chosen individually and which have to be translated into a social preference. One can think of A, B and C as political parties.

The principles with respect to the social preferences are that, if all individuals prefer some alternative (A, for example), to another (say B), then A should also be preferred socially to B. Now assume that people in a society also want society's preferences to be transitive. So, if A is preferred socially to B, and B is preferred socially to C, then A must be preferred socially to C. This will, for example, be the case when all three individuals prefer A to B and B to C: majority voting will indeed lead to the social preference that A is preferred to B, and B to C.

Yet another assumption is that any pairwise choice between alternatives is independent of any other alternative. So, if A is compared to B, it does not matter what the preferences are with respect to C: whether A is preferred to B or not, does not depend on the question of whether A or B are preferred to C.

The final assumption is that social preferences should not be defined by any specific individual's preferences. Obviously, if the preferences of only one individual 'i' define social preferences, this does not correspond to a democracy and majority voting. Such social preferences would coincide with a dictatorship ('i' being the dictator).

We shall now illustrate the general result that social preferences with the above characteristics cannot in general be construed from individual preferences. Suppose individual 1 prefers A to B and B to C; individual 2 prefers B to C to A; and individual 3 prefers C to A to B. This situation is shown in Table 9.3.

Pairwise majority voting will give the following results. If A and B are compared, two out of three individual preferences would lead to the social result that A is preferred to

**Table 9.3** *Preference ordering leading to the Arrow paradox*

| Ranking | Individual 1 | Individual 2 | Individual 3 |
|---|---|---|---|
| 1st | A | B | C |
| 2nd | B | C | A |
| 3rd | C | A | B |

B (individuals 1 and 3 versus 2). If B and C are compared, B is socially preferred to C (individuals 1 and 2 versus 3). If A and C are compared, though, it appears that A is not preferred to C, as the foregoing would suggest if social preferences were transitive, but that C is preferred to A (individuals 2 and 3 versus 1).

Hence, this outcome shows that transitive individual preferences can coincide with intransitive social preferences. This Arrow paradox suggests that making social choices can be manipulated by an individual or interest group that may set the agenda for choices. Basically, this implies that there is a 'dictatorship'.

Note that the pairwise comparison is not fundamental: if each individual merely states her first choice or her total preference ordering, it is still impossible to decide on society's preferred alternative. This is easy to see, because 1 prefers A, 2 prefers B and 3 prefers C, hence there is a tie. This tie is not resolved by comparing the second choices, because 1 then prefers B, 2 prefers C and 3 prefers A. Comparing the third alternative also results in a tie.

Of course, if the assumptions are changed, the result may disappear. For example, is it necessary to have a social preference ordering that is 'transitive'? Society – that is, the majority – might 'vote' for the possibility of non-transitivity. In that case, a dice might be thrown in order to decide which alternatives are to be compared first. For example, to stay within the situation described above, three 'packages' have to be compared: A and B (AB); A and C (AC); and B and C (BC). AB is represented by 1 and 2 on the dice, AC by 3 and 4, and BC by 5 and 6. Throwing the dice will then decide which alternatives are agreed on first – for example, AB. If, in this case, A is preferred to B, as in our example, then A and C may be compared, which in our example implies that C will be chosen. Even though the social preference ordering may not be transitive, society might prefer to have a non-transitive ordering by voting on some rule that will solve the impossibility theorem.

## APPENDIX B: GRAPHICAL ELABORATION OF THE BUREAUCRACY THEORY

As we explained in the main text, politicians strive after different goals compared to civil servants. In Figure 9.2 we assume, in line with the basic bureaucracy theory, that the former desire to optimize social welfare while the latter desire to optimize their budget. The question is how much output, or level of services (L), the civil servants are expected to deliver. Here we simply assume that the total costs (TC) of providing more services increases at a proportional rate, while only the civil servants know the true costs. The total benefits (TB) express the value that the politicians place on each level of services.

The politicians' goal is to provide more services to the public as long as the extra benefits exceed the extra costs, hence the optimal level of services L* will be cost efficient.

The bureaucrats' goal is to work in a department with a size as large as possible so they want to provide more services as long as the total costs cover their expansion in size. At level $L_b$ of services, the allocated budget is just large enough to cover all their expenses. However, from a society's point of view, this is not the efficient level.

Moreover, civil servants may use their informational advantage to try to make the politicians believe that the effects of the bureau's services are higher than they in fact are. If the civil servants succeed in their strategy, this implies that the TB curve will shift upwards, leading to an even higher level of $L_b$. As Rosen and Gayer (2008) argue, this is comparable to misleading advertising strategies in the private sector, which we discussed in Chapter 5.

A related phenomenon is the habit of departments to spend the total budget that is allocated to them before the end of the book year, because otherwise they fear that they will receive a smaller budget for the following year. As a negative side effect, civil servants may spend the remaining budget on purchases that are not so useful (this is called 'slack').

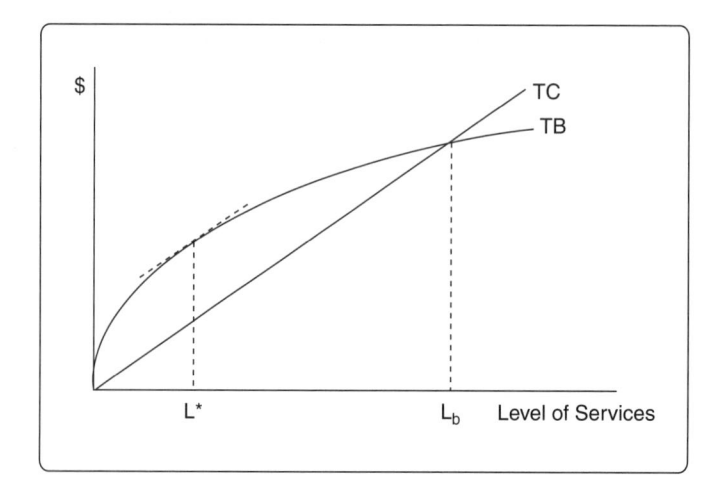

**Figure 9.2** *The different goals of politicians and bureaucrats*

# Epilog

If there is one central message in this book, it is that 'institutions matter'. We hope that we have succeeded in convincing you how Institutional Economics helps to give a better, more fundamental understanding of the economy.

Institutions are a pervasive part of economic life; they comprise all kinds of social rules and accompanying sanctions that can make economic interactions less risky and more predictable, thus smoothing transactions and attaining a higher level of welfare, but they can also be interpreted in terms of vested interests. In that case, inefficiencies generally result.

We have illustrated several points of view, each shedding a different light on economic phenomena and behavior: static and dynamic views, seen both from an efficiency and a vested interest approach. These views are derived from two schools of Institutional Economics: the Original Institutional Economics (OIE) and the New Institutional Economics (NIE). Both schools originated from a dissatisfaction and disappointment with mainstream microeconomics that neglects the fundamental role of institutions in understanding economics. The mainstream, or neoclassical view, can be paraphrased as 'firms are just production functions in a sea of market transactions'.

Coase, North and Williamson are three of the most important founders of NIE. They made rigorous studies of the origins and functioning of firms, markets and hybrids: the basic governance structures described in our book. Generally speaking, they emphasize the efficiency aspects.

Commons and Veblen are two of the most important founders of OIE. In their opinion, the economy is primarily focused on the dynamics of changing institutions that influence economic behavior. In that process technology, values and laws interact, and economic models and theories should capture that aspect of reality. Economic actors operate in specific institutional environments, and markets are institutionalized structures, in which power is as important as efficiency in understanding their performance. In Veblen's renowned analysis of the business world, he described how big business dominated markets and politics, and how business was able to manipulate political decision-making in favor of vested interests.

These days, contributions are made by economists that are viewed by us as belonging to both NIE and OIE, important contributors of this type being Greif and North. This illustrates that the distinction between these two schools of thought is no longer as important. It is their insights into the static and dynamic analysis of institutions, as well as the efficiency approach and the vested interest approach that are most relevant. The central question of Institutional Economics is therefore as much about the explanation of the emergence and change of institutions as about the impact of the institutions on economic behavior.

# Glossary

**Actor** is the general term for any decision-maker in an economic activity (production, distribution, consumption), that can be an individual, a group of individuals, an organization, a firm or a government.

**Adverse selection** (*ex-ante* **opportunistic behavior**) occurs when an information asymmetry (see **imperfect information**) exists before the contract has been signed between parties, so that the party with the better information will be able to use this to his advantage and to the detriment of the other party, with a welfare loss as a consequence.

**Agency** is used differently in different theories. In case of theories related to the interaction between structures and the capacity of individual actors to make choices, agency is used to describe the capacity to choose freely and without constraints. In **principal–agent problems**, agency is used in relation to the costs these problems generate (see **agency costs**). In connection with government, it is a specific entity or bureau that is entrusted by government to carry out a specific task (such as a regulatory agency).

**Agency costs** are the result of **principal–agent problems** and can be divided into three categories: (i) monitoring expenditures, made in order to avoid opportunistic behavior by agents; (ii) bonding costs, incurred by the agent if it pays to spend resources aimed at signaling to the principal that she serves the interests of the principal; and (iii) residual loss, the monetary value of the principal's welfare loss if the agent's economic decisions are not on a par with the principal's interests despite monitoring and bonding.

**Agent**; see **principal–agent problems**.

**Allocative efficiency** is the situation in which goods and services are produced in a technically efficient way (productive efficiency) and according to the preferences of consumers. This is the case at output levels, where prices equal marginal costs. This implies a **Pareto-optimal solution**.

**Arrow's impossibility theorem** (also known as the Arrow paradox) states that it is not possible in general to aggregate individual preferences to a social preference function, so that, by means of voting, the socially preferred outcome will result, as defined by the majority's individual preferences.

**Arrow's information paradox** occurs when an actor thinks information that another possesses is probably of value to him, but he can only decide about its value and price after the information has been revealed to him.

**Asset specificity** is the degree to which an asset is tied to a specific transaction and therefore cannot be put to alternative uses. When the degree of asset specificity is high, the asset cannot be used alternatively without a substantial loss of value.

**Asymmetric information**; see **imperfect information**.

**Authority** refers to the power in a **firm** or government agency to impose decisions on others in the **hierarchy**.

**Autonomy** refers to the ability of private actors to make their own decisions without interference from an **authority**.

**Bounded rationality** is a specific form of rational decision-making (**satisficing behavior**) under the condition of **incomplete information**.

**Bureaucracy theory** is about a principal–agent problem between the government and its civil servants (see **principal–agent problems**).

**Cartel** is an explicit agreement between firms to jointly determine prices, output levels and/or market share (see also **OPEC**).

**Centrally planned economy** is an ideal type of economic system characterized by collective (public) property and a dominant role of government, which takes all important economic decisions.

**Ceremonial institutions** are institutions that protect **vested interests** and strengthen invidious distinctions based on race, gender or income.

**Club goods**; see **types of goods**.

**Coase theorem** states that actors can negotiate an efficient outcome when property rights are clearly defined and no barriers to negotiation exist.

**Collusion** is an explicit or implicit agreement between firms to cooperate in order to avoid competition with respect to parameters such as prices and quantities. See also **implicit collusion**.

**Common property**; see **shared property**.

**Common property resources**; see **types of goods**.

**Comparative static analysis** compares the equilibrium values of an **endogenous variable** related to a change in the value of an **exogenous variable**.

**Consumer surplus** is the difference between the willingness to pay of consumers in a market and the price actually paid for each unit of the product.

**Contract** is an oral or written agreement between two or more parties who consent to exchange **property rights** with respect to goods or services. In a frictionless world, complete contracts are agreements that can be concluded, monitored and enforced without any costs, hence all relevant contingencies may be taken into account (see also **relational contract**). Usually not all contingencies can be specified, leading to incomplete contracts.

**Contingent markets** are markets for commodities that are not characterized by their physical character and availability only at a certain place and time, but also by the environmental and future developments that can occur.

**Conventions** are practical rules that are privately constructed to simplify transactions in complex situations and thus reduce coordination problems.

**Cooperative** is an association of actors united voluntarily to meet a common goal through a jointly owned and controlled organization. See also **hybrids**.

**Countervailing power** is the realization of power by actors on one side of the market to offset existing power on the other side. Examples are trade unions and consumer organizations to offset firms' **market power**.

**Creative destruction** is the phenomenon of investing in new productive capital and the simultaneous depreciation of old capital, because the old capital is not as profitable as the new capital.

**Culture** comprises the aspects of human behavior and society that are shared by all or almost all members of some social group. Culture includes material (buildings, paintings) and immaterial phenomena (values, norms, conventions, laws and governance structures).

**Cumulative causation** is a process of forces that reinforce each other in a cumulative way; that is, changes induce other changes, which push the phenomenon further on its developmental way. This can result in a positive development, such as the agglomeration in an industrial region; or a negative development of increasing poverty in a developing area.

**Darwinian evolution** is the explanation of evolution based on a process of mutation, selection, inheritance and retention.

**Demerit goods** are products that (supposedly) are bad for the direct users, and in addition have negative **externalities**.

**Design perspective** towards institutional change sees institutions as the intended result of individual or collective choice.

**Developmental state**; see **regulatory state**.

**Dynamic efficiency**; see **efficiency**.

**Economic system** is a set of interrelated institutions that influence the ways in which actors organize production, consumption and distribution of goods and services.

**Economic welfare** is the sum of all consumer and producer surpluses; see also **welfare**.

**Efficiency** can be viewed in terms of static efficiency or dynamic efficiency. Static efficiency is **allocative efficiency** and productive efficiency (production at the lowest possible costs given a specific technology and given the level of output). **Dynamic efficiency** arises if, as a result of technological developments (innovation), either production or distribution techniques are improved, or new products and services are produced that better fulfill consumers preferences.

**Enculturation** is the process whereby the members of a group, through formal and informal training, acquire a **culture**.

**Endogenous variable** is the variable whose value is determined by the **exogenous variables** of a (mathematical) **model**. In more general terms, it is the variable that is explained by those factors that are considered to be relevant, but are not themselves explained by the model used.

**Environmental uncertainty** refers to variables about which no actor in the system has information. Examples are developments in technology, climate changes, and natural, political or economic crises.

**Entrepreneur** is an actor who sees and acts upon perceived opportunities and takes the risk of new ventures.

**Entrepreneurial firm** is a firm that is constantly looking for new profit opportunities, especially in unexplored areas.

**Exogenous variable** is a variable whose value is not explained by a (mathematical) **model**, but is supplied from outside the model and is used to explain an **endogenous variable**.

**Externalities** are economic side effects not addressed by the market, which either harm others (in the case of a negative externality) or benefit others (in the case of a positive externality) without compensation taking place. This implies that negative externalities are costs, and positive externalities are benefits that are not reflected in market prices.

**Evolution** is the gradual or incremental change of social or economic phenomena that does not result from the intended behavior of actors.

**Fiat** is the capacity of **actors** to use authoritative command (see **authority**).

**Firm** is the producer in **Neoclassical Economics** (NCE), who transforms inputs into output. In **New Institutional Economics** (NIE) it is a **governance structure** that allocates goods and services by **fiat**. From the point of view of property rights, it is the nexus of contracts. From the point of view of a **principal–agent relationship** the separation of ownership and control is the central element.

**First best solution**; see **perfect competition**.

**First order economizing** is the design of effective and efficient formal public institutions without which actors cannot make optimal decisions in markets.

**Formal contract** is a legally enforceable **contract**.

**Formal institutions** are *public* rules of behavior that are designed by a public authority with legislative power and enforced by (i) a public authority with executive power (the administration or government, making use of police, regulatory agencies and other enforcement agencies); and (ii) a judiciary power (public courts) that have the right and the power to penalize an individual or organization for breaking a rule.

**Franchising** is to **license** a specific business philosophy, including intangible assets such as a brand name.

**Free goods** are goods that are not scarce; that is, when supply exceeds demand at all price levels, hence equilibrium market prices are zero.

**Free rider behavior** is maximizing one's own welfare while profiting uninvited and without compensation from the efforts of others without contributing personally to these efforts.

**Governance structure** is an institutional framework (a system of rules) within which actors coordinate their transactions.

**Government** is in this book a catch-all term for any public authority.

**Government failure** is any type of government intervention that leads to an economic welfare loss.

**Habit** is a recurrent, often unconscious pattern of behavior that is acquired through repetition.

**Hazards** are risks incurred because of imperfect information and the possibility of opportunistic behavior by one of the contracting parties.

**Hicks–Kaldor improvement** is the situation in which at least one actor in the economy can reach a higher level of utility or profit as long as the monetary equivalent of this higher level is larger than the monetary equivalent of the consequent loss in utility or profit by others, so that the loser(s) can be compensated, at least in theory.

**Hierarchy** is the allocation of resources (or coordination of transactions) by **fiat**.

**High-powered incentives** are incentives that encourage an actor to do his utmost; the resulting earnings generally flow to the actor involved. In contrast, **low-powered incentives** do not induce the actor to do his utmost, generally because the resulting earnings do not flow (directly and completely) to the actor himself. This is generally the case in **hierarchies** and government agencies.

**Hold-up** is a situation of *ex-post* **opportunistic behavior** in which one of the parties to an agreement makes transaction-specific investments (the investments have value in this transaction only) that the other party can exploit by threatening to terminate the agreement.

**Hostage** is a form of **self-regulation**, in which parties to a contract are able to impose credible commitments by means of securities such as a down payment or collateral.

**Hybrids** are **governance structures** in which firms cooperate, and in which elements of the governance structure of a **market** and of a **firm** (**hierarchy**) are combined.

**Incomplete contract**; see **contract**.

**Information paradox**; see Arrow's information paradox.

**Imperfect competition** is any market structure in which actors have some degree of **market power**. We distinguish **monopoly, monopsony, oligopoly** and **monopolistic competition**.

**Imperfect information** is a situation in which information is either distributed unequally among the different actors (also known as **asymmetric information**), or none of the actors involved in a transaction is fully informed.

**Implicit collusion** is a form of **collusion** that emerges spontaneously as a result of a self-enforcing mechanism (see **self-enforcement**).

**Indicative planning** is a system by which the government guides economic development by setting indicators that guide the other actors in the economy in the direction of the objectives the government has published in an indicative plan.

**Informal institutions** are private rules of behavior gradually and spontaneously developed that do not need any legal enforcement, because it is either in the interest of the actors to follow the rules spontaneously (**self-enforcement**) or sanctioned by the private actors themselves (**self-regulation**). Examples of informal institutions are social **norms** and **conventions**.

**Innovation** is the creation of new products, production techniques or institutions. Innovations lead to **dynamic efficiency**.

**Institutions** are systems of hierarchical, social rules that structure behavior and social interaction.

**Institution-as-an-equilibrium approach** explains the dynamics towards institutions to which every actor spontaneously adheres.

**Institutional entrepreneur** is an actor who overcomes institutional barriers or who takes the initiative to create new institutions.

**Institutional environment** refers to all rules (both formal and informal) that have an impact on a transaction, ranging from abstract values to norms, conventions to concrete, specific rules.

**Instrumental valuation** is the process of determining which values and norms, and which public and private governance structures, are instrumental with respect to the societal objectives.

**Interdisciplinary approach**; see **multidisciplinary approach**.

**Joint venture** is a governance structure created by two or more other legal actors, in which they combine complementary assets such as equity or knowledge. See also **hybrids**.

**Liberalization** is the process of making a market, formerly reserved for incumbent public or legal monopolies only, accessible to new entrants.

**License** is the permission to use a specific property right in exchange for a fee.

**Lock-in** is a situation in which actors cannot change the organization of economic transactions, because in an economic, institutional or technical sense a change is impossible or too costly.

**Low-powered incentives**; see **high-powered incentives**.

**Market** is the voluntary exchange between individual buyers and sellers of goods and services for other goods and services or money. The exchange is conceptualized differently in the different economic theories.

**Market imperfections** arise when markets do not fulfill the basic assumptions of the standard neoclassical **model** of **perfect competition**, and consequently inefficiencies arise. We distinguish several types of market imperfections: **imperfect information, market power, pure public goods, externalities, (de)merit goods** and **natural monopolies**.

**Market power** is the ability of a seller (or buyer) to set the price above (below) the marginal (factor) cost level. Market power in a dynamic perspective is not only the power to set prices but also to influence consumer preferences.

**Market structures** refer to the number, size and relationships of the actors in the market. The structure indicates the degree of competition on both the demand and supply sides.

**Mental map** is the composition of categories by which actors perceive the world around them.

**Merit goods** are products that (supposedly) are good for the consumers as well as having positive **externalities**.

**Merger** is a **unification** of two or more firms, in which the respective owners agree to combine assets and liabilities.

**Methodological collectivism** explains social phenomena by assigning specific characteristics to social structures that cannot be reduced to the characteristics of individuals.

**Methodological individualism** is the explanation of social phenomena by individual actions.

**Methodological interactionism** is the explanation of social phenomena by simultaneous interaction(s) between actors and social phenomena as well as among the actors themselves.

**Model** is an abstract depiction of reality. The part of reality depicted is then described by those factors desired to be explained by the model (endogenous variables; see **endogenous variable**) in terms of those factors that can explain the endogenous variables and that are assumed to be given (exogenous variables; see **exogenous variable**).

**Monopolistic competition** is a market structure in which suppliers compete with differentiated goods that segment the market. Because of heterogeneity, each firm has some **market power**, but is constrained by the competitive pressure of the firms in the other segments of the market.

**Monopoly** is a market structure, characterized by one supplier only. Generally, this implies that the firm has **market power**. If there is pressure from potential competitive firms (threat of entry), this market power can be constrained.

**Monopsony** is a market structure, characterized by only one buyer, who therefore usually has **market power**.

**Moral hazard** (*ex-post* **opportunistic behavior**) occurs when contracting parties have conflicting interests (goals) in a situation of asymmetric information (see **imperfect information**), so that one of the parties knows that if he does not live up to the agreement, this goes unnoticed.

**Multidisciplinary approach** combines the insights of different disciplines. This is generally done in such a way that the contribution of one discipline (economics) is applied alongside the insight of another (history, or sociology, say). Such an approach has to be distinguished from the case in which insights from different disciplines are integrated. We then speak of an **interdisciplinary approach**.

**Multidivisional organization** (M-form) is an organization (or firm structure) characterized by a division along product lines or geographical areas.

**Multiple Equilibria** refer to the possibility that a (mathematical) model has more than one equilibrium solution. In more general terms, it may also refer to the simultaneous existence of different established rules about how to behave under certain circumstances.

**Natural monopoly** is a situation in which the production technology causes decreasing average costs, so that from the perspective of cost efficiency a single firm in the market is optimal.

**Neoclassical Economics** (NCE) is a term to describe mainstream microeconomic theory. One characteristic of NCE is that there is in general no explicit role for **institutions** in its theories.

**Network** is a hybrid type of governance structure consisting of independent actors that have a mutual interest and coordinate their activities to some extent. The actors in a network can have legal, economic, financial or personal relationships.

**New Institutional Economics** (NIE) is the school in Institutional Economics that builds on the work of Coase, North and Williamson. In general, the approach takes an efficiency perspective and focuses on individual actors, who are characterized by **bounded rationality** and (possibly) **opportunistic behavior**.

**Norms** are generally-held opinions about how to achieve societal **values**. They define the ways in which people ought to behave according to the members of a group.

**Oligopoly** is the market structure characterized by a small number of suppliers that take the reactions of one another into account.

**Original Institutional Economics** (OIE) is the school of Institutional Economics that is built on the insights of authors such as Veblen and Commons. OIE considers the interaction between actors and the dynamics of institutions to be the central question of economics.

**Opportunistic behavior** occurs when actors deliberately take advantage of a situation in the pursuit of self-interest, and this comes at the expense of other people. One can think of lying, cheating, not disclosing relevant information, abusing a dominant position and so on.

**Optimizing behavior** occurs when actors strive to maximize their objective functions or minimize their costs, given the restrictions they encounter.

**OPEC (Organization of the Petroleum Exporting Countries)** is an intergovernmental organization (cartel) that seeks to coordinate petroleum production and pricing policies in petroleum exporting member countries.

**Pareto optimal solution** (Pareto efficiency) is the situation in which no actor in the economy can reach a higher level of utility or profits without another actor suffering a lower level of utility or profits.

**Path dependency** means that economic outcomes at a certain point in time are influenced by events that took place in the past. See also **lock-in**.

**Perfect competition** is a theoretical **model** with many buyers (consumers) and many sellers (producers) on the market for a homogenous product with perfect information: nobody can individually influence the price, but all consumers together determine market demand, and all producers together determine market supply.

**Policy costs** (also refered to as political transaction costs) arise as a result of government intervention and comprise the costs of administration, monitoring and enforcement, compliance, and those resulting from **rent-seeking** behavior and **principal–agent problems** in the public sector.

**Predatory pricing** implies (in general) a short-term pricing policy that is not profit maximizing and sets prices at so low a level that an efficient (potential) competitor is unable to compete at that price and is forced to leave the market (or is prevented from entering).

**Principal–agent problem** occurs when parties to a contract are characterized as a principal and an agent (see **principal–agent relationship**), who have conflicting interests in a situation of asymmetric information.

**Principal–agent relationship** is the situation when two parties conclude a contract in which one party (the principal) gives an assignment and delegates part of her decision-making powers to the other party (the agent).

**Prisoner's dilemma** is a classic in game theory. It describes situations in which each actor in the game chooses one specific course of action that is individually optimal but leads to a non-optimal outcome for all players taken together.

**Private good**; see **types of goods**.

**Privatization** is the process of transfer of collective to private **property rights**.

**Procedural rationality** concerns the procedure of reaching a decision in situations of **uncertainty** based on appropriate deliberation, based on following and applying adequate procedures.

**Producer surplus** is the difference between the price received for each unit sold on the market and the marginal costs of that unit.

**Product life cycle** refers to the pattern of stages of development from rise to decline of products. The concept of the life cycle can also be applied to industries and markets.

**Production function** is the technical relationship between factors of production, such as labor, capital and land, and the output produced with these inputs.

**Productive efficiency**; see **efficiency**.

**Property rights** refer to the rights to decide by whom, when, for what period, and under what conditions an asset can be used. Within the bundle of property rights, a distinction can be made between the right to use, the right to earn an income, and the right to sell an asset.

**Punctuated equilibria** are sudden transformations in the development of a phenomenon after a long period of gradual change.

**Public bureau** is a synonym for a state-owned enterprise, coined by Williamson.

**Public interests** can be defined in different ways. In the economic efficiency approach, the concept concerns the interests of (part of) the population being threatened by market imperfections that cannot be solved by private initiative alone in order to increase welfare. In the vested interest approach (see **vested interests**), public interests are defined by the actors in control. Consequently, the government then seeks to protect **values**, which may be defined differently over time, depending on which interest groups are in power.

**Public property** is property owned by the government.

**Pure market economy** is an ideal type of economic system characterized by private property and market transactions, in which the government confines itself to defining and enforcing the basic rules needed to enable private actors to function optimally.

**Pure public goods**; see **types of goods**.

**Rationality** is consistent, intentional behavior aimed at the realization of explicit objectives.

**Regulation** is state intervention in the free play of market forces with the aim of influencing the economic behavior of private actors in such a way that the public interest is served.

**Regulatory capture** is the phenomenon that the regulator complies with the interest of the regulated (especially in relation to regulated firms) to the detriment of welfare, because of the regulator's dependence on the regulated firm.

**Regulatory risk** is the risk for private actors that the government will change its regulations.

**Regulatory state** is the case in which the government aims only to influence the economic process by setting general rules with which private actors must comply. In the **developmental state**, the government aspires to influence economic activities by giving many more directives to private actors.

**Relational contract** or **open-ended contract** refers to an agreement over an indeterminate period of time. A contract is relational when not all eventualities for the future can be specified.

**Rent-seeking** can be described as a manipulative attempt to transfer resources in order to obtain favors without competitive effort, hence without giving any productive activity in exchange.

**Reputation** is the perception of others about a person, a group of people or an organization based on past performance.

**Revised sequence** is the case where producers influence consumer preferences in order to create demand for their (new) products.

**Risk** is the situation in which the probability of the possible outcomes is known. In this book we sometimes use risk explicitly in this sense, otherwise it is used synonymously with **uncertainty**.

**Risk aversion** means that a person prefers a secure outcome to an insecure one, given that the insecure outcome generates the same expected (monetary) value as the secure one.

**Safeguards** are precautionary measures to prevent contracting parties breaking an agreement. These safeguards can be either of a private nature (such as specific clauses formulated in the contract, and **self-enforcing** mechanisms), or of a public nature, stemming from stipulations in contract law and labor law.

**Sanctions** are enforcement mechanisms which punish when rules are broken or abused (negative sanctions), or which encourage when rules are followed (positive sanctions).

**Satisficing behavior** is aimed at realizing an acceptable aspiration level of utility or profit that is not the **first best solution** because of **bounded rationality**.

**Second best solution** occurs when efficiency is reached after having corrected for **market imperfections**, whereby **transaction costs** are incurred.

**Second order economizing** is the design and execution of institutions that minimize production costs and **transaction costs** in a situation of efficient public **formal institutions**.

**Self-enforcement** implies that the **informal institution** is reinforced by people's individual behavior without enforcement by an external authority, because it is in their own interest to do so.

**Self-regulation** implies that the **informal institution** is reinforced by standards, and possible sanctions that are agreed upon by the private actors involved.

**Separation of ownership and control** is a situation in which the management of the firm is in the hands of actors other than the owners.

**Settled beliefs** in science refers to the established agreement among scientists of a discipline, or of a specific school within a discipline, about what the basic mechanisms are, and how the domain of research should be studied.

**Shared property** is property owned by a group or collective of private actors.

**Social welfare** is an extension of the concept of **economic welfare**. If a government strives to optimize social welfare it does not only take the enhancement of efficiency into consideration but also the question of whether the distribution of wealth can (or should) be improved.

**Spot market** is an archetypal example of an ideal market (see also **pure market economy**), with all the relevant information included in prices. It is composed of one-time buyers and sellers whose only relationship is a single exchange.

**Stakeholders** are people, groups of people, or organizations who have a direct or indirect interest in a particular organization and may be affected by the actions of that organization.

**State** is used in this book as a synonym for **government**.

**State-owned enterprise** is the provision of goods and services by a firm that is owned by the state and operates mainly under the responsibility of a specific ministry.

**Static efficiency**; see **efficiency**.

**Strategic alliance** is an agreement between two or more actors to pool specific resources in order to increase mutual gains. A **joint venture** is a specific form of a strategic alliance.

**Structural economic policy** concerns the policy of changing the structure of the economy; that is, the composition of economic activities. The economic structure consists of different sectors such as agriculture and mining, industry (steel, shipbuilding) and services (banking, insurance).

**Structure** is the configuration of elements that together constitute a system. The structure of the **economic system** can be hierarchical, as in a **centrally planned economy**, or of a network type, as in the Japanese economy. In this book we refer frequently to the structure of (in)formal institutions and to **governance structures**, being the elements that together constitute the **institutional environment** or the economy.

**Tacit collusion**; see **implicit collusion**.

**Theory** is an abstract presentation of the relationship between variables designed to explain facts in reality.

**Third parties** are arbitrators who can enforce the contract when one of the contracting parties does not meet the agreement. This is a form of **self-regulation**.

**Tit-for-tat** is strategic behavior based on the principle of equivalent retaliation; that is, responding in kind to some person's previous behavior. This can lead to **self-enforcement**.

**Tragedy of the commons** occurs when some commonly owned goods characterized by nonexclusiveness (everybody has free access to them) have become rival as a result of scarcity and are under threat of exhaustion. If managed carefully (that is, if the common good is protected and maintained), continuous use could be possible. If not, then increasing rivalry leads to a negative **externality**: the good is overused, or depleted.

**Transactions** take place in the form of an exchange of **property rights** in the sense that products and services (including information) are delivered from one actor to another, either across markets (market transaction), within a firm (managerial transaction), or between government and actors (political transaction).

**Transaction costs** are costs incurred when products and services are exchanged between actors. These comprise search and information costs; costs of drafting, negotiating and concluding contracts; and monitoring and enforcement costs.

**Trust** is a relationship between actors in which one relies on the other in the sense that people expect that promises will be fulfilled; also when no safeguard has been created. A trusted person is presumed to abstain from **opportunistic behavior**.

**Types of goods** are split into four categories. Each type of good can be (intrinsically) characterized as being (non)exclusive on the one hand, and (non)rival on the other. A **private good** is both exclusive and rival: its consumption makes it unavailable to others (rival) and its consumer can prevent others from sharing it (exclusive). A **pure public good** is both nonexclusive and nonrival. **Common property resources** are defined as assets that are nonexclusive yet at the same time rival; while **club goods** are commodities that are nonrival yet at the same time exclusive.

**Uncertainty** is an 'immeasurable' **risk**; that is, a situation in which all of the possible outcomes are not known, and/or a situation in which the probability of a possible outcome is also not known. In this book we sometimes use uncertainty explicitly in this sense, otherwise it is used synonymously with risk.

**Unification** refers to a **merger** (either horizontal or vertical) of two or more firms, so that a **hierarchy** is created.

**Unitary organization** (U-form) is an organization (or firm structure) characterized by a division along functional lines. Examples of functions in a firm are: sales, production or finance.

**Values** are embedded in a society's **culture**. They are generally-held preferences about pursuable goals and embody what most citizens in a certain society consider to be good. Values are standards of judgment.

**Vested interests** refer to the interests of specific individuals or groups in society, who aim to protect their own interests without taking into account of possible adverse effects on the welfare of others.

**Welfare** is synonymous with **economic welfare** in this book. Optimal welfare is equivalent to the 'first best', 'Pareto efficient' or **Pareto optimal solution**. It is the general term to denote the sum of consumer and producer surplus. The concept is to be distinguished from **social welfare**.

# References

Abdul Gafoor, A. L. M. (2002) *Interest-free Commercial Banking*, revd edn (Groningen: Apptec).
Acemoglu, D. and Robinson, J. (2006) 'De Facto Political Power and Institutional Persistence', *American Economic Review* 96(2), 325–30.
Akerlof, G. A. (1970) 'The Market for 'Lemons': Quality Uncertainty and the Market Mechanism', *Quarterly Journal of Economics* 84(3), 488–500.
Alchian, A. A. (1991) 'Property Rights', in J. Eatwell, M. Milgate and P. Newman (eds), *The New Palgrave: A Dictionary of Economics*, Part 3 (London: Macmillan), 1031–4.
Alchian, A. A. and Demsetz, H. (1972) 'Production, Information Costs and Economic Organization', *American Economic Review* 62(5), 777–95.
Amnesty International (2006) *Kimberley Process: An Amnesty International Position Paper* (London: Amnesty International).
Andersson, P., Hultén, S. and Valiente, P. (2005) 'Beauty Contest Licensing Lessons from the 3G Process in Sweden', *Telecommunications Policy* 29(8), 577–93.
Aoki, M. (2000) 'Institutional Evolution as Punctuated Equilibria', in Ménard, C. (ed.), *Institutions, Contracts and Organizations: Perspectives from New Institutional Economics* (Cheltenham: Edward Elgar), 11–36.
Aoki, M. (2001) *Toward a Comparative Institutional Analysis* (Cambridge, Mass.: MIT Press).
Aoki, M. (2007) 'Endogenizing Institutions and Institutional Changes', *Journal of Institutional Economics* 3(1), 1–31.
Armstrong, M. and Sappington, D. (2006) 'Regulation, Competition, and Liberalization', *Journal of Economic Literature* 44(2), 325–66.
Ayres, C. E. (1961) *Toward a Reasonable Society: The Values of Industrial Civilization* (Austin, Tex.: University of Texas Press).
Barr, N. (1998) *The Economics of the Welfare State*, 3rd edn (Stanford, Calif.: Stanford University Press).
Bebchuk, L. A. and Fried, J. M. (2003) 'Executive Compensation as an Agency Problem', *Journal of Economic Perspectives* 17(3), 71–92.
Berle, A. A. and Means, G. C. (1947) *The Modern Corporation and Private Property* (New York: Macmillan).
Bowles, S. (1998) 'Endogenous Preferences: The Cultural Consequences of Markets and Other Economic Institutions', *Journal of Economic Literature* 36(1), 75–111.
Brandl, J. and Bullinger, B. (2009) 'Reflections on the Societal Conditions for the Pervasiveness of Entrepreneurial Behavior in Western Societies', *Journal of Management Inquiry* 18(2), 159–73.
Bromley, D. W. (2006) *Sufficient Reason: Volitional Pragmatism and the Meaning of Economic Institutions* (Princeton, NJ: Princeton University Press).
Brousseau, E. and Glachant, J.-M. (eds) (2008) *New Institutional Economics. A Guidebook* (Cambridge: Cambridge University Press).
Buchanan, J. M. (1965) 'An Economic Theory of Clubs', *Economica* 32(125), 1–14.
Canton, J. (2008) 'Redealing the Cards: How an Eco-industry Modifies the Political Economy of Environmental Taxes', *Resource and Energy Economics* 30(3), 295–315.

Center for Responsive Politics (2009) Lobbying Database, OpenSecrets.Org, accessed 7 May 2009.
Chandler, A. D. (1962) *Strategy and Structure* (Cambridge, Mass.: MIT Press).
Chandler, A. D. (1977) *The Visible Hand: The Managerial Revolution in American Business* (Cambridge, Mass.: Harvard University Press).
Coase, R. H. (1937) 'The Nature of the Firm', *Economica* 4(16), 386–405.
Coase, R. H. (1960) 'The Problem of Social Cost', *Journal of Law and Economics* 3(1), 1–44.
Coase, R. H. (2000) 'The Acquisition of Fisher Body by General Motors', *Journal of Law and Economics*, 43(1), 15–31.
Commons, J. R. (1924) *Legal Foundations of Capitalism* (New York: Macmillan).
Commons, J. R. (1931) 'Institutional Economics', *The American Economic Review* 21(4), 648–57.
Commons, J. R. (1934) *Institutional Economics: Its Place in Political Economy* (New York: Macmillan).
Cusumano, M., Mylonadis, Y. and Rosenbloom, R. (1992) 'Strategic Maneuvering and Mass-Market Dynamics: The Triumph of VHS over Beta', *The Business History Review* 66(1), 51–94.
David, P. A. (1985) 'Clio and the Economics of QWERTY', *American Economic Review* 75(2), 332–7.
Debreu, G. (1959) *Theory of Value: An Axiomatic Analysis of Economic Equilibrium* (New Haven, Conn. and London: Yale University Press).
De Jong, H. W. (1997) 'The Governance Structure and Performance of Large European Corporations', *Journal of Management and Governance* 1(1), 5–27.
Demsetz, H. (1998) 'Property Rights', in P. Newman (ed.), *New Palgrave Dictionary of Economics and the Law*, Part 3 (London: Macmillan), 144–55.
Denzau, A. T. and North, D. C. (1994) 'Shared Mental Models: Ideologies and Institutions', *Kyklos* 47(1), 3–31.
Devereux, M. P., Lockwood B. and Redoano, M. (2008) 'Do Countries Compete over Corporate Tax Rates?', *Journal of Public Economics* 92(5–6), 1210–35.
Doornbosch, R. and Steenblik, R. (2007) 'Biofuels: Is the Cure Worse than the Disease?', Background paper prepared for the 20th meeting of the Round Table on Sustainable Development, Paris, OECD.
Dore, R. P. (2000) *Stock Market Capitalism: Welfare Capitalism: Japan and Germany versus the Anglo-Saxons* (Oxford: Oxford University Press).
Dyer, J. H. (1996) 'Specialized Supplier Networks as a Source of Competitive Advantage: Evidence from the Auto Industry', *Strategic Management Journal* 17(4), 271–91.
Dunleavy, P. (1991) *Democracy, Bureaucracy and Public Choice: Economic Explanations in Political Science* (Hemel Hempstead: Harvester Wheatsheaf).
Elsner, W. and Groenewegen, J. (eds) (2000) *Industrial Policy After 2000* (Dordrecht: Kluwer Academic Publishers).
Estrin, S. and Holmes, P. (1983) *French Planning in Theory and Practice* (London: George Allen & Unwin).
Ferguson, A. (1767) *An Essay on the History of Civil Society* (facsimile edition 1971, New York: Garland Publishing).
Freeman, R. B. and Lazear, E. P. (1995) 'An Econometric Analysis of Works Councils', in J. Rogers and W. Streeck (eds), *Works Councils – Consultation, Representation and Cooperation in Industrial Relations* (Chicago: University of Chicago Press), 27–52.
Furubotn, E. G. and Richter, R. (1998) *Institutions and Economic Theory. The Contribution of the New Institutional Economics.* (Ann Arbor, Mich.: The University of Michigan Press).
Galbraith, J. K. (1952) *American Capitalism; The Concept of Countervailing Power* (Cambridge, Mass.: Houghton Mifflin).
Galbraith, J. K. (1969) *The Affluent Society* (London: Hamilton).
Galbraith, J. K. (1974) *The New Industrial State*, 2nd edn (Harmondsworth: Penguin).
Gertler, M. (1997) 'The Invention of Regional Culture', in R. Lee and J. Wills (eds), *Geographies of Economies* (London: Arnold), 47–58.
Givel, M. (2006) 'Punctuated Equilibrium in Limbo: The Tobacco Lobby and U.S. State Policymaking from 1990 to 2003', *The Policy Studies Journal* 34(3), 405–18.

Graddy, K. (2006) 'The Fulton Fish Market', *Journal of Economic Perspectives*, 20(2), 207–20.
Greif, A. (2006) *Institutions and the Path to the Modern Economy: Lessons from Medieval Trade* (Cambridge: Cambridge University Press).
Groenewegen, J. (1996) *Transaction Cost Economics and Beyond* (Dordrecht/Berlin/Heidelberg/New York: Springer).
Groenewegen, J., Kerstholt, F. and Nagelkerke, A. (1995) 'On Integrating New and Old Institutionalism: Douglass North Building Bridges', *Journal of Economic Issues* 29(2), 467–75.
Gruchy, A. G. (1972) *Contemporary Economic Thought: The Contributions of Neo-Institutionalist Economics* (Clifton, NJ: Augustus Kelley).
Gwin, P. (2007) 'Dark Passage', *National Geographic* 212(4), 126–49.
Handy, C. B. (1985) *Understanding Organizations* (Harmondsworth: Penguin).
Hardin, G. (1968) 'The Tragedy of the Commons', *Science* 162(3859), 1243–8.
Hart, O. (1998) 'Residual Rights of Control', in P. Newman (ed.), *New Palgrave Dictionary of Economics and the Law*, Part 3 (London: Macmillan), 330–5.
Hausmann, R. and Rodrik, D. (2003) 'Economic Development as Self-Discovery', *Journal of Development Economics* 72(2), 603–33.
Hausmann, R. and Rodrik, D. (2005) 'It Is Not How Much But What You Export That Matters', Working paper, Harvard University.
Hayden, F. G. (2005) *Policy Making for a Good Society: The Social Fabric Matrix Approach to Policy Analysis and Project Evaluation* (Dordrecht/Berlin/Heidelberg/New York: Springer).
Hayek, F. A. (von) (1937) 'Economics and Knowledge', *Economica* 4(13), 33–54.
Hayek, F. A. (1979) *The Counter-Revolution of Science. Studies on the Abuse of Reason*, 2nd edn (Indianapolis, Ind.: Liberty Press).
Hodgson, G. M. (1988) *Economics and Institutions* (Oxford: Polity Press).
Hodgson, G. M. (1998) 'The Approach of Institutional Economics', *Journal of Economic Literature* 36(1), 166–92.
Hodgson, G. M. (2006) 'What Are Institutions?', *Journal of Economic Issues* 40(1), 1–25.
Hodgson, G. M. (2007) 'Meanings of Methodological Individualism', *Journal of Economic Methodology* 14(2), 211–26.
Ilias, S. (2008) 'Islamic Finance: Overview and Policy Concerns', CSR Report for Congress, 29 July.
Jacquemin, A. P. and De Jong, H. W. (eds) (1976) *Markets, Corporate Behaviour and the State: International Aspects of Industrial Organization* (The Hague: Martinus Nijhoff).
Jensen, M. and Meckling, W. (1976) 'Theory of the Firm: Managerial Behavior, Agency Costs and Capital Structure', *Journal of Financial Economics* 3(4), 305–60.
Johnson, C. (1982) *MITI and the Japanese Miracle* (Stanford, Calif.: Stanford University Press).
Joskow, P. L. (1998) 'Asset Specificity and Vertical Integration', in P. Newman (ed.), *New Palgrave Dictionary of Economics and the Law*, Part 1 (London: Macmillan), 107–14.
Kapp, K. W. (1976) 'The Nature and Significance of Institutional Economics', *Kyklos* 29(2), 209–32.
Kasper, W. and Streit, M. E. (1999) *Institutional Economics. Social Order and Public Policy* (Cheltenham: Edward Elgar).
Kirzner, I. M. (1973) *Competition and Entrepreneurship* (Chicago and London: University of Chicago Press).
Kirzner, I. M. (1997) 'Entrepreneurial Discovery and the Competitive Market Process: An Austrian Approach', *Journal of Economic Literature* 35(1), 60–85.
Kiss, J. (2008) 'Sony's Blu-Ray wins HD DVD Battle', *Guardian*, 19 February.
Klein, B. (2000) 'Fisher–General Motors and the Nature of the Firm', *Journal of Law and Economics* 43(1), 105–41.
Klein, B., Crawford, R. G. and Alchian, A. (1988) 'Vertical Integration as Organizational Ownership: The Fisher Body–General Motors Relationship Revisited', *Journal of Law, Economics, and Organization* 4(1), 199–213.
Knight, F. H. (1921) *Risk, Uncertainty and Profit* (Boston, Mass.: Houghton Mifflin).
Lambsdorff, J. (2007) *The Institutional Economics of Corruption and Reform. Theory, Evidence and Policy* (Cambridge: Cambridge University Press).
Lamont, D. (2007) 'The McProspects for McDonald's', *Guardian*, 26 March, 9.

Lee, D. (2006) 'The Korean Economy in Transition: In Search for a New Model', *Global Economic Review*, 35(2), 207–30.

Lee, W.-W. (2004) 'US Lessons for Energy Industry Restructuring: Based on Natural Gas and California Electricity Incidences', *Energy Policy* 32(2), 237–59.

Leeson, P. T. (2007a) 'An-*arrgh*-chy: The Law and Economics of Pirate Organization', *Journal of Political Economy* 115(6), 1049–94.

Leeson, P. T. (2007b) 'Pi*rational* choice: The Economics of Infamous Pirate Practices', Working paper, George Mason University, Fairfax, Va.

Li, D. D., Feng, J. and Jiang, H. (2006) 'Institutional Entrepreneurs', *American Economic Review* 96(2), 358–62.

Libecap, G. D. (1989) 'Distributional Issues in Contracting for Property Rights', *Journal of Institutional and Theoretical Economics* 145, 6–24.

McDonough, W. and Braungart, M. (2002) *Cradle to Cradle: Remaking the Way We Make Things* (New York: North Point Press).

Ménard, C. (2004) 'The Economics of Hybrid Organizations', *Journal of Institutional and Theoretical Economics* 160(3), 345–76.

Ménard, C. (2005) 'A New Institutional Approach to Organization', in C. Ménard and M. M. Shirley (eds), *Handbook of New Institutional Economics* (Dordrecht/Berlin/Heidelberg/New York: Springer), 281–312.

Ménard, C. (2006) 'Hybrid Organization of Production and Distribution', *Revista de Análisis Económico* 21(2), 25–41.

Ménard, C. and Shirley, M. M. (eds) (2005) *Handbook of New Institutional Economics* (Dordrecht/Berlin/Heidelberg/New York: Springer).

Menger, C. (1892) 'On the Origins of Money', *Economic Journal* 2(6), 239–55.

Milgrom, P. and Roberts, J. (1992) *Economics, Organization and Management* (Upper Saddle River, NJ: Prentice Hall).

Mueller, D. C. (2003) *Public Choice III* (Cambridge: Cambridge University Press).

Myrdal, G. (1944) *An American Dilemma: The Negro Problem and Modern Democracy* (New York: Harper).

Myrdal, G. (1968) *Asian Drama: An Inquiry into the Poverty of Nations* (New York: Twentieth Century Fund).

Niskanen, W. A. (1971) *Bureaucracy and Representative Government* (Chicago: Aldine-Atherton).

Nooteboom, B. (2002) *Trust: Forms, Foundations, Functions, Failures and Figures* (Cheltenham: Edward Elgar).

Nooteboom, B. (2007) 'Methodological Interactionism: Theory and Application to the Firm and to the Building of Trust', *The Review of Austrian Economics* 20(2), 137–53.

North, D. C. (1981) *Structure and Change in Economic History* (New York: W. W. Norton).

North, D. C. (1990) *Institutions, Institutional Change and Economic Performance* (Cambridge: Cambridge University Press).

North, D. C. (1993) 'The New Institutional Economics and Development', Mimeo, Washington University available at: www.econ.iastate.edu/tesfatsi/NewInstE.North.pdf.

North, D C. (1994) 'Economic Performance through Time', *The American Economic Review* 84(3), 359–68.

North, D. C. (2005) *Understanding the Process of Economic Change* (Princeton, NJ: Princeton University Press).

OECD (2009) 'OECD Tax Database', Centre for Tax Policy and Administration; available at: http://www.oecd.org/dataoecd/26/56/33717459.xls. Accessed 1 February 2009.

Okun, A. (1981) *Prices and Quantities* (Washington, DC: The Brookings Institution).

Olson, M. (1965) *The Logic of Collective Action. Public Goods and the Theory of Groups* (Cambridge, Mass.: Harvard University Press).

Ostrom, E. (1990) *Governing the Commons: The Evolution of Institutions for Collective Action* (Cambridge: Cambridge University Press).

Phelps, E. S. (1985) *Political Economy: An Introductory Text* (New York: W. W. Norton).

Phillips, L. (2008) 'Brussels' Voluntary Lobbyist Register under Fire', *EUobserver*, 23 June; euobserver.com.

Philipsen, N. J. and Maks, J. A. H. (2005) 'An Economic Analysis of the Regulation of Professions', in E. Crals and L. Vereeck (eds), *Regulation of Architects in Belgium and the Netherlands* (Leuven: Lannoo Campus), 11–45.

Porter, M. E. (1980) *Competitive Strategy* (New York: Free Press).
PricewaterhouseCoopers and World Bank (2008) *Paying Taxes 2008: The Global Picture*, Internet report; available at www.doingbusiness.org/documents/Paying_Taxes_2008.pdf.
Qian, Y., Gérard, R. and Chenggang, X. (2006) 'Coordination and Experimentation in M-Form and U-Form Organizations', *Journal of Political Economy* 114(2), 366–402.
RBB Economics (2008) 'Google/DoubleClick: The Search for a Theory of Harm', *RBB Brief* 26, June; www.rbbeco.com.
Rediker, M. (1981) 'Under the Banner of King Death: The Social World of Anglo-American Pirates, 1716 to 1726', *William and Mary Quarterly* 38(2), 203–27.
Rediker, M. (1987) *Between the Devil and the Deep Blue Sea: Merchant Seamen, Pirates and the Anglo-American Maritime World, 1700–1750* (Cambridge: Cambridge University Press).
Richardson, G. B. (1972) 'The Organisation of Industry', *The Economic Journal* 82(327), 883–96.
Rodrik, D. (2004) 'Getting Institutions Right', Working paper, Harvard University.
Rodrik, D. (2008) 'Second-Best Institutions', *American Economic Review: Papers and Proceedings* 98(2), 100–4.
Rodrik, D., Subramanian, A. and Trebbi, F. (2004) 'Institutions Rule: The Primacy of Institutions over Geography and Integration in Economic Development', *Journal of Economic Growth* 9(2), 131–165.
Roider, A. (2006) 'Fisher Body Revisited: Supply Contract and Vertical Integration', *European Journal of Law and Economics* 22(2), 181–96.
Rose, S. (2007) 'Review of Pirates of the Caribbean: At World's End', *Guardian*, 25 May, 8.
Rosen, H. S. and Gayer, T. (2008) *Public Finance*, 8th edn (New York: McGraw-Hill).
Rosen, S. (1985) 'Implicit Contracts: A Survey', *Journal of Economic Literature* 23(3), 1144–75.
Rosenberg, N. (2009) 'Some Critical Episodes in the Progress of Medical Innovation: An Anglo-American Perspective', *Research Policy* 38(2), 234–42.
Rutherford, M. (1994) *The Old and New Institutionalism* (Cambridge: Cambridge University Press).
Sandler, T. and Tschirthart, J. (1997) 'Club Theory: Thirty Years Later', *Public Choice* 93(3/4), 335–55.
Schumpeter, J. A. (1942) *Capitalism, Socialism and Democracy*, 5th edn (London: Allen & Unwin).
Schuster, L. (ed.) (2000) *Shareholder Value Management in Banks* (Basingstoke/New York: Palgrave Macmillan).
Shleifer, A. and Vishny, R. W. (1997) 'A Survey of Corporate Governance', *The Journal of Finance* 52(2), 737–83.
Simon, H. A. (1976) 'From Substantive to Procedural Rationality', in S. Latsis (ed.), *Method and Appraisal in Economics* (London/New York/Melbourne: Cambridge University Press).
Simon, H. A. (1991) 'Satisficing', in J. Eatwell, M. Milgate and P. Newman (eds.), *The New Palgrave: A Dictionary of Economics*, Part 4 (reprinted edn with corrections) (London: Macmillan), 243–5.
Smith, A. (1776) *The Wealth of Nations; An Inquiry into the Nature and Causes of the Wealth of Nations*, ed. E. Canan, 1965 edn (New York: Random House).
Smoke Free Partnership (2006) *Lifting the Smokescreen, 10 Reasons for a Smoke Free Europe*, Research report, Smoke Free Partnership, Brussels.
Soto, H. de (1989) *The Other Path: The Invisible Revolution in the Third World* (New York: Harper & Row).
Spiller, P. T. and Liao, S. (2008) 'Buy, Lobby or Sue: Interest Groups' Participation in Policy Making. A Selective Survey', in E. Brousseau and J.-M. Glachant (eds), *New Institutional Economics: A Guidebook* (Cambridge: Cambridge University Press), 307–27.
Spithoven, A. (2008) 'Surfing the Baby Boom Wave in the Netherlands', *Journal of Economic Issues* 42(3), 649–72.
Spithoven, A. (2009) 'Why U.S. Health Care Expenditure and Ranking on Health Care Indicators Are So Different from Canada's', *International Journal of Health Care Economics and Finance* 9(1), 1–24.
Stern, N. (2006) *Stern Review on the Economics of Climate Change* (Cambridge: Cambridge University Press).

Thaler, R. H. (1988) 'Anomalies: The Winner's Curse', *Journal of Economic Perspectives* 2(1), 191–202.
Tomasevski, K. (2006) *The State of the Right to Education Worldwide: Free or Fee,* Internet report; available at: www.katarinatomasevski.com.
Tool, M. R. (ed.) (1993) *Institutional Economics: Theory, Method, Policy.* (Boston/Dordrecht/London: Kluwer).
Tool, M. R. and Bush, P. D (eds) (2003) *Institutional Analysis and Economic Policy* (Boston: Kluwer Academic Publishers).
Transparency International (2007) *Report on the Transparency International Global Corruption Barometer 2007* (Berlin).
Transparency International (2008) *The Methodology of the TI Corruption Perceptions Index 2008* (Passau: University of Passau).
Truett, L. J. and Truett, D. B. (2007) 'A Cost-based Analysis of Scale Economies in the French Auto Industry', *International Review of Economics and Finance* 16(3), 369–82.
Van den Berg, A. (2004) 'The Contribution of Work Representation to Solving the Governance Structure Problem', *Journal of Management and Governance* 8(2), 129–48.
Vatn, A. (2005) *Institutions and the Environment* (Cheltenham: Edward Elgar).
Veblen, T. (1898) 'Why Is Economics Not an Evolutionary Science?', *Quarterly Journal of Economics* 12(4), 373–97.
Veblen, T. (1899) *Theory of the Leisure Class: An Economic Study of Institutions* (New York: Macmillan).
Veblen, T. (1904) *Theory of Business Enterprise* (New York: Charles Scribner's Sons).
Vlasic, B. and Schwartz, N. D., (2009) 'Chrysler and Fiat Have Hopes for Happy Relationship', *New York Times*, 5 May, B1.
Wallis, J., and North, D. C. (1986) 'Measuring the Transactions Sector in the American Economy', in S. Engerman and R. Gallman (eds), *Long Term Factors in American Economic Growth* (Chicago: University of Chicago Press), 95–161.
Wang, U. (2009) 'What the Green Industry Wants from Obama', *Green Tech Media*, 5 January; www.greentechmedia.com.
Waters, M. (1995) *Globalization* (London and New York: Routledge).
Weber, M. (1964) *The Theory of Social and Economic Organization* (New York: Free Press).
Whitley, R. (1999) *Divergent Capitalisms: The Social Structuring and Change of Business Systems* (Oxford: Oxford University Press).
Williams, J. (2006) 'Surge in Corporate Income Tax Collections Offers Opportunity for Tax Reform', *Tax Foundation*; www.taxfoundation.org.
Williamson, O. E. (1975) *Markets and Hierarchies* (New York: Free Press).
Williamson, O. E. (1983) 'Credible Commitments: Using Hostages to Support Exchange', *American Economic Review* 73(4), 519–40.
Williamson, O. E. (1985) *The Economic Institutions of Capitalism* (New York: The Free Press).
Williamson, O. E. (1991) 'Comparative Economic Organization', *Administrative Science Quarterly* 36(2), 269–96.
Williamson, O. E. (1996) *The Mechanisms of Governance* (New York/Oxford: Oxford University Press).
Williamson, O. E. (1998) 'Transaction Cost Economics: How It Works; Where It Is Headed', *The Economist* 146(1), 23–58.
Williamson, O. E. (1999) 'Public and Private Bureaucracies: A Transaction Cost Economics Perspective', *The Journal of Law, Economics, & Organization* V15(N1), 306–42.
Williamson, O. E. (2000) 'The New Institutional Economics: Taking Stock, Looking Ahead', *Journal of Economic Literature* 38(3), 595–613.
Witt, U. (1999) 'Do Entrepreneurs Need Firms? A Contribution to a Missing Chapter in Austrian Economics', *Journal of Austrian Economics* 11(1), 99–109.
Womack, J. P., Jones, D. T. and Roos, D. (1991) *The Machine That Changed the World: How Japan's Secret Weapon in the Global Auto Wars Will Revolutionize Western Industry* (New York: Harper Perennial).
World Bank (2006) *Where Is the Wealth of Nations? Measuring Capital for the 21st Century,* Report, The International Bank for Reconstruction and Development/The World Bank.

# Index

*Note*: page numbers in *italics* are definitions or key descriptions.

accountability, 82, 277, 333–4
actors, *6*
adverse selection, *109–11*, 132–3, 179–80, 274, 279, 369
advertising, 19, 175, 188–9, 193, 210, 218, 227, 237–8, 245, 278, 298, 356, 366
agency and structures, 57–60
agency costs, *113–14*, 118, 205, 211, 216, 233, 343, 369
  bonding expenditures, *113*–14
  monitoring expenditures, *113*–14, 369
  residual loss, *114*, 205, 343, 369
agency theory, 41, 65, 68, 80, 92, 107–9, 114, 131, 229, 232, 308, 343
agents, *see* principal–agent relationship; principal–agent problem
Akerlof, George, 179
Anglo-Saxon model, 82–4, 136, 155, 166, 169, 195–7, 203, 211, 216, 227, 231–2, 305, 313
  *see also* ideal types
Aoki, Masahiko, 144–5
arbitrage (buying and selling), 179, *184*
arbitrage (mediation), 127–8, 246
Arrow, Kenneth, 81, 328–9
  impossibility theorem, 329, *364–5*, 369
  information paradox, *312*, 369
Asian model, 82, 84, 155
  *see also* ideal types
asset specificity, 92, 114, 119, *120–7*, 132, 161–5, 173–4, 177, 179, 181, 202, 206–7, 209, 211, 215, 233, 245–6, 248–9, 252–3, 257, 303, 319, 369, 372
  dedicated, 121
  human, 121
  intangible, 121
  physical, 121
  site specificity, 121

auctions, 6, 18, 177, 198–200, 291–1, 336–7
  beauty contests, 291–2
  Dutch, 198–9, 336
  English, 198–9, 337
  sealed bid, 198–9, 291
audits, 8, 165, 213–14, 216, 334
  national audit bodies, 333–4, 344–5
Australia, 82, 263, 318, 341, 357
authority (in a hierarchy), 127–8, 160–1, 202, 206–7, 215, 230–1, 248, 267, 369–71
  *see also* fiat
autonomy, 123, 125, 128, 138–9, 160, 175, 213, 233, 236, 241–4, 246–50, 266, 268, 304–6, 308–9, 316–17, 370

Bank of America, *see* system banks
bargaining transactions, *see* transactions, market
battle of the sexes, 329
  *see also* game theory
beauty contests, *see* auctions
behavior
  altruistic, 253
  egoistic, 252–3
  maximizing, 18, 34, 64, 73, 81, 130, 183, 202, 205, 228–9, 237, 372, 375
  opportunistic, *15*
  optimizing, *14–15*, 22, 34, 44, 66, 92, 130, 331, 349, 374
  reciprocate, 253
  satisficing, 69, *73*, 370, 376
  *see also* behavior, optimizing
Belarus, 11
Berle, Adolph, 212
bid rigging, 337
bonding expenditures, *see* agency costs
boycotts, 9–10, 25, 194
branch organizations, 58–9, 128, 180

brand names, 116, 121, 238, 241, 243–4, 247, 371
British Petroleum (BP), 350
budgets (and public agencies), 344–5
Bulgaria, 11, 337
bureaucracy theory, 344–5, 365–6, 370
   *see also* Niskanen

Canada, 63, 82, 144, 299–301, 318, 357
carbon emissions, *see* global warming
cartels, 19, 48–9, 131, 224, 236, 238–41, 250–1, 254, 257–8, 267, 272, 285–8, 317, 342, 370
*ceteris paribus* clause, *125*
Chandler, Alfred D., 127, 138
   *see also* M-form; U-form
China, 11, 33–4, 62, 69, 76, 81–2, 101, 144, 168, 171, 191–2, 244, 279, 301, 306, 309, 313, 354, 355
Citibank, *see* system banks
Coase, Ronald, 102, 104, 118, 161, 181, 182, 202, 206, 367, 374
Coase theorem, *102*–4, 230, 294, 330, 370
Coca-Cola, 105, 194, 245
codetermination rights, *see* works councils
collaboration, 122, 128, 235, 241, 248, 251
collusion, 83, 123, 219, 240, 251, 254, 267, 286–7, 337, 370, 372, 377
   explicit, *251*, 286–7; *see also* cartels
   implicit, 219, *251*, 254, 286–7, 372, 377
commitment, 117, 195, 209, 215, 242, 249, 253, 296, 315, 358, 361
   collective, 153–4
   credible, 116, 162, 242, 372
   mutual, 116, 122, 253
   problem, 358, *361*–2
Commons, John R., 13–14, 27, 64–5, 87, 150, 155, 367, 374
communist regimes, 101, 334
comparative statics, 34, 68
competition
   cut-throat, 140, 166, 224
   imperfect, 18, 44, 48–9, 282, 372;
      *see also* market power
   perfect, 16–18, 45–51, 58, 61, 125–6, 161, 170, 177, 183, 186, 281, 284, 303, 371, 373–4
competition authority, 267, 286–7, 317, 342
   *see also* regulators
competition for the market, 282, 289, 291–3, 336, 358
concessions, 267, 282, 291, 293, 351
conflict diamonds, 176
Continental European model, 83–4, 195–7, 211, 217, 231
   *see also* ideal types
contract law, 7, 25, 109, 116, 170, 207–8, 303, 319, 376

   classical contract law regime, 174, 177
   complex contract law regime (arbitrage), 246, 249
   forbearance contract law regime, 208, 211
contract theories, 40, 92, 107, 118–19, 132, 233
contracting scheme, 92, 123–4
contracts
   classical, *125–6*, 162, 174–5, 177, 246
   complete, 107, 370
   formal, 106–7, 236, 252, 371
   incentive, 213
   incomplete, 107, 114–15, 206, 310
   informal or implicit, 106–7, 115–17
   labor or employment, 106–7, 108, 116–18, 206–9
   market, 32, 41, 65, 69, 122–9, 132, 139, 202, 236, 245, 249, 259
   one-off or simultaneous, 107, 170
   open-ended or relational, 115–*16*, 208, 211, 246, 370, 376
conventions, *26*–28, 40, 66, 69, 71, 94, 137, 142–4, 190, 370, 372
cooperatives, 99, 236, 241–3, 245, 247, 250, 370
copyrights, 105, 302
   *see also* patent rights
corporate governance, 8–9, 18, 83, 211, 216
Corruption Perceptions Index (CPI), 357
costs
   administration, 326
   compliance, *325*–*326*, 327, 345, 375
   crowding, 99
   *ex ante*, *22*–3
   *ex post*, *22*–3, 119
   exclusion, 96
   minimizing, 14, 79, 207, 232;
      *see also* behavior, optimizing
   monitoring and enforcement, *22*–23, 92, 113–14, 119, 213, 278, 326–7, 377
   policy, 326–7, 361, *375*
   search and information, *22*–3, 165, 377
   transaction, *22*–3
countervailing power, 169, 194, 227, 229, 232–3, 236, 257, 356, 370
creative destruction, *188*–9, 197, 370
crowding out, 341
culture, *26*, 63, 71, 74, 77, 79, 136–8, 142, 169, 176, 195, 202–3, 220–1, 227, 313, 370–1, 378
cumulative causation, *148*–149, 154, 191–2, 197, 370

Darwin, Charles, 87, 145
deadweight loss, *49*–50, 131, 238, 273, 282–4, 288, 303, 345, 354–5
   *see also* inefficiencies
Debreu, Gerard, 81, 311

democracy, 27–8, 40–1, 75, 83, 95, 153, 262, 335, 346–7, 364
dependency, 11, 22, 115–16, 120, 122, 182, 243, 247, 249, 341, 362, 376
　*see also* hold-up
design approach (perspective), 60, 68, 115, 142–3, *150*, 155, 157, 371
developing countries, 9, 36–7, 64, 180, 230, 300–1, 327, 340, 357
developmental state, *266*, 268, 305, 313, 376
dikes (pure public goods), 12, 21, 100, 105, 302
diminishing abstraction, 81–2
disciplinary mechanisms, 113, 213–15
disclosure of information, 267, 274–6, 304, 348
discretion, 58, 109, 131, 195, 208, 213, 362
disequilibrium, 46–7, 186–7, 197
diversification, 118, 229, 241
　*see also* M-form
dominance, 123, *184*–5, 193, 211, 219, 227, 237, 267, 284–6, 288–9, 362
　collectively dominant situation, 219
dominant strategy, 237
　*see also* game theory
dynamic approach, 35–6, 38, 61, 130, 140, 157–8, 160, 165–6, 169, 189, 203, 236, 251, 266, 268–9
　dynamic efficiency approach, 35, 235
　dynamic vested interest approach, 35, 235

economic systems, *31*–2, 34, 35, 38, 70–1, 82, 84–5, 101, 128, 136, 148, 151–2, 155, 157, 165–6, 229, 236, 264, 266, 273, 305–7, 348–9, 371
education, 19–20, 23, 37, 87, 100, 119, 149, 168, 195, 300–1, 314, 358
　*see also* positive externalities
efficiency, 16
　allocative or Pareto, *16*–17, 21, 47, 282–3, 289–90, 304, 330, 369, 371, 374, 378
　dynamic, *16*–17, 35, 105, 169, 203, 236, 268, 283, 290, 371–2
　productive, *16*, 369, 371, 375
　static, *16*, 34, 161, 169, 272, 371, 377
emission trading, 33, 72, 297
　*see also* global warming
employees, 14, 63, 83–4, 96, 106, 108, 116–18, 121, 149, 155, 167, 195–6, 206, 209–10, 212–17, 231, 242, 331–2, 345
enculturation, 136–7, 143, 371
Enron, 8, 18, 22, 25, 213–14
entrepreneurs, 71, 76, 80, 118–19, 139, 145, 149, 161, 165–9, 175, 185–8, 190–2, 197, 205, 221–3, 227, 243, 272–3, 276, 283, 306–7, 349, 371
　institutional, 149, *166*, 190, 372
equilibrium, 16, 44–9, 68, 79, 81, 97, 137, 140, 143–5, 148, 155, 157–8, 168, 170, 172, 176, 185, 187–8, 190, 196–7, 239, 254–5, 309–11, 314
　general, 45–7, 51, 81, 311
　partial, 45, 47
　punctuated, 148, 375
European Commission, 10, 193, 218–19, 288, 296, 299, 354
evolutionary approach, 136, 142–3, 145, 148–9, 155, 157–8
*ex ante* opportunism, *see* adverse selection
*ex post* opportunism, *see* moral hazard
excludability, 93, 95–6, 105, 302–3
　full, *93*, 95
expropriation, 349
externalities, 17, *19*–20, 22, 50, 52, 72, 94, 102, 147, 168, 179, 182, 190, 272–3, 294–5, 299–300, 312, 330, 371, 373
　complex, 272, *294*, 319
　negative, 19, 94, 98, 102–3, 272, 278, 294–7, 324, 328–30, 341, 370–1, 377
　positive, 19, 100, 272, 294, 300–1, 331, 371, 373

Fairtrade, 180
fiat, *127*, 129, 162, 202, 206–7, 211, 232, 371–2
financial crisis, 9, 82, 131, 155, 214, 233, 240, 257, 274, 280, 306, 332
financial sector, 277–9, 308, 310, 332
firms (governance structure), *126*–7
　black box, 161, 203
　classical, 203
　limits to expansion, 220
　private, 32, 126, 128, 205, 268, 280, 315, 326, 331, 333, 345, 347, 349–50, 355
　public, *see* state-owned enterprise
first-best solution, 47, 51, 330, 371, 376
fiscal illusion, 346
Fisher Body, 181, 207
fly-by-night, 126, *177*, 209
Ford, 178, 226
franchising, 121, 128, 236, 241, 243, *244*, 245, 250, 371
free riding, 21, 22, 42, *99*–100, 103–5, 212, 237–8, 272, 283, 347, 349, 351, 355, *372*
frequency (of transactions), 79, 119, 122, 125, 161–3, 207, 303, 319

Galbraith, John Kenneth, 166, 193–4, 228
game theory, 79, 115, 144–5, 259, 375
Gazprom, 10–11, 19, 22, 35, 120–1, 181, 350
General Motors (GM), 181–2, 226
Germany, 63, 69, 83, 144, 172, 194, 215–16, 231, 258, 288, 318–19, 338, 352
Global Corruption Barometer, 357
global warming, 12, 19–20, 22, 28, 69, 72, 152–3, 294, 296–7

goods
- club, *95*–6, 98–9, 104, 370, 377
- common property resources, *95*, 97, 98, 377
- credence, *277–8*
- demerit, *19*–20, 300, 370
- exclusive, 21, 92, *95*–6, 377
- experience, *119*, 275, 278
- free, 95, *97*–8, 371
- information, 105, 302, 312
- merit, 17, *19*, 52, 100, 332, 373
- nonexclusive, 21, *95*–7, 100, 105, 129, 272, 301–3, 377
- nonrival, *95*–6, 100, 105, 129, 272, 283, 301–3, 375, 377
- private, 20, *95*–6, 105, 302, 375, 377
- privately owned, *95*–6, 331
- public, 17, 20, 50, 95, 100, 104, 129, 273, 301–2, 319, 330, 333–4, 373, 375
- publicly owned, 100, 130, 266
- pure public, 20–1, 52, *95*–96, 272, 301, 375
- rival, 54, *95*–7, 99, 131, 257, 359, 377
- search, *119*, 275

Gosplan, 307
*see also* (centrally) planned economy
governance structures, *32*, 123–9
government failures, 268, *325*, 327–8, 335, 343–4, 372
Greenpeace, 194, 351, 355

habits, 20, 57–8, 69, 73–4, 77, 87, 122, 137, 142, 146–9, 154–6, 189, 236, 252, 297, 366, 372
Hardin, Garrett, 97–8, 104
Hayek, Friedrich, 142, 149, 186, 311
hazards, 117, 123–5, 176–7, 245, 247, 249, 259, 303, 372
health care, 19–20, 100, 119, 176, 267–8, 272, 300–1, 334–5, 339
- national health care, 105, 111, 334, 338
- National Health Service (NHS), 301, 334
hedge funds, 215
Hicks–Kaldor improvement, 329–31, 372
hidden action, hidden decisions, 109, 179
hidden characteristics, hidden information, 109, 179
hierarchy, 65, 118, 122–3, 125–8, 138–9, 144, 160, 162–5, 174, 181, 202, 207–8, 211, 232–3, 236, 238, 248, 251, 253, 258, 345, 369, 372, 377
historical time, 61, 79–80
hold-up, *120*–1, 123, 126–7, 132, 179, 181–2, 207, 209, 215, 243, 247, 372
hostage, *116*
*see also* commitment, credible
hybrids (governance structure), *128*

ideal types, 31, 82, 85, 155, 162, 170, 177, 195, 216, 306, 370, 375
incentives, *39–40*
- high-powered market, *126*, 129, 162, 228, 247, 305, 331, 334, 373
- low-powered, *127*, 213, 328, 331, 372–3
- monetary, 304
- negative, 113, 213
- nonpecuniary, 214–15
- positive, 113, 213, 334
India, 11, 37, 160, 192, 258
individual freedom, 26, 28
industry life cycles, 314–17
inefficiencies, 17, 49, 50–1, 93, 110, 114, 160, 169, 179, 183, 265, 282–3, 290, 293, 305, 325–8, 344, 363, 367, 369, 373
information, asymmetric, 15, *17*–18, 92, 109, 111, 129, 132, 213, 249, 273, 315, 343, 347, 369, 372, 374–5
information, imperfect, *17*–18, 50, 52, 99, 132, 168, 187, 271, 273–4, 278–9, 328, 335, 360, 369, 372–4
infrastructure, 21, 129, 262, 289, 299, 314, 346
innovations, 16–17, 34, 61–2, 69, 71, 75–6, 166, 168–9, 184, 187–90, 193, 220, 252, 272, 275, 290, 306, 311, 314–17, 360–2, 372
- incremental, 187
- process, 187–8
- product, 57, 187
- R&D, 228, 230, 238, 240, 252, 314–15
- radical, 187
*see also* technology
insider trading, 18
institutional competition, 266, 268, *317*, 319, 339
Institutional Economics, subject matter, 31–3, 56, 80, 151
institutional environment, 17, *26*, 29, 31, 34, 36, 38–9, 42, 62, 64–7, 69–70, 77, 92, 94, 215, 249, 266, 272, 303, 305, 348, 367, 373, 377
institutions, *25*
- effectiveness, 29, 40
- enabling and/or constraining, 30–1, 87, 92
- formal, *25*, 58, 62, 66, 70, 77, 79, 83, 102, 109, 136, 138, 146, 150–1, 188, 313, 371, 376–7
- informal, *25*, 37–9, 42, 69, 94, 99, 102, 105, 116, 264, 354, 372
institutions as an equilibrium approach, 143–5
institutions matter, 36, 38, 62, 64, 92, 367
instrumental value theory, 152–3, 373

insurance, 40, 42, 107–13, 118, 149, 176, 186, 193, 274, 277–80, 297, 301, 314, 331, 335, 338–9, 344
  mandatory, 111, 278–9, 331, 338
intangible capital, 37–8
intangible goods, 96
integration
  backward, 256
  horizontal, 116; *see also* mergers
  vertical, 140, 182, 221, 223; *see also* mergers; hierarchy
International Monetary Fund (IMF), 64, 336
invisible hand, 15–16, 81, 117, 273, 307
Islamic banking, 241, 245, 250

Japan, 37, 60, 62–3, 84, 128, 140, 144, 222, 250, 275, 309, 313, 318–19, 350, 377
  *see also* keiretsu
joint ventures, 6, 69, 150, 316, 350, 373, 377
  *see also* hybrids
just-in-time production, 242, 247

Katrina (hurricane), 12–13, 21–2, 35
*keiretsu*, 60, 128, 241–2, 350
Knight, Frank, 161, 187

language, 24, 30, 74, 249
law
  competition, 83, 128, 139–40, 151, 236, 239–40, 259, 266, 285, 317, 342
  corporate, 69, 71, 80, 128, 151, 205, 215, 259, 267
  private, 276
  public, 276
laws, *27*
  *see also* formal institutions
lean production, 242
  *see also* just-in-time production
learning, 73–5, 88, 145, 148, 169, 191, 253, 301
legal system, *see* system approach; judicial system
levées, 12–13, 21
  *see also* dikes
liability, 106–7, 111, 182–3, 189, 208, 267, 275–7
  limited, 27, *208*, 211–12
liberalization, 294, 308, 313, 333, 349, *358*–60, 362, 373
licensing, 6, 42, 191, 241, *243*–4, 247, 250, 256, 267, 276, 291–2, 317, 336–7, 371, 373
lobbying, 13, 28, 32–3, 64, 136, 184, 190, 193, 227, 229, 250, 268, 296, 326, 348–51, *352*–6, 362

lock-in, *140*, 146–7, 373–4
low-wage countries, 11, 148

Machiavelli, 355
make or buy, 92, 122, 206, 305
managerial power theory, 131
market economy, 17, 75, 82, 93, 150–1, 155, 168, 259, 264–6, 305–7, 309–10, 313–14, 319
  pure (or free) market economy, 31, 83, 95, 231, 375–6
  *see also* economic systems; ideal types
market for lemons, 107, 179, 197, 274, 276
market imperfections, 16–18, 21, 29, 44, 50–1, 169, 179, 264–5, 267, 273, 283, 303, 326, 328–30, 373, 375–6
market power, 10, 17–*18*, 22, 45, 48–9, 52, 105, 122, 129, 169, 183–5, 197, 217–20, 236, 240, 254–5, 267, 272–3, 281–9, 293, 305, 319, 321, 328, 330, 370, 372–4
  administered prices, 183
  mark-up pricing, 184
  predatory pricing, 169, 184–5, 241, 285, 375
  price discrimination, 184, 190, 293
market power theory, 254–7
market process theory, 27–9, 168, 186–7
markets (governance structure), 125–6
  contingent, 169–70, 172–3, 183, 370
  futures, 173, 311
  ideal, 123–5, 162, 170, 175, 246, 376
  institutionalized, 124–5, 162, 197
  spot, 106–7, 169–73, 183, 196–7, 359, 376
McDonald's, 121, 210, 244–5, 247
Means, Gardiner, 212, 287
Menger, Carl, 143
mental maps, 69, 73–4, 77, 136–7, 140, 143, 146–8, 154, 156, 373
merger control, 217, 240
  *see also* competition authority
mergers, 83, 122, 128, 139, 141, 202–3, 210–11, 214, 217–20, 224, 238, 240–1, 245, 247, 285–7, 322, 349, 373, 377
methodological collectivism, 59–60, 373
methodological individualism, *59*–60, 76
methodological interactionism, 59–*60*, 65, 373
M-form, 127, 202, 224–6, 229, 374
Microsoft, 10, 22, 25, 35, 129, 193, 286
mixed economies, 31, 128, 266
  *see also* economic systems
money, 30, 143, 264, 274, 280, 315, 341–2, 353
monitoring expenditures, *see* agency costs
monopolistic competition 18, *49*–50, 58, 282–3, 372–3
  *see also* market power

monopoly, 18, 21, *48*–50, 58, 61, 105, 148, 165, 183–4, 264, 282–5, 288–9, 291–3, 358, 372–4
  legal, 267–*8*, 291, 293–4, 305, 359
  natural, 17, *21*, 48, 52, 100, 272–273, 281–2, 284, 288–9, 291, 294, 323, 336, 358–60, 362, 373
  of coercive power, 264
  *see also* market power
monopsony, *18*, 48, 49, 372, 374
  *see also* market power
moral hazard, 109, *111–12*, 113, 116, 132, 179, 181, 186, 250, 274, 277, 334, 374
mortgages, 9, 116, 281
multidivisional organization, *see* M-form
multiple equilibria, 144, 155, 374
Myrdal, Gunnar, 148–9

nationalization, 101, 268, 281, 306, 309–10, 349
natural environment, 19, 58, 69–71, 76, 262, 275, 295, 327, 350
  *see also* system approach, economic-ecological system
Neoclassical Economics (NCE), 16, 21, 44–5, 61–2, 64–8, 74, 79, 87, 152, 170, 197, 232–3, 265, 371, 374
Netherlands, 83, 111, 172, 213, 215, 318, 327, 339, 357
New Institutional Economics (NIE), 54, 64–9, 74–9, 85, 92, 129, 131–2, 136, 150–2, 352, 367, 371, 374
nexus of contracts, 202–3, 205–6, 211, 232, 371
night watchman state, 264, 325
Niskanen, William, 344–5
norms, 9–10, 15, 24–5, *26–29*, 32–4, 58–60, 66, 71, 74, 82–3, 94, 102, 115–17, 122, 137, 142–4, 149, 252–3, 265, 298, 372–4
North, Douglass C., 23, 26, 36–7, 62, 68, 74, 77, 88–9, 94, 138, 141, 148, 151, 242, 262, 367, 374

oligopoly, 18, *48–9*, 58, 372, 374
  *see also* market power
Olson, Mancur, 351
Ombudsman, 348
OPEC, 19, 49, 236, 251, 254, 257–9, 370, 374
organizational cultures, 221
Original Institutional Economics (OIE), 54, 64–5, 68–71, 74–8, 85, 136, 151–5, 157, 367, 374
Ostrom, Eleanor, 104

Pareto improvement, *47*, 330
Parmalat, 8, 18, 22, 213
patent rights, 6, 48, 105, 165, 223, 247, 256, 283, 302

path dependency, *146*–8, 150, 158, 374
  *see also* lock-in
pay
  fixed, 118, 214, 250
  incentive, 9, 213, 232
  merit, 113, 213, 250, 334
  performance-based, 9, 347
pharmaceutical industry, 230, 277–8
planned economy, centrally, 31, 95, 157, 306–9, 319, 332, 362, 370, 377
  *see also* economic systems; ideal types
planned economy, privately, 193
planning, central, 101, 306, 308–9
planning, indicative, 272, *306*, 309–13, 319, 372
policy
  competition, 272, 282–6, 319
  industrial, 266, 272, 314, 316
  technology, 272, 314–16
Ponzi scheme, 7
pork barrel politics, 355
Porter, Michael, 255
price mechanism, 45, 118, 126, 160, 206, 311
principal–agent problem, 92, *109*, 111, 132, 278, 309, 343, 345–6, 369–70, 375
principal–agent relationship, 112, 308, 315, 343, 371, 375
principal–agent theory, *see* agency theory
principals, *see* principal–agent relationship; principal–agent problem
prisoner's dilemma, 115, 236, *237*–40, 254, 287, 375
private ordering, 51, 123–5, 265, 272–3, 281, 304, 325
privatization, 157, 294, 308, *333*, 340, 349, 358–60, 375
product life cycles, 203, 222–3, 314, 375
production function, *61*, 65–6, 201, 203, 232, 308, 367, 375
property
  intellectual, 105, 189, 244
  private, 28, 31, 34, 82, 93, 95–6, 100–2, 104, 118, 130, 132, 150, 175, 303, 309, 331, 349, 358, 375
  public, 93, 95, 98, 100, 130, 375
  shared (common), 93, 95–9, 104, 132, 309, 370, 376
property rights (bundle), *93*
property rights theory, 68, 92–3, 100, 130–1, 119, 132, 266, 309, 331
prosperity, 26, 28, 36, 186, 204, 300
protectionism, 11, 338
protective function of the government, 264, 273
public agency, 23, 25, 32, 71, 93, 190, 217, 262–3, 276, 278–9, 292, 313, 326, 328, 333, 336, 343, 345, 348, 353, 361, 371–2

public bureaus, *see* state-owned enterprise; public agency
public interest, 32, 123, 129, 133, 193, 227, 264–5, 267, *271*–4, 277, 281, 295, 302, 326, 329, 343–4, 347, 356, 375
public ordering, 51, 123–5, 129, 266, 272, 303–4, 325
public provision, 267, 332–3, 346

quality marks, 116, 126, 175–6, 194

rational ignorance, 346, 362
rationality, 2, 14, 16, 39, 44, 66–7, 73–4, 79–80, 87–8, 97, 127, 146, 151, 153, 249, 370, 375
  bounded, 66–*7*, 77, 119–20, 122–3, 129, 132, 144, 170, 178, 227, 273, 303, 370, 374, 376
  full, 44, 67
  procedural, 69, *73*, 77
rationing transactions, *see* transactions, political
Reagan, Ronald, 231
recoupment, *see* market power, predatory pricing
regulation (governance structure), *128–9*
regulators, 50, 129, 267, 272, 276–81, 290, 293–4, 319, 358–62, 376
regulatory capture, 194, 290, 349, 358, 361–*2*, 376
regulatory state, *266*, 268, 305, 371, 376
rent-creation, 355
rent-seeking, 268, 290, 338, 346–9, *351*, 354, 357–8, 361–2, 375–6
reputation, 11, 25, 41, 94, 115, 117, 163, 170, 175–6, 179–82, 207–9, 211, 230, 232, 246–9, 252–3, 274, 276, 303, 348–*9*, 351, 376
residual claim, 106, 205
residual income, 205
residual loss, *see* agency costs
residual rights of control, 105
revised sequence, 166, 169, 193, 376
right of disposal, 93, 105
risk, *15*
  aversion, *107*–8, 110, 113, 118, 171, 176, 205, 376
  neutrality, *107*–8, 118
  *see also* hazards; uncertainty
Russia, 11, 69, 101, 120, 157, 167–8, 306–7, 341, 350

safeguards, 7–8, 24, 92, 109, 116, 123–7, 132, 162, 165, 175–7, 179–81, 189, 209, 227, 247, 250, 253, 264, 274, 312, 343, 346, 350, 361, 376–7
  administrative, 124–5, 127–8
  market, 124–5, 128

sanctions, 8, 24–5, 29, 31, 40, 99, 104, 109, 123, 127, 180, 239, 248, 252–3, 354, 361, 367, 376
  credible (effective, enforceable), 29, 239
  formal or legal, 26–7, 109
  informal, 95, 105, 354
  negative, 29, 213, 376
  positive, 29, 40, 376
second-best solution, 51, 376
Securities and Exchange Commission (SEC), 280
selection, artificial, 155, 158
self-enforcement, *25*, 115, 144, 237–8, 252, 255, 372, 376
self-interest, 14–15, 25, 116, 130, 144, 213, 227, 233, 252–3, 374
  *see also* behavior, opportunistic
self-regulation, *25*, 115, 126–7, 278, 372, 376–7
self-selection, 111, 347
Sen, Amartya, 358
separation of ownership and control, 211–12, 232, 371, 376
settled beliefs, 154, 156, 376
shareholder model, 166, 202–3, 213, 216, 227, 232
  *see also* Anglo-Saxon model
shareholders, 6–10, 17, 27, 36, 67, 80, 118, 131, 155, 193–5, 202–3, 205, 208–9, 212–17, 222, 226–33, 266–7, 272, 280–1, 306, 309, 315, 332, 347
Shell, 194, 280, 288, 350
shirking, 40, 106, 112, 205, 214
  *see also* behavior, opportunistic
Smith, Adam, 15–16, 37, 48–9, 81, 117–18, 161, 203–4, 211–12, 317–18
smoking, 103–4, 297–8, 329, 356
  *see also* externalities, negative
social surplus, 49
  *see also* welfare, economic
Soviet Union, *see* Russia
Special Economic Zones (SEZs), 309
  *see also* China
specialization, 6, 30–1, 37, 74, 175, 203–4, 208, 224, 228, 232
stakeholder model, 84, 169, 203, 212–15, 217, 231
  *see also* Continental European model
state directives, 139, 266–7, 304–5, 307–9, 376
state-owned enterprise (governance structure), *129*
static approach, 34–6, 91–2, 129, 140, 161, 165, 169, 189, 203, 221, 236, 266, 268, 272, 305
static efficiency approach, 34, 161, 169, 235
static vested interest approach, 34, 165, 169, 235

Stork, 215
strategic alliances, 69, 128, 166, 224, 235, 315, 350, 377
  *see also* hybrids
structures, *see* agency and structures
subsidies, 130, 250, 258, 262, 265, 267, 295, 297, 304, 314–15, 336, 338, 340–1, 345, 351–3, 355
sunk costs, 120, 256, 288–9
supply chains, 31, 218, 236, 250
Switzerland, 37, 317–18, 357
system approach, 70, 75, 82
  economic-ecological system, 76
  judicial system, 36–7, 70–1, 83, 85, 102, 114, 137, 152, 155, 164, 262, 319
  political system, 69, 70–1, 75–6, 82, 85, 150, 153, 157, 262–3, 266, 350, 352
  socio-economic system, 71
  socio-economic-political system, 71, 75
system banks, 193, 240, 281, 332

*tâtonnement*, 46
  *see also* Walras
taxes, 14, 20, 59, 104, 130, 262, 265, 267, 295, 301–2, 304, 314, 326–7, 330, 334, 336, 338–42, 344–6, 349, 351, 354–6
  corporate, 317, 319, 339, 340
  corrective, 297, 299, 324
team production, 202–5, 208
technology, 16, 21, 34, 45, 58, 61, 64, 69, 71, 74–7, 83, 87, 136–40, 142, 146–8, 161, 165, 185, 191, 193, 221, 228, 256, 266, 272, 288–9, 305, 310, 312–17, 352, 367, 371, 374
  general purpose, 163–4, 174
  specific purpose, 163–5, 174
tenders, 291, 333, 336–7
Thatcher, Margaret, 231
theory, 56–7, 78–82
third parties (self-regulation), 115, 117, 127, 239, 377
tit-for-tat, *115*, 175, 239, 254–5, 377
  *see also* game theory
Toyota Company, 241–2
tragedy of the commons, *97–9*, 294, 296, 377
transaction cost economics (TCE), 68, 118–23, 135, 161–5, 173–7, 202, 206–11, 232, 245–9, 303–5
transactions, *13–14*
  managerial, *14*, 23, 304, 377
  market, *13*, 22–3, 164, 174, 202, 208, 236, 238, 367, 375, 377
  political, *14*, 16, 22–3, 304, 319, 377
transaction-specific investments, *see* asset specificity
*trias politica*, 263, 347

trust, 6–7, 15, 27, 30, 36–7, 69, 73, 79, 94, 101, 117, 128, 140, 166, 179, 193, 206, 215, 236, 238, 243, 249–50, *252*–3, 259, 278, 281, 377
two-part tariff, *99*, 290, 293

U-form, 127, 224–6, 378
Ukraine, 11, 120–1, 181
umbrella organizations, *see* branch organizations
uncertainty, *16*
  environmental, 310, 371
  market, 310
  of transactions, 121–3
unemployment, 9, 42, 176, 189, 192, 215, 279, 314, 338–9
unification, 116, 373, 377
  *see also* mergers
unified ownership, 127, 246
unitary organization, *see* U-form
United Kingdom (UK), 27, 82, 210, 231–2, 281, 318, 333
United States of America (USA), 8–11, 13, 15, 23, 27, 62, 64, 82, 131, 144, 153, 155, 158, 179, 181, 190–1, 213, 215–16, 231, 239, 250, 258, 263, 276, 280–1, 285, 287, 297–301, 306, 317–19, 333, 336–7, 340–1, 352–3, 356

valuation, 33, 151–4, 373
values, 15, 25–*6*, 28, 32–4, 36, 56, 58, 60, 65–6, 68, 71, 74–6, 87, 94, 137, 151–5, 157, 189, 252–3, 264–5, 268, 296, 348, 367, 378
  collectivistic, 83–4, 138
  fundamental, 27
  individualistic, 82, 138
variables, endogenous, *47*–8, 60–2, 66–7, 69–70, 72, 76, 79, 136–7, 141–2, 154, 157, 189, 370–1, 373
variables, exogenous or explanatory, *47*–8, 54, 60–2, 64, 66–72, 76–9, 85, 92, 136–40, 155, 157, 165, 257, 311, 370–1, 373
Veblen, Thorstein, 64–5, 87, 148, 153, 367, 374
vested interest approach, *see* static approach; dynamic approach
vested interests, *2*, 25, 28, 33–6, 38, 58, 63, 65, 75, 77, 80, 85, 87, 92, 129–33, 136, 140–1, 151–8, 160–1, 165–6, 192, 202, 211, 220–2, 233, 236, 250, 254, 264–5, 268, 326, 335, 344, 348, 356, 367, 370, 378

Walras, Léon, 46–7, 81
Walt Disney, 148, 243–4
welfare loss, *see* inefficiencies

welfare, economic, *16*, 32, 45, 47, 49, 51, 92, 100, 130–1, 133, 166, 168, 236, 250, 264–5, 285, 294, 299–300, 303, 305, 324, 330, 349, 371–2, 376, 378
welfare, social, *265*, 328, 344, 346, 349, 365, 376
Williamson, Oliver E., 15, 26, 65–6, 68, 92, 116, 118–19, 122–3, 127, 150, 164, 173–4, 207–9, 246, 304, 367, 374–5
winner's curse, *18*
works councils, 214–15, 217
World Bank, 37–8, 64, 313, 327, 336, 357
World Health Organization (WHO), 313
World Trade Organization (WTO), 11, 25, 29